J. Ambrose Raftis

# Early Tudor Godmanchester
## Survivials and New Arrivals

Deserted villages, desolated towns, dwindling population—such conditions were not productive of historical records; small wonder that a former Regius Professor of history at Cambridge University commented upon the fifteenth century as the "dark ages of English historiography." The splendid series of surviving records for Godmanchester have been employed in this study to throw some light on this gloomy historical landscape. Because of its unusual structure—a royal manor yet a place governed by borough customs—Godmanchester also offers to the investigator a rather varied historical experience.

Frankpledge rolls provide the most complete chronological series of records and make possible a yearly reconstruction of the more than 30 elected posts in the town administration for over 150 years. Through information for licensing, these same records supply data about local commerce, especially the food trades. Court rolls covering the same chronological period are particularly useful for listing some 900 individuals granted liberty of the town. An in depth picture of the various levels of wealth in the town becomes available from the 1480s with the survival of several complete lists of names and royal farm rent payments (based upon the size of properties) for the four streets of Godmanchester. Various supplementary records round out the picture from the 1480s, the most noteworthy being bailiffs' accounts, a jurors' notebook, lists of annual property conveyances, wills and lay subsidy rolls.

From all this emerges a picture that is by now familiar to historians in many respects but in many other ways quite different. Familiar enough was the radical decline of population at Godmanchester to probably one half the numbers of the early fourteenth century, the fall in importance of craft trades after the early fifteenth century and the creation of a veritable landless proletariat among poorer residents of the town by the sixteenth century. However, the strategy employed for survival of the town was exceptional. By the third quarter of the fifteenth century impoverishment was such that the size of the royal farm payment had been reduced and over the 1480s Godmanchester was in danger of being taken over by wealthy London merchants. Although constrained by "democratic" customary regulation, more wealthy freemen assumed greater responsibility for administrative insolvency. From the scores of individuals given freedom of Godmanchester, under supply of craft and labour was buffered. More especially by this means regional families and their resources prevented a merchant takeover. This history of Godmanchester demonstrates in detail the capacity for a local community to maintain control of its own destiny and to adapt in the face of fundamental social and economic change.

Owing to the paucity of such materials for this period, extensive appendices make available for specialists' use, editions of bailiffs' accounts and millers' accounts as well as other data supplementary to the text.

STUDIES AND TEXTS 97

# EARLY TUDOR GODMANCHESTER

## Survivals and New Arrivals

BY

## J. AMBROSE RAFTIS

PONTIFICAL INSTITUTE OF MEDIAEVAL STUDIES

## Acknowledgment

This book has been published with the help of a grant
from the Social Science Federation of Canada, using
funds provided by the Social Sciences and Humanities
Research Council of Canada.

CANADIAN CATALOGUING IN PUBLICATION DATA

Raftis, J. A. (James Ambrose), 1922-
  Early Tudor Godmanchester

(Studies and texts, ISSN 0082-5328 ; 97)
Bibliography: p.
Includes index.
ISBN 0-88844-097-9

1. Godmanchester (England) — History.
2. Godmanchester (England) — Economic conditions.
3. Godmanchester (England) — Social conditions.
I. Pontifical Institute of Mediaeval Studies.
II. Title.    III. Series: Studies and texts
(Pontifical Institute of Mediaeval Studies) ; 97.

DA690.G58R33 1990            942.6'54            C89-094393-1

© 1990 by
Pontifical Institute of Mediaeval Studies
59 Queen's Park Crescent East
Toronto, Ontario, Canada M5S 2C4

PRINTED BY UNIVERSA, WETTEREN, BELGIUM

*To the Freemen*
*of Godmanchester*

*Past and Present*

# Contents

CONTENTS

APPENDICES

LIST OF TABLES

# Preface

This is the story of the survival of a small settlement of 1000 to 1200 people over those years of greatest changes in its history between the Norman Conquest and the Industrial Revolution. Godmanchester has an old history. Over the first millenium of our era the place that was to be called Godmanchester figured prominently on the political and military map of that region now designated as the East Midlands. Here the Roman road from Cambridge and the east met another Roman road (Ermine) from the south. For a century and more this was a frontier where the Ouse River filled a role not unlike that of the later Roman Wall to the north. A combination of rich river valley soils and easily cultivable uplands provided a built-in granary for the Roman settlement. Not surprisingly the archaeologist of Godmanchester, H. J. M. Green, has found evidence for the full complement of Roman buildings to be expected from such a mature provincial settlement.[1]

The rather unique polygonal layout of Godmanchester streets was determined by walls and suggests Godmanchester still retained or was revived in its earlier role as late as the time of the Danish invasions. But the political map of England was changing rapidly over the late Anglo-Saxon period. The Ouse River was not permanently bridged at Godmanchester until the twelfth century and so the expanding kingdom found it more convenient to control territory to the north by establishing a borough across the river at Huntingdon. In the meantime Godmanchester retained its status as a royal manor throughout the Anglo-Norman period.

This comparative loss of political visibility vis-a-vis Huntingdon challenged the people of Godmanchester to ensure their independent development by other means. A charter of liberties was purchased from King John for the heavy annual farm of £120. Rather ambiguously the customs developed under the aegis of succeeding kings are able to be classified by modern scholars as borough customs despite the continuing legal status of Godmanchester as a royal manor. For the historian, however, the fortunate feature of

[1] For a general survey of these findings, see H. J. M. Green, *Godmanchester* (Cambridge, 1977).

the independent role of Godmanchester freemen was their decision to retain court records as evidence for their system of self government.[2]

Three-weekly court records survive in an almost unbroken series from the 1270s and have made possible the nominal identification of more than thirteen hundred families. Families too were able to manipulate their customs to ensure survival despite the hazards of replacement and the tensions of entrepreneurial ambitions.[3] Supplementary records for the late thirteenth and early fourteenth centuries, such as the very detailed Hundred Roll for 1279, lay subsidy rolls and subletting lists, also make possible an interesting overview of the settlement pattern of the town as well as the relation of Godmanchester to a local agrarian region and a wider commercial region. With the base provided by some 5000 acres of productive land and an involvement in industries of the region, especially the production of cloth, Godmanchester was able to support over 3000 inhabitants in the early fourteenth century.

Proudly confident of the protection of its privileges and fully familiar with the adaptations possible to its system of customs, thirteenth- and fourteenth-century Godmanchester endured, without any noticeable structural change, new tax impositions by kings, the new economic power of cleric and merchant, the persistent demand for land by outsiders, the dependence upon a regional division of labour, the need to absorb outsiders in the town and even the impact of the Black Death and its immediate aftermath. Godmanchester was clearly very much a part of a greater society and could not expect to escape wider influences. What would happen to the town in the age of "agrarian revolution," "commercial revolution," "religious reformation," and so on?

The materials for this volume derive in great part from records for administration of Godmanchester. Very few of these sources deal directly with the structure and policies of administration. But the variety and volume of extant records that would appear to have survived owing to the financial exigencies of the time are such as to expose much about administrative practice. Re-creating some semblance of order among a mass of detail is further assisted by the fact that each unit of administration had a well defined role and clearly circumscribed records. By the same token, however, the

---

[2] A full study of these records, following the themes to be found in the next two paragraphs, may be found in my volume *A Small Town in Late Mediaeval England, Godmanchester 1278-1400*.

[3] The deployment of smallholdings as a family support system has now been able to be analyzed more thoroughly. See, J. A. Raftis, "The Land Market at Godmanchester c. 1300," *Mediaeval Studies* 50 (1988), 311-332.

scope of this task has dictated the separate treatment in Part One of administration, administrative records and the significant data to be extracted from these.

This study of local records in Part One is not impersonal. Perhaps the most unique feature of local records is the demographic, the wide active or passive involvement of many individuals. Information about many individuals has been painstakingly extracted from thousands of entries in court rolls, frankpledge rolls, rental lists and more subsidiary documents. For reasons of economy of space these lists form the bulk of the Appendices. However, these *acta* from the lives of individuals give the human context to various records so the Appendices present the essential human resource data or "text" for this study.

The social and economic history of any settlement is much more than administration, the role of individuals and their families. Above all in a period of change it is necessary to isolate differing levels of wealth and their relative capacity to respond to and control the elements of change. Since this is a task of reconstruction quite different from the direct derivation of information from records, it has been treated separately in Part Two. Nonetheless the very magnitude of sources for Godmanchester bring disappointments as well as pleasure to the historian. Much of the pretense Godmanchester may have had to the economic status of a town in the fourteenth century may have been lost over the hundred years of contraction prior to the Tudor period. Even during the late fifteenth-century crunch period of important structural economic change at Godmanchester, precipitated in great part by outside merchants, there was no marked shift of power to the great merchants of these Tudor generations. This remained a local story. Those larger questions of urban history, such as the role of the market and relations with other towns, even with Huntingdon, receive no articulation in our sources. One searches in vain, therefore, for further evidence about this manor town in national archives. Such sources as Chancery, Star Chamber, Bequests and State Papers that have added so much to current studies of towns have only occasional references to merchants who listed Godmanchester among their lengthy portfolio of rural investments.

In short the very capacity of this place to control so intimately its own local affairs makes this a story of the evolution of a local community. As is pointed out in the Conclusion, the analysis of the Godmanchester experience in Part Two remains rather unique among published studies of comparable settlements so that the few wider interpretations possible at this time have been limited to this concluding chapter.

*
* *

An apology is no longer necessary for studies of settlements of the size and nature of Godmanchester. I owe a debt of gratitude to Peter Clark for introducing me more fully to the objectives and accomplishments of the Urban History and Pre-Modern Town groups as well as the Centre for Urban History of Leicester University. With the progress of investigations by such scholars no doubt in time Godmanchester, with a royal manor with quasi-borough customs, a community with two feet in the agrarian economy yet a few toes in regional commerce, will become less of an oddity. I do hope that adequate recognition is given in the Conclusion to a number of recent monographs that have been of particular assistance in isolating the more singular qualities of the history of Godmanchester. Among authors of such monographs special mention must be made of Marjorie McIntosh for generously sharing with me over many years the fruits of her vigorous research.

The groundwork for this study was made possible by research assistants funded by a grant from the Social Sciences and Humanities Research Council of Canada over the years 1978-1980. It is pleasant to acknowledge the ready co-operation of Mr. A. D. Hill, Senior Archivist, at every stage of assembling documents from the Godmanchester Borough Records. Mr. Walter Enns is owed a special debt of gratitude for the ordered extraction of names and entries from the frankpledge rolls during the tenure of the above grant. More recently, Dr. John Parsons has edited the bailiffs accounts for Appendix 1. The main burden of this study has fallen upon my research assistant Miss Beryl Wells. Not only has she assisted in extractions from court rolls, farm rentals and other records, but she has tested the arrangement of data by various listings in order to bring out many more significant patterns. Finally, she has developed the structure of the various lists in the Appendices and the Tables throughout the volume.

J. A. RAFTIS
Pontifical Institute of Mediaeval Studies,
Toronto, 1989

# Abbreviations and Notes

| | |
|---|---|
| *Colchester* | R. H. Britnell, *Growth and Decline in Colchester, 1300-1525* (Cambridge, 1986) |
| *Havering* | M. K. McIntosh, *Autonomy and Community: The Royal Manor of Havering, 1200-1500* (Oxford, 1986). |
| *The Peasant Land Market* | *The Peasant Land Market in Medieval England*, ed. P. D. A. Harvey (Oxford, 1984). |
| *A Small Town* | J. Ambrose Raftis, *A Small Town in Late Mediaeval England Godmanchester 1278-1400* (Toronto, 1982). |

Godmanchester three-week courts are referred to by the specific day and year.

The frankpledge rolls, drawn up at Michaelmas, are referred to by year only.

In various references to accounts, "E" signifies the Easter account and "M" the Michaelmas account.

For land measurements, "a" indicates acre and "r" the rod.

Part One


Administration and People

Godmanchester had its own version of the administrative reform that was so common to many levels of government in England at one time or another over the second half of the fifteenth century. Retention of records as evidence for the needs of reform would seem to explain the survival of a cluster of listings for the 1480s of those paying to the royal farm. The administrative method employed for assessing the royal farm has been unravelled in Chapter 2 and provides the basis for the economic analysis of the whole volume. One of the fruits of the reform was the more consistent presentation of information about elections of various officials in the Michaelmas court roll. This information provides a context for various other documents so that much of the town government can be outlined in Chapter 1.

Some of the most difficult data for interpretation are entries by purchase to the liberty of Godmanchester, meticulously recorded in court rolls from the fourteenth to the sixteenth centuries. In Chapter 3 these immigrations can be interpreted as administrative policy and related to the economic strata of Chapter 2. On the other hand the register of wills for Godmanchester only survives from the late fifteenth century. In Chapter 4 an effort is made to describe how families performed their administrative roles through the last will and testament. These wills also relate to the economic status of families to be found in Chapter 2. But it is important that some functions of the wills, more particularly the support of guilds, overlap with the town administration through the involvement of the same personnel.

# 1

# Administration and Government

## A. The Role of Officials

Summary statistics of government at Godmanchester stir images in the modern mind of participation, self-government and indeed a Rousseauian idyllic democracy. For the one year 1486, for example, some 40 officials of one sort or another can be identified from court rolls and frankpledge rolls:

POST STREET: 3 jurors; 2 clerks; 1 collector of farm rents
EAST STREET: 3 jurors; 2 clerks; 1 collector of the farm
WEST STREET: 3 jurors; 2 clerks; 1 collector of the farm
ARNYNG STREET: 3 jurors; 2 clerks; 1 collector of the farm
POST and WEST STREETS: 1 collector of rents; 1 collector of the ale; 1 constable; 1 custodian of the church; 1 collector of the view
EAST and ARNYNG STREETS: 1 collector of rents; 1 collector of the ale; 1 constable; 1 custodian of the church; 1 collector of the view.

In addition, there were also for the vill two bailiffs, one sub-bailiff, one custodian of the seals, one hayward, one bellman, one coroner and one custodian of the horses.

Since some posts were held in several-year cycles, and others more or less frequently, a large number of individuals were involved over the span of a decade or two. Between 1485 and 1505, 135 different individuals were involved in one way or another in this administrative system; from 1506 to 1525, 124 individuals participated in the administration of the town. Large numbers indeed for a town that may have numbered about 1200 people at this period of its history!

The lines of authority among the officers of the town can be clearly established. As was the case with other small towns, and with the villages of Huntingdonshire from the late thirteenth century, superior jurisdiction lay with the twelve jurors. The customs of 1465 directed that "election of all officers belonging to the said Commonalty shall be made in the full court next before the Feast of the Nativity of the Virgin Mary by twelve jurors for the time being for the ensuing year."[1] These same customs of 1465 make perfectly clear that the jurors not only elected the bailiffs and other officials of the town but maintained an overview of their performances in areas of discretion and at the presentation of accounts. Unfortunately scholars have been so fascinated with the identification of power in the feudal hierarchy that the role of the jury in village and small town manorial courts has received little attention.

For Godmanchester, as indeed for the villages of Huntingdonshire, a glance at a frankpledge rolls reveals that jury jurisdiction was not a nominal power. Each surviving frankpledge roll shows the agenda of the regular Michaelmas sessions beginning with the report from the bailiffs on the town proper; that is to say, one bailiff detailed the various persons to be assessed for offences along East and Arnyng Streets and then the other bailiff added names, indictments and fines for Post and West Streets. The intimate inspection of each messuage to discover such public nuisances as improper drains, refuse and wood obstructing the public ways could only have been performed by assistants, very likely the sub-bailiff. The roll then lists the various trespasses in fields and meadows. Although these were likely presented by the hayward through the bailiff, the hayward is not indicated in the frankpledge record as such. In similar fashion, those fined for various breaches of the assizes of ale and bread are listed separately in the frankpledge rolls although the names of aletasters and other assize officers are not given. Those charged with assault and related offences were also listed separately but without indications of the role of the constable.

The frankpledge rolls are, then, the final record of judgement by the jurors on the previous year. Fines for the various offences were determined at this court. This was no mean task. In a typical year such as the Michaelmas view of 1498, there were more than 300 entries. The performance of the bailiffs was reviewed and few frankpledge rolls fail to indicate bailiffs being fined for inadequate performance in one capacity or another. For example, at the view of 1498, the bailiffs William Kyng and William Manipenny were fined 12d for wrongful exercise of their office concerning the assize of bread and ale and smaller fines for failing to repair a common path and a ditch. In 1500, the bailiffs William Kyng and John Ussher were fined about ditches. The jurors exercised final jurisdiction, too, over disposition of surplus and arrears of the bailiffs. Important decisions about allowances for expenses of these and other officials, as well as the cancellation of debts, will be illustrated in the second part of this chapter.

---

[1] *A Small Town*, p. 434.

Finally, the jurors would issue local decrees (*statutum est* in the fifteenth century; *ordinatum est* later). At the foot of the frankpledge roll for 1433, for example, is the entry: "The 12 jurors order that all the sons of freemen living within the liberty are free to amend and repair any tenements, lands, meadows and so forth of the freemen, but not of others, under penalty ...." Over the latter part of the century a great variety of such orders appear, dealing with such interesting items as unlicenced greyhounds, repair of ruined messuages, exclusion from the common meadow of horses with mange and taking wages from outsiders.

An unusual record survives among the court books of Godmanchester[2] that would appear to be a notebook for the use of clerks serving the jurors. This Jurors' Book, as it is called here, gives more detail about various actions of the jurors and thereby serves to complement the frankpledge rolls. From the Jurors' Book it is clear that the various decrees of this body were not idle threats. Over the years 1503-1504, John Wylde, miller, was evicted from the liberty for not bringing his indenture before the jurors. Thomas Lockyngton was evicted for "various matters" concerning John Laxton. Richard Stevens, shoemaker, was fined for cutting willows without permission from the bailiffs and for placing two kine in West Meadow "before the day lymyttd." Richard Robyns was compelled to withdraw a suit in the court of common law by the threat of the loss of his liberty. Some other entries of interest are:[3]

> Memo, that on the day of St. Mary Magdaline in the year of the Lord 1488, William Mundeford came before the 12 jurors and sought re-admission to the liberty of the vill, having been deprived (*exoneratus de libertate sua*) of this the previous year for a certain crime, namely, for having broken the statute in that he kept greyhounds within the said liberty contrary to the letter of the statute therein prescribed. And on the same day William was accepted again (*reacceptus*) by those 12 jurors to that liberty and sworn in. And he paid 6s. 8d. as fine for that offence.

> Memo, that on Tuesday before the feast of St. Michael the Archangel in the 4th year of Henry VII (1488), William Pelle came and bought one yard of arable lying at the end of Shebdenbrooke from the 12 jurors. And he gave the 12 jurors 3s. 4d. for that yard. And it was agreed among them that the said William Pelle should pay halfpenny farthing for his rent at term.

---

[2] This is now catalogued as Court Book No. 3., 1488-1635. Prior to the late fifteenth century, the jurors apparentlty enrolled matters of special concern, as one can see by references to "le dezen rolle."

[3] In the modern pagination of the Jurors' Book, these entries are scattered over pages 9-19 and, as with the evictions noted above, virtually disappear from the later years recorded in this Book.

Memo, that on the same day, John Mathieu intending to completely re-build a house, paid 2s. 4d. to the jurors for placing the foundation of this house next the street. And the said jurors designated the location of this foundation at this was established by the measures agreed upon, namely, that the south end should be built as the house of Thomas Fecas and the north end according to the measure determined by the agreement of the 12 jurors.

On the same day Thomas Balle came before the 12 jurors and asked for a piece of timber lying next the house of John Mynsterchambre to repair some faults in the mills and the said 12 jurors gave the piece of timber to that Thomas.

Memo that on Tuesday at the breaking of the rod before the feast of St. Michael the Archangel, 10 Henry VII (1494), John Steucle came before the 12 jurors and received from the said 12 the empty foundation formerly of John Sterlyng and le Remyng for the payment of three shillings one-halfpenny every year and it was agreed that the said three shillings, one-halfpenny, should be recorded in the roll of the town in perpetuity.

Memo that the 12 men have received and discharged John Clarke and William Melbron for all the contention of the house sometime of John Stokis, which the town seised and distrained the said John and William for contention for the debt of the same John Stokis for the which we quit and warrant harmless the said John and William, in the day of St. Matthew 17 Henry VII (1501).

The customs of Godmanchester referring to the jurors' discretion over expenses that are more than petty and the allowances for entertainment, conclude with reference to a town treasure: "Item that all other persons labouring for the common business shall forthwith out of the Treasure of the said Town be rewarded according to the extent of their labour at the discretion of the said twelve Jurymen."[4] The town treasury was in the common hall (court hall). One entry in the Jurors' Book records the jurors by common consent depositing £16 8s. 8d. of good small gold and silver coins in the common chest in the treasury witnessed by the two bailiffs and the clerk of the court, this taking place in the common hall, Monday after Michaelmas, 1476. For the following year, a memo notes the jurors paying out £8 to the bailiffs and from the latter receiving £16 9s. (of which 19d. was not legal) attested by the jurors.[5]

While the jurors may have had final jurisdiction, their actual role in the town was much less than that of the bailiffs. For the real day-by-day government of Godmanchester was under the jurisdiction of the town bailiffs

[4] *A Small Town*, p. 435.
[5] Both entries are from p. 66 of the modern pagination in the Jurors' Book.

elected annually by the jurors.[6] Surviving customs of the town take these ongoing tasks for granted and are obviously concerned to record only the annual obligations concerning byelaws and accounts. One begins to grasp the real scope of the bailiffs' authority when it is seen that these customs are drawn up by the bailiffs[7] and that these customs are implemented by the three-weekly courts of the bailiffs. That is to say, in the fifteenth century, as they have been from the thirteenth century, the courts are the veritable courts of the bailiffs: courts are headed by reference to place, date and name of bailiffs; properties are conveyed "through the hands" of the bailiffs; debt collection procedures take place with the surveillance of the bailiffs; liberty of the town is granted by the bailiffs; and so on.

As has already been intimated in the few remarks above on the frankpledge rolls, the bailiffs could only perform these tasks with the aid of many assistants. Several accounts[8] survive for the bailiffs and these accounts show the bailiff responsible for payments to many officers of the town. While some payments of a specified nature are spread throughout the bailiffs' accounts, seasonal payments for some officials were listed at the end of the account. For example, in the 1483 account of William Frere for the Easter to Michaelmas period we have the following list:

| | |
|---|---|
| To the bailiff for his fee .............................. | 6s. 8d. |
| To John Mynsterchambre for his fee .................... | 6s. 8d. |
| To the clerk of the court for his fee .................... | 6s. 8d. |
| To the same for writing the view ...................... | 2s. 0d. |
| To the clerk of the court, sub-bailiff and hayward in gifts ..... | 18d. |
| To the sub-bailiff for summoning the view of frankpledge ..... | 12d. |
| To the hayward for repairing the park .................... | 6d. |
| To the bailiff, constable and sub-bailiff for the Hundred ...... | 20d. |
| To the sub-bailiff for his fee .......................... | 6s. 0d. |
| To the constables for their fee ........................ | 6s. 8d. |
| To William Tothe for the office of parchment maker ......... | [    ] |
| To the custodian of the seals .......................... | [    ] |
| For the three hundreds at London and Norwich ............ | [    ] |
| Total: ............................................ | £4 0s. 20d. |

---

[6] "Firstly It is statuted that two principal Bailiffs shall be elected in every year by 12 Jurors whoever they may be for that year and the said Jurors shall have [ *blank* ] from one View to another that is to say, to elect to all offices touching the said Commonalty and to do and ordain all things touching the State of the said Town and that the two principal Bailiffs shall be elected from two Streets that is to say from Post Street and Arnyng Street one year and from West Street and East Street another year." See *A Small Town*, p. 434.

[7] Ibid., pp. 434, 436-437.

[8] See below, Appendix 1, pp. 225-260.

For the term from Michaelmas to Easter, 1527, the bailiff John Page concluded his account with the following items:

| | |
|---|---:|
| To the bailiff for his fee .............................. | 6s. 8d. |
| To the bailiff for his hundreds ......................... | 8d. |
| To the sub-bailiff for his fee .......................... | 5s. 0d. |
| To the sub-bailiff for his gift ......................... | 6d. |
| To the hayward for his garment (*toga sua*) ............... | 6s. 8d. |
| To the hayward for his gift ............................ | 6d. |
| To the clerk of the court for his hundreds ................ | 8d. |
| To the sub-bailiff for his hundreds ...................... | 8d. |
| To the clerk of the court for his gift .................... | 6d. |
| For paper and costs to the same clerk ................... | 12d. |
| Total: ........................................... | 22s. 5d. |

However, the full range of responsibilities of the bailiffs can only be seen in their accounting for revenue and expenses. For the five extant accounts from the fifteenth century there are regular items of revenue: the moneys turned over by the jurors from the previous accounting term; revenues from the town mills; payments collected from ale tolls for the four streets; diverse revenues from the three-weekly courts (usually categorized as entry fines, liberty fines and amercements). Incidental revenues varied widely in scope from year to year: money owed the town by former officials and others; profits from town smallholdings in fields and meadows leased or from which crops were sold; the sale of strays and of goods forfeited for felony. Incidental revenues were often small, but they could sometimes be substantial, as with the 32 shillings received from the goods of Thomas Cambridge, forfeited for felony in 1412, or the eleven shillings fourpence received from the sale of willows in 1445.

Whereas the bailiffs could leave the collecting of most revenues to underlings, the disposition of these revenues towards expenses was a much more complicated matter. The bailiffs reported the expenses of the meetings of the jurors, or "12 men,"[9] as they were called. In 1412 the jurors were paid fourpence for attending a session of the royal justice and 19s. 2d. for the day of the view of frankpledge. During the 1445 year of account the jurors were allowed threepence expenses for attending to the will of "Green," seven pence for (attendance on?) the king, threepence concerning the will of John

---

[9] References in this paragraph are to explicit mention of the 12, although frequently it is implied in parallel entries that expenses of the 12 are involved without these being indicated. The jurors were popularly called "the dozen" according to the designation of their rolls. See above, p. 5, note 2.

Herard and 12s. "for their work" (that is, presumably for the view of frankpledge). From Easter to Michaelmas in 1471, the 12 men were allowed sixpence twice for their meetings at the George, sixpence for their meeting at Nottingham (i.e., the home of Nottingham), sevenpence for their session at Cavys, 6s. 1d. at the breaking of the rod, 2s. to John Gyleman for essoins of the 12 men and 38s. 8d. for expenses at the view of frankpledge. From Easter to Michaelmas in 1483 the 12 men were allowed sevenpence, eightpence and 2s. 4d. from the sessoons for expenses at Bigg', 12d. for a session at Cavys when he went to London, eightpence for a meeting at Sydebottoms, tenpence for a meeting at Scots, fourpence for the view of the house of William Ponder, 8s. 4d. for a further meeting at Bigg' for the breaking of the rod and £4 2s. 10d. for the view of frankpledge. In the bailiffs' account for the Michaelmas to Easter term, 1527-1528, the 12 men met three times at Grene's with expenses of eightpence, 12d. and 2s. 2d.[10] The most expensive session was with the bailiffs and constables and included the "etyng of a hare." The 12 men were also allowed 14d. for costs in taking possession of the goods of Gylbard Walshe and fourpence for settling a property arrangement with Master Sewster.

Among the more interesting features of the bailiffs' accounts are the personalized travel expenses of these officials and of others who frequently accompanied them or carried out work for the bailiffs. The bailiffs, constables and sub-bailiffs were allowed 12d. and a halfpenny for expenses, and a further threepence for ale at Huntingdon during Holy Trinity week, 1412, while attending the royal justice of the peace. Threepence were paid for the sustenance of a man and his horse for carrying the writ from the receipts of the farm of the king. Eightpence were also given on this occasion for expenses of the clerk of the Receiver and another man for a meal, as well as for two horses. An additional fourpence went towards expenses of a servant of the Receiver and his horse for supper and the night after the feast of St. Barnabas. Twopence were expended on ale for men coming from Huntingdon to Godmanchester court for Reginald Queneyeve. The bailiffs, constables and sub-bailiffs were again allowed expenses (12½d.) for their appearance before the justice at Huntingdon on the Wednesday after the feast of St. James the Apostle. In the same account, William Croxton was allowed fourpence

---

[10] It is interesting to note that the building of the Court Hall did not terminate meetings at various houses in the town, much as 200 years earlier (*A Small Town*, pp. 59-60). Several of those places of meetings noted in this paragraph were the homes of clerks. There seems to have been two separate parties at Michaelmas 1508, since the bailiffs accounted for a reception for the 12 jurors (20s.) and another for the officials (16s.).

expenses for going to Higham Ferrers at Michaelmas with a servant of the Receiver and Reginald Queneyeve was paid 2s. 2d. for going to London.

On the 1445 account the bailiffs noted expenses for the sherriff's tourn at St. Neots, Cambridge and Toseland; at Huntingdon for attaching John Myllor and twice for proclaiming strays; for Reginald Quenyeve travelling by horse to the hundred court to present "causes" of the vill; for the sessions at Huntingdon and at Kimbolton, for travelling to London by horse for writs. 1483 included along with the usual trips to London and Huntingdon, travel to Barnwell, Bury, Houghton, Norwich, Ramsey, St. Ives, Stanton and Warboys.

The bailiffs could be kept exceptionally occupied some years by extraordinary business of the town. In the 1412 account there were more than a score of cost items, including much travel, associated with a project to obtain timber from the woods of Potton. During 1471 Godmanchester was caught up in the troubled affairs of the crown and the bailiffs accounted for the costly levy to the crown, payments to a variety of nobles, and much travel. On the other hand, each of the summer term accounts show a great variety of expenses for going about the parish to view goods, houses, lands, meadows, fences, bridges, ditches and so forth.

This responsibility of the bailiffs for the travel expenses and other costs as well as regular fees and wages reached levels of considerable refinement. Gratuities were the order of the day, especially where the royal justices, receivers of the royal farm and other royal officials were concerned. The bailiffs accounted for the parchment and ink of the clerk. In 1445, eightpence was expended on a horn for the hayward. Nor could cultural costs be ignored: sometime during the summer of 1412, fourpence were given to "players for their recitation of a play"; and in the summer of 1445 "two men were paid 12d. for playing in the cemetary of the church."

The personal responsibility of the bailiffs ultimately involved the bailiffs themselves as debtors or creditors. Although the customs do not alert us to this fact, one of the two bailiffs was the head bailiff for each term, that is to say, the bailiff with ultimate responsibility for the accounts of his co-bailiff. In 1412, for example, this head bailiff was Thomas Gyldene. The accounts for that summer show Thomas Gyldene paying 12d. "from his own purse." This same account also shows Thomas finalizing the receipts and expenses of his fellow bailiff, John Howman. On the last portion of this manuscript Thomas Gyldene summarizes his account for the end of the term by listing eight debts that he owes (total: £47 9s. 1d. ob. q.) and 11 debts owed to him (£47 3s. 7d. q.).

In contrast with the bailiffs, those many officials who reported to the bailiffs had quite specific and limited areas of responsibility. A unique document helps to illustrate this point. This is a manuscript[11] entitled "Extraction of the fines for the view held there [Godmanchester] on the feast of St. Michael the Archangel, 1498"; on the top of the manuscript is written "Post Street and West Street." Every one of the 150 entries in this document can be found in the frankpledge roll for that year, although in the latter roll the entries are mixed with those from the other two streets. In short, officials had presented a list of names and charges to the view of frankpledge and the collectors of the fines required an extracted list of the individuals so charged from the streets for which they were responsible together with a specified amount of money to collect.

The small bits and pieces that survive from the accounts of other officials further confirm their limited accounting responsibilities. For example, appended to the frankpledge roll for the year 1433 is the Constable's Roll for that year. This roll indicates, too, that normally the tasks of the constables and coroners were few and occasional by contrast with the bailiffs. There were only 12 entries in the Constable's Roll for 1433, all but one about assault and raising the hue, and five of the 12 about the same assault incident. However, since "Mynstrechambre conestable" appears before that list of outsiders having property in Godmanchester on the 1464 list (discussed in Chapter 3 below) it may be presumed that the constable had collected these names and may have had a special responsibility for such "foreigners."

As will be seen below, the posts of coroner and, to a lesser degree constable were deemed to be suitable only for those townsmen as worthy as bailiffs. These tasks were intimately tied in with the peace keeping of the realm and so did not require special notice in the local Godmanchester customs. Two coroners appear among the elected officials of Godmanchester only from the last quarter of the fifteenth century although the election of constables had been noted from the previous century. While no reference is made in the customs to regulations governing the election of constables, it is clear from one entry with respect to sureties that there are expected to be two constables.

## B. Administrative Personnel

The large number of officials and their varied roles must have challenged to the full the native administrative talents of a small town like Godmanchester. Four qualities can be discerned in the selection of various officials of the town: representation, property, leadership and specialized skills.

---

[11] Huntington Record Office, Godmanchester Borough Records, Box 8, Other Documents of Henry VII, Miscellaneous, no. 4, catalogued as "Copy of Frankpledge fines 14 Henry VII."

Efforts were made by the customs of Godmanchester to maintain a representative base among town administrators: "the two principal Bailiffs shall be elected from two Streets that is to say from Post Street and Arnyng Street one year and from West Street and East Street another year."[12] It should be recalled from the previous section that as a matter of fact each bailiff represented two streets, that is, the bailiffs from either Post or West Street was responsible for both of these streets, just as the bailiff from Arnyng or East Street was responsible for both Arnyng and East Street. The same representative quality was sought for the jurors: "That the Bailiffs for the time being shall elect ordain and empanell twelve honest men that is to say from every Street three to occupy the view and for the year ensuing."[13]

From the very complete information available about officials in fifteenth- and sixteenth-century Godmanchester it is easy to ascertain that these customary regulations were observed to the letter. Here is one example of the actual personnel list obtainable from election entries:

In the first year of the reign of Henry VIII (1509)

*Coroners*
John Brandon for East and Arnyng Streets
William Kyng for Post and West Streets

*Bailiffs*
John Stukeley for East and Arnyng Streets
John Lawe for Post and West Streets

*Constables*
William Orwell for East and Arnyng Streets
Richard Smyth for Post and West Streets

*Clerks of the Farm*
For East Street, William Diggby, his clerk Richard Verly
For Arnyng Street, John Frere, his clerk Thomas Pacy
For Post Street, William Aylred, his clerk [not given]
For West Street, Robert Punt, his clerk William Mynt

*Collectors of the View*
For Post and West Streets, John Salmon, his clerk Robert Punt
For East and Arnyng Streets, John Est, his clerk Richard Verly

*Custodians of the Church*
William Granger and William Pelman

---

[12] See *A Small Town*, p. 434.
[13] Ibid., p. 441.

*Collector of the Ale Toll*
   Thomas Lovell for all the streets

*Hayward*
   William Freman

*Custodian of the Seals*
   William Lord

*Clerk of the Court*
   William Mynt
*Bellman*
   Robert Olyff (Aleyff)

*Sub-Bailiff*
   William Lord

*Jurors*
   Post Street: William Dalton, mercer
                John Robyns
                Robert Whyte

   West Street: John Gybbys
                John Robyns
                John Laxton

   East Street: John Bonfay
                John Page
                Richard Scot

   Arnyng Street: William Arnold
                  William Frost
                  William Mundeford


   This large number of officials, many on a system of rotation, indicates at
once that the administration of Godmanchester involved more than a small
clique of clerks and officials. Unfortunately, that main source of information
about Godmanchester people throughout most of its knowable medieval
history, the court rolls, give only the names of bailiffs for the first two
hundred years (1270s to 1470s) of the extant series. Throughout the greater
part of this period bailiffs appear as specialized officials in the sense that a
few predominated for long periods of time: Henry Rode appeared as a bailiff
at the head of court rolls for at least 25 years between 1292 and 1322; the
names of William Aylred and Godfrey Manipenny dominated the 1330s and
1340s; Alan Aylred and John Manipenny appeared as bailiffs for long
periods of time over the 1350s and '60s; John Curl appeared as bailiff during
the years 1378-1381 and again over 1384-1386.

This same pattern continued well into the third quarter of the fifteenth century through the family Queneve (later more commonly known as Conyff). Although the distinct identity of each Queneve individual cannot be established, the pattern of this family appearance as bailiff is clear enough: Reginald Queneve: 1414, 1418, 1419; Reginald Queneve senior: 1418-1423, 1436; Reginald Queneve junior: 1427, 1428; John Queneve: 1429, 1430, 1443, 1451 (West Street); John Queneve senior (East Street): 1434, 1440, 1451; John Queneve: 1436, 1442; John Queneve, farmer, junior: 1437, 1439; Reginald Queneve: 1441, 1444, 1447, 1452, 1459-1461, 1466; Reginald Queneve (East Street): 1452; Richard Queneve: 1442, 1463-1464; Richard Queneve (West Street): 1452; Reginald Queneve: 1475, 1478; Robert Queneve: 1475. Both court rolls and frankpledge rolls can be used to establish the bailiffs for the fifteenth century. Despite the fact the names of bailiffs cannot be discovered for some half dozen years, the Queneve or Conyff family dominated the post of bailiff from 1414 through the 1460s and indeed on several occasions provided both of the bailiffs for the one year.

The fact that these bailiffs held office for such long stretches of time indicates that they were specially skilled and trained for the task. Although it can be ascertained from further court roll contexts and other records that these leading bailiffs were no doubt among the wealthier individuals of their time, wealth was not a unique criterion. Some wealthier individuals did not appear at all as bailiffs. Some wealthy individuals of the late thirteenth and early fourteenth centuries, such as Adam Grinde, were not prominent as bailiffs. Adam Grinde was a bailiff for three years and in this respect is typical of those "other" bailiffs who served along with long-term bailiffs over the next two centuries. These bailiffs who held office for a year or two would have more curtailed tasks, as we have seen above, and in consequence would not need to be as professional. On the other hand, this system allowed the secondary or short-term bailiff to become a post that would engage a large number of townsmen over the years.

By the 1480s a new pattern is discernible in the election of bailiffs at Godmanchester. From this time, and perhaps from the 1470s, although data are too exiguous during that decade for firm conclusions, no individual dominates the post of bailiff for any great period of time. In order to picture the new election results it becomes necessary to draw on the data available for the election of all officials. With the appearance of the court book register from the mid 1480s to replace the traditional court roll, the names of those elected to various offices were entered around the time of the Michaelmas court session. Prior to this court book, the names of officials elected around Michaelmas were given at the foot of the frankpledge rolls. This is not surprising since, as we have seen in the first section of this chapter, the frankpledge roll was the jurors' roll and the jurors by custom elected these various officials sometime around Michaelmas. Why the clerks began to enter the Michaelmas elections on the court or bailiffs' rolls is not clear. Certainly the bailiffs had a responsibility for appointing the jurors; but the list of jurors is not consistently entered with other elected officials on the court rolls and for the following list the number of officials has often to be supplied from the head of the frankpledge roll.

TABLE 1: NUMBER OF OFFICIALS ELECTED FROM 1421-1548

| YEAR | NUMBER | YEAR | NUMBER |
|------|--------|------|--------|
| 1421 | 39 | 1481 | 35 |
| 1422 | ? | 1482 | 19 |
| 1428 | ? | 1483 | (missing) |
| 1429 | 34 | 1484 | 15 |
| 1433 | 38 | 1485 | 21 |
| 1434 | 38 | 1486 | 23 |
| 1435 | 27 | 1487 | 23 |
| 1436 | 36 | 1488 | 20 |
| 1437 | ? | 1489 | 22 |
| 1438 | 35 | 1490 | 22 |
| 1439 | 35 | 1491 | 23 |
| 1440 | 34 | 1492 | 21 |
| 1441 | 12 | 1493 | 23 |
| 1442 | 17 | 1494 | 23 |
| 1443 | ? | 1495 | 22 |
| 1444 | 38 | 1496 | 23 |
| 1447 | 35 | 1497 | 21 |
| 1448 | 39 | 1498 | 22 |
| 1449 | ? | 1499 | 20 |
| 1450 | 35 | 1500 | 33 |
| 1451 | 39 | 1501 | 23 |
| 1452 | 38 | 1502 | 37 |
| 1453 to 1458 | (missing) | 1503 | 35 |
| 1459 | 33 | 1504 | 37 |
| 1460 | 39 | 1505 | 33 |
| 1461 | 31 | 1506 | 38 |
| 1462 | 35 | 1507 | 34 |
| 1463 | 39 | 1508 | 25 (coroners, |
| 1464 | 36 | | bailiffs and |
| 1465 | 39 | | constables missing) |
| 1466 | 35 | 1509 | 39 |
| 1467 | 40 | 1510 | 39 |
| 1468 | ? | 1511 | 35 |
| 1469 | ? | 1512 | 39 |
| 1470 | ? | 1513 | 37 |
| 1471 | 12 (no elections) | 1514 | 38 |
| 1472 | 12 (no elections) | 1515 | 38 |
| 1473 to 1480 | (missing) | 1516 | 38 |

| Year | Number | Year | Number |
|------|--------|------|--------|
| 1517 | 39 | 1533 | 38 |
| 1518 | 38 | 1534 | 38 |
| 1519 | 38 | 1535 | 38 |
| 1520 | 39 | 1536 | 38 |
| 1521 | 39 | 1537 | 38 |
| 1522 | 39 | 1538 | 38 |
| 1523 | 39 | 1539 | 39 |
| 1524 | 39 | 1540 | 38 |
| 1525 | 40 | 1541 | 39 |
| 1526 | 40 | 1542 | 40 |
| 1527 | 40 | 1543 | 40 |
| 1528 | 38 | 1544 | 40 |
| 1529 | 39 | 1545 | 40 |
| 1530 | (missing) | 1546 | 40 |
| 1531 | 38 | 1547 | 39 |
| 1532 | 37 | 1548 | 39 |

This list shows that frankpledge rolls survive in good series for only two decades, the 1440s and 1460s. For the 1440s the incomplete list of bailiffs for several years makes impossible a sequence of officials for more than five years. While the sequence of elected officials is complete for much of the 1460s, the records are still not adequate for analysis of the rotation system by comparison with the period after 1485.

The more complete election lists on the court book after 1485 makes possible the reconstruction of the rotation of officials over many years.[14] As Appendix 2 shows, most of the officials were elected over periods of time much longer than a decade. The rotation required by the system of representation by street and year explains the changes in official positions every year but it does not explain the variety in sequences among individual officers. Since there was no longer one "professional" bailiff to perform this office for many years, it is not surprising to find that those who were bailiffs more than once were given relief from the onerous task for several years. In the previous section it has been noted that the offices of constables and coroners were not normally very demanding and in consequence it would not have been unduly difficult to be a constable or coroner and even a juror, before and after the year as bailiff. There are many examples of this sequence in Appendix 2, such as William Orwell, Thomas Maryot and John Ussher.

[14] Appendix 2. "The Rotation System for Officials," pp. 261-278.

What does appear as an administrative innovation from the 1480s is the government of the town by a corps of officials. Excluding those who were co-opted into the corps over a few years for two or three posts, there were 57 main officials at Godmanchester between 1480 and 1548. The cycles are individual to a degree, that is to say, these varied from one person to another. But there were common patterns. As the following Rotation List shows, it was the common practice to elect freemen as bailiffs only after some years in apprenticeship with less demanding posts. Furthermore, those with a long tenure among the corps of officials usually maintained this role through other administrative functions, such as collectors of one sort or another (William King, Richard Smith, William Frost senior, William Diggby, John Stukeley, John Armyt, Thomas Lockyngton, William Frere, John Betrych). Since collectors of various sorts required the services of clerks, these responsibilities would seem to indicate individuals with considerable expertise at hand for the normal routine of their lives.

All these chief officers were major property holders, but not all major property holders held office and it is not possible to correlate individual cycles with amounts of property held. Not surprisingly in view of the jealous concern of the townsmen, the larger ecclesiastical property holders such as the Prior of Merton and the vicar of the parish church were never elected. Nor were the knights such as Guido Wulfston, who had bought heavily into Godmanchester but may not have lived there regularly; nor were other wealthy newcomers, such as Thomas Fyncham and John Fisher (alderman from London), perhaps as we shall see below,[15] because they were short-term investers in the town. Some prominent trades people such as Thomas Baker, Matthew Garnet and Marcus Lorydan were also not elected. And of course, women of substance like Anna Plumpton and Margaret Balle were never called.

TABLE 2: THE MAIN CORPS OF OFFICIALS CA. 1480-1548

| NAME | DATE | DUTIES* |
|---|---|---|
| William Snell | 1471-1505 | J. J. J. J. J. J. CF. J + CC. J. CF. J. CO |
| John Aylred | 1472-1503 | CO. CON. BA. BA. CO. CON. BA. CO + J |
| John Robyn | 1477-1509 | J. J. CC. CON. J. BA. CO. J. J. |
| William Aylred | 1481-1515 | J. BA. J. CF + CC. CF. J. CON. BA. CO. |
| William Frere | 1481-1493 | BA. CO. BA. CO. BA. BA |

* BA = Bailiff; CA = Collector of the Ale; CC = Custodian of the Church; CF = Collector of the Farm; CO = Coroner; CON = Constable; CV = Collector of the View; J = Juror

---

[15] Chapter 6, pp. 162-166.

| NAME | DATE | DUTIES |
|---|---|---|
| William King | 1481-1528 | J. CA. CV. CC. CF. J. J. BA. CO. CO. J. CON. BA. CO. CO. CF. J. CF. CON. J. CF |
| John Lockyngton | 1481-1495 | CF. BA. CO. J. CON. CO. CF. J. BA. J |
| William Moundford | 1481-1515 | J. J. CC. CF. J. CF. J. CON. CF. BA. CO. CV. CON. J. CON J. CF. CF. |
| William Orwell | 1481-1510 | J. J. CON. BA. CO. CON. J. BA. CO. BA. CO. CF. J. BA. CO. CF. CON. J. |
| John Stukeley | 1481-1514 | CF. CF. J. CF. CF. J. CF. CON. BA. CO. CV. CON. J. CON. J. CF. CF. |
| Edward Barre | 1485-1491 | J. CC. BA. CO. J. |
| John Bayous senior | 1485-1488 | CON. BA. J. |
| John Bower | 1485-1491 | BA. J. BA. |
| John Sent | 1485-1491 | CON. CON. BA |
| John Smith | 1485-1495 | J. CF. J. BA. CO. |
| Richard Smith (Samt) | 1486-1512 | CON. CO + J. CF. CF. J. CON. CF. J. CO. CF. CO. CF. CON. BA. CO. J. |
| William Stodale | 1486-1491 | J. CON. J. BA. |
| John Bould | 1487-1502 | CON. J. CV. CON. CF + J. J. J. CON. BA. |
| William Frost senior | 1487-1511 | BA. CC. CF. J. CF. BA. J. CON. CF. CC. J. CO. J. J. J. J. |
| Thomas Laxton | 1487-1497 | CC. BA. BA. J. J. |
| Thomas Maryot | 1487-1504 | CF. J. J. CO. BA. CO. CON. CF. BA. |
| John Barnard | 1488-1500 | J. J. CON. BA. CO. J. J. J + SBA. |
| John Bonfay | 1488-1518 | J. J. CF. J. BA. CO. J. CON. J. J. J. J. J. J. J. |
| Thomas Fecas | 1488-1494 | CF. CON. CF + SBA. J. |
| William Diggby | 1489-1528 | J. J. CF. CF. J. J. CON. CF. BA. CO. J. CON. BA. CO. CF. CON. BA. CO. J. |
| William Manipenny | 1489-1501 | BA. CO. J. CON. BA. CO. J. BA. |
| John Page | 1489-1526 | J. J. J. CV. CC. J. BA. J. J. CF. |
| John Laxton | 1490-1525, 1534 | J. J. BA. CO. J. CF. CON. BA. BA. J. J. J. CF. BA. CO. CON. J. J. |
| John Ussher | 1491-1503 | J. CON. CO. CON. BA. CO. CO. CO. J. |
| John Barnard senior | 1492-1494 | CON. CO. |
| Robert Chandeler | 1495-1513 | CF. CON. BA. CO. J. CON. CF. CON. BA. CO. CF. |
| John Armyt | 1496-1520 | CV. CF. J. CC. CF. CC. J. CF. J. CON. CF. CON. BA. |
| William Vyntner | 1496-1513 | CF. CON. BA, CO. J. CON. CF. CON. BA. CO. CF. |
| John Clerk | 1502-1507 | CON. CO. BA. |
| John Frere | 1503-1545 | CF. J. CF. BA. CO. CO. BA. CO + J. CON. BA. CO. J. CF. CON. BA. CO. J. CON. CO. J. CON. BA. CO. CV. CO. CF. BA. CO. J. J. CF. |
| Thomas Lockyngton | 1503-1543 | J. J. J. CF. J. J. CF. J. CC. J. CON. CF + J. J. CF. J. CF. CON. J. CF. BA. CO. CF. CON. |
| William Mynt | 1503,1522 | CV. CO. |
| John Brandon | 1505-1527 | J. CO. J. CF. CF. CF. J. BA. CO. J. |
| William Dalton | 1505-1520, 1534-1536 | CF. J. CF. BA. CO. CON. CON. J. J. |
| John Lawe | 1509-1512 | BA. CO. CON. |
| John Salmon | 1509-1526 | CF. J. CF. J. BA. CO. J. CF. |
| William Stukeley | 1510, 1517, 1519 | CV. CV. CO |

| NAME | DATE | DUTIES |
|---|---|---|
| William Dalton, farmer | 1511-1518 | J. BA. CO. |
| John Punt | 1512-1532 | J. CON. CO. J + CON. BA. CO. CF. J. CON. J. J. CF. BA. CO. |
| William Townshend | 1512-1525 | J. CC + J. BA. CO. BA. CO. CON. CF. |
| Richard Robyn | 1513-1548 | CF. CON. J. BA. CO. CF. J. BA. CO. BA. CO. CF. J. BA. CO. J. CON. J. J. CO. BA. CO. |
| John Page senior | 1493, 1514-1528 | CF + J. CF. J. CO. CC. J. CF. BA. CO. |
| John Boleyn | 1515-1545 | CA. J. CC. J. CC. J. CF. J. CON. J. J. BA. CO. J. J. CON. J. CF. J. CON. |
| Henry Frere | 1515-1548 | CV. J. CON. BA. CO. J. CF. J. CON. BA. CO. J. CF. J. BA. CO. BA. CO. |
| Robert Pelle | 1520-1538 | CF. CO. BA. CO. CON. J. CF. J. |
| Robert Staughton | 1520-1544 | CF. CON. BA. CO. BA. CO. J. CON. BA. J. BA. CO. J. CON. BA. CO. J. CON. J. BA. CO. |
| John Vyntner | 1520-1541 | CF. CON. J. CC. BA. CO. CON. CF. CO. J. CON. J. CF. J. CON. BA. CO. J. CF. |
| John Matthew | 1521-1547 | CF. CV. J. CC. CC. J. J. BA. CO. |
| William Frere | 1522-1543 | CF. BA. CO. J. CON. J. CF. CF. J. J. CF. J. J. J. BA. CO. |
| John Betrych | 1525-1547 | J. CF. CC. BA. CO. J. CF. J. J. CF. J. CF. J. BA. CON. J. CF. |
| Thomas Tryg | 1527-1545 | J. BA. CO. J. J. CON. J. CF. J. CON. CF. J. CF. J. CF. J. BA. CO. CON. |
| John Granger | 1529-1548 | CC. J. J. CF. CON. J. CON. J. CO. BA. BA. |
| William Herdman | 1529-1548 | CF. J. J. BA. CO. J. CON. BA. J. CON. J. CON. |
| Richard Frere | 1531-1535 | CON. J. BA. CO. |
| John Slow senior | 1531-1548 | BA. CO. J. CON. BA. J. CF. J. BA. J. CON. CF. |
| John Grace | 1532-1533 | BA. CO. |
| John Page | 1532-1544 | CON. BA. CO. J. J. J. CF. J. CF. J. CF. J. |
| Thomas Punt | 1538-1548 | J. CF. J. BA. CO. J. CON. CF. |
| William Sewster | 1539-1547 | BA. CO. BA. CO. |
| Robert Croft | 1543-1548 | CON. BA. CO. CF. |

Why does a corps of officials figure so prominently from the 1480s? As far as the records allow, available information points to two explanations. First, as will be seen in the next chapter, there *was* a corps of wealthy townsmen available for such responsibilities. And secondly, the disastrous finances of the town prior to the Tudor period must have made the post of bailiff too heavy for any one person. A large portion of the Jurors' Book, some 50 pages, are dedicated to recording the debts owed by bailiffs at the end of the year and as well from time to time at the Easter term. This record begins at Michaelmas 1474, and for a few years shows the jurors struggling with collection on the farm payment for the king and acknowledging debts owed to bailiffs, most frequently from millers. By 1477 the jurors were making a vigorous effort to recover arrears from the bailiffs themselves within a year after their yearly term of office.[16] In 1477 William Stodale was fined 20 shillings for not having paid off the final arrears (7s.) within the prescribed date. After Michaelmas 1480 John Bayous was able to pay off all of the £5 arrears except 5 shillings and was excused the latter amount on condition that he must pay a 20 shilling fine should he ask for any more expense allowances. At Michaelmas 1491 Thomas Laxton owed £4. 6s. 8d., was allowed 10s. 4d. ob. and paid off 36s. 4d. by 5 October; of the 39s. 11d. ob. still owed, Thomas paid off 26s. 7d. by 18 December but the jurors were still not satisfied and seized two of his horses in distraint.

These three tidbits of information about William Stodale, John Bayous and Thomas Laxton are unusual detail for the Jurors' Book. But even in these three instances we do not know whether the jurors were being unusually harsh. Nor do we know why the jurors were being very lenient in some instances. For example, Edward Barre was able to pay off little more than £1 of the £11 10s. he owed at Michaelmas 1489, yet he was quitted of the £10 3s. arrears. In the following year, Thomas Laxton was quitted of some £2 of arrears. The answer to such decisions lies, no doubt, in missing bailiff rolls and thence in the economy of the town for that year. But it is clear that annual endebtedness had become such a regular feature of the town of Godmanchester that only bailiffs with capital of their own could entertain the possibility of accepting the post. Even those who did accept would be unwise to do so frequently and certainly not for more than one year at a time!

Following is a list of arrears of bailiffs by the Easter (E) term or following Michaelmas (M) of their year as bailiff:

TABLE 3: BAILIFF'S ARREARS[17]

| 1478(M) | William Aylred | £4. |
|---|---|---|
| 1479(M) | William Frere | £4. |
| 1480(M) | John Barnard | £10. 4s. 8d. |
| | John Bayous | £5. |

[16] This ties in chronologically with the issue of a statute by the jurors in 1475 and its re-issue the following year. "Statutes made at a View of Frankpledge in the 15th year of the Reign of King Edward the Fourth also in the 16th year of his Reign by 12 jurors That if either of the Bailiffs or Officers being or dwelling within the Liberty shall be in any arrear of Account concerning his Office in any sum of money due to the Town and Commonalty he shall from henceforth be wholly deprived ... of all Offices within the Liberty until such Officer shall be clearly discharged by the 12 Jurors for the time being and be entirely acquitted of the said Debt within a day and year after his Account under the pain of losing 20s. for every year as often as the said Accountant shall be in any parcel in arrear." *A Small Town*, p. 437.

The Jurors' Book records the immediate application of this new regulation as William Stodale was fined 20s. (17 Ed. IV) for having debts during his term as bailiff and not paying these off by the fixed day (*fregit diem*).

[17] Since these debt entries are too brief for a detailed analysis of the individual bailiffs, these entries are transcribed here as they appear in the Jurors' Book. On some pages the chronologi-

| 1482(M) | William Frere | £4. |
|---|---|---|
| 1482(E) | " " | £7. 8s. 7d. ob. |
| 1483(E) | John Mynsterchambre | £9. 6s. 4d. |
| 1483(M) | " " | £8. |
| 1483(E) | John Aylred | £4. |
| 1483(M) | " " | £4. 0s. 5d. |
| 1484(M) | William Stodale | £5. 11s. 11d. ob. q. |
| 1485(E) | William Aylred | £7. 11s. 11d. ob. q. |
| 1485(M) | John Lockyngton | £5. 14s. 1d. |
| 1486(E) | " " | £5. 2s. 10d. |
| 1486(E) | John Bour | £9. 6s. 4d. |
| 1486(M) | " " | £7. 19s. ob. q. |
| 1486(M) | William Frere | £7. 4s. 7d. ob. |
| 1487(E) | John Mynsterchambre | £6. 16s. 4d. ob. |
| 1487(M) | John Bayous | £2. 1s. 8d. |
| 1488(E) | William Frost | £8. 15s. 4d. |
| 1488(M) | William Frere | £7. 16s. 10d. |
| 1489(E) | Edward Barre | £12. 9s. 9d. ob. q. |
| 1489(M) | " " | £11. 10s. |
| 1490(M) | Thomas Laxton | £9. 9s. 1d. q. |
| 1490(M) | William Manipenny | £10. 1s. 11d. q. |
| 1490(E) | John Aylred | £1. 11s. 6d. ob. |
| 1491(E) | William Orwell | £1. 19s. 9d. ob. |
| 1492(M) | Thomas Laxton | £4. 6s. 8d. |
| 1492(E) | John Bour | £3. 16s. ob. |
| 1494(M) | William Frere | £3. 15s. 1d. |
| 1494(M) | William Frere | £3. 10d. ob. q. |
| 1495(E) | John Smyth | £4. 5s. ob. |
| 1495(M)? | John Aylred | £2. 17s. 7d. ob. |
| ? | Thomas Maryot | 3s. 4d. |
| ? | John Ussher | 17s. 8d. ob. |
| 1497(E) | John Bonsay | £2. 6s. 6d. ob. |
| 1496(M) | John Bayous | £4. 3s. 2d. ob. |
| 1498(E) | William King | £4. 12s. 7d. |
| 1498(M) | William Manipenny | 19s. 5d. ob. |
| 1499(E) | William Orwell | £3. 9s. 4d. ob. |
| 1499(M) | John Laxton | £1. 19s. 5d. ob. |
| 1500(E) | William King | £2. 3s. |
| 1501(E) | William Orwell | 0 |
| 1501(E) | John Robyn | 0 |
| 1502(E) | William Frost | 0 |
| 1502(M) | John Ussher | £1. 18s. 4d. ob. |
| 1503(M) | John Ussher | £1. 13s. 8d. surplus |
| 1503(E) | John Bould | £1. 4s. |
| 1504(M) | John Stukeley | 0 |
| 1504(M) | Robert Chandeler | 0 |
| 1505(E) | William Orwell | 27s. 7d. |

cal order does not appear to be exact. Occasionally, in fact, no date is given with the entry, so the presumed date from the context is given. In a few instances debts may have carried over from previous terms as bailiffs. Where no debt is entered, it may often be presumed that there was a debt but this was paid off prior to the clerk's entry in the Jurors' Book.

| | | |
|---|---|---|
| 1505(M) | Thomas Maryot | 17s. 9d. |
| 1506(E) | William Moundford | 48s. 9d. |
| 1506(M) | John Clerk | £4. 0s. 9d. |
| 1507(E) | William King | £4. 10s. |
| 1507(M) | John Laxton | 15s. 6d. |
| 1508(E) | John Laxton | 35s. 4d. |
| 1508(M) | John Clerk | 13s. 6d. |
| 1508(M) | John Brandon | £4. 16s. 3d. ob. |
| 1509(E) | William King | 22s. 2d. |
| 1509(E) | John Stukeley | 33s. 7d. ob. |
| 1510(M) | William King | 13s. 6d. |
| 1511(E) | William Diggby | 26s. 0d. |
| 1511(M) | Richard Smith | £4. 3s. 6d. |
| 1512(E) | John Stukeley | 46s. 7d. |
| 1512(M) | Robert Chandeler | 23s. 4d. |
| 1513(E) | William Vyntner | £4. 4s. 1d. |
| 1513(M) | John Frere | 36s. 7d. ob. |
| 1513(E) | William Aylred | 29s. 8d. ob. |
| 1514(M) | William Dalton | 35s. 7d. ob. |
| 1514(E) | William Diggby | 22s. 6d. |
| 1515(M) | John Lockyngton | 15d. ob. |
| 1515(E) | John Lockyngton | 46s. 10d. |
| 1516(M) | John Punt | 52s. 0d. |
| 1517(E) | William Vyntner | 33s. 2d. |
| 1517(M) | John Frere | £4. 8s. 5d. |
| 1518(E) | William Dalton, farmer | 40s. 11d. |
| 1518(M) | William Dalton, merchant | £10. 5s. 0d. |
| 1518(E) | John Page | 28s. 1d. |
| 1519(M) | John Laxton | £ 5. 2s. 5d. |
| 1519(E) | William Townshend | £4. 13s. 5d. |
| 1520(E) | Robert Pelle | 29s. 0d. |
| 1521(M) | John Frere | £3. 10s. 7d. ob. |
| 1522(E) | William Townshend | £4. 16d. |
| 1522(M) | William Mynt | 34s. 3d. |
| 1523(E) | Robert Pelle | 28s. 1d. |
| 1523(M) | Richard Robyns | 31s. 5d. |
| 1524(E) | Robert Staughton | 41s. 3d. ob. |
| 1525(M) | John Salmon | 39s. 1d. ob. |
| 1525(E) | John Brandon | 59s. 1d. |
| 1526(M) | William Frere | 13s. 11d. |
| 1526(E) | Robert Staughton | £3. 12s. 10d. |
| 1527(M) | John Vyntner | £3. 5s. 3d. |
| 1527(E) | William Diggby | £3. 8s. 11d. |
| 1528(M) | John Frere | £3. 19s. 8d. |
| 1528(E) | John Page | 30s. 4d. |
| 1529(M) | Henry Frere | 2s. 0d. |
| | John Beterych | 19s. 10d? |
| 1529(M) | Richard Robyns | 40s. 6d. |
| 1539(E) | Richard Howson | 52s. 11d. ob. |
| 1531(M) | Henry Frere | £3. 4s. 0d. |
| 1532(E) | John Vyntner | £4. 8s. ob. |
| 1532(M) | John Frere | £4. 18s. 6d. |

While many of the freemen of Godmanchester performed various administrative tasks early in their career, or had the resources to do so over a longer
period of time, it is clear from a number of career patterns that administration
as distinct from more discretionary roles of government could be a distinct
official pattern. Gathered in the following list are those who were collectors
of the farm, of fines from the view of frankpledge, of fines from the aletoll
and of sub-bailiffs. The sub-bailiffs (William Abram, John Blaxton, Richard
Blaxton, John Holme, William Ibott junior, William Lord, William Osteler)
seem to indicate an increasing tendency towards full-time professionalism.
More will be said of the significance of this tendency in Chapter 6 below.
Even the sub-bailiff, however, could be elected occasionally as custodian of
ale. Others of this secondary group were elected church wardens from time
to time. After two constables became necessary, one of the constables was
frequently taken from this secondary group, as might be one of the jurors,
although Augustine Arnold and John Gybbys became regular jurors. On the
whole then, this secondary corps provided professional services and were
called upon from time to time to participate in the work of the main
governing body of the time.

TABLE 4: THE SECONDARY CORPS OF OFFICIALS

| NAME | DATE | DUTIES* |
|---|---|---|
| Thomas Mayle | 1472-1499, 1505 | J. J. CF. J. J. J. CON. CF. |
| John Gardner | 1481-1487 | J. CC. J. |
| Robert Marshall | 1482-1489 | CA. CV. CV. |
| Thomas Burton | 1485-1504 | CC. CF. J. CF. CF. J. CC. CF. |
| John Gybbys | 1485-1501, 1509, 1517 | CF. CF. J. CON. CF. J. J. J. J. J. |
| William Ibott junior | 1485-1518 | SBA. SBA. J. CV. SBA. SBA. SBA. SBA. SBA |
| John Turneskewe | 1485-1504 | CF. CC. CF. CF. J. CC. CF. CON. |
| William Dey | 1486-1503 | CA. J. CF. CF. CF. |
| William Lessy | 1486-1498 | J. CC. J. |
| John Garlop | 1487-1498 | CA. CV. J. |
| Richard Stukeley | 1487-1492 | CV. CV. |
| John Adam | 1488-1496, 1502 | CV. J. J. J. CF. J. |
| John Miles | 1488-1494 | SBA. CV. CV. |
| John Clerk alias Chese | 1489, 1498 | CA. J + CV. |
| John Foster | 1489-1490 | CV. CA. |
| John Holme | 1489-1497 | SBA. CA. SBA. SBA. SBA. SBA. |
| Robert Vont | 1489-1490 | J. CF. |
| Augustine Arnold | 1490-1505 | CV. CA. CC. J. J. J. J. J. |
| William Gonell | 1490-1492 | J. CF. |
| Richard West | 1491, 1512 | CV. CF. |
| William Frost junior of East Street | 1492-1503 | CF. J. J. |

* CA = Collector of the Ale; CC = Custodian of the Church; CF = Collector of the Farm; CON = Constable;
CV = Collector of the View; J = Juror; SBA = Sub-bailiff.

| Name | Date | Duties |
|---|---|---|
| Thomas Garlop senior | 1492-1498 | CA. CA. CV. |
| John Long | 1492-1504 | CA + CV. CA. CA + CV. CA. CF. |
| William Melbourne | 1493-1517 | CV. CF. CF. J. J. CV. |
| William Basse | 1494-1496 | CF. J. CON. |
| Thomas Monyment | 1497-1522 | CV. J. CC. J. J. CC. |
| Richard Stevens | 1497-1498 | J. CON. |
| Robert Mayle | 1498-1500 | CV. J. |
| William Loveday | 1502-1529 | CA. CF + CV. CV. CA. CC. CF. CON. |
| William Greatham | 1503, 1515-1542 | J. CC. J. CC. J. CF. CON. CF. J. J. CF. J. J. CF. J. |
| Thomas Gybbys | 1503, 1511-1531 | CV. CF. J. CC. CON. CF + J. CF. J. CF. J. |
| William Ibott | 1503, 1527 | J. CA. |
| William Arnold | 1504-1515, 1526 | CC. CF. J. CF. CC. J. CC. |
| William Lord | 1504-1521 | CA. SBA. CA. SBA. SBA. SBA. SBA. SBA. SBA. SBA. SBA. SBA. |
| John Bailey junior | 1505-1513 | CA. SBA. CA. SBA. SBA. SBA. SBA. SBA. |
| William Granger | 1505-1545 | CC. CC. CF. CF. J. J. J. CV. CV. J. CC. |
| John Nottingham | 1505 | CA. J. J. |
| John Barnard | 1506-1507, 1517 | CA. SBA. J. |
| John Manning | 1506-1515 | CV. CV + J. J. |
| Robert Punt | 1506, 1518-1519 | CF. CV. J. |
| Edmund Maryot | 1507-1519 | CF. J. CON. J. CF. |
| Robert Whyte | 1507-1509, 1517 | CF. J. CF. |
| John Hogan | 1508-1524 | CV. J. CF. J. J. CF. CF. |
| John Este | 1509-1526 | CV. CA. CF. CV. J. CF. J. J. |
| William Pelman | 1509-1510 | CC. CF. |
| Richard Scot | 1509-1523 | J. CF. CF. CC. J. J. |
| Thomas Lovell | 1509, 1542 | CV. CA. |
| Robert Nicholas | 1510-1518 | CF. J. CON. CF. |
| William Benet | 1512, 1522-1523 | CV. CV. J. |
| John Dey | 1512, 1523 | CV. CF. |
| John Clerk junior | 1514-1527 | CV. CV. J. J. J. J. J. |
| John Granger junior | 1514-1538, 1548 | CV. CF. CC. CF. CC. J. J. CV. |
| Thomas Pacy | 1514-1526, 1535 | CF. CV. J. CON. CC. J. J. |
| William Dalton, mercer | 1515-1532 | J. BA. CF. J. J. |
| Robert Vyntner | 1515-1529, 1542-1546 | CF. J. CC. CF. J. J. BA. CC. J. CF. |
| Nicholas Gelly | 1516-1520 | J. CF. CON. CC. |
| John Page junior | 1516-1520 | CF. CC + J. CON. |
| Richard Prior | 1516-1541 | J. J. J. CV. J. CC. J. J. |
| John Goodwyn | 1518-1543 | CV. CV. CC. CC. J. J. J. J. J. |
| John Clerk | 1519, 1522 | CA. CC. |
| John Page | 1520-1526 | J. J. J. CF. |
| John Stevens | 1520-1523 | CA. CA. CA. |
| Richard Blaxton | 1521-1526 | CA. SBA. SBA. SBA. SBA. |
| Roger Hawdwyn | 1521-1544 | CV. J. CF. J. CC. CF. J. J. J. |
| William Malden | 1521-1545 | CV. J. CF. J. J. CF. J. CF. J. J. CF. CC. J. CON. J. CF. |
| William Vyntner | 1521-1522 | CON. J. |
| Richard King | 1523, 1531 | CV. CV. |
| William Byrder | 1524, 1527 | CF. J. |
| Thomas Copinger | 1524-1528 | CA. SBA. CV. |
| William Richmond | 1524-1548 | CV. CA. CC. CV. J. CC. CF. CC. J. J. CON. |
| John Wylde junior | 1525-1526 | CC. CF. |
| Thomas Freman | 1527, 1545 | CV. CV. |

| NAME | DATE | DUTIES |
|---|---|---|
| William Osteler | 1527-1542 | CV. SBA. SBA. SBA. SBA. CC. J. CON. |
| Thomas Stevenson | 1528, 1535-1546 | CC. J. CF. CC. J. J. CF. J. CC. |
| Simon Wellys | 1529, 1535 | CA. CA. |
| William Abram junior | 1531-1546 | CV. SBA. SBA. SBA. SBA. SBA. SBA. SBA. SBA. SBA, SBA. J. |
| Thomas Garlop | 1531, 1529, 1545-1547 | CC. CC. CF. CC. |
| William Benet | 1532, 1536 | J. CC. |
| John Clerk | 1532-1548 | CF. J. J. CF. J. J. J. CF. J. CF. BA. |
| John Disney junior | 1532-1545 | J. CF. CON. J. J. J. J. CF. |
| John Byllington | 1533, 1537 | CA. J. |
| Richard Cook | 1533-1545 | J. CF. J. CC. J. CON. J. CON. CF. J. J. |
| William Laxton | 1533, 1537 | CC. J. |
| William Godwyn | 1534-1536, 1542 | CV. CV. CC. |
| John Nelson | 1534-1547 | J. J. CC. J. CF + J. CF. J. CON. J. CF. |
| William Grene | 1535, 1538 | CV. CA. |
| John Croft | 1536-1538, 1542 | J. J. CA. |
| William May | 1536-1537 | J. CF. |
| Walter Colyn | 1537-1542 | J. J. CF. CF. BA. |
| Robert Firmary | 1537-1541 | CV. J. J. |
| William Frost | 1537-1545 | CC. CF. J. J. |
| John Ede | 1538, 1543, 1546 | CV. CV. CA. |
| William Freman | 1540-1541 | CA. CV. |
| Ralph Harrowsby | 1541-1548 | CA. CA. CV. SBA. SBA. |
| Thomas Tryg junior | 1542, 1544, 1548 | CC. J. CF. |
| Robert Bowche | 1543-1546 | J. CC. J. CF. |
| John Robyn | 1543-1545 | CC. J. CON. |
| John Slow junior | 1543-1546 | CC. CF. J. |
| William Aylred | 1544-1548 | J. CF. CC. |
| John Blaxton | 1544-1546 | SBA. SBA. SBA. |
| Thomas Gaddisby | 1544, 1547 | CA. CV. |
| William Normanton | 1544, 1548 | CC. CON. |
| Thomas Collyen | 1545, 1548 | CF. J. |
| John Frost | 1545-1548 | CA. CF + CA. |

## TABLE 5: CUSTODIAN OF THE SEALS

| | |
|---|---|
| William Freman | 1500 |
| William Ede | 1501, 1513-1514 |
| William Ibott junior | 1502, 1512, 1515, 1525-1526 |
| Richard Grene | 1503 |
| Richard Verly | 1504 |
| Thomas Astorwood | 1505-1506 |
| Thomas Blassell | 1507 |
| William Lord | 1509-1510 |
| Robert Marshall | 1511 |
| Robert Nicholl | 1527, 1531-1543 |
| Simon Granger | 1544-1548 |

Some of these secondary corps of officials (William Ibott junior, William Lord) were also elected to the post of the Keeper of the Seals. Despite the pretentious title, this function would not have been laborious, and could readily be performed by those having access to the court house in their more frequent line of duty. Elections to the office of Keeper are only noted regularly after 1500 (see Table 5).

While capital resources and administrative expertise go far to explain the arrangement of officials described in the two corps above, these did not necessarily supply the annual rotation requirements of the customs of Godmanchester. The system of representation by street and year continued to be applied despite changes in the size and composition of the population. Indeed, the system was further extended from 1496 when two constables began to be elected, one from each two-street combination, rather than the traditional single constable for the whole town. In order to fulfill these representational regulations, individuals were co-opted regularly. This occurred less frequently in the higher orders of responsibility and most frequently among the larger body to be elected every year, that is, the jurors. Table 6 shows those co-opted for various tasks for one year only. On the other hand, those listed in Table 7 performed as jurors only for several years.

TABLE 6: LIST OF THOSE ELECTED TO
OFFICES FOR ONE YEAR ONLY

| DATE | NAME | DUTY* |
|------|------|-------|
| 1485 | Robert Conyff | CON |
|      | Thomas Sydebotom | J |
| 1486 | John Lumbard | CF |
|      | Thomas Marshall | J |
|      | Robert Porter | CF |
|      | William Syward senior | CA |
| 1487 | Richard Bayous | J |
|      | Thomas Cokman | CF |
|      | Thomas Frost | J |
|      | Henry Martin | J |
|      | John Stokes | BA |
| 1488 | William Gile | CA |
|      | Thomas Kendale | CV |
| 1489 | John Cave | CV |
|      | Richard Mayle | CC |
| 1490 | John Goodrych | SBA |
|      | Richard King | SBA |
| 1491 | John Brown | CF |
| 1493 | John Breton | CV |
| 1495 | John Caustauns | CV |

* Abbreviations as in Table 4.

| Date | Name | Duty |
|------|------|------|
| 1496 | Steven Clerk | CF |
|  | Thomas May | CV |
| 1497 | Robert Bayous | J |
|  | Richard Motte | CA |
| 1498 | Thomas Bailey | J |
|  | Thomas Mundeford | J |
|  | Thomas Page | CV |
| 1499 | John Wyddyr | J |
| 1501 | Thomas Faldyng | J |
|  | Paul Folkys | J |
| 1502 | Henry Este | CV |
|  | John Gonell | CON |
|  | William Porter | CV |
| 1503 | John Gilby | CC |
|  | John Vyntner | SBA |
|  | William Frost junior | J |
| 1504 | Thomas Paryot | BA |
|  | Thomas Punt | CC |
| 1505 | Thomas Bailey senior | J |
|  | John Clerk, thacher | CC |
|  | John Garlop | J |
|  | John Melbourne | J |
| 1507 | William Ussher | CON |
| 1508 | John Porter | CV |
| 1510 | John Brown | J |
|  | Thomas Matthew | J |
|  | John Robyns junior | CC |
| 1511 | William Broden | CV |
|  | Richard Ibott | CON |
|  | John Smith | J |
| 1514 | Thomas Haplond | CA |
| 1515 | George Hay | CA |
| 1516 | Henry Gybbys | CV |
| 1517 | William Ede | CA |
|  | Thomas Smyth | J |
| 1518 | William Brown | CV |
|  | Richard Clerk | CA |
|  | Richard Frost | CV |
| 1523 | John Marshall | J |
| 1525 | Richard Edmund | CA |
|  | Thomas Lovell | CV |
|  | Gilbert Walsh | J |
| 1526 | Henry Barnard | CA |
| 1527 | Richard Boston | J |
|  | Thomas Frere | J |
| 1528 | William Aston | J |
|  | Richard Grene | CON |
|  | Thomas Holme | J |

| Date | Name | Duty |
|------|------|------|
| 1529 | John Pacy | CC |
| 1532 | William Ingram | CV |
|      | Robert Massy | CA |
|      | Edmund Taverner | CC |
| 1533 | John Garlond | CF |
|      | Thomas Kirby | CV |
|      | John Yattys | CV |
| 1534 | William Abram senior | J |
|      | John Borowe | J |
|      | Robert King | J |
|      | John Wylde | CA |
| 1535 | John Greles | CV |
|      | Thomas Woodward | J |
| 1536 | John Staughton | CO |
|      | William Syward | CA |
|      | John Wilson | CF |
| 1537 | John Sanden | CA |
|      | John White | CV |
| 1539 | John Carles | J |
|      | John Hayward | CV |
| 1540 | Stephen Garlop | CA |
| 1541 | Nicholas Bell | CV |
|      | Richard Smith, alias Bonsay | CA |
| 1543 | Henry Barnard | CV |
|      | William Flesher | CA |
|      | Edward Hayward | CF |
|      | John Herdman | CO |
|      | William Sewster | CO |
|      | William Smith | CV |
|      | Richard Taylor | CV |
|      | Robert Warde | CA |
| 1544 | Richard Smith | CA |
|      | William Nebbes | CV |
| 1545 | Richard Hodgson | CV |
|      | Robert Howell | CA |
|      | John Upchurche | CC |
| 1546 | John Disney senior | CF |
|      | William Thacher | CV |
| 1547 | Henry Este | CV |
|      | John Lockyngton | CC |
|      | Richard Lockyngton | CA |
|      | John Myrgame | CA |
| 1548 | William Glover alias Latysar | CV |
|      | Edmund Peyntner | CA |

TABLE 7: INDIVIDUALS WHO WERE JURORS ONLY

| DATE | NAME |
|------|------|
| 1477, 1489-1496 | Thomas Bailey |
| 1481-1486 | William Godwyn |
| 1481-1487 | John Snell |
| 1485-1495 | John Bayous |
| 1485-1487 | Richard Lockington |
| 1486-1488 | Thomas Benet |
| 1487-1489 | Thomas Emlyn |
| 1487-1489 | John Matthew |
| 1496, 1503 | Henry Smith |
| 1511-1513 | John Lawman |
| 1511-1512 | John Robyn senior |
| 1512, 1522 | William Lessy |
| 1525, 1528 | Thomas Harding |
| 1534, 1536 | Thomas Bell |
| 1542, 1544 | Hugh Hayward |

Since the jury was the highest "review board" for the affairs of the town, it was practical to have all the upper levels of administration function from time to time as jurors. This can be seen in Table 2: The Main Corps of Officals from the first few names: John Lockyngton, William Manipenny, William Orwell, John Ussher and John Laxton. When the freemen had more specialized tasks as one or other of the custodians, as with Thomas Maryot, the total number of years given to administration would tend to be extended and representation on the jury extended. Those in the Secondary Corps level, as we have just seen, were also regularly elected to the juror list. Thomas Burton, John Stukeley and John Turneskewe well illustrate this policy. And so on down the administrative ladder until we meet those who are elected to fill the jury roster (as was John Bonsay) only once. In short, the jury was chosen not only to represent the four streets of the town but also with a view to involving those officials who had performed or were to perform various administrative tasks on these streets. But the post of juror, in particular, by statute could not be held along with another office, so the single year co-opting pattern of the tables above demonstrates no doubt the results of the demand for the jury roster as much as the supply quota exigencies for these various areas of expertise.

With increasing specialization of administration more permanent occupational patterns emerge. Clerks performed their tasks in a less cyclical fashion than the first level officials of the town. As one goes further "down" the scale of officers to the positions of hayward and bellman there are not cycles at all. Such persons were hired for specific competency in these tasks and did not appear to have more general qualities for administration. At the very least, some of these tasks would demand time that excluded the office holder from other commitments. Since these services were well rewarded, there may have been competition for the job. But one can only speculate that some "rule of thumb" was in operation (preference of bailiffs? of the street?) that might explain the variety of individuals to be seen performing these services in Table 8 below.

When clerks moved up the scale to become collectors, and even in the one rare instance of Richard Grene to become a main corp official, others would have to take their places as clerks. No rotational requirements devolved upon the clerks as such, so it is not surprising to find the sequence of their election (Table 8) differing from that of their superior officers. Perhaps the variations to be found in the chronology for clerks might be explained by personal preferences of those for whom they were to work. Elections lists refer specifically to a collector of fines and "his clerk," indicating that the collector chose his clerk and paid him. Bailiffs accounts do not show payments by the town for these clerks. No doubt the bailiffs for the year could have their own preferences too in their choice of the clerk of the court. We know from farm rental lists that the residents on Post Street were almost double those of either Arnyng or West Streets. It is not surprising that the clerks identified with Post Street outnumber considerably those of Arnyng or West Streets, although the basic administrative requirements of each street were the same. Since Post Street was the heart of the "commercial" people of the town who presumably had more accounting experience, one might expect administrative competencies to be more varied as well as more numerous on Post Street. In similar fashion, the heavy concentration of clerical expertise on East Street would explain the larger number of administrators on that street despite a population one third smaller than that of Post Street. Arnyng Street and West Street compensated for inferior numbers of skilled personnel by concentrating responsibilities; that is to say, as may be seen from Table 8, those with five years or more of service on Arnyng and West outnumbered those of the same category on East and Post Streets. On the other hand, it should be recalled that the differing divisions of labour at Arnyng and West Streets, on the one hand, with East and Post on the other, were further compensated by grouping Arnyng with East and West with Post under various officials. Clerks, bellmen and haywards are so infrequently noted in election lists prior to 1500 that it is not possible to tabulate them for the earlier period.

Whether the town was able to preserve these arrangements as a genuine equilibrium in a period of concentration of wealth and power will have to be investigated in more detail below in terms of individuals. Certainly from the broad descriptive point of view of the whole town the system seemed to work

## TABLE 8: SPECIALIZED ADMINISTRATORS: CLERKS

| NAME | POST STREET | WEST STREET | EAST STREET | ARNYNG STREET | CLERK OF COURT | CLERK FOR THE COLLECTOR OF THE VIEW |
|---|---|---|---|---|---|---|
| Augustine Arnold | | | | 1502 | | |
| William Aylred | | | 1503 | 1500-1501; 1503 | | |
| Thomas Benet | | 1517-1523; 1541 | | | | |
| Thomas Benet | | | | 1535-1538 | | |
| Thomas Copinger | 1516 | | 1517-1526; 1528-1533 | 1528; 1529; 1531-1533 | | 1524; 1526; 1528 |
| Thomas Dalton | | | | | | 1525 |
| John Disney senior | 1515 | | 1535-1544 | | | 1529; 1531-1537 |
| William Everard | | | | 1539-1544 | | 1542-1544 |
| Henry Frere | | | 1513-1514; 1516 | 1511-1515; 1517-1524 | 1511-1523 | 1511-1523 |
| Richard Frere | 1508 | | | | | 1506 |
| Robert Granger | | 1506 | 1548 | 1546-1547 | | 1548 |
| George Grene | | | 1545 | | | |
| Richard Grene | 1531-1535 | | | 1525-1527 | | 1503 |
| Richard Grene | | 1500-1503; 1507 | | | 1527-1535 | |
| Thomas Harfreyz | | | | 1510 | | |
| Robert Kyng | 1538-1539 | 1537 | | | | 1537; 1541 |
| Thomas Mayle | | | | 1548 | | |
| William Mynt | 1504 | 1504; 1509; 1512-1516 | 1500 | | 1509 | 1504; 1516 |
| Thomas Pacy[a] | 1520; 1536-1537 | 1508; 1510-1511; 1524-1534; 1538-1540; 1542-1548 | 1534 | 1508-1509 | 1524-1548 | 1537-1538; 1541-1548 |
| William Porter | | | | | | 1525 |
| Robert Punt | 1510-1514; 1516-1529 | | 1515 | 1504-1506 | 1529 | 1507; 1509; 1511-1515; 1517-1525 |
| John Sandon | | | 1546-1547 | 1545 | | 1546-1547 |
| Robert Sandon | 1540-1548 | | | | | 1538-1543 |
| Robert Stoughton | | | 1527 | | | 1527 |
| Richard Verly | 1505 | | 1501-1502; 1504-1512 | | | 1503-1504; 1506; 1509-1512 |
| Robert White | 1500-1507 | | | | | |

[a] Thomas Pacy was involved in being a clerk for over 40 years and was the main clerk of the court.

TABLE 9: BELLMEN AND HAYWARDS

A. BELLMEN

| NAME | YEARS |
| --- | --- |
| John Glover | 1500 |
| Robert Oleyff | 1502-1506; 1509-1518; 1520 |
| Matthew Hedley | 1507 |
| John Barnard | 1519; 1522-1531 |
| R. Book | 1521 |
| Robert Hedley | 1533-1543 |
| Richard Taylor | 1544-1548 |

B. HAYWARDS

| NAME | YEARS |
| --- | --- |
| Richard Kyng | 1500-1501; 1524-1525 |
| John Stokys | 1502 |
| John Barnard junior | 1503; 1505; 1507; 1513; 1515 |
| William Ede | 1504; 1506; 1510-1512; 1519-1521; 1526 |
| Thomas Gybbys | 1507 |
| William Freman | 1509 |
| Christopher Dalton | 1514 |
| Henry Barnard | 1517-1518; 1523 |
| William Brown | 1522; 1527 |
| John Vyntnar junior | 1528-1529; 1532 |
| John Hogan | 1531; 1533-1542 |
| Thomas Kirby | 1540-1543 |
| Richard Kyng | 1544 |
| John Hogan junior | 1545 |
| Thomas Armyot | 1546-1548 |

well until the mid sixteenth century. The town maintained its discretionary power to choose some, and not to choose others, for various posts. An adequate pool of administrative resources seemed to be at hand. Dual tenure of office was so rare that some contingency such as illness or death must have caused the arrangement:

John Turneskewe, juror and collector of the farm in 1485
Richard Smith, coroner and juror 1487
Thomas Fecas, collector of the farm and sub-bailiff 1493
John Bould, collector of the farm and juror 1494
John Clerk, collector of the view and juror 1498
John Barnard, sub-bailiff and juror 1500
William Aylred, collector of the farm and collector of the church 1502 and coroner and juror 1503
John Lockyngton, coroner and juror 1503
John Manning, collector of the view and juror 1512

John Frere, coroner and juror 1517
William Townshende, collector of the church and juror 1517
Thomas Gybbys, collector of the farm and juror 1518
John Punt, constable and juror 1518
John Page junior, collector of the church and juror 1518
William Frere, collector of the farm and juror 1518
Thomas Lockyngton, collector of the farm and juror 1527
John Nelson, collector of the farm and juror 1540

Nonetheless, in nearly all of the above instances it was the post of juror that was the common denominator. Clearly the town found it difficult to fill the quota of three jurors from each street every year. No doubt this would be the reason why for each year a number of individuals were called upon for jury service for the first time, and often for the last time. Perhaps some of these proved to be unable to the task and so were not re-elected. None of our sources indicates a refusal of election as juror or any other post. In any case, the town continued to engage a wide range of its citizens from year to year throughout our period rather than concentrating the office of jurors by a regular cycle of major office holders.

In sum, this chapter has presented evidence for the creation of a main corps of leading officials, especially the bailiffs, following the financial stringencies of the third quarter of the fifteenth century. Is this not just another instance of control in a town of late mediaeval England? For the bailiffs appointed the jurors, and the increasing difficulty in finding jurors may have reflected the attenuated responsibilities of the latter body. Certainly a number of those co-opted for jury duty were already paid servants of the town and even of the bailiffs. Furthermore, from the late fifteenth century there was a permanency about the administration as distinct from the government of Godmanchester, as those more senior administration posts involving the collecting of monies remained within an evermore clearly discernible group.

This easy deduction to an élite group dominating a civil service cannot be accepted at its face value from the evidence presented in this chapter. The jurors were still expressing their final authority over the government of the town in the late fifteenth century. Almost all of those evicted from the town by the jurors were from the wealthiest élite and indeed had functioned as bailiffs. Statutory representational demands for the jurors, that is, three jurors from every street, could not coincide with the relatively easy annual alternative choice of the two bailiffs from the grouping of the streets by twos. We will have to find out more about the possible changing social and economic conditions of those below the major corps of officials in order to explain the locus of power in early sixteenth-century Godmanchester.

# 2

# Farm Rentals and Frankpledge Rolls: Evidence for Economic Activity

The most formidable task facing the administration of Godmanchester, engaging the services of bailiffs, collectors of the farm, clerks and jurors, was the collection of the royal farm. Since this obligation remained fixed from the time of its imposition in the early thirteenth century, the records built up about the farm rental payment system give an aura of permanency about the economic life of the town. In this respect Godmanchester was comparable to those towns and villages throughout England where for centuries it was an administrative facility to list properties in fixed categories in order to have a ready assessment of dues. And so at Godmanchester land alone, without regard for any capital whatsoever, was listed as the basis for payments to the royal farm. Economic historians must remain suspicious about the interpretation of such permanent assessment structures unless comparisons of the final payment lists can be made over short periods of time, and more importantly, the real basis for the rental assessment can be recovered. Happily, the early Tudor records of Godmanchester serve the historian well in both these respects.

Despite the reservations just expressed about the economic interpretation of wealth assessment lists, such lists have taken on a new life for the social historian over recent years. It is now recognized that in an age before the availability of autobiographies, biographies and diaries, these assessment lists introduce us to the names of a multitude of individuals who would otherwise be unknown. By an odd paradox then, those civil servants noted at the beginning of the previous paragraph whose obligations to the Crown involved the most impersonal demands upon town administration, have left us the most useful lists of personal names. Frankpledge rolls, on the other hand, are related to economic roles of tenants, tradespeople and other occupations rather than to wealth assessments as such. Yet the extensive and regular report of so many petty offences in various economic activities will be seen in the third section of this chapter to make possible the gathering of enough data to become a valuable report for a considerable range of economic life of many people.

## A. GODMANCHESTER FARM RENTALS

Students of a modern town most conveniently obtain information about people from such sources as census lists, various tax assessment lists or simply door-to-door interviews of the residents themselves. The people of fifteenth-century Godmanchester can be approached in much the same fashion. Godmanchester owed an annual payment (farm) to the king, or to the recipient designated by the king, of £120.[1] This farm was collected from property holders in the town, both resident and non-resident ("foreign" tenants) according to the property held in the town (messuages, curtilages, enclosures) and in the fields (arable and meadow).[2]

Farm payments were collected by two officials annually elected to the task. As we have seen, to facilitate the collection by these two officials, the streets were always grouped together, Post Street with West Street and East Street with Arnyng Street. In order to have at hand an up-to-date record for the collectors, town officials found it necessary to keep separate lists for each street and a few of these original lists have survived. These lists were headed in a simplified manner such as *Rentale Arnynstrete* with the Easter or Michaelmas feast designation and the year according to the reign of the king. Occasionally, there were variations in the title such as *Rentale de Postrete debite ad festum Sancti Michailis archangeli Anno Regni Regis H. VII X°* (1494) or *Rentale de Westrete renovate ad festum Pasche Anno Regis Edwardi IIII[ti] vicesimo secundo* (1482). The document then listed individuals by street along with the amount of farm owed. For example, the Michaelmas 1494 rental of Post Street begins with the Prior of Huntingdon 9d; William Dey 14$\frac{1}{2}$d; Thomas Kyng 8$\frac{1}{2}$d. At the end of the list of names the farm total is summarized.[3]

The continual turnover of a large number of properties, as detailed in the second section of this chapter, was reason enough for the re-writing of farm rental lists twice a year. By the same process farm rental lists would become obsolete twice a year, so it is difficult to understand why any of these should

---

[1] This amount had been first established by King John and was noted as the standard obligation in the Hundred Roll of 1279. As will be seen below, the amount was lowered in the later fifteenth century but by what amount we do not know.

[2] Other revenues, especially those from the leases of the mills noted in the bailiffs accounts of the previous chapter, were formally to make up the full farm quota. On this point, see the introductory note to Appendix 3: Farm Rental Lists, pp. 279-280.

[3] See further, Appendix 3.

have survived. The fact that nearly all of the extant rental survivals are concentrated in a few years during the late 1480s must surely be related to that administrative re-organization occasioned by the depression of the late fifteenth century and already referred to in the previous chapter. We do know that the town sought and obtained some relief in the form of a reduced farm payment around this time.[4] In any case, a good number of farm assessment lists, or rentals as they were designated, survive for this period. Table 10 indicates the group of survivals employed in the following pages for their comparative value.[5]

TABLE 10: EXTANT RENTALS, 1485-1494

|  | 1485 | 1486 | 1487 | 1488 | 1489 | 1490 | 1491 | 1492 | 1494 |
|---|---|---|---|---|---|---|---|---|---|
| **East Street** | | | | | | | | | |
| Easter | (x) | x | (x) | x | x | (x) | x | x | |
| Michaelmas | x | x | (x) | x | x | (x) | x | x | |
| **Post Street** | | | | | | | | | |
| Easter | | | x | | | x | x | x | x |
| Michaelmas | x | x | x | | | x | (x) | | x |
| **Arnyng Street** | | | | | | | | | |
| Easter | | x | | x | x | x | | | |
| Michaelmas | x | x | | x | x | x | x | | |
| **West Street** | | | | | | | | | |
| Easter | | | | | | x | | | |
| Michaelmas | x | | | | | | | | |

Rentals survive as lists of names together with the money owed by each individual to the farm. But the rentals can be broken down into the size of the property holdings of each tenant since it is clear that all property holdings were assessed at the uniform rate of threepence per acre for farm payments.[6]

[4] There are entries in the Jurors' Book, pp. 68-69, to the effect that the King's Council had indicted Godmanchester at "Estyr Terme," 22 Henry VIII, for withholding from the king from the time of Edward IV under the unlawful title of mitigation an amount that was calculated by the Council to be £16. Godmanchester was ordered to pay the full traditional amount of £120 as well as a further 40 shillings yearly until the £16 be repaid. A number of entries are then made showing the acknowledgement of these full payments for two following years by Richard Throgmorton. Since the payments were acknowledged as received much later than the Easter and Michaelmas dates, and indeed only in December of 23 Henry VIII, the bailiffs and jurors of Godmanchester may have been struggling to obtain the extra levy.

[5] For the more scattered survivals, see Appendix 3. Parentheses for Table 10 and following Tables indicate records where the heading is gone and dating has been derived from internal evidence.

[6] This per acre assessment is lower than that imposed for the farm in 1279 (see introductory note to Appendix 3 p. 280) and may be the means taken to reduce the farm as noted above.

Multiplying the total farm payments at this threepence per acre rate for all streets in September, 1485 gives the following round totals:

East Street:      1469 acres
Arnyng Street:    1173 acres
West Street:      1060 acres
Post Street:      1067 acres

Total:            4769 acres

This total figure would seem to represent quite accurately the town that to this day has approximately 5,000 acres. Farm amounts would include payments for messuages, although the precise number of these in 1485 and their relative assessment cannot be discovered.[7] This total acreage held by tenants apparently included everyone who held land in Godmanchester although the non-free are not distinguished in the rentals. Such individuals, whether resident or outsiders holding property at Godmanchester, had declined greatly in numbers by the fifteenth century.[8] Furthermore, such holdings were usually small, that is, an acre or two, often coming to a non-resident of Godmanchester by bequest of a family relation or for religious purposes. One clear example that such tenure by outsiders still continued may be found in the 1494 rental of Post Street where the Prior of Huntingdon pays a farm of ninepence (that is, for three acres).

A moving picture of this evidence for the next decade or so is given in Table 11. Rental records are not always extant for each street at the same date. However, the property totals can be seen to remain much the same over the years.

For the real variety among the tenants of Godmanchester, then, one must move to the level of individuals. Table 12 lists the specific amounts of property held in Godmanchester on all streets for Michaelmas 1485, the only term for which there are comparable data from the whole town.

---

[7] From various conveyances to be found in the court rolls it is clear that no messuage is assessed by as much as threepence. Messuages are assessed around twopence and there is usually only a halfpenny difference between messuages of the most wealthy and least wealthy of the town. Messuage assessments, therefore, form only a minute percentage of the farm tax revenues. Since there are very few tax assessments below threepence, this means that the messuage has been included with other property. For simplicity, therefore, all tax assessments are broken down into acres for the discussion in these pages. See further the introductory note to Appendix 3, p. 280.

[8] See further below, p. 64.

TABLE 11: Property Totals from Rentals by Streets

| | Post Street | West Street | Arnyng Street | East Street |
|---|---|---|---|---|
| 1485 Michaelmas | 973 acres | 1129 acres | 1150 acres | 1434 acres 2 rods |
| 1486 Michaelmas | 979 acres 3½ rods | | | 1449½ acres |
| 1487 Easter | 1026 acres | | 1120 acres | 1451 acres 2½ rods |
| 1487 Michaelmas | 1026 acres | | 1146 acres | |
| 1488 Easter | | | 1121 acres | 1476 acres |
| 1488 Michaelmas | | | 1186 acres | 1474 acres |
| 1489 Easter | | 1149 acres | 1186 acres | 1504 acres |
| 1489 Michaelmas | | | 1147 acres | 1496½ acres |
| 1490 Easter | 962 acres | | 1131 acres | |
| 1490 Michaelmas | 961 acres 3½ rods | | 1146 acres | 1519 acres |
| 1491 Easter | 1002 acres ½ rod | | | |
| 1491 Michaelmas | (787+ acres) 1½ rods | | 1131 acres | 1453½ acres |
| 1492 Easter | 1001½ acres 3 rods | | | 1508 acres |
| 1494 Easter | 929 acres | | | |
| 1494 Michaelmas | 938½ acres 3½ rods | | | |

TABLE 12: The Disposition
of Agrarian Property at Godmanchester in 1485
as Estimated from the Farm Rental Payments[a]

| Post Street | | | |
|---|---|---|---|
| Dey, William | 1 acre | Stodale, William | 70 acres |
| Manipenny, William | 43 acres | Wright, Isabella | 10½ acres |
| Brown, William | 3 acres | Frost, William | 9 acres |
| Chese, William | 13 acres | Farthing, William | 1 acre |
| Gony, John | 6 acres | Porter, John | 14 acres |
| Goodwyn, William | 32 acres | Arnold, John | 1½ acres |
| Townshend, Richard | 25 acres | Leftub, John | 1 acre |
| Norton, Thomas | 1½ acres | Holme, John | messuage |
| Reygate, John | ½ acre | Turneskewe, John | 12 acres |
| Frere, Alice | 1 acre | Bigge, John | 6½ acres |
| Frere, William | 67½ acres | Willem, Richard | 14 acres |
| Fraternity of Corpus Christi | 19 acres | Stevenson, John | 1½ acres |
| Dey, John | 2 acres | Lessy, William | ½ acre |
| Fisher, John | 122 acres | Cave, John | 9 acres |
| Betriche, William | 12 acres | Lane, Thomas senior | 11 acres |
| | | Motte, Richard | 5½ acres |

[a] In order to show the street residential pattern of small holders and larger tenants, the ordering to be found in the manuscript has been retained in Table 12.

| POST STREET | | | |
|---|---|---|---|
| Garlop, John senior | 5 acres | Whitwick, John | 2 acres |
| Tothe, William | ½ acre | Reed, John | 1½ acres |
| Rumborough, John | 1 acre | Fecas, John | ½ acre |
| Balle, Margaret senior | 25 acres | Feld, John | 2 acres |
| Chicheley, Richard | ½ acre | Sterlyng, John | 2½ acres |
| Bailey, Thomas | 1 acre | Hedley, Matthew | 1 acre |
| Passelowe, Richard | 12 acres | Garlop, Margaret | ½ acre |
| Granger, Simon | 1½ acres | Gardener, John | 14 acres |
| Stalys, John | 12 acres | Marshall, Henry | 18 acres |
| Dawntre, Helen | 1 acre | Vont, Robert | 1 acre |
| Adam, John | 11 acres | Lane, Agnes | 1 acre |
| Barret, Henry | 3 acres | Wyllson, Richard | 1 acre |
| Samt, Richard | 14 acres | Nottyngham, William | 2½ acres |
| Plumpton, William | 47 acres | Balle, Thomas | 4½ acres |
| Garnet, Matthew | 18 acres | Bonsay, John | 42 acres |
| Gonell, William | 8 acres | Faldyng, Thomas | 42½ acres |
| Baron, Thomas | 2½ acres | Lyght, William | 5 acres |
| Kyng, Thomas | 2½ acres | Bayous, Robert | 7½ acres |
| Johnson, Thomas | 2½ acres | Blassell, Thomas | 1 acre |
| Dalton, John | 1 acre | Nicholas, Robert | 38½ acres |
| Garlop, John junior | 20½ acres | Stooke, John | 2½ acres |
| Prior, Cristina | 6½ acres | Punte, Thomas | 1 acre |
| Marshall, Thomas | 1 acre | Davy, Thomas | 2½ acres |
| Fraternity of | | Knaresborough, Godfrey | 1½ acres |
| St. John | 5½ acres | Wright, William | 1 acre |
| Manipenny, John | 1 acre | Matthew, John | ¼ acre |
| Englysh, John | 14½ acres | Osteler, John | 1 acre |
| Reynold, Thomas | 1 acre | Willem, Richard junior | 2 acres |
| Gilby, Richard | 1 acre | Shalford, John | 1 acre |
| Garlop, John junior | 12 acres | Barnard, John junior | 1½ acres |
| Lumbard, John | 28 acres | Edmond, William | ½ acre |
| Byllingford, John | ½ acre | Balle' ( ) | ½ acre |
| Folk, Richard | 1 acre | Number of Tenants: 95 | |

Total acreage: 981

| WEST STREET | | | |
|---|---|---|---|
| Broughton, John | 2 acres | Parker, William | 1½ acres |
| Lockyngton, Richard | 11 acres | Motte, Thomas | 3½ acres |
| Bayous, John | 79 acres | Schylling, Agnes | ½ acre |
| Patten, Henry | 1 acre | Barnard, Henry | 6½ acres |
| Conyff, Robert | 75 acres | Suel, William | 50½ acres |
| Lockyngton, Richard | 107 acres | Kyng, William | 18½ acres |
| Lockyngton, John | 2½ acres | Robyn, John | 75 acres |
| Maryot, Thomas | 33½ acres | Kyng, John | 31 acres |
| Holme, William | 4 acres | Stukeley, Helen | 21½ acres |
| Mayle, Richard junior | 2½ acres | Chese, John junior | 8 acres |
| Mayle, Richard | 88 acres | Pelman, William | 21 acres |
| Mayle, Thomas | 71 acres | Thomson, Agnes | 4 acres |
| Doraunt, Thomas | 7½ acres | Custodian of All Saints | 5 acres |

## WEST STREET

| | | | |
|---|---|---|---|
| Chese, William | 28$\frac{1}{2}$ acres | Stukeley, Richard | 35$\frac{1}{2}$ acres |
| Foly, Paul | 1 acre | Garlop, Thomas | 9 acres |
| Coke, Roger | 33 acres | Allemowthe, John | $\frac{1}{2}$ acre |
| Schylling, John | 26 acres | Barrett, John | 2 acres |
| Gybbys, John | 69 acres | Bennett, Thomas | 51 acres |
| Foster, John | 8 acres | Kyng, Richard | 12 acres |
| Wykyam, Richard | 1$\frac{1}{2}$ acres | Aythroppe, William | 10 acres |
| Smyth, Richard | 44 acres | Brewster, John | 37$\frac{1}{2}$ acres |
| Barre, John | 14 acres | Mayle, Robert | 2 acres |
| Holme, Richard | 1 acre | Loveday, William | 1 acre |
| Welyam, William | 9 acres | Number of Tenants: 47 | |

Total acreage: 1,129

## ARNYNG STREET

| | | | |
|---|---|---|---|
| Aylred, John | 133 acres | Corby, John | 7 acres |
| Garlop, William | 1 acre | Fraternity of | |
| Polle, William | 52 acres | St. James | $\frac{1}{2}$ acre |
| Mayle, William | 48 acres | Bowr, John | 45 acres |
| Prestwode, Simon | 2 acres | Bonsay, John | 43 acres |
| Stukeley, John | 54 acres | Gardiner, William | 48 acres |
| Hawkyn, John | 2 acres | Gardiner, John senior | 41 acres |
| Baker, Thomas | 19 acres | Balle, Thomas | 16 acres |
| Mundeford, Thomas | 45 acres | Brown, John | 44 acres |
| Gardiner, Richard | 14 acres | Mounford, William | 67 acres |
| Frost, Thomas | 44 acres | Marten, Thomas | $\frac{1}{2}$ acre |
| Law, James | 27$\frac{1}{2}$ acres | Slowe, Robert | 3 rods |
| Mateshale, William | 1 acre | Lucas, John | 46 acres |
| Burton, Thomas | 15$\frac{1}{2}$ acres | Frost, William | |
| Arnold, Austen | 46 acres | junior | 2 acres |
| Barnard, John senior | 30 acres | Holy Trinity | 15 acres |
| Grene, John | 8 acres | Fraternity of | |
| Adam, John | 5 acres | St. Mary | 9 acres |
| Marten, Henry | 2 acres | Brown, William | 7$\frac{1}{2}$ acres |
| Scott, William | 1$\frac{1}{2}$ acres | Legge, Richard | 1 acre |
| Robyn, Robert | 13 acres | Gilbert, Thomas | 3 acres |
| Robyn, Henry | 5$\frac{1}{2}$ acres | Howlet, John | 19 acres |
| Suell, John | 96 acres | Holme, William | 1 acre |
| Frost, William senior | 75 acres | Asshe, John | 1 acre |
| | | Number of Tenants: 45 | |

Total acreage: 1,152

## EAST STREET

| | | | |
|---|---|---|---|
| Prior of Merton | 168 acres | Chaplain of | |
| his vicar | 35$\frac{1}{2}$ acres | Blessed Virgin Mary | 73 acres |
| Mynsterchambre, John | 54$\frac{1}{2}$ acres | Tothe, William | 3 rods |
| Chaplain of | | Page, John senior | 58 acres |
| Corpus Christi | 47 acres | Capelle, John | 13 acres |

| EAST STREET | | | |
|---|---|---|---|
| Diggby, William | 3 acres | Ibott, William | |
| Longe, John | 55 acres | junior | 1½ acres |
| Longe, William | 1 acre | Lessey, Thomas | 6 acres |
| Edmond, William | | Ibott, William | |
| Grey, Benet | 8 acres | senior | 7 acres |
| Bones, Alice | 6 acres | | 3 rods |
| Cleyffe, William | 3½ acres | Page, John junior | 7½ acres |
| Lawman, John | 29 acres | Syward, Thomas | |
| Broughton, John | 16 acres | junior | 2 acres |
| Ingraham, William | 2½ acres | Emley, Thomas | 28 acres |
| Aylred, William | 103 acres | Grace, John | 23 acres |
| Hawkyn, John | 1 acre | Porter, Robert | 17 acres |
| Kendale, Thomas | 19½ acres | Andrew, John | |
| Ponder, William | 8 acres | Vincent, John | |
| Orewelle, William | 75 acres | senior | 3½ acres |
| Langham, William | 4 acres | Mannyng, Roger | 5½ acres |
| Syward, William | 24 acres | Syward, Thomas | |
| Wyllam, John | 49 acres | senior | 18½ acres |
| Sydebotom, Thomas | 36 acres | Syward, Alice | 3 acres |
| | 1 rod | Custodian of | |
| Goodwyn, William | 46 acres | St. George | 1 acre |
| Bate, Thomas | 7½ acres | Page, Thomas | 3 acres |
| Barre, Edward | 69 acres | Page, William son | |
| Page, William | 29 acres | of Thomas | 1 acre |
| Newman, Thomas | 62½ acres | Syward, William | |
| Fyncheham, Thomas | 98 acres | junior | 1½ acres |
| Custodian of church | 22 acres | Granger, William | 3½ acres |
| Custodian of | | Pelle, Richard | 34 acres |
| St. Katherine | 6 acres | Warde, Thomas | 1 acre |
| Dangerous, John | 4½ acres | Sparrow, John | 1½ acres |
| Bailiff | 8 acres | Hermyn, John | 2 acres |
| Glover, John | 4 acres | Nottyngham, Thomas | 2 acres |
| | 3 rods | Fol', Marion | 2 acres |
| Ibott, John, | | Bishop, Cristina | 1½ acres |
| aguillar | 6½ acres | Number of Tenants: 64 | |
| | | | Total acreage: 1,434 |

This settlement pattern in Godmanchester looks familiar in so much as there is that telltale scatter of small holdings among larger properties that obtained 200 years earlier. Perhaps the physical structure of the town, that is to say, the "permanent" disposition of roads and lanes dictated this property spread? Upon closer analysis, however, it is quickly apparent from this list that the tenants of Godmanchester were polarized, with 28 holding more than 50 acres of land, 44 holding middling amounts between 21 and 50 acres, only 34 in the 11 to 20 acre bracket and the remainder holding less than 10 acres. This polarization contrasts with information from the 1279 Hundred Roll where the dominant feature was the low profile of the landholding pyramid, that is to say, only three tenants held more than 25 acres of arable in 1279, 77 were bunched between 10 and 25 acres, while 107 held between 5 and 10 acres of arable.[9] A strict comparison between the 1279 Hundred Roll and late-fifteenth-century farm rentals lists may not be valid since the former included much more detail, especially with respect to multifamily tenancies and properties held by nonresidents of the town. Nevertheless, the main pattern of the change is clear: a much larger group of large property holders existed in the late fifteenth century than 200 years earlier.[10]

When this change began to occur is impossible to determine from Godmanchester records. But it is possible to ascertain whether the same changes continued into the late fifteenth century. The 1485 tenant data given above suggest that a first approach to this question must acknowledge some relevance of the street locations since there are as many tenants on Post Street as on Arnyng Street and West Street combined, yet tenants of each of the latter two streets held as much property as the many tenants of Post Street. This point is illustrated below by a summary of tenants according to streets and property range. For comparative purposes, the 1485 tenants are listed first:

|  | UNDER 10 ACRES | 11-20 ACRES | 21-40 ACRES | 41-60 ACRES | OVER 60 ACRES |
|---|---|---|---|---|---|
| Post Street | 64 | 17 | 6 | 1 | 7 |
| West Street | 25 | 4 | 6 | 5 | 7 |
| East Street | 37 | 5 | 8 | 8 | 7 |
| Arnyng Street | 18 | 8 | 2 | 12 | 4 |

Since the settlement pattern at Godmanchester is quite distinct for each street, and records are not always extant for each street at the same date, in Table 23 the property spread summary from these rentals is grouped according to streets.

What was found to be the social and economic character of the God-manchester of ca. 1300 is more important than ever by 1485 in the "commercial" aspect of Post Street with its many small properties. While the number of properties under ten acres was fewer on other streets it remained, nevertheless, a significant category in the land market. The professional preserve of East Street, residence of ecclesiastic persons as well as of those with clerical privilege, explains the larger number of tenants in the over 50 acre bracket. One could also argue for a traditional sturdy core of yeomen

[9] See *A Small Town*, pp. 93ff.
[10] See further below, Chapter 6, pp. 194-198 on comparative tenurial structure.

TABLE 13: THE RANGE OF TENURE

| | UNDER 10 ACRES | 11-20 ACRES | 21-40 ACRES | 41-60 ACRES | OVER 60 ACRES |
|---|---|---|---|---|---|
| POST STREET | | | | | |
| 1485M | 64 | 17 | 6 | 1 | 7 |
| 1486M | 64 | 14 | 4 | 2 | 4 |
| 1487E | 64 | 16 | 4 | 3 | 4 |
| 1487M | 63 | 12 | 5 | 5 | 3 |
| 1490E | 64 | 7 | 7 | 5 | 3 |
| 1490M | 67 | 7 | 7 | 4 | 3 |
| 1491E | 68 | 8 | 7 | 5 | 3 |
| 1492E | 65 | 7 | 7 | 5 | 3 |
| 1494E | 63 | 4 | 9 | 2 | 4 |
| 1494M | 67 | 4 | 9 | 2 | 4 |
| WEST STREET | | | | | |
| 1485M | 25 | 4 | 6 | 5 | 7 |
| 1489E | 24 | 4 | 6 | 6 | 5 |
| ARNYNG STREET | | | | | |
| 1485M | 18 | 8 | 2 | 12 | 4 |
| 1487E | 22 | 6 | 3 | 11 | 4 |
| 1487M | 22 | 6 | 4 | 9 | 4 |
| 1488E | 22 | 5 | 5 | 8 | 4 |
| 1488M | 21 | 7 | 4 | 6 | 7 |
| 1489E | 21 | 7 | 5 | 6 | 7 |
| 1489M | 21 | 8 | 4 | 7 | 6 |
| 1490E | 20 | 8 | 3 | 7 | 6 |
| 1490M | 22 | 7 | 3 | 7 | 6 |
| 1491M | 21 | 7 | 3 | 8 | 5 |
| EAST STREET | | | | | |
| 1485M | 37 | 5 | 8 | 8 | 4 |
| 1486M | 36 | 3 | 8 | 6 | 7 |
| 1487E | 28 | 2 | 7 | 5 | 7 |
| 1488E | 34 | 1 | 10 | 5 | 8 |
| 1488M | 32 | 4 | 10 | 4 | 7 |
| 1489E | 35 | 4 | 10 | 4 | 8 |
| 1489M | 34 | 5 | 9 | 5 | 8 |
| 1490E | 33 | 4 | 7 | 3 | 7 |
| 1490M | 36 | 5 | 7 | 3 | 7 |
| 1491M | 43 | 8 | 8 | 3 | 9 |
| 1492E | 34 | 7 | 8 | 3 | 9 |

at Godmanchester, represented by the old families of Goodwyn (46 acres) and Wyllam (49 acres) on East Street, the Gybbys (68 acres), Chese (49 acres), Cook (33 acres) and Lockyngton (38 acres) on West Street. Arnyng Street is still well established with the older families such as Austin (45 acres), Bonsay (43 acres), Bowre (45 acres), Browne (44 acres), Gardiner (48 acres and 41 acres), Lucas (46 acres), Moundford (67 acres), Pelle (52 acres) and Stukeley (54 acres).

Upon closer analysis, however, the significance of these older categories diminishes. Most striking are those on every street who are newcomers and have accumulated large amounts of property: John Fisher of Post Street (who was an alderman of London) with 122 acres; Thomas Fyncham (over 100 acres) and William Orwell (75 acres) on East Street; two branches of the Mayle family on West Street (88 acres and 70 acres); the Frosts (75 acres) and Suell (Snell) (96 acres) on Arnyng Street. Equally intriguing was the indifferent ability, or desire, to obtain land by the middling family group. On East Street there was actually a wide gap of virtually no tenants in the 11 to 20 acre range. On Post Street, the numbers in the 11 to 20 acre range were actually declining. On Arnyng Street there was a paucity of tenants in the 20 to 49 acre range. West Street, in so far as our data go, may suggest fewer tenants in the 10 to 20 range. On East and Post Streets there were declining numbers in the 41 to 60 acre range. A certain amount of yearly change in some of these categories of properties signifies that processes are at work over these years. In contrast with these negative features of the middle-range property holders, evidence will be adduced in the second section of this chapter to show a lively land market at the top and bottom of the tenurial scale.

## B. THE LAND MARKET FROM RENTALS

The student of the land market at Godmanchester is fortunate in having some conveyance lists for several dates in the late fifteenth century. No doubt the necessity for a record of conveyances throughout the year explains at least the initial reason for retention of the farm rental payment lists, although as has been noted above why such records have been retained for longer periods cannot be determined with any certainty.

The column of payments in the farm lists was corrected over the year by the addition (*receptavit*) or subtraction (*deliberavit*) of properties conveyed since the time of the last farm payment. In turn, on the left hand side of the margin were noted the changes in the total owed by the individual that had been brought about by these conveyances. As a more complete record of these changes two paragraphs were added to the foot of the farm rental list, one paragraph for land conveyed out of the hands of a tenant to a named recipient and another paragraph for land received. The reason for these dual entries about land conveyances would be for the convenience of the final check by bailiff and jurors as well as the provision of names for the collectors of the farm payments. This would be required even though nearly all tenants were listed by name on their "home" address street only since the market in land moved freely among tenants of all streets, that is to say, the farm collectors were responsible for certain streets only, but the personnel of the land market bought and sold properties from people without respect to where they lived.

A considerable number of these land conveyance records have survived, although not always still attached to rental lists.

TABLE 14: EXTANT LAND CONVEYANCE DATA FROM FARM RENTALS

| | 1485 | 1486 | 1487 | 1488 | 1489 | 1490 | 1491 | 1492 | 1493 | 1494 |
|---|---|---|---|---|---|---|---|---|---|---|
| EAST STREET | | | | | | | | | | |
| Easter | | | x | x | (x) | x | | | | |
| Michaelmas | x | x | | x | x | x | x | | | |
| POST STREET | | | | | | | | | | |
| Easter | | | x | | | x | x | x | | x |
| Michaelmas | x | x | x | | | x | x | | | x |
| ARNYNG STREET | | | | | | | | | | |
| Easter | | | x | x | x | x | x | | | |
| Michaelmas | x | | (x) | x | x | x | | | | |
| WEST STREET | | | | | | | | | | |
| Easter | | | | x | | | | | | |
| September | x | | | | | | | | | |

As Table 15 shows, a large number of tenants were involved in the conveyance of land every year. Where spring and autumn lists are extant for one year there is usually a significant difference between the numbers of conveyances early in the year as the new tenants sought to take advantage of the seasonal production schedule.

At first glance these conveyances suggest a bizarre pattern of land marketing, usually in small bits and pieces. When the conveyances are drawn together for a sequence of years and the concentration of activity about certain individuals is indicated by the alphabetical ordering of names a much more meaningful picture emerges.[11] Appendix 4 demonstrates at once that the conveyance data are selective since many of those larger property holders of the town to be found in rentals are not represented, or are represented by

[11] This is organized in Appendix 4.

TABLE 15: COMPARATIVE LIST OF INDIVIDUALS RECORDED
ON TENANT AND CONVEYANCE LISTS

| | TOTAL NUMBER OF TENANTS FROM RENTALS | NUMBER OF TENANTS RECORDED IN CONVEYANCE LISTS |
|---|---|---|
| **EAST STREET** | | |
| 1485 April | – | 22 |
| 1485 September | 63 | 21 |
| 1486 September | 61 | 15 |
| 1487 April | 57 | 16 |
| 1488 April | 62 | 24 |
| 1488 September | 60 | (7) |
| 1489 April | 61 | 17 |
| 1489 September | 63 | 14 |
| 1490 April | 61 | 18 |
| 1490 September | 63 | 15 |
| 1491 September | 60 | 11 |
| 1492 April | 63 | – |
| **ARNYNG STREET** | | |
| 1485 September | 44 | 23 |
| 1487 April | 44 | 15 |
| 1487 September | 43 | 11 |
| 1488 April | 45 | 22 |
| 1488 September | 47 | 11 |
| 1489 April | 45 | 23 |
| 1489 September | 44 | ? |
| 1490 April | 46 | 17 |
| 1490 September | 44 | 10 |
| 1491 September | 47 | ? |
| **POST STREET** | | |
| 1485 September | 92 | 15 |
| 1486 September | 96 | 20 |
| 1487 April | 89 | 24 |
| 1487 September | 86 | 14 |
| 1490 April | 85 | 19 |
| 1490 September | 89 | 19 |
| 1491 April | 89 | 20 |
| 1491 September | 87 | 15 |
| 1492 April | 89 | 16 |
| 1494 April | 82 | 14 |
| 1494 September | 87 | 19 |
| **WEST STREET** | | |
| 1482 April | 57 | ? |
| 1485 September | 48 | 19 |
| 1489 April | 48 | 13 |

only small property exchanges, among the conveyances. The apparent reason for this is that "normal" conveyances among townsmen and women, such as by inheritance[12] or the traditional tally,[13] were not entered in these conveyance lists although in the course of the Easter and Michaelmas list all holdings of tenants must appear in the farm rent rolls. As is suggested below, conveyances noted on the rolls between the Easter and Michaelmas terms must have been largely of the seasonal variety or instigated by the purchases of those "newcomers" who were liable to obtain liberty of the town at any time of the year. Unfortunately there is no description of the properties in these lists, so it is not possible to trace individual units from one season to another although, as we shall see, the cumulative total of the conveyance of small units over several years is such that it can only be explained by a rapid turnover of such units.

The properties on the land market of Godmanchester lists readily break down into several categories. Most striking are the movement of larger blocks of land. Such purchases implied the availability of considerable capital. Significantly, many of those making such purchases had recently acquired the liberty of Godmanchester and these individuals were well able to pay the licence fee for liberty. East Street provides several examples: John Lumbard who paid a licence fee of 6s. 8d. in 1484, purchased 10 acres from John Lawman in the following year. John Lucas paid a licence fee of 10s. in 1481 and by 1489 had accumulated 18 acres of property rents; most of this came from the purchase of 14 acres from John Grace in 1485. William Este with his son Henry paid a licence fee of 6s. in 1489 and rapidly acquired 27 and 15 acres respectively. No doubt the availability of property was an important determinant for the pattern of these purchases. Henry Trayley who purchased his liberty in 1486 (fee: 3s.) had only two acres by 1489 but had augmented his holdings to 19 acres by the next year and to 27 acres by 1492. A major figure among these types in the 1480s was Thomas Fyncham, who obtained his liberty in 1482 (fee: 26s. 8d.) and by 1485 was listed as having 98 acres. When Fyncham began to release some of his land in large parcels towards the close of the decade, it was the property holders of comparable wealth, John Bonsay (60 acres) and John Page junior (20 acres), who purchased the blocks of land. The Bonsay family had only entered the town by 1485, but the Page family are traceable at Godmanchester to the thirteenth century. The capacity to purchase larger blocks of land was not exclusive to newcomers.

This movement of larger blocks of land contrasts with the vigorous land market in smaller properties at Godmanchester from the time of our earliest

---

[12] See below, Chapter 4.
[13] See below, Chapter 6, pp. 183-193.

records in the thirteenth century.[14] At that time, the market was divided in great part among engrossing families, such as Grinde, Millicent and the vicars of the parish church along with interfamily disposition of property in order to strengthen the family estate or support those less propertied, such as unmarried daughters. No doubt family interests in property continued into the fifteenth century.[15] But engrossing through the purchase of many small pieces of property did not seem to be the practice in the late fifteenth century. For example, the wealthy William Aylred dabbled in only eight pieces of property, each of less than one acre. John Aylred purchased four small pieces of property: a curtilege in 1485, one rod in 1487, one-half acre in 1488 and a grove that he sold shortly thereafter in 1489.

Since a messuage actually was a complex of land and buildings and traditionally had "attached" arable and meadow, no doubt those with not much more than a simple messuage residence in Godmanchester would continue to deal in a few acres whenever possible. As we shall see more fully in Chapter 5 below, among those purchasing only small amounts were newcomers who had purchased the liberty of Godmanchester. On East Street examples of this were John Asshe who in 1489 had rents in East Street (3d.) and received rent from Simon Prestwode (ob. q.) and obtained meadow; and in Post Street John Goodrych one acre (3d.). The practice of a trade or occupation must have attracted such people to the town and their property would be most significant as a residence, and perhaps a shop, rather than for the appurtenant arable or meadow.

A very considerable number of smallish property units came onto the market with the gradual or sudden dissolution of family estates by sale. Since there were no family or family name associations with such sales, and the individuals were coming to the term of their active involvement in the town, this phenomenon may indicate the dissipation of property as a maintenance for the disabled or elderly. The relatively large number of such instances lends further support to the probability of a continuing replacement crises for many families of the town.[16]

At the same time, land conveyances recorded in these records are significant amounts, as the following totals indicates. The totals for East Street are 622 acres 2 rods for only 6 years plus one term. Since three terms are missing, and two of these terms were Easter, no doubt the real total exceeded 700 acres. The Post Street conveyance total comes to approximately 620 acres for ten years. However, records for nine terms are missing so that one

---

[14] See *A Small Town*, pp. 119ff.
[15] See below, Chapter 4, the section on wills.
[16] See further below, Chapter 6, pp. 195-198.

might expect more than 1000 acres to have been conveyed for Post Street over these years. Conveyances recorded in Arnyng Street between 1485 and 1489 come to $381\frac{1}{2}$ acres for five years. But the Easter entry for 1485 is missing, as are both entries for 1486, and the Michaelmas entry for 1489, so the real total likely exceeded 500 acres for these five years. The two isolated entries for West Street do not provide a base for extrapolation although the amounts appear much like the norm for other streets. Despite the fact that several hundred acres did not move on this open market, one might extrapolate that over a ten-year period as much land was conveyed on the conveyance market as was to be found altogether in the town, that is, the total farm rent amounts noted in the previous section of this chapter.

The size of the properties on the open market differed from those sizes to be found in the tenurial picture on the rent rolls. If one takes properties over five acres as "larger" units, there were on the three streets providing more complex data (Arnyng, East, Post) the following number of units per approximate acreage size:

| ACREAGE | NUMBER OF CONVEYANCES |
|---|---|
| 6 | 23 |
| 7 | 4 |
| 8 | 1 |
| 9 | 10 |
| 10 | 8 |
| 12 | 7 |
| 13 | 2 |
| 14 | 1 |
| 15 | 2 |
| 16 | 1 |
| 17 | 2 |
| 18 | 2 |
| 20 | 4 |
| 21 | 2 |
| 25 | 1 |
| 40 | 5 |
| 60 | 1 |
| 89 | 1 |

Looking at these data from another perspective, more than 50 percent of conveyanced land moved in these larger units: 379 of 622 acres on East Street, 374 of 620 acres on Post Street and 348 of 382 acres on Arnyng Street. But the larger units only represented a small percentage of the total number of conveyances: 29 of 271 on East Street, 28 of 263 on Post Street and 20 of 144 on Arnyng Street. In short, most of these conveyances were for about an acre or less and in nearly all instances for arable.[17]

Unfortunately, surviving records are not concerned with either the value of the property or the length or nature of the tenure. A memo in the Jurors' Book after the farm rent totals of Easter 1478 describes the location of a property and notes simply that "John Barnard, husbandman, received from the 12 jurors one rod of arable for a halfpenny farthing farm at term." No doubt many bits of land were taken for a season or two, for only a rapid turnover of small units of land can explain so much land falling into this conveyance category over a very few years. As a fuller analysis of the individuals of Appendix 4 becomes possible in Chapter 5, more light may be thrown upon this market in small units of land. For now let it be noted that the land market picture serves as an "action shot" to complement the trends noted on the sequence of rentals in the first section of this chapter. The turnover of so many small units of property demonstrates a different role in the land market for such properties at this stage of an engrossing process and why so many small tenant units were still to be found on every street. The exchange in larger blocks of land demonstrates the break-up of many middling units of land and the manner by which wealthy newcomers were able to build up substantial blocks of holdings.

## C. OCCUPATIONAL SERVICES AND COMMERCIAL GROUPINGS

As we shall see in this section, there were many more people and many other activities at Godmanchester than were discernible through the sources on property analyzed above. For the most part, the information about these further people comes from the frankpledge rolls. Surviving for nearly every year, usually in good condition, the frankpledge rolls average around 90 different names per year. Several names occur in more than one context.

The frankpledge rolls purport to give the names of bakers, butchers and fishmongers who have been licensed for these trades. However, one may doubt that the list is complete, since the numbers are not significantly greater than in the smaller villages of Huntingdonshire at the time.[18] Furthermore, as may be seen in Table 16, the number of those licensed varied considerably from year to year. Such a variation would appear unlikely for standard consumer services. Some of the missing are picked up under separate

[17] The few messuages, curtileges and "swaths" of meadow conveyed have not been included in the conveyance figures given above.

[18] See, for example, E. B. DeWindt *Land and People in Holywell-cum-Needingworth* (Toronto, 1972), p. 235.

frankpledge entries for breach of trade regulations, especially with respect to the sale of bad meat. These have been added to the totals in Table 16. One is left to surmise that many practitioners of these trades were part time only and thereby escaped the frankpledge as an annual list. Those fined for breaking the assize of ale and regulations governing retailers were quite numerous. As has been argued for so long by scholars, therefore, these fines may actually amount to a *de facto* license. In any case, many of the same names occurred year after year.

Changes in the administrative structure of the frankpledge explain some of the variations to be found in the following Table 16. Until the 1460s there were no categories of fines for butchers and fishermen. In 1463 (the 1462 roll is missing) butchers and fishermen began to be fined. Over 1463-1464 two cobblers (John Hawkyn and John Leder) were also fined for selling at "excessive prices." The names of all tradespeople — bakers, brewers, butchers, cobblers, fishermen and sellers of ale — were all mixed up together and not isolated under separate lists until 1466.

Shifts in listing procedure explain part of the variations between brewers and sellers of ale. In the earliest surviving frankpledge rolls of the fifteenth century, the brewer (*pandoxator*) was fined for "wrongly brewing and selling." Gradually, this fine became related to wrong brewing only. Over these same years the helper (*auxiliatrix*) is charged with selling wrongly. By the 1450s the term *auxiliatrix* has changed to a root form of the term (*gannok*) employed rather generally in sixteenth-century England to indicate the keeper of an alehouse. The term brewer or brewing (*brasiatrix* or *brasiavit*) replaces the *pandoxator* occasionally from 1450 and becomes regular from 1466.

There does not seem to be any direct method by which it can be established that the long-term decline in numbers of those brewing over these years indicates a real transformation in the brewing industry in the town. Yet the change must have been related to economic conditions, as would seem to be indicated by many fluctuations in the total numbers of those involved in the ale industry. Furthermore, as will be seen below,[19] when it does become possible to isolate the economic status of brewers by means of wealth recorded on rent rolls from the 1480s, there will be found a definite association of frequent brewers with substantial resources. On the other hand, this process may have evolved very slowly. On the back of the 1464 frankpledge roll is a list of tenants of the town. The names of all those brewing and selling ale were collected for the years 1460-1466 and it was found that only some half-dozen sellers cannot be found identified with the

---

[19] See Chapter 6.

same surname among the tenants or among brewers. In short, these sellers of ale do not represent a substantial new poverty fringe at this time although it will be argued in Chapter 6 below that they did become so. This point can be substantiated by the fact that very few sellers of ale were isolated individuals. Many families both brewed and sold ale, and of these, brewing and selling by different members with the same surname was common. Some families, like the Barnards, would have more than one person selling ale in the same year. These various strategies of what was very likely the family economy component of the brewing industry could buffer over at least the short run the consequences of declining capacity to brew.

TABLE 16: VICTUALLERS IDENTIFIED IN THE FRANKPLEDGE ROLLS

| YEAR | BREWERS | RETAILERS | SUB-TOTAL | BAKERS | BUTCHERS | FISHERMEN | GRAND-TOTAL[a] |
|------|---------|-----------|-----------|--------|----------|-----------|----------------|
| 1422 | 23 | 5 | 28 | 1 | | | 29 |
| 1429 | 23 | 7 | 30 | 1 | | | 31 |
| 1433 | 20 | 4 | 24 | 1 | | | 25 |
| 1434 | 19 | 2 | 21 | 2 | | | 23 |
| 1435 | 20 | 4 | 24 | 1 | | | 25 |
| 1438 | 20 | 11 | 31 | 3 | | | 34 |
| 1439 | 16 | 10 | 36 | 5 | | | 41 |
| 1440 | 17 | 7 | 24 | 4 | | | 28 |
| 1441 | 14 | 8 | 22 | 4 | | | 26 |
| 1442 | 14 | 10 | 24 | 3 | | | 27 |
| 1443 | 12 | 10 | 22 | 2 | | | 24 |
| 1444 | 13 | 8 | 21 | 2 | | | 23 |
| 1448 | 12 | 12 | 24 | 2 | | | 26 |
| 1449 | 10 | 19 | 29 | 3 | | | 32 |
| 1450 | 11 | 13 | 24 | 3 | | | 27 |
| 1451 | 11 | 20 | 31 | | | | 31 |
| 1452 | 13 | 19 | 32 | 4 | | | 36 |
| 1459 | 19 | 22 | 41 | 5 | | | 46 |
| 1460 | 16 | 28 | 44 | 4 | | | 48 |
| 1461 | 18 | 21 | 39 | 4 | | | 43 |
| 1463 | 16 | 26 | 42 | | 4 | 3 | 49 |
| 1465 | 14 | 24 | 38 | | 7 | 4 | 49 |
| 1466 | 12 | 27 | 39 | 5 | 5 | 7 | 56 |
| 1467 | 11 | 24 | 35 | 6 | 4 | 4 | 49 |
| 1468 | 10 | 27 | 37 | 6 | 5 | 3 | 51 |
| 1469 | 12 | 29 | 41 | 5 | | | 46 |
| 1470 | 12 | 29 | 41 | 5 | | | 46 |
| 1471 | 13 | 24 | 37 | 6 | 6 | | 49 |
| 1472 | 18 | 33 | 51 | 7 | 6 | | 64 |
| 1477 | 15 | 29 | 43 | 5 | 3 | 5 | 56 |
| 1481 | 10 | 41 | 51 | 5 | 3 | 5 | 64 |
| 1485 | 11 | 32 | 43 | 9 | | | 52 |

[a] To these totals should be added the less regularly reported candlemakers: three for the years 1495-1503 and one for the years 1525-1526, 1529 and 1532.

| Year | Brewers | Retailers | Sub-total | Bakers | Butchers | Fishermen | Grand-total |
|---|---|---|---|---|---|---|---|
| 1486 | 11 | 24 | 35 | 7 | 2 | 2 | 46 |
| 1487 | 11 | 27 | 38 | 6 | 3 | 3 | 50 |
| 1488 | 11 | 23 | 34 | 7 | 2 | 3 | 46 |
| 1489 | 9 | 25 | 34 | 7 | 3 | 3 | 47 |
| 1490[b] | 10 | (19) | (29) | 5 | 3 | 3 | 40 |
| 1491 | 10 | 26 | 36 | 5 | 3 | 3 | 47 |
| 1494 | 12 | 26 | 38 | 4 | 4 | 7 | 53 |
| 1495 | 11 | 24 | 35 |  | 2 | 8 | 45 |
| 1496 | 11 | 25 | 36 | 7 | 5 | 2 | 50 |
| 1497 | 15 | 21 | 36 | 5 | 4 | 3 | 48 |
| 1498 | 14 | 23 | 37 | 8 | 3 | 6 | 54 |
| 1500 | 11 | 18 | 29 | 6 | 3 |  | 38 |
| 1501 | 11 | 16 | 27 | 7 | 3 | 3 | 40 |
| 1503 | 11 | 18 | 29 | 2 | 4 |  | 35 |
| 1505 | 13 | 14 | 37 | 7 | 5 | 4 | 43 |
| 1509 | 13 | 5 | 18 | 6 | 1 | 1 | 26 |
| 1510 | 16 | 11 | 27 | 5 | 1 | 2 | 35 |
| 1511 | 16 | 7 | 23 | 6 | 1 | 1 | 31 |
| 1512 | 2 | 10 | 12 | 4 |  | 1 | 17 |
| 1513 | 11 | 11 | 22 | 3 | 4 |  | 29 |
| 1515 | 9 | 9 | 18 | 9 | 3 |  | 30 |
| 1516 | 10 | 8 | 18 | 7 | 2 |  | 27 |
| 1517 | 1 | 2 | 3 | 8 | 2 |  | 13 |
| 1518 | 13 | 6 | 19 | 6 | 3 |  | 28 |
| 1520 |  | 5 | ( ) | 9 | 2 | 2 | 18 |
| 1522 | 12 | 4 | 16 | 6 | 3 |  | 25 |
| 1523 | 11 | 7 | 18 | 4 | 3 |  | 25 |
| 1525 | 9 | 11 | 20 | 4 | 3 | 4 | 31 |
| 1526 | 10 | 8 | 18 | 5 | 4 | 3 | 30 |
| 1527 | 10 | 8 | 18 | 6 | 3 | 5 | 32 |
| 1528 | 6 | 5 | 11 | 4 | 3 | 5 | 23 |
| 1529 | 7 | 5 | 12 | 6 | 3 | 4 | 25 |
| 1530 | 9 | 5 | 14 | 6 | 1 | 4 | 25 |
| 1531 | 1 | 1 |  | 1 |  | 4 | 7 |
| 1532 | 9 | 4 | 13 | 6 | 2 | 1 | 22 |
| 1533 | 12 | 5 | 17 | 9 | 4 | 2 | 32 |
| 1534 | 12 | 5 | 17 | 7 | 3 | 2 | 29 |
| 1536 | 13 | 4 | 17 | 7 | 4 | 2 | 30 |
| 1537 | 10 | 4 | 14 | 11 | 4 |  | 29 |
| 1538 | 8 | 4 | 12 | 8 | 2 |  | 22 |
| 1539 | 9 | 5 | 14 | 8 | 2 |  | 24 |
| 1540 | 8 | 4 | 12 | 13 | 2 |  | 27 |
| 1541 | 5 | 4 | 9 | 11 | 1 | 1 | 22 |
| 1542 | 6 | 2 | 8 | 11 | 2 |  | 21 |
| 1543 | 7 | 2 | 9 | 11 | 2 |  | 22 |
| 1544 | 3 |  | 3 | 8 |  |  | 11 |
| 1545 | 5 | 3 | 8 | 9 | 2 |  | 19 |

[b] Parentheses indicate incomplete data.

When these names are checked against property holders from the rentals for the five years 1485-1489, only some 44 of the 74 frankpledge names can be possibly associated with full names or even family names to be found in the rentals. Of the trades people in Godmanchester in 1485, 23 are clearly identifiable with a Post Street residence, eight were on West Street and only four on East and two on Arnyng Street. This identification is made more certain when families engage in multiple operations. On East Street, Agnes Bould would seem to have taken over the whole operation after the apparent death of John Bould around 1486. Agnes was listed as both a baker and brewer from 1487 to 1491 and as a brewer only from 1494 to 1510. On the same street, Thomas Sydebotom was baker in 1485 and his wife Agnes was brewing by the next year. Thomas' name had disappeared and Agnes was listed as a brewer for only one more year (1486). On West Street, Agnes Gybbys was listed as a brewer from 1485 to 1498 (except for 1489 and 1494); her husband John Gybbys was listed as a baker from 1486 to 1491. Post Street still had the old family of Manipenny, with William a baker from 1485 to 1501 and his wife Alice a brewer from 1485 to 1491. And Isabella Manipenny appeared as a brewer from 1494 to 1497 and then was replaced by Elizabeth Manipenny as a brewer from 1498 to 1503. On the same street, Thomas Cokman was licensed as both butcher and a fishmonger from 1485 to 1487, while his wife Alice who had been a brewer in 1494 took over as a butcher to 1496; an Agnes Cokman, possibly a sister of Thomas, remained a brewer from 1487 to 1491 and then was listed simply as a retailer from 1494 to 1496. Post Street also had Thomas Reynold as a butcher and fishmonger from 1486 to 1490; Thomas' wife Alice appeared as a brewer in 1485 and continued to 1491. Alice was listed both as a brewer and retailer in 1490. John Stoke was a butcher from 1485 to 1491 and a Joan Stoke, probably his wife, was a brewer until 1498. Another more brief involvement on Post Street was represented by Godfrey Wright, a butcher between 1487 and 1489. Associated with Godfrey no doubt were Agnes Wright, retailer from 1485 to 1491, and Isabella Wright, retailer from 1486 to 1498 and brewer over 1490 to 1491.

It is clear from several examples given above that merchants found it convenient to combine the trades of butcher and fishmonger. Other individuals with this practice were Thomas Fecas, John Gredley and Richard Sheter. This tendency to combine trades shifted noticeably to baking and brewing in the early sixteenth century. When baking and brewing are combined under presumed "families" as is done in Appendix 5, some of these combinations can be seen to be of longer standing.

No doubt many more labourers and occupations exclusive of fishermen, bakers, brewers, butchers and retailers do not appear on the Appendix 5 below. Over the 15 years after 1485 some 230 individuals appear on the frankpledge whose names cannot be identified with tenants or trades. Of these 230, 67 were charged in the context of trespassing and an equal number in the context of an assault charge. Those trespassing would appear to be engaged as cowherds or shepherds for the most part. While some of those involved in assaults may have been transients, the court records do not say so. Indeed the fact that many of these were charged with trespass and assault in more than one year would suggest a labour force with some continuity. The annual list of those appearing in the context of assault charges and trespassing is the following:

| | | |
|---|---|---|
| 1485: 21 | 1490: 18 | 1497: 43 |
| 1486: 24 | 1491: 20 | 1498: 38 |
| 1487: 9 | 1494: 32 | 1500: 32 |
| 1488: 18 | 1495: 35 | 1501: 30 |
| 1489: 19 | 1496: 36 | 1503: 31 |

It would seem logical to deduce that Godmanchester could draw upon a casual labour pool of at least one hundred men over this time and that one-third of these could have had a more permanent association with the town.

Servants were another distinct occupational group in the fifteenth and sixteenth-century Godmanchester. References to servants appear in the same context as references to labour in the frankpledge rolls so that we cannot even guess at actual totals from this source. Taken from the frankpledge rolls, Table 17 does indicate the identity of servants with the more wealthy townsmen and women:

TABLE 17: MASTERS WITH SERVANTS

| YEAR | SERVANT'S NAME | MASTER |
|---|---|---|
| 1415 | John Balle | Robert Peek |
| 1421 | John Pernell | John Copegray |
| 1443 | William | John Campion |
| ca 1450 | Thomas Mustard | John Aylred |
| 1481 | servant of | Richard West |
| 1482 | John Manning | John Lockyngton |
| 1485 | John Wright | Robert Gony |
| 1487 | Alice | John Bould |
| " | Robert | John Turneskewe |
| 1489 | John Clark | John Draper |
| 1490 | Thomas, super servant | John Turneskewe |
| 1491 | Margaret Frost | Richard Mayle |

| YEAR | SERVANT'S NAME | MASTER |
|------|----------------|--------|
| 1494 | Richard Ostun' | William Pacy |
| 1496 | John | Thomas Gravy |
| 1498 | John | Anna Gravy |
| " | servant of | Thomas Bailey |
| " | Robert | John Nottingham |
| " | Thomas | John Smith |
| " | servant of | Rase |
| " | servant of | Roger, the vicar |
| " | servant of | John Brown |
| 1500 | servant of | John Laxton |
| 1501 | servant of | Thomas Massey |
| " | servant of | Guido Wulfston, knight |
| " | servant of | Marv Grantofte |
| 1501 | servant of | William Melbourne |
| " | servant of | John Stokes |
| 1503 | servant of | Thomas Osse |
| 1509 | servant of | William Cranfield |
| " | servant of | William Awston |
| 1510 | William | Robert Nicholas |
| " | servant of | John Bonsay |
| 1511 | shepherd of | John Lawman |
| 1512 | shepherd of | William Dalton |
| " | servant of | Thomas Faldyng |
| " | shepherd of | Robert Chandeler |
| 1516 | Thomas | William Leffyn |
| 1517 | Gor' | Thomas Wylde |
| 1520 | Elizabeth Kingston | John Laxton |
| 1521 | Robert Harryson | John Boleyn |
| 1523 | William Dorraunt | John Frere |
| 1525 | Agnes | Katherine Monyment |
| " | shepherd of | Robert Pelle |
| " and 1534 | shepherd | Master William Sewster |
| 1526 | servant | John Ha(n)le |
| 1527 | William Ol' | John Est |
| 1528 | servant of | Edmund Archebould, priest |
| " | Elizabeth Page | John Brandon |
| " | servant of | Thomas Decone |
| 1529 | William | Richard Grene |
| 1530 | Robert (Passe) | John Page |
| " | servant of | John Wylde |
| 1531 | William Brown | John Granger |
| " | servant of | John Byllington |
| 1532 | Alice Cromwell | Alice West |
| " | Agnes Richardson | Alice West |
| 1534 | John Watson | William Birdere |
| " | shepherd of | Richard Robyn |
| " | shepherd of | Thomas Woodwared |
| 1537 | Anthony Garlond | Irbyll Corby |
| " | Richard Garlond, prentys of | Irbyll Corby |
| " and 1542 | servant of | Lord Thomas Payton, clerk |
| 1538 | Margaret Bawnye | John Granger senior |

| Year | Servant's Name | Master |
|------|---------------|--------|
| 1539 | Thomas Elways | Robert Pelle |
| " | Edward Menell | Robert Pelle |
| 1540 | Elizabeth | William Benet |
| " | John Jonson | William Benet |
| 1547 | Margaret Morgan | John Frere |

Another source earlier in the fifteenth century does give the number of servants from outsiders, or "foreigners" as they were called. Following the list of tenants with freedom of the vill, the dorse of the 1464 frankpledge roll has the entry: "The names of foreigners called servants who have freedom within etc. in the year given above."[20] There then follows 53 names: 8 on Arnyng Street, 13 on Post Street, 15 on East Street and 17 on West Street. On East Street there was a John noted only as servant of Ponder, on Arnyng Street a Richard noted as servant of Shepyn, on Post Street a Thomas noted only as servant of Waleys and on Arnyng Street a Benett noted as servant of (Light). In all other instances the surname is given but, except for the one instance of John Robyn servant of Conyff, the names of the master are not given. From their official roles we know that Ponder, Waleys and Conyff were leading townsmen. It may be remarked that no names of women are given on this list. Nine names are given as sons, largely from familiar surnames of the town. It is difficult to see "foreigners" in such context as little more than children of Godmanchester families who had not been in tithing, perhaps because of a stay abroad in neighbouring villages with friends or relatives. The question of servants will be treated in more detail under the section by that title in Chapter 5. The full list of servants by street is as follows:

EAST STREET: John Rede junior; William Sebynford; Hugh Gerbeys junior; Thomas Bate; Thomas Lesse; William Ibott; John Beverich; John Sydebotom; Robert Porter; John Gybbys; Thomas Hansen; William Fodrby; William Rede junior; John, servant of Ponder; Edward Marshall.

ARNYNG STREET: Richard Longe; William Snell; Thomas Snell; John Snell, son; Benett, servant of (Light); William Betrich; Richard, servant of Shepyn; Thomas Cole(umb)ur.

POST STREET: William Balle; John Balle, son; Thomas Goodchild; William Corby; John Gra(c'); Reginald son of Olyff; William Porter; John Cave; Thomas, servant of Waleys; William Barnard; Thomas Bailey; Walter Baker

[20] "Nomina forinsici, dicunt servientes, qu' habendam libertatem infra etc. de anno infrascripto."

WEST STREET:        John Robyn, servant of Conyff; John Sylke; John Seynt;
                    John Corby; William Dorraunt; William Foly; George
                    Barre; John Barre, son of William; William Ibott; John
                    Roger; William Whyte; Robert Ely; John Wattison, son
                    of John; Thomas Motte; Walter Motte; John Garlop
                    junior; John Longe.

Information about occupational services and commercial groupings adds
significantly to the land economy noted in Section A above. Only some 60
percent of these people can be identified with property holders of any level
of wealth. Commerce was a distinct avenue to wealth at Godmanchester and
the relative scope of this commercial role and land investment will have to
be analyzed further below. The prospect for further analysis of cowherds,
shepherds and other labouring groups is less encouraging. However, the
existence of this significant group, that did not include those having purchase
of liberty at even the smallest price, adds considerably to our knowledge of
the labour resources of the town.

What was the population of Godmanchester in the early Tudor period?
The second and third sections of this chapter make clear that the 250 odd
people listed for farm payments come nowhere near the true total. Was it
double, or triple the 250? After the Reformation, an appeal for the restora-
tion of the school cited the pastoral needs for "800 houslings." The round
figure of 800 leads to suspicion of the accuracy of the number. However, this
approximation to the number of "adults" requiring sacramental services does
seem plausible given the number of messuages. One could perhaps cite the
number of children below the "pastoral concern" age as 20 per cent. It has
been estimated that children under 12 constituted about 27 percent of the
total English population in the early 1560s.[21] As we shall see in Chapters 5
and 6, one should expect a declining population despite increases in family
size to be noted in Chapter 4. A population of around 1000 by the second
quarter of the sixteenth century, over and against a population of around
1200 or more in the 1480s, would seem to be a reasonable estimation.

Whatever the actual total population for the freemen of the town, there was
an apparent under supply in every category touched upon in this chapter —
land, trade and labour. The following chapter will describe the response to
this phenomenon through admissions to the freedom of the town. Part Two
of the volume will analyze in detail further shifts in economic activities and
the related populations change.

---

[21] See, E. A. Wrigley and R. S. Schofield, *The Population History of England, 1541-1871*
(London, 1981), p. 561 and related Table A3.1.

# 3

# The New Freemen in the Court Rolls of Godmanchester

The concept of freedom as applied to the ancient demense of Godmanchester found its origin in the ancient manorial and feudal organizations of England. Liberty was first and foremost a place; the parish of Godmanchester was the liberty of Godmanchester in the court rolls and customaries of the town from the thirteenth century. Those enjoying the full right to the use and excise of the customs of the town were simply said to have the liberty of Godmanchester. The exercise of jurisdiction over this liberty was commended to "the men" of Godmanchester in royal charters of privilege from the time of King John, although increasingly from the fifteenth century these men were referred to as the "commonalty"; and from this time an individual was occasionally called a "freeman."

The right to the liberty of Godmanchester was acquired by birth, that is to say, as the son of a freeman, and by purchase. The common form for entry by purchase changed little from the fourteenth to the sixteenth centuries. In general, these entries became more terse from the Tudor period, but the main elements did not change. In the sixteenth century most of the fines were paid on the spot so that pledges were not required. Fines were usually required to be paid within the term, or at most, the year. These are typical court roll entries:

> John Howson and his son John are admitted to the liberty of Godmanchester by a special grace of the whole community. They are sworn in according to the customs of the court and pay the fine entered above on the margin (7s.), one-half to be paid at the feast of Easter and one-half at Michaelmas. The pledge is John Godechild. (17 December 1422)[1]

---

[1] Johannes Howson et Johannes filius eiusdem ex speciali gratia totius comitatis admissi sunt ad libertatem de Gumecestre et jurati sunt secundum consuetudinem curie et dederunt pro fine ut supra in margine (viis.) solvenda ad festum Pasche et Michelis equali portione. Plegius Johannes Godechild.

John Kyng of Steeple Gidding is admitted to the liberty of Godmanchester by a special grace of the whole community. He is sworn in according to the customs of the manor of Godmanchester and pays the fine noted above (6s. 8d.). The pledges are Thomas Phille and William Powe to be collected at the feast of St. John the Baptist and Michaelmas. (7 December 1441)[2]

At this court Richard Lofti is admitted to the liberty of the vill and sworn in by pledges Richard Motte and Thomas Fecas for the fine of five shillings. The day for payment is the Sunday after the feast of the Epiphany. (16 December 1448)[3]

Margery Pope and her son Hugh come to this court and by a special grace of the whole community they are admitted to the liberty of the vill and pay the fine (5s.) on the spot. And the said Margery Pope is sworn and the said Hugh is sworn. (7 June 1501)[4]

John Dysney comes to this court and by a special grace is admitted to the liberty of the vill. He is sworn and pays the fine noted above (2s. 8d.). (19 September 1510)[5]

John Walshe, son of Godfrey Walshe, comes to this court and by a special grace of the whole community is admitted to the liberty of the vill, paid the fine on the spot (16d.) and is sworn. (5 December 1532).[6]

To be sworn into the liberty of Godmanchester was not an exceptional phenomenon by 1400. Between 1301 and 1399, 211 individuals are recorded in court rolls as having received the liberty of the town. However, the rate of entry in the fourteenth century posed no great problem of absorption for a town of several thousand residents who became members of the liberty by birth. Over the first half of the century, the entries averaged little more than one a year. The more catastrophic events of the second half of the century brought points of heavy influx — 27 in 1349, 7 in 1350 and 10 in 1380 as the largest — but these peaks were followed by averages of three or

---

[2] Johannes Kyng de Stepulgyddyng ex speciali gratia totius comitatis de Gumecestre admissus est ad libertatem de Gumecestre et juratus est secundum consuetudinem manerii de Gumecestre et dedit pro fine ut supra (vis.viiid.). Plegii Thomas Phille et Willelmus Powe coll(igenda) ad festum Sancti Johannis Baptiste et festum Michelis.

[3] Ad hanc curiam Ricardus Lofti admissus est ad libertatem ville et iuratus per plegios Ricardum Motte et Thomam Fecas pro fine vs. Dies solutio Dominica proxima post festum Epiphanie.

[4] Ad hanc curiam venerunt Margeria Pope et Hugo filius eius ex speciali gracia totius comitatis admissi sunt ad libertatem ville et solvit finem (vs.) in manibus et dicta Margeria Pope iurata est et dictus Hugo iuratus est.

[5] Ad hanc curiam venit Johannes Dysney ex speciali gratia et admissus est ad libertatem ville et iuratus est et solvit pro fine ut patet in capite (iis.viiid.).

[6] Ad hanc curiam venit Johannes Walshe filius Galfridi Walshe et ex speciali gratia totius comitatis admissus est ad libertatem ville et solvit finem (xvid.) in manibus et juratus est.

four a year. Furthermore, if one may judge by the size of the fines, prior to
the last quarter of the century many of those granted liberty of Godmanchester seem to be given the light entry fee expected of those with some
inherited property title in the town.[7]

## A. THE EARLY AND MID FIFTEENTH CENTURY

With the 1390s a new pattern appeared in the court rolls. Between 1392 and
1400 more than 30 individuals were granted entry to the town. This pattern
was to persist at the same high level for at least the next four decades: 49
between 1400 and 1409; 55 between 1410 and 1419; 60 between 1420 and
1429; 63 between 1430 and 1438.

In short, during four decades of the early fifteenth century Godmanchester
took in more newcomers than over the whole of the previous century. As
Table 18 indicates, the number of those given liberty of the town still
continued to occur in a cyclical pattern. For a few years (1412, 1416, 1426,
1427, 1433 and 1439) the paucity of surviving records would seem to
explain the exceptionally few entries. But, on the whole, the number of those
entering was clearly not determined by variations in numbers of surviving
records. Furthermore, the "peaks" of entry were more frequent and, as has
been noted, the cumulative effect dramatic.

Why Godmanchester was willing and able to accept this huge influx of
population is not readily apparent. At first glance it would appear that the
town retained its relatively open market to neighbourhood and region for
land, labour and craftsmen. But a gradual transformation in several features
of the traditional market can be discerned. First, individuals from what has
been called the "greater agrarian zone" of the town continued to get property
by bequest or gift under the formula of a small fine and swearing of the oath.
A few individuals were recorded under such title: John Orold' de Gidding
(20 November 1399);[8] Isabella wife of William Leche, couper de Huntingdon, (9 September 1400);[9] Emma wife of Master Roger Wynston de
Huntingdon (9 september 1400);[10] Margaret wife of Richard Grownde de

---

[7] See *A Small Town*, Chapter 2, Section B.

[8] Johannes Orold' de Gylling iuratus est ut mos est ville et dedit pro fine ut supra (iis.)
In the same court John took seisin of 1/2 acre by bequest of his mother Agnes.

[9] Isabella uxor Willelmi Leche Cowper de Huntyngdon' iurata est ut mos est curie et dedit
pro fine ut supra (xxd.).
This entry and the following (note 10) are for sisters and is followed by seisin of property
in gift from the will of their mother Agnes Millicent: three rods and three swaths of meadow
to Isabella and one acre to Agnes.

[10] Emma uxor Rogeri Wynston de Huntyngdon' iurata est ut mos est curie et dedit pro
fine ut supra in capita (xxd.).

## TABLE 18: INDIVIDUALS ENTERING LIBERTY EACH YEAR

| Year | | Year | | Year | | Year | | Year | | Year | | Year | | Year | | Year | | Year | | TOTAL BY DECADE |
|---|---|---|---|---|---|---|---|---|---|---|---|---|---|---|---|---|---|---|---|---|
| 1400 | 4 | 1401 | 14 | 1402 | 1 | 1403 | 5 | 1404 | 4 | 1405 | 4 | 1406 | 6 | 1407 | 5 | 1408 | 3 | 1409 | 3 | 49 |
| 1410 | 13 | 1411 | 6 | 1412 | MISSING | 1413 | 2 | 1414 | MISSING | 1415 | 14 | 1416 | MISSING | 1417 | 13 | 1418 | MISSING | 1419 | 7 | (55) |
| 1420 | 7 | 1421 | 9 | 1422 | 5 | 1423 | 9 | 1424 | 10 | 1425 | 1 | 1426 | MISSING | 1427 | MISSING | 1428 | 16 | 1429 | 3 | (60) |
| 1430 | 4 | 1431 | 7 | 1432 | 6 | 1433 | MISSING | 1434 | 8 | 1435 | 3 | 1436 | 15 | 1437 | 8 | 1438 | 12 | 1439 | MISSING | (63) |
| 1440 | MISSING | 1441 | 2 | 1442 | 4 | 1443 | MISSING | 1444 | 2 | 1445 | 4 | 1446 | 1 | 1447 | MISSING | 1448 | MISSING | 1449 | 9 | (22) |
| 1450 | 9 | 1451 | MISSING | 1452 | 3 | 1453 | MISSING | 1454 | MISSING | 1455 | MISSING | 1456 | 6 | 1457 | MISSING | 1458 | MISSING | 1459 | MISSING | (18) |
| 1460 | MISSING | 1461 | MISSING | 1462 | MISSING | 1463 | 8 | 1464 | 5 | 1465 | 9 | 1466 | 1 | 1467 | MISSING | 1468 | MISSING | 1469 | MISSING | (23) |
| 1470 | MISSING | 1471 | MISSING | 1472 | 2 | 1473 | 1 | 1474 | 3 | 1475 | 5 | 1476 | MISSING | 1477 | MISSING | 1478 | 1 | 1479 | 7 | (19) |
| 1480 | 8 | 1481 | 6 | 1482 | 15 | 1483 | MISSING | 1484 | 3 | 1485 | 5 | 1486 | 14 | 1487 | 7 | 1488 | 16 | 1489 | 13 | (87) |
| 1490 | 4 | 1491 | 11 | 1492 | 7 | 1493 | 6 | 1494 | 21 | 1495 | 8 | 1496 | 11 | 1497 | 8 | 1498 | 4 | 1499 | 1 | 81 |
| 1500 | 6 | 1501 | 15 | 1502 | 3 | 1503 | 12 | 1504 | 3 | 1505 | 8 | 1506 | 8 | 1507 | 7 | 1508 | 6 | 1509 | 11 | 79 |
| 1510 | 12 | 1511 | 13 | 1512 | 17 | 1513 | 8 | 1514 | 6 | 1515 | 4 | 1516 | 8 | 1517 | 12 | 1518 | 2 | 1519 | 12 | 94 |
| 1520 | 11 | 1521 | 17 | 1522 | 1 | 1523 | 7 | 1524 | 4 | 1525 | 7 | 1526 | 5 | 1527 | 12 | 1528 | 8 | 1529 | 7 | 79 |
| 1530 | 5 | 1531 | 10 | 1532 | 15 | 1533 | 10 | 1534 | 15 | 1535 | 2 | 1536 | 14 | 1537 | 7 | 1538 | 18 | 1539 | 4 | 100 |
| 1540 | 10 | 1541 | 9 | 1542 | 1 | 1543 | 12 | 1544 | 8 | 1545 | 1 | 1546 | 8 | | | | | | | 49 |

GRAND TOTAL: 878

Hemingford Abbots (15 May 1404);[11] William son of Margaret Mychell de Hartford (25 February 1406);[12] John Collyson de Hartford (11 September 1410);[13] Emma daughter of Agnes Grace de Hemingford (11 September 1410);[14] John son of Robert Brendehouse de Hemingford Abbots (6 June 1415);[15] Godfrey Pays de Offord (2 September 1417);[16] Margaret wife of Simon Cowlynsge de Croxton and Agnes wife of Robert Smyth de Potton (2 June 1418);[17] Arthur Ormesby and wife Margaret (17 April 1421);[18] John Aylmar de Hemingford Abbots (17 April 1421);[19] Lord William Motte, vicar of the church of St. Mary de Huntingdon (4 August 1429).[20]

It may be noted that these entries were not to liberty of the vill as were those entry forms exemplified earlier in this chapter. On the other hand, this traditional form of entry by outsiders to property in the town by bequest or gift does not appear in court rolls after the 1420s. Furthermore, that special official designated in the bailiff's roll of 1413 "as collector of the farm from foreigners" does not appear in bailiff's accounts after the early fifteenth century. That there was a policy at work is further demonstrated by the customs of 1475[21] wherein it was forbidden under severe penalty to sell or alienate property to foreigners and the latter were further forbidden to pasture beasts within the liberty under severe penalty.

[11] Margareta uxor Ricardi Grownde de Hemyngforde Abbotis iurata est secundum consuetudinem curie et fecit finem et dedit pro fine ut supra (iis.).

There follows seisin of property of 1/2 acre by gift of her mother.

[12] This entry has the same form as note 13.

[13] Johannes Collyson de Herford iuratus est ut forinsecus secundum consuetudinem curie et fecit finem pro (xxd.).

[14] Emma filia Agnetis Grase de Hemyngford iuratas est ut forinseca secundum consuetudinem curie et fecit finem et solvit pro fine (viiid.).

Emma then took seisin of 1/2 acre property received by bequest.

[15] Johannes filius Roberti Brendhouse de Hemyngford Abbatis iuratus est secundum consuetudinem curie ut forinsecus et dedit pro fine ut supra in capite (xiid.).

In the very next entry John takes seisin of one acre in gift from John Brendehouse his ancestor.

[16] Galfridus Parys de offord admissus est ad libertatem de Gumecestre ut forinsecus et iuratus est secundum consuetudinem curie et dedit pro fine ut supra in margine (iiis.).

No property entry is recorded in court records at this time.

[17] Margareta uxor Simonis Cowlynsge de croxton et Agnes uxor Roberti Smyth de Potton iurate sunt secundum consuetudinem curie ut forinsice et dederunt pro fine ut supra in margine (iis.).

In the very next entry Margaret and Agnes take seisin of one acre, one and one-half rods by bequest.

[18] This entry has the same form as note 13: 4 acres.

[19] Ibid. : 1/2 acres plus 1/2 rod.

[20] Dominus Willelmus Motte vicarius ecclesie Sancte Marie de Huntyngdon' juravit ut forinsecus comitatis de Gumecestre et dedit pro fine ut supra (xiid.).

A following entry indicates Motte taking seisin of property, but the entry is incomplete.

[21] *A Small Town*, p. 438.

A gradual reduction in the numbers of foreign tenants had been occurring at Godmanchester for a long time. If one accepts the suggested division into streets of the 1279 Hundred Roll for the town,[22] then at the end of the Hundred Roll are listed nearly two full columns, that is, over 100 names, of individuals holding small properties in Godmanchester. That these individuals were foreigners is not surprising in view of the fact that some 40 individuals from the borough of Huntingdon alone held small units of land at Godmanchester in the second quarter of the fourteenth century.[23] That list of tenants on the back of the 1464 frankpledge roll[24] gives first the names of 241 tenants by street with liberty, then 57 by street who were servants with liberty and finally 35 names of foreigners (*forinsici*), not by street, as "having land and tenements in Godmanchester." This last group of 35 were undoubtedly the traditional foreigners since they are not listed as residents by street. Names of this group include at least six church-related officials. One of these, John Copegray, chaplain, had the surname of a prominent Godmanchester family. As has been seen above in the examples of this type of entry from the early fifteenth century, women's names occur frequently. No doubt many of the six names of women in the 1464 list were daughters who had married abroad. In some instances this would explain a surname that was unusual for a Godmanchester person. But many of the names (Aylred, Dorraunt, Este, Lawe, Maryot, Reygate) were familiar Godmanchester family names.

An undated list[25] of foreigners paying rent also survives among Godmanchester records. Some half dozen of these names are to be found among those purchasing liberty around 1500, but identification cannot be firm since foreigners were not listed on the regular rent roll. Probably this list can be dated in the last quarter of the century. Numbers of foreigners are about the same as in 1464, but few names come from traditional families of the town. The two lists are arranged in Table 19 to show some continuing tenancies.

A document entitled "Rent Owed from Foreigners on the Feast of St. Michael 1547"[26] has survived and shows the attenuated survival of this form

[22] See below, Chapter 6, p. 194.

[23] *A Small Town*, pp. 131-132.

[24] See above, p. 57.

[25] Currently collected with the Tithing Rolls from Huntington Record Office, Godmanchester Borough Records, Box 8, Bundle 4, other Documents of Henry VII, miscellaneous no. 9. The 1464 list is preceded by the entry "Mynstrechambre Conestable," indicating that the constable collected rents from foreigners.

[26] Rentale de Foreigners debite ad festum Sancti Michaelis Edwardi VI primo. Huntingdon Record Office, Godmanchester Borough Records, Box 1, Bundle 13, Document 12C. A document in the Godmanchester collection, Box 5, Bundle 7, shows officials having difficulty in collecting farm from foreigners in 1603.

of tenure. As can be seen in Table 20, 15 of the 18 names owed the traditional small farm. Why the large payments are entered is not clear since at least two of these individuals had obtained liberty a decade or more earlier. One must surmise that these two persons no longer live in Godmanchester. Chapter 7 will deal with the question of purchase of large blocks of land in Godmanchester by non-residents as a new feature of the late fifteenth and early sixteenth-century land market of the town.

TABLE 19: NAMES OF FOREIGN TENANTS

| 1464 | CA. 1490 |
|---|---|
| Vicar of Hertford | Vicar of Hertord |
| Prior of Canons of Huntingdon | Prior of Canons of Huntingdon |
| Custodian of the Church, attorney | Custodian of Church of Blessed John of Huntingdon |
| Priory of (All Saints?) of Huntingdon | Prior of Brothers of Huntingdon |
| Rector of Church of Blessed | John Copegray, chaplain |
| Mary of Huntingdon | |
| Joan Dorraunt | William Dorraunt |
| John Dorraunt | John Dorraunt |
| William Boleyn, junior | John Boleyn |
| Robert Warwick | John Tempillman |
| Nicholas Overton | Thomas Barber |
| John Parysch | William Pope |
| Arthur Hacneste | William Lincoln |
| John Este | John Carter |
| Elena Este | William Browne |
| Thomas Selde, chaplain | Mayster Horwod |
| Margaret Grown' | Thomas Gardener |
| Cecilia Este | William Bloke |
| John Anton | William Bigh |
| Margaret Scot | John Triklow |
| Emma (At?)wod | William Fald |
| John Ploughwright | John Jeffere |
| Agnes Alred | Thomas Page |
| Emma Mariot | Henry Judd |
| John Dalton | John Clarke de Higham |
| John Reygate | John Smyth de Caxton |
| William Weston | John Foster |
| Richard Booke | John Alkok |
| John Melbourne junior | John Barre |
| Thomas Kent | John V(iz)d |
| John Plumpton | William (Growne) |
| John Fischer | William Kyng de Weston |
| Edward Kent | John [      ] |
| James Lawe | John Page de Caxton |
| Robert Marke | John Bayford de Croxton |
| John Hay' | John Garlop de Offord Cluny |
| | Richard (Plumbe) de Hertford |

TABLE 20: RENTAL OF FOREIGNERS OWED AT MICHAELMAS 1547

| | |
|---|---|
| Albert Mollem of Huntingdon | 12d. |
| Philip Chambre, gentleman | 6d. |
| Custodian of St. John the Baptist | 5d. ob. & 11d |
| Custodian of Church of Hemingford | 3d. |
| Walter Barber of Hemingford | 18d. |
| John Alcoke of Hemingford | 3d. ob. & ob. |
| Robert Porter of Hemingford | 8d. |
| Lawrence Marrame | 3d. ob. |
| Randall Hawle of Cambridge | 2s. 2d. ob. q. |
| Vicar of Hertford | ob. q. |
| William Lockyngton of Earith | 19d. ob. |
| Alice Fermary | 1d. |
| William Latisser | 1d. ob. |
| John Dorraunt | 2s. 8d. |
| Robert William of Earith | 12d. |
| Robert Goddarde | 9d. |
| Robert Cherseye of London | 7s. 4d. ob. q. |
| Thomas Hardyng of Hertford | 1d. ob. q. |
| TOTAL | 22s. 1d. ob. |

Another feature of these records should be noted. When occupations are appended to first name and surname of those entering Godmanchester there are no indications of new occupational demands of the town. Furthermore, in the context of the large numbers entering at the time, and in contrast with occupational identifications for the fourteenth century, occupational identification for those entering the town does not seem to have been considered important. Three butchers were admitted: John Grawnhurst in 1401 and Henry Chamberlayn and Robert Ferwell with his sons John and Thomas in 1428. Other multiple occupations admitted were: two fishermen, John Boys and son in 1420; two millers, Richard Grene in 1401 and William Broke in 1406; three sengilmen, John Barrett, John Cook and John Porter in 1438; two smiths, John Fisher in 1403 and John Freman in 1404; three taylors, Richard West in 1406 and Richard Brace and William Nevsham in 1452; two weavers, Robert Marshall in 1423 and William Marche in 1436. Single representatives of occupations were:

| | |
|---|---|
| scrivener | Richard Taylor, 1399 |
| draper | Walter Rowthe, 1402 |
| *ovillio* | John Wryght with his sons Thomas and William, 1403 |
| potter | William Crandon, 1404 |
| ferrour | John Eston, 1419 |
| glover | William Godeherd, 1419 |
| turner | William Bron, 1419 |

| shether | John Botelmaker, alias shether with his son John, 1434 |
| lockyer | John Swynford, 1434 |
| fuller | John Cula, 1438 |
| wulschem | Godfrey Robyn with his sons Richard and William, 1438 |

A further feature of those entering Godmanchester in the first half of the fifteenth century was the fact that their place of origin does not seem to have been worthy of note. Some of these came from local villages, others from a wider regional radius and others again from a great distance. This pattern was familiar enough to fourteenth-century Godmanchester, but what was new in the fifteenth century was the fact that the provenance of immigrants did not rank as important in the rush for acceptance of the newcomers. Most of those whose place of origin was indicated were local:

| 1401 | John son of William Bryan | Yelling (Hunts.) |
| 1401 | William Everard | Swavesey (Cambs.) |
| 1403 | Richard Ferrour | Raveley (Hunts.) |
| 1407 | William Taylor and son Robert | Brington (Hunts.) |
| 1417 | John Ive | Hilton (Hunts.) |
| 1419 | Robert Boteler | Yelling (Hunts.) |
| 1428 | Bartholomew Sofham and his son Thomas | Cambridge (Cambs.) |
| 1432 | John Smyth junior and son John | Hemingford Abbots (Hunts.) |
| 1434 | John Baron senior | Graveley (Cambs.) |
| 1441 | John Amyson | Wyng (in Rutland) |
| 1445 | John Grene | London |

In the Ramsey Abbey villages of Huntingdonshire, dozens of villeins deserted their traditional homesteads from the 1390s for the promise of more attractive futures elsewhere.[27] This information is clearly available from lists of such villeins on the manorial account rolls as well as lists on rental rolls of vacant properties let at a discount. Since Godmanchester was a royal manor and its people were not villeins, if these people decided to desert the town there would be no reason for proscribing them. At the same time, from

---

[27] See J. A. Raftis, *Tenure and Mobility*, (Toronto, 1964), pp. 160-66. The sole reference to this issue of villeinage comes in the Jurors' Roll, p. 19, under the date before St. Thomas the Apostle, 14 Henry VII when John Foster and Richard Foster make a statement before the bailiffs (William Orwell and John Laxton) to the effect that they are not villeins and bondmen "of blood" of William Knight of Hamerton or Wynwyk. Interestingly enough, in the following year Michaelmas 15 Henry VII, John Foster pays a fine of 2s. 8d. for "pety bryburry" and promises not to do so again. Unfortunately, there is no detail about the amount or purpose of the bribery.

indirect evidence there is no reason to believe that an unusual number of people deserted Godmanchester from the late fourteenth century.[28] Such desertion would be expected to be reflected in the failure to pay farm dues, but in the hundreds of extant court records references to such failure are rare: during September 1429 William Manipenny took seisin of a parcel of land in West Crofts that had fallen into the bailiff's hands through defect of payment; John Donewych had his messuage seized, 16 January 1444, for failing to pay to the farm.[29] Furthermore, as the summary list of entry fines to the liberty of Godmanchester illustrates, until the 1440s at least, the bailiffs of Godmanchester were able to attract sufficient newcomers without discounting the entry fine.[30]

Furthermore evidence to the effect that social and economic intercourse of a more traditional nature was not discontinued may be seen in the hiring of casual labour from beyond the town. Some evidence for this phenomenon is presented below from the list of Ramsey Abbey villeins away from their home manors with, or without, licence of their lord. None of these former Ramsey villeins were listed among those obtaining liberty of the town of Godmanchester:

---

[28] An interesting entry occurs on the court roll of 24 March, 1429, when Thomas Bonis and his son John were granted liberty of the town and their fine condoned because the father of Thomas had been a freeman.

[29] Ad curiam de Gumecestre tentam etc. post festum Wulfstani venit quidam colectorum firme domini Regis in le Postrete in Gumecestre presentandum et ostendum ballivis et curie quod quidem Johannes Donewyche filius et heres Johannis Donewych tenet jure hereditate quoddam messuagium in le Postrete predictam vocatum donewicheplace et non solvit redditum assisum de messuagio predicto pro eo ad festa Pasche et Michelis. Prefatus collector venit ad predictum messuagium ad equitandum redditum inde debitum et consuetum et prefatus Johannes tenens et heres non fuit ad aliquod temporibus terminorum predictorum nec aliquis alius nomine suo parati ad equitandum et exonerandum messuagium predictum de redditu predicto nec aliquo tempore medio terminorum predictorum sufficientes dictrictiones in eodem messuagio invenire potuit. Unde petiit pro exoneratione sua quod dictum messuagium capiatur in manu domini Regis secundum consuetudinem manerii. Unde consideratum est per curiam quod dictum messuagium capiatur in manu domini Regis ita quod ballivi predicti et eorum successores respondeant comitati de exitu et proficiis quamdiu in manu ballivorum remanere contigerit. Eodem die venit Henricus Hildemar et cepit seisinam de quodam messuagio vocato donewicheysplace prout iacet in longatudine et latitudine in le Postrete in Gumecestre cuius unum capud abuttans versus viam regiam vocatam oldlondonweye et aliud capud abbutans versus viam vocatam Newlondonweye empto de ballivis ville de Gumecestre habendo et tenendo sibi et heredibus et assignis suis in perpetuum ad defendendum pro firma debita et de jure consueto.

This entry is added to the court records for 16 January 1444. There was no regular meeting of the court after the feast of St. Wulfston (19 January), so presumably a special session of the court was called to address this issue.

[30] The sole exception is that of John Undyl, granted the liberty on 9 February 1419, but with the fine condoned "since he was unable to pay".

Chircheman, Matilda daughter of Henry Houghton, at Godmanchester 1404-1433;[31]

Bate, Robert of Ellington, at Godmanchester 1405-1407;[32]

Bellond, John son of John of Hemingford, at Godmanchester with Thomas Frost in 1411 and at Holywell in 1419;[33]

Newman, Agnes daughter of Nicholas of Hemingford, at Godmanchester 1423 with her father;[34]

Marshall, Robert of Hemingford, at Godmanchester in 1428 and returned;[35]

Carter, John son of Richard of Houghton, at Godmanchester in 1429-1433;[36]

Dyke, Nicholas of Graveley, at Godmanchester in 1448 to 1458;[37]

Hacon,[38] John, son of Simon of Weston, at Godmanchester in 1450 to 1462; Joan, daughter of Walter of Weston, at Godmanchester in 1455 to 1462, and in 1450 noted with Henry Hildemar; Thomas, son of Walter of Weston, at Godmanchester in 1455 to 1457 and returned in 1461 and noted dead by 1462; Mariota, daughter of John of Weston, at Godmanchester in 1455 to 1457; John son of Walter, *sutor*, of Weston, at Godmanchester in 1455 to 1460 and noted dead by 1460s;

Hacon, Thomas, naif of Weston, lives at Godmanchester 1400-1401;[39]

West, John son of Robert de Graveley at Toseland in 1455 and Godmanchester in 1457 and dead by 1458;[40]

Upton, Thomas of Houghton, at Godmanchester, 1421;[41]

Molt, Alice, daughter of Thomas of Warboys, licence to marry Thomas Scot of Godmanchester, 1421;[42]

Wistow, Margaret of, at Ramsey, widow of John Whyte and daughter of Robert Attegate, naif of the lord by blood, pays six capons for licence

[31] 179/48, 39477, 179/50, 179/53, 179/56, 179/57, 179/59, 179/60, 179/61, 179/62. For this and the following nine notes the 179 indicates the portfolio heading for the Public Record Office court roll collections under SC 2; other five digit references are to Additional Rolls in the British Library.

[32] 179/50, 179/51.

[33] 179/53, 179/56.

[34] 179/57. Nicholas then went to Huntingdon for at least ten years, but there is no further mention of Agnes in the records.

[35] 179/59.

[36] 179/60, 179/61, 179/62.

[37] 179/65, 179/66, 179/67, 34831, 179/68.

[38] 179/66, 34909, 179/67, 39870, 179/68, 39729.

[39] See, Edwin DeWindt, *The Liber Gersumarum of Ramsey Abbey* (Toronto: Pontifical Institute of Mediaeval Studies, 1976), p. 44, fol. 265.

[40] 179/67, 34831, 179/68.

[41] 179/70.

[42] *Liber Gersumarum*, p. 159, fol. 1858. These husbands married to naifs have familiar names in Godmanchester.

to marry Nicholas Morell of Godmanchester — this time (24 October 1445);[43]

George Stocke[44] of Godmanchester and his wife Isabella: one messuage and two quarters of land recently held by Thomas Coole once held by John Howlot in Abbots Ripton (April 1453).

Clearly, what we are witnessing over these decades of the fifteenth century is a two-fold phenomenon. On the one hand, traditional markets were no longer supplying the needs of the town. On the other hand, as the system of supplying needs through entry to liberty took over traditional functions this market management became more impersonal. Blood relationships, neighbourhood, village and town identities as well as craft associations became replaced by categories of entry fines to the liberty of Godmanchester. Fines also required some financial capability since these were to be paid on the spot or fairly quickly. The payment of a substantial fine would imply commitment to some specific and permanent economic interest in the town.

Throughout the whole of the fifteenth and early sixteenth centuries, the largest fines are traceable to those who obtain property in Godmanchester. A breakdown of fines according to year and size is presented in Table 25. For the first half of the century additions of new names to property holders were numerous. The chance survival of a fragment[45] entitled "Tithing Roll [    ] H VI" listing the names of tenants that were resident on East and Arnyng Street, and to be dated probably to around 1436, provides a dramatic picture of the result of the previous decades of immigration. 116 names are listed for the two streets; although about 20 names are indicipherable, 30 of those identifiable can be clearly recognized as having been granted liberty over the previous years. In short, some thirty per cent of the property holders on these two streets were newcomers to the town!

The remaining category of fines at this time were sometimes identified with specific crafts or occupations.[46] If all fines in this group are considered to designate occupations, Appendix 6 has 21 such specialists entering the town over the first four decades of the fifteenth century. Both from the numbers of newcomers taking up land and of those entering to pursue various occupations, one conclusion appears to be inescapable. An exceptionally large number of families were disappearing and perhaps dying out at Godmanchester between the 1390s and 1440s.

[43] Ibid., p. 312, fol. 3740.

[44] Ibid., p. 353, fol. 4158. This is an example, of course, of a Godmanchester individual having moved to a Ramsey manor, perhaps through marrying someone at Abbots Ripton.

[45] Huntington Record Office, Godmanchester Borough Records, Box 1, Bundle 12. Rotulus Decene de [    ] Strete de Anno Regno Regis H. VI [    ].

[46] See below, pp. 137-143.

From the mid 1440s there are clear signs that Godmanchester could no longer attract immigrants with the level of fines that had persisted from the fourteenth century. The most common fine of these earlier decades, as seen in Appendix 7, that is, the half mark (6/8d.), began frequently to be reduced by one half to 3/4d. This policy was not fully successful. Although there is a thinner scatter of surviving court rolls for the 1440s, 1450s, 1460s and 1470s evidence from Table 18 indicates that the level of immigration was not sustained over these two decades.

Fines for immigrants who were to take up property did not fall so drastically at this time. One may presume, therefore, that replacement was not so exigent and when replacement was required for this group there was at hand a ready supply of applicants. It is not possible to obtain a precise picture of the total impact of immigration upon the property scene at Godmanchester since disease could decimate the immigrant as well as the native. Furthermore, to judge by later decades[47] some immigrants would take up property for a short-term commercial advantage only. However, the unique list of tenants and servants of Godmanchester for the year 1464 may be taken as the end-product of more than one-half century of new arrivals at Godmanchester. The following Table 21 shows the date at which certain individuals (or their fathers) were given liberty of the town and the location of such families on the streets of Godmanchester in 1464. This Table shows at least 55 of the 242 tenants listed in 1464 were "newcomers" to the town. The spread of these "newcomers" around the town was fairly even with 14 on East Street 25 on Post Street 11 on Arnyng Street and 7 on West Street.

Data in this table underline the continuing process of outsiders obtaining liberty and land in Godmanchester. But the fact that 29 individuals from outside the town took up land prior to 1440 and only 22 between 1440 and 1464 does not provide a sufficient basis for comparison since many more records are missing during the 1440s and 1450s than over earlier decades. It is interesting to observe that those 30 new names found in the Tithing Roll of 1536, or 60 names if this figure is extrapolated to the four streets, had now become 39 for the whole town. In short, probably one-half of those taking up property at Godmanchester over the first third of the fifteenth century did not survive, or at least did not survive in the town. There is also no possible means, prior to the extant rent rolls from later in the century, to establish whether many of these new names appearing and disappearing were larger or smaller tenants.

---

[47] See below, Chapter 6.

TABLE 21: "NEWCOMERS" ON THE TENANT LIST OF 1464

| NAME | YEAR IN WHICH LIBERTY ACQUIRED | STREET |
|---|---|---|
| Ponder, William | 1401 | East |
| Kyng, Thomas | 1404 | Post |
| Clark, John | 1407 | Post |
| Frost, Thomas | 1409 | Arnyng |
| Frost, John son of Thomas | 1409 | Arnyng |
| Melbourne, John | 1411 | East |
| Campion, John son of John[a] | 1415 | West |
| Campion, Richard son of John | 1415 | West |
| Roper, Henry and son John | 1415 | Arnyng |
| Godeherd, William | 1419 | East |
| Howson, John | 1422 | Arnyng |
| Baron, John son of Thomas | 1423 | Arnyng |
| Gardener, John son of Roger | 1424 | East |
| Chamberlayn, Henry, butcher | 1428 | Post |
| Newman, Thomas | 1428 | Post |
| Chamberlayn, John | 1432 | Post |
| Smyth, John de Hemingford Abbots[b] | 1432 | Post |
| Waleys, John and son Thomas | 1432 | Post |
| Botelmaker, John son of John, alias shether | 1434 | Post |
| Loveday, Richard son of William | 1434 | Post |
| Stalys, John | 1434 | Post |
| Bishop, William | 1435 | East |
| Bishop, John | 1436 | East |
| Allyngham, Thomas and sons John and Robert | 1436 | Post |
| Brawn, John | 1437 | Arnyng |
| Barrett, John, sengliman | 1438 | East |
| Fille, Thomas | 1438 | Post |
| Porter, John | 1438 | Post |
| Wright, Thomas son of Robert | 1438 | East |
| Hanson, George | 1442 | Post |
| Horewode, William | 1442 | West |
| Mayhew, John | 1442 | East |
| Stafford, John son of John | 1442 | Post |
| Corby, John | 1444 | Arnyng |
| Corby, William | 1444 | Post |
| Schylling, John | 1445 | Post |
| Stukeley, Thomas | 1445 | West |
| Gerrard, John | 1446 | Arnyng |
| Folkes, Richard son of John | 1449 | East |
| Mayle, Richard and son Thomas | 1449 | West |
| Baron, John | 1450 | East |
| Folkes, John | 1450 | West |
| Levot, John | 1450 | Arnyng |
| Lushton, John | 1450 | Post |

[a] Not noted as John son of John on the 1464 List.
[b] John Smyth is not designated as coming from Hemingford Abbots on the 1464 List.

| | | |
|---|---|---|
| Vincent, John | 1450 | East |
| Emley, John | 1452 | Post |
| Holme, William | 1456 | West |
| Motte, John senior and John junior | 1456 | East |
| Parysch, John | 1456 | East |
| Bowle, Hugh | 1463 | Post |
| Chycheley, Richard | 1463 | Post |
| Maryot, Thomas | 1464 | Post |
| Misterton, Thomas | 1464 | Post |
| Rede, William | 1464 | East |
| Mayle, William[c] | 1465 | West |

[c] William Mayle would seem to have obtained some property before he purchased his liberty.

## B. THE LATE FIFTEENTH AND EARLY SIXTEENTH CENTURY

From the 1480s those receiving liberty almost doubled in number: 1480-1489: 80; 1490-1499: 76; 1500-1509: 69; 1510-1519: 88; 1520-1529: 80; 1430-1539: 99 and 1540-1549: 64. The yearly spread over each decade remained quite uneven throughout the whole of the period and may suggest a calculated policy of controlled absorption. Nevertheless, the total cumulative picture was dramatic. By 1546, 878 surnames had been added to names existing before 1400 by grants of liberty of Godmanchester, more than two thirds of these coming between 1480 and 1549.

Again, this list of liberties from the 1480s bears no relation to a traditional methods of absorbing local or regional people into the town. Unfortunately, Godmanchester officials did not deem it important to retain consistent records of those sworn into tithing as they came of age.[48] However, a few such records do survive on frankpledge rolls and serve to demonstrate that entries to tithing merely represent sons of freemen coming of age and assuming the tithing responsibilities of adults. Such entries bear no relationship to the category of entry to freedom of the town. That is to say, the admission to tithing is simply noted and there are no pledges, nor is there a fine except for the nominal penny or so that would cover the clerk's expenses for the entry.

---

[48] That there was such a roll is established by the unique entry that on the day of assessing the view of frankpledge 'venit Henricus Frere et iuratus in rotulo decennarie et dat pro fine prout in capite (1d.)'. See also, of course, note 45 above.

TABLE 22: INDIVIDUALS SWORN INTO TITHING

| | |
|---|---|
| *1486* | Richard Vyntner |
| William Aylred | *1529* |
| Reginald Corby | William Benett junior |
| William Frost | Richard Mayle |
| William Holme | John Robyn |
| Thomas Knaresborough | *1530* |
| Robert Mayle | William Bortwe |
| Robert Nottingham | Henry Est |
| Thomas Page | Richard Lockington |
| *1490* | Bernard Tor[  ] |
| William Farthing | *1531* |
| John Page | William Clark |
| John Stevenson | Thomas Copinger junior |
| *1520* | Thomas [Wryght] |
| Henry Frere | *1532* |
| *1521* | William Grace |
| Thomas Garlop | Robert Puryyour |
| *1523* | *1533* |
| William, son of Robert White | John Clark |
| *1526* | William son of John Clark |
| John Ede | Henry Taylor |
| Thomas Punt | John Taylor |

Social historians usually assume a vast increase in geographical mobility in the English countryside of the fifteenth century.[49] May the great numbers of those entering Godmanchester reflect movement from the town as well as entry into it? One index of those moving from the town could be the number of those seeking re-admission. But these were not many: John Schylling 1489; John Wynde 1508; John Lockyngton 1509; John Gredley 1510; John Wylde 1516; John Brandon, Thomas Pacy, Richard Prior, Richard Robyn and Robert Roysely all in 1519; William Koynne, Richard Scot and John Wyllyson in 1520; John Papworth 1521; William Alake 1538 and Thomas Frere 1541. In any case, most of these seeking re-admission were more wealthy and had often lost their liberty by abuse of customs.[50]

Information about the provenance of those coming to Godmanchester continued to be sparse throughout the whole of the period under consideration here. As Table 23 shows, when such information does exist there was no discernible change of pattern except for the increasing importance of London.

---

[49] See, for example, E. F. Jacob, *The Fifteenth Century, 1399-1485* (Oxford, 1961), pp. 366-370.

[50] See below, Chapter 7, p. 213. Indeed those formally ejected from the liberty very likely remained in the town until their free privileges had been recovered.

TABLE 23: OUTSIDERS RECEIVING LIBERTY

| YEAR | VILLAGE | FINE | | YEAR | VILLAGE | FINE | |
|---|---|---|---|---|---|---|---|
| 1401 | Yelling | 20s. | | 1524 | Brampton | 8s. | |
| | Swavesey | 26s. | 8d. | 1525 | Huntingdon | 10s. | |
| 1403 | Raveley | 13s. | 4d. | 1528 | Caxton | 3s. | 4d. |
| 1407 | Brington | 6s. | 8d. | 1529 | London, husbandman | 13s. | 4d. |
| 1410 | Hemingford | 8s. | | 1532 | Stowe | 26s. | 8d. |
| 1417 | Hilton | 8s. | | 1533 | London, merchant | 20s. | |
| | Offord | 3s. | | 1534 | London, grocer | 40s. | |
| 1419 | Yelling | 5s. | | | Doddington | 2s. | |
| 1428 | Cambridge | 8s. | | | Hemingford | 3s. | 4d. |
| 1432 | Hemingford Abbots | 6s. | 8d. | | Huntingdon | 4s. | 8d. |
| 1434 | Graveley | 6s. | 8d. | 1536 | London | 40s. | |
| 1441 | Wynge in Rutland | 8s. | | | Drayton | [ ] | |
| | Steeple Gidding | 6s. | 8d. | 1538 | Houghton | | 12d. |
| 1445 | London | 7s. | | | London | | |
| 1482 | Cambridge | 13s. | 4d. | | pewterer | 13s. | 4d. |
| | Hemingford Abbots | 10s. | | | St. Neots | 6s. | 8d. |
| | Hemingford Abbots | 16s. | 8d. | | Offord, | | |
| 1488 | Buckden | 6s. | 8d. | | subhayward | 2s. | |
| 1493 | Hereford | 6s. | 8d. | | Ramsey | 6s. | 8d. |
| | Ripton | 6s. | 8d. | 1543 | Huntingdon | | |
| 1497 | Croxton | 13s. | 4d. | | sengilman | 6s. | 8d. |
| 1504 | London | 5s. | | 1546 | London, merchant | 20s. | |
| 1509 | Huntingdon | 6s. | 8d. | | London, grocer | [ ] | |
| | Welbe | 3s. | | | Brampton | 6s. | |
| 1511 | London | 3s. | 4d. | 1547 | Kaptone | 6s. | |
| 1513 | Broughton | 5s. | | | London | 5s. | |
| 1517 | Stoughton | 6s. | 8d. | 1549 | London | 13s. | 4d. |

Detail about the occupations of those coming to Godmanchester also remained sparse, although there was a proportionate increase of information from the greater number receiving liberty of the town from the late fifteenth century. Again, as the following list shows, the outreach of the merchants of London was a familiar landmark of Tudor period.

From the third quarter of the fifteenth century the difference widened between those entering the liberty of Godmanchester for property and those not acquiring property. The former became fewer in number and their entry fines were not reduced. The great increase in immigrants, therefore, was among those not expecting to acquire property. This number of immigrants, vast for a town the size of Godmanchester, increasingly acquired the characteristics of a common pool of labour. That is to say, the fines for crafts and occupations lost their distinctiveness as they became smaller and smaller.

TABLE 24: OCCUPATIONS RECEIVING LIBERTY

| YEAR | OCCUPATION | FINE |
|------|------------|------|
| 1400 | baker | 10s. |
| 1401 | butcher | 8s. |
|      | miller | 6s. 8d. |
| 1402 | draper | 8s. |
| 1403 | smith | 6s. 8d. |
|      | *ovilio* | 6s. 8d. |
| 1404 | potter | 7s. |
|      | smith | 10s. |
| 1406 | miller | 6s. 8d. |
|      | taylor | 6s. 8d. |
| 1419 | turner | 6s. 8d. |
|      | farrier | 6s. 8d. |
|      | glover | 6s. 8d. |
| 1420 | fisher | 6s. 8d. |
| 1423 | weaver | 6s. 8d. |
| 1428 | butcher | 8s. |
| 1434 | lockyer | 3s. 4d. |
| 1434 | shether | 5s. |
| 1436 | weaver | 6s. 8d. |
| 1438 | sengilman | 5s. |
|      | sengilman | 6s. 8d. |
|      | fuller | 6s. 8d. |
|      | *wulschev* | 5s. |
| 1452 | taylor | 5s. |
|      | taylor | 8s. |
| 1463 | thatcher | 5s. |
| 1465 | fishmonger | 8s. |
| 1479 | barker | 3s. 4d. |
| 1481 | clerk | 5s. |
| 1488 | cobbler | [   ] |
| 1491 | canon? | 3s. 4d. |
| 1494 | servant | 3s. 4d. |
| 1496 | taylor | 2s. |
|      | clerk | 6s. 8d. |
| 1503 | chaplain | 5s. |
| 1508 | gentleman | 20s. and paid directly |
| 1509 | farmer | 10s. |
| 1510 | carver | 2s. |
| 1521 | shoemaker | 3s. 4d. |
|      | servant | 1s. |
|      | servant | 3s. |
| 1523 | glover | 1s. 8d. |
| 1524 | miller | 6s. 8d. |
| 1525 | two chaplains | paid by hand, amount not stated |
|      | sengilman | paid by hand, amount not stated |
| 1529 | husbandman, de London | 13s. 4d. |
| 1532 | gentleman | 26s. 8d. |
| 1533 | merchant, de London | 20s. |

| YEAR | OCCUPATION | FINE |
|------|------------|------|
| 1534 | grocer, de London | 40s. |
|      | smith | 3s. 4d. |
|      | labourer | 2s. |
| 1538 | pewterer, de London | 13s. 4d. |
|      | sub-hayward, de Offord | 2s. |
| 1539 | taylor | 2s. 4d. |
| 1541 | clerk | [   ] |
|      | yeoman | [   ] |
| 1543 | glover | 2s. |
|      | sengilman, de Huntingdon | 6s. 8d. |
| 1544 | miller | 10s. |
|      | yeoman | 20s. |
| 1546 | merchant, de London | 20s. |
|      | grocer, de London | [   ] |
| 1547 | glover | [   ] |
| 1549 | yeoman | 10s. |
|      | gentleman | 20s. |
|      | merchant, de London | 13s. 4d. |

As may be seen in Table 24 above, in 1534 the smith and labourer paid the same fine of (3/4d.) for liberty of the town. The same Table showes that there were many who paid much less.

In short, most of our evidence for entry to the liberty of Godmanchester after 1480 serves to measure the large supply of labour readily available to the town. Whether the lower purchase price for liberty had triggered this influx cannot be directly deduced since the influx does not coincide with that first lowering of purchase prices from the mid-century. But in this respect the many missing records for the 1460s and 1470s may blurr the evidence. There is some evidence for considerable impoverishment among the poorer classes of England by the 1470s,[51] so that the lowering of purchase prices for liberty would have become more attractive.

The fact that the town was able to absorb so many people during the flood of immigrants from the 1480s would seem to indicate that unusual demographic as well as economic factors were at work. R. S. Gottfried[52] has documented a long-term (1430-1480) series of epidemics for East Anglia.

[51] From a personal communication concerning a work in progress by Dr. Marjorie McIntosh. This was of course a time of financial crisis for Godmanchester too, as has been seen in Chapter 1, perhaps precipitated by the same depression.

[52] See, *Epidemic Disease in Fifteenth Century England: The Medical Response and the Demographic Consequences* (New Brunswick, NJ: Rutgers University Press, 1949), especially p. 129 and also p. 142.

Very likely such infestation would not stop within a few miles of Godmanchester. The location of the town on main transportation routes left
Godmanchester liable to epidemics of regional significance and the marshy
fens of the town made Godmanchester prone to disease of a more local
character.

All this does little to define in economic terms the nature of this pool of
labour! These newcomers are not identifiable among those many occupations, whether commercial or rural, noted in Chapter 2. If so, one might
wonder why they had to pay a fine to have liberty of the town. One suspects
that, from the third quarter of the fifteenth century, there was increasing
pressure to impose liberty of the town on all residents. All available evidence
for the rentals from the 1480s indicates all, or virtually all tenants exercising
the liberties, that is, the use of customs of Godmanchester.

Recalling that *corpus* of officialdom presented in Chapter 1, who implemented town policy about the supply and demand for new freemen? Records
show that decisions about licensing were made in the bailiffs' three-weekly
courts. There is only one reference in the Jurors' Book to the jurors issuing
a license, although jurors could be readily consulted on the matter. Clearly
the bailiffs must have had that discretion signified by those variations within
the different economic levels of fines. But there would be a common town
policy from year to year and from one set of bailiffs to another about the level
of fines for different "classes" of newcomers.

Given the problems bailiffs had from time to time in balancing their
accounts there must have been a temptation to admit those who could pay
hefty fines. After all, a wealthy newcomer would pay a fine that would cover
the salary of the chief bailiff for the year; a craftsman entering the role of
freemen would pay the salary of someone on the administrative level, such
as a clerk. Would this same budgetary rationale help explain the acceptance
of so many small fines as well?

The following list of annual revenues from the sale of liberties does
demonstrate the substantial amounts that could be acquired. For some years
of substantial arrears by the bailiffs, as in the 1480s, such revenues must have
been of significant assistance to the town. But trends could not be controlled
by the actions of bailiffs alone; over a period of years revenues ultimately
depended upon the number of individuals willing to pay fines for the liberty
of Godmanchester.

Over the fourteenth and fifteenth centuries the licensing system for the
liberty of Godmanchester had evolved in a direction almost directly opposite
to that of the larger towns of England at the time. The latter gradually
tightened access to liberty of the town or city in order to retain power in the
hands of crafts or some other commercial élite. From the largest city,

TABLE 25: TOTAL FINES FOR LIBERTY

| YEAR | £ | s. | d. | YEAR | £ | s. | d. | YEAR | £ | s. | d. |
|---|---|---|---|---|---|---|---|---|---|---|---|
| 1400 | 2 | 8 | 8 | 1449 | 2 | 4 | 4 | 1508 | 2 | 7 | -* |
| 1401 | 6 | 5 | - | 1450 | 2 | 1 | 8 | 1509 | 1 | 19 | - |
| 1402 | | 8 | - | 1452 | 1 | 6 | 4 | 1510 | 1 | 11 | 4 |
| 1403 | 1 | 6 | 8 | 1456 | | 16 | 4* | 1511 | 1 | 2 | 2 |
| 1404 | 2 | - | 4 | 1463 | 1 | 18 | 4* | 1512 | 1 | 9 | 10 |
| 1405 | 2 | 8 | 2 | 1464 | 1 | 10 | - | 1513 | | 13 | 4* |
| 1406 | 2 | 8 | - | 1465 | 2 | 3 | 4* | 1514 | 1 | 1 | 4 |
| 1407 | 1 | 10 | - | 1466 | | 5 | - | 1515 | 2 | 16 | 8 |
| 1408 | | 13 | 4 | 1472 | | | 2* | 1516 | 2 | 6 | 4 |
| 1409 | | 13 | 8 | 1473 | | 4 | - | 1517 | 2 | 5 | 8 |
| 1410 | 3 | 12 | - | 1474 | | 10 | - | 1518 | | 7 | - |
| 1411 | 2 | - | - | 1475 | 1 | 14 | 8 | 1519 | 2 | - | 4 |
| 1412 | | 14 | 8 | 1478 | | 5 | - | 1520 | 1 | 3 | 4 |
| 1413 | 4 | 2 | 4 | 1479 | 1 | 18 | - | 1521 | 2 | 16 | - |
| 1414 | 1 | 1 | - | 1480 | 1 | 6 | 8 | 1522 | | 6 | 4 |
| 1415 | 4 | 2 | 4 | 1481 | 1 | 15 | - | 1523 | 1 | 8 | 4 |
| 1417 | 1 | 1 | - | 1482 | 6 | 17 | -* | 1524 | | 17 | 8 |
| 1418 | 1 | 17 | 4 | 1484 | 1 | 6 | 8 | 1525 | | 19 | -* |
| 1419 | 1 | 18 | 8 | 1485 | | 11 | 10 | 1526 | 1 | 2 | 8 |
| 1420 | 1 | 8 | 8 | 1486 | 4 | 17 | 8 | 1527 | 1 | 3 | 8 |
| 1421 | 2 | 7 | 8 | 1487 | | 16 | - | 1528 | 1 | 19 | - |
| 1422 | | 10 | - | 1488 | 2 | 18 | -* | 1529 | 2 | 17 | 8* |
| 1423 | 1 | 15 | - | 1489 | 4 | 2 | 4 | 1530 | | 4 | 4* |
| 1424 | 2 | 8 | 8 | 1490 | | 17 | 8 | 1531 | 1 | 6 | 8* |
| 1425 | | 10 | - | 1491 | 3 | 2 | 4 | 1532 | 4 | 4 | -* |
| 1428 | 3 | 7 | 4 | 1492 | 1 | 6 | 10 | 1533 | 1 | 13 | 2 |
| 1429 | | 13 | 4 | 1493 | 1 | 18 | - | 1534 | 5 | 14 | 4 |
| 1430 | 1 | 2 | - | 1494 | 3 | 4 | - | 1535 | | 9 | 8 |
| 1431 | 2 | 1 | 8 | 1495 | 2 | 5 | 8 | 1536 | 4 | 14 | -* |
| 1432 | 1 | 13 | 4 | 1496 | 1 | 18 | - | 1537 | 1 | 14 | 8 |
| 1434 | 1 | 13 | 4 | 1497 | 1 | 15 | 8 | 1538 | 3 | 5 | 6 |
| 1435 | 1 | 3 | 4* | 1498 | | 4 | -* | 1539 | | 17 | 8 |
| 1436 | 2 | 8 | 8 | 1499 | | 10 | - | 1540 | 3 | - | - |
| 1437 | 2 | 4 | 8 | 1500 | 1 | 1 | 4 | 1541 | | 13 | 8* |
| 1438 | 2 | 10 | 4 | 1501 | 1 | 19 | - | 1542 | | 10 | - |
| 1441 | | 14 | 8 | 1502 | | 13 | 4 | 1543 | 3 | 10 | - |
| 1442 | 1 | 12 | 6 | 1503 | 3 | 19 | 8 | 1544 | 2 | 5 | - |
| 1444 | | 6 | - | 1504 | | 13 | - | 1545 | | 2 | - |
| 1445 | 1 | 2 | 8 | 1505 | 2 | 1 | -* | 1546 | 2 | 4 | 4 |
| 1446 | | 3 | 4 | 1506 | 2 | 7 | - | 1547 | 1 | 3 | 8* |
| | | | | 1507 | 1 | 7 | 4 | 1549 | 3 | 8 | 8 |

* Asteriks indicate years for which some courts are missing.

London,[53] to the smaller, such as Exeter,[54] this pattern was consistent. At Godmanchester on the other hand, the umbrella of liberty was considerably widened from those few outsiders granted the privileges of the town in the early fourteenth century to the hundreds granted access by the 1500s.

However, the licensing system at a small rural town and the cities of the time are not strictly comparable. The closer look at Godmanchester from the thirteenth into the sixteenth century must conclude that the fines of the licensing system introduced after the Black Death indicate a control mechanism. There is no doubt that purchases of freedom at Godmanchester from the time of the Black Death until the mid-sixteenth century provide real indices to the supply of land available in the town and the demand for craft and labour. Further chapters of this volume will serve to present a more complete picture of the whole land and labour markets of the town.

[53] On this and more generally, see Sylvia Thrupp, "Gilds," in *The Cambridge Economic History of Europe* (1963), vol. 3, chapter 5.

[54] See Maryanne Kowaleski, "Local Markets and Merchants in Late Fourteenth Century Exeter," unpublished Ph. D. thesis, University of Toronto, 1982, especially chapter 2.

# 4

# Testamentary Evidence:
# The True Religion of the Freemen

Students of the English medieval village and town have often remarked with
some amazement the strict division of labour between matters ecclesiastical
and civil in surviving records. Godmanchester was in the diocese of Lincoln
and the history of this diocese is well served both by its archives[1] and its
historians.[2] Regrettably, however, the parish registers of Godmanchester only
survive from 1604 so that the splendid demographic work[3] possible with
such records cannot be tied in with the detailed records of early Tudor
Godmanchester. Nor, of course, do there survive sources found useful by our
modern sociologist of religious practice: data for church attendance, reception of the sacraments and so forth.

Nevertheless, the fundamental thrust of Christian teaching has never
allowed true religion to be identified solely with activities within a parish
church building. This is particularly so for two sectors of social life—the
family and social charity or welfare. A central example of relevance to the
family was that somewhat cryptic teaching of Paul in chapter 5 of Ephesians:
"and that is the way Christ treats the Church, because it is his body—and we
are its living parts. For this reason a man must leave his father and mother
and be joined to his wife, and the two will become one body. This mystery
has many implications; but I am saying it applies to Christ and the Church."

---

[1] The invaluable publications of the Lincoln Record Society have made most of these
archives more readily available to the historian.

[2] No collection of records for a single parish come close to representing the great variety
of customs and practices actually at work in one place. For this reason, the gathering of data
from a wider area is essential for the more complete picture of any one village or town. In this
respect, Dorothy M. Owen, *Church and Society in Medieval Lincolnshire*, History of Lincolnshire 5 (Lincoln, 1971), especially the chapter on "The Laity," has much that provides a useful
context for this chapter on Godmanchester.

[3] See the publication of The Cambridge Group for the History of Population and Social
Structure as well as the ongoing journal *Local Population Studies*.

This teaching is glossed today by reference to the family as a mini-church, though how the teaching was interpreted by vicars of fifteenth-century Godmanchester is hard to say. As one of the most vigourous areas of contemporary mediaeval scholarship, family history[4] now shows us that the modern form of marriage was the product of a long evolution. Contemporaneous to the evolution of marriage regulations, and closely related to them in real life, was the last will. The belief in the immortality of the soul as the very *raison d'être* of the Christian church, that whole sphere of expression conveniently called in its archaic form ancestor worship and marriage regulations concerning family responsibility combined to give canon law and thence ecclesiastical courts jurisdiction over the last will.[5] The survival of a good many wills for Godmanchester provides us, then, with considerable data about religious practices and the family economy.

A familiar refrain in the ears of medieval people was the admonition from the letter of James (1:27): "Pure, unspoilt religion, in the eyes of God our Father is this: coming to the help of orphans and widows when they need it and keeping one-self uncontaminated by the world." A recent study presents the dramatic new thesis that guilds were the measure of a vital religion in pre-reformation England.[6] As we shall see in this chapter, the freemen of Godmanchester responded vigorously to this admonition of James—even to the extent of founding a confraternity of St. James!—and guild buildings became indeed mini-churches throughout the town.

## A. WILLS

Among all the actions of the people of Godmanchester there was none more unique to the individual than death. Individuals died, not families, friends, communities or the town. Fortunately for the historian, the pivotal importance of death to the individual in Christian religion lead to the recording of the dying person's intent in the last will and testament. While only 130 wills[7]

---

[4] Something of the scope of data available to the study of peasant families in medieval England may be found in Barbara Hanawalt, *The Ties that Bound* (New York and London, 1985). David Herlihy has considered it possible to re-constitute the broad patterns of family life and organizations in *Medieval Households* (Cambridge, Mass. and London, 1985).

A useful working bibliography is now available: M. M. Sheehan *Family and Marriage in Medieval Europe* (Vancouver: Medieval Studies Committee, Faculty of Arts, University of British Columbia, 1986).

[5] See M. M. Sheehan, *The Will in Medieval England* (Toronto, 1963), For the evolution of marriage forms with particular respect to England, see the many articles of R. H. Helmholz and M. M. Sheehan.

[6] J. J. Scarisbrick, *The Reformation and the English People* (Oxford, 1985).

[7] 130 wills from the *Calendar of Huntingdonshire Wills, 1479-1652*, issued by the British Record Society, vol. 42, N.D., and compiled by W. M. Noble, were used for study. Only 106

survive for the period under study here, these are enough to give us a good grasp of the decisions made by individuals as they lay dying "sick of body" but "whole of mind." The last will was drawn up according to an established legal form but as the last act of an individual this very form became the opportunity for much recording about life. It was the last disposition of those things that would remain a visible memorial of many associations, so the formal structure of the will was bound to record a good number of people as members or friends of the family, witnesses, executors and supervisors. Nearly one thousand (986) names are actually recorded in the 106 wills prior to the 1550s.[8] Generalized references to customs are rare in these wills, and then only in relation to relatively fixed items, such as the *principale* (mortuary) and the use of the tally. Furthermore, as we shall see, personal preferences and differing financial possibilities exposed a wide variety in the disposition of wealth even for religious services and the more normal inheritance practices.

However much the will might be the reflection of the last act of an individual, the written instrument was expected to be implemented in a very public manner. Something of the flavour and scope of the legal and social context of a will in early Tudor Godmanchester can be seen from depositions recorded in the Godmanchester court book under the date of 2 August 1520. The depositions were actually taken at Westminster three years earlier and involved a dispute over a messuage, four score acres of arable, 35 acres of meadow and three groves (estimated as five acres) devised by the will of John Mynsterchambre. The preliminary statement notes that the property had been "willed, devised and given" to "one Anne then this wife" and after her decease to "one John Mynsterchambre his son of the body of the said Anne begotten." The land had then been sold to Sir Robert Drury, knight, who in turn sold the land to John Wynde, claimant against William Mynsterchambre.

First to be examined was John Lockyngton, yeoman of about 60 years of age, who had spent all his life at Godmanchester. John Lockyngton said that John Mynsterchambre had held the property for about 40 years, had died about 21 years ago, that Anne was his second wife, that his son had the land for a year or two, and that time out of mind property could pass and devise and be given at will at the pleasure of the owner. Lockyngton then re-created the scene as follows (the English text is here modernized):

---

of these wills are before the main range of this study, that is, 1548, but the remaining score of wills have also been employed since the major part of the life of the testator occurred before 1548.

[8] This does not include, of course, the frequent reference to unnamed "others" in many wills.

Also he says that on Trinity Sunday evening about 12 o'clock before none before the decease of the said Mynsterchambre, which deceased in the night next following, this deponent being with the said Mynsterchambre lying in his death bed in a high chamber in the said messuage, saw and heard the said Mynsterchambre being of good mind sit up in his bed bidding the said Anne his wife to bring to him his will which she so did. At which time the said Mynsterchambre then looking on the said will, said he could not read it, wherefore, then and there he delivered the said will to William Tothe praying him to read it. Which Tothe then and there read the said will wherein among divers things he willed that after his decease his messuage and lands should wholly remain through the said Anne during her life. And after her decease to remain to John their son in fee simple. But who wrote the said will this deponent knows not, but he remembered well, that after the said reading thereof, the said testator then expressly reported and said, that the said will should stand for his last will and never to be changed. Then present John Borowe, William Stodale, Robert Dobbyns, clerk, Sir John Oxon, clerk, and divers others about the number of 14 persons, which shall all be deceased except this deponent as far as he remembers. And he says, in Lent past William Mynsterchambre, younger son to the said testator, and Anne, being in one West house, read to this deponent a will in paper, which as he said was of his father's handwriting ... to remain to the said John, elder brother to the said William in fee simple in like manner as the said Tothe read beforetime. Which will as this deponent supposes remains still in the hands of the said William. ...

Omitting repetition of references to properties and other forms, the other depositions were as follows:

William Kyng of Godmanchester aforesaid, husbandman, of the age of 58 years ... and knew well John Mynsterchambre, and Anne his second wife with whom this deponent dwell by the space of two years and which had issue together John and William, together with Mary and Dorothy their daughters which John the father occupied the said messuage etc. how many he remembers not by certain years ... which deceased about twenty years past as he supposed. But how the said messuage and lands came to the said Mynsterchambre this deponent otherwise knows not. ... But whether they should remain to John his son by his first wife, or else, to John his son by his second wife, otherwise remembers not. ... After the decease of the said Master, he knew the said Anne occupied the said messuage etc. after whose death the said John son of the said Mynsterchambre occupied the said messuage etc. about a year to his remembrance which was to the time that the said younger John dwelt with Sir Robert Drury as it was reported. ...

William Granger of Godmanchester aforesaid, husbandman of the age of 52 years. ... he knew John Mynsterchambre about the space of 20 years which was to the time of his decease and he occupied these lands etc. at that time. About 16 years passed to his remembrance which was about 12 to 14 days next before the decease of the said John Mynsterchambre, this deponent was in high chamber of the said messuage wherein the said John then lay sick in his deathbed and then and there this deponent in the presence of John Lockyngton and others whom he remembers not, saw and heard the said John Mynsterchambre with his own mouth say and report that after his decease Anne his second wife should have for term of her life all the said messuage and lands and after her decease John their son should have then forever the said messuage and lands, but under what other manner the said John should have them this deponent more and otherwise remembers not, neither this deponent any time saw any will written and read to his remembrance, neither knows not any such will is becoming, but he says that after the decease of the said Testator this deponent knows the said Anne during her life after whose death John entered the said property ... as he his own a certain season how long he remembers not. ...

Thomas Osse, chantry priest of the Chantry of Corpus Christi of Godmanchester aforesaid, of the age of 49 years. ... he has dwelt in Godmanchester about the space 20 years and that the said John Mynsterchambre whom this deponent never knew was deceased before the coming of this deponent to the said town, which John has by common report was owner of this messuage etc. which this deponent believes to be true for so much this deponent knew Anne being called second wife to the said Mynsterchambre by certain years how many he remembers not. Which was to the time of her decease occupying the said messuage and lands to her own use by force of her said husband's will, as the said which Anne divers time said to this deponent that she had full more as much land as belonged to the said Chantry. And he said, that soon after this deponent had heard the confession of the said Anne lying in her deathbed and minister to her the blessed sacrament of the altar which as this deponent remembers was about sevennight or a xiiii night before her decease how long passed he remembers not this deponent at her desire wrote the will of the said Anne at which time she said that she would not intermeddle with this aforesaid messuage and lands which was her said husband's, because as she then said, her said husband had by his last will disposed them to her son John after her decease. ... Then commanding Mary or Elizabeth her daughters to bring to her their said father's [will] whereupon then and there one of the said daughters brought the said will to the said Anne which will then being in paper of whose handwriting he knows not this deponent then and there at the desire of the said Anne openly read wherein among divers things was written etc. ... And there upon this deponent at the desire of the said Anne wrote her will wherein she with other things willed that William her son should have certain meadow and lands which was by her report she had bought of John Mynsterchambre son of her said husband by his first wife as more plainly appears by the said will being of the handwriting of this deponent. ... Then present Robert and Henry Ashton, clerks and others deceased and he knows the custom by report of old men and wills he has made, by report William has the father's will on paper ... and he

says after the decease of the said Anne John her son and one Gladwell servant
to Sir Robert Drury entered the said messuage and lands administered the said
... to the use of the said John to the space of two years. ...[9]

Some initial order can be put into the multitude of detail to be found
in wills by beginning with the demographic factors that framed much of the
strategy lying behind the wills. Excluding the eight wills of single individuals,
some 41 (33.6%) of the remaining 122 wills indicated both sons and
daughters as children, 30 (24.6%) had sons only, 19 (15.6%) had daughters
only while 32 (27%) recorded no children. Of the 30 families with sons only,
19 reported singular sons, and of the 19 families with daughters only, 12
reported singular daughters. In short, given the number of families with no
children and the families with singular sons and daughters, fewer than 50%
of the families were replacing themselves. In common with demographic
patterns throughout England,[10] the size of families increased noticeably in the
second quarter of the sixteenth-century. However, the size of the will sample
would suggest that this evidence for such trends must be employed with
caution and, indeed, this sample may indicate a decline in the size of families
in the late 1540s and throughout the 1550s. These families data from wills
can be summarized as follows (brackets indicate totals):

TABLE 26: FAMILY DATA FROM WILLS

| 1 son | 2 sons | 3 sons | | |
| --- | --- | --- | --- | --- |
| 19 (19) | 8 (16) | 3 (9) | | |

| 1 daughter | 2 daughters | 3 daughters | 4 daughters | 5 daughters |
| --- | --- | --- | --- | --- |
| 12 (12) | 2 (4) | 2 (6) | 2 (8) | 1 (5) |

| 1 son and 1 daughter | 1 son and 2 daughters | 1 son and 3 daughters | |
| --- | --- | --- | --- |
| 17 (34) | 3 (9) | 1 (4) | |

| 2 sons and 1 daughter | 2 sons and 2 daughters | 2 sons and 3 daughters | 2 sons and 5 daughters |
| --- | --- | --- | --- |
| 6 (18) | 5 (20) | 2 (10) | 1 (7) |

| 3 sons and 1 daughter | 3 sons and 2 daughters | 5 sons and 1 daughter | 6 sons and 1 daughter |
| --- | --- | --- | --- |
| 3 (12) | 1 (5) | 1 (6) | 1 (7) |

TOTAL: 211 children from 90 families

[9] The suit was decided in favour of John Wynde. This loss of land to an outsider by an
old family of the town was an important legal indicator at the time. See below, chapter 7.

[10] The most up-to-date study of this recovery of marriage and family over mortality may
be found in E. A. Wrigley and R. S. Schofield, *The Population History of England, 1541-1871*
(London, 1981).

All but 19 of the 122 wills of married persons are wills of the husband. In turn, the fact that all but eight of the these 103 wills of husbands indicate a widow surviving would seem to give a substantive support to the "European pattern of marriage" theory, that is, at the time of marriage the wife was much younger than the husband.[11] This theory is further supported by the fact that in only 13 instances does one of the sons seem to be of age, that is, he qualifies as executor to inherit by the time of his father's will.

The fact that husbands died before their wives does not mean that husbands died young. Frankpledge rolls provide us with a fairly consistent series of entries for property holders at Godmanchester (trespassing in fields, failure to clean gutters about house, etc.). Since property was held by adults only, it may be assumed that these series of frankpledge entries would occur after the Godmanchester individual had reached majority, by custom 20 years of age.[12] If, then, 20 years are added to the number of years between the date of first appearance in the frankpledge rolls and the date of death recorded by the last will, one has a reasonable estimate of age at death. Table 27 presents these ages for 63 individuals; their average age is 58 (58.37). In one instance at least, this age may be an underestimate: Robert Mayle entered tithing in 1486 and therefore was actually 24 when his series of entries began in the frankpledge rolls.

Boys of Godmanchester became subject to frankpledge regulations when they entered the tithing at the age of 12 years, and so technically could appear

---

[11] J. Hajnal, "European Marriage Patterns in Perspective," in *Population in History*, ed. D. V. Glass and D. E. C. Eversley, (London, 1965).

[12] *A Small Town*, p. 432: "When boys have come to the age of twenty, then by the custom of the manor they are of full age, and girls when they are sixteen; and then they can sell, demise, and give their lands and tenements to whom they will." Most wills take for granted entry of the heir when he comes of age. Whether the different age of maturity for men and women could be significant for bequests other than descent of property to the male heir cannot be readily determined. In any case some wills show a variety of ages designated by the testator:

1530 Robert Vynter—son Thomas at 14 years, land
1538 Thomas Bell—son Thomas at 10 years, farming gear
1542 Robert Mayle—son John at 21 years, house
1543 Walter Colyn—son Christopher at 20 years, £20
1543 John Vyntner—grandson John at 16 years, £2
1545 William Freman senior—godson William Everard at 10 years, 6s. 8d.
1545 Hugh Hayward—daughters Alice, Elizabeth and Joan at 15 years, £2 each
1546 John Gybbys—grandson John at 14 years, £2
1546 Marion Hawdwyn—grandson Richard Clerk at 18 years, £1
1546 John Wryght—son Thomas at 18 years, 3 acres
1554 William Paxton—son Edward at 20 years, messuage
1556 William Aylred—son William at 20 years, messuage and lands
1558 John Nelson—son Robert at 21 years, lands

TABLE 27: RECONSTRUCTION OF AGE FOR TESTATORS
FROM FRANKPLEDGE ROLLS[a]

| NAME | FIRST NOTED | DATE OF DEATH | AGE AT DEATH |
|---|---|---|---|
| Archebould, Edmund, priest | 1516 | 1558 | 62 |
| Arnold, William | 1509 | 1535 | 46 |
| Barre, William | 1467 | 1509 | 62 |
| Bailey, John | 1486 | 1506 | 40 |
| Bennett, Thomas | 1494 | 1527 | 53 |
| Bennett, William, son of Thomas | 1498 | 1540 | 73 |
| Bennett, Thomas | 1517 | 1555 | 58 |
| Bonsay, John, son of Agnes Lynsey | 1485 | 1520 | 55 |
| Brown, William | 1485 | 1528 | 63 |
| Bullion (Boleyn), John | 1515 | 1558 | 63 |
| Burton, Thomas | 1469 | 1506 | 58 |
| Byrder, Elena, wife of Robert Nicholas | 1498 | 1538 | 60 |
| Cook, Richard | 1533 | 1553 | 40 |
| Cook, Joan, widow of Thomas | 1485 | 1533 | 68 |
| Corby, Renalde | 1486 (tithing) | 1535 | 61 |
| Dalton, John | 1469 | 1533 | 84 |
| Dalton, William, mercer | 1513[b] | 1541 | 48 |
| Diggby, William | 1497 | 1530 | 53 |
| Este, John | 1509 | 1530 | 41 |
| Este, Henry, son of John | 1530 (tithing) | 1557 | 39 |
| Freman, William, senior | 1500 (Liberty 1496) | 1546 | 70 |
| Frere, John | 1501 | 1548 | 67 |
| Frere, William | 1498 | 1545 | 67 |
| Frost, Thomas | 1460 (Liberty 1463) | 1491 | 51 |
| Garlop, John | 1480s | 1528 | 68 |
| Goodwyn, John | 1509 | 1551 | 62 |
| Goodwyn, William | 1534 | 1550 | 36 |
| Granger, John senior | 1511 | 1538 | 48 |
| Granger, Thomas | 1498 | 1545 | 67 |
| Grene, Agnes, widow of Richard | 1495 | 1544 | 69 |
| Grene, Richard | 1495 | 1536 | 61 |
| Gybbys, Henry | 1498 | 1559 | 81 |
| Hawdwyn (Awdwen), Marion, wife of Roger | ca. 1516 | 1546 | 50 |
| Hays, Katherine, wife of George | 1498 | 1540 | 62 |
| Hays, George | 1520 (Liberty 1496) | 1534 | 56 |

[a] Data for the ten women likely biases averages downwards since women are not presented in Frankpledge Rolls and Court Book entries are not frequent.
[b] Taken from Court Book.

| NAME | FIRST NOTED | DATE OF DEATH | AGE AT DEATH |
|---|---|---|---|
| Hogan (Huggyn), John | 1509 | 1545 | 56 |
| Hogan (Huggyn), Margaret, widow | 1511<sup>b</sup> | 1558 | 67 |
| Ingram, William | 1509 | 1557 | 68 |
| Kyng, William | 1486 (Liberty 1511) | 1530 | 64 |
| Lane, Agnes, widow | 1464 | 1483 | 39 |
| Lawe, John | 1497 | 1518 | 41 |
| Lockyngton, Alice, widow of Thomas | 1518 | 1545 | 47 |
| Lockyngton, Thomas | 1497 | 1544 | 67 |
| Loveday, William | 1497 | 1539 | 62 |
| Marshall, Thomas | 1481 (Liberty 1507) | 1507 | 46 |
| Mayhew, John | 1515 | 1557 | 62 |
| Mayle, Robert | 1486 | 1542 | 67 |
| Mayle, Thomas | 1467 (Liberty 1449) | 1500 | 71 |
| Mayle, William, husbandman and brother of Robert | 1497 | 1549 | 72 |
| Monyment, Thomas | 1491 (Liberty 1493) | 1524 | 53 |
| Nelson, John | 1517 | 1559 | 62 |
| Osteler, William | 1527 | 1557 | 50 |
| Pelle, William, son of Robert | 1490 (Liberty 1520) | 1559 | 56 |
| Pelman, William | 1477 | 1530 | 73 |
| Pryor, Thomas | 1526 | 1554 | 48 |
| Sanden, John senior | 1514 (Liberty 1520) | 1546 | 52 |
| Scott, John | 1503 | 1544 | 61 |
| Seward, William | 1470s | 1530 | 80 |
| Smyth, Richard | 1470 | 1512 | 62 |
| Stukeley, Margaret, widow | 1517 | 1541 | 44 |
| Trege (Tryg), Thomas | 1522 (Liberty 1519) | 1548 | 49 |
| Turneskewe, John | 1464 (Liberty 1465) | 1506 | 62 |
| Vyntner, John | 1512 | 1543 | 51 |
| West, Alice, widow | 1491 | 1532 | 61 |
| Whyte, Robert | 1494 | 1543 | 69 |
| Wryght, John | 1534 | 1550 | 36 |
| Wylde, John senior | 1503 | 1532 | 49 |

in the frankpledge rolls from that age. There are records[13] for 79 entries to tithing scattered over the reigns of Henry VII and Henry VIII. However, for only 14 of these individuals are there wills to indicate the date of death and a further four of these (Frere, Robert and William Mayle, Robyns) present problems of identification because of common family surnames and first names. Furthermore, there is reason to believe that arriving at 12 years of age was not always the operative factor in the entry to tithing. Was it just a

[13] Huntington Record Office, Godmanchester Borough Records, Box 8, Bundle 4, Documents of Henry VII, Miscellaneous no. 9.

coincidence that Henry, son of John Este, was said to be under age at the time of his father's death in 1530 and yet entered tithing at the following Michaelmas? Certainly Renalde Corby must have been more than 12 years of age when he entered tithing in 1486 for he had just received liberty as an adult. In short, the active adult period demonstrated in the frankpledge rolls would seem to provide the better estimate of age at death.

There is further evidence to corroborate the upper mortality ages of the previous table. Three older persons from the labouring and craft group of Giles Lane, selected to give evidence in the court of 3 August 1543, would seem to corroborate that the average age at death for even the less wealthy members of the town could be well over 50 years:

> At this cort came Richard Jermayn of the aforesaid town in the County of Huntingdon, labourer of the age of 60 years or more, William Neel of the said town and county, plummer, age of 50 years or more, John Firmary of the said town and county, labourer, of 52 years or more.

Further corroboration that Godmanchester individuals did live to a good age, is noted in the Jurors' Book (on a non-paginated leaf facing p. 70) where there is a deposition stating that Thomas Freman was 80 years old in 1567 (which means he was born in 1487) and it goes on further to state that Henry Barnard was 80 years old, John Gybbys 67 years old, William Maryot 63 years old, William Taylor 58 years old, Richard Smyth 66 years old, William Besent (Bennett?) 60 years old and Henry Lackie 34 years of age.

Ages cannot be computed with any degree of accuracy from entry to the freedom of the town when there is no supporting evidence from frankpledge rolls. The fact that many of these new freemen had children when they purchased liberty and adult children at the time of their death indicates they were well over 20 at the time of their licensing in the liberty. However, for the general indicative purpose of Table 28, a round figure of 20 is added to those years between entrance to liberty and date of death to obtain a possible age figure. These data would not appear to be of much use for those (marked +) who died young or entered at a rather mature age. Table 28 does retain some value by indicating the considerable minimum age of death of several individuals such as John Betrych and John Laxton.

In addition to the frequency of the widow surviving her spouse, the number of families without any heirs of their own blood and the number of single or multiple daughters all contrived to give the widow a powerful rôle in these many families. Dying husbands recognized this dependence upon their widows by making them sole executors in 60 instances. Indeed there seemed to be nothing hindering the administration of property by the widow. This may simply be taken for granted in most wills under the form "residue to

TABLE 28: RECONSTRUCTION OF THE AGE OF NEW FREEMEN

| NAME | DATE OF LIBERTY | DATE OF DEATH | AGE AT DEATH |
|---|---|---|---|
| Awdwen (Hawdwyn), Roger | 1516 | 1545 | 49 |
| Beatrice (Bettes) (Betrych), John | 1511 | 1558 | 67 |
| Byllington, John | 1527 | 1535 | 28+ |
| Blaxton, Richard | 1515 | 1526 | 31+ |
| Brandon, John | 1495 | 1528 | 53 |
| Dalton, William, mercer | 1513 | 1541 | 48 |
| Dawson, Henry, miller | 1544 | 1555 | 31 |
| Disney, John junior | 1520 | 1559 | 59 |
| Felde, John, goldsmith from Huntingdon | 1482 | 1485 | 23 |
| Frost, William senior | 1486 | 1519 | 53 |
| Gaddisby, Thomas, husband of Agnes, daughter of Margaret Stukeley | 1538 | 1548 | 30+ |
| Garlond, John, miller | 1526 | 1537 | 31 |
| Laxton, John | 1488 | 1540 | 72 |
| Manderston, Thomas | 1526 | 1536 | 30+ |
| Marshall, John | 1517 | 1544 | 47 |
| Mynt, William | 1492 | 1522 | 50 |
| Pelle, Robert, husbandman | 1515 | 1539 | 44 |
| Punte, John, husbandman | 1494 | 1533 | 59 |
| Steylton, William | 1517 | 1535 | 38 |
| Vyntner, Robert, husbandman | 1516 | 1530 | 34 |
| Vyntner (Wynter), Richard | 1517 | 1546 | 49 |
| Warde, Robert | 1535 | 1546 | 31 |
| Woode, Henry | 1517 | 1543 | 46 |

wife." Only in a few instances (Richard Smyth, John Este, William Pelman, John Punte, William Seward) does the will specify "all his lands" are left to the wife. Occasionally, the amount of land left to the wife was noted in detail (John Bailey—30 acres, William Kyng—53 1/2 acres, Robert Mayle—16 acres, Thomas Lockyngton—two messuages and 16 acres). Some idea of the value of "residue" left to the widow may be indicated in those two isolated instances when the value of money left to the widow was given rather than the farm "residue." Joan, wife of Thomas Newman was left £9 in 1485, and Agnes, wife of Thomas Burton, was left 12 marks in 1505. In 1530, Robert Vyntner left 20 marks from the sale of moveables as well as all household goods to his wife Joan who must have been elderly given the time span of her appearance in various records; his brother John who was sole executor received the residue.

While husbands were usually content to leave this general jurisdiction over their property to their wives, care was taken in nearly all instances to specify where the wife could live. This was indicated by the expression "where I now live" or "where she now lives." The word "house" was commonly employed throughout most (47) of these records, but should likely be taken to mean more basically "home" or "homestead." A few of the earliest wills (and those in the 1550s) did indeed employ the traditional term "messuage" for the place where he or she was living. That the term house could have this larger meaning throughout the intervening decades may be seen from the will of John Pownte where the widow could sell two tenements "from the house."

Paradoxically in view of the demographic realities of the time, most of the customary regulations concerning the descent of land between surviving spouses are concerned with the husband's rights over the lands of his deceased wife:[14]

> If a husband should take a wife having any lands and tenements coming to her by any kind of right, and the said husband and wife have children lawfully begotten between them, and the wife die before her husband, the said husband should hold and enjoy all the lands and tenements for the term of his life.

> If no children are begotten of the marriage, the husband shall hold a moiety of all the said tenements of the wife after her death for his life.

The fact that later enrollments of Godmanchester customs repeated these same texts and did not elaborate on the significant role of widows in managing family property would seem to indicate how little such customs reflected demographic change.

As has been noted at the beginning of this chapter, among all these wills the wife seems to have predeceased her husband very rarely. The wills of two of these wives predeceasing their husbands, Elizabeth wife of John Laxton and Agnes Lovell have been preserved. Elizabeth left a place in Newmarket to her husband John for two years to pay funeral expenses; several detailed items were left to Robert Hatch her son; another son Christopher Hatch, received a place in Newmarket on condition that he pay the legacy to his brother Robert that had been determined by their father (Elizabeth's first husband); Christopher was the sole executor. "By sufference of her husband Thomas," Agnes Lovell stated that she was following the will of her late husband William Melbourne and the messuage that she lives in was to go to her daughter Alice. Thomas Lovell could stay on this messuage for duration of his life; and Thomas was one of the executors. In these two instances, then, the second husband would not seem to have obtained any real control over his wife's family property.

The capital required to manage a farming property and a household were essential complements to the descent of property. Yet, as we shall see below, the testator liked to maintain greater freedom over chattels than land. No

---

[14] *A Small Town*, p. 433.

doubt this problem explains a certain ambiquity in the customs whereby the capacity of the testator to make specific bequest of moveables is acknowledged as a general principle but immediately qualified by an attempt to give the male heir title to the best moveables and to make the widow responsible to the male heir should she hold any of these moveables.[15] Frequently, the wills do not reflect this spirit of the customs. At the same time, the customs do lean towards the widow at one point: "If a man dies intestate ... his wife shall have a half of the residue, and the other half shall be divided among the sons and daughters unmarried in his lifetime."[16] It is in this latter spirit that many wills seem to have been written.

In those few wills where the widow was not executrix, but was replaced in that category by a son and heir, the role of the widow still remained strong. That is to say, the widow was not left with some "standard of living" maintenance only, but with a large percentage stake in goods and property. The customs noted above would seem to have been followed, that is, the dividing of one-half of the property between the heir and the widow, if such a generalization can be made from Alice, wife of Robert Pelle (1539), the wife (unnamed) of Walter Collyn (1543) and Florence, the wife of Thomas Tryg (1548). Moreover, these three widows, as well as Marion, wife of Roger Hawdwyn (1545), Joan, wife of Robert Vyntner (where the heir was the brother of her husband) (1530) and Elizabeth, the wife of Harry Gybbys (1546) received all, or nearly all, the household goods. Even where property was divided, some additional animals could be added, as in the following synopses of the Pelle and Tryg wills:

*Robert Pelle*: to wife Alice all her part of crops to be brought in by son William and to be divided equally in sight of Walter Collyn (who gets 6s.8d. for labour) + three bullocks + three yarlyng + three cuppell + three lamhoge + featherbed + wall hangings + $\frac{1}{2}$ pewter and brass. ...

*Thomas Tryg*: to wife Florence five mylch neats + calves, carts, cow and goods of house; to Elizabeth, daughter of his son Thomas, messuage he lives in after death of his wife (Florence)

Only in the one instance of Margaret widow of John Frere (1547) is the mention made of dowry, as she received all goods she brought at marriage plus one gray horse and one bullock, the best gown and dwelling in his house for life with provisions by his son Thomas, if she wishes to live there, if not, he pays 20s. per year. Elizabeth, widow of Henry Gybbys (1546) apparently lived with her son and heir Edmund, with the support of house and goods

---

[15] Ibid., p. 432.
[16] Ibid., p. 432.

and cow and heifer (food from son Edmund), and six acres leys to be tilled by son Edmund. The most detailed arrangement of this sort was for Marion, widow of Roger Hawdwyn (Awdwen) (1545), specifying even a pile of wood and stock of 200 fagotts among household chattels, all the goods of Roger except 26s. 8d. and a few other articles, and concluding with a place for Marion "by the chimney" in addition to her "little chamber."

Despite the fact that widows were treated by their husband's wills with more largesse than might be expected from a strict reading of the customs with respect to heirs, the primary role of the chief heir was clearly maintained. Where there was a son not yet of age the father's will specified that he should inherit from the widow, as was the obligation placed upon Jane, widow of William Dalton to the son and heir of Thomas, and Agnes, widow of William Frost to the son and heir John, and Elizabeth, widow of Thomas Bennet to the son and heir Robert and Agnes, widow of Edmund Maryot to the son and heir William.

When the son was of age he usually was the sole executor. For example, William son of Robert Pelle receives the residue and his mother lives with him; Thomas son of John Frere gets the messuage, lands and residue and his mother lives with him; William son of William Mynt received land and also his mother's house, and if she married he is to sell the house and divide with his sisters; Edmund son of Henry Gybbys receives the house and all lands and his mother lives with him; John, son of Roger Awdwen received the residue, the house in Post Street and all the lands.

Something of the sequence of role of mother and son can be traced in three generations of the Lockyngton family. By the brief will of Thomas Lockyngton (1544) the wife Alice is given the general disposition of property and residue but all is to be disposed "as in the last will of his father, John Lockyngton." Specific designation of property is given by Alice's will in the following year when she leaves five acres to son John; six acres to son Thomas; six acres to son Robert; five acres to son Edmund; one acre to son Richard; one acre to daughter Anne and also to son John she leaves a messuage in Arnyng Street plus a grove in West Street and to son George two horses and many goods. Preferential treatment of the heir is not obvious. Further examples of this function of the widow may be found in the wills of Joan Cowke (Cook), widow, and Margaret Jonson. Joan Cowke wills in 1533 her house on West Street to her son-in-law John Kyng for £8 13s. 4d. per year, and when "the tally of payments for the said house are made between the said John and my executors according to the custom of the town" the last 40s. of the payment will be allowed to John Kyng and this 40s. to go to Alice, her daughter, wife of John Kyng for "performance" of her father's will. Margaret Jonson, widow, in 1527 willed to her son William the

house she is in for 26s. 8d. to be paid to the town of Godmanchester, owed
for the said house and tally she made with him for the house he dwells in
in East Street and moveables on condition that he helps and keep her
daughter Elizabeth during their lives together so long as she does not marry.
In short, as might be expected by their control over residue the widow had
a specific role in the disposition of property.

Concern for the heir was expressed in other ways as well. Some fathers
found it necessary to spell out the order of succession among children. No
doubt it reflects the mentality of that plague-ridden era that Robert Mayle
should detail in his will of 1542 the bequest of 16 acres of land to his son
John when he comes 21 years of age, "then if he dies it goes to his son Henry
and if Henry dies to his daughter Elizabeth and if Elizabeth dies to his
daughter Joan." Because William Dalton owned a valuable town property
(The George) he was careful to indicate in his will of 1518 that his daughter
Agnes and his heirs inherit The George should his son Thomas die: "To wife
Jane, so long as she lives, the messuage called 'The George' and after her
death to his son and heir Thomas and heirs or to daughter Agnes and her
heirs and if not executors to sell."

How far would the people of Godmanchester go beyond their immediate
family in order to retain their property among their kin? Even in this
demographic scene where wives were so often left as widows with young
children, there are examples of real concern for grandchildren. Elena Byrder
left to her grandchild Elena daughter of her son William Nicholas 6s. 8d.
when she married and also to Joan daughter of her son William Nicholas 1s.
(1538); William Benet left one sheep each to John and Agnes son and
daughter of his son William (1540); William Frere, whose daughter Sybil
married Thomas Stevenson, left one acre each of land to their children,
Anne, Henry, John, Thomas and William (1544).

In the same year Thomas Granger left to his grandson Giles, son of John
Granger 10s. and to his other grandson Leonard Gyttons son of his daughter
Jane 10s., this to be received after death of his wife Margaret; Thomas
Upchurche certainly looked after his grandson John who was bequeathed
13s. 4d. for a period of nine years; John Vyntner left to his grandson John
(a son of John Vyntner who was the son of the above John) 40s. and he
receives this when 16 years old and to his other grandson Robert (also the
son of John Vyntner) one quarter of barley (1543).

Nevertheless, concern for an heir never obscured care for the welfare of
all children as well as spouse. Where the family was less wealthy and without
male heir, this could mean *de facto* the same disposition of wealth as to the
male heir. Renalde Corby, labourer, left his house on West Street and three
acres of meadow to his wife Elizabeth. If the house were not sold, both the

house and meadow were to go to their daughter Sybil at the death of Elizabeth. Should Elizabeth become needy she could sell the house, but each payment must be shared equally with Sybil. John Feld, goldsmith, willed that his messuage remain with his wife Isabella and at her death be given to their daughter Joan. Both Corby and Feld left the "residue" to their wives. But Feld was undoubtedly more wealthy since he left 10s. as religious offering for his soul and that of his wife. Apparently, the Feld residue would be adequate for maintenance of his widow and daughter.

The same pattern may be seen when there was more than one daughter. John Byllington, who may have been of much the same economic status as Renalde Corby,[17] left his house on East Street to his wife Agnes to use or sell as she wished on condition that she give 6s. 8d. to each of his daughters, Agnes and Joan. A parallel arrangement is seen in the John Wylde, senior, will when he left his house to his wife Anne for life, and she could sell it if needy, but if sold then she had to give 10s. each to her three daughters, Emma, Agnes and Anne. Margaret Stukeley left two and one-half acres of meadow and one acre arable to her married daughter Agnes (who was married to Thomas Gaddisby). Margaret also left her house on Post Street to both her daughters, that is, to Agnes and her sister Joan, one-half each. The practical resolution of dividing a house into two parts was solved by disposing that Joan could live there by paying one-half of the rent to Agnes. If Joan should marry, one-half of the house could be rented to another who would pay one-half of the rent, presumably to Joan.

Around 1500, as had been the case around 1300,[18] once the family homestead was settled on the main heir there was an obvious equality among sons and daughters. William Frost in 1519 gave to each of his three children 40s., three calves and 13s. 4d. Richard Blaxton left some garments of his trade to his sons John, Robert and Thomas and to his daughter Elizabeth two quarters of barley in 1526. Henry Gybbys in 1546 left to his son John and daughter Elizabeth £3 6s. 8d. a piece. In 1544, John Marshall left one-half of his goods to his wife and the other half were to be distributed equally between his two sons John and Thomas. Edmund Maryot (1519) left a house, four acres, one-half acre of meadow and four quarters of barley to each of his sons Richard and William.

Again, as was the case around 1300, sons tended to receive more than daughters. William Dalton (1518) had a son and heir Thomas, and to the other son William left a tenement along with 10 sheep while his daughter Agnes received two milkbeasts, two "hekforth," 10 sheep and a featherbed

---

[17] See Chapter 5, below.
[18] *A Small Town*, pp. 220-224.

with a mattress. Walter Colen (1543) left the obligation upon his heir, Thomas, to pay £30 to each of the other sons, Edward, John and Walter, and £10 to the daughter Dorothy. William Freman (1545) left six acres to his second son Thomas and the latter was to pay 10s. to each of daughters, Elena and Joan. After arranging for his messuage and lands to go to his heir, William, when he reached the age of 20 years, William Alred (1556) left £10 to his other son, John, and £5 to each of his daughters, Margaret, Elizabeth and Agnes.

As one descends the economic scale the possibility of priority among children would seem to have given away to subsistence concerns. The wealth of John Bailey (1506) was money only, as he left £1 each to his children, Alice, William, John and Agnes. Elizabeth, wife of William Mynt (1522), was to sell her house should she re-marry and divide the revenues evenly among her children, Agnes, Joan and William. After leaving his house and one acre of meadow to his son Simon, Thomas Granger (1544) left 10s. each to a son John, a daughter Jane, the grandson Giles (son of John) and the grandson Leonard (son of Jane). John Huggyn (Hogan) (1545) left 6s. 8d. each to his son John and daughter Beatrice. John Upchurch (1553) left 7 $\frac{1}{2}$ acres apiece to his children, John, William, Harry and Elizabeth. In the same year William Schacher left his messuage to his four children, William, John, Thomas and Margaret. Such equality among girls and boys is not likely to be taken in our current modern sense since it is noteworthy that girls are most often listed last, as in the two examples just given.[19]

This preoccupation with equality makes difficult any generalized deductions about the maintenance allowances for children. John Wright left to his son John one acre in each field, when he reached the age of 18 years and to his daughter Agnes a white bullock now for marriage when it takes place and £3 from his wife and son at marriage when it takes place. Thomas Tryg left in 1548 to his wife Florence livestock and goods of his house; to son Thomas three sheep; to daughter Elizabeth three sheep; to Elizabeth daughter of his son Thomas eight quarters of malt; and to his godsons, Richard Pacy, William Stevenson and Steven Faldyng one quarter of malt to each.

A more intimate and thereby more complex picture of this interplay of concern for family heir and heirs with individual sons and daughters may be found in the disposition of clothing and other moveables. Even where there were broad provisions in the will for division of moveables, few testators could refrain from disposing item by item those personal belongings for which they obviously had a special affection. Alice West, widow, left quite a lot of her personal belongings in 1532: to Alice Cromwell her servant her

[19] On the other hand, listings in some wills may have been according to age.

best gown lined with buckram; to Agnes Richardson her servant 20s. plus a mattress, a bolster and a kirtill and three smocks; to Joan Robyns two silver spoons; to Dorothy Robyns her second featherbed; to her sister, wife of Grace, her best gown; to Richard Robyns her silver plate gilded and a silver and gold plate; to her brother-in-law, John Grace, her "plene silver plate" and silver spoon.

Unfortunately, until the later wills of the early Tudor period and increasingly later in the century, there is little consistency among the listing of such items. It is not possible, therefore, to reconstruct a profile of the standard of living at Godmanchester over these decades. Nor can one attempt an inventory of capital wealth in such items as brass and silver for wealthy men (as Aylreds and Dawsons) tended to leave money rather than goods. These data also defy easy differentiation of wealth groups. For Anne Hedley, from a lower level of wealth than Joan Cook, vied with the latter by leaving to ten persons in her will three brass pots, one pewter pot, two "great pans," eight "harden sheets," one flaxen sheet, four petticoats and a red kirtle.

The disposition of material goods did not stop within the nuclear family. As has been noted above the concern of testators was extended to grandchildren. This widening relationship gave a significant role to sons and daughters-in-law. A nice touch of maternal family management is seen in the will of the widow, Agnes Grene, who specified a bequest to Dorothy King, fiancé of her son George. Particularly was this important where there were no male heirs. One can see the importance of John Dorraunt to his mother-in-law Agnes Burton; of Robert King to his in-laws William and Elizabeth Dalton; of Thomas Stevenson to his in-laws William and his wife Alice Frere; of William Nebbis to his mother-in-law, the widow Alice Frost; and of so many others. Whether of a poorer family, such as that of Richard Edmund and his wife Rose who had a son-in-law Nicholas Swalowe, or wealthier, as were most of the examples in the previous sentence, descent by blood through a daughter was as real as through a male heir.

Whereas the position of grandchildren and their parents in last wills signified the direct descent of wealth through the family cycle, collateral relationships might also be called upon for support at various stages of the cycle. Individuals are noted also with the same surname as the testator, and thereby could be a brother or sister of the deceased. Roger Awdwen noted his brothers, Sir Peter and John in 1545; Sir John Colen was the brother of Walter Colen in Walter's will of 1543; Henry Dawson also bequeathed to his two brothers, a William and John of St. Neots; Richard Edmunds noted his brother John in his will of 1545. More than likely Edward and Richard Este could be the brothers of John Este, husbandman in 1530; John Frere named his sister in his will of 1547 who was Margaret Granger, the wife of Thomas

Granger; John Garlond named his brother William in 1537; and Thomas Herman remembered his sister Ursula Vyntner in 1546, to give a few illustrations of this collateral relationship.

Blood ties continued, then, to exercise a powerful pull in the dispersal of material goods by bequest and to impose a wide circle of obligations in the enforcement of various demands of the last will. The fact that those assuming obligations were well rewarded ought not to be allowed to obliterate the larger social context of the obligation. For example, an executor or executrix was most frequently the chief benefactor from the will but remained personally responsible none the less for the implementation of the family "policy" decreed by the last will and testament.

Nevertheless, the fact that various friends and officials were well paid ought not to be taken as an economic relationship distinct from social ties. That they were paid well is clear: John Laxton as supervisor of John Bonsay's will received 20s.; William Dalton left 40s. to each of his two executors; John Este left 6s. 8d. to each of his two executors, Henry Frere and John Clerk; Margaret Stukeley left 13s. 4d. to her two friends, Dorothy Sudbury and Elizabeth Punt; Thomas Lockyngton noted Thomas Pacy as his overseer and paid him 6s. 8d.; Harry Gybbys left 3s. 4d. to his supervisor, William Richmund; and the same amount was left to William Abraham, supervisor for William Godwyn's will. But these were friends and associates who gathered at the bedside of the dying, as in the evidence concerning the death of John Mynsterchambre given at the beginning of this chapter.

These various sorts of groups and associations were cohesive forces not unlike the family. Only very gradually are social historians challenging the naive evolutionist formula that "society displayed community" by study of the flexible and creative possibilities of communities and small groups. One major advance in this regard has been the use of the term "household" to complement the study of the family.[20] The importance of the household for Godmanchester families is demonstrated by bequests to servants and others who are presumably friends since there is no kinship indication: Roger Hawdwyn bequest to Elena (Hawdwyn), wife of John his servant; William Bennet bequest to Elizabeth his servant and John Jonson his servant; John Bonsay bequest to John Bettres his servant; John Brandon bequest to Elizabeth his servant and also to John Elys of Barn(well) who could have been his friend; Robert Dawle left his looms and shop to his fellow tradesman John Lambert; John Frere bequest to his servant Margaret Morgayn; Thomas Frost bequest to his friend William Basse; John Goodwyn noted his servant

---

[20] It is instructive to follow the gradual employment of this concept in the productive literature of The Cambridge Group for the History of Population and Social Structure.

John Bele; William Goodwyn also had a servant called Margaret Bawyne; Katherine Hays bequeathed to William Olyff, William Lord and William Osteler in 1540, all who were very likely from the same social and economic group. Robert Pelle, husbandman, had two servants who were Edward Menell and Thomas Elways. As noted above, Alice West had two servants Alice Cromwell and Agnes Richardson and besides these she left to numerous individuals who could have been her workers and friends.

In many respects, then, the term household must give way to economic association along petty craft lines and to those personal friendships that criss-cross neighbourhoods or even the whole breadth of smaller towns and villages. Other instruments would be required, of course, to complement the will in this extension of trust to the household and beyond. As will be seen in the following chapters, the common use of the tally "as was the custom of the town" provided an important credit instrument. Unfortunately, data available for the history of Godmanchester at this time do not make possible more extensive network studies.[21] The last column in Appendix 8 ("Families and Other Personnel Recorded in Wills") supplies merely an indicator to the existence of many networks. Nevertheless, the next section of this chapter does demonstrate the creative social potential of the community of Godmanchester.

## B. Guilds and Other Charities

An understanding of the parish community in late medieval and early modern England is still at the pioneer stage despite a long term interest in the question by many scholars.[22] Every will specified those formal payments that had acquired the status of canonical obligations. After stating that the soul was to go to God (and the saints), and the body to the parish church, the will noted that the mortuary (*principale* in Latin wills) was to be paid "according to custom." Then a payment to the diocesan cathedral, the church of Lincoln, was entered. In the will of William Fryer (Frere), 1491, and that of Richard Grene in 1535, this was stated to be for the fabric of the church of Lincoln. These payments were small, and relatively uniform, as the following summary shows. There is no apparent correlation between the size of this payment and the wealth of the testator: 47 at 2d.; 26 at 4d.; 5 at 6d.; 3 at 8d.; 1 at 9d.; 2 at 1s.; 1 at 1s. 8d.; 1 at 2s.

---

[21] For one of the earlier studies, see Richard M. Smith, "Kin and Neighbours in a Thirteenth-Century Suffolk Community," *Journal of Family History*, 4 (1979), 219-256.

[22] For example, many valuable insights to be found in W. O. Ault, "The Village Church and the Village Community in Mediaeval England," *Speculum*, 45 (1970), 197-215, still remain to be explored.

The next formal obligation to be found entered in these wills was an offering to the parish church of the town in compensation for tithe payments "neglected" during the lifetime of the testator. Here, too, the payments are not large, but they do reflect variations in wealth among the testators: 6 at 2d. ; 38 at 4d.; 6 at 6d.; 11 at 8d.; 10 at 1s.; 1 at 1s. 4d.; 6 at 1s. 8d.; 2 at 2s.; 5 at 3s. 4d.; and two gave two bushels of barley; two gave two modes of barley and three gave four modes of barley. But these formal payments are no more adequately descriptive of genuine human concerns than the local taxation records of today serve to describe the local community.

One of the more intimate ways by which religious expression created small communities of interest was through that adoption of spiritual obligations called godchildren. In only three instances are the godchildren named: William Freman left to William Everard his godson 6s. 8d. when he reaches the age of 18 years in 1545; William Bennet left one sheep each to his four godsons, William Ede, William Godwyn(?), William Kyng and William Schacher; and Thomas Tryg left to his three godsons, Stephen Faldyng, Richard Pacy and William Stevenson one quarter of malt. The other testators who left to their godchildren are listed below:

| | |
|---|---|
| Roger Awdwyn | 4d. to each godchild |
| William Dalton | 12d. to each godchild for prayers |
| Richard Edmund | 4d. to each godchild |
| William Godwyn | 4d. to each godchild |
| Robert Pelle | one bushel of barley to each godchild |
| John Stevens | 1d. to each of six godchildren |
| Thomas Upchurche | one bushel of barley to each godchild |
| Robert Vyntner | one bushel of barley to every child in Godmanchester |
| Richard Wynter | 4d. to each godchild |

Special gifts to the church of Godmanchester reflected personal devotion as well as a particular type of adhesion to the parish. A very personal tone is introduced to express anxiety about the spiritual welfare of the testator and his immediate relatives, whatever the cost to rich or poor. Usually it would be an obligation of the executors to arrange for the funeral and oral instructions would have been given by the dying person. A good many of the wealthier townsmen left more detailed written instructions. From their para-liturgical bequests we are able to see the involvement of families in parish service communities. For example, William Kyng asked to be buried by his first wife Agnes and left 4d. to every priest for singing a requiem and 2d. to each of the two parish clerks, and 1d. for the bellman; John Brandon in June of 1528 left to the church wardens one acre of meadow for his wife's anniversary and 2d. to each clerk. But guilds had obviously become the common framework of many varieties of religious commitment, so to these we must now turn in order to give more context to the parish community.

The Merton community whose sub-priory held 75 acres at Godmanchester together with the gift of the Church and its 63 acres according to the Hundred Rolls of 1279,[23] was a product of that twelfth-century religious enthusiasm that has recently attracted much scholarly interest.[24] A well known statute of Edward I signalled the official end to this enthusiasm for twelfth-century religious houses. This statute, "De Religiosis," was carefully preserved in the customs of Godmanchester and, as far as can be observed from court rolls, was meticulously observed from the end of the thirteenth century.[25] Somewhat ironically, the people of Godmanchester then renewed their donations for religious purposes under a different title, that of fraternities and guilds. Certainly there was continuity in the religious gift mentality of Godmanchester since the amount of land given to guilds by the time of their dissolution in the sixteenth century was much the same as that accumulated by Merton from the time of its foundation in the reign of Stephen.

Much of the variety of guilds that had become such a social reality at Godmanchester is clear from surviving records. Five guilds and fraternities are noted in the records: Corpus Christi, Holy Trinity, St. James, St. John the Baptist and St. Mary. There were very likely less formally organized societies behind the devotion to St. George and St. Katherine and the support of their altars and others in the parish church. In the history of the religious life of the people of Godmanchester these guilds must be considered to be of major importance, comparable to the formal religious institutions of the twelfth[26] and thirteenth centuries (especially, of course, Merton) and the religious sects of early modern centuries.

---

[23] *Rotuli Hundredorum*, eds. W. Illingworth and J. Caley, Publications of the Records Commissioners (1812-1818), 1:591.

[24] A valuable recent survey may be found in Brenda Bolton, *The Medieval Reformation* (London, 1983).

[25] This does not mean to say Merton had no other alternatives. See, Sandra Raban "Mortmain in Medieval England," *Past and Present,* 62.1 (1974), 3-26. But any activity on the land market by Merton Priory is totally absent from the court roll conveyances. See further below, p. 168.

[26] The large Black Monk establishments of the fenland region were of a different order of magnitude. The most recent historian of these monasteries makes the point clearly: "Whereas in the tenth century, leading churchmen and nobles contributed whole villages, by the twelfth century it was more often knightly families sparing a few virgates or a small manor from their more limited resources" (Sandra Raban, *The Estates of Thorney and Crowland: a Study in Medieval Monastic Land Tenure* [Cambridge, 1977], p. 33).

The historical identity of the institutions and lives of these guilds is another matter. This expression of religious experience never gained a formal status in either canon or common law. That is to say, no charters of approbation or canonical recognition were issued by ecclesiastical authorities while common law authorities ambiguously[27] identified guilds with canonical religious bodies and ultimately dissolved them under this title. In consequence, it is difficult to discern the formal role of various interests such as Merton Priory, secular clergy (vicars and chaplains) and the laity of the town in these "new" directions given to religious experience at this time. On the other hand, the practical arrangements employed to avoid the necessity for the licenses required of land granted in mortmain by "De Religiosis" are quite clear.

Apparently from early in the fourteenth century[28] gifts of land to guilds came under jurisdiction of the town and by paying to the royal farm avoided the strictures of "De Religiosis." Most of the references to guilds over the ensuing two centuries come from various entries in rentals and court rolls to record obligations to the royal farm. Godmanchester had developed its own distinct economic and administrative structures as reflected in the spread of occupations throughout various streets and the representation by street among the officials of the town. Not surprisingly, therefore, the evidence for guilds until perhaps the late fifteenth or early sixteenth centuries indicates an equal effort to locate guilds throughout the town.

Rentals listed guild farm obligations consistently on different streets or specific locations. In short, there would seem to have been some meeting place identifiable with the guilds. When these rental obligations are broken down into acres, following the approach of Chapter 2 above, the Custodians of All Saints is located on West Street in 1485 with five acres and in 1489 with seven acres. On Arnyng Street were the three Fraternities of St. James (1485, one-half acre); Holy Trinity (1485, 15 acres; 1487, 16 acres; 1490, $18^{1}/_{2}$ acres) and St. Mary (nine acres throughout 1485, 1487 and 1490). On Post Street were the Fraternity of St. John (1485, five and one-half acres)

---

[27] Scholars seem to be generally agreed that this ambiguity is reflected in the very requests of Parliament to identify guilds in 1389 and the fear of the latter that by responding they should be seen as religious institutions. See Toulmin Smith and Lucy Toulmin Smith, eds., *English Gilds: The Original Ordinances of More than 100 English Gilds*, Early English Texts Society, Orig. Ser. 40 (London, 1970); and more recently, William R. Jones, "English Religious Brotherhoods and Medieval Lay Piety: The Inquiry of 1388-89," *The Historian*, 36 (1974), especially, p. 648. For the problem more generally in Europe, see Gabriel Le Bras, "Les Confréries Chrétiennes. Problèmes et Propositions," in *Études de Sociologie Religieuse*, vol. 2 (Paris, 1956), especially p. 447.

[28] *The Victoria County History of Huntingdonshire*, vol. 2, eds. William Page, Granville Proby and S. Inskip Ladds, (London, 1932), p. 295.

and the Fraternity of Corpus Christi (1485, 19 acres; 1486-1490, $18\frac{1}{2}$ acres; 1491-1492, 19 acres; and 1494, 20 acres). On East Street was the Custodian of the Church (1485, 22 acres; 1486 to 1492, 23 acres), the Custodian of St. George (1485-1592, one acre) and the Custodian of St. Katherine (1485-1492, six acres). The older guilds were the wealthier and the use of their funds for more liturgical purposes is well expressed in the fact that some of their wealth was at the disposition of their chaplains who lived on East Street, that is, in the ambience of the church and with other clerical personnel. The rentals of East Street listed a chaplain of Corpus Christi (1485-1488, 47 acres; 1488 Michaelmas, 48 acres; 1489-1490, 49 acres; and 1491-1492, $39\frac{1}{2}$ acres) and a chaplain of the Blessed Virgin Mary (1485, 73 acres; 1486-1488, $73\frac{1}{2}$ acres; 1488 Michaelmas, $77\frac{1}{2}$ acres; 1489, 77 acres; 1490, 79 acres; 1491, 68 acres; and 1492, 72 acres).

The wills of Godmanchester people do not tell us any more about the role of guild meeting places, if such they were, throughout the town, but they do demonstrate the liturgical interests of the various fraternities. The focus of the Fraternity of St. John the Baptist was clearly an altar and statue in the parish church. Although this guild had been formed by the mid-fourteenth century, it remained very small and limited in character.[29] A will of 1526 identified the interest of the guild as "in the church"; the tabernacle is noted in a will of 1483, the altar cloth in 1532, a candle "before him" (that is, his statue) in 1524, and a "light for him" in 1527.

A will of 1534 also informs us that there was an altar dedicated to St. Katherine. By the time of the dissolution no prominence is given to the holdings of the Fraternity behind this devotion, but the commitment had been substantial. John Pownte (Punt) entered in his will of 1532 an obligation from the will of his mother to supply 40s. worth of revenues from a grove for vestments for the altar of St. Katherine. One rod of land had been bequeathed to this fraternity in 1528 along with an obligation on a house to pay 6s. 8d. to the Fraternity of St. Katherine in 1507. A bequest of fourpence in 1534 also establishes the existence of an altar of St. Christopher. This fraternity was also cited as an alternative legatee for a monetary bequest in 1528. The apparent disappearance of the Fraternity of St. James by the sixteenth century may be attributed to the fact that it was a statue only, that is, a sort of mini-shrine. A will of 1528 arranged for a candle before the (statue of) St. Peter "every principal day," that is, on his feast days. The bequest of Roger Hawdwyn in 1545 of five rods for an obit on St. Margaret's day further exemplifies this alternative form of devotional support.

[29] Ibid., p. 296.

Devotion to the patroness of the parish church, the Blessed Virgin Mary, had sponsored early guild development at Godmanchester[30] and was expressed in a variety of forms. From a bequest of 1534 it is clear that there was an altar with a special dedication to Our Lady with child (*in puerperium*). This is perhaps also the object of a bequest of 1526 to "the Fraternity of the Blessed Virgin Mary in the Church." As we shall see below, there was also a Chantry of the Blessed Virgin Mary by the late fifteenth century. A more complex matter is the existence of a reliquary, no doubt along with a statue, apparently within the chapel of the Holy Trinity in the parish church. There was a bequest of 1483 to repair the reliquary of the "Holy Mary of Trinity," a substantial gift of 13s. 4d. in 1519 to the "Blessed Virgin Mary of Trinity of Godmanchester" and a bequest of linen (?) in 1528 to "Our Lady of Trinity." References to the relatively wealthy Fraternity of the Holy Trinity and its chapel occur in wills of 1491 (£2 13s. 4d. for vestments); for the tabernacle of Blessed Trinity in 1522; 40s. "to the Fraternity" in 1512; a small obit for the Fraternity of the Trinity in the Church in 1526; another small obit to Trinity Chapel in 1534; and a reference to the Chaplain of Holy Trinity in 1538.

The late medieval period was a time of rebuilding and embellishment of the parish church of Godmanchester.[31] This was no doubt the reason for attention in wills to altars noted above but there was also reflected a great interest in the parish church as a whole. Around 1500 there was a special interest in the fabric as Thomas Mayle left money towards the tabernacle and screen in 1500 while John Turneskewe gave £6 13s. 4d. for repairs to the chancel in 1505. In 1505 money was also left for repairs to the belfry. Bells played an intimate part in the liturgical interests of the people and indeed money was left in many wills towards bell ringing at funerals. A cluster of bequests around 1530 (1527, 6d.; 1528, 40s.; 1530, 12d.; 1535, 12d.) indicates the repair of bells or even more likely, the purchase of new bells.

It would appear to have been traditional to make funerals and anniversaries "large" liturgical occasions. For example, in 1512 Richard Smyth left land from which the revenues were to be disposed at fourpence for each priest, twopence for each clerk, twopence for the offering and one penny for the bellman for the anniversaries of Richard and his wife Alice. Such arrangements continued, at least into the 1530s, as may be seen by the will of William Kyng in 1530. William left two acres of arable and some meadow to his wife so that on the annual anniversary fourpence should be given to

---

[30] Ibid., p. 295.

[31] Ibid., pp. 292-294. See further below, p. 251, on the bailiff's account for 1508-1509 the three interesting items about selection of an organ player.

every priest in attendance and singing the requiem, twopence to each of the two parish clerks, one penny to the bellman and twopence as an offering. From lands bequeathed to his son Richard, William designated seven swaths of meadow for bell ringing for himself and Adam Barre (from whom the land had been purchased), as well as tenpece for five priests and twopence for each of the two parish clerks. Whether this interest in a grandiose clerical scene continued after the Reformation cannot be determined from wills and may not be expected. Even allowing for an age of inflation, the cost of funerals did remain high. For example, in 1545 Roger Hawdwyn left £3 for funeral and following anniversary expenses to begin with 20s. for mass, dirige and dispensation to the poor at the funeral itself.

Often cited as a "cause" of the anti-clerical feeling that accompanied some elements of the English Reformation, increases in costly masses, especially the Gregorian (30 day sequence) do appear in the 1530s in significant numbers considering the volume of wills for that period. Gregorian masses are designated in the following wills: William Pelman (1529, 3); William Digby (1530, 1); William Kyng (1530, 1); Joan Cowke (1533, 2), William Birdere (1534, 1) and William Stelton (1538, 1). This mass arrangement for Joan Cowke, together with a priest to sing for three months, brought a stipend of 26s. 8d. For the one Gregorian of William Diggby 6s. 8d. was left. In addition to the Gregorian series of masses, William Kyng left six marks for (masses by) a priest for two one-half year periods. Considerable gifts towards the high altar of the parish church accompanied the liturgical interest of this period: five marks for a chalice for the high altar and black vestments (1528); 6s. 8d. for a high altar cloth (1529); 40s. for a specially designed moving image of Christ rising from the dead (1530) and a crossed (altar) cloth (1532).

One should expect, given the history of tensions between secular clergy and the "sectarian" friars over the later medieval period, that this increasing prominence (if such it was) of the parish in the sixteenth century was at the expense of the decentralized guilds. Most certainly the vicar, Edmund Archbould, was a central figure in the wills as chaplain, recipient of Gregorian masses and gifts to the main altar as well as frequent official (supervisor) for implementing the wills. Was there a spirit of rebellion against this centralized control among families like the Daltons? In 1503 John Dalton bequeathed 13s. 4d. to the Corpus Christi Guild for himself and his wife. The Daltons maintained their interest in this guild and in 1541 William Dalton left some meadow for a "sepulcher" light at the guild and, exceptionally, appointed the Keeper of Corpus Christi Guild as the supervisor of his will.

Guardians and Keepers of guilds were for the most part from the major governing families of the town. John Byllingford gave up a cottage in Giles Lane to John Mynsterchambre and John Gardener keeper of the Corpus Christi guild for the use of the bailiffs in 1483. John must have been getting old by this time, since he was noted in the Frankpledge Rolls as early as 1460, as a juror for Arnyng Street in 1469 and 1482, while in 1486 he served as bailiff. John Gardener was well established by 1483 having property in Arnyng Street and also acting as juror for that street in 1481 and 1487. He was given the position of Custodian of the church in 1482. John practiced the trade of ploughwrighte.

William Stodale was noted as a guardian of Corpus Christi in July 1483, when once again John Byllingford gave up a cottage for the use of William Stodale and John Mynsterchambre in Giles Lane. William was active as an official over a period of 12 years: by 1481 he was a juror for East Street, and the same for the years 1483, 1486 and 1488. In 1489 he was a constable, 1490 bailiff, 1499 coroner, 1493 constable, 1495 juror, 1498 bailiff, 1499 coroner and a coroner for East and Arnyng Streets in 1500. William who does not appear to have been married had his abode on East Street. By an entry of 1488 we find John Aylred and William Frere the custodians of Corpus Christi: "John Mundeford son and heir of John Mundeford and wife Isabella surrender to John Aylred and William Frere guardians of Corpus Christi an empty lot with grove." William Frere was no doubt the most active official of the town. As early as 1467 and 1469 we find him elected clerk for Post Street. By 1481 he was a bailiff for Post and West Streets, the next year a coroner, the next year a juror and then in 1485 a bailiff, 1486 coroner, and in 1487, 1493 and 1501 bailiff. William by this time must have been getting on in years and in 1506 it is more than likely that his son William continued the tradition and started off as a collector of the view. The Freres were a very well established old family going back to the 1279 Hundred Rolls as land holders.

The Aylreds were also of the same mould as the Freres, that is, a well established family as far back as 1279. John Aylred may be cited as an example. Like other members of his family he took part in the administrative duties of the town, starting off as a juror in 1467 for Arnyng Street; by 1472 he was a bailiff, a bailiff again in 1483 and the next year a coroner, in 1488 constable, bailiff in 1489 and 1495, and in 1496 coroner for Arnyng and East Streets. John lived on Arnyng Street and he was one of the wealthiest landholders of the town.

By 1507 there appears to have been three guardians for the guild of Corpus Christi and two for the guild of Holy Trinity. On 23 September 1507, William Ussher, William Orwell and John Brandon, guardians of Corpus

Christi and Robert Chandeler and Richard Smyth, guardians of Holy Trinity, surrender to Richard Smyth and wife Joan and their son a messuage in Post Street called the Horseshoe. Unfortunately, our knowledge of William Ussher only covers the year 1507 when he was a constable and held a messuage in Giles Lane; William Orwell, on the other hand, held official posts in the town for many years: 1483, 1486 and 1488 juror, 1489 constable, 1490 bailiff, 1491 coroner, 1493 constable, 1495 juror, 1498 bailiff, 1499 and 1500 coroner for East and Arnyng Streets.

Robert Chandeler the guardian for Holy Trinity was a collector of the farm for 1495, five years later a constable, 1503 collector of the ale, 1504 coroner, 1505 juror, 1506 constable, 1508 collector of the farm, 1510 constable, 1511 bailiff, 1512 coroner and 1513 collector of the farm. Robert's duties varied somewhat from the pattern of his fellow guild guardians given above. Richard Smyth was a constable for 1503, 1504 collector of the farm, 1507 coroner, 1508 collector of the farm, 1509 coroner, 1510 bailiff, 1511 coroner and 1512 juror. Richard held his property on Post Street.

In 1510 John Lockyngton and John Stukeley, custodians of the Holy Trinity, bought a messuage that was formerly Thomas Lockyngton's in West Street. The Lockyngtons were very prominent in Godmanchester and John kept up the tradition: he was a bailiff in 1502 and a coroner in 1503 and continued to act as an official for the town, such as acting as constable, juror and collector of the farm for a number of years. The other custodian of the Holy Trinity, John Stukeley, also was an official of the town, such as bailiff, coroner, and constable from 1503 through to 1514. John held his messuage on Post Street.

Another two officials who were the guardians of the Corpus Christi Guild were John Laxton and John Brandon. They delivered to Alice Bettres in 1512 a messuage in Post Street. John Laxton was an active participant in the town performing his official duties from 1502 through to 1525: 1502 collector of the farm, 1505 constable, 1506 and 1507 bailiff, 1509 bailiff, 1509 juror, 1512 juror, 1515 collector of the farm, 1518 bailiff, 1519 coroner, 1521 constable, 1522 and 1525 juror. John held his property on West Street and he married Elizabeth Hatcher (as her second husband) who in her will left to John land that lay in Newmarket.

John Brandon, the second guardian of the Corpus Christi guild, was of a different calibre from the above officials in so far as in 1495 John was evicted from the vill for malefactions against the vill but was re-instated in 1519. This evidently did not stop John from performing his duties as an official. In 1505 he was a juror, 1509 coroner, 1512 juror, 1513 and 1517 collector of the farm, and the same in 1522, 1523 juror, 1524 bailiff, 1525 coroner and 1526 juror. John was married but he had no children. John's property lay on Post

Street. By 1521 John Punte and John Paye (Page) were the custodians of the guild of the Holy Trinity then delivering to William Leffyn a messuage in West Street. John Punt and John Paye were also active in their official duties of the town like the custodians already mentioned.

The information given in these few paragraphs would seem to leave little doubt that government of the guilds was perceived as the province of the central administration of the town. Indeed this function of the town administration was even extended to the parish church in so far as the church wardens accounted to the 12 jurors. In the Jurors' Book are entered the end of the term accounts for churchwardens from the 1480s. Where these monies originated is not clear. That some came from legacies is indicated by three entries distinct from the accounts as such noting that there are "owed to the church" from the legacies of the wife of William Hallam, John Barret and Joan Pelman the sums of four shillings, one shilling eightpence and one shilling eightpence respectively. Further, as entered below for 27 July 1485, one account simply enters the obligation of the executor, Agnes Sydebotom. Churchwardens tended to be elected from the secondary level of administration and include, therefore, a large number of clerks. Entries from the Jurors' Book are tabulated below.

TABLE 29: CHURCH WARDENS' ACCOUNTS[32]

| DATE | NAME | AMOUNT |
|---|---|---|
| M 1482 | Henry Marshall | 11s. 7d. |
| | William Morell | 14s. 1d. |
| 7 October 1482 | John Page senior | 9s. 4d. |
| | Thomas Mayle | £1 5s. 3d. |
| | William Lessy | 3s. 5d. |
| 13 October 1483 | John Gardner senior | 1s. 2d. |
| | William Plumpton | £2 9s. 1d. |
| 23 April 1483 | Edward Barre | 4s. 6d. |
| 13 December 1483 | William Suell | £2 1s. 3d. |
| 27 July 1485 | Agnes Sydebotom, executor of Thomas Sydebotom | 12s. 2d. |
| | William Goodwyn | £3 1s. 2d. |
| 18 February 1486 | John Robyn | £2 3s. 1d. q. |

[32] According to an entry in the Jurors' Book for 13 October 1490, the 12 men agreed to elect William Lessy and John Adam as churchwardens for the following three years. They were to account every year at Michaelmas and payment "for their labour" was 3s. 4d. each. These two churchwardens only accounted once in the following list.

Most of these entries are to be found in the Jurors' Book, pp. 72ff. Since most of the entries are stroked out without further additional entries, these arrears would seem to have been paid off rather quickly.

| Date | Name | Amount | | |
|---|---|---|---|---|
| E 1489 | William Moundford | nothing | | |
| M 1489 | Thomas Laxton | £3 | 2s. | 4d. |
| M 1490 | John Bould | | 2s. | 6d. |
| | John Townshend | £2 | 2s. | 6d. |
| 21 November 1490 | Richard Mayle junior | £2 | 11. | 5d. |
| 20 December 1491 | John Adam & William Lessy | £3 | 8s. | 6d. |
| M 1492 | William Diggby | | 16s. | 9d. |
| | William Kyng | £3 | 3s. | 5d. ob. |
| 13 December 1493 | Stephen Clerk | £3 | 1s. | 4d. ob. |
| 17 June 1494 | William Barre | | 6s. | 1d. |
| | John Robyn | £3 | 3s. | 1d. ob. |
| 15 December 1495 | Robert Nicholas | £3 | 3s. | 1d. ob. |
| 19 December 1496 | Richard Smyth | £3 | 0s. | 9d. ob. |
| E 1497 | Augustine Arnold | | 6s. | 5d. |
| 14 December 1497 | Robert Chandeler | £2 | 16s. | 9d. |
| E 1499 | William Suell | £1 | 15s. | 1d. ?b. |
| M 1499 | William Melbourne | £2 | 11s. | 1d. |
| E 1500 | William Vyntner | nothing | | |
| M 1500 | Richard Smyth | £1 | 13s. | 1d. ob. |
| M 1501 | John Turneskewe | £2 | | |
| E? 1502 | John Page | | | 6d. ob. |
| M 1502 | John Frere | £1 | 13s. | 8d. |
| M 1503 | William Aylred | | 2s. | 2d. ob. |
| | William Dalton | £1 | 1s. | — |
| 17 December 1504 | John Gybbys | £2 | 7s. | 7d. |
| E 1505 | William Arnold | nothing | | |
| E 1506 | William Granger | | 3s. | 1d. |
| | Thomas Punt | £2 | 1s. | 9d. ob. |
| M 1506 | John Clerk | £2 | 4s. | 8d. |
| M 1508 | John Frere | £2 | 4s. | 3d. |
| | John Arnyot | £1 | 9s. | 9d. |
| M 1511 | Robert Whyte | £1 | 4s. | 6d. |
| | William Granger | nothing | | |
| E 1511 | William Pelman | £2 | 2s. | — ob. q. |
| 18 December 1511 | John Robyn | £2 | 6s. | 4d. ob. |
| ? 1512 | John Stukeley | nothing | | |
| 20 December 1512 | William Frere | £2 | 3s. | 3d. |
| M 1513 | William Melbourne | | 15s. | 3d. |
| M 1514 | William Stukeley | nothing | | |
| | John Granger senior | £2 | 7s. | 3d. |
| M 1515 | Thomas Monyment | £2 | 10s. | 9d. |
| E 1516 | Richard Scot | | 3s. | 2d. ob. |
| M 1516 | Thomas Pacy | £2 | 14s. | 2d. |
| E 1517 | Thomas Lockyngton | £1 | 6s. | — ob. |
| M 1517 | John Holme | £2 | 13s. | 4d. |
| M 1518 | John Clerk | £2 | 19s. 5d. | |
| E 1519 | John Page | | 2s. | 5d. |
| M 1519 | Robert Whyte | £2 | 1s. | — |
| E 1520 | John Boleyn | nothing | | |
| M 1520 | William Loveday | £1 | 12s. | — ob. |
| M 1521 | William Greatham | (10s) | — | |

| Date | Name | Amount |
|------|------|--------|
| E 1521? | John Granger | £1. — 6d. ob. |
| M 1522 | Thomas Pacy | £1 19s. 2d. |
| M 1524 | John Boleyn | 9d. |
| | John Clerk | £2 7s. 8d. |
| M 1525 | John Vyntner | £3 1s. 2d. |
| M 1526 | John Wylde junior | £2 19s. — ob. q. |
| M 1527 | William Greatham | £2 2s. 9d. |
| E 1528 | John Betrych | 11s. 2d. |
| M 1528 | John Goodwyn | £2 7s. 11d. ob. |
| M 1529 | Thomas Stevenson | £2 12s. 11d. |
| E 1530 | John Granger | 13s. 7d. |
| M 1530 | William Richmond | £2 10s. 4d. |
| E 1531 | John Manning | 13s. 5d. surplus |
| M 1531 | John Disney junior | £2 4s. 2d. |
| E 1532 | Thomas Garlop | 14s. 7d. surplus |
| M 1532 | John Goodwyn | £2 10s. 1d. |
| E 1533 | Edmund Taverner | 4s. 4d. |
| M 1533 | Thomas Stevenson | £3 12s. 1d. ob. |
| E 1534 | John Mayhew | 8s. 11d. |
| M 1534 | William Laxton | £2 10s. 4d. |
| E 1535 | Richard Prior | 15s. 8d. surplus |
| M 1535 | Roger Hawdwyn | £2 8s. 10d. ob. |
| E 1536 | John Mayhew | 12s. 5d. |
| M 1537 | William Richmond | £2 9s. — |
| E 1537 | Richard Chycheley | 5s. 9d. surplus |
| M 1537 | William Osteler | £3 4s. 8d. |
| E 1538 | William Frost | 10s. 10d. ob. surplus |
| M 1538 | William Benet | £4 2s. 5d. |
| E 1539 | John Nelson | 7s. 8d. ob. surplus |
| M 1539 | Thomas Stevenson | £2 14s. 5d. |
| E 1540 | Thomas Garlop | 10s. 9d. surplus |
| ? 1541? | William Richmond | £3 12s. 8d. |
| M 1541 | Roger Bowche | £3 18s. 4d. ob. |
| E 1542? | William Granger | 5s. 7d. surplus |
| M 1542 | William Goodwyn | £3 16s. 7d. ob. |
| E 1543 | John Slow | 8s. 5d. ob. surplus |
| M 1543 | Thomas Tryg | £4 1s. 11d. |
| E 1544 | Robert Vyntner | 4s. 4d. surplus |
| M 1544 | John Robyn | £3 8s. — |
| E 1545 | Roger Bowche | 13s. 5d. surplus |
| M 1545 | William Normanton | £3 10s. — ob. |

A further resolution of many questions is difficult owing to the paucity of records for comparison with earlier generations in the history of the guilds and, more importantly, because of the hidden institutional history of guilds. Beyond these altars, chapels and statues in the parish church already discussed, as well as the identification of fraternities with various streets on rentals, some hints to the actual guild institutions throughout the town appear only as reference points in describing the location of neighbouring properties in court rolls. A court roll entry of 29 June 1513 describes the messuage conveyed from John Brandon to John Manning as having Piper's Lane to the north, London Road to the south, to the east the *Puella* (statue or part of a cross?) and to the west the chantry. Chantries were in the same category as the parish church with respect to farm payments and hence there was no mention of any guild association with this part of the town in rental lists.

The only other chantry beyond the precincts of the parish church comes in a court roll conveyance of 24 August 1502, when John Clerk received from the bailiffs a messuage on Post Street backing onto the River Ouse and fronting on the street, with the messuage of John Lockyngton to the south and the messuage of the chantry, formerly John Baron, to the north. In a conveyance of 24 April 1505, and another of 4 July 1508, similar references are made to this chantry, specified as the Chantry of the Blessed Virgin Mary. John Baron had obtained this future chantry messuage in the court of 24 November 1491. In the conveyance description William Light was noted as the former owner and John Tully as his predecessor in the property while Thomas Fecas held the messuage to the north and William Tothe to south. The properties in this area of Post Street are well recorded in conveyances, so that it is possible to deduce that the chantry was the second main messuage south of Mill Lane.[33] In short, the pre-Reformation school was on the same section of Post Street, although not necessarily on the same ground as the Elizabethan Grammar School of today. No records survive for the transfer of this property from John Baron to the Chantry.[34] John Baron would seem to have died around 1495, if one may so judge from the disappearance of his name from the frankpledge rolls.

The Post Street Chantry was no doubt the one described by the Chantry Commissioners of 1548: "One Chantry there founded to assist the curate there being in the town 800 housling people, and to keep a grammar school teaching children in the same and so hath been and still is used."[35] Despite this need, the Post Street Chantry was dissolved[36] by the Commissioners and

---

[33] This is according to medieval messuage locations. Further investigation of the location of medieval messuages with respect to modern counterparts, especially with the assistance of archaeologists, may give more precision to this point.

[34] The founding of this chantry is attributed to the chaplain.

[35] This entry is to be found among the county valuations now at the Public Record Office, London, D.L. 38, No. 5. As in 1389, the local people stressed the religious aspect in order to try to retain the endowment, that is, this was the only living for the incumbent, Thomas Paxton, who assisted the parish priest.

[36] *The Victoria County History of Huntingdonshire*, 2: 295.

disappeared.[37] The town school was not forgotten. Ten years later, Richard Robyns willed funds for a school to be under the supervision of the bishop of Lincoln. By letters patent of 10 May 1561, the Elizabethan School of which Godmanchester was so rightly proud was indeed established.[38] The fourteen men appointed by these letters to govern the school with the vicar were all from old Godmanchester families (Robert Croft, John Goodwyn, William Granger, Thomas Mayle, Thomas Garlop, George Grene, Thomas Wiseman [bailiff], John Nicholls, John Lockyngton, Simon Granger, John Stevenson, William Stevenson, William Laxton, John Richmont).

These men were indeed the twelve jurors elected for that year on 15 August 1559 along with the bailiffs. Furthermore, Richard Robyns had been bailiff, along with Robert Croft, at the time of the dissolution of this chantry as well as in the following year in an interesting court case where it was noted that 60 people were present at the court sitting.[39] Richard was then replaced among officials by John Robyns. Richard left two daughters as heirs, Agnes the wife of Henry Stocker, and Elizabeth the wife of Gilbert Punt. In the court of the last day of February 1559, these heirs turned over "all their fathers property" to the bailiffs to be sold for the grammar school.[40] Unfortunately, we do not have detailed lists of the properties, so the cost of the school cannot be ascertained, nor can we be certain that the new school was built on a former Robyns property. One can be certain, however, that the role of the town administration in a (guild) chancery endeavour was not something new.

The almshouses of the fifteenth and sixteenth centuries are equally hidden behind the normal records. In the conveyance of a property by Thomas Frost, 24 February 1480, one finds the incidental remark that across the road on Arnyng Street was an almshouse. This goes far to explain the listing of the two Fraternities of The Holy Trinity and of the Blessed Virgin in the rentals

---

[37] The chantry may only have disappeared "officially." It is difficult to suppose that the people of Godmanchester should have neglected a well-established tradition of education for their children. J. J. Scarisbrick reminds us that we cannot be certain about whether many schools may not have survived (*The Reformation and the English People*, p. 112). In a court for the last day of February 1554, there is reference to lands in the fields belonging to the chantry whereas some meadow is spoken of as formerly belonging to Corpus Christi. However, for the purpose of locating a proximate messuage, court roll entries of 15 February 1555 and 2 April 1556 refer to a "fundum" (usually a plot without buildings at this time) "formerly the chantry."

[38] *The Victoria County History of Huntingdonshire*, 2: 287.

[39] Richard Robyns was listed at the head of the list of jurors this year.

[40] ... *ea intentione ut de tempore in tempus homines ville predicte, quos domina nostra Elizabet' Regina nominabit in litteris suis patentibus, omnia et singula promissa ad libitum suum disponatur ad pias usum schole gramaticali prout eis vendebitur expedire.*

of this part of Arnyng Street. These fraternities were listed as in the neighbourhood of the holdings of the wealthy Frost family and perhaps next to the Brown holding among the more scattered messuages of the east side of Arnyng Street. Between them, the two fraternities on Arnyng Street were taxed for more than 25 acres in the 1480s so that their resources could well support an almshouse.

In an East Street conveyance of John Page to Edmund Clerk, 9 August 1526, the property is described as having the tenement of Richard West called the Almshouse to the north. Almshouses would not expect to be major homesteads on capital messuages. One can only conjecture that the spread of various fraternities to every street that has been noted above from the rentals may suggest the existence of an almshouse for each street.

The scattered information surviving for the Corpus Christi Guild does not clarify this question of almshouses. In a conveyance of 13 April 1536, a property obtained by John Manning on East Chadleigh Lane is described as having the almshouse of the Chaplain of Corpus Christi to the north and the east end on the meadow of the rector called The Russhes. A rental of the possessions of the Guilds of Corpus Christi of Godmanchester[41] survives for this same year. Apparently this is a fragment from notes taken by the royal commissioners prior to the dissolution of the religious establishments. There are many problems of interpretation with this record but the general thrust is clear. After some 60 acres of meadow are listed there occurs the entry "Item there be land onto the said gyllde of Corpus Christi Alms House to lodge poor people maintained and repaired by the said priest of Corpus Christi." Whether this refers to the previously listed 60 acres of meadow is not clear. The document then continues "Item there be land to pay towards the said almshouse with courtyard and seven little groves to the yearly value of 7s. Item to the maintenance of the prior 5s. 6d." After a detailed listing of eleven more acres and one-half rod of meadow, acres are totalled at 80 plus, that is, more than the actual total in this record as it stands. The total revenue value of the meadow is given as £11 7s. 9d., close to the £11 8s. 8d. of all rents given in the surviving record. From this revenue allocations were noted as: to the king at 6d. per acre, 41s. 10d.; to the priest of the guild yearly, 76s.; to several times in the year spent in bread and ale at meeting of the brothers and of the poor, 13s. 4d.; to the vicar of the church according to a last will and testament, 9s. 8d.; in obits and other deeds of charity to be paid yearly at times appointed by the said widows, 17s. 6d.; to the common bellman yearly, 10d.; distributed yearly in alms on Good Friday, 3s. total: £10 6s. 10d. These allocations actually total some two pounds less than this

---

[41] See note 33 above and copy at the Record Office, Huntingdon.

given total, but the commitment of the major part of the revenues appears to be clear. The actual disposition of all revenues, for example whether the chaplain disposed some of his personal salary to the almshouse, cannot be ascertained without personal records of account.

As various institutions, whether almshouse or school went down with their guilds after the Reformation, there occurred a gap in reference to almshouses for a number of years. That the caring mentality of the people did not change is reflected in increasing references to poor in the wills of men, and gradually to the poor box of the parish.

The amount given directly to the poor is as difficult to assess for individuals as for institutions. In great part this may be explained by the fact that Christian charity involved spiritual giving (prayers) as well as material support and liturgical forms as well as economic realities changed again and again over time. In the wills of Godmanchester people a common form of substantial giving was tied to the disappearance of the family. If direct heirs died instructions were left for the property to be sold and given to the church for the salvation of souls. The occasional reference to "distribution," as in the will of Marion Wylde where money from the sale of a house was "to be distributed for her salvation," may suggest that this common form included giving to the poor. Certainly a variety of giving was possible in these many wills when executors were simply given general discretion "to dispose of the residue as they willed." Over the fifteenth century and into the early sixteenth, when families disappeared at Godmanchester so frequently, this form of giving must have been highly significant.

Among surviving wills, it was only by 1524 that explicit mention is made of a certain amount of money to be distributed to the poor in the liturgical context of masses and so forth. The will of John Garlop in that year bequeathed 40 pence for the poor for his soul and those of his father Thomas and mother Alice. In her will of 1533, Joan Cowke (Cook), widow, left a life obligation upon her son Thomas to pay eightpence every year for her soul, that is, sixpence for the poor and twopence for an offering. By his will of 1530 John Este placed an obligation on "whoever has the house" to distribute 15 pecks of wheat and 15 pecks of malt to the poor every mid-lent. In 1538 Ellen Birdere left an acre of meadow to pay 13d. to poor people every Good Friday and a quarter of wheat for the poor on her burial day, another quarter of wheat for the poor on the seventh day and a quarter of wheat for the poor every year on her obit day as long as the executor (her son-in-law) lives. Late in the same year John Granger, who apparently never married, left his house to be sold by his executor (his brother) for alms to be given to the poor. Margaret Stukeley arranged by her will of 1541 that her heirs give the vicar 3s. 4d. every Good Friday for alms to the poor. She had also left a quarter of wheat for the poor on her day of burial and another on the seventh day.

Roger Awdwyn's will of 1545 gave the more general bequest of 20s. for the mass, dirige and poor at his funeral and the same for seventh and thirtieth day. He also left five acres of meadow for his yearly obit remembrance on the feast of St. Margaret. The bailiffs were to do this should his son John fail to do so. There are fewer specific references to the poor in wills over the 1540s but this may be just a change in style. More references appeaer to family and servants, very likely with real need in mind. The bequest of £2 to the poor by Thomas Herman in 1546 might suggest that attitudes may not have changed.

Another institutional arrangement for alms was gradually coming into place. Well before the statute of 1556 the poor box was being institionalized at Godmanchester.[42] In 1549 William Mayle left eightpence for the "poor man's box," John Wryght left three shillings in 1550, William Goodwyn left two shillings in the same year and Edmund Lockyngton 10s. in 1559.

As we shall see in Chapter 6 below, many people at Godmanchester began to experience a crisis in their supply of capital from the last quarter of the fifteenth century. In this context, it is interesting to find recorded in the Jurors' Book[43] for the year 1488-1489 a gift of money to be employed as a loan for the poor: "Be it remembered that one Arneborough did give to be delivered into the hands of the 12 men of the town of Godmanchester, 20s. to be lent yearly to the poor people of the same town, they putting sufficient sureties to the said 12 men for the repaying of the same again."

The 1532 will of Alice West explains that this type of loan is an attempt to help poorer people retain some property:

> Item I will that my executors shall deliver to the bailiffs and the xii men of the town of Gumecestre for ther tyme beyng IIII£ of good and lawful money of Ynglonde for this intent or purpose that the seid baileffs and xii men for ther tyme beyng shall hayde socure and helpe powere men with all and suche tyme or tymes as they shall save their lande not havynge steide therto everye any of them for to have percell of it so farre as it shall extende for to helpe him or them with all for the space of oone yere fyndyng sufficiente sucurtie to make a

---

[42] I owe this appreciation of the sequence of local practice and royal statute to the unpublished paper of Marjorie McIntosh, "Financing the Relief of the Poor in Tudor England," North American Conference of British Studies, Toronto, October 1984.

[43] Jurors' Book, p. 20: *Memorandum quod XII Jurat' deliberaverunt Thome Laxton et Edwardo Barre ballivis ibidem anno Regni Regis Henrici Septimi quarto xxs quos Willelmus Arnburgh dedit comitati ad prestandum pauperibus perquisitoribus per mensem. ubi necessitas videbitur ne perdant perquisitiones suas. Et voluit quod delibentur semper ballivis de anno in anno pro causa predicta.*

repaymente or deliverye of it agayn at the yere ende to the bayleffs and to the xii men of the seid town of Gumecestre and so for to contynue from tyme to tyme and from yere to yere perpetually and forever.

A later entry in the Jurors' Book,[44] written in English and apparently entered in the 1560s adds seven names to those of Arneborough and West:

Also, Richard Robyns did give likewise £4.

Also, John Boleyn did give his wife to the same intent and purpose, 40s. Memo that John Godwyn and Richard Newman, executors of the last will and testament of the aforesaid John Boleyn have paid and delivered the aforesaid 40s. to the 12 men, the 17 day of December 1560.

Also, Thomas Upchurche did give and bequeath likewise to be lent unto the poor as expressed before, 40s.

Also, Master Nicholas Sewster did likewise give and bequeath to be lent to the poor as expressed before, 40s.

John Nicholas did give and bequeath likewise to be lent, 20s.

Memo that Robert Heaumne did give and bequeath likewise to be lent as aforesaid, £6. 13s. 4d.

Henry Darles did give and bequeath likewise to be lent, 20s.

Total: £23 13s. 4d.

For the town of Godmanchester and its low lying meadow and pasture the clearing and digging of ditches was an ongoing necessity. Since the unkempt ditch affected the drainage for one's neighbours the obligation of care for ditches about his property lay upon the property holder. Indictments for failure to maintain this drainage system are the most numerous among all types of entry in the frankpledge rolls and attest, no doubt, to the heavy burden of this obligation. On the other hand, there is no evidence that responsibility for the care of roads devolved upon the individual property holder. One might have thought that the care of roads was among those "common expenses" of the bailiffs cited in the Customs. But there is no reference to regular expenses in the many surviving bailiff accounts, nor are roads among those exceptional expenses, such as the bridge at Redemede in

[44] Jurors' Book, p. 106. A later hand has added at the foot of the page a further gift £3 6s. 8d. under the year 1620. Gathered in with the dilapidated fragments concerning the disenfranchisement of John Wynde (Box 8, Other Documents) is a scrap of parchment illustrating another charitable practice of the sixteenth century. The first entry is as follows: "First, let to farm to John Newman one milk cow being a brown cow paying in rent for one year 3s. 4d. to the use of the poor in Godmanchester aforesaid and at the year's end to deliver to the bailiff and 12 men 30s. for the same cow, pledge John Stevenson." There then follows the same arrangement with Edward Cox, Thomas Prior, William Stevenson, George Grene, John Benet, Henry Stevenson and Robert Granger. Across the bottom of the scrap are listed several names with the same arrangement for another year.

1412, or the cost of fencing the commons and repairing the penfold in several accounts. The wills of Godmanchester people show that road repair was a charge on the generosity of charitable benefactors. There was continuity in this form of bequest from the fifteenth century through the Reformation:

Agnes Lane: 6s. 8d. to repair of road to rectory (1483)

Thomas Newman: 2s. to repair of bridge (1485)

Thomas Frost: 20s. to repair of roads in Needingworth (1491)

William Frost: 40s. to repair of road in Arnyng Street (1519)

John Bonsay: 6s. 8d. to repair bridge in East Street (1520)

Thomas Bennet, labourer: one combe of barley to repair of the road in West Street (1527)

John Este: 30s. for stone and gravel for the road "between William Aylred's hedge corner and my chamber window" (1530)

Joan Cowke, widow: rest of payments from house (that is 26s. 8d.) for street that is, 6s. 8d. for each street (1533)

Elena Byrder: 3s. 4d. to every street of the town (1538)

William Bennet: 26s. 8d. to repair of road from John Godwyn's bridge to the west end of West Street (1540)

William Frere: 6s. 8d. to repair of road, West Street, and 6s. 8d. to repair of road on Post Street from the cross to the court hall [   ] and to Graveley (1545)

Hewgene Heyworth: 6s. 8d. to repair of highway between the mayday rede cross and the almshouse (1545).[45]

Assuming that the town was responsible for the maintenance of roads but no records of such costs have survived, these wills indicate that road maintenance could not be budgeted from the normal income of the town. There was obviously a general repair fund for each street and most of the bequests were directed towards this necessity. The will of John Este does not mention repair so that it could be assumed that these 30s. were essentially for a new stone and gravel road before his residence. To construct such a road before every messuage of the town would be a formidable task far beyond revenues when it is recalled that the total revenue of the bailiff from Michaelmas to Easter 19 Henry VIII (1527-1528) came to only £7 2s. 2d.[46]

---

[45] This unique reference to an almshouse at this time may suggest some continuity for such institutions during the Reformation years.

[46] The study of public works in sixteenth-century England is an old topic. But the problem of the small budgets of these towns is now being actively addressed, as in The North American Conference of British Studies (see note 42 above), especially the unpublished paper of Robert Tittler, "Finance and Politics in English Towns, 1500-1640," where the pathetically small budgets of several towns in view of needs of the time were documented.

On the other hand, it cannot be assumed from the records available that social charity was adequate to the high costs of public works in sixteenth-century Godmanchester. The earlier religious establishment, the Priory of Huntingdon, had been identified with such public responsibility in the Hundred Rolls of 1279. In this instance it was the "repair of the path (*calcetum*) to Huntingdon" in return for a "certain" meadow. But in the frankpledge roll for 1503 the jurors issued a sharp injunction to the Prior about the repair of the path (*calcetum*) and ordered that it be repaired before the Feast of All Saints under threat of 100 shillings penalty.

*<br>* *

In conclusion, the first section of this chapter has found that key administrative instrument for the continuation of the family, that is, the last will and testament, capable of adaptation to a score of existential variables in the family life of the time. The second section of this chapter would seem to bear out the thesis of Professor J. J. Scarisbrick concerning the vigorous health of lay religious practice over the fifteenth and early sixteenth centuries. Two additional qualifications bearing upon the accepted historical wisdom about this period may be offered from the Godmanchester experience. First, the close co-operation and control by town govenment over so much religious-related activity suggests that we must question[47] further the use of the term "secular" for the time and the role of local government in the changing religious scene. Secondly, the religious experience of a community such as Godmanchester, especially as reflected in the representative spread of "religious" places throughout the town and the hiring or removing of chaplains,[48] must surely have provided a seed bed for sectarian development.

[47] The rather naive conceptualizations by W. K. Jordan have been sufficiently answered to require no further comment here. For a review of some of these strictures on the work of Jordan, see J. J. Scarisbrick, *The Reformation and the English People*, p. 187, note 37.

[48] Rather early in the known history of the guilds at Godmanchester, on the frankpledge roll of 1336, the jurors entered a regulation concerning chaplains "assigned by the community" to sing anniversary masses to the effect that should they fail in these duties they may be removed by the community (*fiat removetur ob officio suo per communitatem*).

Part Two


Socio-Economic Structures and Change

Despite the diverse nature of the records and their contents all of the preceding four chapters have two features in common. First, there were sets of customs, formalities and regulations determining the structure of government, the tenure of property and practise of trades, entry to freedom of the town, the bequest of belongings and the disposition of charity. Secondly, the real life situation of the people of Godmanchester over the decades of the late fifteenth and early sixteenth centuries required adaptations, adjustments and hence a wide range of variations in each administrative sector of the town. Hence, with the evidence adduced for this first part the bias of administrative information leans towards survival of various structures rather than towards the individual. How were individuals of different economic and social sorts able to respond to the changing conditions of the time? In order to attempt an answer to these questions an effort will be made in the following chapters to reconstruct the situation in which fate, fortune and providence had placed most of the people of Godmanchester and to trace their actions in response to these situations.

# 5

# Crises in the Economy
# of the Common Folk

## A. LABOURERS

The convenient title of "labourers" has been applied here to those on the lowest level of wealth in Godmanchester records. On farm rentals these are the individuals paying the smallest farm of around threepence. There were more than a dozen of this category in each of Arnyng and West Streets, more than fifteen on East Street and Post Street has as many as the other three streets combined. Not all of these can be exclusively identified as labourers. As we shall see below, some of these were small craftsmen, some young sons of wealthier families with their first properties and others elder men and widows with residual subsistence properties. But more than 50 of these 80 names were labourers.[1] These labourers are further identified in many instances as those paying the smallest entry fines when they purchased liberty of the town. In the Lay Subsidy Roll of 1523[2] the wealth of this group is

[1] The numnber 50 is a firm figure derived from actual references to labourers for the 1480s period in the following pages of this section as well as the few references to servants as labourers in the next section. This figure does not include wives who were at least part-time labourers in the brewing industry. Nor does this number include those less permanent and identifiable labourers noted at the end of this section.

[2] The student of Godmanchester can agree with an appreciation of the lay subsidies first ordered in the parliament of 15 April, 14 Henry VIII (22 April 1522 to 21 April 1523) to be found in Keith Wrightson and David Levine, *Poverty and Piety in an English Village, Terling, 1525-1700* (New York, 1979), p. 32 and especially their quote from J. Sheail, "it is probably safe to assume that a picture of England based on the lay subsidy returns, while neither complete nor accurate in all its details, does reflect some of the major elements in the distribution of wealth in the 1520's."

Since the local information included in the lay subsidy rolls would have been collected and therefore reflect conditions at Godmanchester for 1523 and 1524, it seemed better for the chronological purposes of this study to employ these dates rather than the dates of the rolls completed for submission to Westminsister, that is, 1524/1525. It would only be practical for the assessors to employ such records as the farm rental lists from the previous year. Indeed, we know from surviving wills that John Disney died on 29 November 1522, and William

indeed identified in wages. There are 54 individuals noted as paying £1 in 1523, 50 of these in wages.

Since the farm payments are entered as total monetary sums in the rentals it is not possible to ascertain whether each small entry indicated a messuage proper. These holdings could be tenements[3] or parts of messuages such as a curtilage. But it is clear from the listing on the streets and the movements from one street to another that these are residences. A rare detail comes from the farm rental lists specifying that the twopence paid by John Holme on Post Street over the 1480s was for a messuage. As we shall see below, many of these labourers added to their property, at least for a time, so that the twopence was a below-average farm rent from labourers. Surviving rental lists totalled farm rent payments from all types of holdings as a final record so the messuage was not indicated. On the other hand, since subtenants had to pay to the farm, these lists are invaluable complements to the leasing or subletting lists given above.[4]

Labourers listed on the farm rentals of Godmanchester may properly be said to form a "pool" in so far as they were very mobile in response to opportunities. Some entered the town by paying entry fines and it may be noted that these were the smallest range among all entry fines. Others moved from one street to another. Assuming economic opportunity to be the reason for such moves within the town, the labourer very likely moved close to his employer. This helps explain, no doubt, the juxtaposition of small farm payments and large in the farm rental lists.[5] On the other hand, distances were not great within the town and change of employment in itself would not always have necessitated a move. Furthermore, as labourers became older, it might have become more opportune for them to move to a less expensive home. Here are some of the patterns to be found in the records.

---

Mynton on 20 November 1522, yet their names are reported in the first lay subsidy list of the 1520s.

The study by Julian Cornwall, "English Country Towns in the Fifteen Twenties," *The Economic History Review*, 2nd. Series, 15 (1962), 54-69, provides a useful introduction to the lay subsidy rolls in country towns. For a more recent appreciation, see B. M. S. Campbell, "The population of early Tudor England: a re-evaluation of the 1522 Muster Returns and 1524 and 1525 Lay Subsidies," *Journal of Historical Geography*, 7.2 (1981), 145-154. Roger Fieldhouse, "Social Structure from Tudor Lay Subsidies and Probate Inventories: A Case Study: Richmondshire (Yorkshire)," *Local Population Studies*, no. 12 (Spring 1974), 9-24, is a useful application of the 1540s lay subsidies and related records to social analysis.

[3] See Chapter 3, above, p. 48. For this problem of standard units of assessments, see Harvey, *The Peasant Land Market*, especially p. 16 with note 30. And see further below in this chapter.

[4] On this point, and this whole paragraph, see Chapter 2, above.

[5] See chapter 2, above, p. 41.

A William Hilton appeared on the Arnyng Street rentals of 1487, paying at Michaelmas 1487 and Easter 1488 only twopence farthing; by Michaelmas 1488 Hilton's farm rent had increased to 2s. 4 $^1/_2$d. He then moved to Post Street and was paying farm of tenpence farthing in his last entry of Easter 1490. A William Holme paid threepence at his first entry on Arnyng Street in 1485, then only one half that amount over later years of the decade and is cited as paying the latter amount on his last appearance on East Street. Richard Legge paid threepence from 1485 on Arnyng Street, but his last entry for the same amount was on East Street. John Templeman was listed on the Post Street rental to 1487, paying twopence, halfpenny farthing but by 1488 he was on Arnyng Street paying a farm of tenpence halfpenny, or enough for more than three acres. Indeed we do have from the conveyance records John Templeman entering to twopence halfpenny farthing rents (of land) in 1488 and releasing the same in 1489. William Parker was on West Street during the 1480s and was to be found on East at a reduced farm rent by the 1490s. Since rather more moved to East and Post Streets from Arnyng and West Streets than in the reverse order and reductions in farm rent payment accompany some of these moves, it may be that East and Post were more suitable for "retirement."

Unfortunately, it is not possible to discover family ties among labourers to assist in understanding their mobility. It would appear that when someone replaced another resident on Godmanchester streets the new farm rent entry would be the same as the former and entered at the same place in the farm rental sequence. For example, on Post Street Robert Chandeler (3d. ob.) appeared on the Michaelmas 1494 rental at the place where John Matthew (3d. ob.) had been entered at Easter 1494. But there is no indication of family relationship between Chandeler and Matthew. Indeed, someone replacing another with the same surname is rare and often a woman's name is involved. For example, in the same two Post Street rentals of 1494 Richard Holme (2d.) replaced Alice Holme (2d.).

Further corroboration that labourers did not retain properties in their families comes from the fact that the great majority of new entries to the labouring group were added at the end of the farm rental roll and not in sequence with a previous tenant. Again on Post Street for example, 10 of the 12 new entries between 1490 and 1492, and five of the eight between Easter and Michaelmas 1494, were added to the end of the farm rent roll by the clerks rather than in the normal residence patterns. Of course, entry to larger properties could also be added at the end of the roll, but as Appendix 3 shows, most of these additions were the small "labourer" tenant.

The inability of labouring families to replace themselves would also explain why the labour pool had to be supplemented from beyond the town. Most of these newcomers paying the smallest entry fines can be identified among the labour group on the rent rolls: John Asshe (1485), William Hermet (1486), Robert Olyffe, Thomas Parker, Robert Rydmer (1487), John Robynson, John Mildenhall (1488), John Schylling (1489), William Pelle (1490), John Harryngton (1492), John Dey, William Ede, John Punt (1494).

These few individuals who can be identified in our labour group reflect only a small percentage of the labour demands of the town. Such labourers worthy of the full attention of the town administrators that are treated in this section were a rapidly disappearing breed. As will be noted more fully at the end of this section and in the summary to this chapter, nearly all the ordinary labour requirements would henceforth be filled by a large revolving army of casual labour, known officially in the town only by the fine of the few pennies required to give them the privilege of remaining for their period of work.

Established occupations no doubt explain why some people did not move. To take Arnyng Street as an example, remaining throughout the period of our extant rentals were Simon Prestwode (sevenpence rental, acquired one rod in 1485) and Henry Martin (obtained a messuage and croft in 1480, added an acre in 1485—paying farm rent of eightpence halfpenny by 1487 and eleven pence halfpenny for the remainder of the decade). William Scott was paying fourpence halfpenny for rent from 1485 until the last entry at Michaelmas 1487 before his disappearance when he paid only one penny halfpence. Robert Slow, whose name appears from two decades earlier in other records, paid farm rent on Arnyng Street of twopence halfpenny until his name was dropped after Michaelmas 1490. Also coming late for surviving rental lists was John Mildenhall who purchased liberty of the town in 1488 for 4s. and paid the modest farm rent of two pence halfpenny thereafter. Richard Spicer was more successful, purchasing a messuage in 1486, adding one-half acre in 1487, another acre the next year and one acre three rods in 1488 so that his farm rent rose from fourpence to fivepence halfpenny.

The continued presence of residents on every street paying a fixed small rent for years, such as John Mildenhall noted in the previous paragraph, needs further attention. Since most residents on every level of wealth tried to add land to their holdings, there is a *prima facie* case for arguing that those with stable farm rent payments never acquired the surplus cash to buy or even lease land. At the same time, it must be allowed that these small payments could indicate a residence with a shop where improvements may have been added to the small working capital.[6] Indeed, the number of these with fixed

---

[6] See further below, p. 146, for this tendency among other tradesmen, especially butchers, not to invest in land.

payments that were to remain stable for East Street was more significant than for Arnyng or West Streets: John Andrew (1d.), Cristina Bishop (4d. ob.), John Grace (3d.), Thomas Hawkyn (3d. ob.), William Ibott junior (4d. ob.) and John Sparrow (3d.) for the year 1486. Post Street had the greatest number, indicating that, along with East Street, shops were concentrated in this part of the town: Thomas Bailey (3d. ob.), John Byllingford (1d. ob.), John Barnard, junior (4d. ob.), Richard Chycheley (1d. ob.), John Dalton (4d.), Helen Dawntry (4d.), William Edmond (ob. q.), William Farthyng (2d. ob.), Thomas Fecas (1d. ob.), John Feld (1d. ob.), Richard Folkys (ob. q.), Margaret Garlop (1d. ob.), John Granger (2d.), Simon Granger (6d.), Matthew Hedley (2d.), John Holme (2d.), William Lessy (1d.), Thomas Marshall (4d.), Thomas Martin (1d. ob.), John Rede (6d.), John Reygate (1d. ob. q.), John Rumborough (4d. q.), John Shalford (3d.) and William Tothe (1d. ob.) to name those from 1487 who continued over all recorded years at the same farm payment.[7]

Despite the turnover of labourers' names, something about the lives of a few labourers can be traced beyond the period of surviving rent rolls and indicate that their economic condition remained much the same. John Asshe purchased liberty in 1485 for 1s. 8d. and was to be found on Arnyng Street in the rentals of that year, paying threepence to the farm. By Easter of 1489 John Asshe had moved to East Street and for the next few years for which the rentals are extant, the farm value of Asshe's property had made a modest increase in value to fivepence. References to trespass and to his East Street messuage occur in frankpledge rolls over the next few years. By the time of the 1523 Lay Subsidy lists a John Asshe senior and a John Asshe junior were noted, each assessed at one pound wages in 1523, though by 1524 John junior's assessment had increased to two pounds.

A Reginald Corby was noted as entering tithing in 1486 and from 1487 paid a farm of threepence on Arnyng Street. In the Lay Subsidy lists of 1523 and 1524 Reginald Corby was assessed one pound for wages. He died on 5 March 1534, and in his will he describes himself as a labourer and left his house on West Street to his wife Elizabeth. He had a daughter Sybil and also owned three acres of meadow. Assuming Reginald to have been 16 at the time of his induction into frankpledge, he would have been 64 years old at the time of his death. It may be recalled that another labourer who had wages assessed at one pound in 1523, that is, Richard Jermayn, was noted as over 60 years of age, when he presented evidence in the court of 3 August 1542.

---

[7] As will be noted in the following sections, five of these residents had occupations other than labourer: John Barnard junior (hayward), Thomas Fecas (fuller), John Feld (goldsmith), John Rede (mason) and William Tothe (clerk).

A John Arnouth who appeared in records after 1509 was very likely a shepherd for frankpledge entries show him trespassing with sheep nearly every year for the next decade. John Arnouth gained entry to a messuage on West Street in the court roll of 15 February 1509. In the Lay Subsidy list of 1523 only, Arnouth was assesseed at the standard one pound wage. Also appearing around this time was Robert Cook who paid a 5s. fine for entry to the liberty in 1513 and was fined frequently for not cleaning about his messuage. He was assessed the one pound in 1524 and two pounds by 1543. Robert Dorraunt paid an entry fine of 3s. to the liberty in 1509, had a messuage on East Street by at least 1512 and was assessed the one pound for wages in 1523. Entries are found to his failure to clean ditches to 1527 when he apparently died, leaving a wife Margaret and a son William who took over the messuage and had been the servant of John Frere in 1523. Although we may know little else about many labourers, it is clear that these continued to be drawn from beyond the town in significant numbers: John Bennet who was assessed one pound wages in 1523 and 1524 had purchased liberty for 1s. in 1519. Lawrence Hogg who had purchased liberty for 1s. 8d. in 1519 was assessed one pound wages in 1523. William Prior who was assessed one pound wages in 1523 and 1524 was one of the three sons of Richard who, with their father, paid 3s. 4d. for the liberty in 1512. Thomas Schylling was assessed at one pound wages in 1523, paid twopence for liberty in 1512 and was noted as having an unkempt messuage in 1517. John Woodberne who was assessed at one pound wages in the subsidies of 1523 and 1524 only paid 2s. for purchase of liberty in 1524.

Some labourers can be followed through several decades prior to the 1480s indicating some stability in their economic status. A good example of this were the Richard Chycheleys, represented in the first identifiable generation by a Richard, to be found in the 1464 list of tenants, with a messuage on Post Street near Mill Lane in the 1470s and with a wife Margaret appearing occasionally as a retailer. When this Richard died cannot be established. The second Richard appears to have been a shepherd, frequently in the frankpledge rolls over the second decade until 1526 for trespassing, and assessed one pound for wages in 1523. Concurrently with the second Richard, a Richard son of Richard appeared in records from 1515 but continued to appear after the second Richard until 1534. The last reference to this family occurs in 1534 when there was noted on East Street a tenement formerly of Richard Chycheley.

What was the actual wealth of labourers? As may be seen from the disposition of wealth in wills, the main capital of the labourer consisted in his dwelling. From surviving tallies it can be seen that these dwellings were "tenements" in the language of the second quarter of the sixteenth century and were of the least valuable of the messuages and tenements listed among the tallies. In 1541 the widow Margaret Dorraunt turned over to William Dorraunt her son a tenement for 33s. 4d. tally. In 1541, William Seward turned over a tenement to Robert Croft for £5 and in 1545 John Osteler, labourer, delivered to Thomas Benet a tenement for the tally of 30s. William Brown, labourer, indicated the worth of his house on East Street as 33s. 4d. when his will of 1528 arranged for the payment of 6s. 8d. to each of his five children should his house be sold. The will of William Gyde, labourer, of the following year specified that his son John should receive the house he lives in on West Street and pay 26s. 8d. (at 6s. 8d. per year) to his daughter Agnes. The latter received some of the furnishings. By a will of 10 November 1529, William Seward, labourer, had left to his son William three one-half acre plots as well as a small grove and to his widow Agnes his house on West Street. The son William had likely received this house by the 1540s and now sold it to Robert Croft. The younger William Seward would seem to have prospered with the assistance of the property left by his father. Another example of improved conditions can be seen in the life of William Prior, assessed at one pound wage in 1523, but purchasing a messuage, close, three and one-half acres, one rod of arable and one acre *frisc'* for £9 13s. 4d. tally in 1543. Another Thomas Bennet, labourer (not the son of the above noted Thomas Bennet) left to his wife Elizabeth in 1527 a house on West Street, three and one half rods of leys and nine acres of arable. Reginald Corby, labourer, who received the liberty of the vill in 1486 and died on 3 October 1538, left to his wife Elizabeth his house on West Street and three acres of meadow, and it was stipulated that if she be needy she could sell the property, but that half of the capital must go to his daughter Sibell. By 1542, Elizabeth had sold the house on West St as was noted in the court of Thursday before Epiphany 33 Henry VIII (1542): "Henry Wood had a messuage in West Street next the plot of Henry Gybbys to east and tenement formerly the wife of Reginald Corby to West."

However small the value of the labourer's chattels might be, in terms of his total resources they were significant. John Scot who was assessed £1 wage in 1523 left in his own will of 1544: to son John, table; to daughter Katherine, two plates; to Christopher Scot, 12d.; to John Mordoke, 6s. 8d.; and to wife Anne, house he lives in for life and then to son John; Anne was sole executor. One year later we find the will of a Robert Hedley, labourer, who apparently married Anne the widow of John Scot. In his will Robert leaves a messuage and all his goods to his wife Anne, and the overseer is John Scot (very likely the son of Anne). The next year, 1546, Anne has died and she leaves quite a few goods to her children: daughters Katherine Knowliss and Jane Bell, petticoats and sheets; Alice Mordoke and Elizabeth Knowliss, another two of her daughters, three sheets; Elizabeth Scot, great pan; Anne Scot, 2nd. best brass pot; Alice Scot, brass pot; Margaret Scot, brass pot; and to son John Scot, great pan; and son John has residue and is sole executor.

The disposition of the wills noted above must be seen as family arrangements. For example, Alice Mordoke was no doubt the daughter of John Scot and Anne Hedley. John Mordoke who was left 6s. 8d. by John Scot was the husband of Alice. After her marriage to John they seemed to have settled elsewhere other than Godmanchester. Another daughter Joan was married to Thomas Bell no doubt the same Thomas Bell who received a messuage from William Thong for a £7 tally in 1540. This same Joan was married to William Arnold, husbandman, who died in 1535 and left to Joan who was his sole executor his house on Arnyng Street. They did not have offspring from their union. William Abram, who was one of the witnesses for Anne Hedley's will, was assessed at the £1 wage in 1523.

What labour did these people actually perform? From evidence at hand it would appear that they did many things. Otherwise, they should have come under the more permanent occupational designations described in the following sections of this chapter. Certainly these people did not have the capital resources for more permanent commercial or industrial activity. John Holme, as well as the wives of Robert Chandler and Simon Prestwode, were licensed to brew ale one year only, perhaps from the harvest of those meagre properties they leased for a crop or two. Significantly, too, when any from this group were licensed to sell ale (retailers) it was only once in our records. Such were Margaret Garlop, Alice Holme, and the wives of Richard Holme, William Ibott junior, William Parker, John Rumborough and John Scot. On the other hand, the fact that these people tried to earn a living in such a fashion does not mean that they were the totally unskilled odd-job persons on the economic fringe of the town. One must remember that they had homes and were not casual labour floating about for subsistence. Rather, the variety of tasks demonstrates the multi-task type of employment that will be found to be common to several levels of wealth at this time.

Thomas Schylling and Robert Folke[8] were paid fourpence in the bailiff's roll, 1527, "for fetching of abbot at Houghton." In many ways the work of the so-called labourers must have overlapped with the personnel to be treated in the following two sections. The lines between labourers and petty craftsmen or others on a proximate wealth level would become more blurred in the context of those more social institutions such as marriage. This has been exemplified on a previous page, where John Scot, who was the servant to

---

[8] The name Folke occurs among the smallholders in rentals, although this Robert Folke's relationship to earlier residents of the same surname cannot be established.

John Draper on his first appearance in records, will be seen below to have been involved with poorer weavers and he had a family who intermarried among others with Arnold the poorest husbandman among those so identified.

A rough index to the number of labourers, as well as others within the lowest range of farm payments, was noted at the beginning of this chapter as around 80 individuals from whom about 50 have been identified as labourers. The only later index available for comparison with the 1480s farm data is that "still shot" of those assessed in wages for the lay subsidy of 1523. Of these 54, ten were familiar names of labourers from the late fifteenth century, at least four were sons of familiar labourers and nine were noted above as labourers after 1509. Of the approximately 20 remaining individuals on this list, nothing else is known about most of them. This fact is significant in terms of that radically declining access of poorer tenants to land to be seen in Chapter 6 below. Perhaps these only acquired a peripheral place in the local economy and were able to remain for a few years. Of those about whom

TABLE 30: LABOURERS ASSESSED AT £1 WAGE
IN THE 1523 LAY SUBSIDY LIST

| | |
|---|---|
| Abram, John | Lessy, Robert |
| Alan, Thomas | Mayle, John |
| Arnouth, John | Morgan John |
| Asshe, John | Nell, William |
| —, John senior | Nelson, John |
| Barnard, John | —, Robert |
| Bennet, John | Parrot, Christopher |
| Carr', Robert | Parish, Robert |
| Carter, William | Parker, William |
| Chycheley, Richard | Prentys, Joan |
| Cook, Robert | Pryor, William |
| —, William | Seward, William |
| Corby, Reginald | Schylling, Thomas |
| Dorraunt, Robert | Smith, Richard |
| Farthyng, William | —, Thomas senior |
| Freman, Thomas | —, Thomas alias denfox |
| Garlop, Margaret | Stacy, John |
| Gybbys, Henry | Swyft, William |
| Gransden, John | Taylor, Richard |
| Harryson, William | Tyllett, Thomas |
| Hedley, Robert | Va'nq, John |
| Hogg, Lawrence | Vyntner, Richard |
| Horsley, William | Walter, John |
| Howman, John | Wause, John |
| Jermayn, Richard | Wyttyngham, Henry |
| Kyng, Richard | Woodberne, John |
| Knolle, Thomas | Yattys, John |

there is further information (Alan, Kyng, Mayle, Stacy, Vyntner and Yattys) it will be seen in the following section that some trade was involved. Although information about this level of wealth is too exiguous to draw general conclusions, this poorer class may have followed the middling group discussed in the third section below, by attempting to compensate for declining opportunities in land by developing petty trades.

In the context of Godmanchester evidence from the later fifteenth century those efforts that continue to be made to deduce a positive condition for labour because of lower food prices and firm demand for labour in the later middle ages do not seem to have much meaning. That is to say, the loss of even short term tenure of a few acres[9] would argue against labourers having advantages by being able to supply their own labour either individually or by pooling of their energies.[10] As we shall see further below, the wealthiest landholders were turning to sheep and many of the less wealthy would have little profit to invest in labour since they too were losing land and struggled to diversify for survival. Some more permanent labourers, that is to say, those with a home who were known to the freemen, were in a position to take advantage of a wider variety of seasonal needs. Even for those more fortunate, however, security as measured by a home and a few rods of land appeared to be at most one generation in duration. Upward mobility was the only true guarantee of longer term survival.

The larger numbers of available labour indicated by low entry fines shows the tendency towards casual labour. In the entry fines for freedom of Godmanchester there were approximately 100 individuals purchasing freedom at that lower labour price of 2s. and less between 1494 and 1523. About one-half dozen of these fines represented discounts for re-entry of scions from wealthier families. About one dozen names can be associated with individuals who can be seen to have improved their condition through occupations so as to be assessed above £1 by the time of the lay subsidies of the 1520s. Of the more than 80 names remaining and to be associated with labourers, only ten appear in the 1520s lay subsidies, and of these, six had obtained liberty over the previous five years. Very few indeed had acquired a foothold in the town. Many other labourers would not have been able to purchase freedom and would escape, therefore, from recognition in the administrative records employed for this section. In Chapter Two above, a

---

[9] Beyond the obvious generalization that inflation would have reduced the labourer's margin for investment in land, there are no details in Godmanchester records to test the impact of the act of 1515 (6 Henry VIII) fixing wages at threepence per day for one half year and fourpence per day for the other half year. For a telling account of the importance of one acre of meadow, leased for a year by a "pore tenaunt," see below p. 214.

[10] This point will be pursued further in the Conclusion below.

general estimate of such casual labour as represented in violations recorded on frankpledge rolls numbered in the hundreds over a few years.

## B. Servants

The servants at Godmanchester in the fifteenth and early sixteenth century have already been encountered in several contexts. In Chapter 3 those intinerant former villeins of Ramsey Abbey were often to be found at Godmanchester as servants. In surviving records these ex-villeins do not seem to have acquired a legal status in the town and from what evidence is available, they do not seem to have stayed long. Another type of servant was found to be mentioned in wills as part of the extended *familia* of wealthier families. This "live-in" character of servants explains no doubt why few servants appear as tenants. Some "live-in" servants appear to have been the daughters or sons of wealthy relatives or neighbours serving for a time for training or some special need. Such would seem to have been the case with William Kyng who stayed with John Mynsterchambre for two years as was recorded in the death-bed evidence of the previous chapter.

The type of arrangement possible to servants is shown in an indenture arrangement from the will of William Bennet. In this will of 1540 it was noted that his servant John Jonson had agreed to stay with him for 12 years but only two years of the 12 had elapsed by the time of the imminent death of William. William Bennet offered 40s. to John Jonson should he stay on with Bennet's son, William Bennet, for another 12 years. This will also gave one sheep to John Jonson. Another variant of this arrangement may be seen in the 1550 will of William Goodwyn. This branch of one of the older families of the town would seem to have come to an end. William left his messuage on West Street and his lands to his wife Elizabeth. After eight years the messuage and lands, together with livestock and implements, were to go to "John Bele his servant." John Bele in turn would then pay £1 a year for 12 years to the widow Elizabeth. Three others with the surname Bele, perhaps nephews of John, were given gifts: Thomas Bele, £2; Bridget Bele, £2 when she married; and John Bele, £2 in two years (when he came of age?).[11]

Occasionally, the servants appearing in Godmanchester seem to be of the same status as labourers, and indeed some labourers were servants for a time at least. Such were John Clerk, John Manning and John Wright who appear in rentals as having property of their own and are listed[12] as servants. As the same list shows, most servants were in the employ of wealthier Godmanches-

---

[11] Gifts to other servants were noted in Chapter 4, p. 99.
[12] See p. 54 and Table 17; see also Wynde's three servants, below, p. 215.

ter people and received their identity from their masters. But the reason these servants were not more fully named comes from the fact this information is in frankpledge rolls and the master is responsible for the fine. As members of wealthier households in the sense that they received gifts in wills along with blood relatives, servants could participate to a degree in the security and standard of living of the household. Indeed, many of those to be found listed as anonymous were shepherds. But in the next section a shepherd is found to be classifiable as a petty specialized occupation, normally of a slightly higher standard of living than the labourers. Two of those servants, William Ruhome (fine 3s.) and Richard Austin (fine 3s. 4d.) of the same list, give further indication of this high standard in so far as they paid fines higher than the usual liberty price for labourers. William Pacy, under whom Richard Austin served, had paid 10s, that is, within the normal payment range for entry to liberty by a major craftsman.

Major contributions have been made over recent years to the study of servants from the later Tudor and Stuart periods of early modern England. Comparable data do not exist for the early Tudor period as the evidence just given for Godmanchester amply demonstrates. But the same patterns are to be found. As has been said for Havering later in the sixteenth century,[13] the social and economic position of servants at Godmanchester varied in accordance with the level of the household in which they worked and no doubt with their own background. One cannot calculate with any degree of precision that servants provided between one-third and one-half of all hired labour as has been done for later generations.[14] But the fact that there were 53 servants in the 1464 list discussed in Chapter 3 above and around the same number of labourers indicated from those tenant lists of 15 to 20 years later, discussed in the previous section, does point to the same conclusion.

Servants could have numbered many more since the 1464 entry lists only males.[15] But given those demographic realities of fifteenth-century Godmanchester sketched at the beginning of Chapter 4, above, one may wonder whether as many children would have been available to assist others as servants at that time. This is not to exclude the practice during earlier generations.[16] Several servants on the 1464 list (Barre, Bate, Cave, Ibott,

[13] Marjorie K. McIntosh, "Servants and the Household Unit in an Elizabethan English Community," *Journal of Family History* (Spring 1984), p. 12.

[14] Ann Kussmaul, *Servants in Husbandry in Early Modern England* (Cambridge, 1981), p. 4 and passim.

[15] Marjorie K. McIntosh, p. 15, found 58 percent of the servants were male in a 1526 list for Romford, Essex.

[16] This relation between servants and family has been described in detail in the context of the late fourteenth-century Poll Tax returns for West Midland parishes by R. H. Hilton, *The English Peasantry of the Later Middle Ages* (Oxford, 1975), p. 31. The appearance of the

Longe, Porter, Rede and Suell) were from long-established families. Nor did their appearance as servants suggest family impoverishment since some of these at least (Bate, Porter, Rede, Suell) became officials over the next decade. On the other hand, of course, some of these names (Barnard, Bennet, Corby, Dorraunt) re-appear on the poorer servants' and labourers' level over later generations. As well, the mention of many young people as legatees in sixteenth-century wills of Godmanchester coincides with evidence for larger families.[17] Servants may indeed have become "buried" in households from this time and escaped lay subsidy records. Such additions to households would also compensate in the workforce of the town for the decline in numbers among the "labourer" class!

### C. The Petty Crafts and Trades Personnel

Throughout the records of Godmanchester there is a consistent picture of a group with wealth slightly above that of the labourers but with a uniformity of wealth not unlike labourers and a level of wealth well below craftsmen and husbandmen. There is no general classification of this group such as the classification of labourers by wages in the Lay Subsidy of 1523. One suspects that the special skills, if not the self-employed nature of this group, prevented the society of the time from developing some general category that could usefully designate the whole group. Only when a more local indentity was required, as was the case with rentals and frankpledge fines, for example, can one expect records to indicate more fully the occupation of individuals in this group. These references do indicate petty crafts and trades as the occupations of the group. So for convenience this bracket has been accepted as the title of this section. By and large, however, the information about this group is given below as it was to be found in the various records.

In the following list may be found a rather large number of individuals at Godmanchester who appeared in tax records as having goods, usually worth more than the wages of labourers. Members of this group also tended to pay more than labourers for entry to the liberty of the town.

---

wider use of the term servant (*servientes*) only in the late fourteenth century and the virtual disappearance of the term in records of the early Tudor period is well described by Cicely Howell (*Land, Family and Inheritance in Transition: Kibworth Harcourt 1280-1700* [New York: Cambridge University Press, 1983], 177-226ff.) in terms that would seem likely applicable to Godmanchester.

[17] See last column, Appendix 8.

TABLE 31: PETTY CRAFTS AND TRADES PERSONNEL
FROM THE LAY SUBSIDIES OF 1523-1524
AND FROM LIBERTY LISTS[18]

| NAME | TAX BASE (GOODS) | | STREET | ENTRY FINE INTO LIBERTY | |
|---|---|---|---|---|---|
| | 1523 | 1524 | | DATE | FINE |
| Aplond, Thomas | 4 | 4 | East | 1501 | 1s. |
| Avys, William | 2 | — | | 1518 | |
| Barnard, Henry | 3 | 2 | Post | | |
| Benett, Oliver, butcher | 2 | 2 | Post | 1519 | 6s. 8d. |
| Benett, Thomas | 3 | 3 | Post | | |
| Blaxton, Richard | 3 | 3 | Post | 1515 | 4s. |
| Borowe, Thomas | 2 | 2 | | | |
| Broughton, Christopher | 2 | | West | | |
| Broughton, Hugh | 4 | | | | |
| Brown, Hugh, carver | 4 | | | 1510 | 2s. |
| Brown, William | 2 | | East | | |
| Carter, John | 3 | | | | |
| Chambre, John | 2 | 2 | Post | | |
| Cook, Joan | 2 | 2 | West | | |
| Cook, Thomas, son of Joan | 5 | 5 | West | 1488 | 5s. |
| Clerk, Edward | 2 | | East | | |
| Collyshawe, William | 2 | 2 | | | |
| Copinger, Thomas | 3 | 2 | | | |
| Dey, William | 2 | 2 | Post | 1494 | 2s. |
| Disney, Agnes, wife of John | 3 | 3 | Post | | |
| Ede, William | 2 | 2 | West | 1494 | 2s. |
| Freman, William | 3 | 3 | | | |
| Frere, Thomas, son of John | 3 | 2 | West | | |
| Gaddesby, Thomas, baker | | 3 | Post | | |
| Gellys, Nicholas | | 2 | | | |
| Glover, William | 2 | 2 | | | |
| Granger, John junior | 2 | 2 | Post | | |
| Granger, Thomas | 2 | | Post | | |
| Hay, George | 3 | 3 | Post | 1496 | 2s. |
| Hebdon, Edward, son of Robert | 2 | | | | |
| Hunt, Richard | 2 | 3 | Post | 1516 | 1s. 8d. |
| Ibott, William | 2 | 2 | Post | | |
| Kendale, Alice, widow | 2 | 1 | East | | |
| Longe, William | 2 | 2 | East | | |
| Loveday, William | 3 | 3 | East | | |
| Mayle, John, baker | 1 | 1 | | | |

[18] Those listed over the early 1520s with £1 in goods (John Abrams, Henry Frost, butcher, Robert Johnson, William Lord) should also be added to this list. See further below in this section on William Lord. Unlike the labourers, many more petty crafts and trades families augmented their revenues from the ale industry. Some were so occupied for one year only, others for several years. See Table 33 below under Carter, Dey, Disney, Hay, Ibott, Kendale, Mynt and Wellys.

| NAME | TAX BASE (GOODS) | | STREET | ENTRY FINE INTO LIBERTY | |
|---|---|---|---|---|---|
| | 1523 | 1524 | | DATE | FINE |
| Mynt, Elizabeth | — | 2 | | | |
| —, Isabella | 2 | — | | | |
| Nicholas, William | 2 | 2 | | | |
| Parker, Thomas | 2 | 1 | West | 1487 | 1s. 4d. |
| Prior, Thomas (with his father) | 3 | 2 | East | 1512 | 3s. 4d. |
| Salmon, Joan, widow | 2 | 2 | Post | | |
| Say'm, William | 2 | | | | |
| Seward, Thomas | 2 | 2 | | | |
| Smith, Thomas | | 2 | | | |
| Stilton, William, candelmaker | 2 | 2 | | 1517 | |
| Tavener, Edmund | 2 | 1 | Arnyng | 1517 | 2s. |
| Wellys, Simon, smith | | 2 | Post | | |
| Wright, John | | 4 | Arnyng | | |
| Wylde, John senior | 2 | 2 | | | |
| Vyntner, John junior | 2 | | | | |
| —, William | 4 | 4 | | | |
| Yattys, John, glover | 1 | 1 | Post | 1523 | 1s. 8d. |

Unfortunately, Lay Subsidy records were not concerned to register occupations with any consistency. Nor is it possible to establish continuity for most of these individuals after the better documented decades of the late fifteenth century. Some incidental references, in great part frankpledge rolls of the late fifteenth century, give the greater occupational detail that is listed below. Property data not shown on this list show the modest scope of the wealth of this group, no doubt largely in messuages, when farm rentals listed these people. All these data given in the following pages suggest that bellmen, carpenters, cobblers, candelmakers and the lowest class of cloth and metal workers tended to make up this economic group.

The economic level of these petty craft and trades people is further demonstrated by their inability to develop sustained commercial or industrial enterprises. Despite their more frequent appearance than labourers in the ale industry, many of these could not brew or retail ale more than once. Such were the "Retailers for One or Two Years" (Table 33). Perhaps many in this list could as readily be on the corresponding list in the first section of this chapter. Some have been placed here simply because there is no association with identifiable labourers and others[19] because their husbands, or unique

[19] As with Hay and Mynt.

TABLE 32: PETTY TRADESMEN 1479, 1485-1525,
LISTED ON OTHER RECORDS

| NAME | OCCUPATION | DATE | STREET |
|---|---|---|---|
| Barnard, John | artisan | 1485-1490 | ? |
| —, John | carpenter | 1495 | Giles Lane |
| —, John senior | carpenter | 1495-1497 | Post |
| —, John | candelmaker | 1492-1502 | Giles Lane |
| —, William | wright | 1494-1498 | Post |
| Bishop, John | artisan | 1479 | ? |
| Brown, John | shoemaker | 1521 | ? |
| Butcher, William | alias wright | 1496 | Post |
| English, John | clothmaker | 1488 | Post |
| Elys, John | fisherman | 1509, 1512 | |
| Feld, John | goldsmith | 1485 | Post |
| Glover, John | common bellman | 1486 | East |
| Hawkyn, John | shoemaker | 1480s | Arnyng |
| Hanson, Thomas | alias cobbler | 1488 | ? |
| Huys, Richard | alias taylor | 1496 | ? |
| Marmion, John | alias juggelar | 1526-1527 | ? |
| Rede, John | mason | 1485 | Post |
| Sent, John | artisan | 1489 | East |
| Schylling, John | smith | 1489 | West |
| Stevens, Richard | shoemaker | 1479, 1490 | ? |
| Taylor, John | tanner | 1479, 1495 | East |
| White, Robert | taylor | 1505 | Post |

family name appears on the earlier list of this section. On the other hand, the fact that few of these names can be associated with streets may indicate single working women who were "live-ins."

In a few instances, knowledge of occupation does give a unique focus in the records and makes possible the reconstruction of a simple profile of the individual. An interesting glimpse of a modest profession may be obtained through the records of John Hawkyn, cobbler. John Hawkyn first appears on the records in 1459 as a resident of Arnyng Street. In the rental of 1485 he was taxed as having two and one-half acres. But by the 1480s Hawkyn would have been advanced in years and was apparently selling off his property. In 1481 there is a reference to his former messuage; in 1485 he let go two holdings of one acre and three rods respectively and there is no further mention of him on Arnyng Street rentals by 1488 and he apparently had died by 1490. The old cobbler had been able to acquire sufficient property to sustain himself in his old age. There are no references to family.[20]

[20] Little is known of other identifiable cobblers such as Richard Stevens.

## TABLE 33: RETAILERS FOR ONE OR TWO YEARS, 1485-1525

| NAME | DATE | STREET |
|---|---|---|
| Adam, wife of John | 1520 | East |
| Aberneley, wife of John | 1498 | ? |
| Annsell, wife of Fremond | 1488 | ? |
| Barbour, Margaret | 1497 | ? |
| Bawdwyne, wife of Thomas | 1501 | ? |
| Beek, wife of William | 1500 | ? |
| Bower, Margaret | 1498 | Arnyng |
| Bryte, Margaret | 1495 | ? |
| Carter, wife of John | 1498 | ? |
| Clerk, Agnes | 1494 | ? |
| —, Isabella | 1496 | ? |
| —, Margaret | 1525 | ? |
| —, Matilda | 1495 | ? |
| Dey, Anna | 1494 | ? |
| —, wife of William | 1491 | Post |
| Dobson, wife of Dyer | 1501 | ? |
| Garlop, Joan | 1485 | ? |
| Goodwyn, Joan wife of Henry | 1510-1511 | ? |
| Goodrych, Agnes | 1489-1490 | Post |
| Gor', Joan | 1510 | ? |
| Halle, wife of John | 1494-1495 | ? |
| Halton, Joan | 1487 | ? |
| Hay, Katherine, wife of George | 1498 | Post |
| Holme, wife of Thomas | 1520 | ? |
| Hope, Alice | 1494 | East |
| Johnson, Isolda | 1497-1498 | Post |
| Lessy, Joan | 1485 | ? |
| —, Margaret | 1494 | ? |
| Lord, Isabella | 1503 | ? |
| Matday, wife of John | 1512 | ? |
| Maynard, wife of John | 1498 | ? |
| Mynt, Isabella | 1494-1495 | Post |
| Nolesham, Beatrix | 1485 | ? |
| Nottingham, Elizabeth, wife of William | 1510 | Post |
| Ocorne, wife of Henry | 1498 | ? |
| Osse, wife of John | 1512 | ? |
| Rumborough, Joan | 1485 | Post |
| Salmon, Margaret | 1503 | Post |
| Scot, Alice | 1485 | East |
| Strynger, wife of William | 1496-1497 | ? |
| Swan, wife of Thomas | 1497 | ? |
| Taylor, wife of John | 1494 | East |
| —, Katherine, heu | 1497 | ? |
| Thompson, wife of Robert | 1512 | ? |
| —, wife of Thomas | 1512 | ? |
| Wilkinson, Katherine | 1485 | ? |
| Willison, Joan | 1494-1495 | ? |
| —, Margaret | 1497 | ? |
| Wydyr, Joan, wife of Thomas | 1503 | ? |
| Wyse of Hunts | 1496 | ? |

At the time the name of John Hawkyn was disappearing from the rentals of Arnyng Street, that is Easter 1488, a John Gony appears on the list paying threepence. John had purchased a curtilege on Arnyng Street in 1487 and this no doubt was the basis for his farm obligation. John Gony had been on the rental list for Post Street paying one penny halfpenny farm, from 1485 through 1487. John also surrendered a small rent in a conveyance list of Easter 1488 and engaged in credit financing as one may gather from a debt of 3s. 4d. in 1488 and a further debt of 12s. in 1489. From his frequent fines in the frankpledge rolls for trespassing it would appear that John Gony was a shepherd.

Near the bottom of the long list of elected officials, and therefore no doubt one of the most humble, was the bellringer. Still, election as an official provided a guaranteed income and must have been a step upward for poorer members of the town so long as they held the job. What the annual stipend for this task was is not specified in any records. But the wills do indicate the source of the stipend in the penny payments (for example, by William Kyng, 1530) left for ringing the bell at funerals and anniversaries as well as in properties left for the same purpose. An example of the latter was the "yard" of land bequeathed "forever" by William Pelman in 1529 to the bellman and his successors, from which the bellman and his successors should also "pay a mass penny every year for his soul." John Glover, who was bellman for a number of years up to 1500, may have typified the resources of this occupational group. On the rental of 1484 John Glover (appropriately on East Street near the parish church!) paid farm for four acres, added another acre in 1486, another in 1489 and a curtilege in 1491. No evaluation is available for the wealth of Robert Olyff who was bellman in 1502, and from 1509 to 1520. John Barnard, who was bellman in 1519, and from 1522 to 1531, and Robert Hedley, who was bellman from 1533 to 1543, were both assessed under the £1 wage in the early 1520s.

Those elected haywards were not recorded at the time of the rentals but would appear to have been of much the same economic status as bellmen. Whether that John Barnard, junior, elected hayward in 1503, 1505, 1507, 1513 and 1515 was actually that John Barnard paying £1 in the lay subsidies and indeed became the bellman, we cannot ascertain. But the William Freman who was hayward in 1509 was assessed for £3 goods in both tax years. And as we can see from Table 31, above, William Ede (hayward, 1504, 1506, 1510-1512, 1519-1521, 1526) had £2 tax base in both years, Henry Barnard[21] (hayward, 1512-1518, 1523) £3 in 1523 and £2 in the following

---

[21] The life of a hayward was not necessarily dull. Henry Barnard appeared before an episcopal visitation to give evidence that in a certain garden of Offord Cluny a woman charged

year, William Brown (hayward, 1521-1522) £2 in 1523 and John Vyntner, junior (hayward, 1528-1529, 1532) £2 in 1523. If the John Hogan who was hayward in 1531 and from 1533 to 1542 was the John Hogan, the younger, then his lay subsidy tax was on £1 in 1543.

William Lord provides us with a different profile for a petty craftsman. In the same year (1495) that William Bennet, labourer, paid one shilling for freedom of Godmanchester a William Lord also purchased freedom for two shillings. Various conveyances among his neighbours over the early sixteenth century (1510, 1520, 1528) reveal that William had a property on Post Street. In the 1524 Lay Subsidy, William was assessed at £1 for goods. During the same year a small plot of saffron ground "formerly belonging to William Lord" was conveyed. William Lord was noted as a brewer in 1525 although this frankpledge tax may more properly have pertained to his wife, Katherine, for the latter paid a fine several times during the 1530s for both baking and brewing. The true occupation of William was only revealed towards the end of his life when in 1538 William Lord, wright, mortgaged "all his goods and moveables to William Caverley on condition that he pay for his shop and houses." The following year William Lord, wright, sold a curtilege next his messuage on Post Street to Richard Kyng. William and Katherine did not have any children and William Lord seems to have died by the early 1540s for an entry in 1542 registers a tally for £2 between a John Clerk, taylor, and Edmund Peynter for the former tenement of William Lord on Post Street.

Just as we have seen labourers sharing their petty corporate wealth by family arrangement at the end of Section One of this chapter, so craftsmen could share their capital. By his will of 1540, Robert Dawle divided one half of his looms and all things "belonging to his occupation" between his wife Cristina and John Lambart. Specific provision was made for allocating hall hangings to Cristina and a mattress with sheets to John Lambart, while wood was divided between them. Robert Dawle had paid 2s. for liberty of the town in 1537 and John Lambart paid 3s. for liberty in 1540. One may suspect that John Hedde (who received liberty in 1503, 6s. 8d.) and Henry Yonge, who were designated by the will of Robert Dawle to view the division of the tools of the trade, were fellow craftsmen of the taylor trade.

Much of the same group arrangement may be seen in the conditions imposed on a debt of William Alanson. Alanson was no doubt a weaver as were Thomas Judd (liberty 1499, 10s.) and John Clerk (liberty 1493, 4s.)

---

with bigamy was heard to say "my father and my mother are against me marrying you but even without their consent I will never forsake you." See *An Episcopal Court Book for the Diocese of Lincoln, 1514-1520*, ed. Margaret Bowker, The Lincoln Record Society, vol. 61, pp. 3, 9.

who witnessed and pledged four looms and working gear and all such gear
that they held that the debt be repayed to a certain Morgroves of Cambridge,
and others of the same town, by 25 June 1499. A bond of 1539 indicates
that John Clerk had purchased the tenement formerly belonging to William
Lord for £2.

Glovers seem to have come into this same category of modest craftsmen:
John Yattys, who received liberty in 1523, 1s. 8d.; Robert Hanson, liberty
in 1543, 2s.; William Frere, received liberty 1545 [    ] and William Glover,
alias latysar noted in 1548. Taylors as such occur also with regularity
especially in frankpledge rolls from Richard West in 1420, John Robyn in
1427, John Baker in 1430, Robert Awynham in 1442, John Browne and
Richard Brace in 1452, to Richard Smith in 1480, Richard Huys with a
liberty fine of 2s. in 1496 and John Clerk a fine of 2s. 4d. in 1539, Robert
Marshall in 1523 and 1542, William Nevsham in 1542. Many of these would
have been no more wealthy than the labourers. Indeed John Yattys was
classified among the £1 wage assessments in 1523. But there was little sign
of security among such craftsmen and perhaps less security than for those
labourers who were able to purchase some land. There is no evidence for
more permanent family commitment to the town and needless to say,
therefore, no sign of upward economic mobility in this group despite the fact
there was obviously a continuing demand for the service of petty textile
craftsmen.[22]

No doubt the line between petty craftsmen and labourers was not always
as clearly drawn in some individual circumstances as has been depicted by
these two sections. The short-term nature of evidence for many of these
individuals often makes difficult the tracing of upward or downward economic mobility to be expected of movements across economic group lines.
Thomas Aplond paid only 1s. for liberty (1501) but by 1523 had a tax base
of £4. John Marshall paid 2s. 8d. for liberty (1507) and had a tax base of
£5 by 1523. But these instances are so beyond the usual liberty fine and tax
pattern that one suspects extenuating circumstances. Thomas Seman and
William Seward had surnames associated with labourers, but their tax (£2)
was not identified as wages. William Freman had a more substantial liberty

---

[22] If the experience of Colchester also typified the Huntingdonshire region, this might
explain the paucity of references to personnel of the cloth industry in Godmanchester records.
See, Britnell, *Colchester*, p. 189: "The conclusion to be drawn from ulnage accounts is that
Colchester entrepreneurs had managed well between the 1390's and the 1460's." And see
further in the same volume, pp. 183-184, where it is stressed that increasing dependence upon
wealthier clothmakers by the last quarter of the fifteenth century left little scope for independent entrepreneurial activity by weavers and others performing only one stage of the
clothmaking operation.

fine of 2s. in 1496 and a tax base of 3s. in the early 1520s, but by the 1540s William (or his son) was more modestly classified as a wage labourer (£2). William Stilton (candelmaker, according to his will of 1535) also fell below the promise of his entry fine (2s.) in later assessments (£2).

## D. The Entrepreneurs

A number of people coming between petty crafts and tradesmen on an economic level below them, and capitalist on a higher economic echelon, are with difficulty characterized as a distinct group or class. For these people stand out as individuals with a great variety of initiatives in the use of credit, flexibility in the direction of their enterprise and capacity to change long-established patterns of economic activity. Since the main occupation of the freemen of Godmanchester had been farming, this flurry of economic activity was as much a struggle for survival among husbandmen as a new "age of amibition." For convenience, then, this most articulated economic activity of the freemen of the town will be distinguished as entrepreneurial.

Information about the metal trade is extremely exiguous for Godmanchester. There is no direct evidence to anyone as a mason or smithy. A number of debt entries over 1507-1509 suggest that Richard Arnouth was functioning as a blacksmith. During 1507 Richard was charged with payments for the purchase of shop gear and bellows 2s. 9d. and a horse 2s. 6d.; in 1508 Richard was charged with the purchase of two quarters of barley, seven pounds of iron and 8s. worth of coal and claimed debts from the sale of a (plough) share, an acult, another share, a blade and an akyrfen; debt data for 1509 reveal that Richard had to pay 19s. 10d. for coal and sold two cartloads of wood for 2s. 8d.

More esoteric metal trades were represented by at least one family over our period. In 1482, John Feld and his son William were granted liberty of Godmanchester for the exceptionally high fine of 26s. 8d. John Feld did not have long to enjoy Godmanchester. His will of 26 February 1485 was probated at the local church on 6 October 1486. In this will John Feld describes himself as a goldsmith and left his messuage[23] to his wife Isabella for her lifetime and after her death to their daughter Joan. There is no mention of the son William who may be presumed to have predeceased his father.

In 1481, shortly before John Feld received liberty of the town, a William Diggby appears on the frankpledge record for a trespass. William was married

---

[23] John Feld's shop on Post Street was one of those low farm rent messuage units listed above, p. 39.

to Elena who appeared frequently as a retailer between 1481 and 1510. William Diggby paid the unusual modest sum of 8d. (3a.) for a holding on East Street in the extant rentals of 1485-1492. This holding was in fact a shop and well placed in the shadow of the ecclesiastical establishment to participate in the embellishments of the Godmanchester church. A certain *quid pro quo* may be seen in the expensive Gregorian masses arranged by the last will of Diggby. For whatever reason, a dramatic change took place in the circumstances of William Diggby over the late 1490s and for the next three decades. By the time of the Lay Subsidies of 1523 and 1524, he was assessed at £9. This chronology suggests an exceptionally long active life, but there is no indication of a son William, who in any case would only give a two-generation dimension to the change.

William Diggby's new economic status was reflected in his higher role in administration, from juror in the years 1489, 1497, 1501, 1512 and 1516 (in 1496 he was church warden) to bailiff in 1511, 1515 and 1517. This administrative function was demonstrated in four debt entries in 1520 when William Diggby combined with Richard Scot as a former (1516) church warden to claim 3s. 8d. from Joan Dalton, executrix of William Dalton, and 6s. 8d. from the sale of meadow to William Say'm; and Diggby combined with Richard Scot as executor of the will of William Long to claim payment for three combs of barley and an unnamed debt from John Page senior.

There is no evidence that William Diggby invested in the agrarian land of Godmanchester, though he was owed payment for two quarters of barley and in fact was referred to as a "yeoman" in a bond of 1497 and John Wylde bonded himself for two payments of malt (five quarters by All Saints in 1521 and four quarters by All Saints, 1522) by a court entry of 25 April 1521. He was brought to court for claims by eight different individuals and entered a suit for debt against seven different people. But in all these, as with the 26s. 8d. owed by Robert Seman on 1516, nothing is known of the contract behind the debt. In his will of 16 July 1530 (probated on 21 October of the same year) William Diggby referred to himself as a craftsman. His property was referred to as "Dyggbys" in conveyances over the next decade and the identity with craft continued when it was sublet (*ad opus*) to William Freppis of London, pewterer, in 1538.

The more generic traditional name of craftsman, that is artificer, is to be found in the fifteenth-century records of Godmanchester among those detailed sources from the 1480s. Presumably, then, this was a traditional occupation in the town. A John Bishop, artificer, who may have obtained liberty of the town as early as 1436, appears in 1478 as acquitted with his wife of eight marks worth of repairs for their messuage on Giles Lane, a messuage formerly belonging to Thomas Longe. John Bishop had died by

1483. John Sent, artificer, appears in the context of several debts in the mid-1480s. John Smyth was living on the messuage formerly belonging to John Sent when this messuage on Post Street near Pekkislane was purchased by Matthew Garnet in 1493. Matthew Garnet, artificer, held 16 acres in the Post Street rental of 1490. Around the same time (1487, 1491) John Garlop, artificer, was entered on the Post Street rental as having the farm payment equivalent for 36 acres. Around the late 1490s, one of the many John Barnards was identified in several debt entries as an artificer.

These artificers were clearly of more substance than the petty craftsmen listed in the previous section. But there is no indication that artificers were able to obtain full time employment at their trade. Some, such as Garlop and Garnet, combined their crafts with farming. John Sent functioned in the administrative capacity of a sub-bailiff and custodian. The artificer of Godmanchester was in a vulnerable position in a period of economic change. Unfortunately, the disappearance of the term from these records cannot be explained. One is only left to hazard the guess that this disappearance indicated the decline in economic stature of those craftsmen so that the parliamentary identification of labourers and artificers did[24] indeed reflect conditions of the time.

Information about major occupations increases rapidly when one's attention is turned to the food trades. Among these trades, that of butcher has the most unique pattern and will be dealt with first. Butchers can be identified as two distinct groups. First were those butchers who shared with other occupations the fact that over much of our period many individuals practised the trade for only a year or two. Some of these would seem to be outsiders, perhaps attempting branch shops from Huntingdon. Others, as with Richard Savage whose wife Margaret was a retailer for the years 1509-1512 were clearly resident but of the less wealthy group discussed in the previous section. In any case, few of these butchers succeeded for long enough to find it worthwhile to purchase liberty of the town.

| 1485 | Hugh Nolesham |
| 1487-1489 | Godfrey Wright (purchase of liberty with son Henry 1486, 8s.) |
| 1490-1491 | Thomas Newman |
| 1494 | Richard Sheter |
| 1496-1497 | Thomas Wodecroft |
| 1496 | Henry Frost |
| 1500-1501 | John Stokes |

---

[24] The artificer was allowed one penny a day more than the labourer. Both groups were required to work the same hours. See J. D. Mackie, *The Early Tudors 1485-1558* (Oxford, 1952), pp. 454-455.

| 1501 | William Hanby |
|---|---|
| 1503, 1516-1518 | Richard Savage |
| 1505 | Richard Bocher |
| 1533 | John Ward (purchase of liberty 1534, 2s.) |
| 1543 | Robert Lovell, flecher |

A second group of butchers becomes apparent with the concentrated evidence from the 1480s. Most of the butcher trade of the group in Godmanchester may be seen as a specialized full-time occupation and not in any way an offshoot of the farming community. One butcher, Thomas Baker, speculated in land, largely those small units recorded on the conveyance lists.[25] The volatile nature of Thomas Baker's land holdings may be seen from the acreages for which he was responsible in payments to the royal farm: 1487 E, 20 acres; 1487 M; 11 acres; 1488 M, 18 acres; 1489-1490 E, $17\frac{1}{2}$ acres; 1490 M, 11 acres. The large number of individuals involved in these conveyances may signify that Baker employed land rather than credit and debt instruments. The purchase of land for the time period indicated above was from four individuals and over the same period Baker sold to 14 different individuals. Thomas Baker's name does not appear as plaintiff or defendant among the numerous debt suits over these years.

The normal practice of these full-time butchers demonstrated a dependance upon the credit system of the town.[26] John Couper, butcher, in the years from 1497 to 1503 was in debt to 18 individuals, and over the same period 27 people owed to John; Thomas Reynold, butcher, was in debt to six individuals from 1483 to 1491 and ten individuals owed to Thomas in the same time span and John Stokes, butcher, was in debt to 25 people from 1485 to 1502 and 18 people had credit with John for the same period of time. Although debts were not cumulative on the court rolls, the dangers inherit in cumulative debts may be seen in the total known debts of a few years. Over four years around the turn of the century John Couper was owed £10 5s. 5d. and owed £17 12s. 9d. Over the late 1480s, Thomas Reynold owed £1 14s. 1d. and was owed £2 1s. 6d. From the mid-1480s to the turn of the century, John Stokes was owed £4 9s. 3d. and owed £10. 3s.

Something more is known about the detail of the credit and debts for John Couper than for the other butchers. Those detail indicate that debts were acquired by the purchase of goods for the trade, that is, produce for the feeding of animals as well as the purchases of animals: five quarters of barley from John Ward in 1504, 24s. worth of fen (hay) from William Orwell in

---

[25] See Appendix 4, p. 321.
[26] See Appendix 8.

1506, a further 2s. 6d. worth of fen from William Kyng in 1507, 16s. 8d. for pigs from John Spere in 1508 and 33s. for a cow and sheep from John Wynde during the same year. Interestingly enough, noticeable among the moneys owed to John Couper over these years were those fellow tradesmen whom we shall meet in these pages: 8s. owed by John Gybbys (1504), 10s. owed by Robert White, taylor (1506) and during the same year, 10s. from Thomas Faldyng. The significance of this pooling of funds among craftsmen will be discussed in the following chapter.

Dependence upon credit would seem to have become too precarious towards the beginning of the sixteenth century and, as we shall see, was the case with other food trades, butchers began to diversify. Before further study can be made of this diversification, a general description of other major food trades becomes necessary. Brewing was largely a full-time occupation of women in the late fifteenth century.[27] Such a consistent commercial commitment would seem to have been possible because of the farming resources of their families. The following wives or widows were outstanding in this respect:

Isabella Bailey, sold ale as a retailer from 1485 onwards and brewed ale after the death of her husband John who had 79 acres at the time of his death in 1499. Agnes Bould, functioned both as a baker and brewer in the late 1480s and brewed ale from at least 1494 to 1510. The husband of Agnes had 39 acres in 1492 and she may have been a widow shortly after that date.

Alice Brandon first appears on the records as a retailer in 1496, but from 1497 to 1510 she appeared as a brewer. Her husband John was noted as a butcher for the year 1496. John Brandon was a prominent member of the town, though the survival pattern of farm rentals does not make it possible to assess the size of his property which was on East Street. In the Lay Subsidy of 1524 John was assessed at £17 and in his will of 1528 he left £11.

Agnes Cokman brewed ale over 1487-1491 and retailed for the last two years of her entries in the frankpledge rolls, 1494-1495. Her husband Thomas has already been noted as a prominent butcher during this time and he was assessed at 32 acres in the farm rentals. Isabella Faldyng had the most consistent set of entries of all these people for brewing from 1485 to 1511. Her husband Thomas had 34 acres and was recorded as a candelmaker over 1495-1496 and a baker for the year 1509.

Agnes Gybbys brewed almost as long as Isabella Faldyng, from 1485 to 1505 and was cited as retailing in the one year, 1488. Her husband John was a baker over 1486-1491 and had 69 acres. Alice Manipenny brewed over the late 1480s and another Manipenny woman over the 1490s until at least

---

[27] This was typical of village in Huntingdonshire from at least the thirteenth century.

1503. Two of these women at least were consecutive wives of William Manipenny who had 32 acres in the rentals. The latter was a baker from 1485 through to 1503. The Manipennys and Gybbys show a pattern emerging in the late fourteenth century that was to become common over subsequent decades, that is to say, the concentration of baking and brewing in one family.

The pattern first appearing in the 1480s as retailing and then finding the resources for brewing was also to be found for Isabella Norton and Margaret Suel: Isabella for brewing and retailing in 1485, and then 1486 to 1491 just brewing and Margaret 1485 to 1491 retailing and by 1494, 1497-1498 brewing. Variations occurred of course. Agnes Rede brewed only over the late 1480s; and Agnes Pacy over the late 1490s; Alice Ussher brewed from the late 1480s through to 1503 while Alice Reginald continued to both brew and retail into the 1490s.

Husbands continued to brew for a year or two as one moves from the late fifteenth into early sixteenth century, as may be seen by the families of Basse, Chandeler, Monyment, Nottyngham and Prior in Appendix 5. Wives not only still dominated the brewing industry but added baking as well: Frere, Ibott, Kyrby, Laxton, Mayle, Salmon, Wellys. Elizabeth wife of John Boleyn even combined retailing with baking and brewing as did some of the Granger women. Other women—Disney, Lovell, Vyntner, Wylde—continued to concentrate on brewing only. In several families where a concentration of occupations began, the husbands did most of the baking. Such were the Glapthorn, Grene, Holme, Lord, Massey, Mayle, Osteler and West.

A further division of labour occurred with alternating baking one year and brewing the following year for nearly all those families noted in the previous paragraph. There seems to have been no obvious technological reason for this sequence although the new technology of brewing beer rather than ale would have reached Godmanchester by this time[28] and added considerably to the cost by the purchase of hops. Perhaps the alternating years may be explained by the timing of the inspections by the officers reporting to the view of frankpledge. But at least one is led to presume that resources were deliberately spread over long periods of time and this factor, together with the concentration of production in fewer hands, would indicate greater bulk production at any one period of time. Licensing practices would not appear to have changed with the concentration of trades since several women

---

[28] Much research still remains to be done on the spread of the use of beer during the fifteenth century. Hops were introduced to East Anglia early in the century, see Britnell, *Colchester*, p. 194. For a more general study of the introduction of beer and relevant economic factors, see Peter Clark, *The English Alehouse, a social history 1200-1830* (London, 1983), especially pp. 31-34, 97.

continued to be fined regularly as retailers through most of the first quarter of the sixteenth century: Arnold, Brampton, Brewster, Couper, Joan Granger, Hilton, Kelson, Punt and Wright.

Prior to the sixteenth century, much of the baking was done by less affluent people than those indicated above. Baking had traditionally attracted many itinerant practitioners, perhaps especially for public events.[29] In Appendix 5 it can be seen that many persons baked for only a year or so. At first, one finds it rather odd that many of these were also fishmongers! Upon closer observation, it can be seen that fishmongers too performed for a year or so, some obtaining liberty ostensibly for only a brief period: John Feltwell (of Hunts 1494), 1486-1504; John Godard, 1498, 1505; William Golding 1494; Richard Sheter 1494; Jacob Barret, 1525-1527; Thomas Disney 1520; John Ely 1496-1512; William Godard 1501; John Hogson 1533-1536; Richard Kesby 1528-1531; John Papworth 1520 (liberty 1512); John Tyme de Hunts 1525-1527; Thomas Tyme 1528-1531; Richard Wynde 1510 (liberty 1510). In short, bakers and fishermongers from beyond the town were much the same type of people if not the same individuals.

By contrast, those permanent residents who sold fish most often developed this trade in relation to their butcher operation. Such were Cokman, Couper, Fecas, Gredley. Not all fall so neatly into patterns. William Manipenny tried selling fish for a year or two along with the baking and brewing of his family as did the Basse family. Some butchers (Fecas, Stokes) combined occasional sales of fish with candlemaking as well as the butcher trade. Candlemaking by itself would seem to have been more important for Thomas Faldyng who was a poorer resident of the town and baked once at least. Both William Dalton and Richard Gybbys sold fish for at least three years over 1525-1531. Neither the selling of fish nor of candles would seem, then, to have supported a permanent occupational trade in the early sixteenth century or earlier. The future of diversification in these trades as with others noted earlier lay with those having more resources. Richard West, of the prominent baking and brewing family already discussed, sold fish at least once (1495) and sold candles along with baking over the 1497-1507 period. Roger Hawdwyn, who was a wealthy baker over much of the second quarter of the sixteenth century, combined the selling of fish with baking over much of his professional career.

Other evidence can be cited to illustrate that the less well endowed people of Godmanchester did not suffer from the lack of entrepreneurial initiative.

---

[29] The earlier fairs of St. Ives had been notable in this respect. See E. W. Moore, *The Fairs of Medieval England: an Introductory Study* (Toronto, 1985), p. 86. Owing to the total lack of material on markets, it is impossible to determine whether these bakers appeared only on market days.

Godmanchester would have participated in the cloth industry of fifteenth-century[30] England through the sale of wool and also by the growing and sale of saffron. There were several acres of open land at the heart of fifteenth-century Godmanchester called Benewal, that is, Arnyng Street lay to the south west, the east end of Giles Lane to the west and Pekkislane (now St. Anne Street) to the north. In this area, and Wigmore Croft which lay to the west of Arnyng Street (now London Street) and "road to London to the north," were what are called "saffron plots" in the court roll conveyance entries. A series of such entries from the court rolls show that those families with only retailer pretensions for the wives (Adam, Balle, Brewster) or less prominent occupations (Barre, Fecas) were purchasing these saffron plots although these began to be succeeded from the late 1480s by the wealthier Aylred, Basse, Laxton and Manipenny families:[31] John English buys saffron plot formerly Thomas Brewster, chaplain, lying in Pekkislane, 20 February 1483; Thomas Balle, saffron plot in Wigmore, 30 October 1483; John Adam, saffron plot in Wigmore, 20 December 1487 and another saffron plot in Wigmore, bought from Alice Caby, ob., 10 March 1491; William Manipenny, saffron ground in Post Street, between his own saffron plot and Edward Barre's saffron plot, $\frac{1}{2}$ d., 29 November 1487; Thomas Fecas, saffron plot in Benewal, 3d., 27 August 1489; Thomas Laxton, saffron ground in Wigmore croft, $\frac{1}{2}$ d. 27 August 1489; William Basse two pieces of saffron ground, formerly William Aylred and surrended by his executors to William Basse, and abutting Pekkislane to north, 26 April 1492; William Basse one piece of saffron ground, from Thomas Fecas, lying in Benewal, $\frac{1}{2}$ d. 17 May 1492.

Unfortunately nothing is known of the sale for these plots. The court entry fine for their conveyance gives only the usual nominal fee of 3d. Nor do we know anything of the extent of the effort to develop the cloth industry at Godmanchester itself. That there was such an effort is clear from the frankpledge entry for 1478 identifying Thomas Fecas as operating a fulling

---

[30] According to the range of responsibility for the ulnager, Godmanchester would be included in the wide area embracing Essex, Suffolk, Norfolk, Cambridgeshire and Huntingdonshire from the mid-fifteenth century. See, Britnell, *Colchester*, p. 187. But the sparse references to personnel of this trade noted early in this section have not made it possible to pursue study of the cloth industry from Godmanchester records. The fulling mill of Thomas Fecas (see the following note) may parallel the same phenomenon of fifteenth-century entrepreneurial activity to be found at Colchester as noted by R. H. Britnell, ibid., p. 185.

[31] The mills of Godmanchester were important to corn growers of the town and region and provided a significant component in the revenues of the town. However, little is available about mills in the sources available to this early Tudor study. Appendix 10 makes some materials available for the larger archaeological and chronological treatment that these mills require.

TABLE 34: FOOD TRADES

| NAME | YEAR | TAX |
|------|------|-----|
| FULL TIME FOOD TRADES | | |
| Boleyn, John | 1524 | £5 |
| Brandon, John | 1524 | £17 |
| Granger, John | 1523 | £17 |
| Grene, Richard | 1523 | £16 |
| Mayle, William | 1523 | £17 |
| Monyment, Thomas | 1524 | £7 |
| Nottyngham, John | 1523 | £14 |
| Stevens, John | 1524 | £6 |
| Vyntner, John | 1523 | £9 |
| West, Richard | 1523-1524 | £13 |
| PART TIME FOOD TRADES | | |
| Arnold, William | 1523 | £4 |
| Benet, Oliver | 1523-1524 | £3 |
| Brampton, John | 1524 | £1 |
| Frost, Henry | 1524 | £1 |
| Kelson, William | 1523-1524 | £3 |
| Kendale, Alice, widow | 1523-1524 | £2 |
| Mayle, John | 1523 | £1 |
| Prentys, Thomas | 1524 | £2 |
| Salmon, Joan, widow | 1523 | £2 |
| Skelton, William | 1523 | £4 |
| Stacy, John | 1523-1524 | £1 |
| Wellys, Simon | 1523 | £2 |
| Wylde, John | 1523-1524 | £2 |
| FULL TIME TRADES AFTER 1524 | | |
| Boleyn, John | 1542 | £10 |
| Frere, Henry | 1542, 1548 | £13 |
| Lorydan, Marcus | 1545 | £5 |
| Lovell, Thomas | 1543 | £9 |
| Massey, Robert | 1543 | £5 |
| Osterler, William | 1543 | £5 |
| Relton, Bryant | 1543, 1545 | £7 |
| PART TIME FOOD TRADES AFTER 1524 | | |
| Barnard, Henry | 1542 | £2 |
| Kyrby, Thomas | 1543 | £2 |
| Laxton, William | 1543 | £4 |
| Prior, Nicholas | 1543 | £3 |
| Wellys, Agnes, widow of Simon | 1543 | £2 |

mill and requesting substantial funding (£3 13s. 4d.) for repairs to this mill (September 1478). One also suspects that the John English who purchased the saffron plot in the entry above in 1483 was a clothing manufacturer since he was asked to evaluate seven and one-half yards of cloth: "Thomas Marshall, John Broughton, William Godwyn evaluated (*appretiaverunt*) a piece of blanket containing seven yards and $\frac{1}{2}$ at 4d. per yard from the goods of Henry Cook, to the use of John English," 29 May 1483.

While rentals are not generally available for the sixteenth century that would allow a comparative resource picture for various trade practitioners, the Lay Subsidy records (Table 34) provide a clear indication of the relative resources for what have been termed above as short term or part time occupations over against the longer term or full time trades people.

Debt instances from Godmanchester court rolls provide further indications that some trades people were only able to spend a few years at the trade owing to a lack of capital. Oliver Bennet was cited as a butcher between 1522 and 1525; he was assessed only £3 over 1523-1524; he was charged with owing Thomas Scot 10s. in 1520 and Margaret Stukeley 39s. 11d. and 3s. 4d. in 1524. John Stacy was assessed on the Lay Subsidy for 1523-1524 at £1 wages; his wife brewed from 1511 to 1515. John certainly was in debt: in 1515 he owed to John Holme of Alconbury 13s. 4d. for a *burso*; in 1516 he owed John Wynde, gentleman, six quarters of barley and in the same year owed to John Wynde and William Kyng 16s. for meadow and also 18s. for arrears of a house and yet again he owed to John Wynde in the very next court 10 quarters of barley; in 1517 he owed to Thomas Gony of Hemingford Abbots 13s. 4d. and payed off 6s. 8d. ; and in the same year he owed to William Diggby six quarters of barley and by 1523 he owed William Kyng 4s. (this very likely from the debt he owed the latter in 1516). There is no record of John Stacy's credits.

Isabella, wife of Thomas Faldyng, had 25 years as a brewer and Thomas had a few successful years as a baker and candelmaker. So it is interesting to note a more balanced credit and debt pattern from 1485 through to 1514. While Thomas Faldyng appeared as plaintiff for 31 debts over this period during the same period he was defendant for 39 debt claims. Here are some examples of Thomas's debts and credits.

| DATE | CREDITS | DEBTS |
|------|---------|-------|
| 1504 | Richard Grene 10s. | Thomas Lockyngton 5s. 4d. |
| 1505 | William Lord 9s. | William Ussher (no amount) |
| 1505 | Helen Frere 13s. 3d. + 2s. | Helen Frere 3s. + 16s. 4d. |
|      |         | William Frere 1s. |
| 1506 | John Gredley 5s. 8d. | William Kyng 10s. 6d. |

| DATE | CREDITS | DEBTS |
|---|---|---|
| 1506 | John Couper, butcher, 3s. 4d. | John Couper, butcher, 10s. |
|  |  | John Gredley 7s. 4d. |
| 1507 | Thomas Walcar, alias Thomas Fuller, 4s. 6d. for service | John Lawrence of Hunts 5s. 6d. |
| 1507 |  | John Stukeley 35s. malt; + 22s. malt |
| 1507 |  | Robert Chandeler 9s. for horse and colt |
| 1508 | William Hilton (no amount) |  |
| 1512 |  | William Aylred 12s. |
| 1514 | William Frost senior trespass with horse 6s. 8d. | Robert Chandeler 8s. malt |
| 1514 | Richard Chycheley 2s. |  |

Elizabeth, the wife of William Kelson, was rather unique in remaining a retailer over the long period 1513-1544. But she never rose to become a brewer. The debt structure of her husband William may be taken as indicative of an equilibrium rather than advance or decline in wealth:

| DATE | CREDITS | DEBTS |
|---|---|---|
| 1514 | Thomas Wylde 1 bushel of malt |  |
| 1517 | Thomas Bennet 3s. 6d. |  |
| 1519 |  | John Clapham, clerk, 3 quarters of barley worth 10s. |
| 1519 | William Packer *burso* 11d. |  |
| 1519 |  | Henry Barnard 1s. |
| 1520 | Henry Lane 6s. 8d. |  |
| 1520 | William Kyng and Thomas Haryson 1 pig 6s. |  |
| 1520 | William Kyng 1s. 2d. |  |
| 1520 |  | Thomas Pacy 4s. |
| 1520 |  | Robert White, damage of a sow 6s. 8d. |
| 1521 |  | William Lockyngton, 4 modes of barley |
| 1527 | William Keym 1s. for 2 bushels of malt |  |

On the other hand, Robert Chandeler began brewing along with his wife during the first decade of the sixteenth century and his credit balance in the court rolls would seem to reflect this economic success, although before this success he owed to 15 individuals from 1495 to 1502. But from 1506 to

1511, 25 individuals owed to Robert, whereas he only owed to nine individuals in this latter period.

| DATE | DEBTS | CREDITS |
|------|-------|---------|
| 1507 | William Vyntner 10 quarters of barley worth 34s. 10d. (20 quarters of barley, original debt) | |
| 1507 | Thomas Faldyng 8s. for malt + 9s. for horse and colt | |
| 1508 | Robert Nicholas 3s. for ma- nure + 26s. 8d. for manure | Robert Nicholas (no amount) |
| 1508 | Richard Grenam 3s. 4d. meadow | |
| 1509 | | Robert Nicholas for a tally £3 + 26s. 8d. + 13s. 4d. |
| 1509 | John Gybbys 4s. 8d. + 9s. | |
| 1509 | Thomas Bennet 8s. | |
| 1510 | Thomas Ingrave 6s. 8d. | |
| 1510 | John Kyng (no amount) | |
| 1511 | William Mayle and his mother 3s. 4d. | |
| 1511 | John Punt (no amount) | |
| 1512 | Robert Nicholas 6s. 8d. for tres- pass with sheep in his grain | |

Somewhat at the other extreme, the Barnards were never able to establish a strong foothold in the food trades. A John Barnard was a fishmonger once and a butcher four times in the 1490s; the wife of Henry Barnard[32] (assessed at £2 in 1545) brewed and baked over four years during the 1530s. But the Barnards remained by and large among those petty occupations described in the previous chapter. While it is not possible to distinguish the various Barnards with John as a first name and so to identify their respective trades, the following list shows the consistency of the debt pattern in the family:

---

[32] Noted in the previous section of this chapter as hayward during the second decade of the century.

| Year | Name | Buys | Sells | Credit | Debt |
|---|---|---|---|---|---|
| 1504 | John, candelmaker | | | | John Suell |
| 1504 | John, husbandman | | | | John Townshend 39s. 9d. ob. q. |
| 1504 | John, hayward with Richard Fawn | | | | John Dymand of London |
| 1504 | John, earthman of West Street | | | | Richard Stevens (dead) |
| 1504 | John junior, hayward | | | | William Kyng 27s. 8d. |
| 1504 | John senior, husbandman | | | | Richard Steven (dead) |
| 1504 | John, hayward | 2 quarters of barley, from John Townshend | | | |
| 1504 | John, hayward | | | | William Kyng 4s. 4d. + 1s. 2d. |
| 1505 | John, earthman | | | John Couper, butcher 3s. 4d. | |
| 1505 | John, candelmaker | | | | William Dalton |
| 1505 | John, candelmaker and John, carpenter | | | | Richard Grene |

| YEAR | NAME | BUYS | SELLS | CREDIT | DEBT |
|---|---|---|---|---|---|
| 1505 | John, candlemaker | | | | John Taylor 5s. 8d. |
| 1505 | John, candlemaker | | | | John Garlop, carpenter |
| 1505 | John junior, carpenter | | | | John Gybbys |
| 1505 | John junior | | | | William Granger and William Aylred 2s. 2d. |
| 1505 | John, redhead | | | | to the same |
| 1506 | John, hayward | | | | John Nottyngham 6s. 8. |
| 1507 | John, carpenter | wood for 3s. 4d. from Master Wynde | | | |
| 1507 | James | | | | Master Wynde |
| 1508 | John, sub-bailiff | | | | William Kingston 2s. 6d. |
| 1508 | John of West Street | | | | Thomas Schylling 1s. 6d. |
| 1508 | John, hayward | | | | William Dalton |
| 1509 | John | | | | William Dalton 7s. 8d. |
| 1509 | Thomas, alias Fylyp | | | | Thomas Roper |
| 1509 | John, now the hayward | | | | William Ussher 2s. |
| 1509 | John | | | | |
| 1510 | John | 1 quarter of malt from William Mayle | | | William Dalton 24s. |

| Year | Name | Buys | Sells | Credit | Debt |
|---|---|---|---|---|---|
| 1510 | John | | | | John Nottyngham and Jane Townshend 3s. 4d. |
| 1511 | John | | | | Thomas Pacy |
| 1511 | John | | | | William Lord |
| 1511 | John | | | | Richard Frere of London and Henry Frere |
| 1512 | John | | | | Henry Gybbys 6s. |
| 1512 | John | | | | William Smyth 7s. 9d. |
| 1514 | John | | | | John Punt, for use of a cow |
| 1514 | John | | | | Thomas Wylde 20s. |
| 1514 | John | | | | Ralph Mansell 16s. 8d. |
| 1516 | John, with Robert Nicholas | | | | John Punt and William Granger 25s. 8d. |
| 1517 | Henry | | 1 bushel of rye to Christopher Manner | | |
| 1517 | John | | | William Kelston 1s. | Nicholas Gelly 26s. 8d. + 10s. |
| 1519 | Henry | | | | John Clapham, clerk 13s. 8d. |
| 1521 | John | | | | John Brandon and Thomas Pacy |
| 1521 | Henry | | 2 bushels of malt to Thomas Tryg | | Thomas Tryg 2s. |
| 1522 | Henry | | | James Chambre 2s. | |
| 1524 | Henry | | | | John Porter for farm of land 2s. |

By contrast with the part time food trades, those ten individuals listed above as full time and having substantial assessments virtually do not appear at all on the court rolls among the debt suits. John Brandon does appear with John Laxton as custodians of the Corpus Christi Guild attempting to collect debts over 1513-1515 and John is a plaintiff for 3s. 8d. owed him by William Anys in 1518. Clearly these trades people had the resources in land to eschew the credit and debt structures of the town as had been the practice over the late fifteenth century.

The overall employment effects of changes in the victualling trades has been dramatized in Chapter 2, Table 16 listing those licensed for major occupations. That table underlines in particular the decline around 1500 by some fifty per cent in the numbers of those employed in the brewing industry and the concomitant control of more branches of the industry by fewer families.[33]

Fines paid for purchase of the liberty of Godmanchester (Appendix 6) provide a general summary index to this chapter. Over the first three decades of the fifteenth century, there were no fines paid below the level of fines for those major craft and trades people just discussed in the last part of this chapter. The 6s. 8d. fine was maintained as the "standard" throughout the whole of our period for such trades and crafts.

6s. 8d. FINES PER DECADE

| | |
|---|---|
| 1400-1409: 20 | 1480-1489: 7 |
| 1410-1419: 22 | 1490-1499: 11 |
| 1420-1429: 8 | 1500-1509: 12 |
| 1430-1439: 19 | 1510-1519: 5 |
| 1440-1449: 2 | 1520-1529: 9 |
| 1450-1459: 1 | 1530-1539: 7 |
| 1460-1469: 6 | 1540-1549: 5 |
| 1470-1479: 5 | |

The heavy concentration of the 6s. 8d. fine in the early years of the fifteenth century suggests that this little "manor-town" may have shared in a peripheral fashion in the "golden age" of the late fourteenth and early

[33] Downward or upward economic mobility among individuals of intermediate wealth cannot be traced over longer periods of time for most families owing to the fact that the wealth of many of these is not properly represented in farm rentals. Furthermore, those with a propensity for trade had much economic mobility within their families. Edward Hebden was assessed for two pounds in 1523; he was the son of Robert Hebden, miller, worth six pounds according to the same assessment. Widows very often took up an occupation upon the deaths of their husbands but their wealth was less substantial in these new roles than the wealth status of their family. Thus Joan Salmon, widow, was worth only two pounds in the tax assessment whereas her son John was worth ten pounds. Agnes, widow of John Disney, and Christine, widow of John Broughton, were further examples of this intrafamily variation in wealth.

fifteenth century cloth industry of East Anglia.[34] Indeed there are several references to fines for participants in the wool trade at this time: draper (1402, 8s.), weaver (1423, 6s. 8d.), fuller (1438, 6s. 8d.). These trades are not noted again but for related trades that are noted again the fine has fallen: glover (1419, 6s. 8d.; 1423, 1s. 8d.; 1433, 2s.), taylor (1406, 6s. 8d.; 1452, 8s.; 1452, 5s.; 1496, 2s.). Even taking into account the gaps among surviving records for the mid and third quarter of the century the number of 6s. 8d. fines had fallen radically.

The increased number of these fines over the last quarter of this century and into the sixteenth would come from what has been described above as the entrepreneurial activity of the local economy and not from a revival of the cloth industry. A miller paid an entry fine of 6s. 8d. in 1401, 1406 and 1524. It is difficult to compare the smith who paid 6s. 8d. in 1403, 10s. in 1404 and 3s. 4d. in 1534. As in the instance of the latter figures, these tradespeople often paid more than 6s. 8d. around 1400. The most that can be said for the later period is that their fine did not tend to fall below the 6s. 8d. level in periods of depression.[35] A baker paid 10s. in 1400. Bakers are not specified in entry fines again. Those who specialized in baking a century later were paying substantial fines although they also became property holders of some significance. A fishmonger paid 6s. 8d. in 1420, 8s. in 1465 and (Robert Seman) paid 6s. 8d. in 1508. A butcher paid 8s. in 1401 and again in 1428.

No doubt many of those traditional devices described in Chapter 3, above, and especially the frankpledge system, had served to control the movement of petty craft and tradespeople as well as labourers over the early decades of the century. The decline in fines for glovers and taylors just noted points to what became a general policy of conflating fines for petty craft and tradespeople with the 3s. 4d. fine as the standard. The amount first appears for a "lockyer" in 1434 and then over the ensuing decades as follows:

3s. 4d. FINES PER DECADE

| | |
|---|---|
| 1440-1449: 4 | 1500-1509: 6 |
| 1450-1459: 3 | 1510-1519: 11 |
| 1460-1469: 2 | 1520-1529: 8 |
| 1470-1479: 4 | 1530-1539: 17 |

---

[34] See, R. H. Britnell, *Colchester*, Part II: "Growth, 1350-1414." As has been noted in Chapter Three, above, the great increase in the number of those entering Godmanchester began in the last decade of the fourteenth century. The fact that many craft payments were for the late fourteenth and early fifteenth century adds further indication of industrial prosperity at this time.

[35] See, Chapter 6, below Table 36: "New Townsmen from the Region," p. 166.

1480-1489: 5                    1540-1549: 7
1490-1499: 10

Around the time of the appearance of the 3s. 4d. fine, there were a few
fines at the 3s. level: 1442, 2; 1445, 1; 1465, 1; 1486, 2; 1488, 1. These were
very likely modifications of the 3s. 4d. fine for some special circumstances.
A policy of fines for the group classified as labourers in this chapter only
began with the heavy influx of immigrants from the last quarter of the
fifteenth century. Payments at the bottom of the scale (1s.) were usually only
one per year, while payments at the top of the scale (2s. 8d.) were less
frequent by year and usually one or two per year.

NUMBERS PAYING 1S. FINE

1 in 1482, 1489, 1491, 1495, 1498, 1500
3 in 1501
1 in 1503, 1512, 1516, 1517
2 in 1521
1 in 1523, 1524, 1525, 1526, 1527
2 in 1532
1 in 1537, 1541, 1544

NUMBERS PAYING 2S. FINE

| | |
|---|---|
| 1 in 1479 | 3 in 1517 |
| 2 in 1480 | 1 in 1518, 1519 |
| 1 in 1482, 1485 | 3 in 1520 |
| 2 in 1486 | 2 in 1521 |
| 1 in 1487 | 1 in 1523, 1524 |
| 4 in 1488 | 2 in 1528 |
| 2 in 1489 | 1 in 1530, 1531 |
| 4 in 1494 | 2 in 1533 |
| 1 in 1495 | 4 in 1534 |
| 5 in 1496 | 1 in 1536 |
| 1 in 1500, 1501 | 2 in 1537 |
| 2 in 1503 | 5 in 1538 |
| 1 in 1506 | 1 in 1539 |
| 2 in 1507 | 4 in 1543 |
| 3 in 1509, 1510 | 2 in 1544 |
| 1 in 1511 | 1 in 1545 |
| 2 in 1516 | 3 in 1549 |

Beyond the fact a few variations (8d., 1s. 2d., 2s. 4d.) were introduced
occasionally from the second decade of the sixteenth century, most labourers

paid entry fines of 1s. 4d., 1s. 8d., or 2s. There was obviously some policy governing the assessment of these fines. After three individuals were assessed 1s. 4d. in 1487 there was a shift to the 2s. fine (1488, 1489, 1494, 1496); the 1s. 8d. fine assumed greater significance in the second quarter of the sixteenth century. Although statistics became less complete as the fines paid immediately ("by hand") were not recorded, by the second quarter of the sixteenth century the volatile nature of the labour market[36] is indicated by the lower fines in 1527 with return to the higher in 1528, the lower in 1532 and the higher in 1534, the lower in 1541 and the higher in 1543, the lower in 1547 and the return to higher by 1549.

| NUMBERS PAYING 1S. 4D. FINE | NUMBERS PAYING 1S. 8D. FINE |
|---|---|
| 1 in 1486 | 2 in 1479, 1481 |
| 3 in 1487 | 1 in 1481, 1485, 1488, 1489, 1490 |
| 1 in 1494, 1500, 1501, 1503, 1505, 1510, 1512 | 2 in 1497 |
| | 1 in 1501, 1505 |
| 3 in 1520 | 2 in 1509 |
| 1 in 1526 | 1 in 1510 |
| 4 in 1527 | 3 in 1511 |
| 1 in 1531 | 2 in 1512 |
| 5 in 1532 | 1 in 1516 |
| 1 in 1533 | 2 in 1517 |
| 2 in 1534, 1538 | 1 in 1519 |
| 3 in 1540 | 2 in 1521, 1523, 1527 |
| 2 in 1541, 1547 | 3 in 1538, 1541 |
| | 1 in 1544, 1546, 1549 |

"What comen folk in all this world may compare with the comyns of Ingland, in ryches, in freedom, lyberty, welfare and all prosperytie ?"[37] boasted an author of 1515. Complementary statutory efforts to enforce the boast upon labourers, artificers and small husbandmen proved a failure. Certainly for Godmanchester, sixteenth-century efforts to reverse conditions for this common folk were far too late, for a new socio-economic order that would make this impossible was already in place.

---

[36] For date on the considerable migration at this time, see the article of B. M. S. Campbell, "Population Early Tudor, England."

[37] For this quote, and the government response, see J. D. Mackie, *The Early Tudors*, p. 450ff.

# 6

# A New Society Evolves

## A. THE CAPITALISTS

Over the fifteenth century, and increasingly in the sixteenth century, it is possible to distinguish individuals in the Godmanchester records who were well provided with capital. These were people who could purchase large blocks of land or quickly engross from many purchases of smaller units of land; they did not depend upon the petty credit system of the town, although many would provide the credit for fellow townsmen; and, of course, they were not dependent upon crafts for their livelihood, although some might venture into agrarian-related brewing or milling for a few years. While the disposition of liquid capital is an entreprenurial activity, those with ready capital stand out so clearly against those who have been described as entrepreneurs in the previous chapter that an attempt must be made to assess this group in terms of the role of capital.

In chronological terms, these capitalists first come to our attention in fifteenth-century records as paying the largest fines (in parentheses below) and usually to be found quickly in leadership roles in the town: 1400, William Rumborough (20s.); 1401, William Everard de Swavesey (26s. 8d.) and William Ponder (20s.); 1405, Henry Waleys (20s.); 1415, John Campion and three sons (20s.); 1421, Thomas Grigge and two sons (15s.); 1435, William Bishop (13s. 4d.); 1437, William Brown (13s. 4d.); 1442, William Horewode (13s. 4d.); 1449, John Folkes and two sons (16s. 8d.); 1452, John Emley (13s. 4d.); 1456, John Motte and son John (13s. 4d.).[1]

With the survival of rentals in the 1480s entry fines and property holdings over the following years can be correlated. As the previous paragraph illustrates, the largest entry fines demanded for the liberty of Godmanchester had become smaller from the second quarter of the fifteenth century through to the 1480s. These smaller fines would seem to indicate a fall in the value

---

[1] See Appendix 6.

of Godmanchester land. Even into the 1480s, as with William Orwell and Richard Samt below, smaller entry fines more typical of previous decades could still mean very significant purchasing power. In the following list, the first date is that for the licensing (date and amount in parentheses) of newcomers who were able to acquire large amounts (quantity with date of rental) of land very quickly. The ready availability of marketable land, rather than the lack of ready capital, would in part explain these differing rates of accumulation: [1470s], John Fisher of London: 122 acres 1485; William Orwell (1480, 16s. 8d.): 75 acres 1485, 79 acres 1486; Thomas Fyncham (1482, 26s. 8d.): 98 acres 1485; Richard Townshende (1482, 13s. 4d.): 25 acres 1485; Richard Samt (1484, 13s. 4d.): 14 acres 1485, $22\frac{1}{2}$ acres 1486, 48 acres 1487 and $56\frac{1}{2}$ acres 1490; Thomas Laxton (1486, 40s.): 72 acres 1489; John Ussher (and son Richard) (1489, 33s. 4d.): 6 acres 1494, [100 acres, *ca.* 1500].

As has already been noted,[2] the court rolls of Godmanchester do not register most of the property conveyances and their reporting is least useful as a record of transfers of arable and meadow lands. Appended conveyance lists do bridge the gap between the two annual rental lists, but very few sequences of conveyances and rentals are extant for more than the one or two terms during one year. The source of the properties accumulated by outsiders in the above list cannot be ascertained to any great degree, therefore, with the exception of a partial glimpse of the holdings of John Fisher.

A court roll of September 1481 registers the purchase of a messuage on East Street, formerly belonging to John Aylred, by John Fisher. In a court entry of 30 January 1483, John Fisher released a messuage on West Street, formerly belonging to Thomas Motte, to John English and purchased a groveage and close on the same street. John Fisher would appear to have died late in 1486. Margaret, the widow of John Fisher, formerly alderman of London, was given possession of a messuage on Arnyng Street with adjacent curtilage, and groveage formerly of Robert Robyns, along with a messuage and adjacent gardens on West Street by the court of 14 December 1486. John Aylred and Robert Robyns were wealthy natives of the town. Whether substantial acreages in the fields went with these conveyances we do now know.

Other records add further to the detail about the property purchase of John Fisher. The rentals from 1485 for Post Street note that John Fisher owed farm of 15d. ob. q. for property from Dorraunt senior, 2d. ob. for a messuage of Wilson, 6d. for a messuage of William Ibott, 14d. from property of William Frere and 2d. for the groveage of John Chese. This was in addition to a farm

---

[2] Chapter 2, p. 50.

payment of twenty shillings tenpence farthing owed for unspecified lands over the next year. A further property was acquired from Lawman worth a farm of two shillings sixpence (i.e., in field terms, 10 acres). Sometime earlier in his career in the town a memorandum was drawn up to report the farm fines for which John Fisher of London, merchant, was responsible. This memo[3] from which part of the heading has broken away, indicates the variety of properties and the former or current tenants for the properties John Fisher was accumulating:

| | |
|---|---|
| For le Bury formerly Thomas Waleys | 21d. ob. |
| For Remyng in le Bury | 3d. ob. |
| For curtilage and grove formerly John Reygate | 21d. |
| For tenement (that) William Butcher holds | 3d. ob. |
| For cageyard | 9d. |
| For gersum $\frac{1}{2}$ acre meadow formerly John Schyllyng | 1d. |
| For le Bury formerly Richard Conyff | 22d. ob. |
| For grove formerly William Manipenny | 18d. |
| For tenement Richard Smyth, taylor, formerly John Reygate | 3d. ob. |
| For gersum 12 acres bought of John Stalys | 2/– |
| For meadow formerly Roper's | 21d. |
| For messuage John Roper | 4d. q. |
| For messuage formerly Richard Smyth | 1d. ob. |
| For $2\frac{1}{2}$ acres formerly John Cleyff | 5d. |

Holdings in this memo represent less than 40 acres, but they do demonstrate engrossing from 11 former tenants of a wide variety of economic status. From all the evidence at hand, at one time or another John Fisher held nine messuages and from the rental records he had at least 122 acres in one year. John Fisher represented a new type of investor at Godmanchester, a type that was to increase in number over subsequent decades. Members of this group paid the highest entry fines to liberty, although it is unlikely that any of these settled in Godmanchester. Their affairs at court were handled

---

[3] Huntington Record Office, Godmanchester Borough Records, Box 2, Roll 1, no. 67. The fact that tenements had been sublet to William Butcher and Richard Smith, taylor, provides further evidence for that short-term leasing of shops and small messuages to labourers and craftsmen discussed in Chapter 5.

Some of the properties obtained by these various capitalists were under the formula *ad opus*. But no particular pattern has been discovered that makes this expression any more useful for isolating properties coming on to an open market than *ad opus* conveyances served to designate the surfacing of a land market among customary holdings. On this latter point, see Harvey, *The Peasant Land Market*, p. 25. Certainly for speculators such as John Fisher the differences between leasing and alienation must have been incidental.

John Fisher has been identified as a merchant, acquiring freedom in 1454, alderman 1481-1483 and dying in 1485. See Sylvia Thrupp, *The Merchant Class of Medieval London* (Ann Arbor, Michigan, 1962), p. 340.

by attorneys. Their purpose was to make profits as a short-term enterprise. The quick turnover of messuages by John Fisher reflects this policy. As will be seen below, profits might be taken from the fields of the town for a number of years, but no effort was made to establish a more permanent family estate. All were given designations, at first usually "merchants" from London and more frequently later, "gentlemen." There follows a list of these individuals:

TABLE 35: MERCHANTS AND GENTLEMEN

| NAME | DATE | FINE |
|------|------|------|
| Baptiste, Borrono, John, de London, merchant | 1546 | £1 |
| Beek, William, de Stowe | 1532 | 26s. 8d. |
| Caldecote, Nicholas, de London | [1530's] | ? |
| Chertsey, Robert, de London, merchant | 1533 | £1 |
| Croft, John, de London, grocer | 1534 | £2 |
| Dormer, Michael, de London | 1546 | £2 |
| Dragner, John, de London, merchant | 1549 | 13s. 4d. |
| Freppis, William, de London, pewterer | 1538 | 13s. 4d. |
| Frere, Richard, de London, grocer | [1530's[ | ? |
| Harforth, Robert, gentleman, de Huntingdon | 1525 | 10s. |
| Langton, William, yeoman | 1544 | £1 |
| Martre, Robert, gentleman | 1531 | ? |
| May, William, clothmaker | 1529 | 5s. |
| Parider, Thomas, de London, husbandman | 1529 | 13s. 4d. |
| Pennyson, William, squire | [15?] | ? |
| Wilson, Edward, yeoman | 1549 | 10s. |
| Wood, John, gentleman | 1508 | £1 |
| Woodward, Thomas and sons James and William | 1534 | 33s. 4d. |
| Woodward, William, gentleman | 1532 | 26s. 8d. |
| Wulfston, Guido, knight | [1480's] | ? |

The tradition[4] represented by Laxton, Orwell and Samt did not disappear when Londoners and gentlemen capitalists came on the scene. When more information about members of this group is available, it would appear that they are from the agrarian and commercial regions about Godmanchester although the place of origin is not always designated. The fact that they already had contacts in the town would explain a support system allowing liberty fines lower than those for merchants and gentlemen. Such associations would also explain the readiness with which this second group was elected to positions of high administrative responsibility in the town. Members of this second group are listed in Table 36. Either through evidence for their role as administrators, or their active personal involvment in commerce,

---

[4] See *A Small Town*, pp. 76ff. Analysis of such regional economies of Huntingdonshire can only be undertaken as a large study in itself.

TABLE 36: NEW TOWNSMEN FROM THE REGION

| NAME | DATE | LIBERTY FINE | LAY SUBSIDY | MAJOR OFFICIAL |
|---|---|---|---|---|
| Adam, John de Cambridge | 1482 | 13s. 4d. | | |
| Barbour, Thomas de Hemingford | 1482 | 10s. | | No |
| Boleyn, John | 1524 | 1s. | 1542, 1545, 1547 £10 | Yes |
| Collyn, William | 1536 | 12s. | | |
| Dalton, William, farmer | 1509 | 10s. | | Yes |
| Dalton, William, merchant | ? | ? | | No |
| Dawson, Henry, miller | 1544 | 10s. | 1543 £10; 1548 £12 | No |
| Disney, John senior | 1530 | 1s. 4d. | 1545, 1547 £10 | Yes |
| Fyncheham, Thomas | 1482 | 26s. 8d. | | No |
| Gaddesby, Thomas, de St. Neots | 1538 | 6s. 8d. | | No |
| Gonell, John, de Caxton | 1497 | 13s. 4d. | | No |
| Grene, Richard | 1511 | 8d. | 1523 £16 | Yes |
| Hawdwyne, Roger | 1514 | 5s. | 1523 £8 | Yes |
| Hawdwyne (Howdene), Roland | 1537 | 16s. 8d. | | No |
| Holme, Thomas | 1518 | 2s. | 1524 £5 | Yes |
| Holme, William | 1491 | 6s. | | No |
| Laxton, John | 1488 | 6s. 8d. | 1523 £29 | Yes |
| Lorydan, Marcus | ? | ? | 1545 £5 | No |
| Massy, Thomas | 1488 | 6s. 8d. | | No |
| Massey, Robert | 1529 | [   ] | 1545 £5 | Yes |
| Monyment, Thomas | 1493 | 4s. | 1524 £7 | Yes |
| Orwell, William | 1480 | 16s. 8d. | | Yes |
| Osteler, William | 1521 | 2s. | 1523 £3; 1524 £1; 1543 £5 | Yes |
| Parrot, John, de London, merchant | 1504 | 5s. | | No |
| Pelle, Robert | 1515 | 26s. 8d. | 1523 £26 | Yes |
| Samt, Richard | 1484 | 13s. 4d. | | Yes |
| Stevens, John | 1507 | 5s. | 1524 £6 | Yes |
| Sewster, Nicholas, gent | 1549 | £1 | 1548 £20 | No |
| Sewster, William, gent | 1527 | 6s. 8d. | 1542, 1543, 1545 £20; 1548 £50 | Yes |
| Townshende, Richard | 1482 | 13s. 4d. | | No |
| Tryg, Thomas, de Brampton | 1540 | 11s. 8d. | | No |
| Trevet, John, de Stanton | 1527 | 10s. | | No |
| Tharsnok, Thomas, de Brampton | 1524 | 8s. | | No |
| Ussher, John and son Richard | 1489 | 33s. 4d. | | Yes (John) |
| Ussher, William and son John | 1505 | 26s. 8d. | | No |
| Wellys, Simon | ? | ? | 1523 £2; 1543 £2 (wife) | Yes |
| Wylde, John | 1520 (re-ad-mitted) | 6s. 8d. | 1523-1524 £2 | Yes |
| Wylde, Thomas | 1506 | 6s. 8d. | | No |

these outsiders of varying degrees of wealth clearly became residents of Godmanchester. Most of these regional people settled in Godmanchester during the period after surviving rental records are available, so it is not possible to assess their property holdings. However, as residents of Godmanchester, this group was taxed in the town for royal subsidies. Where available, these lay subsidy assessments are given below and show by and large how many of this group had prospered.

Common characteristics cannot be forced too strongly on this group. John Parrot of London is commonly designated as a merchant, but he did not invest too heavily and appeared to have lived in the town for a time. Although designated "gentlemen," the Sewster family seems to have settled in the town and even functioned as officials. Not every branch of the families of Dalton, Hawdwyne and Ussher seems to have shared in official duties. Some individuals such as Thomas Gaddesby, who was cited only once for baking, did not seem to stay long, no doubt because of a failure to prosper. Beyond these more individual eccentricities, this group does break down into middling and wealthy sub-groups. On the lower end of the economic scale of this group, many of the individuals in the following group are on the level of those craft and commercial individuals discussed in Chapter 5. Indeed, in terms of this level of wealth, one might question whether many of those in Table 36 ought to be grouped with the wealthy, that is, such as Grene, Laxton, Pelle and Sewster. But the economic impact of this less wealthy group on the town was no less dramatic. For these individuals include the great majority of those families who contributed to that concentration of local commerce discussed in Chapter 5: Boleyn, Dalton, Disney, Hawdwyne (Roger), Ibott, Laxton, Lorydan, Massey, Monyment, Osteler, Prior, Stevens, Ussher, Wellys, Wylde. As will be seen further below, this commercial group of middling wealth had other characteristics in common in so far as they supported one another by a common pool of credit and intermarried.

A third group involved in this "land grab" at Godmanchester were some of the oldest families of the town. It was noted in Chapter 2[5] that much of the rapid accumulation of property in the 1480s was by recently liberated outsiders. However, a few old families of the town had survived the demographic and economic crises of the fifteenth century and profited from their exceptional luck of survival. Over the ensuing decades several of these Godmanchester "natives" were able to react to the new competition and accumulate much land themselves. This local competition forced external land purchases into a circumscribed pattern for the early Tudor period that will be delineated below. Perhaps this competition also explains the increase

[5] See p. 47.

in entry fines for many wealthy outsiders from the 1490s. Following is the list of the most successful local engrossing families as reflected in lay subsidy assessments.

| NAME | LAY SUBSIDY |
|---|---|
| William Aylred | 1543 £6; 1545 £5; 1547 £6 |
| Thomas Bennet | 1543 and 1545 £8 |
| William Bennet | 1523 £11; 1543 £8; 1545 £7; 1547 £8 |
| Henry Frere | 1523 £6; 1524 £5; 1542-1548 £13 |
| John Frere | 1542-1545 £10; 1547 £8 |
| William Kyng | 1523 £42; 1524 £40 |
| John Locktyngton | 1545 £10; 1547 £5 |
| Thomas Lockyngton | 1523 £29 |
| William Mayle | 1523 £17; 1543 and 1545 £6; 1547 £5; |
| John Nottyngham | 1523 £14 |
| Richard Robyns | 1523 £50; 1524 £50; 1542 £12; 1545 £60; 1547 £50; 1548 £50 |
| William Townshende | 1523 £24; 1524 £20 |

The more local in origin were the property engrossers at Godmanchester the more local had to be the capital they generated in order to purchase more property. In consequence, their success became a sort of double jeopardy for other members of the town since capital-producing trades and commerce as well as land became more and more a monopoly of this group. In this respect the older families came to differ little from the more recently arrived families listed in the previous group. Many of the older families of the town—Bennet, Bould, Frere, Holme, Ibbot, Kyng, Mayle, Nottyngham, West, Wylde— participated along with newcomers of the second group in that creation of commercial monopolies described in Chapter 5.

The fact that some of the older families of Godmanchester rose to prominence among wealthy merchants and other outsiders of the early Tudor period was no accident of easy affluence. Various details about the Robyns family may be cited in illustration of the survival pattern of older family of the town. In Godmanchester from the early fourteenth century,[6] the Robyns were revealed in court rolls as versatile people: there was a Henry Robyns noted as a "dicer" in 1400; one, or various, John Robyns identified as launderer (1411), taylor (1416), husbandman (1416); Godfrey was noted as a "wulschem" (1439). This family also had a wider demographic base than

[6] *A Small Town*, p. 378. Even in the second quarter of the fourteenth century there was an association with Hemingford.

the one town over those precarious plague generations. A John Robyns of
Hemingford purchased liberty in 1410; by the 1430s a Henry Robyns who
came from Hemingford was an official for Arnyng Street; a John Robyns of
Huntingdon was noted as an "outsider" in 1432; a Hugh Robyns from
Hemingford was mentioned in 1445. In the Ramsey Abbey *gersuma* roll[7] for
1431 it was noted that a William Robyns of Godmanchester had held land
in Upwood.

Skipping the sparse records of the third quarter of the century, the story
of the Robyns family can be picked up again in the 1480s. From the evidence
in the rentals, there were two branches of the family at that time: a Robert
Robyns on Arnyng Street paying 3s. 4d. for 13 $\frac{1}{2}$ acres, and a John Robyns
on West Street. The latter can be seen taking advantage of land becoming
available at that time. In 1482 he purchased a messuage on West Street
formerly belonging to Richard Conyff together with 44 acres of arable. This
property was still held by John as late as 1510, by which time John became
an official for West Street (1511) and was designated as senior. In the
meantime John junior, no doubt a son of senior, had purchased a messuage
on Post Street from John Bonsay in 1505 and this messuage became the
family home. There was still another John Robyns living on this property, an
official in 1544 and assessed £10 in the Lay Subsidies of 1545 and 1547.

Although no direct linkage between John Robyns of West Street and
Richard Robyns can be discovered in surviving records, a Richard Robyns
did carry on the family association with that street. Richard first appears in
records as a juror for 1516, but had a rather shaky beginning so that he was
deprived of his liberty by the jurors for some un-stated malefaction and had
to re-purchase this status for 6s. 8d. in 1519. Richard was already sufficiently
affluent to become a creditor to fellow townsmen. In 1518 John Nottyngham
had pledged a messuage to Richard for a £5 6s. 8d. debt; in the same year
John Gybbys gave Richard a bond for a £1 debt; in 1520 Joan Townshende
and Katherine Monyment pledged a messuage for a 15s. debt; in 1527
Robert Harforth pledged eight acres one yard of meadow for a £7 debt.

No doubt Richard Robyns was dealing in property over these years
although there are only recorded references to release of a messuage on East
Street to Margery Bonsay (1520) and to his pasture (1521). By the 1530s
Richard clearly launches into real estate to become one of the wealthiest
property holders of the town. On West Street a grove was added to his
property (1531) as well as a close (1533). The farm rental figure for West
Street in 1529 translates into more than 100 acres of arable and/or meadow.
Charges against his shepherd for trespassing with the flock (1533) suggest

[7] E. Dewindt, *The* Liber Gersumarum of *Ramsey Abbey* (Toronto, 1976), p. 221.

a concentration on sheep. Richard purchased one of the most valuable properties of the town, the Horseshoe on Post Street, together with appurtenant orchard and barnyards in 1538. In 1546, Richard Robyns and John Nelson purchased from the wealthy William Sewster, gentleman, a messuage and close on West Street along with 50 acres of arable. Less wealthy townsmen had to pool their resources in the face of the increasingly formidable wealth of Richard. In 1537, the three butchers, Robert Massy, Briant Relton and Simon Wellys had a common pay arrangement with Richard Robyns. In 1548, three men of middling wealth status identified with their occupations, William Grene, William Greatham and William Osteler bound themselves jointly to re-pay £2 13s. 4d to Richard Robyns.

Richard Robyns was first given the title of yeoman in 1527. He was a juror for West Street in 1527, 1538, 1539, 1540, 1542 and a bailiff for 1533 and 1545. The Lay Subsidies reflect the wealth of this family: 1523 £53; 1524 £50; 1542 (£12); 1545 £60; 1547 £50; 1548 £50. It would be extraordinary for one individual to have carried on so actively for more than four decades, but there is no record of succession to another Richard over these years. In any case, there were no male successors by the time of Richard Robyns' last will and testament in 1548. As has been noted in Chapter Four, it was a fitting tribute to one-half century of energetic activity that this leading freeman of the town should make possible by his will the re-establishment of the grammar school at Godmanchester.

## B. Capital, Credit and Debt

No direct correlation can be made between these major shifts in the ownership of property at Godmanchester and the actual amounts of money involved. As has been noted, extant records do not exist for the piece by piece accumulation of property and even when such records do survive, as is the case with John Fisher, the purchase or sale prices of properties are not indicated. But there are three major categories of information that show the operation of the credit system and the valuation of various types of properties so that we are able to obtain a more explicit picture of the role of capital at the time. These three categories are, first the registering of debt amounts in court rolls during the reign of Henry VII, secondly bond arrangements for the collection of debts largely over the same period of time, and thirdly the increasing tendency to register the traditional tally in court rolls from the early sixteenth century.

The traditional form of debt plea entry in the court rolls did not change over the early Tudor period. In nearly all instances court roll entries are clipped to the bare essentials of the lawsuit: the plaintiff, the defendant and the amount owed. In the margin, or inserted above the entry, are the clerks shorthand indicating the legal status or response to the plea, that is to say, brief formulaic indications of essoin, warranty, distraint, pledge and so forth. Typical of such entries are the following:

> John Gybbys enters a plea of debt against Agnes Thomas (margin: essoin W.) (29 June 1413)
>
> John Cabe enters a plea of debt for 18d. against John Suell (p.) (29 June 1413)
>
> John Mathieu enters a plea of debt against John of Oxford, clerk (margin: essoin. W.) (13 December 1492)
>
> Through his attorney John Brewster, Master Wynde enters a plea of debt against Thomas Alan (Po. se) (Margin: essoin) (1 April 1507)

These court records have the entry once only despite the indications of various stages of the legal process.[8]

This information about credit and indebtedness has been tabulated below for that period during which the information about these debts is most useful for this study. Although the reason for registering debts in the court rolls was clearly the fact that many credit arrangements had gone awry, this information reveals much of what had been the traditional scope of credit.

Over the 18 years, 1485-1503, 504 individuals were involved as either debtors or creditors. The use of credit was common among all peoples of the town. 500 years ago, as today, those using or offering credit would seek to avoid lawsuit for indebtedness. At Godmanchester, very few large landholders and prominent officials are listed as having outstanding debts at any time. Such individuals, who could pay substantial licence fees to purchase liberty, and, whether from old families or new, could purchase blocks of property, were not suffering from the lack of liquidity. On the other hand, at the lower end of the wealth spectrum, few of the poorer labourers and craftsmen had the collateral to back an extension of credit for their needs and certainly not to pursue or be pursued for debt by the court.[9]

---

[8] What has been described as "labour-saving reforms in the listing of new pleas" (Britnell, *Colchester*, p. 206 and p. 207 note 9) did seem to occur over the mid fifteenth century for Godmanchester too in so far as pleas were not dragged out so often over those long periods typical of the thirteenth and fourteenth-century lawsuits. However, the economic information from Godmanchester pleas was so exiguous from the thirteenth to the late fifteenth centuries that the counting of pleas would not seem to have much meaning.

The older form "detention of chattels" occurred only rarely for the period under study here, so such pleas have been included with debt pleas (*placita debitorum*).

[9] One can see why the charitable practice of interest free loans, above p. 116, arose at this time. The development of this practice underlines further the use of credit as a "normal" practice of the age.

For the debt entries we do have approximately one-half of those listed in Appendix 9 appearing in court only once in response to a plea of debt. Furthermore, by far the majority of those answering more than one plea of debt can be classified in much the same fashion because of the concentration of their debts in periods of a year or two. For example, Christopher Broughton was charged with two debts (5/- and 1/6d) in 1499. William Melbourne with three debts (4/-, 6/8d and 17/-) in 1495; William Ede with two debts in 1500 (3/- and 6/8d) and one in 1503 (3/-); Richard Fawne with one in 1501 (39/11d) and two in 1503 (9/- and 16/-) and so forth. In short, most of the debt pleas must have typified normal debt arrangements that had broken down for reasons of temporary financial embarrassment.

Of the 504 people known to be involved in the credit system between 1485 and 1503, 179 were creditors only, 133 come to our attention as debtors only, and the remaining (192) were involved in both capacities. That most detailed study to date in the use of credit in rural villages and small towns has discovered that credit was offered by all levels of society from humble labourers to the wealthy.[10] Godmanchester people of the late fifteenth century followed the same pattern. Among those offering credit only were 17 who had occupations beside their name: knight, vicar, two millers, two gentlemen, one servant of John Draper, two chaplains, one labourer, two merchants, two clerks, one mason and one draper. There were 20 individuals who were both creditor and debtor: two artisans, three labourers, two candelmakers, one husbandman, one carpenter, one miller, one shepherd, four butchers, one sub-bailiff, one vicar, two clerks and one wright.

On the other hand, Appendix 9 shows that the credit system at Godmanchester not only touched many lives but had become specialized. There were obviously professional money lenders. Over the 1485-1503 period John Aylred recovered money from 43 people, William Basse from 18, William Gonell from 25, John Lockyngton from 16, Thomas Lockyngton from 34, William Manipenny from 37, Richard Motte from 20, William Orwell from 33 and John Stukeley from 44. This group of lenders were from among the wealthiest property holders of the town and were charged rarely if at all with debts. Townsmen from all levels of wealth borrowed from these professionals. From these debt schedules it may be suggested that professional lenders spread their credit fairly evenly from year to year, that is, made available to borrowers a rather fixed pool of capital.

---

[10] See, Elaine Clark, "Debt Litigation in a Late Medieval English Vill," in *Pathways to Medieval Peasants*, ed. J. A. Raftis (Toronto, 1981), pp. 265-267; but more particularly by the same author, "Medieval Debt Litihgation, Essex and Norfolk, 1270-1490," unpublished Ph. D. dissertation (University of Michigan, 1977), Chapter Four.

Indeed, by the late 1480s the town was still far from exclusive dependence upon the professional lender since efforts were still being made to obtain credit within the context of mutual obligations. That is to say, many more debts were owed to a less wealthy corps of lenders than to the professionals, a less wealthy corps[11] who also might be as frequently borrowers from others: William Basse, John Bayous, Thomas Benett, Thomas Burton, Robert Chandeler, Thomas Faldyng, Thomas Fecas, William Gardener, William Gyle, John Gybbys, William Holme, Richard Kyng, Richard Motte, William Moundeford, William Nicol, John Nottyngham, Thomas Reginald, John Smyth, John Suell, Richard Stevens, John Stokys, John Taylor, John Turneskewe, John Tychemarsh. A further dozen or so of the less wealthy had only debts over a number of years. As has been noted in Chapter 5, there were also those who depended extensively upon credit for their normal business operation; for example, Roger Cook was in debt 37 times, John Couper, butcher, 35 times, John Custauns 25 times, William Godwyn, 18 times and John Gredley, butcher, 73 times.

In Table 37 available information about debts have been summarized from the 1480s to the early sixteenth century. The explosion in indebtedness occurring from the 1480s can only mean that the traditional pools of credit have dried up. The size of debts varied greatly from a shilling or two to 40[12] or 50 shillings. There was a tendency for the less wealthy to have smaller and fewer debts. William Hilton, who held only three and one-half acres on Post Street had the following debts: 3s. 10d (1488), 7s. (1490), 2s. (1490), 2s. + 6s. (1493), 5s. (1495), 3s. 4d. (1496), 5s. (1499) and 3s. 4d. (1502)—all owed to different people. By contrast, John Mayle who came from a family usually holding 40 to 50 acres had a schedule of larger debts: 6s. 8d. (1493, 1496), 10s. and 14s. (1497), 20s, 5s. 4d. and 27s. (1499) and 39s. 11d. (1503). But the debts of William Hilton were substantial for someone in that level of wealth described in Chapter 5 and the mutual resource support system described in that chapter was no longer able to rescue many debtors.

A new source of capital became available from those wealthy individuals noted at the beginning of this chapter who began to compete for Godman-

---

[11] The overall description of the social structure of debt given in this paragraph may be complemented by references to the pools of credit among labourers, petty craftsmen and middle wealth groups noted above, pp. 130, 141, 147.

[12] The 40 shilling rule governing the upper limit of debt to be administered in the local court was followed at Godmanchester. See John S. Beckerman, "The Forty-Shilling Jurisdiction Limit in Medieval English Personal Actions," in *Legal History Studies*, ed. Dafyyd Jenkins (U. of Wales, 1975), pp. 110-117. This rule did not mean of course, that the indebtness of individuals was limited to 40 shillings. Tallies very frequently exceeded this amount.

chester property. For example, William Orwell had the funds to pay a steep
entry fine and purchase nearly 80 acres by 1486, but he also was able to loan
money to a wide variety of individuals. Of the 40 debt pleas concerning
William Orwell between 1486 and 1509, for only two was William the
defendant: 3s. 8d. owed to William Manipenny in 1486 and 2s. owed to
William Ede for some grain and a cart in 1507. Nearly all of the 30
individuals in the following list who owed William Orwell were from the
lower levels of income described in Chapter 5. Nothing could depict more
clearly the collapse of traditional pools of credit and the new dependence
upon capital from outside the town.

#### DEBTS OWED TO WILLIAM' ORWELL

| | |
|---|---|
| 1486 | William Diggby (   ) |
| 1487 | Thomas Emlyn (   ) |
| | John Shalford (   ) |
| | Robert Porter (   ) |
| 1488 | William Hilton 3s. 10d. |
| | Roger Manning (   ) |
| | John Gredley 4s. |
| 1488 | William Gardner (   ) |
| | John Scot (   ) |
| 1489 | William Holme 20s. |
| | Thomas Newman (   ) |
| | William Nicholas (   ) |
| 1490 | Thomas Baker 1s. |
| 1491 | Agnes Butcher Alright, widow (   ) |
| | William Este 10s. |
| 1492 | William Goodwyn 17s. |
| | John Gredley 1s. 3d. |
| 1495 | Robert Caldwell 6s. 8d. |
| 1496 | Robert Caldwell (   ) |
| | William Frere (   ) |
| | John Vincent (   ) |
| | John Foster (   ) |
| | William Goodwyn (   ) |
| 1497 | John Custauns (   ) |
| 1498 | John Mildenhall (   ) |
| | Robert Huston 2s. 2d. |
| | Thomas Faldyng 13s. |
| | John Barnard, sub bailiff 11s. |
| 1500 | Roger Coke (   ) |
| 1501 | John Nottyngham (   ) |
| | John Stacy (   ) |

Richard Fawne (   )
John Barnard, sub bailiff 8s. 8d.
1501    John Gredley (   )
1507    John Hedde 3s. 3d. for one acre meadow
1508    William Farthyngton 2s. 8d.
1509    Richard Lonysdale 2s. 8d.
1515    Thomas Faldyng (   )

As may be seen in the following summary Table 37, the high percentage
of unknown debts together with variations in the size of debts makes
hazardous generalizations about total indebtedness. The total number of
debts seems to have grown steadily over the 1480s from a lower level

TABLE 37: INDEBTEDNESS AT GODMANCHESTER 1484-1514

| YEAR | TOTAL KNOWN DEBT AMOUNTS | NUMBER OF KNOWN DEBTS | NUMBER OF UNKNOWN DEBTS | TOTAL NUMBER OF DEBTS |
|---|---|---|---|---|
| 1484 | £1  3s. 10d. | 4 | 27 | 31 |
| 1485 | £4 10s.  5d. | 15 | 45 | 60 |
| 1486 | £7 17s.  6d. | 12 | 42 | 54 |
| 1487 | £15 10s.  6d. | 25 | 36 | 61 |
| 1488 | £17 14s.  7d. | 25 | 47 | 72 |
| 1489 | £23  1s.  5d. | 26 | 52 | 78 |
| 1490 | £12  5s.  2d. | 15 | 42 | 57 |
| 1491 | £10 10s.  7d. | 21 | 42 | 63 |
| 1492 | £19 17s.  8d. | 22 | 43 | 65 |
| 1493 | £14  2s.  5d. | 24 | 46 | 70 |
| 1494 | £15  2s.  3d. | 17 | 37 | 54 |
| 1495 | £12  4s.  1d. | 22 | 45 | 67 |
| 1496 | £5 11s. 10d. | 11 | 41 | 52 |
| 1497 | £14  5s. 10d. | 23 | 44 | 67 |
| 1498 | £19 16s.  1d. | 28 | 62 | 90 |
| 1499 | £23  4s. 11d. | 32 | 59 | 91 |
| 1500 | £18 11s.  0d. | 28 | 64 | 92 |
| 1501 | £13  3s.  1d. | 22 | 76 | 98 |
| 1502 | £19  3s. 10d. | 26 | 62 | 88 |
| 1503 | £21 13s. 11d. | 23 | 56 | 79 |
| 1504 | £18  5s. 10d. | 36 | 23 | 59 |
| 1505 | £16 10s.  5d. | 39 | 43 | 82 |
| 1506 | £28  3s.  8d. | 56 | 52 | 108 |
| 1507 | £28  8s.  2d. | 51 | 48 | 99 |
| 1508 | £28 11s.  5d. | 67 | 42 | 109 |
| 1509 | £20 14s. 10d. | 31 | 28 | 59 |
| 1510 | £9 13s.  7d. | 23 | 23 | 46 |
| 1511 | £6 16s.  3d. | 16 | 28 | 44 |
| 1512 | £12 11s. 10d. | 33 | 29 | 62 |
| 1513 | £15 10s.  8d. | 33 | 7 | 40 |
| 1514 | £22  8s.  0d. | 33 | 8 | 41 |

common earlier in the century,[13] to have levelled off somewhat in the earlier 1490s and then to have moved upward only to fall again after 1500. Increases in the total known indebtedness tend to follow the increase in the total number of known debts (1488, 1498-1500) but the pattern cannot be interpretated closely owing to the structure of debts described in the previous paragraph and the fact that the number of creditors gradually increased over this whole period. By the second decade of the sixteenth century this summary table no longer serves a useful purpose since data become bunched from year to year and within each year.[14] In short, the debt structures were gradually reflecting the new economic and social realities of the town. Those without resources could not long participate in this new era of extensive credit and debt arrangements. That traditional era of popular involvement in credit arrangement still to be found in the 1480s was drawing to a close. The credit system, as revealed through debt structures, would become largely a direct reflection of the major economic actors of the town.

More substance can be given to these changes occurring in the early sixteenth century from the fact that over the first two decades of the sixteenth century transactions lying behind debt pleas are sometimes entered on the court roll record. For petty occupations indebtedness seemed to be endemic. For example, as has been detailed in Chapter 5, the John Barnards, whether two or three and whether designated variously as carpenter, earthman, hayward or sub-bailiff, were claimants in nine debt pleas between 1505 and 1524. But the same family was brought to court by 40 debt claims against them over this time.

At the other extreme, the involvement of most of the wealthier individuals of the town was largely as creditors only. For example, debts were owed to William Dalton, William Kyng, William Moundeford and John Stukeley as follows:

WILLIAM DALTON:[15] 1504: John Couper, butcher; Richard Fawn; John Holme; 1505: William Foster, labourer; Thomas Granger 39s. 11d. ob. q.; John Gybbys 39s. 11d. ob. q. + 30s. + 36s. 8d. + 23s.; Thomas Granger; Richard Gyenessde; Richard West 12s.; 1506: John Asshe junior; John Couper, butcher 2s.; John Elliott; Thomas Granger; John Hedde; John

---

[13] Precise figures are not available owing to the fact debt amounts are rarely entered over the first three quarters of the century and so it is impossible to know when pleas were continued for more than one court. From a count of names, the 1481 data would appear to be typical of earlier decades.

[14] For example, the larger known debt and number of debt figure for 1516 is to be explained by the fact that only a few owed £22 in 11 different debts.

[15] It has not been possible to distinguish the two William Daltons, farmer from merchant, for many of these pleas.

Mayle; Robert Punt; Thomas Sandon and John Wylde; 1507: Henry Gybbys; Robert Whyte, organist; Robert Whyte 2s. for madder and alum; 1508: John Barnard, hayward, 7s. 8d.; 1510: Richard Fisher 3s. 4d.

WILLIAM DALTON, FARMER: 1509: Nicholas Gelly; Richard Grenam; 1512: Thomas Bennet £1; Richard Clerk; John Foster; 1516: John Gybbys 10s. 8d.

WILLIAM DALTON SENIOR: 1511: William Townshende.

WILLIAM DALTON, MERCHANT: 1509: Richard Arnouth 26s. 8d.; William Farthyngton 2s. 6d. for cloth; 1511: Joan Adam, widow, 6s. 8d.; 1513: Thomas Osteler 6s. 8d.; 1514: Robert Hunt for cloth; 1517: William Stukeley; Margaret Stukeley; William Harryson; 1519: William Anys 8s. 4d.; 1520: William Leffyn 4s.; 1521: John Laxton 8s. + 2s. for timber; Richard Kyng 12s.; 1522: Thomas Tryg 10s. + 26s. 8d.; 1523: John Laxton 2s. 8d.; John Laxton and William Townshend; Richard Scot; William Vyntner; 1524: Thomas Mayle 6s. 8d.

WILLIAM KYNG:[16] 1504: John Barnard junior, hayward, 27s. 8d. + 4s. 6d. + 1s. 10d.; Thomas Gybbys 7s. 8d.; 1505: John Bayous 6s. 8d. + 10s.; John Couper, butcher; John Hedde 9s. 6d.; 1506: Thomas Faldyng 10s. 6d.; Robert Greatham; 1507: John Couper 2s. 6d. for fen; John Wynde, gent.; 1508: John Page senior 35s. 8d. + 10s.; 1509: William Farthyngton; 1512: John Laxton for 1 vern; 1515: Thomas Gybbys one comb of barley worth 2s.; Thomas Hancock for *burso* worth 8s.; 1516: Richard Darcy 6s. 8d.; John Nottyngham 9s. 8d.; John Page junior 26s. 8d.; 1517: William Townshend 6s. 8d.; Thomas Wylde for malt; 1519: William Diggby 3s. 8d.; Richard Robyns 26s. 8d. for damage to a fence and for trespassing on William's "front" 3s. 4d.; 1520: William Ibott 8s. 8s. for willows; Richard Robyns 3s. 4d.; Robert West de Offord 10s. for six sheep; 1521: John Este 6s. 8d. for trespassing on grove; Richard Grenam 2s. 6d.; William Kelson; Roger Seman 13s. 4d. for *burso* and 13s. 4d.; 1522: Thomas Lockyngton 1s.; 1524: John Este 6s. 8d.; Dorothy Wynde 3s. 4d.; 1525: Richard Scot 33s. and William Seward 7s. for a cow.

— WITH JOHN BRANDON AS CUSTODIANS OF CORPUS CHRISTI: 1506: William Vyntner 2s.; 1508: William Anys 6s. 8d. for a horse; and they owed to Richard Grene 39s. 11d. ob.

---

[16] William Kyng was sued for only six debts over this period: (1506) as executor of Edward Barre owing an unspecified debt to William Melbourne and Alice, his wife; (1510) owing an unspecified debt to William Townshende and (1517) owing to the same for two ells of cloth; (1521) owing 1s. 2d. to William Kelson; (1522) owing to Robert Pelle and John Holme 3s.

William Kyng's roles as administrator with others, for the most part of guild affairs, is given below to underline the consistency of this wealth-creditor pattern for public administration by this group. This function may also be seen for John Stukeley, below.

— AS CUSTODIAN OF ALL SAINTS: 1506: Roger Cook 7s. 8d.; William Stukeley 6s.

— WITH ROBERT CHANDELER AS CUSTODIANS OF CORPUS CHRISTI: 1507: Joan Gardener, executor of Thomas Gardener; John Mayle 20d. for fen.

— WITH JOHN STUKELEY: 1510: William Benett 4s. 8d.

— WITH WILLIAM DIGGBY AS CUSTODIANS OF ST. GEORGE: 1511: Thomas Faldyng and John Nottyngham.

— WITH JOHN WYNDE AS CUSTODIANS OF CORPUS CHRISTI: 1516: William Cook 16d.; John Stacy 16s. for meadow.

— WITH THOMAS HARRYSON: 1520: they owed 6s. for trespassing of one pig.

— WITH JOHN NOTTYNGHAM AS CUSTODIANS OF CORPUS CHRISTI: 1524: Dorothy Wynde, executor of John Wynde 33s. 4d. + 10s. for one cow; 1525 William Townshend 10s.

WILLIAM MUNDEFORD:[17] 1504: Thomas Bawdwyne 2s. 6d.; Richard Kellnet 3s. 4d.; William Melbourne 1s. 8d.; Robert Nicholas 3s. 4d.; 1505: Margaret Mayle, widow 3s. 4d.; 1506: John Mateshale 2s.; John Bayous 10s. 8d. for fuel; Thomas Fuller, malter; John Couper, butcher 12s.; John Gredley; William Lacy 12s.; William Ussher 10s. 8d.; 1507: Robert Acton, vicar, and John Brandon, executors of John Suell 6s. 8d.; Robert Acton, vicar 5s. 8d. + 4s. for acre and £1 for a house; John Couper, butcher; Thomas Stowe 5s. 4d.; 1508: Richard Beckwell 3s. 4d.; John Courior; John Vyntner 15s. for barley + malt; 1512: William Arnold; 1513: John Gredley 16s. 8d. for sheep + 10s. for *burso*.

— WITH JOHN CLERK AS BAILIFFS: 1506: Thomas Wylde.

JOHN STUKELEY: 1505: Richard Grenam; John Lawman; 1506: John Elliot; 1507: Thomas Mertall, butcher 6s. 8d. for sheep; Thomas Faldyng 35s. for malt + 22s.; 1508: William Gilderdale 6s. 8d. for a horse + 4s. 6d. for sheep; William Ussher 8d.; Joan Lockyngton; John Gybbys 13s. 4d. for malt; Thomas Gybbys; 1509: William Eyt'bye; William Ussher 12d. q. for barley + 39s. 11d. ob. q.; 1510: William Townshend 7d. q. for malt; 1511: Henry Gybbys 6s. 8d. for farm of a cow; Richard Grenam 5s. 5d. for meadow; Henry Gybbys 6s. 8d.; 1513: William Cook 4s. 2d.; 1514: Robert Clerk, alias couper; Robert Dorraunt 13s. 4d.; William Ibott junior 13s. 4d.

— WITH JOHN LAXTON AS CUSTODIANS OF CORPUS CHRISTI: 1507: John Gredley; John Vyntner;

---

[17] Debts were recorded for William Mundeford (1506) 2s. to William Ussher; (1507) 2s. to Richard Beckwell; (1507) owed to Robert Chandeler, executor of John Aylred, chaplain, 39s. 11d. ob. q. three times. If these are in fact three distinct debts, this may represent one tactic for circumventing the 40 shilling rule.

— WITH WILLIAM KYNG: 1510: William Benett 4s. 8d.; Richard West 13s. 4d.

— WITH JOHN LOCKYNGTON AS CUSTODIANS OF CORPUS CHRISTI: 1511: Thomas Page 2s.; William Townshende.

— WITH WILLIAM DIGGBY: 1511: William Dalton, farmer.

— WITH ROBERT NICHOLAS AS FORMER CUSTODIANS OF CORPUS CHRISTI: 1514: Walter Picard 7s. 8d. for willows.

[John Stukeley is dead by 1517 and William Dalton and William Aylred are his executors].

MARGARET STUKELEY, WIDOW OF JOHN STUKELEY: 1518: John Waytman 1s. 3d. (and Margaret owes William Dalton 15s.); 1523: (Margaret owes Dorothy Wynde 39s. 11d. ob.); 1524: Oliver Benett 39s. 11d. ob. q.

There is some evidence that wealthier individuals could be rather cavalier about paying for their purchases. Again, for tradesmen with little extra capital this would provide a further squeeze. Robert Chandeler gives us one example of how an ordinary tradesman could be placed in this position by his wealthier customers. Robert had not been paid for the sale of 20 quarters of barley to William Vyntner in 1507; in the same year Thomas Faldyng owed 8s. for malt and 9s. for a horse and colt and Joan Lockyngton, executor of Thomas Lockyngton, owed £1 and 16s.; 1508: Robert as executor for John Aylred, chaplain, was owed by William Mundeford 39s. 11d. ob. q. In the same year, Robert was owed 3s. for manure that he sold to Robert Nicholas plus 26s. 8d.; Richard Grenam owed 3s. 4d. for meadow; 1509: John Gybbys owed 4s. 8d. anfd 9s. ; 1510: Thomas Ingrave owed 6s. 8d.; 1511: William Mayle and his mother owed 3s. 4d.; 1512: Robert Nicholas again owed to Robert Chandeler 6s. 8d. for trespassing with sheep in Robert's grain; 1513: John Foster owed 10 bushels of barley; 1514: William Hilton and his wife Agnes owed 3s. 4d. and in 1517 John Stevens owed 2s. 4d. Robert was owed money, no doubt from unspecified sales, by John Hedde (1506), Robert Whyte, taylor, (1507), John Kyng (1510) and John Punt (1511). Most of these debtors were wealthier townsmen. Robert Chandeler only had four debts of his own. He owed an unspecified debt to John Lockyngton in 1506, but seems to have become dependent upon Robert Nicholas to whom he owed an unspecified debt in 1508, a £3 tally in 1509 and again 12s. 4d. in 1513.

Another example of a tradesman becoming dependent upon a wealthy client can be seen over 1512-1513 when Richard Brewster had to come to court to recover malt worth 4s. 8d, one quarter of wheat worth 10s. 8d. and nine combs of malt worth £1 all from Nicholas Gelly one of the wealthiest residents of Godmanchester.

William Kelson and William Loveday illustrate further examples of credit and debt profiles for lower income people. It is noticeable, however, that William Kelson reflects largely an involvement with others on his own income level both in his debts and receivables: 1513 Thomas Wylde owes him one bushel of malt; 1517 Thomas Benett owes 3s. 6d.; Thomas Page 22d.; 1519 William Packer owes 11d. for *burso*; 1520 Henry Lane owes 6s. 8d.; William Kyng and Thomas Harryson owe 6s. for one pig; William Kyng owes 14d. and 1527 William Keym owes 1s. for two bushels of malt. William Kelson owed to Henry Barnard 1s. in 1519; John Clapham 4d. for willows he bought. In 1520 with Thomas Harryson they owed 4s. to Thomas Pacy. In 1521 William owes to William Lockyngton four modes of barley; 6s. 8d. to Robert Whyte for damage of a sow and to William Kyng (amount not stated).

1510 William Loveday with Thomas Aplond as guardians of St. Christopher were owed 5s. 4d. from John Kyng for four yards of russet cloth that he had bought. William Loveday owed to John Gybbys one "tone" that he had bought in 1514, and in the same year John Gybbys owed to William five combs of barley and 6s. 8d. In the next year William owed to John Gybbys 1s. for straw that he bought; 1517 John Gredley owed to William 10s. and 1521 William owed to Robert Whyte one comb of barley.

As might be expected, those regional merchants who settled in Godmanchester would continue their traditional commerce. Something of this is reflected in the debt plea profile of the Wylde family. As a family of middling wealth the Wyldes held many receivables from local people but also reflected in their debts a considerable dependence upon others for credit:

WYLDE FAMILY:

| | MONEY OWED TO THEM | THEIR OWN DEBTS |
|---|---|---|
| John: 1505 dead | William Vyntner<br>Thomas Faldyng<br>John Gredley | |
| Thomas: 1506 executor<br>of John | William Vyntner 12s. | |
| Thomas: 1513 | | Thomas & Richard<br>Sandon |
| | John Barnard £1 | John Barnard, 10s. for<br>death of a horse<br>William Kelson, for one<br>bushel of malt |

| | | |
|---|---|---|
| John: 1514 | William Townshend 12s. William Dalton and William Aylred, executors of John Stukeley (no amount) | |
| Thomas: 1517 | | William Kyng for one quarter of malt + one comb of seko |
| John junior: 1520 | | John Laxton 6s. 8d. + 3s. 4d. sowing on his lot; 3s. 4d. for feeding *burci* |
| | 1521 William Ibott 2s. 6d. | |
| John: 1522 | | Richard Lonysdale and Richard Gaylord 1s.; William Goodwyn (no amount) |
| John junior: 1522 | | Thomas Tharnock of Brampton 39s. 11d. ob. q. |
| | 1523 John Garlop 23s. | |
| John senior: 1523 | | Robert Whyte and wife Anna, one quarter of barley 7s. 4d. |
| John and wife Agnes: 1523 | | John Swame de Threplo (no amount) |
| John: 1523 | John Stevens 4s. | |
| John senior: 1524 | | John Hugyl de Potton (no amount) Robert Whyte; |
| John junior: 1526 | Robert Albon, for three sheep, 6s. 8d. | |
| 1527 | | William Ibott, 6s. 4d. for going on the waters |
| | John Stevens 39s. 11d. ob. q. for peas | John May for 20 quarters of malt |

As can be seen above the debts owed by the Wylde's embraced many individuals from beyond the town.

By contrast with the Wylde family, a representative of the gentlemen class, John Wynde, reveals from the appearance of his name in debt pleas that his investment in the local town was for commercial profit. John Wynde held a number of receivables plainly originating in the sale of traditional farm produce. However, the presence of taylors and draper among those owing him money may indicate debts originating in the sale of wool:

John Wynde, gent, sells in 1507 fuel to William Lacy for 6s. 8d. and also to William Ede for 3s. 8d.; 1508 one cow and sheep to John Couper for 33s.; 1512 meadow to John Stacy for 9s. 8d.; 1516 *burso* to William Cook for 2s. In 1516 with William Kyng, they sell meadow to John Stacy for 16s. and also John owed them 18s. for arrears on a house. 1521 John Wynde sold hay to Richard Kyng for 6s. 8d.

In addition, many isolated debts were owed to John: 1507 John Gredley 4d.; William Wright, taylor (no amount); 1508 John Taylor (no amount); William Hunt (no amount); John Couper, butcher, 9s.; Richard Grenam (no amount); John Clerk, draper, 26s. 8d. in 1510; 1511 Richard Lonysdale (no amount); Thomas Gybbys (no amount); 1512 with John Lawe formerly custodians of Corpus Christi, William Diggby owed them 28s. 9d. John Wynde, 1513, was owed 39s. 4d. by William Kyngston; 1516 William Dalton, farmer, 6s. 8d. In 1519 with Robert Kyng, custodians of Corpus Christi, Richard Darcy owed them 6s. 8d.; John Nottyngham owed 9s. 8d. and John Page junior owed 26s. 8d.; in 1519 Henry Gybbys owed 15s. 8d. to John; 1520 John Maye owed 26s. and 3s. 4d. and 1521 Christopher Houghton owed 13s. 4d. In 1522 John is noted as dead. John did in fact incur a few debts himself: 1504, 4s. to William Dalton; 1507 to William Kyng (no amount); 1508 John Taylor 3s. 4d. and to John Laxton (no amount) and in 1516, 39s. 11d. ob. to William Mynsterchambre.

To close this series of considerations on debt pleas, a brief profile of Thomas Pacy may be taken to demonstrate the type of moneys an ordinary townsman would be handling if he were to flourish in the early sixteenth century. There is no evidence to determine whether Thomas Pacy was the son of Agnes Pacy who brewed and retailed ale briefly in the late 1490s. Thomas appears first as clerk for the collector of the farm on Arnyng and West Streets over the years 1508-1511.[18] Like many of the clerks at the time, Thomas then seems to have moved about to seek employment. He was admitted to freedom of the town for only eightpence in 1512; the fact that John Barnard was recorded as owing him a debt in a 1511 court may have encouraged his seeking this status. In any case Thomas withdrew again and was re-admitted without a fine in 1519.

It was from this time that Thomas Pacy gained consistent employment as a clerk. Indeed he was the most important clerk, that is, clerk of the court for twenty years (1524-1548) and clerk for either a collector of the farm or of the view over the same years. These positions seemed to place Thomas in

---

[18] See above, Chapter 1, p. 31.

the position of being able to compete in the commerce of the town. In addition to an unnamed debt owed to him by John Barnard in 1521, Thomas in the same year owed to Richard Robyns 39s. 11d. q. for eight quarters of barley that he had bought; 1523 Thomas owed to John Salmon 10s. for barley; Richard Grene owed 10s. for 14 sheep that he had bought from Thomas; Thomas again owed to Richard Robyns 16s. 4d. in the same year; 1524 Thomas owed to Thomas Tharnock of Brampton for 10 quarters of malt worth 39s. 11d. ob.; 1525 Thomas owed to Thomas Tame of Hunts for one quarter of malt worth 4s. and 1527 Thomas owes 39s. 11d. ob. q. to William Wiseman for five quarters of barley.

This great amount of indebtedness at Godmanchester in the late fifteenth century seems to have occasioned more expeditious legal facilities for the process, that is, the registering of bond or mortgage[19] payment schedules and the securing of the debt by collateral. Such arrangements begin to be entered more frequently[20] in the court rolls of Godmanchester for the 1480s and are scattered over the next three decades. Table 38 provides a summary of these data. The court entry for these bonds serves as a registry and is not a copy of the full legal instrument that would have been drawn up for these cases. In order to illustrate their variety, entries for some of these arrangements are

[19] Traditionally, debts would not have to be secured at Godmanchester owing to the personal acquaintance situation of a local community and especially since debts were only one component of a credit system operating in great part among those on the same economic level, as has been noted above. Elaine Clark has demonstrated graphically the complicated network to be found in this traditional system; see "Debt Litigation in a Late Medieval English Vill," p. 269. R. H. Hilton, *The English Peasantry in the Later Middle Ages*, p. 46, has found this same phenomenon for the West Midlands. Even for more commercial centres in the late fourteenth century, unsecured loans were the practice. See, Britnell, *Colchester*, p. 104. The movement towards securing debts occurred in other parts of the countryside in the late fifteenth century. See, Cicely Howell, *Land, Family and Inheritance in Transition, Kibworth Harcourt*, p. 61.

[20] In the fragmentary rolls of 25 November 1417, there is some detail about a bond. The next reference to a bond only occurs in the court of 6 February 1442 and reference to bonds remained rare over the following decades.

The incidental appearance of these bond agreements for a few years during the longer tradition of tally and debt information supports the *a priori* presumption that these bonds are temporary legal expedients rather than indicaters of novel financial arrangements involving interest and/or usury. On the other hand, it is difficult to draw firm conclusions about this question owing to the fact that the real transaction, whether simply the lending of money or a sale, has been so inconsistently designated in debt entries and never designated in bond entries. With the presence of professional money lenders noted above, it must be presumed that such lenders would be paid for their loans (for descriptions of one method, see Britnell, *Colchester*, p. 108) and would be paid more in times of greater insecurity. In any case, the upshot was much the same as those conditional bonds and common recovery suits well known to scholars of later generations, that is, the land of Godmanchester was being lost to the new professional classes such as merchants.

TABLE 38: BOND PAYMENTS SCHEDULES

| LENDER | BORROWER | SECURITY | TOTAL | SCHEDULE | DATE |
|---|---|---|---|---|---|
| John Lockyngton and John Stukeley | John Barnard | white horse; 3 mares with cart and gear | £1 | by feast of St. Michael | 6 May 1487 |
| John Matthew | William Gardener | messuage | £4 | £1 on feast of St. Martin; £1 at Easter, etc. | 4 September 1488 |
| William Mundeford | William Godwyn | messuage | £8 | on feast of St. Martin next | 10 January 1493 |
| John Ussher | Thomas Faldyng | messuage | 26s. 8d. q. | 13s. 4d. by feast of Exaltation of Cross; 13s. 4d. by feast of St. Martin | 27 June 1493 |
| William Frere and John Lockyngton | John Barnard junior | messuage | 26s. 8d. | 13s. 4d. on feast of St. Martin; 13s. 4d. at Easter | 9 April 1495 |
| John Mayle | William Gonell | messuage | £2 13s. 4d. | 46s. 8d. on feast of St. Thomas, apostle; 46s. 8d. on feast of Purification of the Blessed Virgin Mary | 10 May 1498 |
| Reginald Corby | Thomas Faldyng | messuage | 25s. | 3s. 4d. on feast Pentecost; 6s. 8d. on feast of St. Peter in chains; 15s. on feast of St. Etheldreda | 10 May 1498 |
| John Dey junior | John Foster | all his goods | | 6 quarters of barley at feast of Epiphany; 6½ quarters of barley at feast of St. Martin; 4s. 2d. on the same feast | 20 December 1498 |
| Alice Cave, daughter of John Cave | John Lawman | all his lands | £2 | 20s. on feast of St. Andrew; 20s. on feast of Nativity of St. John, baptist | 14 March 1499 |
| William Basse | John Vincent | messuage | 8 marks | 6s. 8d. on feast of St. Martin; 6s. 8d. on Finding of the Cross; and so forth, until the full amount has been paid | 4 April 1499 |

| Grantor(s) | Grantee(s) | Property | Amount | Terms | Date |
|---|---|---|---|---|---|
| John Gonell | William Godwyn | his property | 16s. 8d. | 16s. 8d. at Michaelmas | 16 May 1499 |
| Thomas Judd | Henry Gybbys | 5 virgates of arable, 3 virgates of leys; 1 cockaral yard | 9s. | 3s. at next court; 3s. on feast of the Assumption; 3s. at Michaelmas | 25 June 1499 |
| John Clerk and Thomas Judd | William Alanson of Godmanchester | 4 Lomys (looms) + all working gears | ? | that he pays debts to Morgroves and to all others of the said town of Cambridge | 8 August 1499 |
| John Garlop, wright | John Dey | all his property | 53s. 4d. | 40s. on feast of St. James; 33s. 4d. on feast of All Saints [this is stroked out and a sign beside it says "void"] | 9 January 1500 |
| John Stukeley | John Stokes, butcher | his property | £2 | 40s. by Michaelmas | 16 July 1500 |
| William Kyng | John Nottyngham | ? | 5 nobles | 10s. at next court; 6s. 8d. at the following court; and so at each court until 5 nobles has been paid | 19 November 1500 |
| John Robyns junior | John Nottyngham | 2 acres of arable | 13s. | at feast of Pentecost | 4 March 1501 |
| John Harforth and Joan Stukeley | William Aylred | messuage + grove | £20 | 20s. on feast of Nativity of St. John, baptist; 20s. on feast of St. Martin; and so forth, until amount is paid | 3 December 1507, but issued on 18 January 1506 |
| ? | Richard West | messuage called "The Horse-shoe" | ? | regular payments | made 16 July 1506 but entered in court 23 September 1507 |
| John Brandon | John Stukeley | orchard | £2 | 40s. at feast of St. Etheldreda next | 20 April 1508 |
| Thomas Priory, Canon of Huntingdon | William Ussher | messuage | £2 13s. 4d. | 4 marks at Christmas | 29 June 1508 |
| John Foster | William Townshend | goods | 25s. | 26s. at feast of St. Peter in Chains; 2s. 6d. at feast of St. Michael | 4 May 1508 |
| William Arnold | John Godwyn | messuage | £2 | 35s. at Christmas 1513; 35s. on feast of Anunciation of the Blessed Virgin Mary | 25 November 1512 |

| Lender | Borrower | Security | Total | Schedule | Date |
|---|---|---|---|---|---|
| John Lawe | William Kelson | messuage | ? | if he pays the debt to John Lawe that is owed, it will be null and void | 11 August 1513 |
| William Mynt | John Stacy | 3 acres and one yard land in Eastfield; 4 acres in Westfield; 1½ acres of fallow | £5 | £5 at feast of St. Peter next | 15 May 1516 |
| Richard Robyns | John Nottyngham | messuage | £5 6s. 8d. | 4 marks by next feast of St. Peter in Chains; 4 marks on feast of St. Martin | 22 December 1518 |
| Richard Robyns / Richard Robyns | John Gybbys / Joan Townshende and Katherine Monyment | property / messuage | £1 | 20s. on vigil of St. Michael / 15s. by feast of St. Michael, otherwise property will be seized | 10 June 1518 / 29 March 1520 |
| William Diggby | John Wylde | ? | ? | 5 quarters of malt at All Saints; 4 quarters of malt at All Saints the following year (1522) | 25 April 1521 |
| John Hugyl de Potton, wheelwright | Thomas Smith | ? | ? | 9s. 4d. before Translation of St. Edward next | 15 September 1524 |
| William Ibott on behalf of Walter Worlych of Potton | Thomas Pacy | ? | ? | 6 quarters of good barley after feast of Epiphany | 15 December 1524 |
| Walter Worlych of Potton | Thomas Pacy and wife Agnes | ? | £2 | 13s. 4d. at feast of St. Michael; 13s. 4d. following until the amount has been paid | 19 December 1527 |
| John Vynter and Thomas Tryg, wardens of Corpus Christi | Robert Punt and Oliver Benett, bind for debt of Richard Scot | ? | £21 5s. | 10s. at feast of Corpus Christi; £20 at Exaltation of Holy Cross; 15s. at the next feast of Corpus Christi | 15 January 1528 |

given in the following list. All of these are of course court orders[21] and in some entries, as the first and fourth below, officials of the town are named in the entry. Entry 11 shows that others than officials could perform the same role. In the second and third entries below, the one messuage of William Godwyn serves as surety for the payment of debts in sequence. Sometimes a gage is mentioned in the most general terms, as in entries five and six below. Entries seven, eight, nine, ten and twelve indicate the various ways by which an individual's livelihood could be laid on the line whether this to be grain, trade implements or simply all one's property.

The Godmanchester bonds dramatize the economic insecurity of the time lurking behind casual debt entries in court rolls. Those who had to place their homes or all their property or working equipment as surety for debt were Alanson, Barnard, Dey, Faldyng, Foster, Gardener and Vincent from those labourers and petty craftsmen of Chapter 5 above. Despite the impossibility of tracing the economic vicissitudes of individuals, the ominous meaning of this process for such a less wealthy group as a whole would appear in sixteenth-century tenant lists. Mortgages also reflected the economic crunch being felt by families of middling wealth, about which more will be said below.

These bonds are still too scattered in relation to the large number of debts to stand by themselves as indicating trends in the shortage of capital. Information from the bonds serve to complement the debt arrangement discussed in previous pages, in particular the efforts of the less wealthy (Corby, Dey, Faldyng, Foster) to obtain credit from their own limited pool of resources. For the most part, however, these bonds refer to the normal debt patterns of their time.

1. William Frost, Thomas Laxton, William Manipenny are given entry to a messuage (of William Gardener) in Arnyng Street, on condition that William Gardener pay to John Matthew £4, that is, 20s. on the feast of St. Martin, 20s. on Easter, etc.—fine 12d. (4 September 1488)
2. William Mundeford is given entry to a messuage formerly William Godwyn in East Street on condition that William Godwyn pays £8 on the feast of St. Martin next—fine 3d. (10 January 1493)
3. William Mundeford surrenders to John Adam of Cambridge and to William Manipenny one messuage in East Street, formerly William Godwyn, under condition that William Godwyn repays John Adam according to a tally £16 — fine 6d. (21 November 1493)

---

[21] This simple, and apparently efficient form of mortgage did not of course involve the actual transfer of the property unless conditions had remained unfulfilled.

4. Thomas Fecas and William Ibott surrender to William Frere and John Lockyngton a messuage of John Barnard junior in Post Street, under condition that John Barnard pays at the feast of St. Martin 13s. 4d. and Easter 13s. 4d.—fine 2d. (9 April 1495)

5. William Gonell receives as gage from John Mayle a messuage in Arnyng Street, on condition that he pays on the feast of St. Thomas, apostle, 46s. 8d. and on the feast of the Purification of Blessed Mary, 46s. 8d. (10 May 1498).

6. Thomas Faldyng obliges himself to pay to Reginald Corby on the feast of Pentecost 3s. 4d. and on the feast of St. Peter in Chains, 6s. 8d. and on feast of St. Etheldreda 15s. and if he fails the bailiffs can distrain his property for 41s. (10 May 1498)

7. John Foster gages to John Dey junior all his goods on condition that John Foster pay six quarters of barley at feast of St. Martin and at the same feast also pays 4s. 2d. (20 December 1498)

8. John Lawman gages to Alice Cave, daughter of John Cave, all his lands on condition that he pays on the feast of St. Andrew 20s. and on the feast of the Nativity of St. John, baptist, 20s. (14 March 1499)

9. William Alanson of Godmanchester, with John Clerk and Thomas Judd, witness and pledge for four Lomys (looms) along with such working gear and all such other stuff that John and Thomas hold, under condition that he pays debts to Morgroves and to all others of the said town of Cambridge (8 August 1499)

10. John Dey gaged to John Garlop, wright, all his property on condition that he pays to John Garlop on the feast of St. James 40s. and on the feast of All Saints 33s. 4d. [this is stroked out and a sign beside it said "void"] (9 January 1500)

11. William Sweetman and William Bloke bond themselves by the judgment of John Ussher, William Kyng, William Taylor of Somersham and Richard Grimsby, John Grimsby and John Ward under bond of 40s. (17 September 1500)[22]

[22] The bond arrangement with outsiders was a well known commercial device from an earlier period. Only one original record of such an arrangement survives among Godmanchester documents. This comes over the date of 26 July 1497 and summarizes as follows: "David Gysselly of Stamford in Lincolnshire county, Thomas William of the same place, William Dygby of Godmanchester, yeoman, John Clerk, yeoman, Richard Stevens of Godmanchester, William Vyntner of Godmanchester, Richard Grene and Thomas Smyth of Godmanchester give a bond of £100 sterling to Richard Gonell alderman of Stamford."

The unique traditional bond arrangement to be found on the court rolls (that is, no. 11) is listed here among the more local mortgage schedules in order to suggest that the differences between these two forms of arrangement may have closed considerably with the shift in the rôle of "outside" capital that accompanied the change in the economic personnel of Godmanchester described earlier in this chapter.

12. John Stacy of his own free will pledges to William Mynt three acres and one yard of land as it lies in East Field, with the crop of the same and four acres of land as it lies in Westfield with the crop of the same, three one-half acres of land being fallow as it lies against the Renell' under the following conditions: that John Stacy pay or cause to be paid unto the said William Mynt or his assignees £5 at feast of St. Peter next coming without any further delay that then this present pledge to be void or else to stand in all strength and continue and the same William Mynt to enjoy the said land and crop to his own use forevermore. (15 May 1516)

The traditional mortgage arrangements for debt were not these short-term mortgage-bond payments but the tally. Since the tally was, in the words of the court and the will, "the custom of Godmanchester," there was no need to enter tallies on the court roll record. Hence, it should be remembered that the use of the tally would have continued over the period of the conditional bond arrangements in the late fifteenth and early sixteenth centuries and that tally arrangements would far outnumber bond entries on the court rolls.

The use of the tally was indicated incidentally in Chapter 4 in the description of wills by Godmanchester people. These wills are the best record of the wide variety of uses of the tally as a credit instrument. For example, in 1495 Thomas Newman left by tallies £2 to his daughter Agnes and 6s. 8d. to John Taylor. In 1505, Thomas Burton left £7 17s. to his wife Agnes from tallies owed by Alan Ravshall and William Farthyng (who was the father of Agnes), very likely the price of a messuage. By her will of 1528 Margery Armyt left a tally in the custody of Thomas Byrde from which one mark per year was to be paid for expenses on the celebration of her anniversary. During the previous year Margery Johnson indicated in her will that she held a tally from her son for a house in East Street and this tally was to supply support to her daughter. Joan Cook also left (1533) a tally for a house worth £8 to her son-in-law John Kyng with annual payments of a mark to her executors "according to the custom of the town" and the last £2 of the tally to be allowed to John for the use of her daughter Alice who was the wife of John Kyng.

For some unknown reason tally arrangements began to be entered more frequently on court rolls during the second quarter of the sixteenth century. One reason for this exceptional recording of tallies on the court roll may have been the increasing role of non-Godmanchester people in the land market, people for whom "according to the custom of the town" would not have so much meaning. In any case Table 39 gives us 70 of these tallies demonstrating, by contrast with the mortgages and bond agreements, where

TABLE 39: TALLIES

| LESSOR | LESSEE | PROPERTY | AMOUNT | DATE |
|---|---|---|---|---|
| John Adam | William Godwyn | messuage | £16 | 21 November 1493 |
| Nicholas Caldecote | Richard Frere | messuage called "The George" | £30 | 15 September 1524 |
| Joan Salmon, widow | Richard Edmund | messuage | £10 | date of tally May 8 1525, and entered in court 23 March 1525 |
| Thomas Gybbys and John Vyntner senior | Nicholas Caldecote | messuage called "The George" | £38 | 27 July 1525 |
| Robert Hygham | John Wright and Henry Barnard | messuage | ? | 14 November 1527 |
| John Manning | Thomas Smyth | messuage | ? | 5 December 1527 |
| Thomas Wylde of Brampton, father of John | John Wylde and wife Anne | all lands in Godmanchester | £8 | 12 February 1528 |
| William Bekke | Thomas Wolfe | messuage, called "Hyhams" + 100 acres | ? | 27 February 1535 |
| Robert Wright | Roland Hawdwyn | 2 messuages | £36 | 28 March 1538 |
| William Dalton, mercer | John Disney senior, miller | ? | £3 | 11 December 1539 |
| James Chamber | Richard Hodgson | messuage | £9 | 7 October 1540 |
| Richard Edmunds | John Ibott | messuage | £9 | 7 October 1540 |
| Thomas Mease of Ramsey | Robert King | messuage called "fantt'y" | £10 13s. 4d. | 7 October 1540 |
| Christopher May | William May | tenement called "The Swan" | £12 | 7 October 1540 |
| William Thong | Thomas Bell | messuage | £7 | 7 October 1540 |
| Thomas Carnaby | John Croft, grocer of London | messuage | £54 | 7 October 1540 |
| Margaret Punt, widow and executor of John Punt | Thomas Punt | messuage + lands | £20 | 7 October 1540 |
| John Byllington | John Small | tenement | 36s. 8d. | 28 October 1540 |
| William Caverley | John Johnson | tenement | £2 | 28 October 1540 |
| John Howson | Briant Relton | close | £5 6s. 8d. | 28 October 1540 |
| John Howson | Richard Clerk | messuage | £5 | 28 October 1540 |
| Steven Garlop | William Maryot | tenement | £8 | 28 October 1540 |
| William Dalton | William Sewster | croft called "le Thecher" | £6 13s. 4d. | 28 October 1540 |

| | | | | |
|---|---|---|---|---|
| William Dalton | William Glover, alias latysar | 3½ acres of arable | 46s. 8d. | 28 October 1540 |
| William Dalton | John Marshall | messuage | £13 | 28 October 1540 |
| Jane Fallmoii, widow | William Grene | tenement | £6 | 28 October 1540 |
| Katherine Hay, widow | Robert Clapthorne | messuage | £3 | 28 October 1540 |
| John Ashton | Christopher Towton | tenement | £4 | 28 October 1540 |
| William Godwyn | John Wessnawe | messuage | £3 6s. 8d. | 11 November 1540 |
| Thomas Woodward | Thomas Kirby | tenement | £8 | 11 November 1540 |
| Margery Armouth | Thomas Garlop | messuage + 54 acres | £28 | 11 November 1540 |
| William Pelman | John Frere | messuage + 37 acres | £18 | 11 November 1540 |
| Richard Gyleman | Richard Edmunds | tenement | £1 13s. 4d. (5 nobles) | 27 January 1541 |
| James Sandforth of Toseland, clerk | Robert King | ? | 46s. 8d. | 17 February 1541 |
| Margaret Dorraunt, widow | William Dorraunt | tenement | 33s. 4d. | 17 February 1541 |
| William Pennyson, knight | Thomas Tryge | 34½ acres | £10 10s. 0d. | 31 March 1541 |
| William Pennyson, knight | Richard Cook | 2 tenements | £7 | 31 March 1541 |
| William Pennyson, knight | Henry Frere | messuage | £10 | 31 March 1541 |
| William Woodward | Henry Barnard | messuage | £5 | 31 March 1541 |
| William May | John Disney junior | messuage | £13 | 31 March 1541 |
| William Dalton | Alice Mayle, widow | 60 acres + 5 acres swath | £11 | 14 July 1541 |
| John Hawkyn | John Frere | messuage | £11 6s. 8d. | 11 August 1541 |
| Giles Ireland | Richard Glover | messuage | £8 | 15 September 1541 |
| Walter Than'y of Stanton | William Growne | messuage | £8 | 15 September 1541 |
| William Pennyson | Robert Croft | tenement | £40 | 15 September 1541 |
| William May | Thomas Osteler | tenement | 6s. 8d. | 5 October 1541 |
| William Seward | Robert Croft | orchard | £5 | 6 December 1541 |
| John Mays | Simon Wellys | messuage | £7 | 26 January 1542 |
| Roger Awdwyn | William Everard | tenement + 30 acres + 3 acres meadow | £5 13s. 4d. | 9 March 1542 |
| William Kingston | Robert Roysley, alias Staughton | messuage + 6 acres leys | £20 | 11 May 1542 |
| John Sandon | Robert Sandon | tenement | £12 13s. 4d. | 22 June 1542 |
| Robert Pelle | William Cook | tenement | £4 | 24 August 1542 |
| William Dalton | Robert Massy | part of a vacant plot | £14 | 26 October 1542 |
| William Cook | William Pelle | | 23s. 4d. | 26 October 1542 |

| Lessor | Lessee | Property | Amount | Date |
|---|---|---|---|---|
| John Clerk, taylor | Edmund Peyntor | tenement | £2 | 16 November 1542 |
| Thomas Lovell, executor of Alice Lovell | Thomas Pacy | messuage | £13 6s. 8d. | 4 May 1543 |
| William Abram junior | Richard King | shop | 16s. 8d. | 4 May 1543 |
| Thomas Pacy | Thomas Lovell | messuage | £13 6s. 8d. | 29 November 1543 |
| Joan Pelman | William Crowe | messuage + close | £9 13s. 4d. | 6 December 1543 |
| John Manning | William Manning | messuage | £6 13s. 4d. | 5 June 1544 |
| William Leffyn | William Godwyn and Alice Arnold, singlewoman | tenement | £6 | 26 June 1544 |
| Robert Kyng | Henry Dawson | messuage called "Greyhound" | £9 4s. 8d. | 11 September 1544 |
| Thomas and John Granger | Thomas Whitlock | tenement | £5 13s. 4d. | 11 September 1544 |
| John Dalton | Robert Chertsey | messuage called "The George" | £3 6s. 8d.[a] | 7 May 1545 |
| Richard Wynt | Richard Hodgson | messuage | £6 13s. 4d. | 30 July 1545 |
| John Godwyn | William Alan | tenement | £11 | 22 October 1545 |
| John Osteler, labourer | Thomas Bennet | tenement | 30s. | 22 October 1545 |
| William Greatham | James Payet | 10 acres + 3x 1½ acres meadow | 36s. 8d. | 22 October 1545 |
| Richard Greneam | John Nelson | messuage | £6 6s. 8d. | 22 October 1545 |
| Richard Brown | John Morgan | tenement | 53s. 4d. | 25 February 1546 |
| Agnes, Joan and Margery, daughters of Henry Wood | Edmund Gybbys | messuage | £13 6s. 8d. | 18 March 1546 |
| Thomas Freman | William Freman | messuage | £5 | 28 May 1546 |
| Richard Prior | Steven Prior | messuage + 20 acres | £11 | 9 December 1546 |
| Thomas Tryg junior | John Ede | messuage + 30 acres | £10 | 9 December 1546 |
| John Hawdwyn | Thomas Herdman | messuage | £12 | 9 December 1546 |
| Thomas Bennet | Robert Geme (Grene?) | tenement | £4 10s. | 27 January 1547 |
| Richard Hodgson | Richard Chamber | tenement | £4 6s. 8d. | 31 March 1547 |
| John Morgan | Richard Borowe | messuage | £2 | 17 November 1547 |
| Richard Prior | Steven Prior son of Richard | messuage | £11 | 26 July 1548 |
| Thomas Tryge | James Payet | close | £6 13s. 4d. | 18 October 1548 |

[a]  This amount is still owed to John Dalton for "The George" and is not the actual value of the property.

adequate credit seems to have been assured. Not surprisingly, the vast majority of these tallies involve the more substantial people of the market.

Although these 70 rentals are largely for one generation, they are still far from a full record of the land market if one assumes a tally behind every property sale. Furthermore, as evidence for property values, tallies must be employed with caution. As has already been noted in Chapter 4, the terms "tenement" and "messuage" are not distinguished with any consistency. Occasionally, as with the messuage let to William Godwyn (£16), the two messuages let to Robert Hawdwyn (£36), the messuage let to John Croft (£54) and the messuage let to Robert Croft (£40), the tally must have included more than the normal town property with its buildings. In other instances the messuage complicates the value of appurtenant arable and meadow. If we were to assume the messuages let with field property were worth £10, the 54 acres let by Margery Armouth, the 30 acres arable plus six acres meadow let by William Kingston and the $34\frac{1}{2}$ acres let by William Pennyson, squire, seem to be valued at 6s. or more. But by the same calculation the 37 acres let by William Pelman are worth about 4s. 4d. per acre. Where no messuages were involved, the 60 acres of arable and five acres of meadow let by John Hawkyn were worth 3s. 6d. per acre, the ten acres arable and four and one half acres meadow let by William Greatham were worth 2s. per acre but the three and one half acres let by William Dalton were worth more than 13s. per acre. One can never be certain what cash might have passed hands prior to the tally or what important elements of the transfer the clerk may have omitted from the brief court roll registry.

Nevertheless, these tallies do serve to complement the information in the previous pages. Wealthy outsiders like Nicholas Caldecote and Robert Croft would pay around £40 for properties in the town of Godmanchester. About one dozen messuages in Table 39 were each worth £8 to £11. One-half as many messuages were worth £5 to £7. There was a third group of poorer tenements or messuages identified with petty craftsmen and labourers:[23] John Jonson (£2), Robert Clapthorne (£3), Christopher Towton (£4), John Wessnawe (£3 6s. 8d.), Richard Edmunds (£1 13s. 4d.), William Dorraunt (33s. 4d.), Henry Barnard (£5), Thomas Osteler (6s. 8d.), William Cook (£4), Edmund Peyntor (£2) Thomas Benett (30s.), John Morgan (£2 13s. 4d.); the one shop was worth 16s. 8d.

## C. THE TENURIAL TRANSFORMATION

The last two chapters can be brought into summary focus through the tenurial transformation at Godmanchester. List of farm rent payments

---

[23] Again, the majority of these were agreements among those of a similar level of wealth.

provide the information for this summary. Farm rent payments were upon
land and did not include labour and capital resources of the town. But data
obtainable from those other assessments of the time, lay subsidies, and from
the wills as the most detailed inventories of goods available, merely confirm
that land remained the main basis of wealth.

In Chapter 2 the method for deriving the acreage of property held in the
fields and town of Godmanchester has already been described. This method
is here extended to scattered farm rental lists surviving for the two generations and more after the 1480s: 1533 and 1552 for Arnyng Street, 1529 for
West Street and 1554 for East Street.[24]. This method is further extended to
the 1279 Hundred Roll although this requires a description too complex for
full illustration here.[25]

In order to provide a backdrop for the changes that have already taken
place by the fifteenth century Table 40 brings together the tenurial spread on
all Godmanchester streets in 1279. Despite peculiarities to be found for each
street, the remarkable feature of the 1279 tenurial picture was the comparative uniformity of properties held by the majority of tenants. This "family
economy," as it has been described in a previous study, determined that for
three streets some fifty percent of the property was held in units of 20, 30,
or 40 acres. Another 20 to 30 percent was held in units between 11 and 20
acres. If the large blocks of 204 acres held by Merton on East Street were
removed from calculations for this street, all four streets would be found to
have this same pattern of concentration.

By 1485, as Table 41 indicates, those holding property in the 11 to 20 acre
group had practically disappeared, except for Post Street where trade related
enterprise allowed more tenants to retain these holdings. Moreover, when
guild properties and shifting fortunes of petty craftsmen are taken into
consideration within this tenant range, there are not enough tenants to

---

[24] See Appendix 3.

[25] In a study of the layout of Godmanchester buildings and fields, now planned as a joint
endeavour with an archaeologist, field expert and others, it will be demonstrated that the
listing of messuages in the 1279 Hundred Roll can be broken up along the lines of the four
streets of the town. As H. J. M. Green has indicated (*Godmanchester*, [Cambridge, 1977],
p. 32), by the end of the thirteenth century dwellings extended beyond the limits of the four
streets of the town, and in particular extended to the south along London Road. These units
beyond the town, as well as small units of land held by outsiders, were among the more than
100 entries listed at the end of the Hundred Roll. Nearly all of these were smallholdings. For
the purpose of comparing the units held "on the streets" at various times, these units beyond
the streets have been omitted from the 1279 calculation in the following tables. For this
reason, the total number of 1279 small holdings (below five acres) is not as large in the
analysis of this chapter as indicated above in Chapter 2, p. 42, nor is the analysis of the 1279
smallholding structure intended to be complete for the 1279 period.

TABLE 40: THE TENURIAL SPREAD ON GODMANCHESTER STREETS IN 1279

| ACRES | POST | | | WEST | | | EAST | | | ARNYNG | | |
|---|---|---|---|---|---|---|---|---|---|---|---|---|
| | Tenants | Total Acreage | % | Tenants | Total Acreage | % | Tenants | Total Acreage | % | Tenants | Total Acreage | % |
| 1-5 | 26 | 43 | 4 | 13 | 23 | 2 | 47 | 107.5 | 8 | 25 | 68 | 6 |
| 6-10 | 12 | 98 | 8 | 16 | 122 | 9 | 12 | 77 | 5 | 17 | 122 | 11 |
| 11-20 | 24 | 384 | 31 | 22 | 334 | 26 | 36 | 398.5 | 29 | 17 | 229 | 19 |
| 21-30 | 8 | 206 | 17 | 10 | 254 | 20 | 7 | 175.5 | 13 | 7 | 171 | 15 |
| 31-50 | 9 | 377 | 31 | 10 | 405 | 32 | 5 | 206.5 | 15 | 12 | 464 | 39 |
| over 50 | 2 | 114 (54, 60) | 9 | 2 | 141 (65, 76) | 11 | 1 | 93 | 7 | 2 | 114 (52, 60) | 10 |
| over 100 | – | – | – | – | – | – | 2 | 320 | 23 | – | – | – |
| TOTALS | 81 | 1,222 | – | 73 | 1,279 | – | 110 | 1,378 | – | 80 | 1,179 | – |

TABLE 41: THE COMPARATIVE TENURIAL SPREAD ON INDIVIDUAL GODMANCHESTER STREETS

Tenurial Spread on Arnyng Street

| ACRES | 1279 | | | 1485 | | | 1533 | | | 1552 | | |
|---|---|---|---|---|---|---|---|---|---|---|---|---|
| | Tenants | Total Acreage | % | Tenants | Total Acreage | % | Tenants | Total Acreage | % | Tenants | Total Acreage | % |
| 1-5 | 25 | 68 | 6 | 15 | 24 | 2 | 16 | 28 | 3 | 13 | 23 | 2 |
| 6-10 | 17 | 122 | 11 | 5 | 37 | 3 | 6 | 45 | 5 | 6 | 69 | 6 |
| 11-20 | 17 | 229 | 19 | 6 | 98 | 9 | 5 | 74 | 9 | – | – | – |
| 21-30 | 7 | 171 | 15 | 2 | 58 | 5 | 1 | 22 | 3 | – | – | – |
| 31-50 | 12 | 464 | 39 | 12 | 556 | 48 | 2 | 90 | 11 | 8 | 309 | 26 |
| over 50 | 2 | 114 (52, 62) | 10 | 3 | 238 (67, 75, 96) | 21 | 4 | 254 (56, 61.5, 67.5, 69) | 30 | 5 | 335 (57, 60, 68, 81, 89) | 31 |
| over 100 | | | | 1 | 133 | 12 | 3 | 334 (108, 110, 116) | 39 | 3 | 411 (112, 140, 150) | 35 |
| TOTAL | 80 | 1,236 | | 44 | 1,144 | | 37 | 847 | | 35 | 1,147 | |

The Tenurial Spread on East Street

| ACRES | 1279 | | | 1485 | | | 1554 | | |
|---|---|---|---|---|---|---|---|---|---|
| | Tenants | Total Acreage | % | Tenants | Total Acreage | % | Tenants | Total Acreage | % |
| 1-5 | 47 | 107.5 | 8 | 25 | 61 | 4 | 14 | 25 | 2 |
| 6-10 | 12 | 77 | 5 | 10 | 71 | 5 | 1 | 7 | .5 |
| 11-20 | 36 | 398.5 | 29 | 6 | 84 | 6 | 2 | 24 | 2 |
| 21-30 | 7 | 175.5 | 13 | 6 | 155 | 11 | 2 | 46 | 3 |
| 31-50 | 5 | 206.5 | 15 | 7 | 248 | 17 | 4 | 193 | 13.5 |
| over 50 | 1 | 93 | 7 | 7 | 447 (54.5, 55, 58, 62.5, 69, 73, 75) | 31 | 7 | 557 (66, 70, 77, 79, 80, 92, 95) | 39 |
| over 100 | 2 | 320 (116, 204) | 23 | 3 | 370 (98, 104, 168) | 26 | 3 | 571 (153, 208, 210) | 40 |
| TOTALS | 110 | 1,378 | | 62 | 1,436 | | 33 | 1,422 | |

## The Tenurial Spread on West Street

| ACRES | 1279 | | | 1485 | | | 1529 | | |
|---|---|---|---|---|---|---|---|---|---|
| | *Tenants* | *Total Acreage* | *%* | *Tenants* | *Total Acreage* | *%* | *Tenants* | *Total Acreage* | *%* |
| 1-5 | 13 | 23 | 2 | 17 | 35.5 | 3 | 10 | 19 | 1 |
| 6-10 | 16 | 122 | 9 | 7 | 58 | 6 | 8 | 63 | 5 |
| 11-20 | 22 | 334 | 26 | 4 | 55.5 | 5 | 6 | 82 | 6 |
| 21-30 | 10 | 254 | 20 | 4 | 97 | 9 | 4 | 99 | 7 |
| 31-50 | 10 | 405 | 32 | 6 | 214.5 | 21 | 9 | 376 | 29 |
| over 50 | 2 | 141 | 11 | 6 | 483.5 | 46 | 4 | 244 | 19 |
| over 100 | – | (65, 76) | | 1 | 107 | 10 | 4 | 437 | 33 |
| TOTALS | 73 | 1,279 | | 47 | 1,051 | | 45 | 1,320 | |

## The Tenurial Spread on Post Street

| ACRES | 1279 | | | 1485 | | |
|---|---|---|---|---|---|---|
| | *Tenants* | *Total Acreage* | *%* | *Tenants* | *Total Acreage* | *%* |
| 1-5 | 26 | 43 | 4 | 56 | 80 | 8 |
| 6-10 | 12 | 98 | 8 | 9 | 63 | 7 |
| 11-20 | 24 | 384 | 31 | 17 | 241 | 26 |
| 21-30 | 8 | 206[a] | 17 | 2 | 53 | 6 |
| 31-50 | 9 | 377 | 31 | 6 | 245 | 26 |
| over 50 | 2 | 114 | 9 | 2 | 138 | 14 |
| | | (54, 60) | | | (68, 70) | |
| over 100 | – | – | – | 1 | 122 | 13 |
| TOTALS | 81 | 1,222 | | 93 | 942 | |

[a] This enumeration is no doubt too low since some of the 100 and more tenants, mostly smallholders, unable to be identified on streets in the 100 Rolls are actually listed after regular Post Street entries.

suggest a surviving group as such, again except for Post Street. On the two more "rural" streets, that is Arnyng and West, the process had gone farther in so far as an identifiable group with properties between 21 and 30 acres had to all intents and purposes disappeared in 1485. The process had also gone further for the six to ten acre group on these two rural streets. Rather less property had been held within the six to ten acre range on either East or Post Street in 1279, so changes there by the late fifteenth century were not dramatic.

That capacity for labourers, retailers and other petty occupations to retain small units of property as described in Chapter 5 explains the certain degree of concentration still remaining among the tenants of smallest units. How-ever, since it is impossible to identify with any street some hundred tenants appended to the 1279 record and for the most part holding only an acre or less, comparative observations for the 1279 and 1485 records cannot be made for tenants under five acres. The observations made in this paragraph may be summarized in terms of property control in the town. On West Street, those holding property under 31 acres had 57% of all property in 1279, 23% by 1486; on Arnyng Street it was 51% in 1279, 19% in 1485, on East Street, 55% in 1279 and 26% in 1485, on Post Street, 60% in 1279 and 47% in 1485.

The group of tenants holding property between 31 and 50 acres was maintained to a considerable degree on all streets by 1485. Very possibly this 31 to 50 acre range represented the most active and optimum property units over the hundred years after the Black Death. Such may be indicated by the fact that family names for this group were for the most part older families of the town.

However, by the late fifteenth century the viability of property units of this size was being threatened as is indicated by the decline in numbers on Post Street and West Street. While this group actually had increased in numbers and held more property by the late fifteenth-century date on Arnyng and East Streets this increase had taken place in the upper range of the group. In short, by the 1480s the equilibrium in the 31 to 50 acre holdings was more apparent than real and could no longer be maintained as the optimum level for husbandry units. This can be seen by the thrust towards larger units, those indicated in Table 41 as "over 50" acres. In terms of the percentage of property held, this latter group had doubled on Arnyng Street, tripled on East Street and quadrupled on West Street. Post Street had not changed although the fact that Post Street residents held 25% less property in 1485 than 1279 may explain the difference. Furthermore, by 1485 the 31 to 50 acre group had moved upward in so far as nearly all tenants of this group on Arnyng and East Streets now held properties in the 40 acre range while on

West Street few held in either the 30 or 40 acre range but many more now held in the 50 acre range.

When one looks at the individual property holders from 40 to 90 acres it is clear that their variety does not entitle this range of tenants to consideration as one landed "group." Rather, it was the common commercial endeavours of these property holders that had become more significant than the size of their land units. Just as many in the middling group of 30 or 40 acres had apparently maintained their property by subsidiary commercial activity in the fifteenth century, so from the late fifteenth-century holdings of 50 acres and more could only be sustained by commerce. The capacity of this group of "middling tenants" to obtain and retain properties is another side of the entrepreneurial story already told in Chapter 5.

To summarize briefly here, in the late fifteenth century those major commercial occupations in Appendix 5 can be seen associated with properties of the middling range: Bailey (72 acres), Basse (43 acres), Bould (37 acres), Brewster (38 acres), Cokman (32 acres), Faldyng (33 acres), Gybys (68 acres) and Manipenny (43 acres). Into the sixteenth century, the greater concentration of commercial activities to be seen in Appendix 4 was accompanied by larger concentrations of wealth as with the 47 acres of Henry Frere, 46 acres of Robert Stoughton on Arnyng Street (1552) and the 92 acres by Alice, widow of William Mayle (1554) although it is difficult to obtain a coincidence for many rentals and occupations in the skimpy sixteenth-century series. The lay subsidies are more profitable records for this late period, as has already been noted, showing food traders with substantial taxes indicative of large holdings in the 1520s (Brandon £17, Disney £10, Pelle £26, Holme £5, Lorydan £5, Steven £6, West £13, Monyment £7); others were improving (Boleyn £5 in 1524 and £10 by 1540s; Benett £5 in 1523, £8 10s. by 1540s); among more recent taxpayers by the 1540s several were paying £5 in taxes (Massey, Mayle, Osteler), while Henry Frere paid £13 and Hawdwyn £10 by the later date.

Although other commercial activities are less well represented than food trades in the records the pattern is true for these also, as with the 36 acres held by the late fifteenth century by the artificer Garlop and the 40 acres by the goldsmith Diggby four decades later. For some with only a brief flurry in the food trade, success could be found in other occupations. Such was the case for clerks such as of Thomas Benett and Thomas Pacy (41 acres) who were able to obtain full time clerical posts.

With farming so undergirded by commerce, small wonder that the term "husbandman" never became common in the records of Godmanchester. That the term had some traditional status is indicated by its application in the second quarter of the fifteenth century to some of the more prominent townsmen: John Copegray, Thomas Dorraunt, William Fynche, Thomas Matthew and John Porter. During subsequent generations the term was only employed in records when a specific distinction was required. Over the well documented years of the late fifteenth century the term is to be found only three times. There was nothing unique among farmers about the John Barnard, husbandman, who had six acres on West Street, the John Corby on Arnyng Street, husbandman, who had seven acres and the John Garlop on Post Street who had six and one-half acres, except that in each instance there were individuals with the same surname and first name who were not cultivating land as their designated occupations.

At least one dozen uses of the descriptive "husbandman" can be found in the second quarter of the sixteenth century. Nine of these names are old families of the town: Este, Frere, Gybbys, Mayle, Pelle, Punt, Smyth, Upchurche and Vyntner. All of these successful landholders may have shared with the Tudor parliament of the time the concept of the role of the farmer as the backbone of the nation. Seven of these names appear in wills (Arnold, Este [2], Mayle, Pelle, Punt, Vyntner) indicating perhaps a traditional pride in the descriptive. It was still useful in records, of course, to distinguish John Frere, husbandman, from William Frere, glover. But these husbandmen were also among those already noted as involved in commerce. Small wonder, then, that those statutes of early Tudor government, based upon an obsolete ideal of modest holdings as self sustaining could find little practical implementation at Godmanchester.

The "middle class" created by economic events at Godmanchester with one foot on the land and the other in commerce was abetted by family property arrangements. In every instance where information about the disposition of wealth through women is available among wills for this middling group, such disposition is one factor in an improving tenurial wealth situation. For example, John Brandon who died without a family had a £17 assessment in the 1523 Lay Subsidy and by his will of 1528 would appear to have left his wealth to Alice West, one of his executors. Alice West's husband, Richard, came to hold over 100 acres. When Alice died as a widow in 1532 without children from Richard, she left valuable plate and other items to the wealthy Richard Robyns. William Stodale, one of the wealthier townsmen in the 1480s with 70 acres, died in 1494 without sons and left his property to his one daughter Margaret. Margaret married John Punt who would be recognized as one of the wealthiest taxpayers (£18) in the 1520s. The increasing wealth of Richard and William Mayle over the second quarter of the sixteenth century was in part to be explained by the bequest of houses and valuable movables from their mother Margaret (Jonson by her second marriage) in her will of 1528.

The concern of mothers and wives for the success of their families was but one facet of a whole family network system. For example, marriage alliances tied together in one way or another the families of Cook, Dalton, Grene, Gybbys and Kyng. Some salient samples of the evidence are as follows. Joan Cook, widow, willed her house to John Kyng in 1533. John Kyng had married Alice, Joan Cook's daughter. William Dalton's daughter Elizabeth Dalton married Robert Kyng and by his will of 1541 Dalton left a building to Elizabeth. Parts of William Dalton's wealth had in fact come from Robert Kyng's father William. For, in 1530 William Dalton had been witness to the will of William Kyng and had bequeathed the residue of his property. Richard Grene left to his son George the prominent building with the "sign of the Dolfyn." George Grene had been affianced to Dorothy Kyng. Richard Grene's other daughter Elizabeth had married Henry Gybbys. There is also detailed evidence from wills for marriages among the families of Awdwen (Hawdwyn), Clerk, Monyment and Vyntner. The Granger and Frere families also intermarried.

In short, whether it was between older families, newer residents and older resident families, newer residents and more recent resident families, the middle group at Godmanchester had quickly bound themselves together by family ties during the rapid changes of the early Tudor period.

In time, of course, the very success of some of its members would destroy the coherency of the Godmanchester "middle class." That there was no coherent wealthy corps to take its place may have prevented this from happening more quickly. As early as the 1480s the wealthy Aylred family, that is with more than 100 acres, had begun to stand aside from marriage in the town and involvement with local government as jurors. John Wynde, gentleman, who clearly lived in the town in the early sixteenth century, as did his widow from some two decades after his death, did not become involved at all in the government of the town. This phenomenon was abetted towards the mid sixteenth century as the lines dividing gentlemen, wealthy merchants and even yeoman began to separate these classes from more local groups. But this question can only be properly pursued during the period after the chronological scope of this study. The will of Henry Dawson of April 1555, for example, shows how this family had moved beyond the local scene. By this will Henry left monies to daughters of his sisters who were in Baslow, Derby, to one of his brothers John Dawson of St. Neots and to this brother's son Henry of Bedford.

The middling tenurial group, roughly interpreted as over 30 and under 100 acres, held most of the property by 1485 and retained some 50% through the 1530s and the 1550s. This fact would seem to explain the difficulty in discerning any great shift in the governing power of Godmanchester despite the revolutionary shifts in property ownership. Jurors were co-opted infrequently from the salaried professional corps. The corps of those with uniquely concentrated roles as bailiffs, coroners and other leading posts did indeed continue to be identified with most major landholders: John Frere, Henry Frere, Richard Robyns, Robert Stoughton and John Vyntner—as with William Aylred and John Laxton in the late fifteenth century. But their numbers were not large. Furthermore, a few individuals who clearly were not the wealthiest in the town—John Betrych, William Diggby, John Godwyn, John Lockyngton, William Mounford, William Townshend— also had careers as main officials.

Most of the jurors, then, continued to come from townsmen of the middling wealth group. There were an increasing number of tenants who served as jurors but never became leading officials, except for the occasional stint as constables. In the late fifteenth century a few people can be identified in this position (Augustine Arnold, John Bonsay, John Bould, William Suell) but the number increased into the sixteenth century: John Brandon, Richard Cook, John Disney, John Est, John Granger, William Granger, John Hogan, Thomas Lockyngton, William Loveday, William Malden, Edmund Maryot, John Nelson, John Nottingham, Thomas Pacy, William Richmond and Richard Scot. Many of these never attained considerable wealth and indeed were declining relative to those in an upward mobility position. On the other hand, those in the latter position did tend to become bailiffs and coroners as their wealth moved them out of the middling group. Examples of this were John Armyt, John Boleyn, William Herdman and John Page. In short, we may be witnessing here something of a stagnation of the role of jurors and the appearance of control by the wealthiest elite of the town. But confirmation of this trend is not possible within the chronological limits of this volume. In fact, the full confirmation for this evolution may only appear with the incorporation of Godmanchester as a borough in 1604.[26]

Despite the centrifugal forces internal to the middling group at Godmanchester over the first half of the fifteenth century, some sense of solidarity among the middling group must have been sustained by the increasingly formidable power of a few wealthy landowners. If one were to exclude Merton Priory on East Street as wielding little governmental influence in the town, even by 1485 those with more than 100 acres did not hold much more than ten percent of the wealth of the town. Furthermore, in many cases the actual property held in 1485 was not so much over 100 acres as to become a "class apart" from tenants of 70 acres and more. However, by the second

---

[26] For a few comparative comments on earlier incorporations, see further, "7. Conclusion."

quarter of the sixteenth century evidence available for Table 41 shows several tenants far outstripping fellow townsmen in the size of their holdings and these veritable magnates of the town came to hold a proportion of town lands only some ten percent or more less than all the major middling group taken together.

Some of the tenants most outstanding for their success in engrossing holdings at Godmanchester during the second quarter of the sixteenth century can be further identified. The 1554 rental for East Street shows that, in addition to the 210 acres associated with the parish church (the 168 acres in the parsonage farm, that is, formerly the Priory of Merton, plus 40 acres held of the vicarage), John Shepherd, Lawrence Wellered and Luke Ronstall were jointly assessed for 210 acres "for the chancery land, church land, guilds' land, lamp lands and bellman's lands." None of these three tenants appear in the Lay Subsidy lists for the 1540s. Thomas Tryce with more than 153 acres on the East Street listing does appear to be a resident of the town. He was no doubt the "Thomas Tryse of Brampton" who had purchased liberty as recently as 1540 for 11s. 8d.

The Arnyng Street rental for Michaelmas 1552 identifies Edmund Powlter paying a farm rent for 140 acres and Robert Croft paying for 159 acres. Powlter only appears on the scene in the 1550s. Robert Croft was noted as paying £15 (1545) to the lay subsidies of Godmanchester. William Aylred who had acquired 112 acres by 1552 was from an old Godmanchester family. Without farm rent lists for the other two streets it is impossible to identify the exact holdings for the families of Richard Robyns (105 acres in 1529), William Kyng (135 acres in 1529), John Frere (105 acres in 1529), William Sewster (108 acres in 1533) and Slow (110 acres in 1533). Nor can the acreage be discussed for Thomas Dally who paid £20 to the lay subsidy of 1542 and Nicholas Sewster (20s. fine for liberty in 1549) who paid £20 to the Godmanchester lay subsidy on 1545.

For those familiar with early sixteenth-century economic history it will come as no surprise to discover that the boom in the wool trade was the foundation for the comparative explosive growth in the landholdings of a few tenants at Godmanchester. From the Huntingdonshire returns for the Poll Tax on sheep in 1549[27] can be seen listed under Godmanchester William Sewster with 194 sheep on the commons, 60 wethers and 91 ewes at Stukeley, Robert Croft with 120 sheep on the commons as well as Thomas

[27] The collectors' accounts for Huntingdonshire are under the Public Record Office E179/122/146. The analysis of these accounts by M. W. Beresford ("The Poll Tax and Census of Sheep, 1549," *The Agricultural History Review*, 2 [1954] 22-28) have been found useful as a background for the following two paragraphs.

Tryce with 320 sheep on the commons and 60 sheep in the hathe at Wytton. Nicholas Sewster must have been assessed early in 1549 and before he purchased the liberty of Godmanchester, for in this Poll Tax Nicholas was entered under Great Gransden, with 183 sheep on the commons of that village and only 50 sheep in Godmanchester.

While these Poll Tax data illustrate that the new wealth of Godmanchester looked upon pasture anywhere as the base for their enterprise and might be prone to move their residences with fresh opportunities, taken in the wider context of this chapter these Poll Tax data also underline the fact that most of those new residents from the region as well as those older residents of Godmanchester who had thrived in the early sixteenth century concentrated their resources in the town. Although sheep had long been important in the economy of Godmanchester,[28] there is no reason to believe that the Huntingdonshire commissioners were less than thorough. Tillage remained the foundation of Godmanchester's wealth. When the bottom fell out of the cloth export markets of the sixteenth century, the future of Godmanchester would rest more securely in the hands of the traditional freemen, the Frere's, Robyns and their associates.

---

[28] See *A Small Town*, pp. 101-116.

# 7

# Conclusion

At least three quite distinct social and economic structures are revealed in the records of Godmanchester from the thirteenth to the sixteenth centuries. What has been called "the family economy" prevailed around 1300. That is to say, wealth centred about household units and needs for individual family members dominated the land market. While the contractual compulsion of tenants was limited to farm payment rents and there were wide disparities between different levels of wealth, there was a remarkable comparability among tenants of the same level of wealth. Intermarriage and subsequent family networks served to maintain this comparable wealth among villagers. In consequence, such engrossing of property that was possible tended to remain a phenomenon during one stage only of the life cycle giving place to the comparable household[1] over the longer term. Since the Godmanchester family economy was presented in detail in an earlier study[2] further summary remarks would not seem to be necessary here.

By the last quarter of the fifteenth century, families shared the economic and social spotlight with secondary institutions. Every street in the town boasted its almshouse and its favourite guild. Every street in the town featured a series of brewing and retailing outlets. The concentration of petty craftsmen on St. Giles Lane is only one geographical reference to the tendency towards communal commercial settlements. Town leadership now lay in the hands of an official corps rather than the unique individuals of earlier generations. Custom requirements of representation by streets had also generated common patterns of participation.

---

[1] The brilliant thesis of David Herlihy, *Medieval Households* (Cambridge, Mass., 1985), suggests a framework of analysis for this earlier Godmanchester society.

[2] See *A Small Town*. Since the publication of this volume several Godmanchester records that were in private hands have become known. Among these is a list of tenants on Post Street, ca. 1300. In a recent article ("The Land Market at Godmanchester c. 1300," *Mediaeval Studies*, 50 [1988] 311-332), this Post Street list is placed in a land market context with the 1279 Hundred Roll and records from the second quarter of the fourteenth century.

Records surviving for Godmanchester from the mid fourteenth to the mid fifteenth century are too few and scattered to provide a precise chronology for these developments. Obviously some of these institutions, such as the consumer trade pattern lying behind the ale industry, would have existed from the thirteenth century. Local guilds were an old phenomenon in the religious sociology of Europe, although at Godmanchester as elsewhere in England they came more into fashion after the Black Death and gradually took the form of a new lay expression of religious institutional revival. Despite the impossibility of tracing short term economic change,[3] it would seem clear that the great burst of immigration to Godmanchester from the late fourteenth century coincided with the participation of East Anglia in the thriving cloth industry of the time. Indeed, some of the immigrants can be identified with the cloth industry, and as well, the apparent decline in their numbers and in the levels of their fines coincided with the general collapse of the industry in the early fifteenth century.

On the whole, however, where records are available one is struck by the unique characteristics of the social history of Godmanchester. For example, although the function of the bailiffs at Colchester in the fourteenth century[4] was not unlike that of Godmanchester, the fee farm due from Godmanchester was three and one-half times that of Colchester and correspondingly required a more elaborate administrative structure. On the other hand, as a formally acknowledged borough Colchester followed the common oligarchic path when new constitutions were adopted in 1372.[5] Despite having customs that Mary Bateson[6] found comparable to borough customs, Godmanchester remained formally a royal manor and its administrative evolution took place within this formality.

As another royal manor, one might have expected Havering, Essex, to be rather comparable to Godmanchester. But Havering of the thirteenth and fourteenth centuries was much more like the normal manor of the age within a demense of 391 acres and administration controlled from without.[7] When Havering did acquire its charter of liberties in 1465 this was in no way comparable to the charter held by Godmanchester since the time of King

---

[3] For some detail possible to studies of other areas, see for example, Christopher Dyer, *Lords and Peasants in a Changing Society: The Estates of the Bishopric of Worcester, 680-1540* (Cambridge, 1980), chapters 7ff. The paucity of town-related research for this period and something of the scope of more recent research is well demonstrated by the chapters of A. F. Butcher and R. B. Dobson in *The English Rising of 1381*, eds. R. H. Hilton and T. H. Aston (Cambridge, 1984).

[4] Britnell, *Colchester*, pp. 28ff.

[5] Ibid., Chapter 8.

[6] *Borough Customs*, Selden Society, 21 (London, 1906).

[7] McIntosh, *Havering*, p. 283.

John. For the Havering charter, not unlike the New Constitutions of Colchester, was required by economic forces beyond the traditional town. Indeed at Havering, three prominent citizens of London obtained the Charter of Liberties in order to protect their economic interests at Havering.[8]

In order to assess these different if not rather unique qualities of the Godmanchester records, then, we must look more closely at the decisions[9] of the town. Since our contemporary social historians tend to focus their interests about external innovative forces of change rather than the more humanistic emphasis upon initiative and independence of decision the underlying current at Godmanchester should no doubt today be identified as conservative. That is to say, for the freemen of Godmanchester the proud heritage of their customs, their *Magna Carta* from the time of King John,[10] remained virtually an unchallenged framework of administration throughout changes of the fifteenth and sixteenth centuries. Indeed, the obligations of representation by streets and of office holding limited by one post to one year may most properly be seen in the order of political liberties.

When Godmanchester attempted its version of administrative reform during the 1460s, this was done by putting more teeth into the frankpledge control of tradesmen rather than favouring external trade. In the face of bankrupcy by the 1470s, responsibilities of bailiffs were given a wider base among the wealthier members of the town. Not unlike the much older story of the Crown borrowing from Jews, Italians and other merchants, this system virtually mortgaged a freeman for a year. But, in contrast to the long term of office of earlier bailiffs, no individual held the post for two years in succession and most bailiffs were elected for only three to five years in all. As long as

---

[8] Ibid., p. 363. In some respects, particularly the open relationship with merchants and yet the capacity for local people to retain their independence, Leighton Buzzard was more comparable with Godmanchester. See Andrew Jones, "Bedfordshire: Fifteenth Century," in Harvey, *The Peasant Land Market*, pp. 245-251.

[9] A theoretical discussion of this point could most usefully begin with the recent volume of Jack Goody, *The Logic of Writing and the Organization of Society* (Cambridge, 1986), for example, p. 136: "But such changes do not require the intervention of a deliberate process of organized decision-making. ... What happens is a gradual adjustment. ... I do not argue that such adjustments are inevitable, nor that deliberate 'legislative' decisions do not occur, but that there is a greater flexibility in the oral context." Unfortunately, the historiography available to Jack Goody has not directed him to follow the role of custom through institutions of later medieval England. As we shall see further below, his theoretical perceptions are applicable to a society that is no longer simply "oral."

[10] Although submerged in a rather too dense and complex presentation, it is encouraging that R. M. Smith has begun to challenge a historiography that has isolated villagers from the Crown. See his "Modernization and the corporate medieval village community in England: some sceptical reflections" in *Explorations in Historical Geography: Interpretative Essays*, eds. Alan R. H. Baker and Derek Gregory (Cambridge, 1984).

economic and social realities would allow, the "political logic" of the
Godmanchester administration was pushed as far as it would go.

The same forces that brought about a wider resource base for balancing the
budget of the town also lead to the pooling of capital in every economic
sector of the town. That customary credit instrument especially adaptable for
the control of capital within the family network, that is, the tally, remained
and its use was more widely extended beyond the family. But the immediate
press of indebtedness could only be met by credit support among participants
in the same occupations. The economic crunch was felt first, of course, by
those with little in the way of capital resources in property. Just as money was
the poorer man's wealth for disposal by his last will, so money was the last
line of defence among petty occupations and trades. For occupations of more
major economic importance, such as butchers, where there was no vertical
control of supplies[11] the credit system depended upon an equilibrium
between debts to the supplier and the purchaser of the commercial product.

Pooling of capital among labourers, poorer artisans and tradespeople had
become more necessary as the landholding base of this group declined. This
virtual disappearance of small tenants at Godmanchester by the late fifteenth
century was predominately the result of secular demographic trends. Immigration patterns show that there was a market for labour. When labourers and
others on the same economic level did replace themselves, they did retain
some property. But the economic well being of this poorest level of tenants
depended directly upon the elemental physical resources supplied by
members of the family. Hence, this group were more immediately sensitive
to demographic factors than any more wealthy sector of the economy. Fewer
hands meant less resources. Again, no chronology can be placed upon this
transformation. Godmanchester people may have shared in that modest
spread of landholding to be found a generation after the Black Death among
the small tenants of Ramsey vills[12] throughout the county. But, if so, such
tenurial patterns had disappeared by the early fifteenth century at Godmanchester as it had for Ramsey vills.

Supporting evidence for this sort of phenomenon is necessarily negative,
if not "from silence," but, it is consistent. There was a marked decline in the
number of smallholdings by "foreign" tenants, especially those of the poorer
sort. The foreign tenant arrangement had been particularly useful for extending the family patterns of land use beyond the town into those neighbouring
settlements that have been charactized as the "greater" agrarian zone" of

---

[11] The cloth trade offers the most detailed examples of this credit interdependence, but to
a degree it was traditional in other processing trades.

[12] See J. A. Raftis, *The Estates of Ramsey Abbey* (Toronto, 1957), Chapter IX.

Godmanchester around 1300. The radical decline in numbers of foreign tenants by the late fifteenth century is a sensitive indicator, therefore, to the replacement problem for multi-branched regional families.

No doubt for Godmanchester as for the English economy as a whole, the increasing geographical mobility of labour during the fifteenth century buffered much of the impact of local demographic strictures. There was a paucity of familiar Godmanchester names among the scores of herdsmen, servants and casual labourers to be found in frankpledge rolls and when familiar names do occur almost never were there indications of more than one male with the same surname. By the last quarter of the century, the short-term activity on the small-property land market demonstrated very little capacity to retain land by smallholders beyond the active career of one family member. When the wills finally give us some access to vital statistics, there is no reason to believe that the lowest economic group did not share in the negative replacement rate of all families from the town. Moreover, for the majority among those poorer ranks of villagers, the lack of an economic base rarely encouraged establishment of a household with full family cycle pretensions.

For the traditional husbandman of Godmanchester, those directly dependent upon a land economy whose main taxable wealth around 1300 would be measured in heaps of grain, the chronic depression in grain prices gradually undermined their economic way of life. Godmanchester had rich meadow and pasture so that it is not surprising to find, through evidence of shepherds for the larger landholders, that more sheep were introduced to the town over the later medieval period. But in the view of sixteenth-century observers Godmanchester remained famous as a cereal producing centre. Sheep stinting on the commons was strictly controlled by byelaw, so one is not surprised to find wealthy sheep raising specialists of the early sixteenth century being forced to maintain flocks on the Ouse fen commons of the neighbouring villages of Brampton and Houghton.

Diversification tended to develop within the lines of the open field country economy. Consistently, traditional families of Godmanchester survived by enlarging the size of their holdings and, at the other end of the process, engaging in the commercial sale of grain products, especially through the brewing industry. The fact that those many "middle wealth" group from the region who settled in Godmanchester are immediately identified with industry, again usually the brewing industry, while they were gradually accumulating land, confirms the pivotal role of such commerce for economic survival in the countryside.

The strong role of the brewing industry in fifteenth-century Godmanchester is just one piece of evidence that the commercial and craft industries remained reasonably strong despite depression in other sectors of this local economy. In the long series of entry fines to Godmanchester there was a small but steady stream[13] of immigrants to the town either directly or indirectly identifiable as craftsmen and their fine payments fell less than for other immigrant group during the mid-century. The recruiting of craftsmen from the region was a phenomenon extending back to the thirteenth century,[14] so that a rather traditional reward pattern no doubt qualifies them as in the "wage-stickiness" bracket rather than an active component of the wider wage movements of the time. Even further, Godmanchester records prior to the last quarter of the fifteenth century show a perduring individual and no doubt social character to craft practices that are more familiar to students of modern centuries.[15] For example, despite pestilence and plague John Stalys appeared in frankpledge rolls as a baker from 1438 to 1477 and John Hawkyn pursued his modest cobbler trade from at least the early 1460s well into the 1480s. On the whole, however, data about Godmanchester are of a more general sort. There is some evidence that fallen demand for crafts by the second quarter of the century is reflected in the decline in numbers of those entering Godmanchester. But certainly new craft trades, such as those introduced by the cloth industry, declined radically in licence-fee level from the second quarter of the fifteenth century. This country town did not participate in the golden age of craftsmen found for the European economic history of this time.[16]

---

[13] This seems to correspond with the "small but significant influx of craftsmen" into many village communities over the late fourteenth and fifteenth centuries noted by P. D. A. Harvey. See *The Peasant Land Market*, p. 342. On the other hand, it should be noted that surviving records of Godmanchester contain practically no data for reconstructing the institutional nature of town trade. There are a few records testifying to the importance of trade for the town. An exemplification of 5 Elizabeth I (Godmanchester Borough Accounts, Box 5, Bundle 7) recalls that tenants of Godmanchester were quit of toll at Peterborough, Harborough and Northampton. A document dated 26 July 1497, associated Godmanchester residents John Clerk, William Diggby, Richard Grene, David Gysselly, Thomas Smyth, Richard Stevens, William Vyntner and Thomas William of Stanford, Lincs., in a bond of £100 sterling given to Richard Gonell of Stanford, alderman. (Godmanchester Borough Records, Box 8, Other Documents of Henry VII, Miscellaneous, no. 5). And more importantly, a settlement of 17 May 1417 (Godmanchester Borough Records, Box 8, Other Documents in Box) over disagreement with Huntingdon about pickage and stallage refers to the traditional rights of "merchants, artificers and victuallers" in the market and fairs of the borough of Huntingdon. And arrangements for the fee refer to trestles and tables of cloth, meat, shoes, leather goods, "irembugers" (iron), ropers, "peddlers" and others. One searches in vain for any reference to markets in the courts and frankpledge rolls.

[14] See *A Small Town*, p. 135 ff.

[15] See, the useful description of stereotypes in Ronald Blythe, *Akenfield, Portrait of an English Village* (London, 1969).

[16] W. Abel, *Agricultural Fluctuations in Europe from the Thirteenth to Twentieth Centuries*, trans. O. Ordisch, (London, 1980).

The lack of price and wage data for Godmanchester makes it impossible to enter directly into current revisionist discussion turning upon such sources. But every facet of information available from Godmanchester records, the patterns to be found for licence fees among different immigrant groups, administrative reforms from the 1460s through to the 1480s, collapse of the late fourteenth-century revival as well as a lifeless open field economy in th whole region,[17] suggest a prolonged and deepening depression from the 1430s to the 1480s. Analyses of the various price and wage indices now becoming available for many parts of the country conform decade by decade with evidence for depression from Godmanchester: "... the price index plunged again during the 'bullion famine' era of the 1440s and 1450s, rising only slightly during the debasements of the 1460s (4.9%), then starkly dropping in the 1470s to reach its late medieval nadir (76.4), with an overall 40-year decline of 18.0%." And again, "The combined agricultural money wage series begins to fall in the 1440s, the first to do so. From the 1430s peak to the 1450s, it fell 4.8%; but then declined more steeply and without a break, until the 1480s, for an overall slump of 21.0% in the index."[18]

The first movements towards the foundation of what may be called *early modern Godmanchester* can be traced to the 1480s. By this time the people of Godmanchester were "capital poor" in every field of wealth. There were indeed a few individuals who functioned as professional money lenders but their resources were sharply circumscribed. Most individuals must still depend for their capital arrangements upon disposition by tally of various resources and productive activities of the town. But the casual tally instruments employed for such arrangements were difficult to implement on every level of society and required enforcement by the court through short-term mortgage registrations. The threat that this system presented to the elementary living resources of individuals was recognized by a new form of social assistance, the annual interest free loan.

By the 1480s, then, this small provincial community was extremely vulnerable to economic intrusion by those sectors of the English economy that were beginning to generate surplus capital. Within a very few years some of these "capitalists" moved into the economy of Godmanchester, purchased hundreds of acres of land and became prominent money lenders. However, from the 1490s the pace of this economic occupation began to level out and remained so until the second quarter of the sixteenth century. The only

---

[17] See, J. A. Raftis, *The Estates of Ramsey Abbey*, Chapter x.

[18] I am grateful to John H. Munro for bringing these data to my attention. References in this paragraph are taken from his forthcoming study, "The Behaviour of Wages During Deflation in Late-Medieval England and the Low Countries."

perceptible explanation for this levelling process was the degree to which regional immigrants became a force for equilibrium. These regional people settled in Godmanchester, became part of its government, intermarried with local families and brought their resources to supplement and accelerate the increasing vertical integration of husbandry and commerce. The small holders were already long disappeared as a group. But somewhat paradoxically, this middle group hastened the disappearance of tenants holding ten to thirty acres of land.[19]

Outside investors in Godmanchester, especially London merchants, brought with them more than capital: "To be a merchant, in the particular occupational sense in which that term was used, was to be known, wherever one went, as belonging to a group with a distinctive economic position, referring to the conduct of wholesale trade, and with a distinctive political position, that of controlling municipal government."[20] As was amply demonstrated in the Peasants' Revolt of 1381, English countrymen were sensitive to intrusion by outsiders into their way of life.[21] With their proud tradition of self government one can be certain that the freemen of Godmanchester reacted strongly to the capital-laden newcomers of the 1480s. Were there protests from William Manipenny, with one of the oldest surnames in Godmanchester history, as the name took on less prominence from the late fifteenth century? Certainly by this time the Manipenny family were on the lower half of the middle wealth group, failed to improve their wealth and

[19] Very Likely the disappearance of this lower middle group was much more drastic than depicted in Chapter 6. The analysis of this Chapter 6 did not take fully into account all those in the one-half mark range who very likely entered Godmanchester as craftsmen and brought with them money for investment in the ten to thirty acre range and so to a degree perpetuated this group. But the estimates of Chapter 6 remained on the cautious side since craftsmen were infrequently identified by occupation at the time of their purchase of liberty.

The most recent and thorough demonstration of the difficulties facing an explanation of engrossing by peasants in late mediaeval England may be found in Christopher Dyer, "Warwickshire Farming 1349-c.1520, Preparations for Agricultural Revolution," *Dugdale Society Occasional Papers*, No. 27 (Oxford, 1981). Dyer's description offers some comparison for Godmanchester: "The majority of the cultivators of the land in Warwickshire were neither gentry nor demesne farmers but peasants—contemporaries called them husbandmen and yeoman—the majority of whom, as we have seen, towards the end of our period held a yardland or more but rarely more than three yardlands, say between twenty-four and a hundred acres." (Ibid., p. 22).

[20] Sylvia Thrupp, *The Merchant Class of Medieval London, 1300-1500* (Ann Arbor, Michigan, 1948), p. IX. Reference has already been made in this chapter to the case of London merchants successfully imposing their will upon the royal manor of Havering.

[21] This is a common phenomenon in peasant history, of course. A suggested sketch of how the 1381 Peasants' Revolt may be seen in this light can be found in J. A. Raftis, "Social Change versus Revolution: New Interpretations of the Peasants' Revolt of 1381," in *Social Unrest in the Middle Ages*, ed. F. X. Newman (Binghamton, New York, 1986), pp. 3-22.

disappeared over the next generation. A cluster of evictions only appears in the records at this time, but these may be explained by the new tough financial administration of the town.

Another possible indicator of the internal struggle at Godmanchester over these years could be the well documented case of John Wynde. The entry of John Wynde, gentleman, upon this local scene would seem to have begun in mid June 1504, when he appeared before the court in person and presented a royal writ of close (dated 6 May 1504) that he be seized of one messuage, 90 acres (of arable), 40 acres of meadow, 12 acres of wood and appurtenants deforced by William Mynsterchambre. The latter was called to respond at the next court. Both John and William appeared in person at the following court. William called John Mynsterchambre to warranty and this John in turn called Richard Sterlyng. The latter at first placed himself on the great assize but later in the day lost the case by not re-appearing in court. Whether the disenfranchment of John Wynde sometime afterwards was related to revenge cannot be determined. He regained liberty status in 1508.[22]

William Mynsterchambre entered a claim to this traditional family estate in 1516 under the form of death of ancestor. John Wynde then appealed to Wolsey to hear the case in chancery. Evidence[23] brought forth in the ensuing Westminster hearing has already been summarized at the beginning of Chapter 4 above for its interesting information on wills. The local court does not seem to have been in a hurry to implement the Westminster decision and it may not have been until July 1520 when summary accounts of the proceedings were recorded at his request that John Wynde was finally seized of this estate. Behind this delay was a violent local feud. From about this time may be dated three badly torn away and dilapidated parchment fragments now catalogued as "Disenfranchisement of John Wynde of Godmanchester."[24] Owing to the condition of this record the following account must be

[22] See below, Appendix 7.

[23] This suit does clarify that John Wynde, gentleman, had purchased this property from Sir Robert Drury. From the practice of the time, it would seem that the property had been let to the use of Drury while John Mynsterchambre, the heir, was under age. Robert Drury was no doubt a member of a prominent family by that name, and with many Roberts, from Bury St. Edmunds. See Robert S. Gottfried, *Bury St. Edmunds and the Urban Crises: 1290-1539* (Princeton, 1982), pp. 159-164, for a valuable treatment of this family at Bury St. Edmunds. Bury St. Edmunds was a sophisticated market centre far above Godmanchester, but Professor Gottfried's study does have many useful analytical comparisons, as on the demographic basis for decline (pp. 70-71), and his isolation of the land dealing rôle of burgesses (p. 136). Actually on the court for the first week of January 1516, a messuage on Post Street (between the path to the mill and the land of the chantry) was let to the use (*ad opus*) of John and Dorothy Wynde.

[24] Huntington Record Office, Godmanchester Borough Records, Box 8, Other Documents.

largely in the nature of a summary. Nevertheless, the nature of the charges by the freemen, and the counter charges by Wynde are clear.

The top half of the sheet listing the charges by the freemen is torn away and the first decipherable charge is as follows (in a somewhat modernized English):

> Item the said John Wynde doth manesse and thretten many pore tenaunts of the seid town which do nothing offend ageynst hym but only seke for the maintenance of their seid customs. In such wise that many of them for fear of his words be mynded to forsake the said town and to dwelle in other places far from thence. By reason whereof the seid complainant shall not be able to pay the kings fee farm unless the good maistership so provided some remedy that the seid pore tenaunts may dwell still there quyetly and in peace without fear or threatening of the seid John Wynde.
>
> Item whereas one William Townsend a pore tenaunt of the seid town hyred an acre of meadow for his whole yeres store of hay. At such time as he had mowed the same and made it up ready to the cart havyng no more but only that. Came the servant of the seid John Wynde in forcible manner with swords bukles and pitchfork and carried away all the pore mans seid hay wherewith he should have fed his cattle all the winter season which be like now rather to famish in cold weather than otherwise by reason of the great extraction of the seid John Wynde. Which is a piteous case and to the most perilous example that hath be seen seying that he is in such authority and put in trust the pore mens wrong redress and amended.

The freemen further charge that when the bailiffs (no doubt as plaintiffs for the town) went to the sessions they were fined 6s. 8d. although they should have been in the king's peace. And they charged further that the king's lete was held in traditional fashion and the 12 jurors instructed the collectors to collect the fines. But when they went to John Wynde to collect a fine, he refused. The collectors then seized a horse. But John Wynde recovered the horse through the sheriff and even further seized the collectors book so that he was unable to complete his collection. The townsmen plead for remedy since Wynde is likely to become worse.

From the testimony of John Wynde it can be seen that the first article of complaint by the town concerned William Mynsterchambre's "cause." Little can be deciphered about the response except for the fact John Wynde had purchased this property for £100 sterling, held the land peacefully for 13 years and was forced to (go to Westminster) for a fair trial. Article 2 of the bill of complaint must have concerned the customs of the town, for John Wynde flatly states that "such customs are no laws but are against the law, reason and good conscience." Wynde then denies the charge concerning poor tenants, countercharging waste by the town administration (of funds levied for the poor?).

Concerning the charge that he has abused his power, John Wynde notes that he was Justice of the Peace and often fined Godmanchester people for misdemeanours. Then he makes personal charges against leading town officials. William Diggby and William King are both untrustworthy. Indeed William King is a known drunk. Persons of extreme malice got Mynsterchambre to act. Unruly people leave Wynde in fear for his life. Finally, an interesting scenario is described: "On 21 October last in the house of Ibbott which is a house of much ill rule as well as supporting of diverse card table players as other misruled persons who passed the time together in the seid house till XI of the clocke in the night, Ibbott himself checked at the door from time to time. When Christopher Towton came by Ibbott rushed out and struck him with a stave. ... Towton told this to John Caldecot, William Brown and Edmund Knight, servants of John Wynde whom he met. ... These servants returned to the Ibbott house and were attacked by Ibbott, William Aves, John Ashton and Richard Savage so that Edmund Knight was badly hurts. ... Yet the constable jailed John Caldecote and William Brown for two days !"

The animosity between the town and John Wynde even entered the precincts of the parish church. Dorothy, the wife of John Wynde, was involved in charges before the episcopal visitor (22 May 1518) concerning failure to give the kiss of peace during mass and other disturbances with three men of the town.[25] Although the Wynde's lived on East Street there is no evidence, except for the brief appearance of John as one of the guardians of the Corpus Christi guild, that the family became integrated with the local society. In any case, John Wynde had not long to enjoy unchallenged his Godmanchester holdings. He would appear to have died late in 1522 for from that time Dorothy Wynde alone is named in court roll entries and an entry after Pentecost 1523 cites Dorothy as widow and executor of John Wynde.

Dorothy Wynde was herself engaged prominently in lawsuits over the 1520s. But whether this involved traditional claims to the estate cannot be determined. More than likely it was just another feature of a series of legal wrangles among the wealthier freemen (Hartford, King, Punt, etc.) that filled most of the court book for this period. Dorothy proved to be a redoutable "gentlewoman" as she was called in the court records. Her taxable wealth was assessed at £30 in the early 1520s. Court entries of 1524 suggest that she had added two more properties on Post Street along with a messuage purchased by John in 1516. She sublet the disputed East Street messuage in 1524 and continued active in the property market until her death in 1543.

[25] *An Episcopal Court Book for the Diocese of Lincoln, 1514-1520*, folio 57, p. 63.

By this time most of the lands were held for life by William Sewster, gentleman, and the court acknowledged that she had a son and heir named Frank.

Beyond personal tensions, by the time one gains as much intimate acquaintance with the fifteenth-century experience of the people of Godmanchester that extant records make possible, violent social reaction to the deterioration of the traditional society is not to be expected. For those poorer levels of society whose landed estate had dissolved by the late century the process was long-term and based upon mortality from disease. This collapse in their way of life must have gradually become "natural" and as much part of the Divine order of things as the deteriorating climate in late mediaeval England and the decimation of flocks by the corresponding chronic "murrain" among animals. No leadership of the Jack Strawe sort could be expected from people where social and economic life had lost that economic base required for the whole tissue of extended household, trade association and friendship grouping summarized in Chapter 4 above. But for families that did survive the story would be quite different.

For this latter group, the survival of a good number of families assisted by the extraordinary internal capacity of the family to adapt through the role of widows and such customary usages as the tally, must have preserved the sense of corporate continuity. In no way did Godmanchester develop a "deserted village" syndrome. Individual families might disappear, but this had become a common phenomenon for long beyond the range of human memory. Neighbours might disappear, but for a town this size the ambience of acquaintance and friendship could be the street and even the whole parish. Some families remained on their "home" streets in Godmanchester from the thirteenth to the sixteenth centuries. Such were the Aylred, Balle, Frost, Gardiner and Legg families on Arnyng Street; the Bennett, Cook, (Fryer, Freer), Hilton and Lockyngton families on West Street; Garlop, Gony, Manipenny and Nottyngham families on Post Street; and the Clerk, Newman, Nicholas, Page and Syward families on East Street, to give but a few examples. For these wealthier and long-established families very deliberate attention was given to passing on the old family homestead. If, as we have seen from the wills, heirlooms were personal items, how much more must have been the attraction of the familiar home! The customs of the town had long expected the main heir to inherit the main home on the capital messuage. The messuage was still associated in farm rental payments of the fifteenth century with the family holdings of arable and meadow. Few messuages traded separately from other properties. Furthermore, a quick glance at the land estimates derived from rental payments in Appendix 3 for Post Street covering some ten years and slightly less for Arnyng Street and

East Street, might suggest that over this period of time the size of some 90% of the properties remained the same.

In one way or, another, many families continued for a considerable period in the Godmanchester of the late fifteenth and early sixteenth centuries. Exact evidence for continuation varies widely among families owing to such features as the replacement patterns noted in Chapter 4, the regional structure of families and the uneven survival of extant records such as wills. Table 42 merely gives family surnames continuing for many generations in order to demonstrate the "corporate bulk" of continuity in the town.

TABLE 42: FAMILY CONTINUITY PERIODS FROM RECORDS

| Surname | Date | Surname | Date |
|---|---|---|---|
| Abram | 1522-1547 | Bishop | 1436-1483 |
| Adam | 1482-1520 | Blaxton | 1515-1546 |
| Alam | 1494-1545 | Boleyn | 1517-1548 |
| Alcock | 1440-1503 | Bonde | 1416-1482 |
| Aleyn | 1400-1498 | Bonsay | 1485-1538 |
| Allyngham | 1437-1470 | Bonis | 1420-1492 |
| Andrew | 1485-1543 | Borowe (Boro) | 1522-1548 |
| Anton | 1440-1535 | Boulde | 1463-1510 |
| Aplond | 1488-1527 | Bour | 1407-1489 |
| Armouth | 1497-1545 | Branden | 1497-1543 |
| Arnold | 1485-1535 | Brewster | 1472-1510 |
| Asshe | 1485-1524 | Broun (Brown) | 1418-1548 |
| Aylmar | 1421-1493 | Bulward (Bullard) | 1486-1545 |
| Aylred | 1409-1545 | Burton | 1445-1507 |
| Aythroppe | 1464-1484 | Butcher | 1419-1505 |
|  |  | Byllyngton | 1527-1537 |
| Bailey | 1424-1547 | Byrd | 1525-1543 |
| Baker | 1405-1524 | Bydrer | 1510-1534 |
| Balle | 1400-1501 |  |  |
| Barbar | 1418-1460 | Campion | 1406-1482 |
| Barker | 1445-1489 | Carter | 1424-1545 |
| Barnard | 1407-1545 | Cave | 1415-1515 |
| Baron | 1402-1495 | Chamberlayn | 1411-1481 |
| Barre | 1403-1525 | Chamber | 1516-1548 |
| Barret | 1422-1527 | Chandeler | 1494-1527 |
| Bartlelot | 1402-1425 | Chese | 1405-1488 |
| Basse (Baseley) | 1487-1543 | Chycheley | 1437-1526 |
| Bate | 1402-1485 | Clerk | 1400-1548 |
| Bawdwyne | 1498-1502 | Cokman | 1486-1513 |
| Bayous | 1450-1500 | Collins | 1537-1545 |
| Beek | 1490-1512 | Cook | 1402-1548 |
| Bell | 1480-1543 | Copegray | 1422-1469 |
| Benet | 1401-1548 | Corby | 1429-1548 |
| Betrich | 1464-1548 | Couper | 1497-1533 |
| Bettes (Betteson) | 1511-1545 |  |  |

| Surname | Date | Surname | Date |
|---|---|---|---|
| Dalton | 1481-1545 | Gredley | 1485-1512 |
| Davy | 1485-1499 | Grene | 1401-1548 |
| Dawntre | 1420-1487 | Gretham | 1490-1540 |
| Desney | 1511-1548 | Grome | 1408-1423 |
| Dey | 1486-1534 | Gybbys | 1464-1544 |
| Dicer | 1400-1442 | | |
| Dobbyn | 1437-1511 | Hacfeld | 1423-1491 |
| Donwaich | 1421-1441 | Hall (Aula) | 1490-1540 |
| Dorraunt | 1411-1545 | Hanson | 1442-1484 |
| | | Harleston | 1400-1441 |
| Ede | 1400-1432, | Harryson | 1495-1548 |
| | 1494-1544 | Hawdwyn | 1538-1548 |
| Edmund | 1472-1548 | Hawkyn | 1449-1492 |
| Eliot | 1494-1506 | Hay | 1520-1538 |
| Ely | 1440-1464, | Hildemar | 1400-1465 |
| | 1494-1520 | Hilton | 1460-1535 |
| Emlyn | 1463-1492 | Hogan | 1507-1543 |
| Englysh | 1451-1534 | Holme | 1456-1534 |
| Est | 1489-1548 | Howden | 1516-1547 |
| | | Howman | 1401-1439 |
| Faldyng | 1481-1523 | Hunt | 1494-1548 |
| Farthyng | 1485-1538 | | |
| Fauk | 1407-1419, | Ibott | 1460-1524 |
| | 1452-1472 | Ingram | 1473-1523 |
| Fecas | 1479-1499 | Ive | 1406-1418 |
| Feld | 1429-1494 | Johnson | 1463-1524 |
| Fisher | 1407-1489 | | |
| Folkys | 1449-1499 | Kelson | 1512-1545 |
| Foster | 1460-1526 | Kendale | 1485-1527 |
| Freman | 1404-1547 | King | 1443-1546 |
| Frere | 1411-1547 | Kyrby | 1527-1545 |
| Frost | 1409-1545 | | |
| Fuller | 1400-1500 | Lane | 1400-1498 |
| Fylle | 1438-1477 | Lavenham | 1419-1432 |
| | | Lawrence | 1485-1502 |
| Gardener | 1424-1524 | Laxton | 1486-1543 |
| Garlond | 1521-1537 | Ledder | 1422-1464 |
| Garlop | 1405-1544 | Legge | 1485-1490 |
| Garnet | 1485-1502 | Lessy | 1422-1494 |
| Gilby (Gilbert) | 1490-1534 | Lessyn (Leffyn) | 1509-1546 |
| Gyle | 1480-1494 | Locksmyth | 1405-1464 |
| Glover | 1413-1464, | Lockyngton | 1400-1548 |
| | 1481-1490, | Long | 1404-1497 |
| | 1523-1533 | Lord | 1460-1543 |
| Godwyn | 1400-1547 | Loveday | 1463-1524 |
| Goneld (Gonell) | 1486-1501 | Lovell | 1500-1548 |
| Gony | 1400-1498 | Lucas | 1441-1497 |
| Grace | 1485-1533 | Lyte | 1438-1492 |
| Granger | 1464-1547 | | |
| Gray | 1474-1494 | | |

| Surname | Date | Surname | Date |
|---|---|---|---|
| Manipenny | 1401-1505 | Rede | 1406-1514 |
| Manning | 1461-1546 | Reygate | 1410-1479 |
| Marshall | 1429-1545 | Robyn | 1400-1547 |
| Martin | 1461-1545 | Rumborough | 1464-1491 |
| Maryot | 1428-1548 | | |
| Mason | 1413-1469 | Salmon | 1494-1524 |
| Massy | 1487-1546 | Samt | 1485-1494 |
| Matthew | 1442-1548 | Sandon | 1514-1545 |
| May | 1495-1543 | Schepin | 1440-1472 |
| Mayle | 1449-1547 | Schylling | 1442-1523 |
| Maynard | 1488-1532 | Scot | 1401-1523 |
| Michele | 1518-1532 | Seman | 1495-1524 |
| Miller | 1444-1511 | Sewster | 1525-1548 |
| Mileward | 1402-1432 | Slow | 1486-1545 |
| Monys | 1449-1466 | Smith | 1400-1545 |
| Monyment | 1493-1534 | Snell | 1438-1500 |
| Morel | 1404-1452 | Spruntyng | 1400-1461 |
| Motte | 1434-1501 | Squier | 1500-1547 |
| Mounford | 1464-1511 | Stafford | 1434-1472 |
| Mynt | 1494-1534 | Stalis | 1434-1487 |
| | | Stevenson | 1466-1545 |
| Neel | 1513-1543 | Stodale | 1486-1494 |
| Newman | 1466-1497 | Stokes | 1467-1503 |
| Nichole | 1497-1524 | Stoughton | 1517-1547 |
| Nottyngham | 1459-1520 | Stukeley | 1445-1538 |
| | | Syward | 1417-1545 |
| Oliver | 1419-1446, 1539-1548 | Taylor | 1493-1543 |
| Orwell | 1480-1516 | Thomson | 1488-1547 |
| Osse | 1494-1545 | Tryg | 1540-1548 |
| Osteler | 1485-1548 | Tully | 1429-1470 |
| Page | 1418-1545 | Upchurch | 1400-1547 |
| Parker | 1512-1543 | Ussher | 1489-1505 |
| Paryse | 1440-1532 | | |
| Passelowe | 1484-1494 | Valey | 1413-1434 |
| Pasy (Pacy) | 1494-1526 | Vincent | 1450-1543 |
| Peek | 1406-1417 | Vyntner | 1492-1544 |
| Pelle | 1485-1545 | | |
| Pelman | 1479-1544 | Waleys | 1405-1477 |
| Pennyman | 1423-1472 | Wellys | 1516-1543 |
| Pernell | 1401-1496 | West | 1472-1525 |
| Peyton | 1527-1534 | Whyte | 1493-1545 |
| Pope | 1481-1511 | Wood (Wode) | 1495-1543 |
| Porter | 1419-1543 | Wright | 1403-1540 |
| Prior | 1505-1548 | Wylde | 1505-1534 |
| Punt | 1485-1545 | Wynde | 1508-1543 |
| Quenyng | 1402-1497 | | |

Survival also meant demographic success in replacement and a frequent pattern of multiple branches. While it is difficult to give precise figures to this family survival pattern since so many of these families had regional branches, it is impossible to follow families that might have continued outside Godmanchester and then returned after a generation or two. Nevertheless, it was the very regional nature of such families that provided the model for their transitional economic survival. As has been noted above, the injection of outside money and personnel on this wealth level gave the pattern, and gradually an integrated pattern, for the survival and then revival of the middle wealth group. With such an active option those freeman at Godmanchester who had the resources to rebel against the new order of things were least likely to do so as a group.

It has already been noted in Chapter 3 that the Godmanchester courts no longer bothered to record the place of origin of most of those purchasing liberty of the vill. This may have been a tacit way of avoiding the requirements of the Statute of Labourers for some newcomers. But more generally, the courts would not have required identity of place of origin because the town was already familiar with the newcomers in one way or another. The wide number of townsmen giving surety for newcomers suggest a previous economic contact.[26] Even though entries no longer specified outsiders inheriting property according to the custom of the town, that is through family ties, some identity with a wider district would continue to be fed by exogamous marriages. Godmanchester wills show this continued commitment to a native parish, perhaps from as close at hand as Offord Cluny or as distant as Newmarket.

One must be cautious, therefore, in ascribing the decline and disappearance of any particular family to the plague. A family such as the Newman family at Godmanchester were active in the vill from 1466 to 1497, although they maintained a strong presence at Hemingford Abbots. The same can be said of the Dorraunt family who originated from Hemingford Abbots, and still kept ties with this neighbouring village; but one branch of the family took Godmanchester as their abode from 1411 to 1547. Unfortunately, the paucity of records for some vills neighbouring Godmanchester, such as Offord Cluny, do not allow a thorough study of this phenomenon. One must be content to acknowledge that continuity was a social function of regional as well as local life.

---

[26] References in Godmanchester records to people from outside the parish occur largely in the fifteenth and early sixteenth centuries for economic relations only. Appendix 11 derived from property contracts and trespass suits in court and frankpledge records illustrates a continuing commerce with a region much as in the thirteenth century. The incidental nature of this source in no way indicates the total variety or density of such communication patterns.

For most of the families that continued at Godmanchester, therefore, change from the late fifteenth century must have been rather imperceptible. Such an attitude is familiar enough to oral societies.[27] But the line between oral and literate culture may be too strongly drawn.[28] For at Godmanchester it was the capacity for adjusting within the customary structures of byelaws, administration, tallies and so forth that gave the character of "gradualism" to the whole process.[29] In so far as Godmanchester was concerned, the freemen still ran the town. Analogies to this situation are numerous throughout history. One analogy of considerable current interest is the possibility for successful introduction of intermediate technology and related economic structures to developing nations since traditional cultures can adapt, control and survive such interventions.

Emphasis has been placed upon the notion of continuity in the last few pages in order to better understand the capacity of Godmanchester to survive. In no way is this notion meant to minimize the realities of change and the often calamitous effects of change upon the lives of individuals, families and institutional support systems. A full scale study of the physical changes in the town must await more detailed archaeological-historical research. But evidence for even physical "desolation"[30] is not hard to find. The following two sketches, together with the list of changing tenants for the various properties, shows the physical transformation that had taken place on St. Giles Lane over two generations. Actually the changes may have been more dramatic than the disappearance of all the artisans along the south of Giles Lane, since there is some evidence for the decay of at least one property to the north of this lane and information about other properties becomes suspisciously vague.

[27] "While shifts in this latter kind [deliberate process of organized decision making ... gradual adjustment ... the deliberate removal of "anomalies"] take place in non-literate societies, there is less room for direct conflict, for open confrontation, between the old and the new. The old fades more quickly into the background; it is, quite simply, forgotten." Jack Goody, *The Logic of Writing and the Organization of Society*, p. 137.

[28] See, for example, ibid., p. 139: "The process [of adjustment of norms that constantly takes place in oral societies in response to external pressures or internal forces] is imperceptible because norms have only a verbal, or oral existence, so that rules that are no longer applicable tend to slip out of "the memory store."

[29] The masterful treatment by P. D. A. Harvey of legal institutions within the context of the gradual evolution of new institutions over the longer span of English medieval history in *The Peasant Land Market*, offers another example of analysis of this process.

[30] Charles Pythian-Adams, *Desolation of a City, Coventry and the Urban Crisis of the Late Middle Ages* (Cambridge, 1979) is rapidly becoming the classic study of this phenomenon.

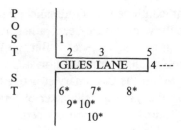

SEQUENCE OF PROPERTY HOLDINGS IN GILES LANE, CA. 1487-1500

1. Messuage: John Holme; John Barnard, candelmaker; William Lord, wright
2. Messuage: Thomas Cokman, butcher; John Garlop, wright (possibly decayed thereafter)
3. Messuage: John Porter; William Greatham; John Granger
4. Messuage plus two rentals: William Frost senior; William Corby
5. Messuage: John Garlop, carpenter
6*. Tenement: Robert Dobbyn, chaplain; William Stodale; Edith Grene; Richard Grene; George Grene
7*. Messuage, later known as the "sign of the Dolphin": Thomas Balle; John English; Alice English; John Barnard, candelmaker; John Barnard, wright; John Stokes, butcher; John Ussher; Richard Stevens, shoemaker; Richard Grene; George Grene; "Sign of the Dolphin"
8*. Messuage: John Bishop; Richard Gilby; Henry Lane; George Grene
9*. Fundum: Robert Hunt; George Grene
10*. Two cottages: Richard Kyng; George Grene

*Property owned by George Green in the 1540s.

The juxtaposition of radical change in various human conditions with the sense of continuity can be illustrated in other ways. The less formal identification of less wealthy people with religious institutional structures would have minimized for these some of the religious changes of the time. That is to say, those individuals and families who found religious identity through special affection for certain altars and statues may not have experienced great changes in such para-liturgical practices. For the more wealthy, the destruction of the guilds was a massive institutional revolution. But as we have seen this traditional religious sociology was able to develop new expressions. The laity of Godmanchester would seem to have conformed to an assessment of the general spirit of the diocese: "Yet it seems reasonably certain than when [Bishop John Longland, 1521-1547] died in May 1547, he left a diocese with priests and laity as conservative as he was."[31]

Finally, current research would suggest that further generalizations about the Godmanchester experience would be premature. First the rôle of local

---

[31] Margaret Bowker, *The Henrician Reformation in the Diocese of Lincoln under John Longland, 1521-1547* (Cambridge, 1981), p. 181.

change in the evolution of late medieval English society is under review.³²
Analysis of comparative differences and similarities among local communities
from the thirteenth to the sixteenth centuries must be further developed.³³
Secondly, while it was impossible to study Godmanchester without those
wonderful pages of R. H. Tawney recurring to one's mind again and again,
the moral indictment of an age as calvinistic and capitalistic is no longer
accurate, nor is it helpful. One could as usefully deplore the failure of Tudor
government and local societies to develop micro-mercantilist policies for
their protection! Rather, the importance of these studies is to isolate ever
more clearly and comprehensively an experience of our culture that is still
very much with us. With only slight adjustments for perspective, the following
set of observations about modern society apply equally as well to early Tudor
Godmanchester: "... capital must be concentrated in the local system if local
specialization and industry are to develop; ... the low-energy cycle of the
undeveloped [traditional] system is dramatically broken by world [wider]
demand for one or more of its products ...; underdevelopment [local capacity
for adaptation] is a dynamic, active process, not a passive, receiving one ..."³⁴

³² See, for example, Marjorie K. McIntosh, "Local Change and Community Control in England, 1465-1500," *The Huntingdon Library Quarterly* 49 (1986), 219-242.
³³ See for example, Judith M. Bennett, "Gender, Family and Community. A Comparative Study of the English Peasantry, 1287-1349," unpublished Ph. D. thesis (University of Toronto, 1981), and M. Spufford, *Contrasting Communities: English Villagers in the Sixteenth and Seventeenth Centuries* (Cambridge, 1974).
³⁴ Carol A. Smith, "Regional Economic Systems: Linking Geographical Models and Socioeconomic Problems" in *Regional Analysis, 1: Economic Systems,* ed. Carol A. Smith (New York, 1976), pp. 53, 54, 56. The bracketed portions have been interposed by this writer.

# Appendix 1

## Accounts for the Bailiffs of Godmanchester

### INTRODUCTORY NOTE

The general context for these accounts has been set in Chapter 1. Accounts of this nature throw some light on local budgets at a time of changing political economy and are sufficiently rare that it has been thought useful to edit such records for Godmanchester. That is to say, the economic data here, for example, the price of ink and parchment, are of wider interest than the range of this volume. Another resource to be found in these records and not developed in this study is the range of contacts of local government officials. These regional features of local government are not something new, as Anne and Edwin DeWindt have amply demonstrated for the late thirteenth century in *Royal Justice and the Medieval English Countryside* (Toronto, 1981). But description of the regional nature of the society of Huntingdonshire for every century from the thirteenth to the sixteenth is a large task for which material can only be assembled from more detailed local studies.

Payments for various officials were assessed equally for the Easter and Michaelmas terms. From the time of the first account in 1412 to the last surviving account for this period in 1532 the amount of the stipend allowed each official does not seem to have varied. Owing to the great difference among the various offices in scope and prestige it is surprising to find "main" officials (bailiff, constable) paid the same stipend of one mark a year, the clerk of the court rewarded also by one mark and the chief assistants, collectors of the farm and sub-bailiffs paid only slightly less at 10s. a year. But it must be recalled that various officials recovered "expenses," which no doubt included a stipend, for *ad hoc* tasks. For example, the clerk of the court received 12d. for writing the roll of the view of frankpledge in 1446 (called "roll of fines" that year) and two shillings for the same task in 1471. The same clerk received sixpence for writing the bailiff's roll in 1446 and 1528. Looked at from the lower end of the spectrum the same point can be made by noting that the collector from "foreigners" (later remyng') until 1446 at least received the substantial amount of four shillings despite the few for-

eigners on the rolls; and for the one term of Michaelmas 1471 the keeper
of the seals received three shillings, fourpence. But neither one of these
officials were given extra expenses.

It is only in the earliest surviving account that much detail is given about
the relationship between the accounts of the two bailiffs and the term-end
indebtedness. From the late fifteenth century the Jurors' Book was clearly
complementing the bailiffs' accounts, and the latter becomes more useful for
the study of account balances, as has been seen in Chapter 1. One also
suspects that the jurors also maintained a more immediate control over the
reception of funds in the town treasury and the disposal of funds after the
reforms of the late fifteenth century. But the sequence of surviving bailiff
accounts is too broken to reveal any pattern for the delivery of funds from
the treasury to the bailiffs beyond the occasional entry recording smallish
amounts "received from the jurors."

### A. Account of the Bailiffs of Godmanchester
### 3 April 1412–29 September 1412

(Godmanchester Borough Records, Box 1, Bundle 10)

#### Gumecestere

Compotus Thome Gylden' et Johannis Howman' Balliuorum ville a festo Pasche
Anno regni regis Henrici quarti post conquestum xiij° usque ad festum sancti
Michaelis

| | |
|---|---|
| In primis receperunt de remanenti ultimi compoti | viij.*li.*vj.*s.*x.*d.* |
| Item receperunt de exitu molendinorum | xxiij.*s.*ij.*d.* |
| Item de Collect' de Remyng'[1] | xxiij.*s.*iiij.*d.* |
| Item receperunt de collect' Altollagii de Estrate et Arnyng-strate | iij.*s.*vij.*d. ob'* |
| | seruic' alloc'[2] |
| Item receperunt de collect' altollagii de postrete et Westrate[3] | xiiij.*s.*iij.*d.* |
| Item receperunt de Gersumis et libertatibus[4] Curie | xiij.*s.*vj.*d.* |
| Item receperunt de Amerciamentis Curie | xiij.*s.*vj.*d.* |
| Item receperunt pro[5] vestura unius frisci de West lays dimissi Henrico Ede | vj.*d.* |

---

[1] Possibly "Remyngf'."
[2] Uncertain to which entry "seruic' alloc'" is meant to refer.
[3] postrete, Westrate: *sic* MS.
[4] "libertatibus" seems to have been struck out.
[5] pro: *sic* MS ("de" in other entries).

Item receperunt de[6] vestura unius Swath' iuxta nouum fossatum ex parte de Offord'     vj.*d.*

Item receperunt de bonis Thome Cantebrigg' forisfactis pro quodam felonia     xxij.*s.*

Item receperunt de bonis eiusdem Thome pro eodem de Johanne Fuller' ex debitis dicti Thome     x.*s.*

[7]Item receperunt de lane vij.li. et di'[8] prec'     v.*d.*

[7]Item receperunt de uno vitulo     ij.*s.*viij.*d.*

Item remanent in manibus domini Thome Dale nuper vicecomitis ij. blanket' et j. linth*eamentum*     ---------[9]

Item de exitu redditus regii[10]     ij.*s.*ij.*d.qua*'

Item receperunt de Alano Parkyn' pro quodam fine facto cum Balliuis     xvj.*d.*

Summa totius recepti xiiij.*li.*viij.*s.*ij.*d.*ob'qua

## EXPENSE

In primis in minutis expensis ad diuersas vices iiij.*d.* Item in vino dato seruienti domini Bewmont' v.*d.* Item solut' collectori firme pro redditu regio de Pekkisgroue viij.*d.* Item in expensis Clerici Receptoris Regis .vj.*d.* Item in expensis circa compotum Rotulorum redditus regii iiij.*d.* Item dat' custodi silue de Potton' .xl.*d.* Item in vino et ceruisia datis dicto custodi .vj.d.*ob*'. Item dat' seruienti eiusdem custodis viij.*d.* Item solut' pro cecacione arborum in Silua de Potton' ij.*s.*viij.*d.* Item in expensis Johannis Howman et R. Quynyzene versus Potton' et ibidem ix.*d.* Item dat' portantibus hastas circa campos .iiij.*d.* Item dat' lusoribus in recitacione ludi .iiij.*d.* Item in expensis Johannis Howman et R. Quynyzene et carpent' in cecacione meremii apud Siluam de Potton' .xvj.*d.* Item dat' seruienti custodis Siluarum de Potton' .xx.*d.* Item dat' pro factura unius paludis in via a Potton' .ij.*d.*[11] Item in expensis *eadem*[12] vice apud Potton' vij.*d.* Item solut' Marg*arete* Baker' pro ceruisia data carett*ar*' eadem vice ij.*s.*iiij.*d.* Item pro[13] caseo eodem tempore viij.*d.* Item in expensis Balliuorum Constabularii et subball*iui* Hunt' in septimana sancte Trinitatis coram Justiciariis domini Regis de pace .xij.*d.ob*'.[14] Item in vino dato dictis

---

[6] de: *sic* MS (see preceding note).

[7] These two entries connected by a marginal bracket with "straye" in left margin.

[8] The amount is conjectural; MS creased and stained.

[9] No amount entered in MS.

[10] MS omits "receperunt" in this entry.

[11] "ij.d." interlineated.

[12] Possibly "alia vice"; MS creased here.

[13] "Item pro" conjectural; MS creased.

[14] "ob'" interlineated.

Justiciariis .viij.*d.* Item dat' xij. Juratis de assisa[15] in sessione Justic*iariorum* domini Regis iiij.*d.* Item in ceruisia Hunt' eadem vice iij.*d.* Item solut' Johanni Sly' pro factura unius sere et unius Stapyl pro arn' j.*d.ob'.* Item in expensis apud Potton' in Arnald' Holker' et aliis offic' vj.*d.* Item alia vice apud Potton' .ij.*d.* Item in expensis ad ludum in virid*i* in ceruisia data patro[16] .xv.*d.* Item in factura poncium versus Redemade solut' Johanni Wryght' et suis sociis .x.*d.* Item in expensis ibidem dictorum operiatorum in cibis et potis .xj.*d.ob'.* Item in ceruisia ad luttacionem de Paxton' .iij.*d.* Item dat' agillar*io* j. par sotularium prec*ium* viij.*d.* Item in expensis Johannis Howman versus Potton et ibidem die Sabbati proximo post festum sancti laurentii[17] ij.*d.* Item in expensis bonorum hom' ad reducend*um* frangentes le Bilawe augusti iiij.*d.* Item in expensis ad reducendum meremium poncium de Redemade .iiij.*d.* Item in prandio unius hominis et sui equi de Sutton' portantium litteram a Receptore pro firma regia .iij.*d.* Item in expensis clerici Receptoris tempore recepcionis firme regie ad Pascham in prandio cum uno alio homine et duobus equis .viij.*d.* Item in ceruisia data hominibus Hunt' venientibus ad Curiam pro Reg*inaldo* Quyn*yzene* .ij.*d.* Item in ceruisia in emendacione de Howlondfogrth' .ix.*d.* Item in expensis vnius seruientis Receptoris firme in cena per noctem cum equo circa festum sancti Barnabe[18] .iiij.*d.* Item solut' Thome lister' et in potu circa scalas de Westmade .iij.*d.*[19] Item in potu dato Johanni Basset et aliis ad videndum dictum pontem .j.*d.ob'.* Item in expensis Balliuorum constabularii et subballiui ac alio[20] die mercurii in crastino sancti Jacobi apostoli[21] Hunt' coram Justiciariis delib*erantibus* .xij.*d.ob'.*[22] Item solut' pro emendacione de le Pondfoldwal' xj.*d.*[23] Item in pergameno empto .iij.*d.* Item in incausto .vj.*d.* Item dat' lusoribus xx.*d.* Item in expensis circa compotum Balliuorum .xij.*d.* Item in expensis circa factur*am* pontis de Redemade[24] et cariagium meremii versus pontes de Redemade .xij.*d.* Item dat' Thome Bernewell' pro remuneracione sua ad narrand*um* de bonis Thome Cantebrigg' xx.*d.* Item in cariagio scal*arum* versus diuersa prata .ij.*s.* Item in expensis xij. Jur*atorum* in die visus franciplegii .xix.*s.*ij.*d.* Item[25] in expensis Johannis H*owman* versus Potton' et ibidem et Hunt' iiij.*d.ob'.*

  Summa Expensarum iij.*li.*vij.*s.*v.*d.ob'.*

[15] MS "asis'."
[16] Possibly "patre."
[17] = 13 August 1412.
[18] = about 11 June 1412.
[19] "et memorandum" in left-hand margin here.
[20] "alio": *sic* MS.
[21] St. James fell on Monday, 25 July, in 1412; the morrow was thus Tuesday 26 July, and the Wednesday was 27 July.
[22] "ob'" interlineated.
[23] "xj.*d.*" is found in the left-hand margin.
[24] "pontis de Redemade" interlineated.
[25] MS repeats "Item" from the end of one line to beginning of another.

[dorse]

| | |
|---|---|
| *Allocaciones.* Johanni Styucle pro feodo suo | x.*s.* |
| Item Balliuis Gumecestr' pro officiis suis | xiij.*s.*iiij.*d.* |
| Item Constabulario pro eodem | vj.*s.*viij.*d.* |
| Item Collectori firme | .xx.*s.* |
| Item Collectori firme forinsece | ij.*s.* |
| Item Clerico Curie | vj.*s.*viij.*d.* |
| Item Subballiuo pro eodem | v.*s.* |
| Item Balliuo pro cariagio scalarum[26] | ij.*s.* |
| Item Balliuo Constabulario et subballiuo pro diuersis Hundredis | xx.*d.* |
| Item in oblacione clerici et subballiui | .xij.*d.* |
| Item ... [Cu?]rie[27] | vj.*d.* |
| Item in diuersis Hundredis [Johanni How?]man et *Reginaldo Quynyzene*[28] | xx.*d.*[29] |
| Item in Johanne Howman et Reginaldo Quyn*yzene* et Johanne Aylred' pro diuersis Hundredis versus Potton' et ibidem existentibus ad siluam pro cecacione meremii | iij.*s.* |
| Item solut' executor*ibus* Willelmi Peck' pro uno gronag' empto de dictis executoribus communitati | vj.*li.* |
| Item solut' pro Willelmo Herford' pro quodam fine facto coram Justic*iariis* de pace | xij.*d.*[30] |
| Item solut' vicecomiti pro fossura luti in communi via usque Offord' | ij.*s.* |
| Item alloc*atur* Thome Gylden' pro amerciamento Johannis Purqwey | iiij.*d.* |

Summa allocacionum ix.*li.*xiij.*s.*ij.*d.*

Et remanet ultra expensas xxvij.*s.*vij.*d.*

Et remanet in manibus Johannis Copegray de bonis Johannis Basset Junioris xj.*s.*vij.*d.* insolut' nec in isto compoto prescripto comput'

[A new hand continues:]

| | |
|---|---|
| Et remanet in manibus Thome Gylden' remanens Redditus Regii de termino Michaelis prescripto | xv.*d.* |
| De quibus in expensis Willelmi seruientis Receptoris per ij. vices semel per noctem et alio prouidendo. ac Pis*e* ad equum | vj.*d.* |

---

[26] Everything in this entry from "Balliuo" to "scalarum" is struck out, but the amount opposite is not deleted.

[27] Most of this entry is obscured by an apparently accidental spill of ink.

[28] Entire entry is underlined as if for deletion.

[29] Amount struck through.

[30] "*d.*" interlineated.

Item in expensis ball*iuorum* et collectoris firme per tres vices
ac ultimo[31] xij. iur*atorum*                                                    x.*d.*
Item remunerat' Willelmo Croxton' agill*ario* ex conuencione
pro itinere suo versus Hyham Ferer' cum seruiente Receptoris firme ad terminum Michaelis ultimum                        iiij.*d.*
Item pro uno equo ad Reginaldum Quenezene versus Lond'
ex conuencione                                                                  ij.*s.*ij.*d.*
Item deliber' Lond' ad festum Purificacionis beate Marie[32] per
manus .W. Arneburgh'                                                           .x.*s.*
Item eodem tempore per manus Johannis Fuller .ij.*s.* Et de
bursa mea propria xij.*d.*
Item eodem tempore de mutuo                                           xl.*d.*
Item petimus remuneracionem bonorum domini Thome Can-
t*ebrigg*                                                                         -----[33]

[The following memoranda are on a scrap sewn to the original membrane; in the
same hand as the original *compotus.*]
Memorandum quod Thomas Gylden' recepit de Johanne Howman' de suo remanent*ibus* Compoti dicti Johannis anno regni regis xiij° usque Michaelis[34]

In primis In par' bedys prec*ium* iij.*s.*iiij.*d.*[35]
Item in j. qwiylt' prec*ium*                                              iij.*s.*j.*d.*
Item in expensis factis pro Johanne Howman a festo Pasche
anno regni regis xiij° usque ad festum Michaelis proximo
sequentem                                                                  xxxiij.*s.*ij.*d.ob'.*
Item in expensis Johannis Howman' in visu franciplegg'       v.*s.*vij.*d.*
Item in diuersis Hundredis pro Potton' et Hunt'               ij.*s.*iiij.*d.*
Item de cariagio scalarum et pro labore circa pontes versus
Redemade                                                                  xviij.*d.*
Item solut' Thome Bernewell'                                       xx.*d.*
Item alloc' pro seruicio suo                                          vj.*s.*viij.*d.*

      Summa Lvj.*s.*iiij.*d.ob'.*

Item solut' executoribus W. Peek pro Le Groue[36]          iiij.*li.*vij.*s.*v.*d.ob'.*

      Summa totalis vij.*li.*iij.*s.*x.*d.*

Et sic omnibus computatis et allocatis Johannes *Howman* debet xxiiij.*s.*iiij.*d.* Et pro
uno vitulo Comelyng' precium ij.*s.*viij.*d.*

---

[31] ultro?
[32] = 2 February 1412.
[33] Blank in MS.
[34] "usque Michaelis" seems to have been written in later.
[35] The amount is here written directly next to the entry, not opposite.
[36] "Peek" occurs elsewhere in the MS as "Peck."

Et de exitu firme                                          ij.*s*.ij.*d.qua'*.

[The following seems to be written on the dorse from the top:]

Memorandum quod hec sunt debita que Thomas Gylden debet de compoto suo Balliue sue infrascripta

| | |
|---|---|
| In primis dictus Thomas debet Reginaldo Quynzene pro seruicio suo | iij.*s*.iiij.*d.*[37] |
| Item debet dicto Reginaldo pro Hundredis versus Potton' et Hunt' | x.*d.* |
| Item Johanni Aylred pro seruicio et Hundred*is* suis | iiij.*s*.ij.*d.* |
| Item Ricardo Skryuen*er*' pro seruicio et oblatione et incausto | vij.*s*.viij.*d.* |
| Item debet executoribus Willelmi Peek[38] | xxxij.*s*.vj.*d.ob'*. |
| Item Johanni Styuecle pro feodo | x.*s.* |
| Item Just*iciariis* pro quodam fine facto coram Justic*iariis*[39] | xij.*d.* |
| Item vicecomiti pro fossura luti | ij.*s.* |
| Item debet arrerag*ia* compoti Balliue sue | xxvij.*s*.vij.*d.qua'*. |

        [40]Summa iiij.*li.*ix.*s*.j.*d.ob'.qua'*.

Memorandum quod hii sunt debitores Thome Gylden de compoto suo infrascript*i*

| | |
|---|---|
| In primis Johannes Howman omnibus computatis et allocatis debet dicto Thome | xxix.*s*.ij.*d.qua'* |
| Item Willelmus Arnyngborw debet de exitu molendinorum | xxiiij.*s*.ij.*d.* |
| Item Thomas Ede debet de Altollag' | xv.*d.* |
| Item Willelmus in the bowr' omnibus computatis et allocatis | vij.*s*.ij.*d.* |
| Item Henricus Ede debet pro j. laye | vj.*d.* |
| Item Johannes Shyllyng' pro j. laye | vj.*d.* |
| Item Johannes lane iuxta cimiterium debet pro panno empto | vj.*s*.vj.*d.* |
| Item Johannes Fuller' debet pro debitis T.C.[41] | x.*s.* |
| Item Johannes Wryght' Sheperd' pro lana | v.*d.* |
| Item Alanus Parkyn debet[42] | xvj.*d.* |
| Item Johannes Freman' pro Gersum*a* | iiij.*s*.vij.*d.* |

        [43]Summa iiij.*li.*iij.*s*.vij.*d.qua'*.

---

[37] "*s.*" interlineated.

[38] Elsewhere in MS "Peck".

[39] Entry originally read "Item vicecomiti," but the second word is struck out.

[40] The sum is entered in a different hand.

[41] Presumably Thomas Cantebrigg', whose goods are mentioned elsewhere in the MS.

[42] The surname is possibly "Perkyn"; no reason given in MS for the debt.

[43] Summa appears in different hand identical to that of the earlier Summa (see note 40).

B. Account of the Bailiffs of Godmanchester
29 September 1413–8 April 1414

(Godmanchester Borough Records, D/1)

The document is in an excellent state of preservation and few "guesses" have had to be made. Because of some later antiquary's jottings and a few adjustments by the original scribe, however, it has not been possible to avoid some editorial footnotes. Briefer editorial adjustments have, as usual, been noted in the text in squared brackets.

The scribe's punctuation (scanty) and orthography have been allowed to stand. Capitalization has not been standardized. The form of the account is reproduced as it stands in the document—the receipts each as single entries, the expenses in paragraph form, and the allocations again as single entries.

*m. 1*

Compotus[1] Thome Gylden et Johannis Copegray Ballivorum ville de Gumecestere a festo sancti michaelis archangeli anno regni regis Henrici V[ti] [primo, *interlineated*] usque ad festum Pasche proximo sequens.

| | |
|---|---|
| In primis recept' de exitu molendin*orum*[2] | .iij. *li*.xvj. *s.*iij.*d.* |
| Item recept' de amerciamentis visusfranciplegg' de Estrete et Arnyngstrete[3] | .xiij. *s.* |
| Item recept' de Postrete et Westrete pro eodem | .xxvij. *s.*ij.*d.* |
| *servic' alloc'.* Item recept' de altollag' de Estrete et Arnyngstrete | .ij. *s.*v.*d.* |
| *sequid'* [?] *alloct' debet .iij.s.* Item recept' de Postrete et Westrete pro eodem | .x. *s.*ij.*d.* |
| Item recept' de amerciamentis curie | .vij. *s.*vj.*d.* |
| Item recept' de libertatibus[4] | .vj. *s.*x.*d.* |
| Item recept' de Gersumis Curie | .ij. *s.*vj.*d.* |
| [Item recept' de remanentibus xv[me] pro duobus terminis videlicet Martini et Pasche anno predicto][5] | |

---

[1] Each entry, including the heading, is marked with a small a-type marginal sign not reproduced here. Above the heading, an eighteenth or nineteenth-century hand has added "A festo Sancti Michaelis Anno Henry 5th," without a regnal year, and "Thomas Sylden [ *sic* ] & John Copegry Bailiffs".

[2] An eighteenth or nineteenth-century hand has written "Mill" between the end of this line and the sum of money across from it.

[3] The same hand adds "East Street Arynyng Street" between the end of the entry and its sum.

[4] The same hand adds "Freedoms 6[s]10[d]" in the corresponding location.

[5] The entire entry is struck out; no sum has been entered for it.

| | |
|---|---|
| *Weif'*. Item recept' pro quadam forisfactura unius feloni | .iij.*s*.iiij.*d.* |
| [Item recept' de fratribus Gilde omnium sanctorum per Willelmum Taylour ad emendandum vias ubi maxima egestas exigit | .iiij.*s.*][6] |
| Item recept' de Johanne Ive pro communi tauro | .ix.*s.* |
| Item recept' de quodam fine facto etcetera | .xij.*d.* |
| Item recept' de collectore de Remyng' | .xxiij.*s*.iiij.*d.* |
| Item recept' de Taxa forinseca integra[7] | .iiij.*s.* |
| Item[8] recept' de remanentibus xv^me de Estrete et Arnyngstrete de termino Martini | .xj.*s.* |
| Item recept' de remanentibus xv^e de Estrete et Arnyngstrete pro [eodem, *struck out*] termino Pasche | .ij.*s*.ix.*d.* |
| Item recept' de remanentibus xv^me de Postrete et Westrete pro termino Martini | .xiiij.*s*.x.*d.* |
| Item recept' de remanentibus xv^me de Postrete et Westrete pro termino Pasche | .x.*s*.ix.*d.* |
| Item recept' de exit*ibus* firme | .ij.*s*.iij.*d.* |

Summa recept' xj.*li*.ix.*s*.j.*d.*

## EXPENSE

In primis in expensis Balliuorum [et, *omitted*] Constabularii in posicione ceruisie ad asisam .j.*d.ob'.* Item solut' pro agitacione [*sic*] bouorum Johannis leenthorp' in Essex .ij.*s*.iiij.*d.* Item in Balliuis Constabulario et aliis bonis hominibus apud Hunt' ad habendum colloquium cum Balliuis de Hunt' pro tolloneo .iij.*d.* Item in expensis Balliuorum Constabularii et aliorum bonorum hominum pro posicione taxe ad festum sancti Martini .ij.*s*.j.*d.ob'.* Item in expensis operariorum in factura calceti citra Polebrigg' .iiij.*d.ob'.* Item in Balliuis Constabulario et aliis bonis hominibus apud Hunt' coram Justic' domini Regis de pace .ij.*s*.ij.*d.* Item dat' xij. Juratis eiusdem sessionis .iiij.*d.* Item apud Hunt' in expensis Balliuorum Constabularii et aliorum hominum ad habendum colloquium cum Rogero Hunt et aliis viris pro certis negociis communitatis faciendis .iij.*d.* Item in expensis .xij. Juratorum eodem die quo appreciati fuerunt .ij. Stott' .iiij.*d.* Item dat' Ricardo Chaloner'[9] de le Polebrigg' .j.*d.* Item in ceruisia data viris de Offord' pro die amoris facienda cum Thoma Nicole .vij.*d.ob'.* Item dat' Clerico Johannis Boteler .iiij.*d.* Item in Balliuis Constabulario et aliis bonis hominibus coram Justic' domini Regis de pace apud Hunt' .ij.*s.* ix.*d.* Item in vino dato dictis Justic' in eadem sessione .xv.*d.* Item dat' .xij. Juratis dicte

---

[6] This entry is marked "vacat" in left margin.

[7] "integra" was written in by the original scribe after the line had been drawn connecting the entry with its sum.

[8] An unexplained marginal "sol'" is written next to this entry.

[9] An unexplained marginal "emd'" is written in the left margin with apparent reference to this entry.

sessionis .ij.*d.* Item in Balliuis Constabulario et aliis bonis hominibus apud Hunt'
coram Justic' domini Regis de asisa .xxij.*d.ob'.* Item in expensis .xij. Juratorum in
posicione taxe ad terminum Pasche .ij.*s.* Item solut' pro obstupacione le Gappe iuxta
Johannem atthegrene .iiij.*d.* Item in Balliuis Constabulario et aliis ad habendum
colloquium cum Balliuis de Hunt' .ij.*d.ob'.* Item in pergameno empto .iiij.*d.* Item
apud Hunt' coram iustic' domini Regis .ij.*d.* Item in expensis Balliuorum Constabularii et aliorum bonorum hominum circa compotum [apud Johannem Baron',
*interlineated*] .vij.*s.* Item dat' Johanni Wafrer' pro suo labore versus Potton' ad
loquendum cum Johanne Leeu—— [remainder illegible] et Arnaldo Holker' .vj.*d.*
Item dat' pro turno vicecomitis tento apud sanctum Neot' .iij.*d.* Item Johanni
Copegray transeunti ad sanctum Neot[10] pro turno vicecomitis tento post Pascham
.vj.*d.* Item in expensis eadem vice .v.*d.* pro eodem turno. Item in expensis clerici
receptoris apud Hunt'. in deliberacione firme .xj.*d.* Item in expensis .xij. Juratorum
in ebdomada Pentecostis .iij.*d.* Item in Balliuis Constabulario et aliis bonis hominibus coram iustic' domini Regis de asisa apud Hunt' .vj.*d.* Item in pergameno
empto .vj.*d.* Item apud Hunt' in Johanne Styuecle Balliuis et aliis bonis hominibus
pro die amoris habenda pro tolloneo .viij.*s.vj.d.ob'.* Item dat' Johanni Boteler pro
sua remuneracione laboranti pro dicto tolloneo .vj.*s.viij.d.* Item in expensis vicecomitis pro certis negociis cum dicte vicecomite habendis .ij.*s.iij.d.ob'.*

Summa .xlix.*s.*ix.*d.*

*m. 2*[11]

Item solut' pro cibo militum .xij.*s.* Item dat' captori carett' ... expen*sis* eiusdem
captoris .xvj.*d.* Item in expensis factis dicti capt*oris* const*abul'* .xvj.*d.* Item in ceruisia
expendita de hominibus Hunt' tempore equitacionis cum Rege .xix.*d.* Item dat'
hominibus de Offord' et sancti Neoti [*sic*] eodem tempore .xij.*d.ob'.* Item in Balliuis
Constabulario et aliis bonis hominibus coram Justic' domini Regis de asisa apud
Hunt' .ij.*s.j.d.* Item .xij. juratis eiusdem Sessionis .iiij.*d.* Item in expensis .xij.
juratorum circa appreciacionem sotularium et unius selle Weif' .iiij.*d.* Item dat'
Thome Milleward' pro transitu suo ad Howton' pro retraccione de lez flodegat' [*sic*]
.j.*d.* Item in vino dato Arnaldo Holker' .vj.*d.* Item dat' lusoribus .iij.*s.* Item in
ceruisia expendita. pro Johanne How——[torn at right edge] in hominibus *patrie*
ad eundem ludum .vij.*d.* Item in ceruisia data Nicholao Styuecle et viris Hunt' et
patrie in redeundo a luctacione de Offord' .xiiij.*d.* Item in potu expendito pro
fraccione unius Goule in *houdepole*[12] .iiij.*d.* Item dat' Guydoni nuncio[13] ducatus

---

[10] Here a large hole deforms the left edge of the parchment; the scribe wrote around it for
the next six lines. Nothing appears to be lost as a result of the hole.

[11] The top of m. 2 is slightly folded over, losing the end of the first line; there is a small
tear at the right edge, losing the end of the second line. Ellipsis indicates words that cannot
be recovered or conjectured; underlined expansions are conjectural.

[12] This reading is conjectural.

[13] If "nuncio" is the correct reading, the word is lacking the "i." It is just possible that some
surname such are "Minco" is intended.

.xij.*d.* Item in expensis eius et in prandio equi Sui .vj.*d.* Item in carpentar' et in conduccione nauicule et in clauis emptis circa posicionem poncium ad diuersa prata per duas vices .vj.*d.* Item in .j. tauro empto pro communi[14] .x.*s.*vj.*d.* Item pro scripcione rotulorum visus suprascripti----.xij.*d.* [ *sic* ] Item alloc' Johanni Ive pro remuneracione unius tauri empti de Communitate minus cari .vj.*s.*

[The word "summa" is lacking] xliij.*s.*iiij.*d.ob'*.

| | |
|---|---|
| *Allocaciones.* Johanni Styuecle pro feodo suo | .x.*s.* |
| Item collectori firme | .xx.*s.* |
| Item collectori firme forinsece | .ij.*s.* |
| Item Balliuis Constabulario et subballiuo pro diuersis hundredis | .ij.*s.*viij.*d.* |
| Item Clerico curie pro officio suo | .vj.*s.*viij.*d.* |
| Item subballiuo pro eodem | .v.*s.* |
| Item clerico et subballiuo pro oblacione eorum [ *sic* ] | .xij.*d.* |
| Item solut' pro custodia communis tauri tempore iemali | .ij.*s.* |
| Item collectori amerciament*orum* visusfranciplegg' | .vj.*s.*viij.*d.* |
| Item solut' xij. iuratis clerico et subballiuo pro labore tempore visusfranciplegg' | .xiiij.*s.* |
| Item solut' pro redd*itu* le Greuage quondam W.P. [ *sic* ] | .iiij.*d.ob.quad'*. |
| Item solut' pro firma de termino Martini ultimo preterito a retro existente | .vj.*d.* |
| Item circa compotum Balliuorum | .xx.*d.* |

["Summa" again lacking] iiij.*li.*xij.*s.*   .*d.ob'*.   [ *quad'.* ][15]


### C. Account of the Bailiffs of Godmanchester
### 29 September 1445–17 April 1446

(Godmanchester Borough Records, Box 1, Bundle 10)

Compotus Ricardi Caue et Reginaldi Quenyene Balliuorum Ville de Gummecestr' a ffesto Michaelis Anno regni regis Henrici Sexti post conquestum Vicesimo quarto usque ad festum Pasce proximo sequens[1]

| | |
|---|---|
| [2]Item receperunt de exitibus molendinorum | xxvij.*s.*[2] |
| In primis receperunt de salicibus | xj.*s.*iij.*d.* |

---

[14] Possibly "communitate," but there is no suspension mark.

[15] The bottom of the membrane is turned up and the edges slightly damaged; the entire sum cannot be made out although "x.*d.*" is a possible reading. The "*quad'*" is entirely invisible but since only one sum among the allocations included a quad, there must have been one.

[1] From 29 September 1445 to 17 April 1446.

[2] Entire entry probably written in after the other entries completed.

Item receperunt de colect' le rermyng'                                              xxij.*s.*

Item receperunt de alltol' Estrete et Arnyngstrete et seruicia
allocantur[3]                                                                        iij.*s.*ij.*d.*

Item receperunt de altoll'[4] Postrete et Westrete et seruicia
allocantur[3]                                                                        x.*s.*

Item receperunt de Amerciamentis Curie                                              ix.*s.*vj.*d.*
                                                                                    et seruicia
                                                                                     allocantur[5]

Item receperunt de Gersmis[6] Curie                                                 ij.*s.*ij.*d.ob'.*

Item receperunt de Amerciamentis Visu[7] ffranci plegge Estrete
et Arnyngstrete[8]                                                                   v.*s.*v.*d.*

Item receperunt pro eodem Postrete et Westrete et seruicia
allocantur                                                                           xxj.*s.*iiij.*d.*

Item receperunt de Johanne Grene pro libertate sua                                  vij.*d.*

Item receperunt de T. Abildon' pro eodem[9]                                         vj.*s.*viij.*d.*

Item receperunt de Johanne Gerard' pro eodem[9]                                     iij.*s.*iiij.*d.*

Item receperunt de Willelmo Powe                                                    vj.*d.*

Item receperunt de assh' et Weche                                                   xiiij.*d.*

Summa recept' vj.*li.*x.*s.*vj.*d.ob'.*

In primis in expensis per manus R. Quenyene ad sanctum
Neotum apud Scheryuys[10] torn et Cantabirg'                                         iiij.*s.*

Item in expensis ante equitabat ad iantaculum[11]                                   v.*d.*

Item expen' apud *Hunt'* cum Willelmo Castelle                                      ij.*d.*

Item expen' apud Tadeselond' ad vicecomit*is* torn' per[12]
manus R. Quenyene                                                                   xxij.*d.*

Item expen' super illos qui ceperunt j stray                                        j.*d.*

Item expen' super illos qui colligebant sinos'[13]                                  iiij.*d.*

Item in expensis circa inquissisionem unius copule sygnorum
per manus R. Weuer'                                                                  j.*d.*

Item in diuersis expensis                                                           j.*d.*

Item solut' Johanni Bernard pro factura de muro cartabili                           xvj.*d.ob'.*

Item in expensis apud Hunt' quando Johannes Myllor fuit
attachiatus                                                                          v.*d.*

---

[3] "et seruicia allocantur" added later, in a new hand.
[4] *sic* MS, though "alltoll'" in preceding entry.
[5] "et seruicia allocantur" added later.
[6] *sic* MS.
[7] *sic* MS.
[8] "Estrete et Arnyngstrete" added later.
[9] *sic* MS, although "eadem" (i.e., "libertate") would seem better.
[10] I.e., sheriff's?
[11] I.e., ientaculum?
[12] MS clearly has "pro."
[13] Swans? (but *cf.* succeeding entry).

Item in expensis super clamorem de uno stray bis clamato
    apud Hunt'                                          ij.*d.*

Item in expensis in die sabati proximo post festum sancti
    Martini[14] cum diuersis                             ij.*d.*

Item in expensis Willelmi[15] Garloppe quia abigababat peccora
    extra Westemed'[16]                                ij.*d.*

Item in expensis in die sancti nicolai[17] super Radulfum
    Ramseye                                        ij.*d.ob'.*

Item in expensis super vxorem T. Pays de sancto Ivone    j.*d.*

Item in expensis super xij[cim] Homines pro testamento Grene
    et homine                                      iij.*d.*

Item solut' pro uno cornu empto pro agillaro          viij.*d.*

Item in expensis per manus Willelmi ffysscher' cum calcroft'    iij.*d.*

Item idem Willelmus expendebat apud Hyllyng' cum episcopo    iiij.*d.*

Item in expensis pro R. Quenyene quando equitabat lund'
    causa necessitatis ville                          vij.*s*.v.*d.*

Item in expensis in die sabati ante festum sancti T. apostoli[18]
    cum sub vicecomite                             xij.*d.*

Item dat' eodem vicecomiti[19] pro causa ville          iij.*s*.iiij.*d.*

Item solut' pultero domini regis[20]                 ij.*s*.viij.*d.*

Item in expensis super illos qui portauerunt stalas pratorum    j.*d.*

Item solut' ij. hominibus qui ludebat in cimiterio ecclesie    xij.*d.*

Item in expensis quando ponderauerunt panem in diuersis
    temporibus                                      vj.*d.*

Item in expensis quando Reginaldus Atnborowh' equitabat ad
    loquendum cum Gerard de lay[21]               vj.*d.*

Item solut' Gerardo de laye pro causa ville      xiij.*s*.iiij.*d.*

Item dat' xij[cim] Iuratorum pro domino rege          viij.*d.*

Item dat' Willelmo Castel'                       xij.*d.*

Item in expensis ad jentaculum eodem die et aliis expensis    ij.*d.*

Item eodem die in Vino                             vj.*d.*

Item in expensis per manus Willelmi Herr'wode ad sanctum
    neotum et ad T. et aliis locis               xiij.*d.*

Item in expensis quando consiliauerunt in die veneris ante ibant Hunt' et multi cum
illis totidem Rowseys vj.*d.* Item in die sabbati quando venirent domum in pane et

---

[14] 13 November 1445.

[15] MS has "Willelmo."

[16] The verb is perhaps derived from the adj. "abigeus," cattle-rustling.

[17] 6 December 1445.

[18] 18 December 1445.

[19] *sic* MS, although the undersheriff alone is mentioned in preceding entry.

[20] MS reads "domino regis."

[21] This name is written "Gerarddelay" to fit all on the same line, *cf.* next entry.

seruisia iiij.*d.* Item in carnibus emptis de W. Horr'wode et R. Oliue et in pane
seruisia .W.[22] iiij.*d.*[23] Item in expensis apud *Hunt'* quando balliui iste ville et eodem[24]
ceperunt consilium pro sessiones iiij.*d.* Item in expensis circa xij$^{cim}$ hominibus pro
iestyng' Johanni Garard' iij.*d.* Item in[25] expensis quando cessiones[26] fuissent pro ill*is*
de Kymbolton' ij.*d.* Item solut' pro ffacs' de stauulo et cepe ad finem le Holme iiij.*d.*
Item solut' T. Mathewe pro iemacione tauri[27] de Estrete ij.*s.* Item in expensis quando
R. Arnborgh' equitabat usque lund' pro Wryit' vij.*s.*vj.*d.* et pro labore xx.*d.*

| | |
|---|---|
| Item solut' pultero domini[28] regis | iij.*s.*vj.*d.* |
| [29]Item in expensis per manus R. Couyf' in paruis expensis | vj.*d.*[29] |
| Item in expensis diuersis vicibus | viij.*d.* |
| Item in expensis paruis | vj.*d.* |
| Item in expensis circa compotum balliuorum | ix.*d.ob'.* |
| Item in expensis quando balliuis venit[30] vicecomitem apud Croftum pro Wrytt' | ij.*s.*iij.*d.* |

[dorse]

| | |
|---|---|
| Alloc*atur* in primis Reginaldo Arneborgh' pro feodo suo | xiij.*s.*iiij.*d.* |
| Item Ricardo Este pro eodem | iij.*s.*iiij.*d.* |
| Item alloc*atur* balliuo pro officio suo | vj.*s.*viij.*d.* |
| Item clerico curie pro officio suo | vj.*s.*viij.*d.* |
| Item subbaliuo pro officio suo | v.*s.* |
| Item alloc*atur* collectori[31] firme reg*ie* | xx.*s.* |
| Item alloc*atur* collectori[31] le rermyng' | ij.*s.* |
| Item pro scriptura rotuli de amerciamentis | xij.*d.* |
| Item pro scriptura compoti balliui | vj.*d.* |
| Item pro incausto | iij.*d.* |
| Item alloc*atur* clerico et subbaliuo pro oblacione | xij.*d.* |
| Item alloc*atur* pro hundred' apud Cantabirg' balliuo[32] | xij.*d.* |
| Item alloc*atur* pro hundred' apud sanctum neotum balliu*o* et constabul*ario* | xij.*d.* |
| Item alloc*atur* balliuo pro hundred' apud Towselond' | iiij.*d.* |
| Item alloc*atur* balliuo et constabulario et subballiuo apud H*unt'* | x.*d.* |

---

[22] *sic* MS.
[23] The sum is interlineated.
[24] I.e., the bailiffs both of Godmanchester and of "that city"?
[25] MS omits "in" here.
[26] *sic* MS.
[27] See the entry on dorse below for a similar reference.
[28] MS again has "domino regis" (cf. note 20).
[29] Entire entry interlineated.
[30] "venit" conjectural.
[31] MS reads "colect'" in both cases.
[32] Expansion of "balliuo" conjectural.

Item alloc*atur* pro ij. Gr' empt' de Johanne Arneborgh'        xx.*d.*
Item pro percamino empto                                        v.*d.*
Item alloc*atur* Reginaldo Couyf pro hundred' usque lond'       iij.*s*.vj.*d.*
Alloc*atur* agillar' pro labore                                 xx.*d.*
Alloc*atur* Johanni Couyf pro custodia tauri in tempore yemali  ij.*s.*
Alloc*atur* xij^{cim} iuratorum pro labore[33]                  xij.*s.*
Alloc*atur* pro scriptura Rotuli firm*e* reg*ie* de postr*ete*  iiij.*d.*

  Summa expens' xvij.*s*.vj.*d*.ob'.

Et sic omnibus computatis et allocatis expens' extendunt recept'
  xxvij.*s.*


## D. Account of the Bailiff of Godmanchester
### 14 April-29 September 1471

(Godmanchester Borough Records, Box 1, Bundle 10)

Compotus Roberti       [1] a festo Pasche anno regni Regis Edwardi quarti post conquestum undecimo ad festum Michaelis Archangeli ex tunc proxim*o* sequentem[2]

### Recepta

In primis recept' de xij. hominibus                        ij.*li*.xix.*s.*
Item recept' de dictis xij. hominibus                      xxviij.*s.*
Item recept' de bonis A ...[3]                             xx.*d.*
Item recept' de bonis Johannis Polter[4]                   xxij.*d.*
Item recept' remanent' Thome Froste[5]                     xiiij.*s*.iiij.*d.*
Item recept' remanent' Willelmi Alred'                     xij.*s.*
Item recept' de le Caws ...[6]                             xv.*s*.x.*d.*
Item recept' de xij. hominibus                             xlix.*s*.xj.*f.*
Item recept' remanent' Thome Froste                        vj.*s*.viij.*d.*
Item recept' de Reginaldo Couyff' pro le Cawsre ...[7]     xiij.*s*.iiij.*d.*
Item recept' de Willelmo Stoday pro eisdem                 xiij.*s*.iiij.*d.*
Item recept' de Thoma Froste pro eisdem                    xiij.*s*.iiij.*d.*

---

[33] iuratorum: *sic* MS.

[1] MS blind.
[2] = from 14 April 1471 through 29 September following.
[3] MS illegible.
[4] "Polter" conjectural.
[5] Meaning unclear: possibly "recept*um de* remanent*ibus*"?
[6] MS not clear.
[7] MS not clear; probably same name as at note 6.

| | |
|---|---|
| Item recept' remanent' Willelmi Stoday | vj.*s*.viij.*d.* |
| Item recept' remanent' Reginaldi Couyff' | vj.*s*.viij.*d.* |
| Item recept' pro eodem Thom*e* Froste[8] | vj.*s*.viij.*d.* |
| Item recept' de Johanne Gardener Juniore pro communi frisci[9] | xij.*d.* |
| Item recept' de Roberto ... yott' pro eodem | x.*d.* |
| Item recept' de Ricardo Mannyng' pro dimidio acre frisci empto | xx.*d.* |
| Item recept' de dicto Ricardo pro vestura dicti dimidii acre | viij.*d.* |
| Item recept' de Thoma Balle | xx.*s.*[10] |
| Item recept' remanent' Willelmi Alred | viij.*d.* |
| Item recept' remanent' Reginaldi Couyff' | x.marc' |
| Item recept' de Willelmo Chisle | x.*s.* |
| Item recept' de amerciamentis Curie | xvij.*s*.ix.*d.* |
| Item recept' de diuersis libertatibus diuersorum hominum | xxj.*s*.iiij.*d.* |
| Item recept' de Gersumis Curie | xv.*d*.*ob'*. |
| Item recept' remanent' Johannis Suell | iiij.*s.* |
| Item recept'[11] de uxore Thome Longe | vj.*s*.viij.*d.* |
| Item recept' pro sign*etto* | xij.*s.* |
| Item recept' remanent' Roberti Couyff' per xij. homines | xxij.*s.* |
| Item recept' de Aletolle Postrete et Westrete et seruicia alloc*entur* | viij.*s.* |
| Item recept' de Aletolle Estrete et Arnygstrete et seruicia alloc*entur* | ij.*s*.viij.*d.* |
| Item recept' de priore Canonicorum Hunt' pro redditu de Causeholm' | xij.*d.* |
| Item recept' pro firma molendinorum | xiij.*li.* |

Summa tocius recepte xxxviij.*li*.v.*d*.*ob'*.

### *ROTULUS* EXPENSARUM ET DELIBERACIONUM

In primis expend' super le Cawgerus ij.*li*.xvj.*s.* Item Henrico Marshall pro le leryng de Wagys ad dictum le Cawgerus xx.*d.* Item Roberto Smyth pro eodem ij.*s.* Item expen' in delyng de le Almuscorn*er* vj.*d.* Item super xij. homines apud Georg' vj.*d.* Item apud Hunt' iiij.*d.* Item apud Hug' Bowlde super le Cawgerus ij.*d.* Item dat' le Cawgerus xxviij.*s.* Item in Capcione monete Hugon*is* Bowlde ij.*d*.*ob'*. Item super Cawgerus et in Weethyng' apud Ricard' *W*elia x.*d.* Item apud Cauys pro eodem

---

[8] Meaning unclear; received for the identical Thomas Frost, or received *from* Thomas for the same reason?

[9] "communi" conjectural.

[10] This amount is accompanied by a small indecipherable marginal notation.

[11] At this point there is an illegible interlineation.

x.*d*.[12] Item in diuersis expensis vj.*d*. Item Thome Samson' pro le dichyng' viij.*d*. Item pro Cariagio de Silua communi grene et pro heggyng' xiiij.*d*. Item super xij. homines quando appreciauerunt bona Johannis Pouders viij.*d*. Item super viam[13] apud Cauys pro Blakke Robyn viij.*d*. Item in vino dato Wake et Steuecle apud Mustr' vij.*d*. Item pro eodem super Cullam et alios generosos domini de Wylchyr' vj.*d*. Item expen' eodem die super vicecomitem et balliuum Hunt' vj.*d*. Item ball*iuo* Hunt' pro le Cagarde xiij.*s*.iiij.*d*. Item eodem tempore ibidem x.*d*. Item expen' super Wake Steuecle Tailard et Cullam xx.*d*. Item expen' apud Boleys super Homines Cantabrg' quando seruus Henrici barrett fuit impe*tratus*[14] iiij.*d*. Item pro *scriptura* Rotuli Redditus Regis de Postrete viij.*d*. Item expen' apud Hunt super Wolmer' quando iuit Lond' vij.*d*. Item apud Georg' super xij. homines vj.*d*. Item pro rakett' le Caw*gerus circa* festum Pasche v.*s*.x.*d*. Item apud Hunt' super Counte de Kente ij.*s*. Item super Wolmer' quando venit Lond' vj.*d*. Item apud Hunt' iij.*d*. Item apud Ball' in deliberacione monete le Cawgerus vj.*d*. Item apud Hylton'[15] super Cawgerus' istius ville et Hunt' quando transier*unt* Regi vj.*d*. Item dat' Wolmer' quando iuit lond' pro rumoribus vj.*s*.viij.*d*. Item Thome Samson' pro stryng salic' iiij.*d*.[16] Item dat' Cawgerus v.*li.*v.*s*.iij.*d*. Item Johanni Fuller pro beryng' le Wayt de Cawgerus lond' ij.*s*. Item Reginaldo Couyff' pro uno equo lond' viij.*d*. Item expen' apud ludum in die dedicacionis xj.*d*. Item expen' super sapcote viij.*d*. Item pro *fabricacione* de le Poundfold j.*d*. Item Rogero Mannyng pro stryng' salic' ex parte orientali viij.*d*.[16] Item Johanni Manypeny pro eodem ex parte occidentali iij.*d*. Item in die Sessionis Gaol' super vic*ecomite*m et extraneos apud Johann' Draperys ij.*s*. Item in vino dato Justiciariis vicecomiti et diuersis generosis ij.*s*. iiij.*d*. Item in die electionis coronatoris comitatus xiiij.*d.ob*'. Item apud Hunt' super Balliuum de Brampton' et alios vj.*d*. Item apud Cauys super xij. homines vij.*d*. Item in die Curie apud Notyngham vj.*d*. [End of recto or of m. 1]

Item super Capcione Bigarum domini Regis et constat xiiij.*d*. Item dat' le Carters vj.*d*. Item Thome Brygthwell pro stipendo xv.*s*. Item in Electione nouum Officiar' iij.*s*.iiij.*d*. Item Thome ffyss' et socio suo pro expensis apud Stylton' et Staumford quando equitauerunt cum le *gunnys'* xiiij.*d*. Item apud Hunt' super balliu*os* et vicecomitem quando generos*i* obuiauerunt ibidem vj.*s*. Item expen' in takyng sign' ad diuersa tempora xx.*d.ob*'. Item expen' apud Hunt' quando rex fuit ibidem super Capter' bigarum et aliorum iiij.*s*.vij.*d.ob*'. Item in Caponibus iij.*s*.x.*d*. Item expen' quando balliui et vicecomes equitauerunt Hertford' Regi xxviij.*s*.vj.*d.ob*'. Item in regard' diuers' generosis x.*marc*' et x.*s*. Item super xij. Homines in fractione virge vj.*s*.j.*d*. Item in pargameno et incausto xv.*d*. Item pro scriptura computi[17] Balliui vj.*d*. Item circa compotum[17] balliui x.*d*. Item expen' quando balliui et Gylmyn' equi-

---

[12] MS not easily legible here; "*d*." likely but possibly could be "*s*."

[13] "viam" conjectural; if Black Robin was an outlaw "vicecomitem" would be plausible reading.

[14] Conjectural reading from "impe⁹."

[15] "Hylton'" interlineated, replacing "Hunt'" which is struck out.

[16] "salic'" is *definitely* a willow, but "stryng" is obscure.

[17] *sic* MS.

242 APPENDIX 1

tauerunt Sapcote viij.*d.*[18] Item pro iac' stalar'[19] ij.*s.* Item solut' Johanni Gylmyn' pro Eas' xij.*li.*ij.*s.* Item dat' in regard' Thome Gylmyn' vj.*s.*viij.*d.*[20] Item dat' fil' Johanni Albyngham iij.*s.*iiij.*d.* Item expen' in visu ffranciplegii xxxviij.*s.*viij.*d.* Item Thome Bryhtwell' pro stipendio xv.*s.*

Summa totius expense xxvj.*li.*vj.*s.*v.*d.ob'.*

| | |
|---|---|
| Allocatur Balliuo pro officio suo | vj.*s.*viij.*d.* |
| Willelmo Hussey pro feodo suo | iij.*s.*iiij.*d.* |
| Johanni Mynstr' chaumbr' pro feodo suo | vj.*s.*viij.*d.* |
| Johanni Gylmyn' pro feodo suo | iij.*s.*iiij.*d.* |
| Clerico Curie pro[21] officio suo | vj.*s.*viij.*d.* |
| Clerico Curie pro scriptura visus | ij.*s.* |
| Subballiuo pro summonicione visus | xij.*d.* |
| Balliuo Constabulario et Subbaliuo pro Hundredo apud Hunt' | xx.*d.* |
| Balliuo pro Hundredo apud Lond' | iij.*s.*iiij.*d.* |
| Subbaliuo pro officio suo | v.*s.* |
| Agillar' pro ...[22] patr*ie* | vj.*d.* |
| Constabulario pro officio suo | vj.*s.*viij.*d.* |
| Thome *Bates Beonde*[23] pro custodia sign*etti* | iij.*s.*iiij.*d.* |
| Clerico *Curie* subballiui et agillar' pro oblacionibus suis | xviij.*d.* |

Summa tocius alloc*acionum* ij.*li.*xj.*s.*viij.*d.*

Et sic omnibus computatis in computandis et allocatis allocandis per manus de Clerico[24] Comitatus ix.*li.*ij.*s.*iiij.*d.*

Inde de amerciamenta per villam ad communem aulam per xij. Homines xxv.*s.ob'.* in vigilia sancti Georgii Martyris anno regni regis Edward iiij.*ti* xij.[25]

Item deduct' in pecunia ...[26] dicto die xviij.*s.*ix.*d.*

Inde deduct' die jouis proximo ante festum sancti Michaelis Archangeli anno suprascripto[27] xl.*s.*

Item deduct' die dominica in vigilia sancti Thome apostoli anno supradicto[28] xiij.*s.*iiij.*d.*

Item deduct' die veneris ante festum sancti Michaelis archangeli anno regni regis Edwardi iiij.*ti* xiij° pro fine Willelmi Horrewod'[29] iij.s.

---

[18] "viij.*d.*" interlineated, replacing "vj.*d.*" which is struck out.
[19] The form "pro iactura stalarum" occurs written out fully in the 1527-1528 roll.
[20] Everything from "Thome" to the end of the entry has been struck out.
[21] "pro" interlineated.
[22] MS illegible.
[23] "Beonde" conjectural.
[24] *sic* MS.
[25] = 22 April 1471.
[26] MS indecipherable.
[27] = 26 September 1471.
[28] = 20 December 1471, unless referring to the feast of St. Thomas' translation on 3 July, in which case the vigil would be 2 July. The former, however, is the more likely.
[29] = 24 September 1473.

E. ACCOUNT OF BAILIFF OF GODMANCHESTER
30 MARCH 1483–29 SEPTEMBER 1483

(Godmanchester Borough Records, Box 1, Bundle 10)

Compotus Willelmi ffrer' balliui a festo Pasche usque festum Michaelis anno regni regis Edwardi quarti xxiij.°

Recept*a*

| | |
|---|---|
| In primis recept' de *Willelmo Many*peny[1] | xl.*s.* |
| Item de Edwardo Barre *et* ...[1] | vj.*s.*viij.*d.* |
| Item for Payeforow | xvj.*s.* |
| Item recept' de ffinibus | iiij.*li.*viij.*s.*viij.*d.* |
| Item recept' de Gersumis | iiij.*s.*vj.*d.ob'.* |
| Item de Amerc*iamentis* visus de E. et A. seruic*iis* allocat*is*[2] | xj.*d.* |
| Item de Amerc*iamentis* visus de P. et W. seruic*iis* allocat*is*[3] | iij.*s.* |
| Item de Amerc*iamentis* Curie | xvj.*s.* |
| Item recept' de Thoma Maille | x.*s.* |
| Item recept' de Thoma Mowinforde | iij.*s.*iiij.*d.* |
| Item de ffirma molendinorum | xij.*li.* |
| Item de Alletolle .E. et .A. seruic*iis* allocat*is*[2] | -----[4] |
| Item de Alletolle .P. et .W. seruic*iis* allocat*is*[3] | iiij.*s.*iij.*d.* |
| Item recept' de prato Trelowe | -----[4] |
| Item recept' de Willelmo Maille pro .ij. frisc*is* | ---.*d.*[5] |
| Item de Willelmo ffrost socio meo pro uno frisco | ---.*d.*[5] |
| Item for scabydhorsolasur' | vj.*s.*iij.*d.* |

Summa xxj.*li.*viij.*s.*iiij.*d.ob'.*[6]

liberaciones et expensa

...[7] in die Parasceues xij.*d.* Item super Wulfe ...[7] *in* vigilia Pasche .x.*d.* Item Henrico Pikforke quando equitauit Bury x.*d.* Item apud Bigg' super Wulfe et at generosis xij.*d.* Item apud Hunt' in die sessionis pacis v.*s.*iiij.*d.* Item in die Curie apud Cauys ix.*d.* Item super xij. homines apud Bigg' vij.*d.* Item in delyng of Almescorn' iiij.*d.* Item Willelmo Ybotte pro le Fellyng' salic*iarum* iiij.*d.* Item pro Rayles for the Grene .ix.*d.* Item for Settyng' de dictis Rayles iiij.*d.* Item Willelmo Ybotte pro labore quando iuit Wardboys ij.*d.* Item super .xij. homines apud Bigg' viij.*d.* Item super xij. homines

---

[1] A broad diagonal stain obscures roughly the first third of the receipts; words underlined are conjectural.

[2] Probably the "Arynyngstrate" and "Estrate" of the other accounts.

[3] Probably the "Postrate" and "Westrate" of the other accounts.

[4] No sum in MS.

[5] These sums are rubbed out, perhaps deliberately.

[6] The summa is in a new hand.

[7] A stain obscures the first words in the first two lines of expenses.

apud Cauys quando veni Lond' xij.*d.* Item in die Curie et in ponderac*ione* panis iij.*d.*
Item pro factura lees Dampne et pylys x.*s.* Item Willelmo Ybotte pro carryyng[8] le
bote ij.*d.* Item apud Sanctum Yvonem super vicecomitem et extraneos die lune
Pent*ecoste*[9] vij.*s.* Item in Regard' Regi pro piscibus et in expensis apud Hunt'
diuersis temporibus xx.*s.* Item pro iactur*a* stalarum iij.*s.* Item in Regard' in die
dedicacionis Stephano Sygar' xx.*d.* Item Thome Lesse quando iuit Howghton' j.*d.*
Item super xij. Homines apud Sydebotoms viij.*d.* Item pro le takyng uppe duorum
sign*orum* ij.*d.* Item Willelmo Nottyngham pro le Swanhoke ij.*d.* Item Roberto Weber
quando transiuit Howghton' ij.*d.* Item in regard' le Messenger .xiij.*s.*iiij.*d.*. Item in
expensis super eundem et vicecomitem diuersis temporibus iiij.*s.* Item ad parues apud
Bat' iij.*d.* Item apud Hunt' in die Gaole deliberac*ion*' super vicecomitem et extraneos
et in vino dato iusticiar*iis* vj.*s.*vj.*d.* Item apud Scott' super xij. Homines x.*d.* Item pro
dortores iij.*d.* Item for leyng' up of tymbr' xiij.*d.* Item apud Will' Taylour ad le parues
iij.*d.* Item super xij. homines pro visu domus Willelmi Pouder iij.*d.* Item in expensis
in electione offic' apud biggys v.*s.*ij.*d.* Item pro fedyng duorum signorum et pro
labore ij.*s.*x.*d.* Item for Wynteryng of a bulle ij.*s.* Item for taking up trium signorum
iiij.*d.* Item transende ad Barnwell' xij.*d.*[10] Item to the Berewarde x.*d.* Item Thome
Embey et Willelmo Ybotte pro cariagio duorum signorum ball*iuo* de Stanton' pro
labore et expensis vj.*d.* Item super xij. homines apud Bigg' ij.*s.*iiij.*d.* Item super
Robertum Pulter quando venit lond' iij.*d.* Item apud Will' Manypeny quando Mr
Stodalfe fuit Hunt' iiij.*d.* Item Johanni Sent quando equitauit Ramesey mecum ad
loquendum cum dicto Magistro Stodalfe et per[11] horsemet' ibidem vj.*d.* Item apud
le parueys apud Faldyng' v.*d.* Item Johanni Inglysshe pro equo lond' xij.*d.* Item
Thome Sidebotom' pro eodem xij.*d.* Item Johanni Capell' quando iuit cum le
Carttaker iij.*d.* Item to the cartetaker'[12] xij.*d.* [13]Item circa compotum x.*d.* Item
clerico curie pro incausto et pergameno xv.*d.* Item pro scriptura compoti vj.*d.* Item
apud Biggys super xij. Homines frangendo virgam viij.*s.j.d.* Item in expensis in
tempore visus franciplegii iiij.*li.*ij.*s.*x.*d.* Item apud le leete xx.*d.*

Summa ix.*li.*xviij.*s.j.d.*

[Dorse:]

## Allocaciones

| | |
|---|---|
| In primis allocatur balliuo pro feodo | vj.*s.*viij.*d.* |
| Item Johanni Mynstrchaumbr' pro feodo | vj.*s.*viij.*d.* |

---

[8] *sic* MS.
[9] = 19 May 1483.
[10] Should "transende" be read "transeude" and conjecturally expanded to some form of, e.g., "transeundo"?
[11] *sic* MS.
[12] "Carttaker" is differently spelled in two successive entries.
[13] The following entries, though in the same hand, would appear to have been written in later.

Item clerico curie pro feodo suo                                              vj.*s*.viij.*d*.
Item pro scriptura visus                                                       ij.*s*.
Item clerico curie subballiuo agillar' pro oblationibus suis                  xviij.*d*.
Item subbaliuo pro summonicione vis*u* franciplegii                           xij.*d*.
Item agillar' pro emendacione petre[14]                                       vj.*d*.
Item balliuo constabulario et subbaliuo pro hundreda                          xx.*d*.
Item subballiuo pro feodo                                                     vj.*s*.
Item constabulario pro feod*is* suis[15]                                      vj.*s*.viij.*d*.
Item Willelmo Tothe pro officiis ergamste[16]                                 -----[17]
Item custodi signorum                                                         -----[17]
Item pro iij. hundredis london' et Norwic'                                    -----[17]

    Summa iiij.*li*.xx.*d*.

Summa remanent vij.*li*.viij.*s*.vij.*d*.*ob*'.
Inde allocatur die mercurie proximo ante festum Michaelis anno regni regis Ricardi tercii[18] primo pro diuersis expensis ut deliberacionibus et donacionibus pro xij. iuratis xxviij.*s*.vij.*d*.*ob*'. unde remanent die et anno prescriptis de remanentibus predictis vj.*li*.

## F. ACCOUNT OF A BAILIFF OF GODMANCHESTER
## CA. 1495

(Godmanchester Borough Accounts, Box 8,
Other Documents, Miscellaneous, no. 3)

Fragment of an account of a bailiff of Godmanchester, perhaps late Henry VII.

This document was clearly written by an inexperienced scribe who wanders back and forth between English and very poor Latin. No attempt has been made to impose uniformity of spelling or syntax since this would have resulted in an apparatus longer than the account itself. Particularly striking departures from standard usage have been noted only by "*sic*" and diplomatic events (interlineations, etc.) by footnotes. Spelling and capitalization have been reproduced as carefully as possible despite the resultant confusion (e.g., "vigilaverunt" and "wigilaverunt" in successive entries).

The entries for expenses are written firstly in linear fashion, one by one, then go into paragraph form, return to linear form and conclude in paragraph form. This has been reproduced here.

[14] MS possibly "pecre" or "pacre".
[15] "feodis" is expanded to agree with "suis" which is written out in full.
[16] [P]ergamste is a form of pergamina (parchment).
[17] A stain obscures these sums.
[18] = 24 September 1483.

Almost every final sum in the account was altered, in one case three times. It is rarely possible to decipher the original sums that were deleted. Whether these alterations indicate a mathematician as clumsy as the scribe is unclear.

Despite the scribal atrocities, some 21 names appearing in this account are familiar to other Godmanchester records of the 1490s: John Adam de Cambridge, (William) Basse, John Bowlde, John Brewster, Stephen Clerk, Robert Chandeler, Thomas Fecas, (Robert) Feltwell, William Frere, John Gredley, William Gybbys, John Holmes, William Ibott, William Kyng, John Lockyngton, William Manipenny, Thomas Marshall, John Smyth, Henry Smyth, John Turneskewe, John Ussher. The earliest date possible to this document would be the end of the 1480s since William Basse purchased liberty in September, 1487. Many of the other names begin to disappear shortly after 1500, so this account is roughly dated here as ca. 1495. Other names on the record are likely outsiders: John Comyn, Foster de Huntingdon, John Marham, Master David Philip, Master Taylord.

| | |
|---|---|
| Item recepit de aletoll' de E et a ...[1] | v.s ... |
| Item recepit de Willelmo Kyng' pro toga | iiij.d. |
| Item recepit de Iohanne Comyn' pro tallia | vj.s.viij.d. |
| Item recepit pro salucibus diuersorum hominum | xx.s.xj.d. |

Summa recepcionis viij.li.iij.s.iiij.d.ob'[2]

deliberationes et expense

| | |
|---|---|
| Item In expencis super cariagium meremii ville apud Iohannem vschars in pane et potu et alijs victualibus[3] | iij.s.xj.d. |
| Item In expencis apud Iohannem vschars die sessiones [sic] pacis tente apud hunt' | vij.d. |
| Item In expencis datis Stephano Clarke pro labore suo et pro Instrumentis apud synt marigrowe | xvj.d.[4] |
| Item in expencis apud Iohn vschars pro unitate faciendo [sic] Inter Willelmum Kyng et Robartum Wolfe[5] | v.d.[5] |
| Item In expencis super ballivis de Hunt' ad habendum copiam Convencionis pro schot'[6] | xj.d.[6] |

Item In expencis super diversos homines qui vigilaverunt ignem apud Chawretre pro labore pane et potu ij.s. Item solvit iiij[or] homines [sic] qui wigilaverunt [sic] super le leche et pro aquietando ad habendum talem de morbus suys xix.d. Item soluit quinstabulare [sic] pro pro [sic] labore suo advigilandum et Equitandum pro dicto leche vj.d. Item In expencis pro cariagio dicti leche apud huntyngdon' xij.d. Item pro

---

[1] Top edge of fragment crumbled, losing much of the first line.
[2] Original sum written here is scratched out.
[3] "victualibus" and the sum were added below the line.
[4] Sum added below the line.
[5] "Wolfe" and sum added below the line.
[6] "pro schot'" and sum added below the line.

facticione le stylys aput kynwale iij.*d.* Item In expencis super balliuis et aliis pro
diversis cavsis communicandis apud bassis iiij.*d.* Item In vino dato priori de hunt'
quando sacrificavit altaria xvj.*d.* Item pro emendacione le pinfolde et pro meremio
pertinente dicto [*sic*] x.*d.* Item pro loppyng de salucibus et pro hedgyng et cariagio
apud grenagium qui nuper fuit gillis xix.*d.*[7] Item In vino dato magistro morres' et
magistro malari apud hunt' die eleccionis militum de scher' viij.*d.* Item In expencis
super magistrum r. morres apud manypenyes ij.*d.* Item In expencis super seruientes
magistri davit philyp apud Bassys ij.*d.* Item In expencis super Iohn Adams de
Cambrygg' apud Iohn' Grydleys ij.*d.* Item In expencis die sessiones [*sic*] tente apud
hunt' super generosos et vicini et apud Iohn' vschars ij.*s.*v.*d.*

| | |
|---|---|
| Item In expencis super commissiones domini regis super lone apud hunt' | xxj.*d.* |
| Item pro exclamacione le equa de lechys et pro feno sibi apud hemmynford' | ix.*d.* |
| Item In expencis pro unitate faciendo Inter Willelmum Iobet Thomam Marschall' et fost' de hunt' | xij.*d.* |
| Item In expencis super duodecym et alijs[8] apud Willelmum Iobott' quando mittebant pecuniis [*sic*] domino regi | xiiij.*d.* |
| Item In expencis super conuinciones de granis apud huntyng- don' | xj.*d.* |
| Item payd pro beryng up ye lone to london xl.*d.* et expencis ye sam tim | iij.*d.ob'.* |
| Item soluit Willelmus [*sic*] manipeny quinstabullario pro cariagio de homine qui periurit regnum regis ad proximum quinstabularium et super capciones de granis | vij.*d.ob'.* |

Item In expencis die sessiones [*sic*] et deliberaciones apud hunt xxij.*d.* In vino dato
Iudico et magistro Taylord xij.*d.* Item In expencis pro vnitate faciendo [*sic*] apud
Ivonem et apud Iohn' boldes viij *s.*v.*d.* Item In expencis super Willelmum fryr' et
Iohn' lobryngton' et alijs pro labore apud magistro [*sic*] taylor' per remedium illis
[*sic*] qui fuerunt Indicati apud Iohn' Grydleys.[9] Item in expencis super Iohannem
Marham et henrico [*sic*] Smyth et alijs pro laboracione Inter festwell' et aliis istius
ville apud Iohn' holmys iiij *d.* Item In expencis super Takar of horsys xix.*d.*

| | |
|---|---|
| Item In expencis super seruum recepercionis[10] | ij.*d.* |
| Item for wyntryng of ye comyn bull' | ij.*s.*[11] |
| Item In expencis super deliverey super almystor' | ij.*d.* |
| Item payd to aman that caw w$^t$ ye tacar of horsys | viij.*d.* |

Summa totalis expense ij.*li.*vj.*s.*x.*d.*[12]

---

[7] "xix.*d.*" added below the line.
[8] "et alijs" interlineated.
[9] There seems to be an interlineation here, but it is indecipherable.
[10] "recepercionis" conjectural.
[11] The sum appears originally to have read "ij.*s.*iiij.*d.*" but the 4*d* is erased.
[12] Original sum written here was scratched out.

| | |
|---|---|
| Item In expencis apud Primis Curiis et per visum tentum apud Iohn holmys | v.*d.* |
| Item In expencis apud Curiam et per visum tentum apud Iohn Turnskewe | v.*d.ob*'. |
| Item In expencis apud Curiam et per visum tentum apud Iohn vschars | vj.*d.* |
| Item In expencis apud Curiam et per visum tentum apud bassys et pro duobus [*sic*] questionibus pro diversis cawsis communicandys | iij.*s*.iiij.*d.* |
| In expencis apud curiam et per visum tentum apud Iohn grydeys | xj.*d.* |
| Item In expencis apud Curiam et per visum tentum apud Iohn' brewstarr' | iij.*d.* |
| Item In expencis apud Curiam et per visum tentum apud Willelm' Iobott' | xij.*d.* |
| Item In expencis apud Curiam et per vysum tentum apud Robartum schawnlars | x.*d.* |

summa istius parcelle vij.*s*.viij.*d.ob*'.

| | |
|---|---|
| Item In expencis super equitando [*sic*][13] magistro [*sic*] david[14] philyp cum Willelmo manypeny et Thoma fecas super ballivum Clerc et subballivum apud harbrow | x.*s*.ix.*d.* |
| Item subballivo pro Equo et pro labore suo ibidem[15] | xviij.*d.* |
| Item pro vino datto [*sic*] magistro davitie philyp ibidem | iiij.*d.* |
| Item In expencis equitando apud london cum predicto Willelmo manipeny super ballivum Iohn' Smyth' Willm' Gigby et subballivum et pro labore | xviij.*s*.x.*d.* |
| Item In expencis super magistr*um* daviti phylyp apud huntynton' | xxij.*s.* |
| Item In expencis super magistr*um* davit' predict*um* apud Iohn' vschars | xiiij.*s.* |

summa istius parcelle xxxvj.*s*.iiij.*d.*[16]

Alocatur [*sic*]

| | |
|---|---|
| Item In primis Ballivus pro feodo | vj.*s*.viij.*d.* |
| Item ballivus quinstabularius et subballivus pro hundryd' | xl.*d.* |
| Item subballivo et agillario pro oblacionibus | xij.*d.* |
| Item subballivo pro feodo | v.*s.* |
| Item custodes sygnorum pro feodo | iij.*s*.iiij.*d.* |

[13] After "equitando" there are perhaps two or three words scratched out.
[14] "david" interlineated.
[15] "ibidem" interlineated.
[16] Original sum written here was scratched out.

Item agillario pro Toga et feodo                                vj.*s*.viij.*d.*
Item eidem agillario pro sotularibus                           viij.*d.*

       summa xxix.*s*.iij.*d.*

Omnibus computatis et allocatis debet declaro comitatur [*sic*] x.*li*.vj.*s*.x.*d.ob*'[17]

Item recepit de Thome marschall' et Willelmo Iobot pro redditu de[18] lese of ye[19] next ye pondyerde viij.*d.* Item recepit de Willelmo Iobot pro stondyng' of hys best ad finem ... ...j.*d.ob*'.[20]

## G. Account of the Bailiff of Godmanchester
### 29 September 1508–8 April 1509

(Godmanchester Borough Accounts, Box 8,
Other Documents, Miscellaneous, no. 7)

The accounts are in a mixture of Latin and English, the receipts mostly in Latin with a few English words and the expenses largely in English. Latin resumes for the allocations. In the English sections where the expansion was not beyond all doubt, the suspension has been retained since the intended spelling could not be determined.

    There is some damage at the beginning of the document. This is indicated by a system of asterisks and by ellipsis; the starred entries are mutilated. Entries that have been deleted, interlineations, etc., have been noted in footnotes.

Compotus Iohannis Branden vnius Ballivorum a festo sancti michaelis archangeli in anno Regni Regis henrici septimi vicesimo quarto vsque pascha ex tunc proximo sequenan' [*sic*]

Item In primis Recepi de duodecim homines [*sic*] ad festum
    sancti michaelis                                            xx.*s.*
Item Recepi de amerciamentis Curie                         xv.*s.* ...*
*.....Curie                                                              xiiij.*d.ob*'.
*......                                                                   xxv.*s*.viij.*d.*
*......        [original sum struck out]     xx.*s.*
*.... [?exitu] de pondyerd et ....                                ....*
*.... et ... suis ...                                                    ....*
Item Recepi ... visus de ....                                       nichil
*.... visus .... alloc'                                                 viij.*s*.viij.*d.*

---

[17] Perhaps three trial sums originally written here have been scratched out.
[18] "de" interlineated.
[19] A word has apparently been omitted here, perhaps something like "house".
[20] Bottom edge crumbled, losing most of last line; it cannot be certain that the "j.*d.ob*'." belongs with the "standing of William Iobot's beast."

Item Recepi de vicario Eound [?] pro fino de eo quod Emebat
unum Messuagium de Iohanne Clarke contra statutum ville    xx.*s.*

Item Recepi for a stray Calfe    ij.*s.*vij.*d.*[1]

[Item Recepi of Bassys Tayll' Whyche forfet to ye Town at
Estr'    xl.*s.*][2]

[Item Recepi de Willelmo Ingram pro salucibus    x.*d.*][3]

Item Recepi de Iohanne foxyn pro salucibus    x.*d.*

Item Recepi de Willelmo Brywer' pro salucibus    xij.*d.*

Item Recepi de Iohanne Barnard' Wryght' pro salucibus    xvj.*d.*

Item Recepi de Thoma Marten pro salucibus    xij.*d.*

Item Recepi de Iohanne Bryte pro salucibus    viij.*d.*

Item Recepi de Iohanne Robyns iunior' pro salucibus    xvj.*d.*

Item Recepi de Willelmo seward' pro salucibus    xj.*d.*

Item Recepi de Thoma Byrdar' pro salucibus    xx.*d.*

Item Recepi de Willelmo hylton' pro salucibus    ij.*s.*iiij.*d.*

Item Recepi de Thoma Tomson pro salucibus    ij.*s.*iiij.*d.*

Item Recepi de Thoma Gybbz pro salucibus    iij.*s.*

Item Recepi de Thoma Chishale pro salucibus    viij.*d.*

Item Recepi de Willelmo parcar' pro salucibus    x.*d.*

Item Recepi de Ricardo fostar' pro salucibus    xvj.*d.*

Item Recepi de Willelmo fryre pro salucibus    ij.*s.*

Item Recepi de Roberto alassz pro salucibus    viij.*d.*

Item Recepi de Thoma Seward pro salucibus    xj.*d.*

Item Recepi de Willelmo Frost iunior' pro salucibus    xix.*d.*

Item Recepi de Henrico Cranfeld' pro salucibus    xviij.*d.*

Item Recepi de Ricardo Prour[4] pro salucibus    iij.*s.*

Item Recepi de Ricardo Bekwell' pro salucibus    viij.*d.*

Item Recepi de Willelmo Isbett senior' pro salucibus    vj.*s.*viij.*d.*

Item Recepi de Roberto punt pro salucibus    xvj.*d.*

Item Recepi de Willelmo freman pro salucibus    xvj.*d.*

Item Recepi de Iohanne Holme pro salucibus    xx.*d.*

[5]Item Recepi of Robert pont For ye surplus of ye kyngis rent'    xx.*d.*[5]

Summa totalis Rec*epcionis* vij.*li.*xv.*s.*v.*d.*[6]

---

[1] The sum originally had a different number of pence that was struck out and then followed by "vij.*d.*" Possibly the original number was "x.*d.*"

[2] Entry marked in left margin by a cross, probably to indicate deletion since the sum is struck out.

[3] Entire entry struck through.

[4] *sic*, perhaps for "Prior."

[5] Added in a different hand. The original has "curplus."

[6] Sum originally had a different number of pounds that was struck out and "vij.*li.*" interlineated.

Item in primis In Expencis apon the xij men on Michalmas day at Night — iiij.*d.*

Item In Expencis apon ye xij men Anodyr tyme at Asemli — x.*d.*

Item In Expencis at Cowrt et per visum holde at John' Holmys — xiiij.*d.*

Item In Expencis apon ye Bayllyffz and odyr honest neygbors when Roodes came to Town — iiij.*d.*

Item In Expencis apon ye xij men at Willm' vschars — x.*d.*

Item In Expencis at Cowrt and pervisum hold at Richard West' — x.*d.*

Item In Expencis at Weyng of Bred — ij.*d.*

Item In Expencis at ye Iaylars at Huntyngdon' and apon ye Bayliffz of Hunt' whan we browte Roodes to ye yayle — v.*d.*

Item In Expencis apon owr company that went w$^t$ vs. that time at West' — v.*d.*

Item In Expencis whan we chose ye organ playar — iij.*d.ob'.*

Item gewyn in reward to Aman that browte the letter from ye organ playar — xij.*d.*

Item In Expencis whan we came hom' from Maystr' Wynd' for Asking of Cowncell' for A matter for Robert Roodes — iiij.*d.*

Item payd for ij pec' of Tymbar' for palys for ye rynfold' — ix.*d.*

Item payd for sawyng' of ye same palis — ix.*d.*

Item In Expencis at Cowrt and per visum at Ione Salmons widowe — xxij.*d.*

Item payd to ye heyward of hemyngford for reward — j.*d.*

Item payd to Thom' Chycheley for serchyng of panturs — j.*d.*

[Item payd for Cryyng of a stray geldyng — iij.*d.*][7]

[Item payd to ye heyward for taking up of ye same stray geldyng — ij.*d.*][8]

Item In Expencis for Weyng of bred ye sonday after synt Katryns day — ij.*d.*

Item In Expencis apon ye Crownars and apon ye Enquest for ye Myllars matter at dyuers timis — ij.*s.*ij.*d.*

Item In Expencis at Cowrt and per visum hold at Willm' Isbetts — xvj.*d.*

Item In Expensis apon ye Comissari whan he sate w$^t$ us — x.*d.*

Item In Expencis apon a tacar of fowlis for ye kyng and apon ye offisars at hunt' and at godmynchest' — x.*d.*

Item payd for wyne gevyn to mayster Wynd' — x.*d.*

Item payd for ij hennys and for a dosen larkis gevyn to mayster Wynd' — vij.*d.*

Item In Expencis apon Kethe of hemyngford' and odyr whan he labord for our myllis — iiij.*d.*

[7] Entry marked in left margin with cross, probably for deletion since sum is struck out.
[8] Entry marked in left margin with cross, probably for deletion since sum is struck out.

Item In Expencis at ye sealyng of ye perpetuite of ye organ
   pleyar                                                                iiij.*d.*

Item In Expencis apon mayster Wod' at ye hors showe at
   Cristynmas                                                           ij.*d.*

Item In Expencis apon Thomas Wynd' whan he Came to
   chaleng Welawyd men goods[9]

Item payd to Willm' Kyng' for ye hyre of a hors ij days                 viij.*d.*

Item In Expencis at hunt' in ye day of ye sessyons of pas after
   Cristynmas and in wyne gevyn to ye Iustyvis and for seyng
   of our Chartyrs                                                      v.*s.*iiij.*d.*

Item In Expencis at hunt' ye morowe aftyr ye sessyons apon
   Mayster Wod' and Mayster Wynd' and apon our honest
   neygbors                                                             iij.*s.*vj.*d.*

Item In Expencis apon Mayster Wynd' at West' ye same day                iiij.*d.*

Item payd to Richard Grene for his cost and labor for ridyng
   to mayster Wod' for Cowncell ij days                                 xvj.*d.*

Item payd for tymbyr and makyng of ye style at harstorp                 xvij.*d.*

Item In Expencis at Cowrt and per visum hold at Thom'
   Monymynts                                                            xiij.*d.*

Item In Expencis at Cowrt and per visum hold at Iohn
   Nottyngams [and apon ye xij men][10]                                 ij.*s.*ij.*d.*

Item In Expencis whan we went to london and for Corde to
   bynde ye hampyrs and apon ye xij men the same tyme                   vj.*d.*

Item In Expencis whan we went to huntyng' at Willm' lords               vj.*d.*

Item In Expencis at Cowrt and per visum hold at Richard
   Grenys                                                               xvij.*d.*

Item In Expencis whan we Came from london at West'                      xiij.*d.*

Item In Expencis apon ye xij men and odyr dyvers' honest
   men at huntyngdon at ye wyne whan we dynyd w^t mayster
   Wynd'                                                                xxj.*d.*

Item payd for vj busshells [and dimid'][11] of Barly for swannys        ij.*s.*ij.*d.*

Item In Expencis apon Mayster Wynd' and his brodyr and
   apon ye Bayliffz and dyvers of ye xij men at West' aftyr we
   Came from london'                                                    xiiij.*d.*

Item In Expencis at mayster Wynde and his brodyr and apon
   divers of ye xij men at West' whan the millars wyfe delyverd
   hur Indenture of ye myllis                                           xviij.*d.*

Item In Expencis apon mayster Wynd' apon Afryday whan we
   Askyd him Cowncell for dyvers Cawsis for ye Towne                    iij.*d.*

---

[9] I.e., the goods of the men of Wellwood?
[10] Words in brackets interlineated.
[11] Words in brackets interlineated.

Item In Expencis apon ye xij men whan they sate for ye
Townys Causis at grenis     ij.*s.*

Item In Expencis at ye Bayli Swetnams at hunt' ye day of
sessions of delivere at dyner and apon our honest neygbors
and apon strayngers [and In wyne][12]     iiij.*s.*

Item In Expencis at ye bayly morewyns ye same day and at
Nuells apon strangers and In wyne     xj.*d.*

Item In Expencis at Cowrt and per visum hold' at Willm'
lordis     xiiij.*d.*

Item In Expencis apon maister Wynd' and apon ye crownars
quest at West'     ij.*d.*

Item In Expencis apon ye servants of ye Clarke of ye Market
at West'     ij.*d.*

Item In Expencis at Cowrte and per visum hold at Richard
Priowrs     xxij.*d.*

Item payd for the Cryyng of Astray Calfe     iij.*d.*

Item payd to ye heyward for Takyng up of ye same Calfe     ij.*d.*

Item payd for Wyntryng of ye Comyn bull     ij.*s.*

Item payd for the kyngs rent of ye howse that was deysternyd[13]     xxij.*d.ob'.*

Item payd for heggyng of ye same to Thom' Gybbz     vj.*d.*

Item payd to ye Bayly for his hundyrd to london     iij.*s.*iiij.*d.*

Item In Expencis at Nottyngams whan ye hennys were delyverd to london     ij.*d.*

Item payd for Wyntryng of a stray Calfe     viij.*d.*

Item payd for makyng of the wallis at Cowrt hall     iij.*s.*ij.*d.*

Item payd to Richard grene for hys Iorne to london' w^t ye
Bayli     iiij.*s.*

Summa totalis Expense iij.*li.*x.*s.*ix.*d.ob'.*

### Allocationes

Item Inprimis alloc*atur* Ballivo pro feodo suo     vj.*s.*viij.*d.*

Item alloc*atur* Ballivo Constabulario et subballivo pro les
hundred     iij.s.iiij.d.

Item alloc*atur* subballivo pro feodo suo     v.*s.*

Item alloc*atur* subballivo pro oblac*ionibus*     vj.*d.*

Item alloc*atur* agillario pro Toga sua     vj.*s.*viij.*d.*

Item alloc*atur* agillario pro sotularibus suis     viij.*d.*

Item alloc*atur* agillario pro oblac*ionibus*     vj.*d.*

Item alloc*atur* Custodi signorum pro feodo suo     iij.*s.*iiij.*d.*

Summa allocacionum xxvj.*s.*viij.*d.*

[12] Words in brackets interlineated.
[13] In the final word, "-ternyd" is interlineated.

Omnibus computatis dictus Ballivus restat in arreragiis declaro  ij.*li*.xvj.*s*.iij.*d.ob'*.
Payd to ye xij men at Ester last[14]  xv.*s*.
Payd at ij tymys Iur^d Boyll' howysse[14]  xvj.*s*.iij.*d.ob'*.

## H. Account of the Bailiff of Godmanchester
### 29 September 1527–12 Arpil 1528

(Godmanchester Borough Records, Box 1, Bundle 10)

### Gumecestr'

Compotus Johannis Page unius Balliuorum ibidem a festo Sancti Michaelis Archangeli in anno Regni Regis Henrici octaui decimo nono usque festum Pasche ex tunc proximo sequentem[1]

### Recepciones

Item in primis[2] Recepi de xij. hominibus[3] ad festum sancti
  Michaelis Archangeli  xx.*s*.
Item Recepi de Johanne Treuet pro Garsuma Tenementi  iij.*d*.
Item Recepi de Willelmo Richemont pro Garsuma Tenementi  iij.*d*.
Item Recepi de Reginaldo ...[4] pro Garsuma Tenementi  iij.*d*.
Item Recepi de Willelmo ...[4] pro Garsuma Tenementi  iij.*d.ob'*.
Item Recepi de Roberto Boston pro Garsuma Tenementi
  nuper dyglyer[5]  iij.*d*.
Item Recepi de Johanne Treuet pro Garsuma de una otherall'
  yarde prati  j.*d.ob'*.
Item Recepi de Ricardo Grene et Georgio[6] filio suo pro
  Garsuma ij^as acr' et dimid' et una virga  v.*d.ob'*.
Item Recepi de Roberto Boston[7] pro Garsuma Tenementi
  nuper Thomas pacies  j.*d*.
[8]Item Recepi de Ricardo Robyns et Roberto Boston pro
  Garsuma Tenementi Thome Wolde  ij.*d*.[8]

---

[14] The last two entries were added in a different hand, probably identical to the hand that added the entry noted in 5 above.

[1] = from 29 September 1527 until 12 April 1528.
[2] *sic* MS (the first entry usually begins "In primis," not "Item in primis").
[3] MS clearly has "homines" here.
[4] The MS is stained at this point.
[5] This is just possibly "dyghyer."
[6] MS has "Georgeo."
[7] After "Robarto" another surname was originally written, but has been struck out.
[8] Entire entry struck out.

| | |
|---|---|
| Item Recepi de Johanne dosue juniore pro salucibus | ij.*s*.viij.*d.* |
| Item Recepi de Johanne dosue seniore pro salucibus | viij.*d.* |
| Item Recepi de Willelmo Arnold pro salucibus | ij.*s*.j.*d.* |
| Item Recepi de Roberto Peryth' pro salucibus | iiij.*d.* |
| Item Recepi de Thoma Carnabe pro salucibus | iiij.*d.* |
| Item Recepi de uxore Johannis Holme pro salucibus | iiij.*d.* |
| Item Recevyd[9] de Johanne Page pro salucibus | xvj.*d.* |
| Item Recepi de Johanne Page pro salucibus apud puteos | xvj.*d.* |
| Item Recepi de xij. hominibus ad unum tempus | xiiij.*s*.iiij.*d.* |
| Item Recepi de Johanne Page de meremio apud Maydyhed | x.*d.* |
| [10]Item Recepi de Johanne Page pro una pecia meremii jacente apud West leys | xij.*d.*[10] |
| Item Recepi pro uno equo de Colore de Grey videlicet a Wesse | ix.*s*.ij.*d.* |
| Item Recepi de Johanne Page pro uno vitulo extrani[11] | xxij.*d.* |
| Item Recepi de magistro Ricardo Frere pro firma aque | xx.*s*.vj.*d.ob'.* |
| Item Recepi pro amerciament*is* curie ibidem | xlij.*s.* |
| Item Recepi de Roberto Horforth' gent' pro Garsuma unius Clawsi | xj.*d.ob'.* |
| Item Recepi de dicto Roberto Horforth' pro Garsuma de octo acris et dimid' Rode prati | xvj.*d.ob'.* |
| Item Recepi de Johanne dosue seniore pro Garsuma Tene-menti sui | ij.*d.* |
| Item Recepi de Thoma Grouecie[12] pro Garsuma unius acre prati | ij.*d.* |
| Item Recepi de Johanne Gybyz de paxton' pro Garsuma dim' acre prati | j.*d.* |
| Item Recepi de Roberto Same de Caxton' pro fino libertatis ville | iij.*s*.iiij.*d.* |
| Item Recepi de Ricardo Hutton et lawrencio filio suo pro fino libertatis ville | iij.*s*.iiij.*d.* |
| Item Recepi de Johanne Berie de Hemyngforth' pro salucibus | iij.*d.* |
| Item Rec*evyd* of Symon Smyth et Willm' Ibot for Welows | xxij.*d.* |
| Item Rec*evyd* of Thomas Freman for Hobbys at bassy ley | iiij.*d.* |
| Item Rec*evyd* of John' Wylde ye yongar for a garsum' | vj.*s.* |

Summa totalis Recept' vij.*li*.xiij.*s*.ij.*d.*

| | |
|---|---|
| Item In Expens*is* apon the Baylyff' Constabull' et odyr of our honest neybors whan we kepte sessyons of statute laborars | iiij.*s*.ij.*d.* |
| Item In Expens*is* apud Curiam et per visum tentum apud Ricardum Grenys | iij.*s*.ij.*d.* |

---

[9] *sic* MS.
[10] Entire entry struck out.
[11] *sic MS.*
[12] Reading uncertain.

Item In Expens*is* apud Curiam et per visum tentum apud
Oliuerum Benett'                                                                iij.*s*.ij.*d.*

Item In Expens*is* apud Grenys super xij. homines quando
sedebant pro diuersis Cawsis ville                                    xviij.*d.*

Item In Expens*is* super seruientem domini Johannis Hosy qui
facit nobis noticiam a london de Capcione latronum qui
soliauebant[13] Ecclesiam nostram                                      ij.*d.*

Item In Expens*is* super diuersos vicinos at eadem[14] tempus
apud West'                                                                        iiij.*d.*

Item solui agillare pro sotularibus suis                              viij.*d.*

Item In Expens*is* apon the xij. homines at grenis               viij.*d.*

Item In Expens*is* super Ricardum Wynde quando mittebamus
pro eo ad habendum consilium                                              vj.*d.*

Item In Expens*is* super duodecim homines alia vice apud
grenys                                                                                 xij.*d.*

Item payd to Nicholas Hyll for clausyng' of the Base at Curte
Hall' Wall'                                                                          j.*d.*

Item In Expens*is* apud Curiam et per visum tentum apud
Aliciam West'                                                                      iiij.*s.*

Item In Expens*is* apud Curiam et per visum tentum apud
Holmys                                                                               iiij.*s*.vij.*d.*

Item In Expens*is* apud Curiam et per visum tentum apud
Aliciam West'                                                                      v.*s*.iij.*d.*

Item In Expens*is* super xij. homines quando ceperunt pos-
sessionem In bonis Gylbardy Walsche                              xiiij.*d.*

Item gevyn In reward' to men that toke the Watyr              ij.*d.*

Item payd to John' Cart' for Wachyng of Willm' lawnden'    ij.*d.*

Item In Expenc' the day of sessions of deliuere at Willm'
Hornwodd'                                                                          v.*s.*

Item In Wyne gevyn to Maystr' Gaskyn et odyr Iustyssis of
pese                                                                                    viij.*d.*

Item payd to Annes grene for fagotts to ye Cowrt hall'       j.*d.*

Item payd to Thomas shyllyng and to Robert Fokke for
fachyng of Abott at Howrton                                               iiij.*d.*

Item In Expens' apon my fellow and me and ye constabull'
Whan Maystr' Hall' send for us                                           iij.*d.*

Item In Expens' the nyght that we kepte prime wache for the
Kynge and apon ij. men of Hunt' that was w! us In the same
Wache                                                                               ij.*s*.iij.*d.*

Item In Expens' apon the Baylygg' and Constabull' Whan the
wachyd a nodyr nyght                                                      viij.*d.*

---

[13]  *sic* MS.
[14]  *sic* MS.

Item In Expens' the day of ye sessions hold' at Hunt' after xij tyde — xvj.*d.*

Item In Expens*is* apud Curiam et per visum tentum apud Ricardum Grenys — v.*s.*vij.*d.*

Item In Expens*is* apud Curiam et per visum tentum apud Johannem bolens — v.*s.*iiij.*d.*

Item In Expens' apon the Baylyffz constabullis and apon dyvers of ye xij homines at Etyng of a hare at Richard Grenys — ij.*s.*ij.*d.*

Item In Expens' Whan maystr' Sewstar greyd w! ye xij. homines for rente of maners lond — iiij.*d.*

Item In Expens' at Weyng of bred at grenys diuers tymys — viij.*d.*

Item In Reward Gevyn to the pleyars on Candylmas day — xvj.*d.*

Item In Expens' Whan maystr' Hall' send for my felow and me Whan we shuld vewe corne — v.*d.*

Item in Expens' apon y^e Baylyffz constabull' and y^e clarke Whan we vewyd ye corne — xiij.*d.*

Item In Expens' the laste day that we vewyd the corne at dyn*er* and supper — xix.*d.*

Item In Expens' apon maystr' Hall at Grenys — iiij.*d.*

Item In Expens' at Cowrte et per vjs'[15] hold' at John' Holmys — iiij.*s.*viij.*d.*

Item In Expens' at Curt et per vis' hold' at Grenys — v.*s.*viij.*d.*

Item In Expens' apon y^e myller et hys warkmen what they tok y^e watyr[16] — vj.*d.*

Item In Expens' at Hunt' the day of y^e sessions of delyuerans and In wyne gevyn to ye Jug*es* — viij.*s.*viij.*d.*

Item payd to the Clarke for Wrytyng of myne A Cownte — vj.*d.*

Summa totalis Expens' iiij.*li.*vj.*d.*

## Allocacione[17]

Item allocatur Balliuo pro feodo suo — vj.*s.*viij.*d.*

Item allocatur Balliuo pro les Hundred' suis — viij.*d.*

Item allocatur subbaliuo pro feodo suo — v.*s.*

Item allocatur subbaliuo pro oblacione sua — vj.*d.*

Item allocatur agillare pro toga sua — vj.*s.*viij.*d.*

Item allocatur agillare pro oblacione sua — vj.*d.*

Item allocatur Clerico pro Hundredis suis — viij.*d.*

Item allocatur subbaliuo pro Hundredis suis — viij.*d.*

---

[15] *sic* MS.
[16] "what" in this entry is probably an error for "when."
[17] *sic* MS.

Item allocatur Clerico Curie pro oblacione sua                    vj.*d.*
Item allocatur pro papir et In Cawsto predicto clerico            xij.*d.*

      Summa totalis alloc' xxij.*s*.x.*d.*

Summa omnibus allocatis et allocandys dictus Balliuus restat
  In Arreragiis                                         xxxviij.*s*.x.*d.*[18]

### I. ACCOUNT, IN ENGLISH, OF THE BAILIFF(S) OF GODMANCHESTER
### 29 SEPTEMBER 1531–31 MARCH 1532

(Godmanchester Borough Records, Box 1, Bundle 10)

This MS is severely damaged and the following system has been adopted to indicate as clearly as possible the manner in which the text has been affected by the damage :

    Ellipsis (...) shows a passage of more than one word lost.
    Dashes at the beginning or end of a fragmentary word (e.g., Jo——,——pril) show the loss of some letters in that word *only*, although this may be followed or preceded by ellipsis indicating the loss of additional words.
    Squared brackets ([ ]) identify editorial supplements, which have been effected only when there was reliable evidence from the text to suggest the words to be supplied. Where the missing words were not beyond reasonable doubt, ellipsis has been inserted.

    The scribe consistently used long majuscule and miniscule "i" for initial "j"; this has been rendered using "j" as the most sensible choice. The scribe was fairly consistent in distinguishing "u" and "v", but the few times he slipped are reproduced exactly as in the MS.
    Although the heading is gone, this fragmentary account can be dated as the Easter account for 1532 since William Woodward, gentleman, is entered on the court book under the date 15 February 1532 as paying the fine of 26s. 8d. for liberty.

*m. 1*

... Jamys Chambyr' for Go——                                      .j.*d.*
[Item] Recevyd of Willam Rychemont for ...Akyrslond'             .xij.*d.*
[Item] Recevyd of Willam Wodward gent—— for the fyne of
  the lyberte                                              .xxvj.*s*.viij.*d.*
[Item] Recevyd of the subballi for mercime[nts] of the Curte
  for tyme of the Cownte                                   .xxiij.*s*.viij.*d.*
Item Recevyd of Rychard Frere ... ——matyr' for the halfe
  yere                                                     .xx.*s.*

---

[18] MS originally had "xxx.*s*.xviij.*d.*," which was struck out and the final reading substituted.

[Item Recevyd of] Rychard [?G——] ... yard and for standyng
   of his bote                                                         .xj.*d*.*ob*.

[Item] Recevyd for Welows at Logg' garn—— ... ——ayly
   Willam Ingram in latisar'                                       .iiij.*s*.viij.*d*.

[Item] Recevyd of Willam Richemont for [Welows]      .xvj.*d*.

Item Receuyd of Rychar*d* Grene for Welows        .ij.*s*.viij.*d*.

[Item Recevyd of] John Grace for Wel[ows]         .iiij.*s*.iiij.*d*.

[Item Recevyd of] ... Frere for Welows              .ij.*s*.

[Item Recevyd of] ... Cokke for Wel[ows]          [.viij.d.?]

[Item Recevyd] of John Morgan for Welows         .xij.*d*.

[Item] Recevyd of Robert Massy for Welows         .vj.*s*.

Item Recevyd of Christofer Toppan for Welows      .vj.*s*.iiij.*d*.

Item Recevyd of sir Richard Bill[yngton] for Welows   .v.*s*.iiij.*d*.

Item Recevyd of Richard Sam—— ...               .iij.*s*.

Item Recevyd of Squiars Wyffe for Welows        .viij.*d*.

Item Recevyd of Harry Barnard for Welows         .xij.*d*.

Item Recevyd of sir Richard Billyngton ... tyme for Welows  .iiij.*s*.iiij.*d*.

Item Recevyd of Christofer Thowgharton [for We]lows   .ij.*s*.viij.*d*.

[Item Recevyd] of Symon Wellys for Welows        .ij.*s*.

[Item Rece]vyd of John Byllyngton for Welows      .xij.*d*.

Item [Recev]yd of John Stacy for Welows          .xvj.*d*.

[Item] Recevyd of forthe the fisicion for Welows      .xv.*d*.

Item Recevyd of Thomas Kyrby for [Welows]       .xvj.*d*.

Item Recevyd of John Bolen for ...               .ij.*s*.iiij.*d*.

Item Recevyd of Richard Fryre ...                .xx.*d*.

Item Recevyd of sir Edmund Archebold' and sir Thomas
   Dycons for Welows                                      .xvj.*d*.

[Item Recevy]d of sir Thomas Peyton for Welows     .viij.*d*.

Item Recevyd of John Granger for the garsom of Notynghams
   howse                                                .ij.*d*.

[Item Recevyd?] for a stray geldyng colt wh——...    .vij.*s*.iiij.*d*.

[A summa was entered, but is lost through damage]

*m. 2*

### Allocaciones

Item alowd to the Bayly for [hys] Fee               .vj.*s*.viij.*d*.

Item alowd to the Bayly for ... hundyrd ...         .viij.*d*.

Item alowd to the subball' [for hys] Fee           v.*s*....

Item alowd to the subbally for ... hundyrd'        .viij.*d*.

Item alowd to the subbally for [hys] offryng       .ij.*d*.

Item alowd to the Clarke for papyr and inke      .xij.*d*.

Item alowd to the Clarke for hys hund*yrd*                    .viij.*d.*
Item allowd to the Clarke for hys offryng'                    .vj.*d.*
Item alowd to the heyward for hys Gowne                       .vj.*s.*viij.*d.*

Omnibus computatis computandis allocatis et allocandis [ *sic*] dictus Ball*ius*
Restat in arreragiis Communitati declaro .iij.*li.* ...

# Appendix 2

## The Rotation System for Officials

The derivation of these data from annual election lists has been described in Chapter 1. No election list survives for 1530, and elections for bailiffs were not recorded for 1499 and 1508. All elected officers, particularly for minor officials are noted in Table 9 (p. 32), were by no means fully reported every year at Michaelmas. On the other hand, there is no reason to believe that all elected positions were not filled every year. Since minor officials were under the jurisdiction of such major officers as bailiffs, perhaps from time to time the "election" of minor officials simply consisted in their appointment by superior officials.

| | | | |
|---|---|---|---|
| BA | bailiff | CON | constable |
| CA | collector of the ale | CV | collector of the view |
| CC | custodian of the church | J | juror |
| CF | collector of the farm | SBA | sub-bailiff |
| CO | coroner | * | continued on into other years |

| NAME | 1485 | 1486 | 1487 | 1488 | 1489 | 1490 | 1491 | 1492 | 1493 | 1494 | 1495 | 1496 | 1497 | 1498 | 1499 | 1500 |
|------|------|------|------|------|------|------|------|------|------|------|------|------|------|------|------|------|
| William Frere | BA | CO | BA | | | | | BA | BA | | | | | | | * |
| John Lockyngton | CO | J | CON | CO | CF | J | | BA | | J | CLERK | | | | | * |
| Edward Barre | J | | CC | BA | CO | | | | | | | | | | | |
| William Ibott jr. | SBA | | | | | | SBA | | | J | | | | | | BA |
| John Robyn | J | | | | | | | | CC | | CON | | J | | | |
| Robert Conyff | CON | | | | | | | | | | | | | | | |
| John Gybbys | CF | CF | | | J | | CON | | OF | | J | | J | | | * |
| Thomas Sydebotom | J | | | | | | | | | | | | | | | |
| Thomas Burton | CC | | | CF | | J | | | CF | | | CF | J | | | CC* |
| William Godwyn | J | J | | | | | | | | | | | | | | |
| John Turneskewe | J+CF | | | CC | | CF | CF | | | CF | | J | | | | CC* |
| John Bayous sr. | CON | BA | | J | | J | | | | | J | BA | | | | |
| John Bayous | J | | | J | | | | | | | | | | | | |
| Richard Lockyngton | J | | J | | CF | | J | | | CF | J | CON | | | | * |
| William Mundeford | J | | | CC | | | | | | | | | | | | |
| John Snell | J | | J | | | J | | | | BA | CO | | | | | * |
| John Smith | J | | CF | J | | | | | | | | | | | | |
| John Sent | CON | | | | | CON | | | | | | | | CON | | |
| John Stukeley | CF | J | | | | CF | | | | | CF | J | | CF | | CON |
| Thomas Mayle | CF | | | | J | | J | | | | | J | | J | CON | * |
| John Bower | BA | | | | J | | BA | | | | | | | | | * |
| Richard Smyth (Samt) | | CON | CO+J | CF | CF | J | | | CON | | | CF | | BA | CO | J* |
| William Orwell | | J | J | J | BA | BA | CO | | CON | | J | | | BA | CO | BA* |
| John Lumbard | | CF | | | | | | | | | | | | | | |
| Thomas Marshall | | J | | | | | | | | | | | | | | |
| William Stodale | | J | | CON | J | | BA | | | | | | | | | |
| William Dey | | CA | | J | | | | | | CF | | J | | J | CF | * |
| William Snell | | J | | J | | J | | | | | | J+CC | | J | CF | J* |

| Name | Offices (in sequence) |
|---|---|
| Thomas Bennet | J |
| William Frost | CF — J |
| Robert Porter | CF |
| William Syward sr. | CA — J — CF — * |
| William Frost sr. | BA — J |
| John Mynsterchambre | BA |
| William Kyng | CA — CV — CC — CF — CF — BA — CO — CO* |
| John Bould | CON — J — CC — CON — BA — CF+J — J — J — CF — CF* |
| Thomas Laxton | CC — BA — BA — J — J |
| William Lessy | J — CC |
| Thomas Maryot | CF — J — J — CO — CO — CON — CF — * |
| Thomas Emlyn | J — J — J |
| John Matthew | J — J |
| Richard Bayous | J |
| John Gardiner | J — * |
| Henry Martin | J |
| Thomas Frost | J |
| William Aylred | CV |
| William Gardiner | CF |
| Thomas Cokman | CV |
| Richard Stukeley | CV — CV |
| John Garlop | CA — CV — BA — J |
| John Stokes | BA |
| Thomas Fecas | CF — CON — CF+SBA — J |
| John Aylred | CON — BA — J — BA — CO — BA — CO — * |
| Thomas Reginald | J — J |
| John Bonfay | J — J — J — BA — J — J* |
| William Gile | CA — CF — CF — * |
| John Adam | CV — J — J — CF — * |

| NAME | 1485 | 1486 | 1487 | 1488 | 1489 | 1490 | 1491 | 1492 | 1493 | 1494 | 1495 | 1496 | 1497 | 1498 | 1499 | 1500 |
|---|---|---|---|---|---|---|---|---|---|---|---|---|---|---|---|---|
| Thomas Kendale | | | | CV | | | | | | | | | | | | |
| John Page junior | | | | CV | | | | | | | | | | | | |
| Robert Marshall | | | | CV | CV | | | | | | | | | | | |
| John Barnard | | | | J | | J | | CON | BA | CO | | | | J | | J + SBA* |
| John Miles | | | | SBA | | | CV | | | CV | | | | | | CV* |
| John Page | | | | | | J | J | | | | | | | | | |
| John Foster | | | | | | CV | CA | | | | | | | | | |
| John Holme | | | | | | SBA | CA | | | SBA | SBA | SBA | SBA | | | |
| John Cave | | | | | | CV | | | | | | | | | | |
| Robert Vont | | | | | | CA | J | | | | | | | | | |
| John Clerk, alias Chese | | | | | CA | | | | | | | | | J + CV | | |
| Thomas Bailey | | | | | | J | | | | | | | | | | |
| William Diggby | | | | | | J | | | | J | | J | J | CF | CF | * |
| William Manipenny | | | | | BA | | CO | | | | J | CON | BA | CO | | J* |
| Richard Mayle | | | | | CC | | | | | | | | | | | |
| John Laxton | | | | | | | J | | | | | | J | BA | CO | J* |
| John Goodrych | | | | | | SBA | J | | | | | | | | | |
| William Gonell | | | | | | | | CF | | | | | | | | |
| Richard Kyng | | | | | | | CA | | | | | | | | | |
| Augustine Arnold | | | | | | | CV | | | CC | J | | J | | | J* |
| Robert Nicholas | | | | | | | CF | | | | | | | | | * |
| John Brown | | | | | | | CF | | | | | | | | | * |
| Richard West | | | | | | | CV | | | | | | | | | |
| John Ussher | | | | | | | J | CON | CO | CON | BA | | | | | CO* |
| Thomas Garlop sr. | | | | | | | | CA | | CA | | | | CA | | |

|  | | | | | | |
|------|---|---|---|---|---|---|
| John Longe | | | | | | |
| John Barnard, sr. | | | | | CA+CV | CA * |
| William Mayle | | | | | CON | |
| William Frosts jr. of East Street | | | | | CF | |
| William Melbourne | CF | | | J | CF | CF |
| John Breton | | CV | | | | |
| John Page sr. | | CV | | | | |
| Robert Stevens | | CF | CF | | | * |
| William Basse | | | J | | | |
| Robert Chandeler | | | CF | J | | CON* |
| John Caustans | | | CON | CF | | * |
| William Vyntner | | | CC | CV | J | |
| Henry Smith | | | J | | | |
| Steven Clerk | | | CF | | | |
| William Pelman | | | CV | | | |
| John Armyt | | | CV | CA | CF | * |
| Richard Motte | | | | J | | J* |
| Robert Bayous | | | | J | | |
| Richard Stevens | | | | CV | CON | * |
| Thomas Monyment | | | | | | |
| John Bailey | | | | | J | |
| Thomas Mundeford | | | | | J | |
| Robert Mayle | | | | | CV | |
| Thomas Page | | | | | CV | |
| John Wyddyr | | | | | J | |
| Thomas May | | | | | CV | |

| Name | 1501 | 1502 | 1503 | 1504 | 1505 | 1506 | 1507 | 1508 | 1509 | 1510 | 1511 | 1512 | 1513 | 1514 | 1515 | 1516 | 1517 | 1518 |
|---|---|---|---|---|---|---|---|---|---|---|---|---|---|---|---|---|---|---|
| William Frere | BA | | | | | | | | | | | | | | | | | |
| William Orwell | CO | CF | J | BA | CO | CV | | CF | | CA | | | | | | | | CF+J* |
| John Robyn | CO | | | | J | | | | CON | J | | | | | | | | |
| John Aylred | CON | BA | CO+J | | | | | | | | | | | | | | | |
| William Frost sr. | J | | | CON | | | | CF | | CC | | | | | | | | BA* |
| John Page | CC | | | | | | | | | | | | | | | | | |
| William Kyng | J | | | | CON | BA | CO | | | | | | | CF | J | CF | | J* |
| John Bould | CON | BA | | | | | | | | | | | | | | | | |
| John Adam | J | | | | | | | | | | | | | | | | | |
| William Diggby | J | | | | | J | | CON | CF | BA | CO | J | CON | BA | CO | CO | CF | * |
| William Manipenny | BA | | | | | | BA | | | | | | | | | | | |
| John Ussher | | CO | J | | | | | | | | | | | | | | | |
| William Frost | | CO | J | | | | | J | | | | | | | J | | J | * |
| John Clerk | BA | CON | CO+J | | | CO | | | | | | CF | | BA | BA | CO | | |
| John Lockyngton | | BA | | | | | | | CON | | CON | CON | BA | CO | | | | |
| John Gonell | | CON | | | | | | | | | | | | | | | | |
| William Aylred | | CF+CC | | | | | | CF | CF | J | | J | | | CF | | | BA* |
| John Laxton | | CF | | | CON | BA | BA | | J | | | | | | | | | |
| John Turneskewe | | CF | | | CON | | | | | | | | | | | | | |
| Henry Este | | CV | | | | | | | CV | | | | CA | | | | | |
| William Loveday | | CA | | CF+CV | | | | | | | | | | | | | | * |

| NAME | 1503 | 1504 | 1505 | 1506 | 1507 | 1508 | 1509 | 1510 | 1511 | 1512 | 1513 | 1514 | 1515 | 1516 | 1517 | 1518 | 1519 | 1520 |
|---|---|---|---|---|---|---|---|---|---|---|---|---|---|---|---|---|---|---|
| John Stukeley | BA | CO | | CON | | | BA | CO | BA | CO | J | CON | | | | | | |
| Robert Chandeler | BA | CO | J | CON | | | | CON | BA | CO | CF | | | | | | | |
| William Vyntner | CON | | | | | CF | | | | | | | | BA | | | | * |
| Richard Smith | CON | CF | | | CO | CF | CON | BA | CO | BA | | | | | | | | |
| William Dey | CF | | | | | | | | | | | | | | | | | |
| William Mayle | CF | | | | | | | | | | | | | | J | | | * |
| William Mundeford | CF | | BA | CO | | CON | | CON | J | CF | | | CF | | | | | |
| John Frere | CF | | J | | | | CF | | | BA | CO | | CO | BA | | | CON | BA* |
| John Vynter | SBA | | | | | | | | | | J | CF | | CON | CO+J | | | * |
| Thomas Gybbys | CV | | | | | | | | CF | J | J | CC | | CON | CF+J | | | * |
| William Mynt | CV | | | | | | | | | | | | | J | J | | | J* |
| John Armyt | CC | CF | | | | | | J | | | | CF | | J | CON | CF | | BA |
| John Gilby | CC | | | | CC | | | | | | | | | | | CF | CON | |
| Henry Smith | J | | | | | | | | | | | | | | | | | |
| William Greatham | J | | | | | | | | | | | | | | | | | |
| Thomas Lockyngton | J | | | | | | | J | | | J | CF | | | | J | | |
| Augustine Arnold | J | | | | | | | | | | | | J | | | | CF | |
| William Ibott | J | | J | | | | | | | | | | | | | | | * |
| William Frost jr. | J | | | | | | | | | | | | | | | | | * |

| Name | 1504 | 1505 | 1506 | 1507 | 1508 | 1509 | 1510 | 1511 | 1512 | 1513 | 1514 | 1515 | 1516 | 1517 | 1518 | 1519 | 1520 | 1521 |
|---|---|---|---|---|---|---|---|---|---|---|---|---|---|---|---|---|---|---|
| Thomas Maryot | BA | | | | | | | | | | | | | | | | | |
| Thomas Burton | CF | | | | | | | | | | | | | | | | | |
| John Longe | CF | | | | | | | | | | | | | | | | | |
| John Bailey jr. | CF | | | | | | | | | | | | | | | | | |
| William Lord | CA | SBA | | CA | | SBA | SBA | SBA | SBA | SBA | | | | | | SBA | SBA | SBA |
| William Arnold | CC | CF | | | | | CF | | CC | | | J | | | | | | * |
| Thomas Punt | CC | | | | | | | | | | | | | | | | | * |
| William Snell | | CO | | | | | | | | | | | | | | | | |
| Thomas Mayle | | CF | | | | | | | | | | | | | | | | |
| William Dalton | | CF | | | | J | | CF | | BA | CO | CON | | | | | CON | * |
| John Nottyngham | | CA | | | | | CF | | J | | | | | | | | | |
| William Granger | | CC | | | | CC | CF | J | J | | | J | | J | | | | J* |
| John Clerk, thatcher | | CC | | | | | | | | | | | | | | | | |
| John Garlop | | J | | | | | | | | | | | | | | | | |
| John Melbourne | | J | | | | | | | | | | | | | | | | |
| Thomas Bailey sr. | | J | | | | | | | | | | | | | | | | |
| John Bonfay | | J | | | | J | | J | | J | | J | | | | | | |
| John Brandon | | J | CA | | | CO | | J | | CF | | | | CF | J | | | |
| John Barnard | | | | SBA | | | | | | | | | | J | | | | |
| Robert Punt | | | CF | | | | | | | | | | | CV | CV | | | |
| William Melbourne | | | | | | | J | | | | | | J | | | | | * |
| John Manning | | | CV | | | | | CV+J | | | | J | | | | | * | |

| NAME | 1507 | 1508 | 1509 | 1510 | 1511 | 1512 | 1513 | 1514 | 1515 | 1516 | 1517 | 1518 | 1519 | 1520 | 1521 | 1522 | 1523 | 1524 |
|---|---|---|---|---|---|---|---|---|---|---|---|---|---|---|---|---|---|---|
| William Ussher | CON | | | | | | | | | | | | | | | | | |
| Robert Whyte | CF | | J | | | | | | | | | | CC | | | | | |
| Edmond Maryot | CF | | | | J | | CON | | | CF | | | CF | | | J | | |
| John Porter | | CV | | | | | | | | | | | | | | | | |
| John Hogan | | CV | | J | CF | | | | | J | | | | J | CF | | | CF |
| John Gybbys | | | J | | J | | | | | | | | | | | | | |
| John Lawe | | | BA | CO | | CON | | | | | | | | | | | | |
| Thomas Lovell | | | CA | | | | | | | | | | | | | | | * |
| John Salmon | | | CV | | | J | | | | | | | CF | | | | BA | |
| John Este | | | CV | | CA | | CF | | | | CV | | | J | | CF | | CO* |
| William Pelman | | | CC | CF | | | CF | | | | | | | J | | | | |
| Richard Scot | | | J | CF | | | CF | | CC | | | J | | | J | | | |
| Robert Nicholas | | | | CF | | | J | | CON | | CF | | | | | | | |
| John Browne | | | | J | | | | | | | | | | | | | | |
| William Stukeley | | | | CV | | | | | | | CV | CO | | | | | | |
| John Robyns jr. | | | | CC | | | | | | | | | | | | | | |
| Thomas Matthew | | | | J | | | | | | | | | | | | | | |

| NAME | 1511 | 1512 | 1513 | 1514 | 1515 | 1516 | 1517 | 1518 | 1519 | 1520 | 1521 | 1522 | 1523 | 1524 | 1525 | 1526 | 1527 | 1528 |
|---|---|---|---|---|---|---|---|---|---|---|---|---|---|---|---|---|---|---|
| Richard Ibott | CON | | | | | | | | | | | | | | | | | |
| William Broden | CV | | | | | | | | | | | | | | | | | |
| John Robyn sr. | J | J | | | | | | | | | | | | | | | | |
| John Lawman | J | J | J | | | | | | | | | | | | | | | |
| Thomas Monyment | J | | | CC | J | | | | | | | CC | | | | | | |
| John Smith | J | | | | | | J | | | | | | | | | | | |
| William Ibott jr. | CV | | | SBA | SBA | SBA | SBA | SBA | | | | | | | | | | |
| Richard West | | CF | CV | | | | | | | | | | | | | | | |
| Richard Brewster | | CA | CV | | | | | | | | | | | | | | | |
| William Bennet | | CV | | | | | | | | | | CV | J | | | | | * |
| William Lessy | | J | | | | | | | | | | J | | | | | | |
| John Punt | | J | | CON | | CO | CON+J | CO | BA | | | CF | J | CON | J | | J | CF* |
| Richard Prior | | J | | | | J | | | | | | J | J | CON | CV | | | * |
| William Townshend | | J | | | | | CC+J | | BA | CO | | CO | | CON | CF | | | |
| William Dalton, farmer | | | | | | | BA | CO | BA | BA | BA | | | | | | | |
| Richard Robyns | | J | | CON | | J | BA | | | | | BA | CO | | CF | | J | BA* |
| John Dey | | | CF | | | | | | | | | | | | | | | |
| John Page sr. | | | CV | CF | | J | CON | J | CO | | | CC | J | CF | | J | BA | CO |
| Thomas Pacy | | | | CF | CV | | | | | | | | | | | J | | * |
| Thomas Haplond | | | | CA | | | | | | | | | | | | | | |
| John Granger jr. | | | | CV | | | | | | | CC | | | CF | CC | J | | * |

| NAME | 1515 | 1516 | 1517 | 1518 | 1519 | 1520 | 1521 | 1522 | 1523 | 1524 | 1525 | 1526 | 1527 | 1528 | 1529 | 1531 | 1532 | 1533 |
|---|---|---|---|---|---|---|---|---|---|---|---|---|---|---|---|---|---|---|
| Robert Vyntner | CF | | | J | | CF | | | CF | | | J | | | BA | | CON | CF* |
| George Hay | CA | | | | | | | | | | | | | | | | | |
| William Greatham | CC | | | | | | | | | | | | | | | | | |
| Henry Frere | CV | | | | | | | | | | | CC | BA | CO | | | CF | J* |
| William Dalton, merchant | J | | BA | | | | | | | | | | | | | | | |
| John Page jr. | | CF | | CC+J | | CON | | | | | CF | | | J | | | J | |
| John Boleyn | | CA | J | | CC | | | | CC | | | | | | | | | |
| Henry Gybbys | | CV | | | | | | | | | J | | CF | J | CON | | | J* |
| Nicholas Gelly | | J | CF | CON | | CC | | | | | | | | | | | | |
| William Ede | | | CA | | | | | | | | | | | | | | | |
| William Freman | | | CV | | | | | | | | | | | | | | | |
| Thomas Smyth | | | J | | | | | | | | | | | | | | | |
| Richard Clerk | | | | CA | | | | | | | | | | | | SBA | | |
| William Brown | | | | CV | | | | | | | | | | | | | | |
| John Goodwyn | | | | CV | | | | | | | | | | | | | | |
| John Laxton | | | | | CO | | CON | J | | | J | CV | CC | | | CC | | J* |
| John Clerk | | | | | CA | | | CC | | | | | | | | | | * |
| Robert Frost | | | | | CV | | | | | | | | | | | | | * |
| William Loveday | | | | | CC | CF | | | CON | | | J | | CF | | | | * |

| NAME | 1520 | 1521 | 1522 | 1523 | 1524 | 1525 | 1526 | 1527 | 1528 | 1529 | 1531 | 1532 | 1533 | 1534 | 1535 | 1536 | 1537 | 1538 |
|---|---|---|---|---|---|---|---|---|---|---|---|---|---|---|---|---|---|---|
| Robert Pelle | CF | | | | | | | | | | | | CF | J | CO | CON | J | CO* |
| Robert Staughton | CF | CO | CON | BA | CO | BA | CO | J | CON | BA | J | | BA | CO | J | CON | BA | * |
| John Page | J | | J | | | | | J | CON | | | | | | | | J | * |
| William Kyng | CF | | CON | CON | | | | | CF | | | | | | | | | |
| Thomas Cook | CV | | | | | | | CF | | | | | | | | | | |
| John Stevens | CA | | CA | CA | | | | | | | | | | | | | | |
| John Frere | | CO | J | CF | | CON | BA | CO | J | CON | CO | J | CON | BA | CO | J | CON | J* |
| William Vyntner | | CON | J | | | | | | | | | | | | | | | * |
| John Vyntner | | CF | CON | J | CC | BA | CO | CON | CF | CON | CO | J | CON | J | CF | J | CON | BA* |
| William Mayle | | CF | | | CF | CF | | J | | CF | | | | | | | | * |
| Richard Blaxton | | SBA | | SBA | SBA | SBA | SBA | | | | | | | | | | | |
| William Malden | | CV | J | CF | | | J | | J | | CF | CF | J | | CF | J | | J* |
| Roger Hawdwyn | | CV | | | | | J | | | | CF | J | | CC | | | | |
| Thomas Gybbys | | CF | J | | | | | | | CF | J | | | | | | | CF* |
| William Mynt | BA | | CO | | | | | | | | | | | | | | | |
| John Brandon | | | CF | J | BA | CO | J | CON | J | CF | CF | J | | J | CF | J | | * |
| William Frere | | | CF | | BA | CO | J | CON | J | CF | CF | J | CC | J | CF | J | | J* |
| John Matthew | | | CV | CV | CV | J | J | | J | | | J | CC | | CC | | | * |
| Thomas Lockyngton | | J | J | CC | CC | J | CON | CF+J | J | CF | CF | J | CF | CON | | J | CF | BA* |

| NAME | 1523 | 1524 | 1525 | 1526 | 1527 | 1528 | 1529 | 1531 | 1532 | 1533 | 1534 | 1535 | 1536 | 1537 | 1538 | 1539 | 1540 | 1541 |
|---|---|---|---|---|---|---|---|---|---|---|---|---|---|---|---|---|---|---|
| John Este | J | | | | | | | | | | | | | | | | | |
| William Diggby | CON | | | BA | | | | | | | | | | | | | | |
| John Manning | CF | | | | CO | | | | | | | | | | | | | |
| Richard Kyng | CV | | | | | | | CV | J | | | | | | | | | |
| John Marshall | J | | | | | | | | | | | | | | | | | |
| William Byrder | | CF | | | J | | | | | | | | | | | | | |
| Thomas Copinger | | CA | | | SBA | CV | | | | | | | | | | | | |
| William Richmond | | CV | | | | CA | CC | | CV | J | | CC | CF | | | CC | | |
| Richard Edmund | | | CA | | | | | | | | | | | | | | | |
| Thomas Lovell | | | CV | | | | | | | | | | | | | | | |
| John Wylde jr. | | | CC | CF | | | | | | | | | | | | | | |
| John Salmon | | | J | CF | | | | | | | | | | | | | | |
| Gilbert Walshe | | | J | | | | | | | | | | | | | | | |
| John Betrych | | | | CF | CC | BA | CO | J | CF | J | | J | CF | J | CF | J | BA | CON* |
| Thomas Harding | | | J | | | J | | | | | | | | | | | | |
| William Granger | | | | CV | | | | | | | | CV | | CV | | | | * |
| Henry Barnard | | | | CA | | | | | | | | | CV | | | | | * |
| William Arnold | | | | CC | | | | | | | | | | | | | | |

| Name | 1527 | 1528 | 1529 | 1531 | 1532 | 1533 | 1534 | 1535 | 1536 | 1537 | 1538 | 1539 | 1540 | 1541 | 1542 | 1543 | 1544 | 1545 |
|---|---|---|---|---|---|---|---|---|---|---|---|---|---|---|---|---|---|---|
| William Ibott | CA | | | | | | | | | | | | | | | | | |
| Thomas Tryg | CF | | | | | J | CF | | | | | | | | CF | J | BA | CO* |
| Thomas Freman | CV | | | | | | | | | | | | | | | | | |
| William Osteler | CV | SBA | SBA | | SBA | SBA | | | CC | | | | | | CON | | | |
| Thomas Frere | J | | | | | | | | | J | | | | | | | | |
| Robert Boston | J | | | | | | | | | | | | | | | | | |
| Richard Grene | | CON | | | | | | | | | | | | | | | | |
| William Glover | | CV | | | | | | | | | CV | | | | | | | |
| Thomas Stevenson | | CC | | | | | | J | CF | | CC | | | | | | CF | J* |
| Thomas Holme | | J | | | | | | | | | | | J | | J | | | |
| William Aston | | J | | | | | | | | | | | | | | | | |
| John Granger | | | CC | | | | | CON | J | | | CON | | J | | CO | | |
| Richard Robyns | | | CO | J | BA | CO | CF | J | BA | CO | J | CON | J | J | | | BA | CO* |
| William Herdman | | | CF | | | J | CF | | BA | | J | | CON | BA | | J | CON | J* |
| Simon Wellys | | | CA | | | | | CA | | | | | | | | | | |
| John Punt | | | | BA | CO | | | | | | | | | | | | | |

| Name | 1531 | 1532 | 1533 | 1534 | 1535 | 1536 | 1537 | 1538 | 1539 | 1540 | 1541 | 1542 | 1543 | 1544 | 1545 | 1546 | 1547 | 1548 |
|---|---|---|---|---|---|---|---|---|---|---|---|---|---|---|---|---|---|---|
| John Slouth sr. | BA | CO | J | CON | BA | | J | CF | | J | BA | | J | | | CON | | CF |
| Richard Frere | CON | J | | BA | CO | | | | | | | | | | | | | |
| William Abram jr. | CV | | | SBA | SBA | SBA | SBA | SBA | SBA | SBA | SBA | SBA | SBA | | | J | | |
| Thomas Garlop | CC | | | | | | | | CC | | | | | | CF | | CC | |
| John Grace | | BA | CO | | | | | | | | | | | | | | | |
| John Page | | CON | BA | CO | J | | J | J | CF | J | CF | | | J | | | | |
| John Clerk | | CF | J | | J | | | CF | J | J | J | | J | CF | | CF | | BA |
| William Ingram | | CV | | | | | | | | | | | | | | | | |
| William Bennet | | J | | | | CC | | | | | | | | | | | | |
| Robert Massy | | CA | | | | | | | | | | | | | | | | |
| Edmund Taverner | | CC | | | | | | | | | | | | | | | | |
| John Disney jr. | | J | | | CF | CON | J | J | J | J | J | J | J | J | CF | | | |
| Richard Prior | | J | CF | CC | | | | | | J | J | | | | | | | |
| John Garlond | | | CA | | | | | | | | | | | | | | | |
| John Byllington | | | CV | | | | J | | | | | | | | | | | |
| Thomas Kyrby | | | CV | | | | | | | | | | | | | | | |
| John Yattys | | | CV | | | | | | | | | | | | | | | |
| Richard Cook | | | J | CF | J | CC | J | CON | | J | CON | CF | J | | J | | | |
| William Laxton | | | CC | | | | J | | | | | | | | | | | |

| NAME | 1534 | 1535 | 1536 | 1537 | 1538 | 1539 | 1540 | 1541 | 1542 | 1543 | 1544 | 1545 | 1546 | 1547 | 1548 |
|---|---|---|---|---|---|---|---|---|---|---|---|---|---|---|---|
| Henry Frere | CON | BA | CO | J | CON | BA | CO | J | CF | J | J | BA | CO | BA | CO |
| William Dalton | J | | | | | | | | | | | | | | |
| John Laxton | J | | | | | | | | | | | | | | |
| John Nelson | J | | | J | CC | J | CC+J | CF | CF | J | CON | J | | CF | |
| William Abram sr. | J | | | | | | | | | | | | | | |
| William Goodwyn | | CV | | | | | | | CC | | | | | | |
| John Borowe | J | | | | | | | | | | | | | | |
| Robert Kyng | J | | J | | | | | | | | | | | | |
| Thomas Bell | CA | | | | | | | | | | | | | | |
| John Wylde | J | | J | CF | J | | J | CF | J | | | | | | |
| William Greatham | | | | | | | | | | | | | | | |
| John Greles | | CV | | | | | | | | | | | | | |
| William Grene | | CV | BA | CO | CA | J | | | | | | | | | |
| John Boleyn | | | J | | J | | J | CON | | CF | J | CON | | | |
| Thomas Pacy | | | J | | | | | | | | | | | | |
| Thomas Woodward | | | J | | | | | | | | | | | | |

| NAME | 1536 | 1537 | 1538 | 1539 | 1540 | 1541 | 1542 | 1543 | 1544 | 1545 | 1546 | 1547 | 1548 |
|---|---|---|---|---|---|---|---|---|---|---|---|---|---|
| John Staughton | CO | | | | | | | | | | | | |
| John Wilson | CF | | | | | | | | | | | | |
| William Syward | CA | | | | | | | | | | | | |
| William May | J | CF | | | | | | | | | | | |
| John Croft | J | | | J | | | CA | | | | | | |
| John Goodwyn | | J | | J | | J | | J | | | | | |
| John Sanden | | CA | | | | | | | | | | | |
| William Frost | | CC | CF | | | | | J | | | | | |
| John Whyte | | CV | | | | | | | | | | | |
| Robert Firmary | | CC | | J | | | | | | | | | |
| Walter Colyn | | J | J | | CF | | BA | | | | | | |
| John Ede | | | CV | | | CV | | | | | CA | | |
| John Granger jr. | | | J | | | | | | | | | CV | |
| Thomas Punt | | | J | | CF | | | BA | CO | J | | CON | CF |

| Name | 1539 | 1540 | 1541 | 1542 | 1543 | 1544 | 1545 | 1546 | 1547 | 1548 |
|---|---|---|---|---|---|---|---|---|---|---|
| Thomas Lockyngton | CO | CF | | | CON | | | | | |
| John Vyntner | CO | J | CF | | | | | | | CC |
| John Frere | CF | BA | CO | J | | J | CF | | | |
| Robert Staughton | J | CON | | J | BA | CO | | | | |
| John Hayward | CV | | | | | | | | | |
| William Malden | CF | CC | J | CON | | J | CF | | | |
| William Sewster | BA | CO | | | | | | BA | CO | |
| John Robyn | J | | CF | | CC | J | CON | | | |
| John Carles | J | | | | | | | | | |
| William Mayle | J | | | | | | | | | |
| Roger Hawdwyn | J | | J | | J | | | | | |
| William Frere | | J | | BA | CO | | | | | |
| John Matthew | | J | | | | | J | BA | CO | |
| Stephen Garlop | | CA | | | | | | | | |
| William Freman | | CA | CV | | | | | | | |
| Nicholas Bell | | CV | | | | | | | | |
| Ralph Harrowsby | | CA | CA | | | | | CV | SBA | SBA |
| Richard Smith, alias Bonsay | | | CA | | | | | | | |

| Name | 1542 | 1543 | 1544 | 1545 | 1546 | 1547 | 1548 |
|---|---|---|---|---|---|---|---|
| Thomas Tryg jr. | CC | | | | | | |
| Hugh Hayward | J | | | | | | |
| William Richmond | | J | | J | | | CON |
| William Slough | | CO | | | | | |
| John Herdman | | CO | | | | | |
| William Smith | | CV | | | | | |
| John Slough jr. | | CC | | CF | J | | |
| Robert Vyntner | | CC | J | | CF | | |
| William Granger | | J | | CC | | | |
| Robert Croft | | CON | | BA | CO | | CF |
| Edward Hayward | | CF | | | | | |
| Robert Warde | | CA | | | | | |
| William Flesher | | CA | | | | | |
| Richard Taylor | | CV | | | | | |
| Henry Barnard | | CV | | | | | |
| Robert Bowche | | J | CC | J | CF | | |
| William Aylred | | | J | | | CF | CC |
| John Beterych | | | J | | | CF | |
| Thomas Gaddisby | | | CA | | | CV | |

| NAME | 1544 | 1545 | 1546 | 1547 | 1548 |
|---|---|---|---|---|---|
| Richard Smith | CA | | | | |
| John Blaxton | SBA | SBA | SBA | | |
| Thomas Collye | CF | | | | |
| William Nebbes | CV | | | | |
| William Normanton | CC | | | | CON |
| John Upchurche | | CC | | | |
| Robert Howell | | CA | | | |
| John Frost | | CA | | | CF + CA |
| Thomas Freman | | CV | | | |
| Richard Hodgson | | CV | | | |
| Thomas Collins | | J | | | |
| Richard Robyns | | | BA | CO | |
| John Disney sr. | | | CF | | |
| William Thatcher | | | CV | | |
| Thomas Stevenson | | | CC | | |
| Thomas Tryg | | | | CON | |
| Henry Este | | | | CV | |
| John Lockyngton | | | | CC | |
| Richard Lockyngton | | | | CA | |

| NAME | 1547 | 1548 |
|---|---|---|
| John Myrgame | Cl | |
| William Herdman | | CON |
| John Granger | | BA |
| Edmund Peynter | | CA |
| William Glover, alias latysar | | CV |

# Appendix 3

## Farm Rental Lists for Godmanchester Streets

A description of the meaning of these lists and the method by which the size of property holdings can be derived from them has been given in Chapter 2, above. As noted there, the Latin heading to many of the surviving lists as some form of *rentale* is ambiguous since these are not lists of real rent payments for various properties but rather lists of the tax assessments to be paid towards the royal farm. The amounts to be found in the following lists are the final figures of payments to be made at the indicated year and term. That is to say, the various inter-term conveyances to be found at the foot of these records are summarized in Appendix 4 and the complex marginal notations to be found when properties were added or subtracted from the list for the previous term were too bulky to be repeated here. The individuals are shown in the order they appeared in the Farm Rental document, and, therefore, are not in alphabetical order.

The sum total for farm payments has not survived on the extant rental manuscripts for Post Street (except for Easter 1490, and Easter 1494) and West Street. In these instances the total has been obtained from adding all the entries. Where the total has survived on the original manuscripts (Arnyng Street and East Street and the two dates for Post Street noted above) this total has been used to derive the total acreage figures even though there are small variations from time to time from the actual totals to be derived from adding each entry in the manuscript.

Manuscripts for surviving farm rental lists are gathered in Godmanchester Borough Records, Box 1, Bundle 11. Appendix 3 does not include farm rentals for all the streets in 1485 since these have been given in property units in Table 11 (p. 38). Farm rentals still extant for the period after the 1540s are not given in the Appendix except for 1550s farm rentals for Arnyng and East Streets, entered here for comparison. There are no extant farm rentals from the other two streets for the 1550s and later farm rentals are so abbreviated as to be of little comparative value.

Farm rent payments for one term usually amounted to around £60 (between £14 to £15 for Arnyng Street, between £18 and £19 for East Street, between £12 and £13 for Post Street and between £14 and £15 for West Street). So for both terms farm rent payments would supply the £120 farm owed annually to the king. The late fifteenth and sixteenth-centuries assessment was sixpence per acre (threepence at each term) in contrast with the eight pence per acre in 1279. Whether this reduction was the beneficial farm rent allowance because of poverty during the reign of Edward IV cannot be determined. In any case the whole budget situation of the town had changed over the two centuries. Even with the eight pence per acre, revenues indicated in the 1279 Hundred Roll required revenues from the mills to make up the £120. But the revenues from the mills would seem to have been absorbed in the town administrative costs (cf. Bailiffs' accounts) by the late fifteenth century.

A. ARNYNG STREET RENTAL LISTS, 1487-1488

| NAME | 1487E | 1487M | 1488E | 1488M |
|---|---|---|---|---|
| John Aylred | 33/7d ob. (135½a) | 33/7d ob.q. (135½a) | 33/7d ob.q. (135a) | 33/7d ob.q. (135a) |
| William Garlop | 3d (1a) | 3d (1a) | 4d (1a) | 3d (1a) |
| William Pelle | 11/11d ob. (48a) | 11/11d ob. (48a) | 11/11d ob. (48a) | 11/6d ob.q. (46a) |
| William Mayle | 12/- ob. (48a) | 12/- ob. (48a) | 12/6d ob. (50a) | 15/7d ob. q. (62½a) |
| Simon Prestwode | 7d (2a) | 7d (2a) | 7d (2a) | 7d (2a) |
| John Stukeley | 14/- (56a) | 15/2d (61a) | 14/10d ob.q. (59a) | 16/- ob.q.(64a) |
| John Hawkyn | 8d (3a) | 8d (3a) | — | — |
| Thomas Baker | 5/- ob. (20a) | 2/10d q. (11a) | 2/10d q. (11a) | 4/6d ob.q. (18a) |
| Thomas Mundeford | (6/3d) (25?a) | — | — | — |
| Richard Gardner | 3/8d ob.q. (14½a) | 3/8d q. (14a) | 3/8d q. (14a) | 3/8d q. (14a) |
| Thomas Frost | 11/1d (44a) | 11/1d (44a) | 10/6d (42a) | 10/9d (43a) |
| James Lawe | 6/8d q. (26½a) | 6/3d ob.q. (25a) | 6/3d ob.q. (25a) | 5/6d (22a) |
| William Mateshale | 3d ob.q. (1a) | 3d ob.q. (1a) | 3d ob.q. (1a) | 3d ob.q. (1a) |
| Thomas Burton | 3/10d ob. (15½a) | 3/10d ob. (15½a) | 3/10d ob. (15½a) | 4/3d ob. (17a) |
| Austin Arnold | 11/6d ob. (46a) | 12/6d ob. (50a) | 12/7d q. (50½a) | 12/7d q. (50½a) |
| John Barnard sr. | 7/7d ob.q. (31a) | 7/5d ob. (30a) | 7/5d ob. (30a) | 7/5d ob. (30a) |
| John Grene | 2/1d (8a) | 2/1d (8a) | 2/1d (8a) | 2/1d (8a) |
| John Adam | 17d (5a) | 17d (5a) | 17d (5a) | 17d (5a) |
| Henry Martin | 8d ob. (2½a) | 11d ob. (4a) | 11d ob. (4a) | 11d ob. (4a) |
| William Scott | 4d ob. (1½a) | 1d ob. (½a) | — | — |
| Robert Robyn | 3/4d q. (13½a) | 3/4d q. (13½a) | — | — |
| Henry Robyn | 16d ob. (5½a) | 16d ob. (5½a) | 12d (4a) | 12d (4a) |
| William Gile | 8/3d ob.q. (33a) | 8/3d ob.q. (33a) | 8/3d ob. q. (33a) | 8/3d ob.q. (33a) |
| John Snell | 15/9d ob. (63a) | 15/11d ob.q. (64a) | 15/11d ob.q. (64a) | 15/11d ob.q. (64a) |
| William Frost sr. | 21/6d ob. (86a) | 21/6d ob. (86a) | 22/1d ob.q. (85a) | 22/2d ob. (85a) |
| John Corby | 20d ob.q. (7a) | 19d q. (6½a) | 19d q. (6½a) | 19d q. (6½a) |
| Fraternity of St. James | 1d ob. | 1d ob. | 3d (1a) | 3d (1a) |

| NAME | 1487E | 1487M | 1488E | 1488M |
|---|---|---|---|---|
| John Bowre | 11/4d ob.q. (45a) | 11/4d ob.q. (45a) | 11/4d ob.q. (45a) | 11/4d ob.q. (45a) |
| John Bonsay | 12/3d q. (49a) | 7/3d q. (29a) | 17/6d q. (30a) | – |
| William Gardiner | 12/2d q. (48a) | 12/2d q. (48a) | 11/11d q. (48a) | 11/11d q. (48a) |
| John Gardiner sr. | 10/3d (41a) | 10/3d (41a) | 10/3d (41a) | 10/3d (41a) |
| Thomas Balle | 4/2d ob.q. (17a) | 4/2d ob.q. (17a) | 4/2d ob.q. (17a) | – |
| John Browne | 11.2d ob. (44a) | 11/2d ob. (44a) | 11/4d (45a) | 12/1d ob.q. (48½a) |
| William Mownford | 16/9d (67a) | 16/9d (67a) | 16/9d (67a) | 16/9d (67a) |
| Robert Slow | 2d ob. | 2d ob. | 2d ob. | 2d ob. |
| John Lucas | 10/7d q. (42a) | 10/7d q. (42a) | 9/6d q. (38a) | 9/- q. (36a) |
| William Frost jr. | 16d ob.q. (5½a) | 23d (8a) | 23d (8a) | 3/5d ob.q. (14a) |
| Fraternity of Holy Trinity | 4/- q. (16a) | 4/4d (17a) | 4/7d (18½a) | 4/8d q. (19a) |
| Fraternity of St. Mary | 2/3d ob.q. (9a) | 2/3d ob.q. (9a) | 2/3d ob.q. (9a) | 2/3d ob.q. (9a) |
| William Browne | 21d ob.q. (7a) | 21d ob.q. (7a) | 21d ob.q. (7a) | 21d ob.q. (7a) |
| Richard Legge | 3d (1a) | 3d (1a) | 3d (1a) | 3d (1a) |
| John Howlett | 4/9d ob.q. (19a) | 11/1d ob.q. (44½a) | 6d q. (2a) | 3d ob.q. (1a) |
| William Holme | 6d ob.q. (2a) | 1d ob. (½a) | 1d ob. (½a) | 1d ob. (½a) |
| John Asshe | 3d (1a) | 3d (1a) | 3d (1a) | 3d (1a) |
| Reginald Corby | 3d (1a) | 3d (1a) | 3d (1a) | 3d (1a) |
| John Barnard jr. | 12d (4a) | – | – | – |
| William Cleyff | 10d q. (3½a) | 11d ob.q. (4a) | 1d ob. (½a) | 1d ob. (½a) |
| John Schylling | 2d | 2d | 2d | 2/1d (8a) |
| Richard Spicer | – | 4d (1a) | 4d (1a) | 5d ob. (2a) |
| William Hilton | – | 2d q. | 2d q. | 2/4d q. (9½a) |
| Margaret Balle | – | – | – | 4/1d (16a) |
| John Foster | – | – | 2/7d q. (10a) | 3/4d q. (13½a) |
| John Gony | – | – | 3d (1a) | 3d (1a) |
| John Templeman | – | – | 2d ob.q. | 2d ob.q. |
| John Barnard | – | – | – | 10d ob. (3a) |
| TOTAL: | £14 (?s.) 1d. | £14 6s. 8d. | £14 0s. 12 ob. | £14 16s. 7d ob.q. |

B. Arnyng Street Rental Lists, 1489-1491

| Name | 1489E | 1489M | 1490E | 1490M | 1491M |
|---|---|---|---|---|---|
| John Aylred | 33/7d ob. (135½a) | 33/4d ob.q. (134½a) | 33/4d ob.q. (134½a) | 33/4d ob.q. (134½a) | 33/4d ob.q. (134½a) |
| John Garlop | 4d ob. (1½a) | 4d ob. (1½a) | 4d ob. (1½a) | 4d ob. (1 ½a) | 4d ob. (1½a) |
| William Pelle | 11/7d ob. (46½a) | 11/7d ob. (46½a) | 11/7d ob. (46½a) | 11/7d ob. (46½a) | 11/7d ob. (46½a) |
| William Mayle | 15/7d ob. (62½a) | 15/6d ob. (62a) | 15/6d ob. (62a) | 15/5d ob.q. (61a) | — |
| Robert Mayle | | | | | 13/2d q. (52a) |
| Simon Prestwode | 7d (2a) | 6d (2a) | 6d (2a) | 6d (2a) | 6d (2a) |
| John Stukeley | 15/9d ob.q. (63a) | 16/1d (64a) | 15/10d (63a) | 16/3d q. (65a) | 16/4d (65a) |
| Thomas Baker | 3/5d q. (17½a) | 3/5d q. (17½a) | 3/5d q. (17½a) | 2/9d ob. (11a) | — |
| Richard Gardner | 3/8d ob.q. (14½a) | 3/9d (15a) | 3/9d (15a) | | |
| Agnes Gardner | | | 3/9d ob. (15a) | 3/9d ob. (15a) | 3/9d ob. (15a) |
| Thomas Frost | 10/6d (42a) | 10/6d (42a) | 10/6d (42a) | 10/6d (42a) | 10/6d (42a) |
| James Lawe | 5/3d (21a) | 5/- (20a) | 5/- (20a) | 4/10d ob. (20a) | 4/10d ob. (20a) |
| William Mateshale | 3d ob. q. (1a) | 3d ob. (1a) | 3d ob.q. (1a) | 3d ob.q. (1a) | 3d ob.q. (1a) |
| Thomas Burton | 4/3d ob. (17a) | 4/3d ob. (17a) | 4/3d ob. (17a) | 4/10d ob. (20a) | 4/10d ob. (20a) |
| Austin Arnold | 12/7d q. (50½a) | 12/7d q. (50½a) | 12/7d q. (50½a) | 12/7d q. (50½a) | 12/7d q. (50½a) |
| John Barnard sr. | 7/5d ob. (30a) | 7/5d ob. (30a) | 7/5d ob. (30a) | 7/5d (30a) | 7/10d (31a) |
| John Grene | 2/1d (8a) | 2/1d (8a) | 2/1d (8a) | 2/1d (8a) | 2/1d (8a) |
| John Adam | 17d (5a) | 17d (5a) | 17d (5a) | 17d (5a) | 17d (5a) |
| Henry Martin | 11d ob. (4a) | | | | |
| John Cave | | 11d ob. (4a) | 2/10d ob. (11a) | 2/10d ob. (11a) | 2/10d ob. (11a) |
| William Gile | 12d (4a) | 13d (4a) | 12d (4a) | 8d ob. (2a) | 8d ob. (2a) |
| John Snell | { 8/3d ob.q. (33a)<br>{ 15/9d ob.q. (63a) | — | — | — | — |
| Marcus Lorydan | — | 13/11d q. (55a) | 13/8d q. (54a) | 13/8d q. (54a) | 13/8d q. (54a) |
| William Frost sr. | 22/11d ob. (88a) | 23/6d ob.q. (93a) | 23/6d ob.q. (93a) | 24/1d q. (96a) | 24/- ob. (96a) |
| John Corby | 18d (6a) | 17d q. (5½a) | 17d q. (5½a) | 17d q. (5½a) | 17d q. (5½a) |
| Fraternity of St. James | 3d ob.s. (1a) | 3d ob.q. (1a) | 3d ob.q. (1a) | 4d ob. (1½a) | 4d ob. (1½a) |
| John Bowre | 11/4d ob.q. (45a) | 11/4d ob.q. (45a) | 11/4d ob.q. (45a) | 11/4d ob.q. (45a) | 11/4d ob.q. (45a) |
| John Smith | | 18/10d q. (75a) | 18/10d q. (75a) | 18/10d q. (75a) | 24/5d ob. (97a) |
| William Gardiner | 11/8d (47a) | 11/1d q. (46a) | 11/1d q. (46a) | 10/10d q. (43a) | 5/3d ob. (21a) |
| John Gardiner sr. | 10/3d (41a) | 10/3d (41a) | 10/3d (41a) | 10/3d (41a) | 10/3d (41a) |

| Name | 1489E | 1489M | 1490E | 1490M | 1491M |
|---|---|---|---|---|---|
| John Browne | 12/1d ob.q. (48a) | 12/1d ob.q. (48a) | 12/5d ob. (49a) | 12/8d ob. (50a) | 13/- (52a) |
| William Mownford | 16/9d (67a) | 16/9d (67a) | 16/9d (67a) | 16/9d (67a) | 16/9d (67a) |
| Robert Slow | 2d ob. | 2d ob. | 2d ob. | 2d ob. | – |
| John Lucas | 9/- q. (36a) | 9/- q. (36a) | – | – | – |
| William Frost jr. | 3/9d q. (15a) | 5/10d ob. (22a) | 5/10d ob. (22a) | 7/6d ob.q. (23a) | 7/8d q. (23a) |
| Fraternity of Holy Trinity | 4/8d q. (18¼a) | 4/8d q. (18¼a) | 4/8d q. (18¼a) | 4/8d q. (18¼a) | 4/8d q. (18¼a) |
| Fraternity of St. Mary | 2/3d ob. (9a) | 2/3d ob. (9a) | 2/3d ob. (9a) | 2/3d ob. (9a) | 2/3d ob. (9a) |
| William Browne | ? | 20d (7a) | 18d ob.q. (6a) | 18d ob.q. (6a) | 18d ob.q. (6a) |
| Richard Legge | 3d (1a) | 3d (1a) | 3d (1a) | 3d (1a) | – |
| William Holme | ? | 1d ob. (½a) | – | – | – |
| Reginald Corby | ? | 3d (1a) | 3d (1a) | 3d (1a) | 3d (1a) |
| William Cleff | ? | 10d (3a) | 1d ob. (½a) | 1d ob. (½a) | 1d ob. (½a) |
| John Schylling | ? | 23d ob.q. (8a) | 3d ob. (1a) | 9d (3a) | 9d (3a) |
| Richard Spicer | ? | – | – | – | – |
| Richard West | 3/9d ob. (15a) | 3/10d q (15½a) | 5d ob. (2a) | 5d ob. (2a) | 5d ob. (2a) |
| Margaret Balle | 3/- q. (15a) | 4/- ob. (16a) | 3/9d ob. (15a) | 3/5d (14a) | 3/5d (14a) |
| John Foster | 5/3d ob.q. (21a) | 5/3d ob.q. (21a) | 4/- ob. (16a) | 4/- ob. (16a) | 4/- ob. (16a) |
| William Nicol | 3d (1a) | 3d (1a) | 5/3d ob.q. (21a) | 5/3d ob.q. (21a) | 5/3d ob.q. (21a) |
| John Smith | – | – | 15d (5a) | 16d (5a) | 15d (5a) |
| Thomas Bonsay | | | 18d (6a) | 18d (6a) | 15d (5a) |
| John the servant of John Stukeley | – | | 1d ob. (½a) | 1d ob. (½a) | 1d ob. (½a) |
| John Mildenhall | – | | 2d ob. | 2d ob. | 2d ob. |
| Thomas Lessy | – | | – | 6d ob.q. (2a) | 8d q. (2¼a) |
| Robert Mayle | – | | – | – | 10/5d q. (42a) |
| William Longe | – | | – | – | 2d. |
| Thomas Parker | – | | – | – | 1d ob. (½a) |
| TOTAL: | not given | £14 6s 10d ob. | £14 2s 10d | £14 6s 6d ob.q. | £14 2s 10d |

## C. Arnyng Street Rental List,
### 25 Henry VIII (1533) Easter (Doc 43A)

| | |
|---|---|
| William Aylred | 29s. ob. (116a) |
| John Parrot | 4d. (1a) |
| Thomas Gybbys | 6d. (2a) |
| William Arnold | 10s. 3d. ob.q. (41a) |
| Fraternity of Blessed Virgin Mary in puerp' | 13d. q. (4a) |
| Fraternity of St. James | 2d. q. ($\frac{1}{2}$a 1r) |
| Thomas Manyfeld | 17s. 2d. ob.q. (68$\frac{1}{2}$a 1r) |
| William Sewster | 26s 11d. ob. (108a) |
| John Millicent | 8d. ob. (2$\frac{1}{2}$a 1r) |
| Thomas Borowe | 8d. q. (2$\frac{1}{2}$a 1r) |
| Richard Grenam | 2d. q. ($\frac{1}{2}$a 1r) |
| John Vincent | 4d. (1a 1r) |
| William Malden | 15s. 4d. q. (61$\frac{1}{2}$a) |
| John Slow | 27s. 8d. ob.q. (110$\frac{1}{2}$a) |
| Robert Staughton | 16s. 11d. (67$\frac{1}{2}$a) |
| Richard Prior | 2s. 3d. (9a) |
| Edmund Tavener | 2s. 11d. ob.q. (11$\frac{1}{2}$a) |
| John Dey | 20d. ob.q. (6$\frac{1}{2}$a) |
| William Abraham | 3d. (1a) |
| John Morgan | 16d. ob. (13$\frac{1}{2}$a) |
| Robert Frost | 2d. ob. ($\frac{1}{2}$a 1r) |
| Jone Jolly | 10d. (3a 1r) |
| Thomas Freman | 2s. 5d. (9$\frac{1}{2}$a 1r) |
| Richard Brown | 8d. ob. (2$\frac{1}{2}$a 1r) |
| Richard Taylor | 2d. ($\frac{1}{2}$a) |
| John Horwood | 1d. ob. ($\frac{1}{2}$a) |
| Thomas Kirby | 4s. 3d. ob.q. (17a) |
| John Careless | 5s. 6d. (22a) |
| William Greatham | 14s. 1d. q. (56a) |
| John Manning | 12s. 2d. (48$\frac{1}{2}$a 1r) |
| Thomas Smyth, husbandman | 18d. ob. (6a) |
| Thomas Smith, alias Bonsay | 18d. ob.q. (6a) |
| Richard Glover | 7d. ob. (2$\frac{1}{2}$a) |
| John Wright | 3s. 5d. q. (14a) |
| Richard Smyth | 23d. (7$\frac{1}{2}$a 1r) |
| John Small | 3d. (1a) |

Sum of Total: £10. 7s. ob.q. and 7s. ob.q. stroked out and replaced by 5s. 8d. ob.q.

Sum after receipts: £10s. 11s. 5d.

| | |
|---|---|
| Hewgney Howard | 4s. 9d. (19a) |
| John Frost | 5d. ob.q. (2$\frac{1}{2}$a 1r) |

## D. Arnyng Street Rental List,
### 1552 Michaelmas

| | |
|---|---|
| Edmund Powlter | £3 ob. (240a) |
| William Aylred | 28s. 5d. ob.q. (113½a) |
| Thomas Borowe | 6d. ob. (2a) |
| John Slow | 22s. 10d. q. (91a) |
| Richard Prior | 7s. 9d. (31a) |
| James Payet | 8s. 10d. ob. (35a) |
| Richard Taylor | 2d. (1r) |
| Richard Taylor as bellman | 4d. q. (1a 1r) |
| Thomas Freman | 4d. 9d. q. (19a) |
| James Dixon | 15s. q. (60a) |
| James Dixon | 4d. q. (1a 1r) |
| Pernell Carles | 5s. 6d. (22a) |
| William Greatham | 2s. 2d. ob.q. (8½a 1r) |
| Thomas Cook | 8s. 5d. ob.q. (33½a 1r) |
| William Flecher | 3d. ob. (1a) |
| Robert Staughton | 11s. 8d. ob.q. (46½a 1r) |
| John Morgrove | 14d. (4½a) |
| John Frost sr. | 2s. 3d. (9a) |
| William Malden | 19s. 4d. q. (77a 1r) |
| John Small | 1d. ob.q. (½a) |
| Steven Farthyng | 2d. (½a) |
| Edmund Tavener | 4d. q. (1½a) |
| John Scot | 8s. 6d. ob. (34a) |
| Roger Bowche | 12s. 3d. ob. (49a) |
| Henry Este | 14s. 4d. ob.q. (57½a) |
| Richard Prior jr. | 1d. ob. (½a) |
| Elizabeth Gybbys, widow | 21d. (7a) |
| John Lockyngton | 11s. 6d. ob.q. (46a 1r) |
| Robert Mortyme | 3d. (1a) |
| Richard Borrowe | 1d. ob. (½a) |
| Thomas Mayhew | 17s. ob.q. (68a 1r) |
| Steven Prior | 8s. 6d. ob. (34a) |
| Ann Albome | 3d. (1a) |
| Robert Croft | 39s. 9d. (159a) |
| John Stevenson | 4s. 6d. ob.q. (18a 1r) |
| Thomas Collyns | 2s. 11d. ob. (9a) |
| Total: | £16. 20d. |

E. EAST STREET RENTAL LISTS, 1486-1488

| NAME | 1486M | 1487E | 1488E | 1488M |
|---|---|---|---|---|
| Prior of Merton | 42/2d ob. (169a) | 42/2d ob. (169a) | 42/2d ob. (169a) | 42/2d ob. (169a) |
| His vicar | 10/8d q. (43a) | ? | 8/8d q. (35a) | 8/8d q. (35a) |
| John Minsterchambre | 13/7d ob. (54½a) | ? | 13/7d ob. (54½a) | 13/7d ob. (54½a) |
| Chaplain of Corpus Christi | 11/9d q. (47a) | ? | 11.9d q. (47a) | 12/- q. (48a) |
| Chaplain of Blessed Virgin Mary | 18/4d ob.q. (73½a) | ? | 18/7d ob.q. (73½a) | 19/4d ob.q. (77½a) |
| Lord John Oxen | – | – | 9d ob.q. (3a) | 9d ob.q. (3a) |
| William Tothe | 2d ob. | ? | 2d ob. | 2d ob. |
| John Page sr. | 17/6d ob. (70a) | ? | 17/3d ob. (71a) | 17/3d ob. (71a) |
| John Capelle | 2/6d q. (10a) | ? | 2/1d (8a) | 19d (6a) |
| William Diggby | 9d ob. (3a) | 9d ob. (3a) | 9d ob. (3a) | 8d (3a) |
| John Longe | 7/9d ob. (31a) | 7/9d ob. (31a) | 6/9d ob. (27a) | 6/9d ob. (27a) |
| William Longe | 6/3d (25a) | 6/3d (25a) | 6/6d (26a) | 6/6d (26a) |
| Benet Grey | 2/2d (8a) | 2/2d (8a) | 23d (8a) | 22d q. (7a) |
| Alice Bones | 18d ob.q. (6a) | 18d ob.q. (6a) | 18d ob.q. (6a) | 18d ob.q. (6a) |
| William Cleyfe | 10d. (3½a) | – | – | – |
| John Lawman | 7/6d ob. (30a) | 7/11d ob.q. (32a) | 7/10d q. (31½a) | 7/10d q. (31½a) |
| John Broughton | 14d ob.q. (5a) | 14d ob.q. (5a) | 14d ob.q. (5a) | 8d ob.q. (3a) |
| William Ingram | 7d ob. (2½a) | 14d ob.q. (5a) | 14d ob.q. (5a) | 17d q. (5½a) |
| William Aylred | 25/5d q. (102a) | 25/5d q. (102a) | 25/5d q. (102a) | 25/6d ob.q. (102a) |
| Thomas Hawkyn | 3d ob. (1a) | 3d ob. (1a) | 3d ob. (1a) | 3d ob. (1a) |
| Thomas Kendale | 4/10d ob.q. (19½a) | 4/9d q. (19a) | 4/9d q. (19a) | 4/9d q. (19a) |
| William Ponder | 23d q. (8a) | 2/11d q. (12a) | 23d q. (8a) | 2/2d q. (9a) |
| William Orwell | 19/10d q. (79a) | 19/10d q. (79a) | 19/10d q. (79a) | 19/10d q. (79a) |
| William Langham | 12d ob. (4a) | 12d ob. (4a) | 12d ob. (4a) | 12d ob. (4a) |
| William Syward | 5/7d q. (22½a) | 5/7d q. (22½a) | 5/7d q. (22½a) | 5/5d (21a) |
| John Willem | 12/3d ob. (49a) | 12/3d ob. (49a) | 12/3d ob. (49a) | 12/3d ob. (49a) |
| John Bould | 9/3d ob.q. (37a) | 9/3d ob.q. (37a) | 9/5d q. (37½a) | 9/5d q. (37½a) |
| William Goodwyn | 10/5d (41½a) | 10/5d (41½a) | 10/2d q. (40½a) | 5/2d q. (20½a) |
| Thomas Bate | 22d ob.q. (7½a) | 19d ob.q. (6½a) | 19d ob.q. (6½a) | 13d (4a) |
| Edward Barre | 17/11d (72a) | 17/11d (72a) | 18/2d ob. (72½a) | 18/2d q. (72½a) |
| William Page | 7/3d q. (29a) | 7/3d q. (29a) | 7/3d q. (29a) | 7/3d q. (29a) |
| Thomas Newman | 16/3d ob.q. (65a) | 16/1d q. (64a) | 17/1d ob. (68½a) | 17/11d (72a) |
| Thomas Fyncham | 24/6d (98a) | 24/6d (98a) | 5/8d ob.q. (23a) | 3/3d ob. (13a) |

| NAME | 1486M | 1487E | 1488E | 1488M |
|---|---|---|---|---|
| John Bonsay | — | — | 23/9d ob.q. (95a) | 35/9d (143a) |
| Custodian of church | 5/8d ob.q. (23a) | 5/8d ob.q. (23a) | 5/8d ob.q. (23a) | 5/8d ob.q. (23a) |
| Custodian of St. Katherine | 18d ob. (6a) | 18d ob. (6a) | 18d ob. (6a) | 18d ob. (6a) |
| John Dangerous | 14d ob. (4½a) | 14d ob. (4½a) | 14d ob. (4½a) | 14d ob. (4½a) |
| Bailiff | 2/- ob. (8a) | 2/- ob. (8a) | 15d (5a) | 15d (5a) |
| John Glover | 18d ob.q. (6a) | 18d ob.q. (6a) | 18d ob.q. (6a) | 18d ob.q. (6a) |
| William Ibott jr. | 4d ob. (1½a) | 4d ob. (1½a) | 4d ob. (1½a) | 4d ob. (1½a) |
| Thomas Lessy | 19d q. (6½a) | 17d ob.q. (5½a) | 17d ob.q. (5½a) | 17d ob.q. (5½a) |
| William Ibott sr. | 22d q. (7½) | 22d q. (7½a) | 22d q. (7½a) | 22d q. (7½a) |
| Thomas Syward jr. | 16d ob. (5½a) | 16d ob. (5½a) | 16d ob. (5½a) | 16d ob. (5½a) |
| Thomas Emley | 6/9d (27a) | 6/9d (27a) | 6/9d (27a) | 6/5d q. (25a) |
| John Grace | 3d (1a) | 6d ob.q. (2a) | 6d ob.q. (2a) | 6d ob.q. (2a) |
| Robert Porter | 6/6d ob. (26a) | 6/6d ob. (26a) | 6/5d (26a) | 6/5d (26a) |
| John Andrew | 1d | 1d | 1d | 1d |
| John Vincent sr. | 14d ob.q. (5a) | 14d ob.q. (5a) | 18d ob. (6a) | 18d ob. (6a) |
| Roger Manning | 18d (6a) | 16d ob. (5a) | 16d ob. (5a) | 12d ob.q. (4a) |
| Thomas Syward sr. | 5/1d ob. (20a) | 5/1d ob. (20a) | 5/- ob. (20a) | 4/11d q. (20a) |
| Alice Syward | 9d ob.q. (3a) | 9d ob.q. (3a) | 8d ob. (2½a) | 8d ob. (2½a) |
| Custodian of St. George | 4d (1a) | 4d (1a) | 4d (1a) | 4d (1a) |
| Thomas Page | 10d q. (3a) | 10d q. (3a) | 10d q. (3a) | 10d q. (3a) |
| William Syward jr. | 13d q. (4a) | 13d q. (4a) | 16d (5a) | 16d (5a) |
| William Granger | 11d q. (4a) | 11d q. (4a) | 11d q. (4a) | — |
| Richard Pelle | 11/6d q. (46a) | 11/2d ob. (45a) | 11/2d ob. (45a) | 11/3d ob. (45a) |
| John Sparrow | 3d (1a) | 3d (1a) | 3d (1a) | 3d (1a) |
| John Hermyn | 6d ob.q. (2a) | 6d ob.q. (2a) | 6d ob.q. (2a) | 6d ob.q. (2a) |
| Thomas Nottingham | 8d (6½a) | — | — | — |
| Cristina Bishop | 4d ob. (1½a) | 4d ob. (1½a) | 4d ob. (1½a) | 4d ob. (1½a) |
| Reginald Folkys | 20d q. (6½a) | — | — | — |
| Robert Martin | 4d ob. (1½a) | — | — | — |
| John Barnard | — | — | 12d (4a) | — |
| Robert Vont | — | — | 5d ob.q. (2a) | 19d (6a) |
| Richard Willem | — | — | 6d (2a) | 6d (2a) |
| TOTAL: | £18 5s. 0d. | £18 2s. 6d. | £18 3s. 9d. | £18 9s. 1d. |

F. EAST STREET RENTAL LISTS, 1489-1492

| Name | 1489E | 1489M | 1490E | 1490M | 1491M | 1492E |
|---|---|---|---|---|---|---|
| Prior of Merton | 42/2d ob. (168a) | 42/2d ob. (168a) | 42/2d ob. (168a) | 42/2d ob. (168a) | 42/2d ob. (168a) | 42/2d ob. (168a) |
| His vicar | 8/8d q. (35a) | 8/4d q. (34a) | 8/4d q. (34a) | ? | 8/10d (35a) | 8/10d (35a) |
| John Minsterchambre | 13/7d ob. (54½a) | 13/7d ob. (54½a) | 13/7d ob. (54½a) | ? | 20/4d (80a) | 20/4d (80a) |
| Chaplain of Corpus Christi | 12/3d q. (49a) | 12/3d (49a) | 12/3d (49a) | ? | 9/10d (39½a) | 9/10d (39½a) |
| Chaplain of Blessed Virgin Mary | 19/4d ob. (77a) | 19/4d ob. (77a) | 19/9d (79a) | ? | 17/- (68a) | 18/1d (72a) |
| Lord John Oxen | 9d ob.q. (3a) | 17d q. (6a) | 17d q. (6a) | ? | 7d ob. (2a) | 8d ob. (2½a) |
| John Page sr. | 17/3d ob. (71a) | 17/3d ob. (71a) | 17/3d ob. (71a) | ? | 17/2d (71a) | 17/2d (71a) |
| John Capelle | 19d (6a) | 19d (6a) | 19d (6a) | ? | — | — |
| John Snell | — | 10/9d ob.q. (43a) | 11/- ob.q. (44a) | 11/- ob.q. (44a) | 11/1d ob. (44½a) | 11/1d ob. (44½a) |
| John Aylred | — | 13d (4a) | 13d (4a) | 13d (4a) | 13d (4a) | 13d (4a) |
| William Diggby | 8d (2½a) | 8d (2½a) | 8d (2½a) | 8d (2½a) | 8d (2½a) | 8d (2½a) |
| John Longe | 4/3d ob. (17a) | 4/3d ob. (17a) | 4/3d ob. (17a) | 4/3d ob. (17a) | 4/2d (17a) | 4/2d (17a) |
| William Longe | 9/- (36a) | 9/- (36a) | 9/- (36a) | — | — | — |
| Benet Grey | 22d q. (7a) | 22d q. (7a) | 22d (7a) | 22d q. (7a) | 22d q. (7a) | 22d q. (7a) |
| Alice Bones | 18d ob.q. (6a) | 18d ob.q. (6a) | 18d ob.q. (6a) | 18d ob.q. (6a) | 18d ob.q. (6a) | 18d ob.q. (6a) |
| John Lawman | 7/10d q. (31a) | 7/10d q. (31a) | 7/5d q. (29a) | 7/5d q. (29a) | 7/5d q. (29a) | 7/5d q. (29a) |
| William Ingram | 17d q. (6a) | 2/2d q. (8½a) | 2/2d q. (8½a) | 2/2d q. (8½a) | 7d ob. (2½a) | 2/2d q. (8½a) |
| William Aylred | 25/6d ob.q. (102a) | 22/5d ob.q. (99a) | 22/2d ob.q. (98½a) | 22/2d ob.q. (98½a) | — | — |
| John Aylred | 3d ob. (1a) | 3d ob. (1a) | 3d ob. (1a) | — | 3/9d ob.q. (15a) | 3/9d ob.q. (15a) |
| Thomas Hawkyn | — | — | — | 5/1d q. (20a) | — | — |
| William Mayle | 4/9d q. (19a) | 4/9d q. (19a) | 4/9d q. (19a) | 4/9d q. (19a) | 7/3d q. (29a) | 7/3d q. (29a) |
| Thomas Kendale | — | 4/6d q. (18a) | 4/6d q. (18a) | 3/11d (16a) | 4/9d q. (19a) | 4/9d q. (19a) |
| John Lucas | — | — | — | 3d (1a) | 5d ob. (2a) | 5d ob. (2a) |
| Richard Legge | — | — | — | — | — | — |

| Name | 1489E | 1489M | 1490E | 1490M | 1491M | 1492E |
|---|---|---|---|---|---|---|
| William Ponder | 2/2d q. (8½a) | 2/2d q. (8½a) | 2/2d q. (8½a) | 23d q. (7a) | 19d ob. (6½a) | 18d ob. (6a) |
| William Orwell | 19/9d ob. (79a) | 19/10d ob. (79½a) | 19/10d ob. (79½a) | 19/10d ob. (79½a) | 19/10d ob. (79½a) | 19/10d ob. (79½a) |
| William Langham | 12d ob. (4a) | 12d ob. (4a) | 12d ob. (4a) | 15d ob. (5a) | 15d ob. (5a) | 15d ob. (5a) |
| William Syward | 5/5d (21½a) | 5/3d (21a) | 5/3d (21a) | 5/1d ob.q. (20a) | 5/- (20a) | 5/- (20a) |
| Robert Stevenson | | | | 14d q. (5a) | 22d (7a) | 22d (7a) |
| John Willem | 12/3d ob. (49a) | 12/3d ob. (49a) | 12/3d ob. (49a) | 12/3d ob. (49a) | 12/3d ob. (49a) | 12/3d ob. (49a) |
| John Bould | 9/5d q. (37½a) | 9/5d q. (37½a) | 9/5d q. (37½a) | 9/5d q. (37½a) | 9/8d q. (39a) | 9/10d ob. (39a) |
| William Goodwyn | 5/2d q. (20½a) | 5/2d q. (20½a) | 5/2d q. (20½a) | 5/2d q. (20½a) | 4/11d (20a) | 4/11d (20a) |
| Thomas Bate | 13d (4a) | 6d (2a) | 3d (1a) | — | — | — |
| Edward Barre | 18/2d q. (72a) | 18/2d q. (72a) | 18/2d q. (72a) | 18/2d q. (72a) | 18/2d q. (72a) | 18/2d q. (72a) |
| William Page | 7/3d q. (29a) | 7/3d q. (29a) | 7/3d q. (29a) | 7/3d q. (29a) | 7/3d q. (29a) | 7/3d q. (29a) |
| Thomas Page | — | — | — | — | — | — |
| Thomas Newman | 17/11d (71a) | 18/6d q. (74a) | 18/6d q. (74a) | 18/10d ob. (75a) | 18/10d ob.q. (75a) | 18/10d ob.q. (75a) |
| Thomas Fyncham | 3/3d ob. (13a) | 3d (1a) | 3d (1a) | 3d (1a) | 3d (1a) | — |
| John Bonsay | 36/3d (145a) | 37/11d ob. (151a) | 33/- ob. (133a) | 31/6d ob. (125a) | 31/11d (127a) | 31/7d (126½a) |
| Custodian of the church | 5/8d ob.q. (23a) | 5/8d ob.sq. (23a) | 5/8d ob.q. (23a) | 5/8d ob.q. (23a) | 5/8d ob.q. (23a) | 5/8d ob.q. (23a) |
| Custodian of St. Katherine | 18d ob. (6a) | 18d ob. (6a) | 18d ob. (6a) | 18d ob. (6a) | 18d ob. (6a) | 18d ob. (6a) |
| John Dangerous | 14d ob. (4½a) | 14d ob. (4½a) | 14d ob. (4½a) | 14d ob. (4½a) | 14d ob. (4½a) | 14d ob. (4½a) |
| Bailiff | 2/- ob. (8a) | 2/- ob. (8a) | 15d (5a) | 2/- ob. (8a) | 23d q. (8a) | — |
| John Glover | 18d ob.q. (6a) | 21d ob.q. (7a) | 21d ob.q. (7a) | 21d ob.q. (7a) | | |
| William Ibott jr. | 4d (1a) | 3d (1a) | 4d ob. (for amessuage) | 3d ob. (1a) | 3d (1a) | 3d (1a) |
| Thomas Lessy | 14d ob.q. (5a) | 14d (5a) | 14d ob.q. (5a) | 14d ob.q. (5a) | 11d ob.q. (4a) | 11d ob.q. (4a) |
| William Ibott sr. | 22d q. (7a) | 22d q. (7a) | 22d q. (7a) | 4d (1a) | 4d (1a) | 4d (1a) |
| Agnes Light | 1d | 1d | 1d | 1d | 1d | 1d |
| Thomas Syward jr. | 10d ob. (3½a) | 9d (3a) | 9d (3a) | 10d (3a) | 9d (3a) | 9d (3a) |
| Thomas Emley | 6/3d ob.q. (25a) | 6/2d q. (24½a) | 6/2d q. (24½a) | 6/2d q. (24½a) | 6/2d q. (24½a) | 5/9d (23a) |
| John Grace | 6d ob.q. (2a) | — | — | — | — | — |

|  | | | | | | |
|---|---|---|---|---|---|---|
| Robert Porter | 6/9d ob. (27a) | 20d q. (6½a) | 20d q. (6½a) | 20d q. (6½a) | 17d (6a) | 17d (6a) |
| John Andrew | 1d | 1d | 1d | 1d | 1d | – |
| Robert Archebould | – | – | – | – | – | 1d |
| John Vincent sr. | 18d ob. (6a) | 18d ob. (6a) | 18d ob. (6a) | 18d ob. (6a) | 18d ob. (6a) | 18d ob. (6a) |
| Roger Manning | 12d ob.q. (4a) | 12d ob.q. (4a) | 12d ob.q. (4a) | 12d ob.q. (4a) | 12d (4a) | 10d (3a) |
| Thomas Syward sr. | 4/11d q. (20a) | 5/6d (22a) | 6/- (24a) | 6/- (24a) | 5/3d ob.q. (21a) | 5/3d ob.q. (21a) |
| Alice Syward | 8d ob. (2½a) | 8d ob. (2½a) | 8d ob. (2½a) | 8d ob. (2½a) | 8d ob. (2½a) | 8d ob. (2½a) |
| Custodian of St. George | 4d (1a) | 4d (1a) | 4d (1a) | 4d (1a) | 4d (1a) | 4d (1a) |
| Thomas Page | 10d q. (3½a) | – | – | – | – | – |
| William Syward jr. | 16d (5a) | 16d (5a) | 16d ob. (5½a) | 16d (5a) | 15d (5a) | 15d (5a) |
| Richard Pelle | 11/3d ob. (45a) | 11/7d ob.q. (46½a) | 11/7d ob.q. (46½a) | 11/7d ob.q. (46½a) | 13/1d ob.q. (52a) | 13/1d ob.q. (52a) |
| John Hermyn | 9d (3a) | 16d (5½a) | 14d ob.q. (5a) | 14d ob.q. (5a) | – | – |
| Robert Vont | 21d q. (7a) | 3/5d ob.q. (14a) | 4/11d ob.q. (20a) | 3/9d (15a) | 5/9d ob. (23a) | 5/9d ob. (23a) |
| Richard Willem | 6d (2a) | 6d (2a) | 6d (2a) | 6d (2a) | 6d (2a) | 6d (2a) |
| John Asshe | 3d (1a) | 5d (2a) | 2d | 2d | 2d | 2d |
| John Snell | 8/3d q. (23a) | – | – | – | – | – |
| John Bonsay | 2d q. | – | – | – | – | – |
| Henry Est | 6d ob.q. (2a) | 2d q. | 2d q. | 2d q. | 6d ob.q. (2a) | 3/9d ob.q. (18a) |
| William Holme | – | 1d ob. (½a) | – | – | – | – |
| Henry Trayley | – | 7d ob. (2½a) | 7d ob. (2½a) | 4/11d ob.q. (20a) | 6/10d q. (27¾a) | 4/2d ob. (16½a) |
| William Est | – | 3d (1a) | 3d (1a) | 9d ob.q. (3a) | 6/6d ob.q. (26a) | 5/2d q. (21a) |
| Alice Motte | – | – | 4d ob. (1½a) | 4d ob. (1½a) | – | – |
| William Parker | – | – | – | – | 2d q. | 2d q. |
| Richard Brewster | – | – | – | – | 4d ob. (1½a) | 4d ob. (1½a) |
| Margaret Folkys | – | – | – | – | ob.q. | ob.q. |
| William Basse | – | – | – | – | – | 10/11d q. (44a) |
| Thomas Lessy | – | – | – | – | – | 8d (3a) |
| Adam Lessy | – | – | – | – | – | 4/1d q. (16a) |
| John Haryngton | – | – | – | – | – | 9d (3a) |
| TOTAL: | £18 8s. 6d.ob. | £18 15s. 0d. | no sum | £18 14s. 6d. ob.q. | £18 2s. 11d. ob. | £18 3s. 4d. ob. |

G. East Street Rental List,
1-2 Phillip and Mary (1554) Michaelmas (Doc. 51A)

| | |
|---|---|
| Farm of Parsonage | 42s. 2d. ob. (184a) |
| Dorothy Wilson, widow | 20s. ob.q. (80a) |
| Vicary of the church | 10s. (40a) |
| Robert Gyune | 3d. (1a) |
| Alice Mayle | 23s. 1d. ob. (92a) |
| William Granger | 10s. 1d. (40a) |
| Robert Cook | 5d. (2a) |
| John Mayhew | 18s. 3d. q. (77a) |
| Thomas Garlop | 13s. 11d. (56a) |
| Robert Vyntner | 23s. 8d. ob. (95a) |
| John Beterich | 22s. 1d. ob.q. (48a) |
| William Garlop | 1d. ob. (½a) |
| John Bullyn | 16s. 6d. (66a) |
| William Dorraunt | 5d. (2½a) |
| Agnes Whyttington | 14d. (4½a) |
| John Granger | 17s. 5d. ob. (70a) |
| William Ingram | 2s. 8d. ob. (11a) |
| Thomas Prior | 2d. ob. (1a) |
| William Glover | 6s. 3d. (25a) |
| William Frost | 18s. 3d. (77a) |
| Agnes Wellys, widow, for Remyng | 3d. ob. (1a) |
| John Byrde | 10d. (3a) |
| and same John Byrde | 5s. 4d. ob. (21a) |
| Robert Harryson | 3d. (1a) |
| Thomas Exyre | 38s. 4d. (153a) |
| the same Thomas for Remyng | 8d. ob. (3a) |
| the same Thomas for parcel of ground of late Thomas Welle | 1d. |
| William Seward | ob. |
| Robert Granger | 3s. 2d. ob. (13a) |
| Thomas Kyrby | 20d. ob.q. (7a) |
| James Chambre | 2d. (1r) |
| John Harryson | 2d. ob. (1a) |
| William Smyth | 12s. 2d. ob. (49a) |

John Shepherd, Lawrence Wellered and Luke Ronstell for the chancery land, church land, guilds land, lamp lands and for the Bellman's lands all that together 52s. 8d. ob.q. (210a)

| | |
|---|---|
| Robert Martyne | 3d. (1a) |
| Thomas Mayle | 6d. ob.q. (2a) |
| Total | £18. 9s. 7d. ob. |
| and sum of Total after receipts | £18. 9s. 4d. |

## H. Post Street Rental Lists, 1486-1494

| Name | 1486m | 1487e | 1487m |
|---|---|---|---|
| William Dey | 1d | 1d | 1d |
| William Manipenny | 17/7d ob. (70a) | 17/7d (70a) | 17/3d (69a) |
| William Browne | 10d (3a) | 11d (3½a) | 20d (7a) |
| William Chese | 3/5d ob.q. (14a) | 3/5d ob.q. (14a) | 13d ob. (4½a) |
| John Gony | 1d ob. (½a) | 1d ob. (½a) | 1d ob. (½a) |
| William Goodwyn | 8/- (32a) | 8/- (32a) | 9/10d (39a) |
| Thomas Norton | 4d ob. (1½a) | 4d ob. (1½a) | 4d ob. (1½a) |
| John Reygate | 1d ob.q. (½a) | 1d ob.q. (½a) | 1d ob.q. (½a) |
| Alice Frere | 5d ob.q. (2a) | 5d ob.q. (2a) | 5d ob.q. (2a) |
| William Frere | { 16/9d ob. (67a) | 16/9d (67a) | 16/9d (67a) |
| | { 8d q. (2a) | 8d q. (2a) | 8d q. (2a) |
| Fraternity of Corpus Christi | 4/8d (18½a) | 4/8d 18½a) | 4/8d (18½a) |
| John Dey | 10d q. (3a) | 10d q. (3a) | 11d (4a) |
| John Fisher | 33/1d q. (132a) | 33/1d q. (132a) | 33/1d q. (132a) |
| William Betriche | 3/2d ob. (12a) | 3/2d ob. (12a) | 5/9d q. (23a) |
| William Stodale | 17/5d (70a) | 17/3d ob. (69a) | 17/3d ob. (69a) |
| Isabella Wright | 2/8d ob.q. (10½a) | 2/8d ob.q. (10½a) | 2/8d ob.q. (10½a) |
| William Frost | 2/3d ob.q. (9a) | — | — |
| Isabella Wright | — | — | 2/8d ob.q. (10½a) |
| William Farthing | 2d ob. (1a) | 2d ob. (1a) | 2d ob. (1a) |
| John Porter | 2/4d ob.q. (9½a) | 2/4d ob.q. (9½a) | 2/4d ob.q. (9½a) |
| John Templeman | 2d. ob.q. (1a) | 2d ob.q. (1a) | 2d ob.q. (1a) |
| Robert Gony | 3d (1a) | 3d (1a) | 2/11d ob.q. (11a) |
| John Holme | 2d (messuage) | 2d (messuage) | 2d (messuage) |
| John Turneskewe | 3/1d (12a) | 3/2d ob. (12a) | 3/5d ob. (13a) |
| John Bigge | 22d ob. (7a) | 18d (6a) | 18d (6a) |
| Richard William | 3/6d (14a) | 3/6d (14a) | 3/6d (14a) |
| John Stevenson | 7d ob.q. (3½a) | — | — |
| John and Robert Stevenson | — | 10d (3a) | 10d (3a) |
| William Lessy | 1d | 1d | 1d |
| John Cave | 8d (3a) | 8d (3a) | 8d (3a) |
| Richard Motte | 18d (6a) | 18d (6a) | 4d ob. (1½a) |
| John Garlop sr. | 15d ob.q. (5a) | 10d ob.q. (3½a) | 15d ob.q. (5a) |
| William Tothe | 1d ob. (½a) | 1d ob. (½a) | 1d ob. (½a) |
| John Rumborough | 4d q. (1½a) | 4d q. (1½a) | 4d q. (1½a) |
| Richard Chycheley | 1d ob. (½a) | 1d ob. (½a) | 1d ob. (½a) |
| Thomas Bailey | 3d. ob. (1a) | 3d ob. (1a) | 3d ob. (1a) |
| Richard Passelowe | 3/3d (13a) | 3/4d ob. (13½a) | 3/1d ob. (13a) |
| Simon Granger | 6d (3a) | 6d (3a) | 6d (3a) |
| John Stalys | 3/- ob. (12a) | 3/- ob. (12a) | 3/- ob. (12a) |
| Helen Dawntre | 4d (1a) | 4d (1a) | 4d (1a) |
| John Adam | 2/11 q. (12a) | 2/11d q. (12a) | 2/11d q. (12a) |
| John Page jr. | 11d ob.q. (4a) | 23d (8a) | 23d (8a) |
| Richard Samt | 5/4d ob. (21½a) | 5/6d (22a) | 11/11d q. (48a) |
| William Plumpton | 12/- ob. (48a) | 11/8d ob.q. (46½a) | 11/8d ob.q. (46½a) |
| Matthew Garnet | 4/10d q. (19½a) | 4/10d q. (19½a) | 4/10d q. (19½a) |
| William Gonell | 2/- (8a) | 2/- (8a) | 2/- (8a) |
| Thomas Baron | 8d ob.q. (2½a) | 8d ob.q. (2½a) | — |
| Thomas Kyng | 8d q. (2½a) | 8d q. (2½a) | 8d q. (2½a) |

| NAME | 1486M | 1487E | 1487M |
|---|---|---|---|
| Thomas Johnson | 8d q. ($2\frac{1}{2}$a) | 8d q. ($2\frac{1}{2}$a) | 8d q. ($2\frac{1}{2}$a) |
| John Dalton | 4d (1a) | 4d (1a) | 4d (1a) |
| John Garlop jr. | 5/5d ob.q. (21a) | 5/5d ob.sq. (21a) | 5/5d ob.q. (21a) |
| Thomas Deyn | [17d ob.q.] (6a) | 18d ob.q. (6a) | 12d (4a) |
| Thomas Marshall | 4d (1a) | 4d (1a) | 4d (1a) |
| Fraternity of St. John | 17d q. ($5\frac{1}{2}$a) | 17d q. ($5\frac{1}{2}$a) | 17d q. ($5\frac{1}{2}$a) |
| John Manipenny | 3d (1a) | 3d (1a) | 3d (1a) |
| John Englysh | 3/10d (15a) | 3/9d (15a) | 3/8d q. (14a) |
| Thomas Reynold | 6d ob. (2a) | 6d ob. (2a) | 6d ob. (2a) |
| Richard Gilby | 5d (2a) | 5d (2a) | 8d ($2\frac{1}{2}$a) |
| John Garlop, son of John sr. | 3/- ob. (12a) | 3/- ob. (12a) | 3/- ob. (12a) |
| John Lumbard | 5/- (20a) | 5/- ob. (20a) | 5/- ob. (20a) |
| John Byllingford | 1d ob. ($\frac{1}{2}$a) | — | — |
| Richard Folkys | ob. q. | ob. q. | — |
| Thomas Cokman | 6d (2a) | 6d (2a) | 15d (5a) |
| John Reed | 4d (1a) | 4d (1a) | 4d (1a) |
| Thomas Fecas | 1d ob. ($\frac{1}{2}$a) | 1d ob. ($\frac{1}{2}$a) | 3d ob. (1a) |
| John Feld | 1d ob. ($\frac{1}{2}$a) | 1d ob. ($\frac{1}{2}$a) | 1d ob. ($\frac{1}{2}$a) |
| John Sterlyng | 9d ob.q. (3a) | 8d q. (3a) | — |
| Matthew Hedley | 2d ($\frac{1}{2}$a) | 2d ($\frac{1}{2}$a) | 2d ($\frac{1}{2}$a) |
| Margaret Garlop | 1d ob. ($\frac{1}{2}$a) | 1d ob. ($\frac{1}{2}$a) | 1d ob. ($\frac{1}{2}$a) |
| John Gardner | 3/6d ob. (14a) | 3/2d q. (13a) | 3/2d q. (13a) |
| Henry Marshall | 13d q. ($4\frac{1}{2}$a) | 13d q. ($4\frac{1}{2}$a) | 13d q. ($4\frac{1}{2}$a) |
| William Nottyngham | 11d (4a) | 11d ob.q. (4a) | 11d ob.q. (4a) |
| Thomas Balle | 13d (4a) | 17d ob. (6a) | 19d (6a) |
| John Bonsay | 10/- ob.q. (40a) | 10/8d ob. (43a) | 10/8d (43a) |
| Thomas Faldyng | 12/2d (48a) | 12/2d q. (48a) | 14/9d (59a) |
| William Lyght | 16d ($6\frac{1}{2}$a) | 16d q. ($6\frac{1}{2}$a) | 16d q. ($6\frac{1}{2}$a) |
| Robert Bayous | 23d (8a) | 23d ob.q. (8a) | 23d ob.q. (8a) |
| Thomas Blassell | 3d ob.q. (1a) | — | — |
| Robert Nicholas | 9/7d ob.q. ($38\frac{1}{2}$a) | 9/7d ob.q. ($38\frac{1}{2}$a) | 12/8d ob. (51a) |
| John Stooke | 7d ob. ($2\frac{1}{2}$a) | 6d (2a) | 6d (2a) |
| Thomas Punte | 3d (1a) | 6d (2a) | 6d (2a) |
| Agnes Page | 8d (3a) | 8d ob.q. (3a) | 8d ob.q. (3a) |
| Thomas Knaresborough | 9d ob. (3a) | 9d ob. (3a) | 9d ob. (3a) |
| William Wright | 3d ob.q. (1a) | 2d (1a) | 2d (1a) |
| John Matthew | 3/1d ob.q. ($12\frac{1}{2}$a) | 3/3d ob.q. (13a) | 1d |
| John Osteler | 2/8d ob.q. (9a) | 2/8d ob.q. (9a) | 20d (7a) |
| Richard Willam jr. | 6d (2a) | 6d (2a) | 6d (2a) |
| John Shalford | 3d (1a) | 3d (1a) | 7d (2a) |
| John Barnard jr. | 4d ob. ($1\frac{1}{2}$a) | 4d ob. ($1\frac{1}{2}$a) | — |
| William Edmond | ob.q. | ob.q. | ob.q. |
| Balle' | 1d ob. ($\frac{1}{2}$a mea) | 1d ob. ($\frac{1}{2}$a) | 1d ob. ($\frac{1}{2}$a) |
| Thomas Martin | 1d ob. ($\frac{1}{2}$a) | 1d ob. ($\frac{1}{2}$a) | 1d ob. ($\frac{1}{2}$a) |
| John Barnard | 4d ob. ($1\frac{1}{2}$a) | 4d ob. ($1\frac{1}{2}$a) | 4d ob. ($1\frac{1}{2}$a) |
| William Page | 4d ob. ($1\frac{1}{2}$a) | 4d ob. ($1\frac{1}{2}$a) | 4d ob. ($1\frac{1}{2}$a) |
| John Page jr. | 11d ob. (4a) | 11d ob. (4a) | 11d ob. (4a) |
| John Granger | 2d ($\frac{1}{2}$a) | 2d ($\frac{1}{2}$a) | 2d ($\frac{1}{2}$a) |
| TOTAL: | £12 3s 9d q. | £12 16s 8d | £12 16s 8d |

I. Post Street Rental Lists, 1490-1492

| Name | 1490E | 1490M | 1491E | 1491M | 1492E |
|---|---|---|---|---|---|
| Thomas Norton | 4d ob. (1½a) | 4d ob. (1½a) | 4d ob. (1½a) | ? | 4d ob. (1½a) |
| Prior, Canon of Hunts | – | – | – | ? | 9d (3a) |
| Thomas Kyng | 8d q. (3a) | 8d q. (3a) | 8d q. (3a) | ? | 8d q. (3a) |
| Matthew Garnet, artificer | 4/10d q. (19½a) | 4/10d q. (19½a) | 4/10d q. (19½a) | ? | 14/10d q. (19½a) |
| William Gonell | 2/- (8a) | 2/- (8a) | 2/- (8a) | ? | 2/- (8a) |
| Richard Samt | 14/1d ob. (56½a) | 14/1d ob. (56½a) | 14/1d ob. (56½a) | ? | 14/1d ob. (56½a) |
| Anna Plumpton | 11/4d q. (45½a) | 11/4d q. (45½a) | 11/4d q. (45a?) | ? | 9/4d ob. (37½a) |
| Thomas Coke | 6d (2a) | 6d (2a) | 6d (2a) | ? | [4d] (1a?) |
| William Melbourne | – | – | – | – | 2d (1a) |
| Agnes Reed | 4d (1a) | 4d (1a) | 4d (1a) | ? | 4d (1a) |
| Godfrey Grace | 1d | 1d | 1d | ? | 1d |
| John Adam | 7d ob. (2½a) | 7d ob. (2½a) | 7d ob. (2½a) | ? | 7d ob. (2½a) |
| Thomas Marshall | 12d (4a) | 4d (1a) | 4d (1a) | ? | 4d (1a) |
| John Dalton | 4d (1a) | 4d (1a) | 2d ob. (1a) | ? | 2d ob. (1a) |
| Simon Granger | 6d (2a) | 6d (2a) | 6d (2a) | ? | 6d (2a) |
| Thomas Johnson | 9d (3a) | 9d (3a) | 9d (3a) | ? | 9d (3a) |
| Thomas Bailey | 3d ob. (1a) | 3d ob. (1a) | 3d ob. (1a) | ? | 3d ob. (1a) |
| Richard Passelowe | 3/10d (15½a) | 3/10d (15½a) | 3/10d (15½a) | ? | 3/4d (13a) |
| John Page | 10/5d ob. (42a) | 10/5d ob. (42a) | 10/5d ob. (42a) | ? | 10/5d ob. (42a) |
| Richard Chycheley | 1d ob. (½a) | 1d ob. (½a) | 1d ob. (½a) | ? | 1d ob. (½a) |
| Margaret Chycheley | – | – | – | – | 1d ob. (½a) |
| William Manipenny | 5/2d q. (20a) | 3/6d (14a) | 3/6d (14a) | ? | 3/6d (14a) |
| John Feld | 1d ob. (½a) | 1d ob. (½a) | 1d ob. (½a) | ? | 1d ob. (½a) |

| NAME | 1490E | 1490M | 1491E | 1491M | 1492E |
|---|---|---|---|---|---|
| Helen Rumborough | 2d q. (1a) | 2d q. (1a) | – | – | – |
| Thomas Balle | 19d ob. (6½a) | 2/- (8a) | 2/- (8a) | ? | 23d (7a) |
| Thomas Massey | 2d (1a) | 2d (1a) | 2d (1a) | 2d (1a) | 2d (1a) |
| Agnes Light | 8d (2a) | 8d (2a) | 6d (2a) | 1d ob (½a) | |
| John Baron | – | – | – | – | 4d ob. (1½a) |
| William Tothe | 3d (1a) | 3d (1a) | 3d (1a) | 3d (1a) | 3d (1a) |
| John Matthew | 6d (2a) | 6d (2a) | 14/5d (55a) | 14/5d (55a) | 10/10d ob.q. (43a) |
| Thomas Fecas | 4d q. (1a) | 8d q. (2a) | 12d (4a) | 12d (4a) | 12d (4a) |
| Robert Gony | 23d (8a) | 23d (8a) | – | – | – |
| Alice Gony | – | – | 21d ob. (7a) | ? | 18d ob. (6a) |
| Richard Motte | 4d ob. (1½a) | | | | – |
| Richard Kyng | 6/9d (27a) | 3/8d (14a) | 3/8d (14a) | ? | 10d ob.q. (3½a) |
| Thomas Reynold | 5d (2a) | 6d (2a) | 6d (2a) | ? | 6d (2a) |
| John and Robert Stevenson | 12d q. (4a) | 15d (5a) | | | |
| John Stevenson | – | – | 1d | 1d | 1d |
| John Shalford | 4d ob.q. (1½a) | 4d ob.q. (1½a) | 4d ob.q. (1½a) | 4d ob.q. (1½a) | 4d ob.q. (1½a) |
| Robert Willem | 3/- q. (12a) | 3/- q. (12a) | 3/- q. (12a) | 2/4d ob.q. (9½a) | 2/4d ob.q. (9½a) |
| Robert Nicholas | 13/6d ob.q. (54a) | 13/8d ob.q. (54½a) | 14/- ob. (56a) | 14/11d (59a) | 14/11d (59a) |
| John Ussher | 18d (6a) | 19d q. (6a) | 19d q. (6a) | 19d q. (6a) | 22d q. (7a) |
| John Turneskewe | 3/4d ob.q. (13½a) | 3/4d ob.q. (13½a) | 3/4d ob.q. (13½a) | 3/4d ob.q. (13½a) | 3/5d ob. (13½a) |
| John Holme | 2d | 2d | 2d | 2d | 2d |
| Thomas Cokman | 6/3d ob.q. (25a) | 6/8d q. (26a) | 6/8d q. (26a) | 8/6d (34a) | 9/- (36a) |
| Isabella Wright | 19d (6a) | 19d (6a) | 19d (6a) | 19d (6a) | 22d (7½a) |
| William Farthing | 4d (1½a) | – | – | – | |
| Agnes Farthing | – | 2d ob. (1a) | 2d ob. (1a) | 2d ob. (1a) | 2d. ob. (1a) |
| Richard Gilby | 5d ob.q. (2a) | 4d q. (1½a) | 4d q. (1½a) | 4d q. (1½a) | 4d q. (1½a) |
| John Porter | 20d ob. (6½a) | 10d (3a) | 22d (7a) | 22d (7a) | 22d (7a) |

| | | | | | |
|---|---|---|---|---|---|
| William Walcote | 3d ob. (1a) | 3d ob. (1a) | 3d ob. (1a) | — | — |
| John Sente | 1d ob. (½a) | 1d ob. (½a) | — | — | — |
| John Osteler | 12d (4a) | 12d (4a) | 1d ob.q. (½a) | 1d ob.q. (½a) | 2d (½a) |
| John Barnard | 2d ob. (1a) | 2d ob. (1a) | 2d ob. (1a) | 2d ob. (1a) | — |
| Richard Holme | 2d (1a) | 2d (1a) | 2d (1a) | 2d (1a) | 2d (1a) |
| Henry Marshall | 13d q. (4½a) | 13d q. (4½a) | 13d q. (4½a) | 13d q. (4½a) | 13d q. (4½a) |
| William Stodale | 17/3d (69a) | 17/3d (69a) | 17/3d (69a) | 17/3d (69a) | 17/2d ob.q. (69a) |
| William Nottingham | 5d ob.q. (2a) | 5d ob.q. (2a) | 2/- (8a) | 2/2d q. (8½a) | 2/2d q. (8½a) |
| William Beterich | 6/- q. (24a) | 6/- q. (24a) | 6/- q. (24a) | 5/10d ob. (23½a) | 5/10d ob. (23½a) |
| Thomas Knaresborugh | — | 9d ob. (3a) | 9d ob. (3a) | 9d ob. (3a) | 9d ob. (3a) |
| John Lumbard | 5/- ob. (20a) | 5/- ob. (20a) | 5/- ob. (20a) | 5/- ob. (20a) | 5/- ob. (20a) |
| Guido Wulfston, knight | 33/2d q. (132a) | 33/2d q. (132a) | 33/2d q. (132a) | 33/2d q. (132a) | 33/2d q. (132a) |
| Fraternity of Corpus Christi | | | | | |
| William Frere | 4/8d (18½a) | 4/8d (18½a) | 4/9d ob. (19a) | 4/9d ob. (19a) | 4/9d ob. (19a) |
| Alice Frere | 17/5d ob. (69½a) | 17/5d ob. (69½a) | 17/5d ob. (69½a) | 17/5d ob. (69½a) | 17/5d ob. (69½a) |
| William Frere | 5d ob.q. (2a) | 5d ob.q. (2a) | 5d ob.q. (2a) | 5d ob.q. (2a) | — |
| John Granger | — | — | — | — | 5d ob. q. (2a) |
| John Gardner | 2d | 2d | 2d | 2d | 2d |
| Matthew Hedley | 2/5d q. (10a) | 2/9d ob. (11a) | 2/9d ob. (11a) | 2/3d (9a) | 2/1d ob. (8½a) |
| John Dey | 2d | 2d | 2d | 2d | 2d |
| Thomas Faldyng | 11d (4a) | 11d (4a) | 11d (4a) | 11d (4a) | 11d (4a) |
| John Garlop, artificer | 12/3d ob.q. (49a) | 9/2d ob. (36a) | 8/7d ob. (34½a) | 8/7d ob. (34½a) | 8/8d (35a) |
| William Goodwyn | 9/2d q. (36a) | 9/1d (36a) | 9/1d (36a) | 9/1d ob.q. (36½a) | 10/9d ob. (43a) |
| William Wright | 8/8d ob. (35a) | 9/4d ob. (37½a) | 8/5d ob. (33a) | 7/11d (32a) | 7/11d (32a) |
| Robert Bayous | 4d (1a) | 4d (1a) | 4d (1a) | 4d (1a) | 4d (1a) |
| William Page | 2/1d q. (8½a) | 2/1d q. (8½a) | 2/1d q. (8½a) | 2/4d q. (9½a) | 2/4d q. (9½a) |
| Agnes Page | 4d ob. (1½a) | 4d ob. (1½a) | 4d ob. (1½a) | | — |
| John Davy | 18d q. (6a) | 18d q. (6a) | 18d q. (6a) | 18d q. (6a) | 18d q. (6a) |
| John Manipenny | | | | 3/8d ob.q. (15a) | 3/7d q. (14½a) |
| | 3d (1a) | 3d (1a) | 3d (1a) | 3d (1a) | 3d (1a) |

| Name | 1490E | 1490M | 1491E | 1491M | 1492E |
|---|---|---|---|---|---|
| William Browne | 22d (7½a) | 19d (6½a) | 22d (7½a) | 22d (7½a) | 22d (7½a) |
| Thomas Punt | 3d (1a) | 3d (1a) | 3d (1a) | 3d (1a) | 3d (1a) |
| John Bonsay | 5/7d ob.q. (22½a) | 5/7d ob.q. (22½a) | 5/7d ob.q. (22½a) | 5/10d ob.q. (23½a) | – |
| John Smith | – | – | – | – | 5/10d ob.q. (23½a) |
| John Barnard jr. | 21d (7a) | 2/- (8a) | 2/5d (10a) | 2/2d q. (8½a) | 2/3d q. (8½a) |
| Bailiff | 1d ob. (½a mea.) | 1d ob.q. (½a mea.) | 1d ob.q. (½a mea.) | 1d ob.q. (½a mea.) | 1d ob.q. (½a mea.) |
| Thomas Martin | 1d ob. (½a) | 1d ob. (½a) | 1d ob. (½a) | 1d ob. (½a) | 1d ob. (½a) |
| Thomas Knaresborough | 9d ob. (3a) | – | – | – | – |
| Edmund Manning | 2d q. (1a) | 2d q. (1a) | 3d (1a) | 3d (1a) | – |
| John Reygate | 1d ob.q. (½a) | 1d ob.q. (½a) | 1d ob.q. (½a) | 1d ob.q. (½a) | 1d ob.q. (½) |
| John Garlop sr. | 12d ob.q. (4a) | 19d ob. (6½a) | 19d ob. (6½a) | 19d ob. (6½a) | 19d ob. (6½a) |
| Fraternity of St. John | 17d q. (6a) | 17d q. (6a) | 17d q. (6a) | 17d q. (6a) | 17d q. (6a) |
| William Granger | 11d q. (4a) | 11d q. (4a) | 11d q. (4a) | 11d q. (4a) | 11d q. (4a) |
| William Hilton | 10d q. (3½a) | – | – | – | – |
| Richard Foster | 1d ob. (½a) | 1d ob. (½a) | 1d ob. (½a) | 1d ob. (½a) | 1d ob. (½a) |
| William Fraunceys | 2/9d ob.q. (11a) | 2/9d ob.q. (11a) | 21d ob.q. (7a) | 18d ob. (6a) | – |
| John Bayous | – | 3d (1a) | 3d (1a) | 3d (1a) | 3d (1a) |
| John Goodrych | – | 1d ob. (½a) | 1d ob. (½a) | 1fd ob. (½a) | 1d ob. (½a) |
| Thomas Baker | – | 21d (7a) | 2/7d ob. (10½a) | 2/9q. (11a) | 2/9 q. (11a) |
| Margaret Folkys | – | ob.q. | ob.q. | ob.q. | – |
| Alice Motte | – | 4d ob. (1½a) | 3d (1a) | 3d (1a) | 2d (1a) |
| William Gretham | – | – | 12d ob. (4a) | 18d q. (6a) | 18d q. (6a) |
| John Passelowe | – | – | 2d | – | – |
| Steven Clerk | – | – | ob | ob | ob |
| William Schylling | – | – | – | – | 3d (1a) |
| William Barnard | – | – | – | – | ob.q. |
| Total: | No sum given | £12 0s. 6d. | No sum given | No sum given | No sum given |

## J. Post Street Rental List, 1494

| NAME | 1494E | 1494M |
| --- | --- | --- |
| Prior of Huntingdon | 9d (3a) | 9d (3a) |
| William Dey | 14d ob. (5a) | 14d ob. (5a) |
| Thomas Kyng | 8d q. (2a) | 8d q. (2a) |
| Matthew Garnet | 4/10d q. (19½a) | 4/10d q. (19½a) |
| William Gonell | 2/- (8a) | 2/- (8a) |
| John Smith | 18d (6a) | 18d (6a) |
| Anna Plumpton | 5/4d ob. (21½a) | 5/4d ob. (21½a) |
| John Stokys | 5d ob. (1a) | 5d ob. (1a) |
| William Melbourne | 2d | 2d |
| John Barnard, carpenter | 4d (1a) | 4d (1a) |
| John Salmon | 1d | 1d |
| John Adam | 7d ob. (2½a) | 7d ob. (2½a) |
| Thomas Marshall | 1d ob. (½a) | 1d ob. (½a) |
| John Dalton | 2d ob. (1a) | 2d ob. (1a) |
| Simon Granger | 6d (2a) | 6d (2a) |
| Thomas Bailey | 3d ob. (1a) | 3d ob. (1a) |
| John Passelowe | 8d q. (2a) | 8d q. (2a) |
| Alice Dawe | 2d | 2d |
| John Page | 10/2d ob. (40½a) | 10/2d ob. (40½a) |
| Richard Chycheley | 1d ob. (½a) | 1d ob. (½a) |
| William Manipenny | 8/1d q. (32½a) | 8/2d q. (32½a) |
| Thomas Balle | 2d | 2d |
| Thomas Massey | 2d | 2d |
| William Pacy | — | 2d q. |
| John Baron | 4d ob. (1½a) | 4d ob. (1½a) |
| John Clerk | 1d ob. (½a) | 1d ob. (½a) |
| John Matthew | 3d ob. (1a) | — |
| | | |
| Robert Chandeler | — | 3d ob. (1a) |
| Thomas Fecas | 9d (3a) | 9d (3a) |
| Alice Conyff | 9d (3a) | 9d (3a) |
| Richard King | 10d ob.q. (3½a) | 10d ob.q. (3½a) |
| William Lessy | 7d ob.q. (2½a) | 9d q. (3a) |
| John Stevenson | 1d | 1d |
| John Shalford | 4d (1a) | 4d (1a) |
| Robert Nicholas | 15/6d ob.q. (62a) | 15/6d ob.q. (62a) |
| John Ussher | 2/4d q. (9½a) | 2/4d q. (9½a) |
| John Turneskewe | 3/3d q. (13a) | 3/3d q. (13a) |
| John Holme | 2d | 2d |
| Thomas Cokman | 8/- (32a) | 8/- (32a) |
| Isabella Wright | 17d ob. (6a) | 17d ob. (6a) |
| Agnes Burton | 2d ob. | 2d |
| Richard Gilby | 7d q. (3½a) | 5d ob.q. (2a) |
| John Porter | 4d q. (1½a) | 4d q. (1½a) |
| William Walcote | 2d ob.q. (1a) | 3d q. (1a) |
| John Osteler | 2d | 2d |
| Alice Holme | 2d | — |

| Name | 1494e | 1494m |
|---|---|---|
| Richard Holme | — | 2d |
| Richard Stevens | 5d (1a) | 5d (1a) |
| Margaret Stodale | 17/9d ob. (71a) | 17/8d (71a) |
| William Bekke | 2/2d q. (8½a) | 2/2d q. (8½a) |
| William Betrich | 6/8d q. (26½a) | 6/8d q. (26½a) |
| John Lumbard | 2/6d ob. (10a) | 2/- ob. (8a) |
| Guido Wulfston, knight | 33/8d ob. (135a) | 33/8d ob. (135a) |
| Fraternity of Corpus Christi | 5/1d (20a) | 5/1d (20a) |
| William Frere | 18/- q. (72a) | 18/- q (72a) |
| Simon Granger | 2d | 2d |
| Matthew Hedley | 2d | 2d |
| John Dey | 11d (4a) | 11d (4a) |
| Thomas Faldyng | 8/5d (34a) | 8/5d (34a) |
| William Goodwyn | 2/3d (9a) | 2/3d (9a) |
| John Garlop | 10/6d ob.q. (42a) | 10/6d ob.q. (42a) |
| William Wright | 4d (1a) | 4d (1a) |
| Richard Bayous | 2/2d ob.q. (9a) | 2/2d ob.q. (9a) |
| John Davy | 7/6d ob.q. (30a) | 7/6d ob.q. (30a) |
| William Page | 4d ob. (1½a) | 4d ob.q. (1½a) |
| John Manipenny | 3d (1a) | 3d (1a) |
| William Browne | 22d (7½a) | 22d (7½a) |
| Thomas Punte | 3d (1a) | 3d (1a) |
| John Barnard jr. | (7? q.) (?) | 2/8d ob.q. (10a) |
| Bailiff | 7d q. (2½a) | 7d q. (2½a) |
| Thomas Martin | 1d ob. (½a) | 1d ob. (½a) |
| John Reygate | 1d ob. (½a) | 1d ob. (½a) |
| John Garlop sr. | 19d ob. (6½a) | 19d ob. (6½a) |
| Fraternity of St. John | 17d q. (6a) | 18d (6a) |
| William Granger | 5/8d (22½a) | 5/8d (22½a) |
| John Laxton | 10/6d ob. (42a) | 10/6d ob. (42a) |
| John Goodrych | 1d ob. (½a) | 1d ob. (½a) |
| Thomas Baker | 8d ob. (3a) | 8d ob. (3a) |
| William Gretham | 6/5d (26a) | 6/6d ob. (26a) |
| Richard Motte | 2d | 2d |
| Steven Clerk | 6d ob. (2a) | 9d ob. (3a) |
| William Schylling | 3d (1a) | 3d (1a) |
| William Barnard | 3d q. (1a) | 3d q. (1a) |
| John Barnard, candlemaker | 13d (4a) | 13d (4a) |
| William Este | — | 4/4d q. (17½a) |
| Edmond Page | — | 4d ob. (1½a) |
| Haryngton | — | 9d (3a) |
| Richard Brewster | — | 4d ob. (1½a) |
| John Gredley | — | 3d ob. (1a) |
| John Dnons | — | ob |
| **Total:** | £11 12s. 5d. ob. | No sum given |

## K. West Street Rental List, 1489 Easter

| | |
|---|---|
| John Broughton | 6d ob. (2a) |
| Richard Lockyngton | 25/- 1d (100a) |
| John Bailey | 18/1d ob. (72a) |
| John Lockyngton | 11/3d (45a) |
| Richard Mayle jr. | 8d (2½a) |
| Thomas Lockyngton | 5/9d ob. (23a) |
| Thomas Maryot | 9/7d (38a) |
| William Holme | 13d (4a) |
| Richard Mayle | 21/10d ob. (88a) |
| Thomas Mayle | 18/6d ob. (74a) |
| Thomas Dorraunt | 5d ob. (2a) |
| William Parker | 6d ob. (2a) |
| William Suel | 11/- ob. (44a) |
| William Kyng | 8/2d ob.q. (32½a) |
| John Robyn | 21/4d q. (85½a) |
| John Kyng | 7/9d ob.q. (31a) |
| Helen Stukeley | 2/2d q. (9a) |
| John Chese jr. | 22d ob.q. (7½a) |
| William Pelman | 5/- (20a) |
| Agnes Thomson | 11d ob.q. (4a) |
| Custodian of All Saints | 20d ob.q. (7a) |
| William Chese | 7/11d q. (32a) |
| Paul Folkys | 9d q. (3a) |
| Roger Coke | 4/8d q. (19a) |
| John Gybbys | 17/5d q. (69½a) |
| Richard Wykyam | 2d q. |
| Richard Smyth | 12/2d ob. (48½a) |
| John Barre | 3/2d q. (12½a) |
| William Willem | 2/4d q. (9½a) |
| Richard Stukeley | 11/1d ob. (44½a) |
| Thomas Garlop | 2/1d (8a) |
| John Allemowthe | 1d ob.q. (½a) |
| John Barrett | 1d ob. (½a) |
| Thomas Bennett | 12/9d (51a) |
| William Aythroppe | 2/6d (10a) |
| John Brewster | 5/5d q. (22a) |
| Robert Mayle | 22d ob. (7½a) |
| William Loveday | 6d ob. (2a) |
| Thomas Leffyn jr. | 6d ob. (2a) |
| John Bayous jr. | 3d (1a) |
| Thomas Gybbys | 4d ob. (1½a) |
| Henry Gybbys | 3d (1a) |
| John Sterlyng | 8d q. (3a) |
| Thomas Laxton | 18/1d (72a) |
| John Garlop | 2/3d ob.q. (9a) |
| John Mannyng | ob.q. |
| John Goodrych | 1d ob. (½a) |
| TOTAL: | £14 7s. 5d. q. |

| | | |
|---|---|---|
| William Hilton | 1d. | |
| William Kyng | { 26s. 5d. q. | |
| | { 7s. 3d. q. for Edward Barre | (135a) |
| John Granger | 3d. ob.q. (1a) | |
| John Laxton | ( 19s. 7d. (ob.q.) | |
| | { 14d. for Bolton | (92a) |
| | ( 2s. 3d. q. for Gardiner | |
| John Wylde jr. | { 13s. 7d. q. | |
| | { 15d. for Judd | (59a) |
| William Lockyngton | 14s. 7d. (58a) | |
| John Clerk sr. | 3s. 9d. q. (15a) | |
| William Seward | 2s. 3d. ob.q. (9a) | |
| John Clerk jr. | 8s. 11d. (36a) | |
| William Ede | 5s. 3d. (21a) | |
| Reginald Corby | 11d. ob. (4a) | |
| John Coke | 3s. 10d. (15a) | |
| William Pelman | 3s. q. (12a) | |
| Anne William | 12d. (4a) | |
| Richard William | 9d. ob.q. (3a) | |
| Thomas Pacy | 10s. 2d. ob.q. (41a) | |
| John Frere | 27s. 4d. q. (105a) | |
| Robert Semar | 4d. ob. (1½a) | |
| Thomas Bennet | 2s. 1d. q. (8a) | |
| John Arnouth | 1d. ob.q. (¼a) | |
| William Loveday | 3s. 1d. q. (12a) | |
| William Richmont | 11s. 5d. ob. (46a) | |
| John Hogan sr. | 11s. 10d. q. (47a) | |
| Fraternity of All Saints | 21d. ob. (7a) | |
| William Frere | 10s. 4d. (41a) | |
| Thomas Coke | 9s. 4d. q. (37a) | |
| William Kyme | 3s. 8d. (14a) | |
| William Leffyne | 16s. 1d. ob.q. (65a) | |
| Henry Gybbys | 12s. 6d. ob. (39a) | |
| Richard Robyn | 26s. 4d. q. (105a) | |
| John Godwyn | 12s. 6d. ob.q. (50a) | |
| William Bennet | 9s. 10d. q. (39a) | |
| John Wylde sr. | 2s. 5d. (10a) | |
| William Kelson | 7s. ob.q. (26a) | |
| William Godwyn | 6s. 3d. ob.q. (25a) | |
| John Ede | 19d. ob. (7a) | |
| William Freman | 16d. ob. (6a) | |
| Thomas Frere | 15s. 5d. (62a) | |
| Thomas Parker | 1d. q. (¼a) | |
| William Bennet jr. | 7d. ob. (3a) | |
| John Marshall | 2d. (1a) | |
| John Hogan sr. | 22d. ob. (8a) | |
| John Kyng | 6s. 8d. (27a) | |
| Roger Bowche | 2s. (8a) | |
| John Howson | 3s. 5d. (14a) | |

| | |
|---|---|
| Sum of Total: | £16 14s. 5d. |
| Sum received from West Street: | £16 16s. 11d. ob.q. |

# Appendix 4

## Conveyance Lists for Arnyng, East, Post and West Streets

A. ARNYNG STREET

| NAME | DELIVERED TO | RECEIVED FROM | LAND (FARM PAYMENT) | YEAR |
|---|---|---|---|---|
| Adam, John | | William Hilton | mess (1d.ob.) | 1489E |
| Arnold, Austen | (Thomas) Sander | | 1r (ob.q.) | 1487M |
| | | | 3a ad.t. (12d.) | 1487M |
| Asshe, John | | John Hosteler | 1a (3d.) | 1485M |
| | | John Sparrow | (3d.) | 1489E |
| Aylred, John | rents in East St. | | curtilage (q.) | 1485M |
| | William Ponder | | 1r (ob.q.) | 1487E |
| | Thomas Maryot | | ½a (1d.ob.) | 1488E |
| | Thomas Bate | | | 1489E |
| | Richard Pelle | | gronage (3d.q.) | 1489E |
| Baker, Thomas | *Thomas Gilbert | | 1r (ob.q.) | 1485M |
| | Thomas Faldyng | | 6a ad.t. (18d.) | 1487E |
| | Thomas (Cokman) | | 2a (6d.) | 1487E |
| | William Brown sr. | | 3a (9d.) | 1487E |
| | | Thomas Barnard | 1½a 1r (7d.ob.q.) | 1487E |
| | | | (1r) (ob.q.) | 1487E |
| | | | 1½r (1d.q.) | 1487E |
| | John Stukeley | | mess (1d.ob.) | 1487E |
| | William Polle | *William Polle | 2a (6d.) | 1488E |
| | | Thomas Syward jr. | ½a (1d.ob.) | 1488M |
| | John Bonsay sr. | | ½a ad.t. (1d.q.) | 1489E |
| | Roger Cook | John Osteler | ½a (1d.ob.) | 1489E |
| | John Smith | | 1r ad.t. (ob.q.) | 1490E |
| | John Brown | | 1a ad.t. (3d.) | 1490E |
| | William Longe | | 1a (3d.) | 1490E |
| | William Est | | 2a 1r (6d.ob.q.) | 1490E |
| | William Frost sr. | | 1a (3d.) | 1490E |
| | rents ad.t. | | (3d.) | 1490M |
| | delivered in the street to William Longe | | | |
| | | | curtilage ad.t. (2d.) | 1490M |

* Indicates that this is duplicated in the chart.

| Index | Sub-name | Name | Amount | Date |
|---|---|---|---|---|
| Balle, Margaret | *John Stukeley | | ½a (1d.ob.) | 1487E |
| | William Frost sr. | | 1a (3d.) | 1488M |
| | John Brown | | 1r (ob.q.) | 1489E |
| Barnard, John sr. | Thomas Burton | | 1½a (4d.ob.) | 1490E |
| | John Stukeley | | 3r (2d. q.) | 1487E |
| Barnard John jr. | | John Lucas | 1½a (4d. ob.) | 1490E |
| | | John Longe | 2½a (7d.ob.) | 1487E |
| | rents | | (12d.) | 1487M |
| | | rents in the street | (10d.ob.) | 1488M |
| | | Thomas Hawkyn | 3½a (10d.ob.) | 1489E |
| | | *Robert Mayle | 1a ad.t.(10d.ob.) | 1490M |
| Bonsay, John jr. | John Bonsay sr. | | 20a (5/-) | 1487E |
| Bonsay, John | | *John Smith | 1a ad.t. (3d) | 1488M |
| | | William Godwyn | 1a (3d.) | 1485M |
| | | John Barnard, artificer | 4a (12d.) | 1485M |
| | | *John Stukeley | 40½a (10/1d.) | 1487M |
| | | Roger Cook | 3a (9d.) | 1488E |
| | | *John Lucas | 2a ad.t. (6d.) | 1488E |
| | | John Howlette | ½a 1r (2d.ob.) | 1488E |
| | | *John Lucas | 6a. (18d.) | 1489E |
| | | William Gardener | 20a 3r curt (5/4d?) | 1490M |
| Bonsay, John sr. | | *William Frost sr. | *mess ad.t. | 1490M |
| Bonsay, Thomas | | *Thomas Baker | ½a (1d.ob.) | 1488M |
| Bowre, John | | Robert Fowe | 1a. (3d.) | 1490E |
| Brown, John | | John Schylling | ½a (1d.ob.) | 1485M |
| | | John Hawkyn | 3r (2d.q.) | 1485M |
| | | John Schylling | ½a (1d.ob.) | 1485M |
| | | Robert Mayle | ½a (1d.ob.) | 1487M |
| | | *Margaret Balle | 1r (ob.q.) | 1489E |
| | | James Lawe | 1a (3d.) | 1489E |
| | | ? | 7 swaths ad.t. (3d.ob.) | 1490M |
| Browne, William | John Armyt | | ½a ad.t. (1d.ob.) | 1489E |
| Browne, William sr. | *Thomas Baker | | 3a (9d.) | 1487E |
| | | Richard Baker | ½a (1d.ob.) | 1488E |

| Name | Delivered to | Received from | Land (Farm Payment) | Year |
|---|---|---|---|---|
| Burton, Thomas | | James Lawe | ½a (1d.ob.) | 1485M |
| | | *Robert Howlett | ½a (1d.ob.) | 1485M |
| | | Richard Wyllam | 3r leys (2d.q.) | 1488E |
| | | *Margaret Balle | 1½a (4d.ob.) | 1490E |
| Cam, James | William Snell | | ½a (1d.ob.) | 1490E |
| Cleyff, William | Roger Jacob | | 1½a (4d.ob.) | 1487M |
| | Robert (Farh...) | | mess (10d.ob.q.) | 1487M |
| Corby, John sr. | Thomas Frost | William Frost sr. | ½r (1d.q.) | 1488M |
| | | | 1r (ob.q.) | 1488E |
| Foster John | | rent | (2/7d.) | 1488E |
| | | Thomas Baret | 2a (6d.) | 1488E |
| | | William Manipenny | 1a (3d.) | 1488E |
| | | William Manipenny | 3a 1r (?) | 1488E |
| | | | ½a (?) | 1488E |
| | John Corby | | ½a (1d.ob.) | 1488M |
| | William Hilton | William Schylling | ½a (1d.ob.) | 1489E |
| Fraternity of Holy Trinity | | Richard Ibott | ½a (1d.ob.) | 1487E |
| | | William Gardener | 1a leys (3d.) | 1487M |
| | | Thomas Frost | 3a leys (2d. q.) | 1487E |
| | | Richard Wyllam | 1r mea. (1d.q.) | 1488E |
| Fraternity of St. James | | John Gardener | 3r (2d.q.) | 1487M |
| | | William Polle | 1a ad.t. (ob.q.) | 1490E |
| Frost Thomas | | *Fraternity of Holy Trinity | 3a leys (2d.q.) | 1487E |
| | | William Chese | ½a ad.t. (1d.ob.) | 1488E |
| | | *John Corby sr. | ½a (1d.q.) | 1488M |
| | | *Richard Spycer | mess (4d) | 1487M |
| | | William Godwyn | ½a (1d.ob.) | 1488E |
| Frost, William | | William Godwyn | 2½a (7d.ob.) | 1485M |
| | | John Lucas | mess + 1a (3d.) | 1487M |
| | | Thomas Baker | 1a ad.t. (3d.) | 1490E |
| | | William Gardener | ½a (2d.) | 1490E |
| | | William Syward sr. | ½a mea. (1d.ob.) | 1490M |

| | | | |
|---|---|---|---|
| Frost, William sr. | William Frost jr. | ½a (1d.ob.) | 1485M |
| | Thomas Mundeford | 3r (2d.q.) | 1485M |
| | Thomas Manipenny | 1r leys (ob.q.) | 1487M |
| | Richard Kyng | 1r (ob.q.) | 1488E |
| | John Osteler | 1a. (3d.) | 1488M |
| | *Margaret Balle | 1a (3d.) | 1488M |
| | William Gardener | 1a (3d.) | 1488M |
| | William Syward sr. | ¾a (1d.ob.) | 1490E |
| | *Thomas Baker | ⅔a (3d.) | 1490E |
| | John Bonsay | 1r ad.t. (ob.q.) | 1490M |
| Frost, William jr. | *William Frost sr. | ¼a (1d.ob.) | 1485M |
| | Thomas Syward | 1r (ob.q.) | 1487E |
| | Thomas (B)eme | ⅔a (2d.q.) | 1487E |
| | John Corby sr. | ⅔a (1d.ob.) | 1487E |
| | Roger Cook | 3r (2d.q.) | 1488E |
| | John Schylling | 1½r (1d.q.) | 1488M |
| | William Godwyn | 1½a (4d.ob.) | 1488E |
| | John Corby sr. | 1½r (1d.q.) | 1488M |
| | Richard Kyng | 4a (12d.) | 1488E |
| | Thomas Mayle | 3a (9d.) | 1489E |
| | William Manipenny | 4a 1r (12d.q.) | 1489E |
| | Richard Kyng | 1a r (3d.ob.q.) | 1489E |
| | William Manipenny | 6a 3r (20d.q.) | 1490E |
| Gardener, Agnes | Thomas Notyngham | (?) (ob.) | 1487E |
| | Robert Porter | 1r ad.t. (ob.q.) | 1489E |
| | executors of William Aylred | ½ land ad.t. (ob.) | 1490E |
| Gardener, William | in ye trent chepers | 1a leys (3d.) | 1487M |
| | *Fraternity of Holy Trinity | 1a leys (3d.) | 1487M |
| | Thomas Balle | 1r (ob.q.) | 1490E |
| | *John Bonsay | 3r curt + 20a + mess (5/4d.) | 1490M |
| | *William Frost | ½a (2d.) | 1490E |

| NAME | DELIVERED TO | RECEIVED FROM | LAND (FARM PAYMENT) | YEAR |
|---|---|---|---|---|
| Garlop, John | | Thomas Emley | 1½r (1d.q.) | 1488E |
| | | *John Schylling | mess (2d.) | 1488E |
| | | *John Schylling | 2a ad.t. (6d.) | 1490E |
| Gony, John | rent | | (2d.) | 1488E |
| Gilbert, Thomas | Thomas Baker | | 1r (ob.q.) | 1485M |
| Gyle, William | Fyrgys | | curtilage (1d.) | 1489E |
| | East St. in Benewal | | mess ad.t. (2d.ob.) | 1490E |
| Hilton, William | John Stayls | *John Foster | 8a (2/-) | 1488E |
| | rent Post St. | | ½a (1d.ob.) | 1488M |
| | *John Adam | | (2/4d?) | 1488M |
| | Thomas Burton | | mess (1d.ob.) | 1489E |
| Howlette, Robert | | *Thomas Mundeford | ½a (1d.ob.) | 1485M |
| Howlett, John | | Thomas Mundeford | 17a 1r (4/3d.ob.) | 1485M |
| | | | 6 swaths (3d.q.) | 1487E |
| | *John Stukeley | | 42½a (10/7d) | 1487M |
| | *John Bonsay | | ½a 1r (2d.ob.) | 1488E |
| | John Fyn( ) | | 1a (3d.q.) | 1487E |
| | William Snell | | 1r ad.t.(ob.q.) | 1487E |
| Lawe, James | | Richard Stukeley | ½a (1d.ob.) | 1488M |
| | John Smyth | | 1a ad.t. (3d.) | 1488M |
| | Robert Porter | | 1r (ob.q.) | 1489E |
| | Richard Sent | | 1½r (1d.q.) | 1489E |
| | | William Syward | ½a (1d.ob.) | 1489E |
| | | rent Arnyng St. | (3d.ob.q.) | 1490M |
| | | Thomas Lessy sr. | ½a (1d.ob.) | 1490M |
| Lessy, Thomas | | rents | 10d.q. (?) | 1487E |
| Lessy, William | John Snell | | 9a (2/3d.) | 1489E |
| Lorydan, Marcus | | William Plumper | 1½a (4d.ob.) | 1489E |
| Lucas, John | William Mayle | | 2½a (7d.ob.) | 1487M |
| | *William Frost | | mess (4d) + 1a (3d.) | 1487M |
| | John Bonsay | | 2a ad.t. (6d.) | 1488E |
| | Thomas Cokman | | 12a (3/-) | 1489E |
| | John Bonsay | | 6a (18d.) | 1489E |
| | *John Barnard | | 1½a (4d.ob.) | 1490E |

| Name | | | Property | Year |
|---|---|---|---|---|
| Lyden, William | | John Gardener | 3r (2d.q.) | 1487M |
| Marten, Henry | | John Hawkyn | 1a (3d.) | 1485M |
| Marten, Thomas | rent Post St. | | (1d.ob.) | 1485M |
| Mayle, Robert | *John Brown | *William Mayle | ½a (1d.ob.) | 1487M |
| Mayle, William | | | 40a + mess ad.t. (10/5d.q.) | 1490M |
| | | John Barnard jr. | 1a ad.t. (3d.) | 1490M |
| | | *John Lucas | 2½r (7d.ob.) | 1487M |
| | | William Godwyn | 12a 1½r (3/1d.q.) | 1488E |
| | Thomas Fecas | | 1½r mea. (1d.q.) | 1489E |
| | Robert Mayle | | 40a + mess ad.t.(10/5d.q.) | 1490M |
| Mounford, Thomas | John Howlette | | 17a 1r (4/3d.ob.) | 1485M |
| | *William Frost sr. | | 3r (2d.q.) | 1485M |
| Nicoll, William | | rent ad.t. from Robert Porter | 21a (5/3d.ob.q.) | 1489E |
| Plowryghte, John | Thomas Garlop (son) | | 1swath (ob.) | 1490E |
| Polle, William | Roger Cook | | 1 swath (q.) | 1485M |
| | William Cleyff | | 1 mess (1d.ob.) | 1487E |
| | *Thomas Baker | | mess (1d.ob.) | 1487E |
| | William Ponder | | 1a (3d.) | 1488E |
| | Thomas Baker | | ½a (1d.ob.) | 1488E |
| | John Roke | | 1a (3d.) | 1489E |
| | John Stukeley | | 3r ad.t. (2d.q.) | 1490E |
| | Fraternity of St. James | | 1r ad.t. (ob.q.) | 1490E |
| Prestwode, Simon | | Thomas Deyne | 1r (ob.q.) | 1485M |
| Robyn, Robert | | John Robyn | 9a (2/4d.ob.) | 1487M |
| Schylling, John | *John Browne | | 2 × ½a (3d.) | 1485M |
| | | rents | (2d.) | 1487E |
| | | John Garlop | mess (2d.) | 1488E |
| | William Frost jr. | | 1½r (1d.q.) | 1488M |
| | Richard Mayle | | 6a 1½r (19d.q.) | 1489E |
| | John Foster | | ½a (1d.ob.) | 1489E |
| | | John Garlop | 2a. ad.t. (6d.) | 1490E |

| NAME | DELIVERED TO | RECEIVED FROM | LAND (FARM PAYMENT) | YEAR |
|---|---|---|---|---|
| Smith, John, labourer | | James Lawe | 1a (3d.) | 1489E |
| Smyth, John | | Thomas Bate | ½a (1d.ob.) | 1488M |
| | John Bonsay | | 1a ad.t. (3d.) | 1488M |
| | | *Thomas Baker | 1r (ob.q.) | 1489E |
| | Richard Stukeley | | 1r (ob.q.) | 1489E |
| Snell, John | | Edward Barre | ½a (ob.) | 1485M |
| | rent Post St. | | (8/3d. ob.q.) | 1489E |
| | | | 9a (2/3d.) | 1489E |
| Spycer, Richard | | *Marcus Lorydan | mess (4d.) | 1487M |
| | | Thomas Frost | ½a (1d.ob.) | 1488E |
| | | William Brown sr. | | |
| Stukeley, John | William Holme | Margaret Balle | 3 × ½a (4d.ob.) | 1485M |
| | | | ½a (1d.ob.) | 1487E |
| | | *John Barnard sr. | 3r (2d.q.) | 1487E |
| | | *Thomas Baker | 1r (ob.) | 1487E |
| | John Bonsay | Thomas Ibott | (40½a) (10/1d.ob.) | 1487M |
| | | John Howlett | ½a ad.t. (1d.ob.) | 1487M |
| | | Elena Stukeley | no details (10/7d.ob.) | 1487M |
| | | William Manipenny | 1a (3d.) | 1488E |
| | | William Godwyn | ½a (1d.q.) | 1488E |
| | | Agnes Light | 1a 1r (3d.ob.q.) | 1488E |
| | | John Halford | ½a (1d.ob.) | 1488E |
| | | Richard Wyllam | 3r mea. (2d.q.) | 1488E |
| | | Thomas Fanden | 3r leys (2d.q.) | 1488E |
| | | Agnes Light | ½a (1d.ob.) | 1488M |
| | | Thomas Faldyng | 1a (3d.q.) | 1489E |
| | | Agnes Light | 1a (3d.) | 1490E |
| | | William Polle | ½a (ob.) | 1490M |
| | | rent | 3r (2d.q.) | 1490E |
| Templeman, John | rents in foren' | | (2d.ob.q.) | 1488E |
| | | | (2d.ob.q.) | 1489E |

B. East Street Conveyances

| Name | Delivered to | Received from | Land (Farm Payment) | Year |
|---|---|---|---|---|
| Asshe, John | | *Thomas Fyncham rents East St. | mea. (1d.q.) | 1489E |
| | | | (3d.) | 1489E |
| | | Simon Prestwode | rent (ob.q.) | 1489E |
| | William Est | | 1a (3d.) | 1489M |
| Aylred, William | | John Adam | mea (1d.) | 1489E |
| | Robert Nicholas | | 3r mea. (2d.q.) | 1489E |
| | Thomas Maryot | | 3r (2d.q.) | 1489E |
| | William Walcote | | ½a (1d.ob.) | 1489E |
| | William Dey | | ½a (1d.ob.) | 1489E |
| | John Lockington | | ? (?) | 1489E |
| | John Matthew | | 7 swaths mea. (2d.ob.q.) | 1489E |
| | John Matthew | | 3r (2d.ob.) | 1489E |
| Executors of William Aylred | John Lockington | | 1a (3d.) | 1489M |
| | John Lockington | | 1a (3d.) | 1490M |
| | Agnes Gardener | | ½r (ob.) | 1490E |
| Balle' ( ) | John Oxen, chaplain rents Arnyng St. | | 3a 1r mea. (9d.ob.q.) | 1487E |
| Barnard, John | | | (10d.ob.) | 1488M |
| | Robert Vont | | ½a (1d.ob.) | 1488M |
| | | *Thomas Hermyn | ½a (1d.ob.) | 1489E |
| Barre, Edward | | William Pelman | 1¼a 1½r (5d.ob.q.) | 1485M |
| | | William Manipenny | ½r (ob.) | 1487E |
| | | Richard King | 1½r (ob.) | 1487E |
| | | John Barre | 3r (2d.q.) | 1487E |
| | William King | | mea. (2d.) | 1488E |
| | | John Gybbys | 2a mea. (6d.) | 1488E |
| | | Agnes Page | 1r (ob.q.) | 1488E |
| | John Robyn | | swath of mea. (ob.) | 1489M |

| Name | Delivered to | Received from | Land (Farm Payment) | Year |
|---|---|---|---|---|
| Bate, Thomas | Mayst' Sent | Henglys | 2r (2d.q.) | 1485E |
| | John Sternel | | ¾a (1d.ob.) | 1486M |
| | John Aylred | | ¾a (1d.ob.) | 1486M |
| | John Smith | | ¾a (1d.ob.) | 1488E |
| | in le Foren broke | | 1½a 1r (5d.) | 1488E |
| | | | 1a (3d.) | 1489M |
| | Thomas Foke | | curtilage (3d.) | 1490E |
| Bonsay, John sr. | | John Bonsay jr. | 20a (5/-) | 1487E |
| | | | 20a + mea. + ½ mea. (5/4d.) | 1489M |
| | | John Garlop | 1r mea. (ob.q.) | 1489M |
| | John Bonsay jr. | | 1a (3d.) | 1490E |
| | Thomas Baker | | ½ (?) (3d.ob.) | 1490E |
| Bonsay, John | | *Thomas Fyncham | 60a etc. (15/-) | 1487E |
| | | John Brewster rent East St. | 2a 1½r (7d.q.) | 1488E |
| | | | 42a 3r (10/8d.ob.) | 1488E |
| | | *William Syward sr. | 3a (2d.q.) | 1488E |
| | | John Lucas | 2a (6d.) | 1488E |
| | | John Lopeler | 1½r mea. (1d.ob.) | 1488M |
| | | Thomas Baker | ¾a (1d.ob.) | 1488M |
| | | John Smyth | 1a (3d.) | 1488M |
| | | John Lucas | 6a (18d.) | 1489E |
| | | John Bayous | 1r (ob.q.) | 1489E |
| | | *William Longe | 1½a (4d.ob.) | 1489M |
| | Thomas Bonsay | | 6a (18d.) | 1490E |
| | John Garlop rents Post St. | | gronage (4d.) | 1491M |
| Bonsay, John jr. | | | 3r (2d.q.) | 1489M |
| Bould, John | | Thomas Dene | ¾a (1d.ob.) | 1487E |
| | John Dalton | | for a close (1d.ob.) | 1490M |
| | | *Thomas Emlyn | 3r leys (2d.q.) | 1491M |

| Name | Tenant / note | Holding (payment) | Date |
|---|---|---|---|
| Broughton, John | | 2½r (2d.) | 1485E |
| | Thomas Sydebotom Chaplain of Blessed Virgin Mary | 2a mea. (6d.) | 1488E |
| | rents in Arnyng St. | ¼a (1d.ob.q.) | 1489E |
| Brown, William | William Snell | ¼a (1d.ob.) | 1485E |
| Chaplain (Capell'), John | Robert Porter | 2a (6d.) | 1485E |
| | *Robert Porter | 1r (ob.q.) | 1488E |
| Cleyff, William | William King | ¼a (1d.ob.) | 1486M |
| | William Beterich | 1a 1r (3d.ob.q.) | 1487E |
| | William Beterich | 1a (3d.) | 1488E |
| | William Nottingham | 1a (3d.) | 1488E |
| | William Nottingham | 6a 1r (19d.) | 1490M |
| Corby, William | John Page sr. | curtilage (ob.q.) | 1485E |
| | | (10d.q.) | 1487E |
| | rents Arnyng St. | ¼a (1d.ob.) | 1485E |
| Custodian of Church | John Lawman | 1r mea. (3d.) | 1485M |
| Custodian of St. George | John Dey | 1½r mea. (1d.q.) | 1485E |
| | Margaret Charter | 1r (ob.q.) | 1485E |
| | Thomas Blassell | 1½r (1d.q.) | 1485E |
| | Thomas Balle | 3½a (10d.ob.) | 1490E |
| Dangerous, John | Henry Trayley | ¼a (1d.ob.) | 1488E |
| Diggby, William | John English | 6a (18d.) | 1485E |
| Edmond, William | Robert Bayous | 2a 1r (6d.ob.q.) | 1485E |
| | William Plumpton | 1½a 1r. (3d.ob.) | 1485E |
| | rents Post St. | (ob.q.) | 1485M |
| Ely, Richard de | John Lockington | 2a (6d.) | 1488E |
| Emlyn, Thomas | John Garlop | 1½r (1d.q.) | 1488E |
| | Robert Vont | 1½r (1d.q.) | 1488E |
| | John Goodrych | 1½r (1d.q.) | 1488E |
| | William Gardener | ¼a (1d.ob.) | 1488M |
| | John Matthew | ¼a (1d.ob.) | 1491M |
| | John Bould | 1r (ob.q.) | 1491M |
| | rents East St. | 3r leys (2d.q.) | 1491M |
| Est, Henry | Thomas Benet | 3r (2d.q.) | 1489M |
| | John Marshall | 13a + mea. of leyes (3/3d.) | 1491M |

| Name | Delivered to | Received from | Land (Farm payment) | Year |
|---|---|---|---|---|
| Est, William | John Mayle | | 9a 1r (2/3d.ob.q.) | 1491M |
| | William Fraunceys | | 1r (ob.q.) | 1491M |
| | | Henry Trayley | 4a (12d.) | 1491M |
| | | Thomas Baker | 1a (3d.) | 1490E |
| Folk, Marion | | rents East St. | (6d.ob.q.) | 1485M |
| | | rents East St. | (ob.q.) | 1491M |
| Folk, Richard | | rents East St. | (ob.q.) | 1487E |
| Foly, Paul | rents West St. | | (6d.ob.q.) | 1486M |
| Foly, Reginald | John Brewster | | 6a 3r (20d.q.) | 1486M |
| Fyncham, Thomas | John Page jr. | | 9a 3r (2/5d.q.) | 1488E |
| | John Page jr. | | 10a 3r (2/8d.q.) | 1489E |
| | John Asshe | | 1½r (1d.q.) | 1489E |
| Glover, John | | Agnes Light | 1a (3d.) | 1489E |
| | | John Aylred | curtilage (1d.ob.) | 1491M |
| Goodwyn, William | John Snell | | ½a (1d.ob.) | 1485E |
| | William Snell | | 2a (6d.) | 1485E |
| | Thomas Sydebotom | | 3r (2d.q.) | 1485E |
| | Thomas Newman jr. | | 1a 1r (3d.ob.q.) | 1485M |
| | Thomas Newman jr. | | 1a mea. (3d.) | 1487E |
| | John Stukeley | | 1a 1r (3d.ob.q.) | 1488E |
| | William Mayle | | 12a 1½r (3/1d.ob.q.) | 1488E |
| | William Frost jr. | | 1½a (4d.ob.) | 1488E |
| | John Gybbys | | 1½a (4d.ob.) | 1488E |
| | Robert Mayle | | 3r (2d.q.) | 1488E |
| | Thomas Frost | | ½a (1d.ob.) | 1488E |
| | William Syward jr. | | swath (ob.) | 1488E |
| | John Hermyn | | 2a (6d.) | 1488E |
| Grace, John | John Lucas | | 14½a 1r (3/6d.ob.q.) | 1485M |
| | Richard Pelle | | 7a (21d.) | 1485M |
| | William Tothe | | ½a (1d.ob.) | 1489E |
| | Lord John Oxen | | ½a (1d.ob.) | 1489E |

| Name | | | Holding | Date |
|---|---|---|---|---|
| Granger, William | rents Post St. | | (11d.q.) | 1488E |
| Gray Benet | Thomas Cokman | | 1r (ob.q.) | 1488E |
| Hawkyn, Thomas | John Brown | | 7 swaths mea. (3d.ob.) | 1490M |
| Hermyn, John | | John Schylling | 1r (ob.q.) | 1485E |
| | Robert Dobbyn, chaplain | | 1a (3d.) | 1488E |
| | Robert Dobbyn, chaplain | | 1a (3d.) | 1488M |
| | | Isabella Penyth | ½a 1½r (2d.ob.q.) | 1489E |
| Hermyn, Thomas | John Barnard | | ½a (1d.ob.) | 1489E |
| Hermyn, Edmund | rents in le broke | | 1a (3d.) | 1489E |
| Holme, William | | rents East St. | ½a (1d.ob.) | 1489M |
| | rents in le Foren | | ½a (1d.ob.) | 1490E |
| Horbell, William | | Margaret Balle | 1a (3d.) | 1485M |
| Houghton, John | John Hosteler | | ½a (1d.ob.) | 1485M |
| Ibott, William jr. | Thomas Reynold | | mess (1d.ob.) | 1490E |
| Ibott, William | John Smyth | | ½a (1d.ob.) | 1485M |
| Ibott, William sr. | Robert Vont | | 6a (18d.) | 1485M |
| Ingram, William | | William Manipenny | 3a 1r (9d.ob.q.) | 1488E |
| | | *Henry Trayley | 6a 1r (18d.ob.q.) | 1491M |
| Kendale, Thomas | Robert Nicholas | | 2½a (7d.ob.) | 1485E |
| | Robert Mayle | | 1a (3d.) | 1485E |
| | Robert Mayle | | ½a (ob.q.) | 1486M |
| | William Horwell | | ½a (1d.ob.) | 1486M |
| | | Thomas Baker | 1a (3d.) | 1490E |
| | | *Cristina Prior | 1a (3d.) | 1485E |
| | | *William Corby | ½a (1d.ob.) | 1485E |
| Langham, William | John Lombard | | 10a (2/6d.) | 1485E |
| Lawman, John | | William Snell | 2a (6d.) | 1485E |
| | | John English | 1a (3d.) | 1485E |
| | | William Manipenny | 1r (ob.q.) | 1485E |
| | | William Polle | 1½a (4d.ob.) | 1486M |
| | | William Manipenny | 1r (ob.q.) | 1486M |
| | Thomas Page | | curtilage (q.) | 1491M |
| | Thomas Cokman | | 1½a (4d.ob.) | 1490E |

| NAME | DELIVERED TO | RECEIVED FROM | LAND (FARM PAYMENT) | YEAR |
|---|---|---|---|---|
| Legge, Richard | rents East St. | | (3d.ob.) | 1490M |
| Lessy, Thomas | Thomas Lessy son of Thomas | | 1½a (1d.ob.) | 1486M |
| | Thomas Lessy son of Thomas | | 1a (3d.) | 1488M |
| Lessy, Thomas sr. | Thomas Lessy (son) | | ½a (1d.ob.) | 1490M |
| Long, John | *John Sparrow | | ½a (1d.ob.) | 1485E |
| | John Barnard jr. | | 2½a (7d.ob.) | 1487E |
| | William Longe | | 1a (3d.) | 1487E |
| | William Longe | | 10a land + mea. (2/6d.) | 1488M |
| Longe, William | John Bonsay | | mea. (4d.ob.) | 1489M |
| Lucas, John | *William Ponder | *John Grace | 4a (12d.) | 1486M |
| | | | 7a (12d.) | 1485M |
| | *John Bonsay | rents East St. | 2a (6d.) | 1488E |
| | | | (4/6d.) | 1489M |
| | John Barnard sr. | | 1½a (4d.ob.) | 1490E |
| | John Husser | | 1½r leyes (1d.q.) | 1490E |
| | Richard Smith | | ½a leyes (1d.ob.) | 1490E |
| Manning, Roger | Richard (Slowe?) | | ½a (1d.ob.) | 1486M |
| | Richard Stukeley | | 1r (ob.q.) | 1488E |
| | John Manning | | 1r (ob.q.) | 1488E |
| | Edmund Manning | | 3r (2d.q.) | 1488E |
| | Edmund Manning | | 1r (ob.q.) | 1490M |
| | Edmund Manning | | ½a (1d.ob.) | 1491M |
| Mayle, William | rents East St. | *William Goodwyn | 12a 1½r (3/1d.q.) | 1488E |
| | John Schylling | | (5/1d.q.) | 1490M |
| Merton, Robert | rents Post St. | | 1½a (4d.ob.) | 1486M |
| Motte, Alice | | rent East St. | (4d.ob.) | 1490M |
| | | William Stodale | (4d.ob.) | 1490E |
| Mynsterchambre, John | | | messuage in Byllingford | |
| | William Farthing | | (1d.ob.) | 1486M |
| | | | mea. (1d.ob.) | 1488E |

| Name | | | Property | Year |
|---|---|---|---|---|
| Nottingham, Thomas | Roger Cook | | ½a (1d.ob.) | 1485M |
| | in le Foren broke | | 2a 3r (8d.) | 1487E |
| | *Robert Vont | | 3a (9d.) | 1488E |
| Newman, Thomas | | *Cristina Prior | mea. (ob.q.) | 1485E |
| | | John Barnard | 1a (3d.) | 1485M |
| | | Roger Cook | 1a (3d.) | 1486M |
| | | John Bigge | 1½a (4d.ob.) | 1486M |
| Newman, Thomas jr. | *William Page | | ¾a (1d.ob.) | 1485M |
| | | *William Goodwyn | 1a 1r (3d.ob.q.) | 1485M |
| | | *William Goodwyn | 1a mea. (3d.) | 1487E |
| Orwell, William | Thomas Faldyng | | 1½a (4d.ob.) | 1490E |
| | Richard Pelle | | ½r (ob.) | 1490M |
| Oxen, Lord John | Robert Vont | | 1r leyes (ob.q.) | 1488M |
| | | *William Syward | ½a (1d.ob.) | 1489E |
| | | Cristina Barret | 1a (3d.) | 1487E |
| | | *Balle' (?) | 3a 1r mea. (9d.ob.q.) | 1487E |
| | | John Derward | 1a mea. (3d.) | 1487E |
| | | Richard Mayle | 1r mea (3d.) | 1489E |
| | | *John Grace | ½a (1d.ob.) | 1489E |
| | | Thomas Frost | 1r (ob.q.) | 1491M |
| Page, William | William Frost | | 1r (ob.q.) | 1485M |
| | Thomas Newman jr. | | ½a (1d.ob.) | 1485M |
| Page, Thomas | *John Sparrow | | 3r (2d.q.) | 1485E |
| | | Henry Marshall | 3r (2d.q.) | 1485E |
| | rents Post St. | | (10d.q.) | 1489M |
| Page, John jr. | rents Post St. | *John Lawman | curtilage (q.) | 1491M |
| | | | (11d.q.) | 1486M |
| Page, John | John Shalford | Agnes Lane | 1½a (4d.ob.) | 1485E |
| | | *Thomas Fyncham | 9a 3r (2/5d.q.) | 1488E |
| | | *Thomas Fyncham | 10a 3r (2/8d.q.) | 1489E |
| | | executors of Agnes Lane | 10½a (2/7d.ob.) | 1485M |
| | | executors of Agnes Lane | 1a (3d.) | 1485M |
| | | | messuage (3d.) | 1487E |

| NAME | DELIVERED TO | RECEIVED FROM | LAND (FARM PAYMENT) | YEAR |
|---|---|---|---|---|
| Page, William jr. | rents Post St. | | (4d.ob.) | 1486M |
| Pelle, Richard | | *John Grace | 7a (21d.) | 1485M |
| | | William Manipenny | 1r (ob.q.) | 1485M |
| | | Austen Arnold | 1r (ob.q.) | 1485M |
| | John Grace | | 1a 1r (4d.ob.q.) | 1486M |
| | | John Kerke | 1r (ob.q.) | 1488E |
| | | Isabella Derych | ½r (ob.) | 1488E |
| | | John Aylred | gronage (3d.ob.) | 1489E |
| | | John Aylred | gronage (3d.) | 1489M |
| | | *Thomas Newman | ½r (ob.) | 1490M |
| Ponder, William | | *John Sparrow | ⅔a (1d.ob.) | 1485E |
| | Richard Smith | | 1½a (7d.ob.) | 1486M |
| | | John Lucas | 4a (12d.) | 1486M |
| | | William Pelle | 2⅔a (7d.ob.) | 1486M |
| | Richard Smith | | 3¾a (10d.ob.) | 1487E |
| | | William Pelle | 1a (3d.) | 1488E |
| | John Brown | | 1r leyes (ob.q.) | 1491M |
| | Robert Porter | | curtilage (ob.) | 1491M |
| | William Freneens | | 1a (3d.) | 1490E |
| | *William Brown | | 2a (6d.) | 1485E |
| Porter, Robert | | John Vont | 3a 1r (9d.ob.q.) | 1485E |
| | | John Porter | 4a 1½r (13d.q.) | 1485M |
| | Cristina Bishop | | messuage (4d.ob.) | 1485M |
| | William Browne | | 1r (ob.q.) | 1488E |
| | | John Garlop | 1r (4d.ob.) | 1488M |
| | rent to William Nicol | | 21a (5/3d.ob.q.) | 1489E |
| | Agnes Gardener | | 1r (ob.) | 1498E |
| | | rent from Remyngs Law | (ob.q.) | 1489E |
| | | *William Ponder | curtilage (ob.) | 1491M |

| | | | | |
|---|---|---|---|---|
| Prior, Cristina | John Lawman | | 1a (3d.) | 1485E |
| | Thomas Newman | | mea. (ob.q.) | 1485E |
| | rents Post St. | | (14d.ob.q.) | 1485E |
| Snell, John | | *William Goodwyn | ½a (1d.ob.) | 1485E |
| | | rent East St. | (8/3d.ob.q.) | 1489E |
| | | Thomas Reynold | ½a (1d.ob.) | 1489E |
| | | *Henry Trayley | 1r (ob.q.) | 1490M |
| Sparrow, John | John Lombard | | 3r (1d.ob.) | 1485E |
| | | John Longe | ½a (1d.ob.) | 1485E |
| | | Thomas Page | 3r (2d.q.) | 1485E |
| | William Ponder | | ½a (1d.ob.) | 1485E |
| Stevenson, Robert | | *Thomas Syward | 1r (ob.q.) | 1490M |
| | | rent East St. | (14d.q.) | 1490M |
| | | Thomas Faldyng | ½a (1d.ob.) | 1490M |
| Sydebottom, Thomas | | *William Goodwyn | 3r (2d.q.) | 1485E |
| | | *John Broughton | 2½r (2d.) | 1485E |
| | | Henry Marshall | ½a (1d.ob.) | 1485E |
| | | Roger Cook | 1a (3d.) | 1485M |
| Syward, Alice | son of William Syward | | 3r (2d.) | 1485E |
| Syward, Thomas | John Manning | | 1r (ob.q.) | 1489E |
| Syward, Thomas sr. | Roger Cook | | ½a (1d.ob.) | 1485E |
| | | William Frere | ½a (1d.ob.) | 1485E |
| | | William Frost jr. | 1r (ob.q.) | 1487E |
| | William Syward jr. | | ½a (1d.ob.) | 1487E |
| | Thomas Baker | | ½a (1d.ob.) | 1488E |
| | | John (Knalis) | 2½a (7d.ob.) | 1489E |
| | Robert Stevenson | | 1r (ob.q.) | 1490M |
| | | Margaret Heydrop | 2a (6d.) | 1490E |
| Syward, Thomas jr. | | John Brewster | ½a (1d.ob.) | 1485E |
| | | William Pelman | ½a (1d.ob.) | 1485M |
| | | Thomas Baker | 2a (6d.) | 1488E |
| | John Brewster | | ½a (1d.ob.) | 1489M |
| Syward, William | in le Remyng | | ½a (1d.ob.) | 1489E |
| | William Orwell | | ½a (1d.ob.) | 1489E |

| Name | Delivered to | Received from | Land (Farm Payment) | Year |
|---|---|---|---|---|
| Syward, William sr. | William Syward jr. | | 3r (2d.) | 1485E |
| | William Syward jr. | | 1½a 1r (5d.q.) | 1485E |
| | John Bonsay | | 3a (2d.q.) | 1488E |
| | William Frost jr. | | ¾a mea. (1d.ob.) | 1490M |
| | Henry Est | | 1a + 1r (3d.ob.q.) | 1490M |
| | William Frost jr. | | ¾a (1d.ob.) | 1490E |
| Trayley, Henry | | *John Dangerous | 3¼a (10d.ob.) | 14990E |
| | | Richard King | 12a 1½r (3/1d.q.) | 1490E |
| | | William Hilton | 1½a (4d.ob.) | 1490E |
| | | William Hilton | 1a (3d.) | 1490M |
| | John Snell | | 1r (ob.q.) | 1490M |
| | William Ingram | | 6a 1r (18d.ob.q.) | 1491M |
| | *William Est | | 4a (12d.) | 1491M |
| Executors of Alice Tully | Simon Granger | | ¾a mea. (1d.ob.) | 1485M |
| The Vicar | | John Slow | messuage ad.t. (2d.ob.) | 1490M |
| Vincent, John | Matthew (?) | remyngs law | 3a (9d.) | 1485E |
| | | *William Ibott | 1a 1r (3d.ob.q.) | 1487E |
| | | *William Orwell | 6a (18d.) | 1485M |
| | | *Thomas Emlyn | 1a (3d.) | 1487E |
| | | William Manipenny | 1½r (1d.q.) | 1488E |
| | | Thomas Nottingham | 1a (3d.) | 1488E |
| | | *John Barnard | 3a (9d.) | 1488E |
| Vont, Robert | | Richard Kyng | ½a (1d.ob.) | 1488M |
| | | Robert Gony | 1r (ob.q.) | 1489E |
| | | | 3r (2d.ob.) | 1489E |
| | Richard Hiche | | ½a (1d.ob.) | 1489E |
| | John Lockington | | 4a ½r (12d.ob.) | 1490E |
| | Thomas Burton | | 1a (3d.) | 1490E |
| | | Thomas Faldyng | 1r (ob.q.) | 1490E |

C. POST STREET CONVEYANCES

| NAME | DELIVERED TO | RECEIVED FROM | LAND (FARM PAYMENT) | YEAR |
|---|---|---|---|---|
| Adam, John | John Page jr. | | 6a 3½r (20d.q.) | 1487M |
| Bailiffs | | Agnes Lane | ½a (1d.ob.) | 1485M |
| | Thomas Lockyngton | | ½a 1½r mea. ad.t. (2d.ob.q.) | 1494M |
| | John Stukeley | | ½a mea. (1d.ob.) | 1494M |
| | William Frere | | 1a mea. (1d.) | 1494M |
| Baker, Thomas | John Barnard jr. | | 1½a (4d.ob.) | 1485M |
| | *William Brown | | ½a (1d.ob.) | 1485M |
| | *Thomas Faldyng | | 6a (18d.) | 1487E |
| | | *Thomas Baron | 2a 3½r (8d.ob.q.) | 1487E |
| | *Thomas Cokman | | 2a (6d.) | 1487E |
| | *William Brown | | 3a (9d.) | 1487E |
| | | rent Post St. | 7a (21d.q.) | 1490M |
| | | *John Osteler | 3a 1½r (10d.q.) | 1490M |
| | | | 1r (ob.q.) | 1491E |
| | *John Brown | *John Barnard | mess (2d.ob.) | 1491E |
| | Thomas Syward | | 3½a 1½r (11d.ob.q.) | 1492E |
| | (?) Est sr. | | ½a (1d.ob.) | 1492E |
| | Robert Nichols | | 1a ad.t. (3d.) | 1492E |
| | Richard Stevens | | 1a mea. (3d.ob.) | 1494M |
| Balle, Margaret, widow | Richard Smith | | 1a (3d.) | 1485M |
| | William Horbelle | | 1a (3d.) | 1485M |
| | William Syward jr. | | 1a (3d.) | 1485M |
| Balle, Thomas | John Gony | John Brewster | ½a ad.t. (1d.ob.) | 1487E |
| | | | mess ad.t. (1d.) | 1487M |
| | | John Brewster | ½a ad.t. (1d.ob.) | 1490E |
| | | Thomas Garlop | ½a mea. ad.t. (1d.ob.) | 1490E |
| | | William Gardener | 1r. mea. (ob.q.) | 1490E |
| | Thomas Syward | John Brewster | 1r (ob.q.) | 1490E |
| | | | 1r (ob.q.) | 1491E |

| Name | Delivered to | Received from | Land (Farm Payment) | Year |
|---|---|---|---|---|
| Barnard John jr. | rent Arnyng St. | Thomas Baker | 1½a (4d.ob.) | 1485M |
| | | | (4d.ob.) | 1487E |
| | | Margaret Bishop | 1a (3d.) | 1490E |
| | | *William Godwyn | mess (8d.) | 1490M |
| | Robert Stevenson | | 1a (3d.) | 1491E |
| | | William Godwyn of East St. | 1r (ob.q.) | 1491E |
| | | John Lockyngton | 1½a 1r ad.t. (5d.q.) | 1494E |
| | | John Barre | 3r (2d.q.) | 1494M |
| Barnard, John | Robert Mayle | | 1a ad.t. (3d.) | 1490M |
| | Thomas Baker | | mess ad.t. (2d.ob.) | 1491E |
| | | | 6a 3r (20d.q.) | 1494E |
| Barnard, John, candlemaker | Richard Stevens in the Street | *homines curie* | mess ad.t. (2d.) | 1494M |
| Barnard, William | | John Page sr. | 1r mea. ad.t. (ob.q.) | 1492E |
| | | John Brown | 9a + mess (2/3d. + 4d.) | 1494M |
| Bayous, John jr. | | Richard Wyllam | ½a (1d.ob.) | 1486M |
| | | William Wright | ½a (1d.ob.) | 1494E |
| | | | 18a 3r (4/8d q.) | 1494M |
| Bayous, John | *John Garlop | rent | (1a?) (3d.) | 1490M |
| | | *Steven Clarke | 1a (3d.) | 1494E |
| Bayous, Robert | Roger Cook | | ½a (1d. ob.) | 1492E |
| Beteryche, William | | John Chaplain | 1a 1r (3d.ob.q.) | 1487E |
| | William Frost sr. | | ½a (1d.ob.) | 1491E |
| | | *William Chese | 9a (2/3d.) | 1494E |
| Bigge, John | Thomas Newman | | 1½a (4d.ob.) | 1486M |
| | William Fraunceys | | 1a (3d.) | 1492E |
| | William Schylling | | 1a (3d.) | 1492E |

| Name | Grantee | Holding | Date |
|---|---|---|---|
| Boys, John | rent Post St. | (ob.q.) | 1494M |
| Brewster, Richard | rent Post St. | (4d.ob.q.) | 1494M |
| Brown, William | Thomas Baker | ½a (1d.ob.) | 1485M |
|  | Thomas Baker | 3a (9d.) | 1487E |
|  | William Hilton | 1a (3d.) | 1490E |
|  | Lawrence Brown | 1a ad.t. (3d.) | 1490M |
|  | William Brown, his brother | 1r (ob.q.) | 1491M |
|  | William Brown | 1r (ob.q.) | 1491E |
| Chese, William | rent in West St. | 4a 1r. (13d.ob.q.) | 1487M |
|  | William Beterych in the St. | 9a (2/3d.) | 1487E |
| Clerk, Steven | John Bayous | 1a ad.t. (3d.) | 1494E |
| Cokman, Thomas | *William Nottingham | 3a (9d.) | 1485M |
|  | Thomas Baker | 2a (6d.) | 1487E |
|  | *Richard Passelowe | 1a (3d.) | 1487E |
|  | *John Deyn | 1r (ob.q.) | 1487M |
|  | Benet Grey | 1a (3d.) | 1487M |
|  | John Lawman | ½a (1d.ob.) | 1487M |
|  | John Lawman | 1½a (4d.ob.) | 1490E |
|  | Thomas Syward sr. | 2½a (7d.ob.) | 1491E |
|  | Thomas Dorraunt | 1r mea. (ob.q.) | 1491E |
|  | *John Porter | ½a (1d.ob.) | 1491E |
|  | *John Matthew | 15a 1r (3/9d.ob.q.) | 1491E |
| Conyff, Alice | Isabella Wright in the Street | 1a (3d.) | 1491M |
|  | *Richard Kyng | 3a (9d.) | 1491M |
| Dalton, John | John Matthew in the St. | 4a (12d.) | 1492E |
|  | John Asshe | 1a ad.t. (3d.) | 1494M |
|  | John Lockyngton | 1½a (4d.ob.) | 1494M |
|  | John Bould | 1 croft (1d.ob.) | 1490M |

| NAME | DELIVERED TO | RECEIVED FROM | LAND (FARM PAYMENT) | YEAR |
|---|---|---|---|---|
| Davy, John | William Hilton | | ½a (1d.ob.) | 1491M |
| | Edward Barre | | mess ad.t. (2d.) | 1492E |
| | Edmund Page | | ½a (1d.ob.) | 1494E |
| | | John Barre | ½a ad.t. (1d.ob.) | 1494E |
| | | 12 men | 1a (1d.) | 1494E |
| Dawe, Alice | William Gretham | | (½a?) (1d.) | 1494M |
| Dey, John | Custodian St. Marie in Reminy | Cristina Barrett | 1r mea. ad.t. (ob.q.) | 1487E |
| Deyn, Thomas | John Bould | | 1r mea. ad.t. | 1494M |
| | William Frost jr. | | ½a (1d.ob.) | 1487E |
| | Thomas Cokman | | 1½a (5d.q.) | 1487E |
| | | | (1r) (ob.q.) | 1487M |
| Edmund, William | | his rent | (1r?) (ob.q.) | 1485M |
| English, John with Richard Kyng | *John Shalford in the St. | | mess (4d.) | 1487E |
| English, John | William Pelman | | 2a 3½r (8d.ob.q.) | 1487M |
| | | Thomas Garlop de West St. | ½a (1d.ob.) | 1486M |
| | Paul Foly | | ½a (1d.ob.) | 1486M |
| | Thomas Faldyng | | 1r (ob.q.) | 1487E |
| | | rent | (4/4d.) | 1494E |
| Este, William | John Armyt | | 2a ad.t. (6d.) | 1494M |
| | Edmund Page in the St. | | 5½a 1½r (17d.ob.q.) | 1494M |
| | rent | | (4/4d.q.) | 1494E |
| Faldyng, Thomas | | Thomas Baker | 6a (18d.) | 1487E |
| | | *John English | 1r (ob.q.) | 1487E |
| | Austen Arnold | | 1r (ob.q.) | 1487M |
| | John Boleyn | | (1a 1r?)(3d.ob.q.) | 1487M |
| | William Manipenny | | saffron ground (2d.ob.) | 1487M |
| | Thomas Newman | | 1½a (4d.ob.) | 1490E |

| Index | Occupant | Grantee | Property | Date |
| --- | --- | --- | --- | --- |
| | William Fraunceys in St. | | 6a 1r ad.t. | 1490E |
| | John (vacant), servant of John Stukeley | | ½a (1d.ob.) | 1490E |
| | Robert Vont | | 1r ad.t.(ob.q.) | 1490E |
| | John Garlop, artificer, in Street | | 1r ad.t. (ob.q.) | 1490E |
| | William Godwyn | | mess ad.t. (8d.) | 1490E |
| | Robert Stevenson | | 1a (3d.) | 1490M |
| | Robert Nicholas | | 1a 1r (3d.ob.q.) | 1490M |
| Farthing Agnes | | *John Reygate | gronage (q.?) | 1491M |
| Fecas, Thomas | John Porter | | mess ad.t. (1d.ob.) | 1490E |
| | | Thomas Bate | saffron ground in Benewal, ad.t.(3d.) | 1490E |
| Feld, John | William Pacy in St. | | mess ad.t. (1d.) | 1494M |
| Foly, Margaret | Richard Passelowe in St. | rent | 1a (3d.) | 1485M |
| Foly, Richard | rent East St. | | (ob.q.) | 1490M |
| Foster, John | rent East St. | | (ob.q.) | 1491M |
| | | | (ob.q.) | 1487E |
| | | Thomas Dorraunte rent Post St. from West St. | 1a ad.t. | 1486M |
| Foster, Richard | rent | *William Godwyn | 9a 1r (2/8d.ob.q.) | 1487E |
| | | | 1a (3d.) | 1490M |
| Fraternity of Corpus Christi | | | (1d.ob.) | 1494E |
| Fraternity of St. John the Baptist | | Thomas Frost | ½a mea. (1d.ob.) | 1492E |
| Fraunceys, William | | William Chese | 1r (ob.q.) | 1494E |
| | | William Ponder | 1a ad.t. (3d.) | 1490E |
| | *John Porter | *Thomas Faldyng | 6a 1r (18d.ob.q.) | 1490E |
| | rent Arnyng St. ad. t. | *John Porter | 4a (12d.) | 1490E |
| | | | 4a (12d.) | 1490M |
| | | | (18d.ob.) | 1491M |

| NAME | DELIVERED TO | RECEIVED FROM | LAND (FARM PAYMENT) | YEAR |
|---|---|---|---|---|
| Frost William | rent Arnyng St. | | (2/3d.ob.q.) | 1486M |
| Gardener, John | John Lockyngton | | 3r (2d.q.) | 1486M |
| | John Granger in Street | | mess (2d.) | 1486M |
| | William Hilton | | 3r ad.t. (2d.q.) | 1487M |
| | Fraternity of St. James | | 3r (2d.q.) | 1487M |
| | John Boleyn | | (1a 1r)(4d.ob.) | 1487M |
| | Thomas Johnson in Street | | 1r ad.t. (ob.q.) | 1490E |
| | Robert Stevenson | | 1a (3d.) | 1491E |
| | Richard Stukeley | | 1½r (1d.q.) | 1491M |
| Garlop, John, artificer | William Kyng | | 1r ad.t. (ob.q.) | 1487M |
| | | *Thomas Faldyng | 1r | 1490E |
| | | Thomas Dorraunte | 1r mea. (ob.q.) | 1490M |
| | | William Frost | ½a ad.t. (1d.ob.) | 1494M |
| | | John Bayous jr. | 18a 3r (4/8d.q.) | 1494M |
| Garlop, John | | John Bonsay | gronage (4d.) | 1491M |
| Godwyn, William | | John Hawkyn | 3½a (10d.ob.) | 1486M |
| | | Thomas Motte | (3½a.1r)(11d.ob.) | 1487E |
| | John Barnard jr. | | mess ad.t.(8d.) | 1490M |
| | | *Thomas Faldyng | mess (8d.) | 1490E |
| | Richard Foster | | 1a (3d.) | 1490M |
| | John Foster | | 2a ½r ¼r (6d.ob.) | 1491E |
| | *Robert Nicholas de East St. | | 3r (2d.q.) | 1491E |
| Gony, Alice | John Foster | | ½a 1½r + 1½r mea. (3d.) | 1491E |
| | William Frost | | 1 curtilage (ob.) | |
| | | | (a piece) | 1487M |
| Gony, Robert | John Lockyngton | rent Post from West St. | 10a 3r (2/8d.ob.q.) | 1487E |
| | | *William Manipenny | land of John Bate | |
| Goodrych, John | | rent | 1a 1r (4d.) | 1485M |
| Granger, Simon | | executors of Alice Tully | 1a (3d.) | 1490M |
| | | | ½a mea. (1d.ob.) | 1485M |

|  | | | | |
|---|---|---|---|---|
| Granger, William | | *John Matthew | 4a (12d.) | 1491E |
| | | *John Page | 4a (12d.) | 1494M |
| Gredley, John | | Edmund Manning | 1½a (4d.ob.) | 1494M |
| Gretham, William | | William Ibott | mess (3d.) | 1491E |
| | | William Hilton | 1½a 1½r (5d.ob.q.) | 1491E |
| | | William Polle | 12a ad.t. (3/-) | 1492E |
| | | *William Walcote | ½a (1d.ob.) | 1494E |
| | | *Alice Dawe in the Street | (½a?) (1d.) | 1494M |
| Gybbys, Richard | John Mayle | | ½a (1d.ob.) | 1490E |
| Gylby, Richard | John Stukeley | | ½a (1d.ob.) | 1494E |
| Haryngton, John | rent West St. | rent in Post St. | (9d.) | 1494M |
| Hilton, William | | *John Gardener | 3r (2d.q.) | 1487M |
| | | | (10d.q.) | 1490E |
| | | *William Brown | 1a (3d.) | 1490E |
| Holme, John | *William Gretham | *John Davy | 1½a 1½r (5d.ob.q.) | 1491E |
| | William Levedane | | ½a (1d.ob.q.) | 1491M |
| | | John Barnard, artificer | 3r (2d.q.) | 1486M |
| Kyng, Mariota | William Frost | | ½a (4d.ob.) | 1485M |
| | Henry Trayley | | 1 curtilage (3d.) | 1494M |
| | William Frost jr. | | 12a 1½r (3/1d.q.) | 1490E |
| Kyng, Richard | John Garlop, artificer in the Street | | 3a (9d.) | 1491E |
| Lane, Agnes | John Brown | Thomas Cokman | 5a ad.t. (15d.ob.q.) | 1491M |
| | | | ½a (1d.ob.) | 1491M |
| | Bailiffs | | 3a ad.t. (9d.) | 1491M |
| Lessy, William | John Page | | ½a mea. (1d.ob.) | 1485M |
| | John Page | | 10½a (2/7d.ob.) | 1485M |
| | | | messuage of Robert Vont (3d.) | 1485M |
| | John Stukeley | | ½a ad.t.(1d.ob.) | 1490M |
| | | John Latyzden | ½a mea. (1d.ob.) | 1494E |
| | Thomas Cokman | Thomas Cokman | 1r (ob.q.) | 1494M |

| Name | Delivered to | Received from | Land (Farm Payment) | Year |
|---|---|---|---|---|
| Lumbard, John | John Bould | John Robyn | ½ (virgate)(ob.) | 1486M |
| | | | 2a (6d.) | 1494E |
| Lyght, Agnes | Thomas Mariot | | 3r ad.t.(2d.q.) | 1491E |
| | John Stukeley | | 1a mea. (3d.) | 1491E |
| Manipenny, William | | executors of Alice Tully | ½a mea. (1d.ob.) | 1485M |
| | Robert Gony | | land of John Bate (4d.) | 1485M |
| | John Lawman | | 1r (ob.q.) | 1485M |
| | Thomas Syward sr. | | 1r (ob.q.) | 1485M |
| | Richard Pelle | | 1r (ob.q.) | 1485M |
| | John Lawman | | 1r (ob.q.) | 1486M |
| | Edward Barre | | ½r (ob.) | 1487E |
| | | *Thomas Faldyng | saffron ground (2d.ob.) | 1487M |
| | William Frost sr. | | 6a 3r ad.t.(20d.q.) | 1490E |
| | | William Frost jr. | 1½a (4d.ob.) | 1492E |
| | | Roger Manning | 1r (ob.q.) | 1492E |
| | | Thomas Fyncham | 1a mea.(3d.) | 1492E |
| | | the vicar | (2d.ob.) | 1494M |
| | | John Foster | 4a 1r (12d.ob.q.) | 1494M |
| | | Richard Walcote | 1r ad.t. (ob.q.) | 1490M |
| Manning, Edmund | rent in West St. | | 1a (3d.) | 1491M |
| Marshall, Henry | Thomas Maryot | | 1a 3r (5d.q.) | 1485M |
| | William Kyng | | 1½a (4d.ob.) | 1485M |
| | Fraternity of All Saints | | ½a (4d.ob.) | 1485M |
| | Fraternity of Corpus Christi | | | |
| | Matthew Garnet | | ½a (4d.ob.) | 1485M |
| | | | 4a 1r (12d.ob.q.) | 1485M |
| Marshall, Thomas | Robert Nicol | Roger Manning | messuage (1d.ob.) | 1492E |
| Massey, Thomas | | | 1r (ob.q.) | 1492E |
| Matthew, John | Robert Nicholas | | 12a 1r (3/- ob.q.) | 1487E |
| | | William Aylred | 89a 1½r (22/- 5d.q.) | 1491E |
| | William Mayle | | 3a + messuage (2/1d.) | 1491E |
| | William Mayle | | 15a 1r (3/9d.) | 1491E |

| Holder | | Property | Date |
|---|---|---|---|
| | Thomas Cokman | 4a 1r (12d.) | 1491E |
| | William Granger | 3¾a 1r (11d.q.) | 1491E |
| | William Snell | 1a (3d.) | 1491E |
| | John Cave | 1a (3d.) | 1491E |
| | Richard Stukeley | ½a (1d.ob.) | 1491E |
| | William Walcote in Street | | |
| | Henry Est | 1r + 1½r (1d.q.) | 1491M |
| | William Basse | 13a (3/3d.) | 1491M |
| | | curtilage in Benewal (2d.) | 1491M |
| | Thomas Emley | 1r (?) | 1491M |
| | William Mayle | messuage (4d.) | 1492E |
| | *Thomas Cokman in Street | | |
| Motte, Alice | rent East Street | 4a (12d.) | 1492E |
| | | (4d.ob.) | 1490E |
| Motte, Richard | rent | (ob.q.) | 1490M |
| | Fraternity of St. Trinity | ½a (1d.ob.) | 1487E |
| | Thomas Faldyng | 4a (12d.) | 1487E |
| | William Basse | curtilage in Benewal (1d.) | 1491M |
| Nicholas, Robert | Robert Porter | ½a (1d.ob.) | 1487M |
| | John Long | 1r (ob.q.) | 1487M |
| | *John Matthew | 12a 1r (3/- ob.q.) | 1489E |
| | Roger Cook | ½a ½r (2d.) | 1490E |
| | *Thomas Faldyng | 1a (3d.) | 1490M |
| | William Godwyn de East Street | 3r (2d.q.) | 1491E |
| | *John Porter | 1r (ob.q.) | 1491E |
| | *Richard Wyllam | 2¼a (7d.ob.) | 1491E |
| William Pelman | | ½a 1½r (2d.ob.q.) | 1492E |
| | *Thomas Baker | 1a (3d.) | 1492E |
| | Benedict Grey | ½a (1d.ob.) | 1492E |
| | *Thomas Marshall | ½a (1d.ob.) | 1492E |
| | *John Passelowe | ½a (1d.ob.) | 1492E |
| | *John Page | ½a mea. (1d.ob.) | 1494M |

| NAME | DELIVERED TO | RECEIVED FROM | LAND (FARM PAYMENT) | YEAR |
|---|---|---|---|---|
| Nottingham, William | Thomas Cokman | | 3a ad.t. (9d.) | 1487M |
| | | John Capelle for his land | (19d.) | 1490M |
| | | Roger Cook | ½a (1d.ob.) | 1490M |
| Nottingham, Thomas Osteler, John | | John Broughton | ½a (1d.ob.) | 1485M |
| | Austen Arnold | | 4a ad.t. (12d.) | 1487E |
| | Thomas Baker | | 3a 1½r ad.t. (10d.q.) | 1490M |
| Passelowe, John | Robert Nicholas | *Richard Passelowe | mess (2d.) | 1491E |
| | | | mess (1d.ob.) | 1492E |
| Page, Edmund | | John Davy | 1a ad.t. (3d.) | 1494E |
| | | *John Davy | ½a (1d.ob.) | 1494E |
| | | *William Est in St. | 5½a 1½r (17d.ob.q.) | 1494M |
| Page, John | | *Agnes Lane | 10a + messuage of Robert Vont (2/7d.ob.) | 1485M |
| | William Granger | | 4a land + mea. (12d.) | 1494M |
| | Robert Nicholas | | ½a mea. (1d.ob.) | 1494M |
| Page, John jr. | | rent | (11d.q.) | 1486M |
| Page, William | | rent of 1½a | 4d.ob. | 1486M |
| Passelowe, Richard | | *John Feld in the St. | 1a (3d.) | 1485M |
| | | Roger Manning | ½a (1d.ob.) | 1486M |
| | Thomas Cokman | | 1a (3d.) | 1487E |
| | William Pelman | | 1½a 3½r mea. (5d.q.) | 1491M |
| | John Gardener, plowrighte | | 1½a 3½r (5d.q.) | 1491M |
| | John Passelowe | | mess ad.t. (2d.) | 1491E |
| Plumpton, Anna | John Davy | | 7a + mess (21d. + 2d.ob.q.) | 1491E |
| | John Davy | | 16a (4/-) | 1492E |

| Name | Holder | Property | Date |
|---|---|---|---|
| Plumpton, William | Thomas (surname omitted) | 1a (3d.) | 1485M |
| Porter, John | Paul Foly | 1a 1r (3d.ob.q.) | 1486M |
| | Robert Porter | 4a 1½r (13d.q.) | 1485M |
| | William Farthing | 1r ad.t.(ob.q.) | 1487M |
| | William Fraunceys | 4a (12d.) | 1490E |
| | *Agnes Farthing | ¼a (1d.ob.) | 1490E |
| | William Fraunceys | 4a (12d.) | 1490M |
| | Thomas Cokman | ½a (1d.ob.) | 1491E |
| | Robert Nicholas | 1r (ob.q.) | 1491E |
| | William Gretham | mess + 3¼a (2d. + 12d.ob.) | 1491E |
| Reynold, Thomas | William Ibott | mess, parcel (1d.ob.) | 1491E |
| Reygate, John | Richard Stukeley | gronage ad.t (q.) | 1490E |
| | Thomas Faldyng | gronage ad.t(q.) | 1491M |
| Saint (Samt, Sent), Richard | Thomas Bate | ½a ad.t (1d.ob.) | 1491M |
| | Paul Foly | 25a 3r (6/5d.q.) | 1486M |
| | Fraternity of Corpus Christi | ½a mea. (1d.ob.) | 1487E |
| Shalford, John | John Page and John English | mess formerly Robert Vont (4d.) | 1490M |
| | | curtilage, benewal (ob.q.) | 1487E |
| Sterlyng, John | Thomas Frost | ½a (1d.ob.) | 1491E |
| | Paul Foly | (8d.q.) | 1486M |
| | rent West St. | 3r virgate (2d.q.) | 1487E |
| Stevenson, Robert | Roger Cook | (14d.q.) | 1486M |
| | rent East St. | 1a (3d.) | 1490M |
| | *Thomas Faldyng | 1a (3d.) | 1490M |
| | *John Barnard jr. | 1a (3d.) | 1491E |
| | *John Gardener | | 1491E |
| Stodale, Margaret | William Frost sr. | 1 piece of curtilage (1d.ob.) | 1494E |

| Name | Delivered to | Received from | Land (Farm Payment) | Year |
|---|---|---|---|---|
| Stodale, William | John Turneskewe | | 1r ad.t. (ob.q.) | 1491M |
| | Thomas Mariot | | ½a ad.t.(1d.ob.) | 1492E |
| Stokys, John | John Bonsay | | 1r (1d.ob.) | 1486M |
| | | William King | 2a (6d.) | 1487M |
| Tothe, William | Robert Chandeler | | ½a mea. (1d.ob.) | 1494M |
| | John Oxen, chaplain of St. Mary | | ½a mea. (1d.ob.) | 1492E |
| Turneskewe, John | | Thomas Benet | 1a (3d.) | 1487E |
| Ussher, John | | Thomas Bate | ½a (1d.ob.) | 1486M |
| | John Lucas | | 1½r (1d.ob.) | 1490E |
| | | Robert Vont | 1r mea. (3d.) | 1491M |
| | | William Mounford | 1r mea (3d.) | 1491M |
| | | *John Matthew | 1r + 1½r (1d.ob.) | 1491M |
| Walcote, William | William Gretham | | ½a (1d.ob.) | 1494M |
| Wright, William | John Bayous jr. | | ½a (1d.ob.) | 1486M |
| Wulfston, Guido, knight | | Richard Stukeley | curtilage (ob.q.) | 1490E |
| | | Richard Stukeley | curtilage (ob.) | 1491M |
| | | William Pelman | curtilage (ob.) | 1492E |
| Wyllam, Richard | John Bayous jr. | | ½a (1d.ob.) | 1486M |
| | Robert Nicholas | | 2¼a (7d.ob.) | 1491E |
| 12 men | John Davy | | 1a (3d.) | 1494E |

## D. West Street Conveyances

| Name | Delivered to | Received from | Land (Farm Payment) | Year |
|---|---|---|---|---|
| Barnard, John | John Holme | | 1¼a (4d.ob.) | 1485M |
| Bas, John | John Bonsay sr. | | 1r (ob.q.) | 1489E |
| Benet, Thomas | William Horwyth | | 1r (ob.q.) | 1489E |
| | | *John Robyn | ½a (1d.ob.) | 1489E |
| | Richard Stukeley | | 1r (ob.q.) | 1489E |
| Bonsay, Richard | | Margaret Balle | 1a (3d.) | 1485M |
| Bould, Roger | | Thomas Baker | ½a (1d.ob.) | 1489E |
| Brewster, John | William Manipenny | | 13a + mea.(3/3d.) | 1485M |
| | Thomas Mayle | | curtilage (ob.q.) | 1485M |
| Brust', John | Thomas Balle | | ½a (1d.ob.) | 1489M |
| Cook, Roger | Thomas Nottingham | | ½a (1d.ob.) | 1485M |
| | Thomas Sydebotom | | 1a (3d.) | 1485M |
| | John Brown | | 1r (ob.q.) | 1485M |
| | William Bocher | | 1r (ob.q.) | 1485M |
| | Margaret Marshall | | 1¼a (4d.ob.) | 1485M |
| | William Kyng | | 3r (2d.q.) | 1485M |
| Conyff, Robert Fraternity of All Saints | | Cristina Bate | 1¼a (4d.) | 1485M |
| Garlop, Thomas | Thomas Brewster | Margaret Marshall | 1¼a (4d.ob.) | 1485M |
| | | | 1a (3d.) | 1485M |
| Gybbys, John | Henry Gybbys | *Richard Kyng | ½a (1d.ob.) | 1485M |
| | | | 3r (2d.q.) | 1489E |
| Hilton, William (Hilton), Thomas | | rent | 2a 3r (8d.ob.q.) | 1489E |
| | | Thomas Faldyng | ½a (1d.ob.) | 1489E |
| Hust', John | | | 1¼a (4d.ob.) | 1485M |
| Kyng, Richard | John Lockyngton | Henry Marshall | ½a (1d.ob.) | 1485M |
| | Thomas Garlop | *Roger Cook | 1¼a (4d.ob.) | 1485M |
| Kyng, William | | William Kyng | 3r (2d.q.) | 1485M |
| | | | 1a 1r (3d.ob.) | 1485M |
| | | *John Schylling | ½a (1d.ob.) | 1485M |
| | John Garlop | | ½a (1d.ob.) | 1489E |
| | John Garlop | | 21a (5/3d.) | 1489E |

| NAME | DELIVERED TO | RECEIVED FROM | LAND (FARM PAYMENT) | YEAR |
|---|---|---|---|---|
| Lockyngton, John | | William Manipenny | 6½a (19d.q.) | 1489E |
| | | *John Hust' | 1½a (1d.ob.) | 1489E |
| | | William Aylred | 2a mea. (6d.) | 1489E |
| Loveday, William | John Bonsay | | 3r (2d.q.) | 1489E |
| Manning, John | | Thomas Syward | 1r (ob.q.) | 1489E |
| | | *William Pelman | 1r (ob.q.) | 1489E |
| Mariot, Thomas | | Henry Marshall | 1½a (5d.q.) | 1485M |
| | | the executors of William Aylred | 3r (2d.q.) | 1489E |
| | | William Manipenny | 1a (3d.) | 1489E |
| Mayle, Richard | | John Schylling | 6a 1½r (19d.q.) | 1489E |
| Mayle, Thomas | | *John Brewster | curtilage (ob.q.) | 1485M |
| | | | 1r (ob.q.) | 1489E |
| | | | 3a (9d.) | 1489E |
| Pelman, William | Elizabeth (Wysorld) | | ½a (1d.ob.) | 1485M |
| | William Frost jr. | | 1½a 1½r (5d.ob.q.) | 1485M |
| | Thomas Syward jr. | | ? (ob.) | 1489E |
| | Edward Barre | | 1r (ob.q.) | 1489E |
| | Henry Gybbys | | | |
| | John Manning | | | |
| Robyn, John | Thomas Benet | | ½a (1d.ob.) | 1489E |
| Schylling, John | Richard Motte | | ½a mea. (1d.ob.) | 1485M |
| | Marion Foly | | 2a 1r rent (6d.ob.q.) | 1485M |
| | William Kyng | | ½a (1d.ob.) | 1485M |
| | *Richard Mayle | | 6a 1½r (19d.q.) | 1489E |
| Stukeley, Richard | | John Schylling, smith | 1r (ob.q.) | 1489E |
| Stukeley, Robert | rent | | 3a (15d.ob.) | 1485M |
| Wyllam, William | Robert Mayle | | 3r (2d.q.) | 1485M |

# Appendix 5

# The Victualling Trades People

| NAME | YEAR(S) | BREWER | BAKER | BUT-CHER | FISH-MONGER | RETAILER | CANDLE-MAKER |
|---|---|---|---|---|---|---|---|
| Abram, wife of William | 1512-13, 15, 20, 22-23, 25-30, 32 | | | | | x | |
| ——, wife of William jr. | 1533-34, 36-38, 40-45 | | | | | x | |
| ——, wife of William sr. | 1533-34, 36, 38-43 | | | | | x | |
| Abuelly, wife of John | 1498 | | | | | x | |
| Adam, wife of John | 1520 | | | | | x | |
| Alam, wife of William | 1538-42, 44-45; | | x | | | | |
| | 1543 | x | | | | | |
| Alam, wife of Thomas | 1497-98, 1500-01, 03 | | | | | x | |
| ——, Elena* | 1494-96 | | | | | x | |
| Alax, Thomas | 1501 | | | | | | x |
| Alconbury, Thomas | 1485 | | x | | | | |
| Ansell, wife of Fremond | 1488 | | | | | x | |
| Anton, Alice | 1530-34, 36 | x | | | | | |
| Anys, wife of William | 1523-28 | | | | | x | |
| Aplond, Cristina | 1497-98 | | | | | x | |
| Arnold, John* | 1533-34 | | | | | x | |
| ——, wife of William | 1522-23, 25-30 | | | | | x | |
| ——, William | 1515 | x | | | | | |
| Aylred, tenant of John | 1496, 1500 | | | | | x | |
| Bacar, John de Hunts | 1498 | | x | | | | |
| Bailey, Isabella | 1485-91, 94-96; | | | | | x | |
| | 1497; | x | | | | x | |
| | 1498; | x | | | | | |
| | 1500-01 | | | | | x | |
| Baker, Ka' de St. Neots | 1515 | | x | | | | |
| Balle, Margaret | 1485-91 | | | | | x | |
| Barbour Margaret | 1497 | | | | | x | |
| Baret, Jacob | 1525-27 | | | | x | | |
| Barnard, John | 1491; | | | | x | | |
| | 1494; | | | x | | | |
| | 1496-98 | | | | | | x |
| ——, wife of Henry | 1536; | x | | | | | |
| | 1537-39 | x | x | | | | |
| Basse, Margaret | 1495; | x | | | | | |
| | 1496; | | x | | | | |
| | 1497-98, 1500 | x | | | | | |

* indicates duplication of name, e.g., wife of Thomas Alam and then Elena Alam, who very likely is the wife of Thomas.

| NAME | YEAR(S) | BREWER | BAKER | BUTCHER | FISH-MONGER | RETAILER | CANDLE-MAKER |
|---|---|---|---|---|---|---|---|
| ——, William | 1495; | | | | | x | |
| | 1496 | x | | | | | |
| Bate, Marion | 1485-89 | | | | | x | |
| Bawdwyne, wife of Thomas | 1501 | | | | | x | |
| Bekke, Helen wife of | 1491; | x | | | | | |
| | 1496 | | | | | x | |
| Bellyngton, Anne | 1530 | | | | | x | |
| Benet, Oliver | 1522, 23, 25 | | | x | | | |
| ——, Thomas | 1501 | | | | x | | |
| ——, wife of Thomas | 1526-27 | x | | | | | |
| Berde, wife of John | 1540; | x | x | | | | |
| | 1541-42 | | x | | | | |
| Beytun, William | 1529 | | x | | | | |
| Bigge, Alice | 1485-88 | x | | | | | |
| Blaxton, wife of Richard | 1515, 23-26 | | | | | x | |
| Bocher, Richard | 1505 | | | x | | | |
| ——, wife of Richard | 1505 | | | | | x | |
| Boleyn, Elizabeth wife of John | 1515-17; | | x | | | | |
| | 1518; | x | x | | | | |
| | 1520; | | x | | | | |
| | 1525; | | | | | x | |
| | 1526; | | x | | | x | |
| | 1527; | x | x | | | x | |
| | 1533-34 | x | x | | | | |
| Bollard, wife of Henry | 1540-45 | x | x | | | | |
| Bonfay, Agnes | 1511 | x | | | | | |
| Borowe, Alice | 1533-34 | x | | | | | |
| ——, John | 1533-34 | | x | | | | |
| Bould, Agnes | 1487-91; | x | x | | | | |
| | 1494-98; 1500-01, 03, 09-10 | x | | | | | |
| Bower, Margaret | 1498 | | | | | x | |
| Brampton, Margaret wife of John | 1523, 25-28 | | | | | x | |
| Brandon, Alice* | 1496; | | | | | x | |
| | 1497-98, 1500-01, 03 | x | | | | | |
| ——, John | 1496 | | | x | | | |
| ——, wife of John | 1505, 09-10 | x | | | | | |
| Brewster, Elena | 1494-98, 1500-01, 03, 10 | | | | | x | |
| ——, John | 1496-98, 1500 | | x | | | | |
| ——, Agnes | 1485 | | | | | x | |
| Brown, wife of Nicholas | 1491 | | | | | x | |
| Bryte, Margaret | 1495 | | | | | x | |
| Bysele, John | 1501 | | | | | | x |
| Carter, wife of John | 1498 | | | | | x | |
| Cawdwell, Alice wife of Robert | 1494-96 | | | | | x | |
| ——, Robert | 1494-95 | | | x | x | | |
| Chandeler, Joan* | 1494-96; | x | | | | | |
| | 1498; | x | | | | x | |
| | 1503 | x | | | | | |

| NAME | YEAR(S) | BREWER | BAKER | BUT-CHER | FISH-MONGER | RETAILER | CANDLE-MAKER |
|---|---|---|---|---|---|---|---|
| ——, John | 1497 | x | | | x | | |
| ——, Robert | 1510-11 | x | | | | | |
| ——, wife of Robert | 1505, 11, 13 | x | | | | | |
| Chycheley, Jane | 1501, 03 | x | | | | | |
| ——, Margaret | 1485-89, 91 | | | | | x | |
| ——, wife of John* | 1505, 09-19 | x | | | | | |
| Clark, Agnes | 1494 | | | | | x | |
| ——, Anys widow | 1539 | x | | | | x | |
| ——, Isabella | 1496 | | | | | x | |
| ——, Margaret | 1525 | | | | | x | |
| ——, Matilda | 1495 | | | | | x | |
| ——, wife of John | 1494; | | | | | x | |
| | 1503; | x | | | | | |
| | 1540-41 | | x | | | x | |
| Cleworth, Richard | 1530, 32 | | x | | | | |
| Cokman, Agnes wife of ? | 1487-91; | x | | | | | |
| | 1494-95 | | | | | x | |
| ——, Alice widow of Thomas | 1494; | x | | | | | |
| | 1495 | | | x | | | |
| ——, Thomas | 1487; | | | x | | | |
| | 1488-91, 94 | | | x | x | | |
| Cook, John | 1501; | | | x | | | |
| | 1515 | | x | | | | |
| ——, Margaret | 1513 | | | | | x | |
| ——, wife of Walter | 1513 | | | | | x | |
| Corbet, John | 1520 | | x | | | | |
| Coryar, John of Hunts | 1513, 22-23, 25-27 | | | x | | | |
| Couper, Agnes | 1501, 03 | | | | | x | |
| ——, John | 1497; | | | x | | | |
| | 1498; | | | x | x | | |
| | 1500-01, 03, 05 | | | x | | | |
| ——, wife of John | 1497-98, 1500, 05 | | | | | x | |
| Dalton, William | 1525-28, 31 | | | | x | | |
| ——, wife of William | 1510 | x | | | | | |
| Dey, Anna | 1494 | | | | | x | |
| ——, Margaret | 1485-87, 94 | | | | | x | |
| ——, wife of William* | 1491 | | | | | x | |
| ——, William | 1495 | | | | | | x |
| Denysse, Thomas | 1520 | | | | x | | |
| Diggeby, Elena wife of William | 1485-98, 1501, 03, 10 | | | | | x | |
| Dyar, wife of Dobson | 1501 | | | | | x | |
| Dynet, wife of John | 1496, 1500, 03 | | | | | x | |
| Dysney, Agnes | 1528-29 | x | | | | | |
| ——, wife of John | 1511, 13, 15, 18, 22-23, 25-27 | x | | | | | |
| Ely, John | 1496-97, 1509, 11-12 | | | | x | | |
| English, Marion | 1485-1486 | | | | | x | |

| NAME | YEAR(S) | BREWER | BAKER | BUTCHER | FISHMONGER | RETAILER | CANDLEMAKER |
|---|---|---|---|---|---|---|---|
| Faldyng, Isabelle wife of Thomas | 1485-91, 94-98, 1500-01, 03, 05, 09-11 | x | | | | | |
| ——, Thomas | 1495-96; | | | | | | x |
|  | 1509 | | x | | | | |
| Fawn, Elizabeth | 1497-98, 1500 | | | | | x | |
| ——, Richard | 1500 | x | | | | | |
| Fecas, Thomas | 1491; | | | | x | | |
|  | 1494; | | | x | x | | |
|  | 1495-96; | | | | x | | |
|  | 1497 | | | | | | x |
|  | 1498 | | | | x | | x |
| Feltwelle, John | 1486, 90-91, 95, 1505 | | | | x | | |
| Feltwelle, John of Hunts | 1494 | | | | x | | |
| Foster, John | 1485 | | | x | | | |
| Frere, Elizabeth | 1530; | x | | | | | |
|  | 1532-34, 36-39; | x | x | | | | |
|  | 1540-45 | | x | | | | |
| ——, wife of Henry | 1530; | x | | | | | |
|  | 1540-42; | | x | | | | |
|  | 1543; | x | x | | | | |
|  | 1544-45 | | x | | | | |
| Frost, Henry | 1496 | | | | x | | |
| Gaddisby, Thomas | 1543 | | | x | | | |
| Gardiner, Thomas | 1498, 1500-01 | | | x | | | |
| Garlop, Alice | 1485-87 | | | | | x | |
| ——, Jane | 1501 | x | | | | | |
| ——, Joan | 1485 | | | | | x | |
| ——, John | 1501 | | | x | | | |
| Gibbys, Agnes wife of John | 1485-87; | x | | | | | |
|  | 1488; | x | | | | x | |
|  | 1490-91, 95-98, 1505 | x | | | | | |
| ——, John | 1486-91 | | | x | | | |
| ——, Richard | 1525-28, 31 | | | | x | | |
| Glapthorne, wife of Robert | 1526, 33-34 | x | | | | | |
| ——, Robert | 1529, 33-34, 36 | | | | x | | |
| Goddard, John | 1498, 1505 | | | | x | | |
| ——, William | 1501 | | | | x | | |
| Godwyn, Joan wife of Henry | 1510-11 | | | | | x | |
| Goldyng, William | 1494 | | | | x | | |
| Gonell, Elizabeth | 1500 | | | | | x | |
| Gony, Margaret | 1485-91, 94-98 | | | | | x | |
| Goodrych, Agnes | 1489 | | | | | x | |
| Gor, Joan | 1510 | | | | | x | |
| ——, Richard | 1515 | | | | x | | |
| Granger, Joan | 1530, 32-36; | x | | | | | |
|  | 1537 | x | x | | | | |
| ——, John | 1540 | | x | | | | |
| ——, Margery | 1500-01, 03, 28-30, 32 | | | | | x | |
| Granger, wife of John | 1520-23, 25; | | | | | x | |
|  | 1541-42 | | x | | | | |
| ——, wife of John sr. | 1526-27 | | | | | x | |

| NAME | YEAR(S) | BREWER | BAKER | BUT-CHER | FISH-MONGER | RETAILER | CANDLE-MAKER |
|---|---|---|---|---|---|---|---|
| Gredley, Joan | 1485-91, 94-98, 1500-01, 03, 10; | | | | | x | |
| | 1512 | x | | | | | |
| ——, John | 1491-94; | | | | x | | |
| | 1495; | | | x | x | | |
| | 1496-97; | | | x | | | |
| | 1498; | | | x | x | | |
| | 1500, 03, 05, 09-11, 15, 18 | | | x | | | |
| Grene, Agnes wife of Richard | 1509-11; | x | | | | | |
| | 1522-23; | x | x | | | | |
| | 1532-33 | x | | | | | |
| | 1534, 36-37 | x | x | | | | |
| | 1538-39; | x | | | | | |
| | 1541 (widow) | | x | | | | |
| ——, Richard | 1509; | | x | | | | |
| | 1529; | x | x | | | | |
| | 1533 | x | | | | | |
| ——, wife of William | 1533-34, 36-39 | | | | | x | |
| ——, William | 1533, 36-45 | | | x | | | |
| Gugg, Joan | 1503, 05 | | | | | x | |
| Gylle, Agnes | 1485-90 | | | | | x | |
| Haccar, wife of John | 1511, 13 | | | | | x | |
| Halle, wife of John | 1494-95 | | | | | x | |
| Halton, Joan | 1487 | | | | | x | |
| Hanby, William | 1501 | | | x | | | |
| Hassope (no first name) | 1537 | | | x | | | |
| Hawdwyn, Roger | 1516; | | x | | | | |
| | 1527-28, 31-32; | | | | x | | |
| | 1533-34, 36; | | x | | x | | |
| | 1537, 39, 40; | | x | | | | |
| | 1541; | | x | | x | | |
| | 1542-45 | | x | | | | |
| Hay, Katherine | 1498 | | | | | x | |
| Heddyngley, Thomas | 1530, 32-33 | | x | | | | |
| Herforth, John | 1485-91, 94-96 | x | | | | | |
| ——, John de Hunts | 1498 | x | | | | | |
| Heynis, Roger | 1500-01 | | | | | | x |
| Higdon, William | 1485 | | x | | | | |
| Hilton, Agnes wife of William | 1494-98, 1501, 03, 05, 09-13 | | | | | x | |
| Hogson, John | 1533-34, 36 | | | | x | | |
| Holme, Agnes | 1491, 94 | | | | | x | |
| ——, Alice | 1501, 03 | | | | | x | |
| ——, Joan | 1485-91, 95-98, 1503 | | | | | x | |
| ——, John | 1505, 09, 10, 33 | | x | | | | |
| ——, Margaret | 1495-96; | x | | | | | |
| | 1498 | | | | | x | |
| ——, wife of Jacob | 1515 | | | | | x | |

| NAME | YEAR(S) | BREWER | BAKER | BUT-CHER | FISH-MONGER | RETAILER | CANDLE-MAKER |
|---|---|---|---|---|---|---|---|
| ——, Margaret, wife of John | 1505, 09-12; | x | | | | | |
| ——, John | 1513, 15-16; | x | x | | | | |
| | 1517; | | x | | | | |
| | 1518; | x | x | | | | |
| | 1520; | | x | | | | |
| | 1522-23, 25-27, 29-34 | x | x | | | | |
| ——, wife of Richard* | 1500, 05 | | | | | x | |
| ——, wife of Thomas* | 1520 | | | | | x | |
| Hope, Alice | 1494 | | | | | x | |
| Hunt', Joan | 1528 | | x | | | | |
| Ibott, Alice | 1503 | x | | | | | |
| ——, Rosa | 1485-91, 95-96, 98, 1500-01, 03 | | | | | x | |
| ——, wife of William* | 1505, 10-11, 13; | x | | | | | |
| | 1515-17; | | | | | x | |
| | 1518; | x | | | | | |
| | 1520; | | x | | | | |
| | 1522-27 | x | | | | | |
| ——, wife of William jr. | 1511-12, 15-16 | | | | | x | |
| ——, William | 1505 | | x | | | | |
| Johnson, Isolda | 1497-98 | | | | | x | |
| Kelson, Elizabeth wife of William | 1513, 15-16, 18, 22-23, 29-30, 32-34, 36-41 | | | | | x | |
| Kendale, wife of Thomas | 1503 | x | | | | | |
| Kessby, Richard | 1528-31 | | | | x | | |
| Kyng, Agnes | 1502 | x | | | | | |
| ——, Marion | 1487-91 | | | | | x | |
| ——, Robert | 1536-38 | | x | | | | |
| ——, wife of Robert | 1536-1537 | x | | | | | |
| ——, wife of Richard | 1545 | | | | | x | |
| Kyrby, wife of Thomas | 1538; | x | | | | | |
| | 1540-45 | x | x | | | | |
| Lawe, Marjorie | 1485-89 | | | | | x | |
| Laxton, wife of William | 1536; | x | | | | | |
| | 1537; | x | x | | | | |
| | 1538 | x | | | | | |
| ——, William | 1538 | | x | | | | |
| Lessy, Joan | 1485 | | | | | x | |
| ——, Margaret | 1494 | x | | | | | |
| Leverett, Alice | 1495-98 | | | | | x | |
| Lord, Catherine, wife of William | 1529-30, 33-34, 36; | x | | | | | |
| | 1537; | x | x | | | | |
| | 1538; | | x | | | | |
| | 1539-40 | x | x | | | | |
| ——, Elizabeth, wife of William | 1532 | | | | | x | |

| Name | Year(s) | Brewer | Baker | Butcher | Fishmonger | Retailer | Candlemaker |
|---|---|---|---|---|---|---|---|
| ——, Isabella | 1503 | | | | | x | |
| ——, William | 1505; | x | | | | | |
| | 1509-11, 13, 15, 16, 18, 20, 25-27; | | | | | x | |
| | 1528, 32 | x | | | | | |
| Lorydan, Marcus | 1509; | x | | | | | |
| | 1510 | x | x | | | | |
| | 1511 | x | | | | | |
| Lovell, Maude, wife of Thomas | 1510-11, 13, 15-16, 18, 22 | x | | | | | |
| Manipenny, Alice | 1485-91 | x | | | | | |
| ——, Elizabeth | 1498, 1500-01, 03 | x | | | | | |
| ——, Isabella | 1494-97 | x | | | | | |
| ——, wife of William* | 1505 | | | | | x | |
| ——, William | 1485-91; | | x | | | | |
| | 1494-96; | | | | x | | |
| | 1500-01, 03 | | x | | | | |
| Massey, Agnes | 1489-91 | | | | | x | |
| ——, Joan | 1494-98, 1500-01, 03; | x | | | | | |
| | 1510; | x | x | | | | |
| | 1511-13, 15; | x | | | | | |
| | 1516; | x | x | | | | |
| | 1518 | x | | | | | |
| ——, Robert | 1529-30 | x | | | | | |
| | 1532-34, 36-45 | | | x | | | |
| ——, Thomas | 1505 | | x | | | | |
| ——, wife of Thomas* | 1505 | x | | | | | |
| Matday, wife of John | 1512 | | | | | x | |
| Matthew, Joan | 1485-91 | | | | | x | |
| May, William | 1537-38 | | x | | | | |
| ——, wife of William | 1536; | x | x | | | | |
| | 1537-42 | x | | | | | |
| Mayle, Alice | 1510, 12-13, 15, 18, 20, 28 | x | | | | | |
| ——, John | 1505, 09-11, 15; | | x | | | | |
| | 1525 | x | | | | | |
| ——, wife of John | 1505; | | | | | x | |
| | 1516-18, 22-23, 26-27 | x | | | | | |
| ——, wife of William | 1539 | x | | | | | |
| Maynard, wife of John | 1498 | | | | | x | |
| Mayse, wife of John | 1516-17; | x | x | | | | |
| | 1518; | x | | | | | |
| | 1520 | | x | | | | |
| Melbourne, Emma | 1494-96, 1500-01; | | | | | x | |
| | 1503 | x | | | | | |
| Miles, Elizabeth* | 1497-98 | x | | | | | |
| ——, wife of John | 1491, 1501 | | | | | x | |
| Miller, Margery wife of John | 1510-11 | x | | | | | |
| ——, William | 1494-95 | x | | | | | |
| Monyment, Thomas | 1509 | x | | | | | |
| ——, wife of Thomas | 1510-11, 13, 15-16, 18, 22-23, 25 | x | | | | | |

| NAME | YEAR(S) | BREWER | BAKER | BUT-CHER | FISH-MONGER | RETAILER | CANDLE-MAKER |
|---|---|---|---|---|---|---|---|
| Motte, Alice | 1486-89 | | | | | x | |
| Mynte, Isabella | 1494-95 | | | | | x | |
| | | | | | | | |
| Nelle, wife of Robert | 1513, 15 | | | | | x | |
| Newman, Joan | 1489 | | | | | x | |
| ——, Thomas | 1490-91 | | | x | | | |
| Nicol, Joan | 1485-91 | | | | | x | |
| Nolesham, Beatrice | 1485 | | | | | x | |
| ——, Hugh | 1485 | | | x | | | |
| Norton, Isabella | 1485; | x | | | | x | |
| | 1486-91 | x | | | | | |
| Nottyngham, Alice | 1485-91 | | | | | x | |
| ——, Elizabeth | 1510 | | | | | x | |
| ——, Isabella | 1497; | x | | | | | |
| | 1498 | | x | | | | |
| ——, John | 1497; | | | x | | | |
| | 1498; | | | x | | | |
| | 1509 | x | | | | | |
| ——, wife of John* | 1500; | x | | | | | |
| | 1505; | | | | | x | |
| | 1511; | x | | | | | |
| | 1512; | | | | | x | |
| | 1513; | x | | | | | |
| | 1516, 18 | | | | | x | |
| | | | | | | | |
| Ocorne, wife of Henry | 1498 | | | | | x | |
| Oliver, William | 1545 | | | x | | | |
| Osse, wife of John | 1512 | | | | | x | |
| Osteler, Elizabeth wife of William | 1533-34; | x | | | | | |
| | 1536; | x | x | | | | |
| | 1537-45 | x | | | | | |
| ——, William | 1534, 37-38, 40-45 | | | x | | | |
| | | | | | | | |
| Pacy, Agnes | 1494-95; | x | | | | | |
| | 1496; | | | | | x | |
| | 1497-98 | x | | | | | |
| Page, wife of John | 1511; | | | x | | | |
| | 1545 | | | | | x | |
| Papworth, John | 1517; | | | x | | | |
| | 1520 | | | | x | | |
| ——, wife of John | 1518 | x | | | | | |
| Parker, Alice | 1485-87, 1500-01, 03 | | | | | x | |
| Passelowe, John | 1486-91 | | | x | | | |
| Pelle, Robert | 1520, 25, 27-33 | | | | | | x |
| ——, William | 1537-38 | | | | | | x |
| Peynton, William | 1527-29 | | | x | | | |
| Pope, Margaret | 1501, 03, 05 | x | | | | | |
| ——, Marion | 1509, 11 | x | | | | | |
| Porter, Joan | 1485-87 | | | | | x | |
| ——, wife of William* | 1503 | | | | | x | |
| Prentys, wife of Thomas | 1522-23 | x | | | | | |

| Name | Year(s) | Brewer | Baker | Butcher | Fishmonger | Retailer | Candlemaker |
|---|---|---|---|---|---|---|---|
| Prestwode, Joan | 1497-98 | x | | | | | |
| ———, wife of Simon* | 1485-86 | x | | | | | |
| Prior, Nicholas | 1539-40 | | | x | | | |
| ———, Richard | 1505; | x | | | | | |
| | 1509 | x | x | | | | |
| ———, wife of Richard | 1505; | | | | | x | |
| | 1511; | x | | | | | |
| | 1512 | | | | | x | |
| | 1513; | x | | | | | |
| | 1515-18 | | | | | x | |
| Punt, wife of Robert | 1516, 20 | | | | | x | |
| Rede, Agnes | 1485-89 | x | | | | | |
| Reginald, Alice | 1485-89; | x | | | | | |
| | 1490; | x | | | | x | |
| | 1491 | | | | | x | |
| Reginald (no first name) | 1536-37 | | | x | | | |
| ———, Thomas | 1486-90 | | | | x | | |
| Relton, Bryant | 1498, 1500 | | | x | | | |
| Rumborough, Elena | 1485-91 | | | | | x | |
| ———, Joan | 1485 | | | | | x | |
| Saddeler, Nicholas | 1485-89 | | | x | | | |
| Salmon, Joan wife of John | 1505; | | | | | x | |
| | 1509; | x | | | | x | |
| | 1517-18, 20; | | | x | | | |
| | 1522-23, 25 | x | x | | | | |
| ———, Margaret | 1503 | | | | | x | |
| Savage, Richard | 1503, 16-18 | | | x | | | |
| ———, Marjorie wife of Richard | 1509-10, 12 | | | | | x | |
| Scot, Alice | 1485 | | | | | x | |
| Seman, Robert de Hunts | 1495 | | | | | | x |
| Sheter, Richard | 1494 | | | x | x | | |
| Skelton, wife of William | 1525, 27-28 | | | | | x | |
| ———, William | 1527 | | | | | | x |
| Stacy, wife of John | 1511; | x | | | | | |
| | 1515 | | | | | x | |
| Staughton, John of St. Neots | 1518, 20, 22-23, 26-28 | | | x | | | |
| Stekke, wife of William | 1500 | | | | | x | |
| Stevens, John | 1515; | | | x | | | |
| | 1516-17; | | | x | x | | |
| | 1518, 20, 22-23, 25-29, 32-34 | | | x | | | |
| ———, wife of Richard | 1503 | | | | | x | |
| Stoke, wife of John* | 1500-01 | | | | | x | |
| ———, Joan | 1485-87 | | | | | x | |
| ———, John | 1485-91; | | | x | | | |
| | 1498; | | | | x | | x |
| | 1500; | | | x | | | x |
| | 1501 | | | x | | | |
| Strynger, wife of William | 1496-97 | | | | | x | |

| Name | Year(s) | Brewer | Baker | Butcher | Fishmonger | Retailer | Candlemaker |
|---|---|---|---|---|---|---|---|
| Suel, Margaret | 1485-91; | | | | | x | |
| | 1494, 97-98 | x | | | | | |
| Swan, wife of Thomas | 1497 | | | | | x | |
| Sydebotom, Agnes | 1485-86 | x | | | | | |
| ——, Thomas | 1485 | | | x | | | |
| Taylor, Margery wife of William | 1503, 05, 09-11 | | | | | x | |
| ——, wife of John | 1494 | | | | | x | |
| ——, wife of Richard | 1525 | | | | | x | |
| ——, Katherine | 1497 | | | | | x | |
| Thompson, wife of Robert | 1512 | | | | | x | |
| ——, wife of Thomas | 1512 | | | | | x | |
| ——, wife of William | 1501; | | | x | | | |
| | 1503 | | | | x | | |
| Tothe, William de Brampton | 1496 | | | x | | | |
| Turneskewe, Alice | 1486-91, 94-98, 1500-01, 03 | | | | | x | |
| ——, Joan | 1485 | | | | | x | |
| Tym, John de Hunts | 1525-27 | | | | x | | |
| ——, Thomas | 1528-31 | | | | x | | |
| Ussher, Alice | 1489-91, 94-98, 1500-01, 03 | x | | | | | |
| Vontte, Isabella | 1488-91 | | | | | x | |
| Vynter, wife of John | 1513, 16, 18, 22-23, 25-27 | x | | | | | |
| Warde, John | 1533 | | | | x | | |
| Warener, Margaret | 1529 | | | | | x | |
| Watteson, Thomas | 1485-86 | | | x | | | |
| Wellys, Agnes wife of Simon | 1525-29, 32-34, 36-37; | x | | | | | |
| | 1543, widow | | | x | | | |
| Welyam, Beatrix | 1485 | | | | | x | |
| West, Agnes wife of Richard | 1487-91 | x | | | | | |
| ——, Alice | 1526-30, 32 | x | x | | | | |
| ——, Joan* | 1494-96 | | | | | x | |
| ——, Joan wife of Richard | 1500-01, 03, 05, 09-13 16, 22-23, 25 | x | | | | | |
| ——, John | 1518 | x | | | | | |
| ——, Richard | 1494; | | | x | | | |
| | 1495; | | | | x | | |
| | 1496; | | | x | | | |
| | 1497, 1500-01, 03; | | | x | | | x |
| | 1505, 09, 13, 15-18, 20, 22 | | | x | | | |
| Whyte, wife of Robert | 1542-43 | | | x | | | |
| Whytghthede, Thomas of Hunts | 1494, 96-98, 1501 | | | x | | | |
| Wilkinson, Katherine | 1485 | | | | | x | |
| Willison, Joan | 1494-95 | | | | | x | |
| ——, Margaret | 1497 | | | | | x | |

| Name | Year(s) | Brewer | Baker | But-cher | Fish-monger | Retailer | Candle-maker |
|---|---|---|---|---|---|---|---|
| Wode, Robert (Oud) Villa | 1522 | | x | | | | |
| Wodecroft, Thomas | 1496-97 | | | x | | | |
| Woodward, John | 1485-89 | | x | | | | |
| Wright, Agnes | 1485-91 | | | | | x | |
| ——, Godfrey | 1487-89 | | | x | | | |
| ——, Isabella | 1486-91 | | | | | x | |
| ——, wife of William | 1512-13, 16-18, 20 | | | | | x | |
| Wydyr, Joan wife of Thomas | 1503 | | | | | x | |
| Wyld, Marion* | 1503 | x | | | | | |
| ——, wife of John | 1505, 13, 15-16, 18, 30, 32-34 | x | | | | | |
| ——, wife of Thomas | 1522 | x | | | | | |
| Wynd, Richard | 1510 | | | | x | | |
| Wyre, John | 1501 | | | x | | | |
| Wyse of Hunts | 1496 | | | | | x | |
| Yattys, wife of John | 1525; 1538-42 | x | | | | x | |

# Appendix 6

## Individuals Receiving Liberty of the Town of Godmanchester, 1400-1549

An asterisk (*) indicates that the children are noted as being under 12 years of age.

| Year | Name | Pledged | Not Pledged | Amount | |
|------|------|---------|-------------|--------|---|
| 1400 | Harleston, Richard, baker | | x | 10s. | |
| | Hosyer, John | | x | 6s. | 8d. |
| | Rumborough, William | | x | 20s. | |
| | Wafrere, John | x | | 12s. | |
| 1401 | Alleyson, John | x | | 13s. | 4d. |
| | Benet, Thomas | x | | 6s. | 8d. |
| | Bryon, John son of William de Yelling | x | | 10s. | |
| | Everard, William, de Swavesey | | x | 26s. | 8d. |
| | Grawnhurst, John, butcher | | x | 8s. | |
| | Grene, Richard, miller | | x | 6s. | 8d. |
| | Hancock, John | x | | 6s. | 8d. |
| | Heyrypp, John and son Richard | | x | 7s. | |
| | Horteyrs, Nicholas | | x | 6s. | 8d. |
| | Myrydew, William, chaplain | | x | 6s. | 8d. |
| | Ponder, William | | x | 20s. | |
| | Ryngwood, Roger | x | | 6s. | 8d. |
| | Scharp, John | | x | 10s. | |
| 1402 | Rowthe, Walter, draper | | x | 8s. | |
| 1403 | Ferrour, Richard, de Raveley | x | | 13s. | 4d. |
| | Fisher, John, smith | | x | 6s. | 8d. |
| | Wright, John, shepherd, and sons Thomas and William | | x | 6s. | 8d. |
| 1404 | Crandon, William, potter | | x | 7s. | |
| | Freman, John, smith | x | | 10s. | |
| | Herd, Henry | x | | 10s. | |
| | King, Thomas | | x | 6s. | 8d. |
| 1405 | Nobyl, William | | x | 6s. | 8d. |
| | Ovyrton, Nicholas | | x | 10s. | |
| | Rede, John | | x | 12s. | |
| | Waleys, Henry | | x | 20s. | |
| 1406 | Broke, William, miller | | x | 6s. | 8d. |
| | Ponder, John | | x | 6s. | 8d. |
| | Porter, John jr. and son John | | x | 8s. | |

| Year | Name | Pledged | Not Pledged | Amount | |
|------|------|---------|-------------|--------|--|
| | Taylor, Roger | | x | 20s. | |
| | West, Richard, taylor | | x | 6s. | 8d. |
| 1407 | Clerk, John | | x | 6s. | 8d. |
| | Couryour, John | | x | 10s. | |
| | Dally, Lord John, chaplain | | x | 6s. | 8d. |
| | Taylor, William, | | | | |
| | de Brington and son Robert | | x | 6s. | 8d. |
| 1408 | Grome, Richard | | x | 6s. | 8d. |
| | Prior, Thomas | | x | 6s. | 8d. |
| | Underwode, Robert | | x | 6s. | 8d. |
| 1409 | Frost, Thomas and sons | | | | |
| | John and William | | x | 7s. | |
| 1410 | Andrew, John | x | | 6s. | 8d. |
| | Athewode, Richard | x | | 6s. | 8d. |
| | Bourwelle, John | x | | 6s. | 8d. |
| | Cossale, Robert | | x | 8s. | |
| | Donham, John | | x | 13s. | 4d. |
| | Porthos, John | x | | 7s. | |
| | Pyke, Thomas | | x | 6s. | 8d. |
| | Reygate, William and son Thomas | | x | 10s. | |
| | Robyn, John, de | | | | |
| | Hemingford and son Robert | x | | 8s. | |
| | Wright, Phillip sr. | | | | |
| | and son William | | x | 7s. | |
| 1411 | Barnwell, Thomas | | x | 6s. | 8d. |
| | Grome, William | | x | 6s. | 8d. |
| | Ive, Henry | | x | 6s. | 8d. |
| | Melbourne, John | | x | 6s. | 8d. |
| | Wych, John | | x | 6s. | 8d. |
| | Wythlokke, William | | x | 6s. | 8d. |
| 1413 | Porter, John sr. | | | | |
| | son of John, fisher | x | | 8s. | |
| | Scot, Thomas | | x | 6s. | 8d. |
| 1415 | Burcote, Robert | | x | 6s. | 8d. |
| | Cave, Richard | | x | 6s. | 8d. |
| | Campion, John and | | | | |
| | sons John, Richard | | | | |
| | and Robert | | x | 20s. | |
| | Colles, Isabella | | x | 6s. | 8d. |
| | Gatele, John | | x | 8s. | |
| | Hill, Walter atte | x | | 7s. | |
| | Lavenham, William | x | | 7s. | |
| | Leighton, John | x | | 6s. | 8d. |
| | Morale, Nicholas | x | | 7s. | |
| | Wythirlee, Robert | | x | 6s. | 8d. |
| 1417 | Ade, Lord William de | | | | |
| | Godmanchester | | x | no fine | |
| | Howlond, John | | x | 10s. | |
| | Ive, John, de Hilton | x | | 8s. | |
| | Parys, Godfrey de Offord | | x | 3s. | |

348　　　　　　　　　　　　　　APPENDIX 6

| YEAR | NAME | PLEDGED | NOT PLEDGED | AMOUNT |
|------|------|---------|-------------|--------|
| 1418 | Barbat, John and son Thomas | | x | 8s. |
| | Barber, John and son John | x | | 8s. |
| | Newman, Nicholas and | | | |
| | sons John and John | | x | 8s. |
| | Turner, Simon | x | | 6s. 8d. |
| | Warner, Richard | x | | 6s. 8d. |
| 1419 | Boteler, Robert, de Yelling | x | | 5s. |
| | Bron, William, turner | | x | 6s. 8d. |
| | Chambre, William | x | | 6s. 8d. |
| | Eston, John, farrier | | x | 6s. 8d. |
| | Godeherd, William, glover | x | | 6s. 8d. |
| | Mapyl, William | | x | 7s. |
| | Undyll, John | | x | fine condoned as unable to pay |
| 1420 | Boys, John, fisher, | | | |
| | and son John | x | | 6s. 8d. |
| | Braban, Henry | x | | 8s. |
| | Dawntre, Walter and son Thomas | | x | 7s. |
| | Hornyngtoft, Richard | | | |
| | and son John | x | | 7s. |
| 1421 | Aylmar, John son of Richard | | x | 8s. |
| | Bayngton, William and | | | |
| | sons John and John | x | | 10s. |
| | Grigge, Thomas and sons | | | |
| | John and John | x | | 15s. |
| | Shirham, Lord Henry | | x | 6s. 8d. |
| | Smyth, Robert | x | | 8s. |
| 1422 | Brendehouse, Joan wife | | | |
| | of Robert, de Hemingford, | | | |
| | Abbots and daughter Agnes | | x | 3s. |
| | Bronnyng, John | x | | ? |
| | Howson, John sr. and | | | |
| | John jr. | | x | 7s. |
| 1423 | Baron, Thomas and son John | | x | 7s. |
| | Colles, Richard and | | | |
| | sons John and William | | x | 8s. |
| | Marshall, Robert, weaver | | x | 6s. 8d. |
| | Upholder, John sr. and sons | | | |
| | John jr. and Richard | | x | 13s. 4d. |
| 1424 | Bailey, Thomas and sons | | | |
| | John and Ralph | | x | 8s. |
| | Belcher, Elias and | | | |
| | son William | x | | 7s. |
| | Carter, John | | x | 6s. 8d. |
| | Gardener, Roger and sons | | | |
| | John and William | x | | 7s. |
| | Wappelode, John | | x | 10s. |
| 1425 | Hynle, William | x | | 10s. |
| 1428 | Chamberlayn, Henry | x | | 8s. |
| | Ferwel, Robert, butcher | | | |
| | and sons John and Thomas | | x | 8s. |

| Year | Name | Pledged | Not Pledged | Amount | |
|------|------|---------|-------------|--------|--|
| | Kenynghal, Thomas and son John | x | | 7s. | |
| | Maryot, Edmund and son John | | x | 8s. | |
| | Newman, Thomas and son Robert | x | | 8s. | |
| | Newport, John | | x | 6s. | 8d. |
| | Porthos, John | x | | 6s. | 8d. |
| | Sofham, Bartholomew, de Cambridge and son Thomas | x | | 8s. | |
| | Storme, Robert and son John | x | | 7s. | |
| 1429 | Bonis, Thomas and son John | | ? | 6s. | 8d. |
| | Cale, John | x | | 6s. | 8d. |
| 1430 | Alstrapp, Richard | | x | 8s. | |
| | Chamberlayn, Thomas | | x | 7s. | |
| | Owithwik, Thomas and son Thomas | | x | 7s. | |
| 1431 | Baber, William | | x | 6s. | 8d. |
| | Gottes, William and son Robert | | x | 8s. | |
| | Herneys, John | x | | 6s. | 8d. |
| | Suel, Thomas | | x | 6s. | 8d. |
| | Suel, John | x | | 7s. | |
| | Tulyet, John | x | | 6s. | 8d. |
| 1432 | Chamberlayn, John and sons William and Robert | x | | 6s. | 8d. |
| | Smith, John jr. son of John de Hemingford Abbots | x | | 6s. | 8d. |
| | Waleys, John and son Thomas | x | | 10s. | |
| 1434 | Baron, John sr. de Graveley | | x | 6s. | 8d. |
| | Botelmaker, John alias Sheter and son John | x | | 5s. | |
| | Loveday, William and sons John and Richard | | x | 13s. | 4d. |
| | Stalys, John | x | | 5s. | |
| | Swynford, John, lockyer | x | | 3s. | 4d. |
| 1435 | Bishop, William | x | | 13s. | 4d. |
| | Roseby, Thomas | x | | ( ) | |
| | Stokker, Robert | x | | 10s. | |
| 1436 | Allyngham, Robert and sons John, Robert, Thomas and William | x | | 7s. | |
| | Bishop, John and sons Henry and Thomas | x | | 6s. | 8d. |
| | Cestremaker, Richard and son Thomas | | x | 6s. 8d. | |
| | Gefferyson, Thomas | | x | 8s. | |
| | Marche, William, wever | x | | 6s. | 8d. |
| | Sly, Robert and son William | | x | 7s. | |
| | Sly, Thomas | x | | 6s. | 8d. |
| 1437 | Brawn, John | x | | 13s. | 4d. |
| | Chycheley, John and sons John and William | x | | 10s. | |
| | Dobbyn, Robert and son Richard | x | | 6s. | 8d. |
| | Lucas, John | x | | 8s. | |
| | Ripple, Henry | x | | 6s. | 8d. |

| Year | Name | Pledged | Not Pledged | Amount | |
|------|------|---------|-------------|--------|---|
| 1438 | Baret, John, sengliman | | x | 5s. | |
| | Cook, John, sengilman | x | | 6s. | 8d. |
| | Cula, John, fuller | x | | 6s. | 8d. |
| | Eclde, Thomas, chaplain | | x | (2s.) | |
| | Fille, Thomas | x | | 6s. | 8d. |
| | Herryson, Walter | x | | 6s. | 8d. |
| | Porter, John | x | | 6s. | 8d. |
| | Robyn, Godfrey, *wulshev* and | | | | |
| |    sons Richard and William | x | | 5s. | |
| | Wryght, Robert and son Thomas | x | | 5s. | |
| 1441 | Amyson, John de Wynge Rutland | x | | 8s. | |
| | Kyng, John de Steeple Gidding | x | | 6s. | 8d. |
| 1442 | Blake, Walter | x | | 5s. | 10d. |
| | Hanson, George | | x | 3s. | 4d. |
| | Horewode, William | x | | 13s. | 4d. |
| | Mayhew, John | x | | 10s. | |
| 1444 | Corby, John | x | | 3s. | |
| | Corby, William | x | | 3s. | |
| 1445 | Abyngdon, Thomas | | x | 6s. | 8d. |
| | Grene, John de London | | x | 7s. | |
| | Schylling, John | x | | 6s. | |
| | Stukeley, Thomas | | x | 3s. | |
| 1446 | Gerard, John | | x | 3s. | 4d. |
| 1449 | Bokyngham, John | x | | 3s. | 4d. |
| | Folkes, John and sons | | | | |
| |    John and Richard | x | | 16s. | 8d. |
| | Lomb, John | x | | 3s. | 4d. |
| | Mayle, Richard and sons | | | | |
| |    John and Thomas | x | | 11s. | |
| | Vande, John | | x | 6s. | 8d. |
| 1450 | Baron, John | x | | 6s. | |
| | Deeke, Nicholas | x | | 3s. | 4d. |
| | Folkys, John | x | | 8s. | |
| | Huesson, Robert | x | | 3s. | 4d. |
| | Levot, John | x | | 3s. | 4d. |
| | Lushton, John | x | | 7s. | |
| | Marke, Robert | x | | 4s. | |
| | Vincent, John and son Richard | x | | 6s. | 8d. |
| 1452 | Brace, Richard, taylor | x | | 8s. | |
| | Emley, John | x | | 13s. | 4d. |
| | Nevsham, William, taylor | x | | 5s. | |
| 1456 | Dyconsen, Richard | | x | 4s. | |
| | Holme, William | x | | 5s. | |
| | Lynsey, James | | x | 4s. | |
| | Motte, John sr. and son John | | x | 13s. | 4d. |
| | Parysch, John | | x | ( ) | |
| 1463 | Beet, John | | x | 10s. | |
| | Bowle, Hugh and sons | | | | |
| |    John and Richard | | x | 6s. | 8d. |

| Year | Name | Pledged | Not Pledged | Amount |
|------|------|---------|-------------|--------|
| | Chycheley, Richard | | x | 10s. |
| | Frost, Thomas | | x | 6s.  8d. |
| | Goodman, John | | x | fine not stated |
| | Vincent, John, thatcher | | x | 5s. |
| 1464 | Druell, Robert | | x | 10s. |
| | Maryot, Thomas | | x | 6s.  8d. |
| | Misterton, Thomas | | x | 3s.  4d. |
| | Rede, William | | x | 3s.  4d. |
| | Sheter, Richard | | x | 6s.  8d. |
| 1465 | Baker, John, fisher | | x | 8s. |
| | Blokke, William | | x | 6s.  8d. |
| | Burton, John | | x | ( ) |
| | Hoggekyns, Richard | | x | 6s.  8d. |
| | Mayle, William | | x | 3s. |
| | Rede, John | | x | 5s. |
| | Turneskewe, John | | x | 4s. |
| | Wryghte, William | | x | 5s. |
| | Younge, John | | x | 5s. |
| 1466 | Roof, John | x | | 5s. |
| 1472 | Bottersmyth, John | | x | 2d. |
| | Smyth, John | | x | ( ) |
| 1473 | Ingram, William | | x | 4s. |
| 1474 | Eydrop, William | | x | 3s.  4d. |
| | Gray, Thomas | | x | 3s.  4d. |
| | Williamson, John | | x | 3s.  4d. |
| 1475 | Barnard, Robert | | x | 10s. |
| | Fecas, Thomas | | x | 10s. |
| | Gressop, John | | x | 4s. |
| | Johnson, John | | x | 4s. |
| | Rowne, William | | x | 6s.  8d. |
| 1478 | Daniel, John | | x | 5s. |
| 1479 | Broke, Henry | | x | 6s.  8d. |
| | Dixi, John | | x | 8s. |
| | Hedley, Matthew | | x | 1s.  8d. |
| | Leftrik, John | | x | 10s. |
| | Nicholas, Robert | | x | 6s.  8d. |
| | Taylor, John, barker | | x | 3s.  4d. |
| | Wryght, William | | x | 1s.  8d. |
| 1480 | Bunn, John | x | | 2s. |
| | Davy, John | x | | 6s.  8d. |
| | Gille, William | x | | 3s.  4d. |
| | Gyllane, John | x | | 4s. |
| | Hiche, William | | x | 2s. |
| | Nicholle, William | x | | 10s. |
| | Orwell, William | x | | 16s.  8d. |
| | Wryght, William | x | | 2s. |
| 1481 | Arnborough, John | x | | 1s.  8d. |
| | Blassell, Thomas | x | | 1s.  8d. |
| | Brewster, Thomas, clerk | x | | 5s. |
| | Grene, Henry | x | | 6s.  8d. |

| Year | Name | Pledged | Not Pledged | Amount |
|------|------|---------|-------------|--------|
|  | Lucas, John | x |  | 10s. |
|  | Warde, Thomas | x |  | 10s. |
| 1482 | Abney, Robert |  | x | ( ) |
|  | Adam, John jr. |  | x | 5s. |
|  | ——, John of Cambridge |  | x | 13s. 4d. |
|  | Barbour, Thomas of Hemingford Abbots |  | x | 10s. |
|  | Feld, John and son William | x |  | 26s. 8d. |
|  | Fyncheham, Thomas |  | x | 26s. 8d. |
|  | Gurreny, Robert |  | x | 12d. |
|  | Kyng, John |  | x | 1s. 8d. |
|  | Lolam, John | x |  | 13s. 4d. |
|  | Matthew, John |  | x | 3s. 4d. |
|  | Pope. Thomas of Hemingford Abbots with his son |  | x | 16s. 8d. |
|  | Townshende, Richard | x |  | 13s. 4d. |
|  | Wallse, Richard | x |  | 6s. |
| 1484 | Tothe, William |  | x | 6s. 8d. |
|  | Lumbard, John |  | x | 6s. 8d. |
|  | Samt, Richard |  | x | 13s. 4d. |
| 1485 | Adam, Thomas |  | x | 2s. |
|  | Asshe, John | x |  | 1s. 8d. |
|  | Bayous, John |  | x | 3s. 2d. |
|  | Feld, William |  | x | no fine |
|  | Tothe, Richard | x |  | 5s. |
| 1486 | Baron, John |  | x | 2s. |
|  | Bulward, John | x |  | 3s. 4d. |
|  | Clarke, Steven | x |  | 5s. |
|  | Cokman, Thomas | x |  | 10s. |
|  | Hermet, William |  | x | 1s. 4d. |
|  | Laxton, Thomas | x |  | 40s. |
|  | Marten, Robert | x |  | 3s. |
|  | Miles, John | x |  | 8s. |
|  | Mody, John | x |  | 5s. |
|  | Shalford, John | x |  | 2s. |
|  | Trayley, Henry | x |  | 3s. |
|  | West, Richard | x |  | 7s. |
|  | Wryght, Godfrey and son Henry | x |  | 8s. |
| 1487 | Archeboulde, Robert | x |  | 2s. |
|  | Basse, William |  | x | 3s. 4d. |
|  | Goodwyn, William |  | x | no fine |
|  | Massey, Thomas | x |  | 6s. 8d. |
|  | Olyff, Robert |  | x | 1s. 4d. |
|  | Parker, Thomas |  | x | 1s. 4d. |
|  | Rydmer, Robert |  | x | 1s. 4d. |
| 1488 | Ansell, Fremandus | x |  | 8s. |
|  | Boswell, Thomas | x |  | 3s. |
|  | Clarke, John de Buckden |  | x | 6s. 8d. |
|  | Coke, Thomas and son John | x |  | 5s. |
|  | Goodrych, John |  | x | 2s. |

| Year | Name | Pledged | Not Pledged | Amount | |
|------|------|---------|-------------|--------|---|
| | Hanson, Thomas, alias cobbler | | x | ( ) | |
| | Herlle, Thomas | | x | 5s. | |
| | Laxton, John | x | | 6s. | 8d. |
| | Melbourne, William jr. | x | | 3s. | 4d. |
| | Mildenhall, John | x | | 4s. | |
| | Pope, William son of | | | | |
| |     Thomas Prepositus | | x | 2s. | |
| | Robynson, John | | x | 1s. | 8d. |
| | Smyth, John | | x | 2s. | |
| | Stevens, Richard | x | | 6s. | |
| | Thomson, John | | x | 2s. | |
| 1489 | Breton, Thomas | | x | 2s. | 4d. |
| | Est, William and son Henry | x | | 6s. | |
| | Frances, John and son William | x | | 6s. | |
| | Garnet, John | | x | 2s. | |
| | Horn', Robert | x | | 20s. | |
| | Reginald, John | | x | 2s. | |
| | Salmon, John | x | | 8s. | |
| | Schyllyng, John[1] | | x | | 12d. |
| | Smyth, William, chaplain | | x | | 20d. |
| | Ussher, John and son Richard | x | | 33s. | 4d. |
| 1490 | Beeke, William | x | | 10s. | |
| | *Gretham, William and sons | | | | |
| |     Robert, Thomas and William | x | | 6s. | |
| | Pelle, William | | x | 1s. | 8d. |
| 1491 | Bryce, John | x | | 6s. | |
| | Cawdwell, Robert | | x | | 12d. |
| | Holme, Bartholomew | | x | 10s. | |
| | Holme, William | x | | 6s. | |
| | Hope, Thomas | x | | 4s. | |
| | Michelson, Patrick | x | | 5s. | |
| | Mymmes, William | x | | 5s. | |
| | Orwell, John, canon | x | | 3s. | 4d. |
| | Sare, Valentine | x | | 3s. | 4d. |
| | Sewale, Thomas | x | | 12s. | |
| | Taylor, John | x | | 6s. | 8d. |
| 1492 | Barnard, William | x | | 3s. | 4d. |
| | Bellhorn, Robert | x | | 3s. | 4d. |
| | Chycheley, Robert | x | | 2s. | 8d. |
| | Haryngton, John | x | | 2s. | 6d. |
| | Mynt, William | x | | 4s. | |
| | Passlowe, Godfrey | x | | 3s. | |
| | Vyntner, William | x | | 8s. | |
| 1493 | Axtun, Master Robert, | | | | |
| |     vicar of the vill | | x | 10s. | |
| | Brown, William de Hereford | x | | 6s. | 8d. |
| | Clerk, John | | x | 4s. | |

[1] John Schylling was re-admitted to the Liberty.

| Year | Name | Pledged | Not Pledged | Amount |
|------|------|---------|-------------|--------|
| | Judde, John de Ripton | x | | 6s. 8d. |
| | Monyment, Thomas | | x | 4s. |
| | Tadlowe, Godfrey | x | | 6s. 8d. |
| 1494 | Bewe, Alexander | x | | 2s. |
| | Clerk, Richard | x | | 3s. 4d. |
| | *Charte, John sr. and sons John jr. and Henry | | x | 3s. 4d. |
| | Dey, John | | x | 2s. 4d. |
| | Devette, John and son William | | x | no fine |
| | Ede, William | | x | 2s. |
| | Elson, Robert | x | | 4s. |
| | Fawn, Richard | x | | 3s. 4d. |
| | Goneld, Master John | x | | 2s. |
| | Goneld, John | | x | 6s. 8d. |
| | Lyveret, Robert | x | | 6s. 8d. |
| | Ostun', Richard, servant of William Pacy | x | | 3s. 4d. |
| | Pacy, William | x | | 10s. |
| | Punt, John | x | | 1s. 4d. |
| | Verly, Richard and two children | | x | 2s. |
| | Walke, William | x | | 10s. |
| | Whyte, Robert | | x | 1s. 8d. |
| | Wytham, Richard | | x | 1s. 4d. |
| 1495 | Aplond, John | | x | 3s. |
| | Bennet, William | | x | 12d. |
| | Brandon, John | | x | 6s. 8d. |
| | Edward, Thomas | x | | 6s. 8d. |
| | Gravy, Thomas | | x | 10s. |
| | Lord, William | x | | 2s. |
| | May, Thomas | x | | 3s. |
| | Smyth, Henry | x | | 13s. 4d. |
| 1496 | Avery, John | x | | 2s. |
| | Bryddar, Thomas | | x | 2s. |
| | Croxton, John | x | | 3s. 4d. |
| | Freman, William | x | | 2s. |
| | Grene, Henry | | x | 1s. 8d. |
| | Hay, George | x | | 2s. |
| | Huys, Richard, alias Taylor | x | | 2s. |
| | Osse, Thomas, clerk | x | | 6s. 8d. |
| | Palgrave, William | x | | 1s. 8d. |
| | Truplosse (first name not noted) | | x | 8s. |
| | Wodecroft, Thomas | | x | 6s. 8d. |
| 1497 | Alanisthaw | | x | 1s. 8d. |
| | Cubye, John | | x | 3s. 4d. |
| | Couper, John | | x | 4s. 8d. |
| | Gonell, John de Caxton | | x | 13s. 4d. |
| | Johnson, William | | x | 1s. 8d. |
| | Myghton, John | x | | 2s. 8d. |
| | Smyth, Thomas | x | | 6s. 8d. |
| | Smyth, William | | x | 2s. 8d. |

| Year | Name | Pledged | Not Pledged | Amount |
|------|------|---------|-------------|--------|
| 1498 | Bawdwyn, Thomas and son William | | x | 3s. |
| | Gibson, James | | x | ( ) |
| | Wane, Ralph | x | | 12d. |
| 1499 | Judd, Thomas | | x | 10s. |
| 1500 | Lovell, John and son Thomas | | x | 7s. |
| | Parker, William jr. | | x | 12d. |
| | Sparhawke, Thomas | | x | 10s. |
| | Squire, John | | x | 2s. |
| | Squire, Thomas | | x | 1s. 4d. |
| 1501 | Aplond, Thomas | x | | 12d. |
| | Chycheley, John | | x | 6s. 8d. |
| | Coke, John | x | | 2s. |
| | Dorraunt, John and son John | | x | 6s. 8d. |
| | Dorraunt, Robert and son William | x | | 3s. |
| | Effranges, James | x | | 1s. 8d. |
| | Gilby, Rase | x | | 1s. 4d. |
| | Henby, William | x | | 2s. 8d. |
| | Judd, Thomas de Ripton | x | | 7s. |
| | Laxton, Thomas son of John | x | | 12d. |
| | Manipenny, William jr. | x | | 12d. |
| | Pope, Margery and son Hugh | | x | 5s. |
| 1502 | Austin, Robert | x | | 3s. 4d. |
| | Barbour, Thomas | | x | 3s. 4d. |
| | Bukk, John | | x | 6s. 8d. |
| 1503 | Acton, Henry, chaplain | | x | 5s. |
| | Alcock, John | | x | 10s. |
| | *Crispin, Thomas and sons John and William | x | | 6s. 8d. |
| | Hedde, John | | x | 10s. |
| | Kyreketon, William | | x | 12d. |
| | Masse, William | | x | 13s. 4d. |
| | Page, Adam | | x | 2s. |
| | Plumer, Thomas | | x | 4s. |
| | Punt, Thomas | | x | 3s. 4d. |
| | Smyth, William | | x | 1s. 4d. |
| | Thomson, Thomas | | x | 2s. |
| | Whytyng, William | x | | 20s. |
| 1504 | Beneham, Richard | | x | 4s. |
| | Parrot, John of London | | x | 5s. |
| | Woodcock, Richard | | x | 4s. |
| 1505 | Astewood, Thomas | | x | 1s. 4d. |
| | Gredley, John | | x | fine not stated |
| | Lacy, William | x | | 2s. |
| | Martin, John | x | | 6s. 8d. |
| | Matersay, John | | x | 1s. 8d. |
| | Townshende, William | | x | 2s. 8d. |
| | Ussher, William and son John | x | | 26s. 8d. |
| 1506 | Eliot, John and sons Richard and John | | x | 5s. |
| | Harforth, John | | x | 6s. 8d. |

| Year | Name | Pledged | Not Pledged | Amount |
|------|------|---------|-------------|--------|
|  | Johnson, Andrew |  | x | 13s.  4d. |
|  | Kyng, John |  | x | 13s.  4d. |
|  | Roke, John |  | x | 2s. |
|  | Wylde, Thomas | x |  | 6s.  8d. |
| 1507 | Farthyngton, William |  | x | 5s. |
|  | Gyldyrdale, William |  | x | 2s. |
|  | Hogan, William |  | x | 3s.  4d. |
|  | Hyham, Robert |  | x | 2s. |
|  | Marshall, Thomas | x |  | 6s.  8d. |
|  | Roper, Thomas |  | x | 3s.  4d. |
|  | Steven, John |  | x | 5s. |
| 1508 | Buknell, John |  | x | fine not stated |
|  | Large, John |  | x | 6s.  8d. |
|  | Polle, John |  | x | 6s.  8d. |
|  | Seman, Robert |  | x | 6s. 8d. |
|  | Wood, John, gentleman |  | x | 20s. and paid directly |
|  | Wynde, John[2] |  | x | 7s. |
| 1509 | Dalton, William, the farmer of the rectory |  | x | 10s. |
|  | Goodwyn, Henry |  | x | 1s.  8d. |
|  | Laddysdale, Richard | x |  | 2s. |
|  | Lawres, James de Huntingdon | x |  | 6s.  8d. |
|  | Leffyn, William | x |  | 6s.  8d. |
|  | Lockington, John[3] | x |  | 2s. |
|  | Oldham, William |  | x | 1s.  8d. |
|  | Spenser, Robert and son John from Welbe |  | x | 3s. |
|  | Swyman, Robert | x |  | 2s. |
|  | Vayyse?, John |  | x | 3s.  4d. |
| 1510 | Barford, Richard |  | x | 1s.  4d. |
|  | Brown, Hugh, carver |  | x | 2s. |
|  | Desney, John |  | x | 2s.  8d. |
|  | Faxon, John |  | x | 1s.  8d. |
|  | Gredley, John[4] |  | x | 4d. |
|  | Haber, John | x |  | 2s. |
|  | Ingrave, Thomas |  | x | 2s. |
|  | Jaye, Edmund |  | x | 6s.  8d. |
|  | Lovell, Thomas |  | x | fine not stated but states did pay the fine |
|  | Taylor, Amys, widow |  | x | 6s.  8d. |

[2] John Wynde had been evicted from the Liberty of Godmanchester for crimes against the vill, but in 1508 he was re-admitted.

[3] John Lockyngton was re-admitted into the Liberty in 1509, after having been evicted from the town for malfactions against the Liberty and neighbour.

[4] John Gredley was re-admitted to the Liberty in 1510.

| Year | Name | Pledged | Not Pledged | Amount |
|------|------|---------|-------------|--------|
| | Taylor, Thomas | | x | 3s. 4d. |
| | Wynde, Richard | | x | 2s. 8d. |
| 1511 | Abram, William | | x | 1s. 8d. |
| | Adych, John | | x | 2s. |
| | Ayr, Robert de London | x | | 3s. 4d. |
| | Bettes, John and John Hosteler[5] | | x | 2d. |
| | Grene, Richard | | x | 8d. |
| | Grene, Robert | | x | no fine |
| | Jordan, William | | x | no fine |
| | Kyng, William | | x | 1s. 8d. |
| | Smyth, William heir of Henry | | x | 2s. |
| | Stacy, John | | x | 4s. |
| | Thornhec, Thomas | | x | 1s. 8d. |
| | Wynge, Thomas | | x | 5s. |
| 1512 | Beeke, Walter | x | | 4s. |
| | Cokman, Edward | | x | 2d. |
| | Dyttynsall, Thomas | | x | 3s. 4d. |
| | Gene, Robert | | x | 1s. 8d. |
| | Gryne, William with Peter Sawton | | x | 2s. 8d. |
| | Hancock, Thomas | x | | 1s. 8d. |
| | Kelson, William | x | | 3s. 4d. |
| | Lane, Henry | | x | 1s. 4d. |
| | Orwode, John | | x | 2s. |
| | Pacy, Thomas | | x | 8d. |
| | *Prior, Richard and sons Nicholas, Thomas and William | | x | 3s. 4d. |
| | Richardson, William | x | | 3s. 4d. |
| | Schylling, Thomas | | x | 2d. |
| | Tokton, Christopher | | x | 1s. 2d. |
| | Woodkooke Christopher with John Woodkooke | | x | 12d. |
| 1513 | Bayttam, John | | x | ( ) |
| | Clark, Richard | | x | 12d. |
| | Clark, Richard formerly of Broughton | x | | 5s. |
| | Coke, Robert | | x | 5s. |
| | Lawncester, William with Robert Norreys and Robert Neel | | x | 2s. 4d. |
| | Nicholas, Robert | | x | ( ) |
| 1514 | Gracyon, John | | x | 2s. 4d. |
| | Hawdwyn, Roger | | x | 5s. |
| | Meyerson, John | | x | 2s. 4d. |
| | Rede, Robert | | x | 3s. 4d. |
| | Sandon, John | | x | 5s. |
| | Styll, George | x | | 3s. 4d. |

[5] Now and again, it is noted that a individual asking for Liberty of the town brings another person with him, and they share the fine. Such were John Bettes and John Hosteler.

| YEAR | NAME | PLEDGED | NOT PLEDGED | AMOUNT |
|------|------|---------|-------------|--------|
| 1515 | Blaxton, Richard | | x | 4s. |
| | Manners, Jasper | | x | 20s. |
| | Pelle, Robert | | x | 26s. 8d. |
| | Wylson, John | | x | 2s. |
| 1516 | Bekynsall, Adam | | x | 10s. |
| | Ensham, John | | x | 3s. 4d. |
| | Graveny, Thomas | | x | 12s. |
| | Hunt, Richard | | x | 1s. 8d. |
| | May, John | x | | 10s. |
| | Moryent, John | | x | 3s. |
| | Stryven, Thomas | | x | 2s. 4d. |
| | Sufhweke, Thomas | | x | 2s. |
| 1517 | Bennett, Robert | | x | 2s. |
| | Dawloke, James | | x | 10s. |
| | James, Robert | | x | 13s. 4d. |
| | Marshall, John | | x | 2s. 8d. |
| | Papworth, John | | x | 3s. 4d. |
| | Porter, Robert | | x | 1s. 8d. |
| | Stilton, William | | x | 3s. 4d. |
| | Roysseley, Robert, alias Stoughton | | x | 6s. 8d. |
| | Tanner, Edmund | | x | 2s. |
| | Taylor, Richard | x | | 12d. |
| | Vyntner, Richard | | x | 2s. |
| | Wood, Henry | x | | 1s. 8d. |
| 1518 | Adam, John | | x | 5s. |
| | Anys, William | | ? | ? |
| | Holme, Thomas | x | | 2s. |
| 1519 | Bennet, John | | x | 1s. 8d. |
| | Bennet, Oliver | x | | 6s. 8d. |
| | Brandon, John[6] | | ? | no fine |
| | Clement, Richard | | x | 13s. 4d. |
| | Manderston, George | x | | 2s. |
| | Pacy, Thomas[7] | | x | no fine |
| | Prior, Richard[8] | | x | 8d. |
| | Robyn, Richard[9] | | x | 6s. 8d. |
| | Royssley, Robert[10] | | x | no fine |
| | *Tryg, Thomas and son Thomas | | x | 4s. 8d. |

[6] John Brandon was re-admitted to the Liberty. Previously he had been evicted for crimes against the vill.

[7] Thomas Pacy was re-admitted to the Liberty after having been evicted for crimes against the vill.

[8] Richard Prior was re-admitted to the Liberty.

[9] Richard Robyn was evicted for malfactions against the bailiffs, and then re-admitted in 1519.

[10] Robert Royssley was evicted for crimes against the vill and then re-admitted in 1519.

| Year | Name | Pledged | Not Pledged | Amount |
|------|------|---------|-------------|--------|
| | Wynter, John and sons, John Robert, Adam and William, as well as Richard Clark[11] | | x | 6s. 8d. |
| 1520 | Bryerley, Robert | | x | 2s. |
| | Desney, John | | x | 1s. 4d. |
| | Desney, John[12] | | x | 1s. 4d. |
| | Hawkyns, John and Richard | | x | 2s. 8d. |
| | Koynne, William[13] | | x | 2s. |
| | Pelle, William | | x | 1s. 4d. |
| | Rossew, John | | x | 4s. |
| | Scot, Richard[14] | | x | no fine |
| | Wylde, John[15] | x | | 6s. 8d. |
| | Wylsson, John | x | | 2s. |
| 1521 | Berde, Thomas, vicar of church | | x | 6s. 8d. |
| | Brown, John, shoemaker | | x | 3s. 4d. |
| | Carter, John | | x | 2s. |
| | Dalton, Thomas | | x | 10s. |
| | Garlond, Richard | | x | 1s. 8d. |
| | Haryson, Robert servant of John Boleyn | | x | 12d. |
| | Hoge, Lawrence | x | | 1s. 8d. |
| | Hosteler, William | x | | 2s. |
| | Kyngston, Christopher | | x | 2s. 8d. |
| | *Moroke, Robert and son Robert jr. | | x | 6s. 8d. |
| | Papworth, John[16] | | x | 12d. |
| | P'at, Christopher | | x | 2s. 8d. |
| | Ruhome, William, servant of John Frere | | x | 3s. |
| | Scorbe, John | | x | 5s. |
| | Tomkyn, John | x | | 3s. 4d. |
| | Younge, Thomas | x | | 3s. 4d. |
| 1522 | Janson, Robert | x | | 3s. 4d. |
| | Knyghton, Thomas | | x | 3s. 4d. |
| 1523 | Anton, John | | x | 3s. 4d. |
| | Berder, William | | x | 13s. 4d. |
| | Brown, Richard | | x | 12d. |
| | Bushe, Ralph | | x | 2s. |
| | Hardyng, Thomas | | x | 5s. |

[11] John Wynter must have brought his own clerk with him, as Richard Clark's fine was included in John amount of 6/8d. Also, John's children were all under 12 years of age.

[12] This is not a duplication of names: Thursday before the feast of St. Matthew 12 Henry VIII (20 September 1520), John Desney 16d + John Desney 16d. (i.e., 1/4d).

[13] William Koynne was re-admitted to the Liberty.

[14] Richard Scot was re-admitted to the Liberty.

[15] John Wylde was re-admitted to the Liberty.

[16] John Papworth was re-admitted to the Liberty.

| Year | Name | Pledged | Not Pledged | Amount |
|---|---|---|---|---|
| | Kyng, John | | x | 1s. 8d. |
| | Yeatt', John, glover | x | | 1s. 8d. |
| 1524 | Boll', John | x | | 12d. |
| | Hebden, Robert, miller | | x | 6s. 8d. |
| | Thasnok, Thomas de Brampton | | x | 8s. |
| | Woodberne, John | | x | 2s. |
| 1525 | Archebould, Edmund, chaplain | | x | amount not stated, paid by hand |
| | Bruar, Thomas | | x | 12d. |
| | Bydre, William, sengilman | | x | amount not stated, paid by hand |
| | Cardar, Thomas | | x | 8s. |
| | Harforth, Robert de Huntingdon | x | | 10s. |
| | Kokkys, John, chaplain | | x | amount not stated, paid by hand |
| | Scyrpley, Robert | | x | amount not stated |
| 1526 | Boston, Robert | x | | 7s. |
| | Garlond, John | | x | 3s. 4d. |
| | Glapthorne, Robert | | x | 10s. |
| | Howson, John | | x | 1s. 4d. |
| | Key, John | | x | 12d. |
| 1527 | Aperke, James | x | | 2s. |
| | Batte, William | | x | 12d. |
| | *Boro, John and son Simon | | x | 3s. |
| | Byllington, John | | x | 1s. 4d. |
| | Byllington, Richard, priest | | x | 1s. 8d. |
| | Cross, John | x | | 2s. 4d. |
| | Firmary, Robert | | x | 1s. 4d. |
| | Kyrby, Thomas | | x | 1s. 4d. |
| | Nobyl, Thomas | | x | 1s. 8d. |
| | Sewster, William jr. | | x | 6s. 8d. |
| | Toppan, Christopher | | x | 1s. 4d. |
| | Trevet, John de Stanton | | x | 10s. |
| 1528 | Bardd, Nicholas | | x | 6s. 8d. |
| | Herdman, William | | x | 2s. |
| | *Hutton, Richard and son Lawrence | | x | 2s. |
| | M'my, John | | x | 7s. 8d. |
| | Reymant, John | | x | 4s. |
| | Same, Robert de Caxton | | x | 3s. 4d. |
| | Syman, John | x | | 6s. 8d. |
| | Tykson, Thomas | | x | 6s. 8d. |
| 1529 | Allen, William | | x | 2s. 8d. |
| | Goddard, Robert | | x | 6s. 8d. |
| | [Gony?], William | | x | 10s. |
| | May, William | | x | 5s. |
| | Massey, Robert | | x | (  ) |
| | Parider, Thomas de London, husbandman | | x | 13s. 4d. |
| | *Passe, John and son William | | x | 20s. |
| 1530 | Grene, William atte | | x | 2s. |

| Year | Name | Pledged | Not Pledged | Amount | |
|---|---|---|---|---|---|
| | Gyleman, Richard | x | | ( ) | |
| | Manyfeld, Thomas | x | | ( ) | |
| | Parny, Robert | | x | 1s. | 2d. |
| | Wynde, Jarne' | | x | 1s. | 2d. |
| 1531 | Abram, William jr. | | x | 3s. | 4d. |
| | Byllington, John sr. | x | | 3s. | 4d. |
| | Cokkys, Richard | x | | 13s. | 4d. |
| | *Flesshar, John and sons | | | | |
| | Robert and Thomas | | x | 13s. | 4d. |
| | Glover, Richard | x | | 1s. | 4d. |
| | Hutton, Henry | | x | ( ) | |
| | Ke[l]om, Thomas | | x | 2s. | |
| | Martre, Robert, gentleman | | x | ( ) | |
| | Peyton, Thomas, priest | | x | ( ) | |
| | Slowe, Robert | | x | ( ) | |
| 1532 | Ballivawat, Thomas | | x | 1s. | 4d. |
| | Beeke, William de Stowe | | x | 26s. | 8d. |
| | Byrryngton, George | | x | | 12d. |
| | Forth, Henry | | x | 6s. | 8d. |
| | Hoggeson, John | | x | 4s. | 8d. |
| | Michel, John | | x | 1s. | 4d. |
| | Parys, John | | x | 4s. | |
| | Peynton, William | | x | 3s. | 4d. |
| | Skathur, William | | x | 1s. | 4d. |
| | Stele, Thomas | | x | | 10d. |
| | Walshe, John son of Gilbert | | x | 1s. | 4d. |
| | Warener, William | | x | 1s. | 4d. |
| | Willem, John | | x | 3s. | 4d. |
| | Woodward, William, gentleman | | x | 26s. | 8d. |
| | Wythnowe, John | | x | | 12d. |
| 1533 | Chambre, Robert | | x | | 14d. |
| | Chersey, Robert, alias Chertsey | | | | |
| | de London, merchant of | | x | 20s. | |
| | Coknyrley, William | | x | 2s. | |
| | Dicous, John, priest | | x | ( ) | |
| | Ebbys, William | | x | 3s. | 4d. |
| | Greneleff, Henry | | x | 1s. | 4d. |
| | Small, John | x | | 2s. | |
| | Stilton, Richard | | x | 1s. | 8d. |
| | Toll, William | | x | 1s. | 8d. |
| | Yey, Thomas sr. | | x | 6s. | 8d. |
| 1534 | Crofter, John de London, grocer | | x | 40s. | |
| | Hall, John de Doddington | | x | 2s. | |
| | Harrys, Robert | | x | 2s. | 4d. |
| | Hayward, Hewgeny | | x | 13s. | 4d. |
| | Jekys, Thomas | | x | 2s. | |
| | Kelton, Thomas | | x | 1s. | 4d. |
| | Mewar, John | x | | 1s. | 4d. |
| | Plumer, Robert | | x | 3s. | 4d. |

APPENDIX 6

| Year | Name | Pledged | Not Pledged | Amount |
|------|------|---------|-------------|--------|
| | Pope, John and William sons of Hugh Pope de Hemingford | | x | 3s. 4d. |
| | Randell, John, smyth | | x | 3s. 4d. |
| | Walis, William de Huntingdon | | x | 4s. 8d. |
| | Ward, John | | x | 2s. |
| | *Woodward, Thomas and sons James and William | | x | 33s. 4d. |
| | Woodward, William, labourer | | x | 2s. |
| 1535 | Venell, John | | x | 3s. |
| | Warde, Robert | x | | 6s. 8d. |
| 1536 | Collyns, William | | x | 12s. |
| | Dormer, Michael de London | | x | 40s. |
| | Edward, Renold | | x | (  ) |
| | Flesher, William | | x | (  ) |
| | Goostwyke, Agnes | x | | 3s. 4d. |
| | Laxton, William, son of Thomas | | x | 3s. 4d. |
| | Manderston, Thomas | x | | 3s. 4d. |
| | Melbron, John | | x | (  ) |
| | Mydylton, William | | x | 3s. 4d. |
| | Salmon, William son of John de Drayton | | x | (  ) |
| | Sanford, John | x | | 2s. |
| | Stokell, William | x | | 20s. |
| | Willem, Robert son and heir of Richard | | x | 3s. 4d. |
| | Wyttyngton, Edward | x | | 3s. 4d. |
| 1537 | Dawlaye, Robert | | x | 2s. |
| | Hawslope, Richard | | x | 12d. |
| | Hawdwyn, Rowlond | | x | 16s. 8d. |
| | Normanton, William | | x | 6s. 8d. |
| | Oliver, William | | x | 3s. |
| | Rowlond, Robert | | x | 3s. 4d. |
| | Wryght, Edmund | | x | 2s. |
| 1538 | Alake, William[17] | | x | no fine |
| | Brown, Thomas | | x | 1s. 8d. |
| | Dalton, John son of William | | x | 2d. |
| | Desney, Robert | | x | 1s. 4d. |
| | Dorraunt, John jr. son of John de Houghton | | x | 12d. |
| | Everard, William | | x | 1s. 4d. |
| | Feppis, William de London, pewterer | | x | 13s. 4d. |
| | Gaddisby, Thomas de St. Neots | | x | 6s. 8d. |
| | Gate, Robert | | x | 2s. |
| | Herdman, John | | x | 2s. |
| | Hobson, Walter | | x | 2s. |
| | Kent, Rafele | | x | 2s. |

[17] William Alake was re-admitted to the Liberty.

| Year | Name | Pledged | Not Pledged | Amount | |
|---|---|---|---|---|---|
| | Lawrence, William, subhayward de Offord | | x | 2s. | |
| | Merpe, Thomas de Ramsey | x | | 6s. | 8d. |
| | Peakbowche, Thomas | | x | 3s. | 4d. |
| | Smyth, Robert | | x | 1s. | 8d. |
| | Smyth, Richard, alias Bonsay | | x | 1s. | 8d. |
| | Thornbane, Christopher | | x | 6s. | 8d. |
| 1539 | Clarke, John, taylor | | x | 2s. | 4d. |
| | Ferland, Giles | x | | 3s. | 4d. |
| | Lawrence, Thomas | | x | 10s. | |
| | Payet, James | | x | 2s. | |
| 1540 | Barber, Walter | | x | 3s. | 4d. |
| | Borowe, Edward | | x | 3s. | 4d. |
| | Caxsem, Phillip | x | | 1s. | 4d. |
| | *Halle, Thomas and son Thomas | x | | 5s. | |
| | Hogesone, Richard | x | | 1s. | 4d. |
| | Lambard, William | x | | 3s. | |
| | Lambard, John | | x | 3s. | |
| | Sargent, Richard | x | | 1s. | 4d. |
| | Tryse, Thomas de Brampton | | x | 11s. | 8d. |
| | Wyntryngham, William | x | | 6s. | 8d. |
| 1541 | Andrew, John | | x | 5s. | |
| | Bygge, William | x | | 1s. | 4d. |
| | Frere, Thomas[18] | | x | 12d. | |
| | Ingrome, John | | x | 1s. | 8d. |
| | Osteler, John | | x | 1s. | 8d. |
| | Osteler, John[19] | | x | 1s. | 8d. |
| | Rokis, Christopher, clerk | | x | ( ) | |
| | Robard, Richard, yeoman | | x | ( ) | |
| | Squire, William | | x | 1s. | 4d. |
| 1542 | Gravend, Robert | x | | 6s. | 8d. |
| | Thody, Walter | | x | 3s. | 4d. |
| 1543 | Collyne, Thomas | | x | 20s. | |
| | Freman, John | | x | 2s. | |
| | Crage, John | | x | 3s. | 4d. |
| | Hammund, Thomas | x | | 3s. | 4d. |
| | Harson, Robert, glover | | x | 2s. | |
| | Jenys, John | | x | 2s. | |
| | Peras, John | | x | 3s. | |
| | Tage, John | x | | 2s. | |
| | Tage, Anthony | | x | 4s. | |
| | Watson, John de Huntingdon, sengilman | | x | 6s. | 8d. |
| | Worlond, John | x | | 5s. | |
| | Wytehed, Mychell | x | | 6s. | 8d. |

[18] Thomas Frere was re-admitted to the Liberty.
[19] Sic; there were two John Ostelers receiving the Liberty (15 September 1541 = 33 Henry VIII)

| YEAR | NAME | PLEDGED | NOT PLEDGED | AMOUNT | |
|------|------|---------|-------------|--------|---|
| 1544 | Bulle, William | | x | 5s. | |
| | Crowbe, William | | x | | 12d. |
| | *Dawson, Henry, miller, | | | | |
| | and sons John, Robert and William | | x | 10s. | |
| | Langton, William, yeoman | | x | 20s. | |
| | Mawlaye, Robert | x | | 3s. | 4d. |
| | Shepherd, John | | x | 2s. | |
| | Squire, Christopher | | x | 1s. | 8d. |
| | Watson, William | | x | 2s. | |
| 1545 | Foster, John | | x | 2s. | |
| 1546 | Baptiste, John, Borrono, | | | | |
| | de London, merchant | | x | 20s. | |
| | Boor, John de London, grocer | | x | ( ) | |
| | Hardyng, Thomas and son John | | x | 13s. | 4d. |
| | Herdman, Thomas | x | | 1s. | 8d. |
| | Ibbote, John de Brampton | | x | 6s. | |
| | Kok, Thomas | | x | ( ) | |
| | Warde, Martin | | x | 3s. | 4d. |
| 1547 | Skote, John of de Kaptone | | x | 6s. | |
| | Norton, John de London | | | | |
| | and son Arthur | | x | 5s. | |
| | Nicholason, John | | x | 6s. | |
| | Leston, John | | x | 1s. | 4d. |
| | Frere, William, glover | | x | ( ) | |
| | Mason, John | | x | 1s. | 4d. |
| | Selby, Christopher and son Thomas | | x | 4s. | |
| 1549 | Allyne, Richard | | x | 1s. | 8d. |
| | Amore, John | | x | 2s. | |
| | Beeman, Thomas | | x | 2s. | |
| | Bennett, Edward | | x | 2s. | 8d. |
| | Crayforthe, John | | x | 2s. | |
| | Dragner, John of London, merchant | | x | 13s. | 4d. |
| | Ferne, Robert | | x | 6s. | 8d. |
| | Lyne, Randall | | x | 6s. | |
| | Sewster, Nicholas, gentleman | | x | 20s. | |
| | Smarfote, John | | x | 2s. | 8d. |
| | Wilson, Edward, yeoman | | x | 10s. | |

# Appendix 7

## Breakdown of Fines for Liberty in Chronological Order

| YEAR | 6/8d | 7/- | 8/- | 10/- | 12/- | 13/4d | 20/- | 26/8d | TOTAL |
|---|---|---|---|---|---|---|---|---|---|
| 1400 | 1 | | | 1 | 1 | | 1 | | 4 |
| 1401 | 6 | 1 | 1 | 2 | | 1 | 1 | 1 | 13 |
| 1402 | | | 1 | | | | | | 1 |
| 1403 | 2 | | | | | 1 | | | 3 |
| 1404 | 1 | 1 | | 2 | | | | | 4 |
| 1405 | 1 | | | 1 | 1 | | 1 | | 4 |
| 1406 | 3 | | 1 | | | | 1 | | 5 |
| 1407 | 3 | | | 1 | | | | | 4 |
| 1408 | 3 | | | | | | | | 3 |
| 1409 | | 1 | | | | | | | 1 |
| | 20 | 3 | 3 | 7 | 2 | 2 | 4 | 1 | 42 |

| YEAR | 3/- | 5/- | 6/8d | 7/- | 8/- | 10/- | 13/4d | 20/- | no fine | TOTAL |
|---|---|---|---|---|---|---|---|---|---|---|
| 1410 | | | 4 | 2 | 1 | 2 | 1 | | | 10 |
| 1411 | | | 6 | | | | | | | 6 |
| 1413 | | | 1 | | 1 | | | | | 2 |
| 1415 | | | 5 | 3 | 1 | | | 1 | | 10 |
| 1417 | 1 | | | | 1 | 1 | | | 1 | 4 |
| 1418 | | | 2 | | 3 | | | | | 5 |
| 1419 | | 1 | 4 | 1 | | | | | 1 | 7 |
| | 1 | 1 | 22 | 6 | 7 | 3 | 1 | 1 | 2 | 44 |

| YEAR | 3/- | 6/8d | 7/- | 8/- | 10/- | 13/4d | 15/- | not legible | TOTAL |
|---|---|---|---|---|---|---|---|---|---|
| 1420 | | 1 | 2 | 1 | | | | | 4 |
| 1421 | | 1 | 2 | | 1 | | 1 | | 5 |
| 1422 | 1 | | 1 | | | | | 1 | 3 |
| 1423 | | 1 | 1 | 1 | | 1 | | | 4 |
| 1424 | | 1 | 2 | 1 | 1 | | | | 5 |
| 1425 | | | | | 1 | | | | 1 |
| 1428 | | 2 | 2 | 5 | | | | | 9 |
| 1429 | | 2 | | | | | | | 2 |
| | 1 | 8 | 8 | 10 | 3 | 1 | 1 | 1 | 33 |

| YEAR | [2/-] | 3/4d | 5/- | 6/8d | 7/- | 8/- | 10/- | 13/4d | not legible | TOTAL |
|---|---|---|---|---|---|---|---|---|---|---|
| 1430 | | | | | 2 | 1 | | | | 3 |
| 1431 | | | | 4 | 1 | 1 | | | | 6 |
| 1432 | | | | 2 | | | 1 | | | 3 |
| 1434 | | 1 | 2 | 1 | | | | 1 | | 5 |
| 1435 | | | | | | | 1 | 1 | 1 | 3 |
| 1436 | | | | 4 | 2 | 1 | | | | 7 |
| 1437 | | | | 2 | | 1 | 1 | 1 | | 5 |
| 1438 | 1 | | 3 | 5 | | | | | | 9 |
| | 1 | 1 | 5 | 18 | 5 | 4 | 3 | 3 | 1 | 41 |

| YEAR | 3/- | 3/4d | 5/10d | 6/- | 6/8d | 7/- | 8/- | 10/- | 11/- | 13/4d | 16/8d | TOTAL |
|---|---|---|---|---|---|---|---|---|---|---|---|---|
| 1441 | | | | | 1 | | 1 | | | | | 2 |
| 1442 | | 1 | 1 | | | | | 1 | | 1 | | 4 |
| 1444 | 2 | | | | | | | | | | | 2 |
| 1445 | 1 | | | 1 | 1 | 1 | | | | | | 4 |
| 1446 | | 1 | | | | | | | | | | 1 |
| 1449 | | 2 | | | 1 | | | | | 1 | 1 | 5 |
| | 3 | 4 | 1 | 1 | 3 | 1 | 1 | 1 | 1 | 1 | 1 | 18 |

| YEAR | 3/4d | 4/- | 5/- | 6/- | 6/8d | 7/- | 8/- | 13/4d | not legible | TOTAL |
|---|---|---|---|---|---|---|---|---|---|---|
| 1450 | 3 | 1 | | 1 | 1 | 1 | 1 | | | 8 |
| 1452 | | | 1 | | | | 1 | 1 | | 3 |
| 1456 | | 2 | 1 | | | | | 1 | 1 | 5 |
| | 3 | 3 | 2 | 1 | 1 | 1 | 2 | 2 | 1 | 16 |

| YEAR | 3/- | 3/4d | 4/- | 5/- | 6/8d | 8/- | 10/- | fine not stated | not legible | TOTAL |
|---|---|---|---|---|---|---|---|---|---|---|
| 1463 | | | | 1 | 2 | | 2 | 1 | | 6 |
| 1464 | | 2 | | | 2 | | 1 | | | 5 |
| 1465 | 1 | | 1 | 3 | 2 | 1 | | | 1 | 9 |
| 1466 | | | | 1 | | | | | | 1 |
| | 1 | 2 | 1 | 5 | 6 | 1 | 3 | 1 | 1 | 21 |

| | 2d | 1/8d | 3/4d | 4/- | 5/- | 6/8d | 8/- | 10/- | not legible | TOTAL |
|---|---|---|---|---|---|---|---|---|---|---|
| 1472 | 1 | | | | | | | | 1 | 2 |
| 1473 | | | | 1 | | | | | | 1 |
| 1474 | | | 3 | | | | | | | 3 |
| 1475 | | | | 2 | | 1 | | 2 | | 5 |
| 1478 | | | | | 1 | | | | | 1 |
| 1479 | | 2 | 1 | | | 2 | 1 | 1 | | 7 |
| | 1 | 2 | 4 | 3 | 1 | 3 | 1 | 3 | 1 | 19 |

| YEAR | 12d | 1/4d | 1/8d | 2/- | 2/4d | 3/- | 3/2d | 3/4d | 4/- | 5/- | 6/- | 6/8d | 7/- | 8/- | 10/- | 13/4d | 16/8d | 20/- | 26/8d | 33/4d | 40/- | no fine | TOTAL |
|---|---|---|---|---|---|---|---|---|---|---|---|---|---|---|---|---|---|---|---|---|---|---|---|
| 1480 |  |  |  | 3 |  |  |  | 1 |  | 1 |  | 1 |  |  | 1 |  | 1 |  |  |  |  |  | 8 |
| 1481 |  |  | 2 |  |  |  |  |  |  | 1 |  | 1 |  |  | 2 |  |  |  |  |  |  |  | 6 |
| 1482 | 1 |  | 1 |  |  |  |  | 2 |  |  | 1 | 1 |  |  | 1 | 3 | 1 |  | 2 |  |  | 1 | 13 |
| 1484 |  |  |  |  | 1 |  |  |  |  |  |  | 2 |  |  |  |  |  |  |  |  |  |  | 3 |
| 1485 |  |  | 1 | 1 |  |  | 1 |  |  | 1 |  |  |  |  |  |  |  |  |  |  |  | 1 | 5 |
| 1486 |  | 1 |  | 2 |  | 2 |  |  | 1 | 2 |  | 1 |  | 2 | 1 |  |  |  |  |  | 1 |  | 13 |
| 1487 |  | 3 |  | 1 |  |  |  |  |  |  |  | 2 | 1 |  |  |  |  |  |  |  |  |  | 7 |
| 1488 |  |  | 1 | 4 |  | 1 |  | 1 | 1 | 2 | 1 |  |  | 1 |  | 1 |  | 1 |  |  |  | 1 | 15 |
| 1489 | 1 |  | 1 | 2 |  |  |  | 1 |  |  | 2 |  |  | 1 |  |  |  |  |  | 1 |  | 1 | 10 |
| | 2 | 4 | 6 | 13 | 1 | 3 | 1 | 5 | 2 | 7 | 4 | 7 | 1 | 4 | 5 | 4 | 2 | 1 | 2 | 1 | 1 | 4 | 80 |

| YEAR | 12d | 1/4d | 1/8d | 2/- | 2/4d | 2/6d | 2/8d | 3/- | 3/4d | 4/- | 4/8d | 5/- | 6/- | 6/8d | 8/- | 10/- | 12/- | 13/4d | no fine | TOTAL |
|---|---|---|---|---|---|---|---|---|---|---|---|---|---|---|---|---|---|---|---|---|
| 1490 |  |  | 1 |  |  |  |  |  |  |  |  |  |  | 1 |  | 1 |  |  |  | 3 |
| 1491 | 1 |  |  |  |  |  |  |  | 2 | 1 |  | 2 | 2 | 1 |  | 1 | 1 |  |  | 11 |
| 1492 |  |  |  |  |  | 1 |  | 1 | 2 | 2 |  |  |  |  | 1 |  |  |  |  | 7 |
| 1493 |  |  |  |  |  |  |  | 2 |  | 1 |  |  |  | 2 |  | 1 |  |  |  | 6 |
| 1494 |  | 2 |  | 4 |  |  | 1 | 1 | 4 | 1 | 1 |  |  | 2 |  | 1 |  |  | 1 | 18 |
| 1495 | 1 |  |  |  |  |  | 2 |  |  |  |  |  |  | 2 | 1 | 1 |  | 1 |  | 8 |
| 1496 |  |  | 2 | 5 |  |  |  |  | 1 |  |  |  |  | 2 |  | 1 |  |  |  | 11 |
| 1497 |  |  | 2 | 1 |  |  |  |  | 1 |  |  |  |  | 2 |  |  |  | 1 | 1 | 8 |
| 1498 | 1 |  | 1 |  |  |  |  |  |  |  |  |  |  |  |  | 1 |  |  |  | 3 |
| 1499 |  |  |  |  | 1 |  |  |  |  |  |  |  |  |  |  |  |  |  |  | 1 |
| | 3 | 2 | 6 | 10 | 1 | 1 | 3 | 4 | 10 | 5 | 1 | 2 | 2 | 12 | 2 | 7 | 1 | 2 | 2 | 76 |

## Table 1

| YEAR | 12d | 1/4d | 1/8d | 2/- | 2/8d | 3/- | 3/4d | 4/- | 5/- | 6/8d | 7/- | 10/- | 13/4d | 20/- | 26/8d | fine not stated | TOTAL |
|---|---|---|---|---|---|---|---|---|---|---|---|---|---|---|---|---|---|
| 1500 | 1 | 1 |  | 1 |  |  |  |  |  |  | 1 | 1 |  |  |  |  | 5 |
| 1501 | 3 |  | 1 | 1 | 1 | 1 | 2 |  |  | 2 | 1 |  |  |  |  |  | 12 |
| 1502 |  |  |  | 1 |  |  | 1 | 1 |  | 1 | 1 |  |  |  |  |  | 5 |
| 1503 | 1 |  | 2 |  |  |  |  | 2 | 1 | 1 |  | 1 | 1 | 1 |  |  | 10 |
| 1504 |  |  |  | 2 |  |  |  |  | 1 |  |  |  |  |  |  | 1 | 3 |
| 1505 |  | 1 | 1 |  | 1 |  | 1 |  | 1 | 2 |  |  |  |  |  |  | 7 |
| 1506 |  |  |  | 2 |  | 1 |  |  |  | 2 |  |  |  |  |  |  | 5 |
| 1507 |  | 2 |  |  |  |  |  |  | 2 |  |  |  | 1 | 1 |  |  | 6 |
| 1508 |  |  |  | 1 |  |  |  |  |  | 3 |  | 1 |  |  |  |  | 5 |
| 1509 |  | 1 |  | 3 |  |  | 2 |  |  | 1 |  | 1 | 1 |  | 1 |  | 10 |
|  | 5 | 4 | 4 | 11 | 2 | 2 | 6 | 3 | 5 | 12 | 3 | 4 | 3 | 2 | 1 | 1 | 68 |

## Table 2

| YEAR | 2d | 4d | 8d | 12d | 1/2d | 1/4d | 1/8d | 2/- | 2/4d | 2/8d | 3/- | 3/4d | 4/- | 4/8d | 5/- | 6/8d | 10/- | 12/- | 13/4d | 20/- | 26/8d | fine not stated | not legible | TOTAL |
|---|---|---|---|---|---|---|---|---|---|---|---|---|---|---|---|---|---|---|---|---|---|---|---|---|
| 1510 | 1 |  |  |  |  | 1 | 1 | 2 | 2 | 3 | 2 |  |  |  |  |  |  |  |  |  |  | 1 |  | 12 |
| 1511 | 1 | 1 |  |  |  |  | 3 |  | 1 | 2 | 1 | 1 | 1 |  |  |  |  |  |  |  |  | 2 |  | 12 |
| 1512 | 2 | 1 | 1 | 1 |  | 1 | 2 | 1 | 1 | 1 | 4 |  | 1 |  |  |  |  |  |  |  |  |  | 2 | 15 |
| 1513 |  |  |  |  |  |  |  | 1 |  |  |  | 2 |  | 2 | 2 |  |  |  |  |  |  |  |  | 6 |
| 1514 |  |  |  |  |  |  |  |  |  | 2 |  |  |  | 2 | 2 |  |  |  |  |  |  |  |  | 6 |
| 1515 |  |  |  |  |  |  | 1 | 1 |  |  | 1 |  | 1 |  |  |  |  |  |  |  | 1 |  |  | 4 |
| 1516 |  |  |  |  |  |  | 1 | 1 |  | 1 | 1 |  |  |  |  |  |  | 2 | 1 |  |  |  |  | 8 |
| 1517 |  |  | 1 |  |  |  | 2 | 1 |  | 3 | 2 |  |  |  | 1 | 1 |  | 1 | 1 |  |  |  |  | 12 |
| 1518 |  |  |  |  |  |  |  |  |  | 1 |  | 1 | 1 |  | 1 | 1 | 1 |  | 1 |  |  |  |  | 2 |
| 1519 |  | 1 |  |  |  |  | 1 |  | 1 |  | 1 |  | 2 |  |  | 1 | 1 | 1 | 1 |  |  | 3 |  | 11 |
|  | 3 | 1 | 3 | 1 | 2 | 10 | 13 | 4 | 4 | 1 | 11 | 3 | 7 | 2 | 4 | 3 | 1 | 2 | 1 | 1 | 1 | 6 | 2 | 88 |

## Table 1 (1520–1529)

| YEAR | 12d | 1/2d | 1/8d | 2/- | 2/4d | 2/8d | 3/- | 3/4d | 4/- | 5/- | 6/8d | 7/- | 8/- | 10/- | 13/4d | 20/- | no fine | TOTAL |
|---|---|---|---|---|---|---|---|---|---|---|---|---|---|---|---|---|---|---|
| 1520 |  | 3 |  | 3 |  | 1 |  |  | 1 |  | 1 |  |  |  |  |  | 1 | 10 |
| 1521 | 2 | 2 |  | 2 |  | 2 | 1 |  |  | 1 | 2 |  |  | 1 |  |  |  | 16 |
| 1522 |  |  |  | 1 |  |  |  | 2 |  |  |  |  |  |  |  |  |  | 2 |
| 1523 | 1 |  | 2 | 1 |  | 1 |  | 1 |  | 1 |  |  |  |  | 1 |  |  | 7 |
| 1524 | 1 |  |  | 1 |  |  |  |  |  |  | 1 |  | 1 |  |  |  |  | 4 |
| 1525 | 1 | 1 |  |  |  |  |  |  |  |  |  |  | 1 | 1 |  |  | 4 | 7 |
| 1526 | 1 |  |  |  |  |  |  | 1 |  |  |  | 1 |  | 1 |  |  |  | 5 |
| 1527 | 1 | 4 |  | 1 | 1 |  |  | 1 |  |  | 1 |  |  | 1 |  | 1 |  | 12 |
| 1528 |  |  | 1 | 2 |  | 1 |  | 2 |  |  | 3 | 1 |  |  |  |  |  | 10 |
| 1529 |  |  |  |  |  | 1 |  | 2 | 2 | 1 | 1 |  |  | 1 | 1 |  | 1 | 7 |
|  | 7 | 8 | 6 | 10 | 1 | 4 | 2 | 9 | 3 | 3 | 9 | 1 | 2 | 5 | 2 | 1 | 6 | 80 |

## Table 2 (1530–1539)

| YEAR | 2d | 10d | 12d | 1/4d | 1/8d | 2/- | 2/4d | 2/8d | 3/- | 3/4d | 4/- | 4/8d | 6/8d | 7/8d | 10/- | 12/- | 13/4d | 16/8d | 20/- | 26/8d | 33/4d | 40/- | no fine | TOTAL |
|---|---|---|---|---|---|---|---|---|---|---|---|---|---|---|---|---|---|---|---|---|---|---|---|---|
| 1530 |  |  |  | 2 |  | 1 | 2 |  |  | 2 |  | 1 |  |  |  |  |  |  |  |  |  |  | 2 | 5 |
| 1531 |  | 1 | 2 | 1 |  | 1 | 2 |  |  |  |  | 1 |  |  |  |  | 2 |  |  |  |  |  | 4 | 10 |
| 1532 |  |  |  | 5 | 2 |  | 1 | 1 |  |  | 1 |  |  |  |  |  |  | 2 |  |  |  |  |  | 15 |
| 1533 |  |  | 1 | 1 | 2 |  | 1 | 1 |  |  |  |  |  | 1 |  |  |  | 1 |  |  |  | 1 | 10 |
| 1534 |  |  |  | 2 |  | 4 | 1 | 3 |  | 1 |  |  |  |  | 1 |  |  |  | 1 | 14 |
| 1535 |  |  |  |  |  |  |  | 1 |  |  | 1 |  |  |  |  |  |  |  |  |  | 2 |
| 1536 |  | 1 |  |  | 1 | 1 |  | 6 |  |  | 1 |  |  |  |  |  |  | 4 | 14 |
| 1537 |  | 1 |  | 2 | 2 | 1 | 1 | 1 |  | 1 |  |  |  |  |  | 1 |  |  | 7 |
| 1538 | 1 | 1 |  | 2 | 3 | 5 | 1 | 1 |  |  | 3 |  | 1 |  |  | 1 | 18 |
| 1539 |  |  |  | 1 |  |  | 1 | 1 | 1 |  | 1 |  |  |  |  | 4 |
|  | 1 | 1 | 4 | 1 | 13 | 5 | 17 | 2 | 2 | 17 | 1 | 2 | 7 | 1 | 2 | 5 | 2 | 4 | 1 | 2 | 2 | 1 | 6 | 99 |

99

## Table 3 (1540–1549)

| YEAR | 12d | 1/4d | 1/8d | 2/- | 2/8d | 3/- | 3/4d | 4/- | 5/- | 6/- | 6/8d | 10/- | 11/8d | 13/4d | 20/- | fine not stated | TOTAL |
|---|---|---|---|---|---|---|---|---|---|---|---|---|---|---|---|---|---|
| 1540 |  | 3 |  | 2 | 2 | 1 |  |  | 1 |  |  |  | 1 |  |  |  | 10 |
| 1541 | 1 | 2 | 3 |  |  |  | 1 |  |  | 1 |  |  |  |  |  | 2 | 9 |
| 1542 |  |  |  |  | 1 |  |  |  |  |  | 1 |  |  |  |  | 2 |
| 1543 |  |  |  | 4 | 1 | 2 | 1 | 1 |  | 1 | 1 |  | 1 |  |  | 12 |
| 1544 | 1 | 1 |  | 2 | 1 | 1 |  | 1 |  | 2 | 1 | 1 |  | 1 |  | 8 |
| 1545 |  | 1 |  | 1 |  |  |  |  |  |  |  |  |  |  | 1 |
| 1546 |  |  | 1 |  |  |  | 1 |  | 1 |  | 1 | 1 |  |  |  | 5 |
| 1547 |  | 2 |  |  | 1 | 1 | 1 |  | 1 |  |  |  | 1 | 1 |  | 6 |
| 1549 |  | 1 | 3 | 2 |  |  |  |  | 1 | 1 | 1 | 1 |  | 1 | 11 |
|  | 2 | 7 | 6 | 10 | 3 | 7 | 2 | 5 | 4 | 4 | 2 | 1 | 2 | 4 | 3 | 64 |

# Appendix 8

## Families and Other Personnel Recorded in Wills

| TESTATOR | DATE OF WILL | DATE OF PROBATE | WIFE | SON(S) | DAUGHTER(S) | OTHERS |
|---|---|---|---|---|---|---|
| ALRED, William | 22 Apr. 1556 | 21 Oct. 1556 | | John* William | Agnes Elizabeth Margaret | |
| ARCHEBOULD, Edmund | 29 Mar. 1558 | 29 Apr. 1558 | | | | **Christopher Squire; Margaret of Warboys, his kinswoman |
| ARMET, Margery, widow | 20 Nov. 1528 | 7 Apr. 1529 | | | | John Howman; Thomas Howman and his wife Alice; Agnes Howman; oldest son of Thomas Howman; **Thomas Lovell and wife Alice; Anne & Robert Lovell; Alice Melbron jr.; Thomas Byrde, vicar; Thomas Garlop |
| ARNOLD, William, husbandman | 15 Aug. 1535 | 27 Sept. 1535 | Joan** | | | |
| AWDWEN (HAWDWYN), Roger | 30 Sept. 1545 | 20 Oct. 1545 | Marion | John | | **Sir Peter, brother; John, his brother; Elena Awdwen, wife of John his servant; Maria & Katherine Beam |
| BAILEY, John | 12 May 1506 | 20 July 1506 | Marion** | John* William* | Agnes* Alice* | |
| BARRE, William | 12 Jan. 1509 | 20 July 1509 | | | | |
| BEATRICE, John | 4 Oct. 1558 | 16 Dec. 1558 | Margaret | Gilbert Nicholas** Thomas* | Elizabeth Awdrie Agnes Elizabeth Joan Isabel | Alice & William Melbron; Agnes Howman* |
| BELL, Thomas | 8 June 1538 | 3 Oct. 1538 | Joan, daughter of Anne Hedley | | | |

* indicates a person under 20 years of age.
** indicates an executor.

| TESTATOR | DATE OF WILL | DATE OF PROBATE | WIFE | SON(S) | DAUGHTER(S) | OTHERS |
|---|---|---|---|---|---|---|
| BENET, Thomas, labourer<br>BENET, Thomas | 4 May 1527<br>14 June 1555 | 29 July 1527<br>29 July 1555 | Elizabeth**<br>Alice**<br>(nee Granger) | William<br>Thomas | Elizabeth Norton | Robert Firmary, son of Elizabeth Benet; William Granger, his father-in-law |
| BENET, William | 2 Sept. 1540 | 13 Dec. 1540 | Margaret** | William | | Agnes and John, son and daughter of his son William; John Ede; Elizabeth, his servant; John Jonson, his servant; William Ede, John Godwyn, William Kyng and William Scharhed, godsons; John Armouth |
| BILLINGTON, John | 5 Aug. 1535 | 27 Sept. 1535 | Agnes** | | Agnes<br>Joan | |
| BIRDERE, William | 28 July 1534 | last day of Feb. 1534 | Elena | | | Elena Firmary; John Watson, his servant; Thomas Cowke |
| BIRDERE, Elena[1] | 27 Apr. 1538 | 3 June 1538 | | William Nicholas | | Robert Nicholas, her husband; Robert Firmary[2], her son-in-law; Elena and Joan, daughters of her son William Nicholas |
| BLAXTON, Richard | 10 Oct. 1526 | 17 Dec. 1527 | Elizabeth** | John<br>Robert<br>Thomas | Elizabeth | |
| BONSAY, John | 20 Jan. 1520 | 16 May 1520 | Margaret** | | | Emma Bonsay; Margaret Finch; Margaret Mortymer; John Betres, his servant |
| BRANDON, John | 20 June 1528 | 27 July 1528 | Alice (nee West) | | | Elizabeth Page, his servant; John Elys of Barn(well) |

[1] This could be her maiden name

[2] Robert Firmary is the son of Elizabeth Benet; see BENET 1527 above

| Name | Date 1 | Date 2 | Relict / widow (**) | Other persons | Children | Beneficiaries / notes |
|---|---|---|---|---|---|---|
| BROWN, William, labourer | 17 Nov. 1528 | 25 Jan. 1529 | Agnes** | Agnes; Joan | John; Richard; William | |
| BULLION (BOLEYN), John | 28 Oct. 1558 | 7 Nov. 1558 | | | | John Goodwyn of Godmanchester; **Richard Newman of Hemingford |
| BURTON, Thomas | 30 Sept. 1505 | ? | Agnes** | Margaret Dorraunt | | John Dorraunt |
| CARLES, John | 2 May 1546 | 20 June 1546 | Parnell** | Agnes Laxton | Henry; Harry | Alice jr., Christopher, Elizabeth and Thomas Laxton, all her grandchildren |
| CARLES, Parnell | 25 Oct. 1558 | 4 Feb. 1559 | | | | |
| CLERK, John | 12 Oct. 1557 | 10 Dec. 1557 | Agnes** | | Thomas; William | |
| COLEN, Walter | 9 Aug. 1543 | 23 Oct. 1543 | | Dorothy | John; Edward; Christopher*; Thomas*; Walter | Sir John, his brother; Henry Frere; William Frere son of other wife; John Page; John, Walter and William Robyn |
| COOK (COCKS), Richard | 28 July 1553 | 21 Oct. 1553 | Margaret** | | Edward; Edmund; William | |
| COOK (COWKE), Joan, widow | (12) June 1533 | 22 Sept. 1533 | | Alice King, wife of John | Thomas** | to every child of John King, her son-in-law; to every child of Thomas Cook |
| CORBY, Renalda, labourer | 6 Mar. 1534 | 29 Nov. 1535 | Elizabeth** | Sybel | William** | |
| DALTON, John | 15 Nov. 1503 | 16 Feb. 1506 | Joan | Agnes | John | |
| DALTON, William | 26 Nov. 1518 | ? | Jane** | | Thomas | |
| DALTON, William, mercer | 6 May 1541 | 19 Sept. 1541 | Elizabeth** | | | |
| DAWLE, Robert[3] | 7 May 1540 | 14 June 1540 | Cristina** | Agnes daughter of Elizabeth King | | John Lambert |

[3] Robert Dawle, could have been a weaver, as he left his looms and shop to John Lambert

| Testator | Date of Will | Date of Probate | Wife | Son(s) | Daughter(s) | Others |
|---|---|---|---|---|---|---|
| Dawson, Henry | 15 Apr. 1555 | 24 May 1555 | Agnes (nee Kirke) | | | Henry Dawson's sister's children, Elizabeth, Emma and Robert Wright from Boslow, Derby; William Wright their father; John Kirke, his brother-in-law; William Kirke, his brother; John of St. Neots, his brother; Henry son of John Dawson of Bedford |
| Desney, John | 29 Nov. 1522 | 26 Feb. 1522 | Agnes** | ** John sr. John | Joan Bron | |
| Desney, John | 17 Apr. 1559 | 20 June 1559 | Joan** | Thomas** | | |
| Digby, William, craftsman | 16 July 1530 | 21 Oct. 1530 | Rose** | | | |
| Edmunds, Richard | 2 Dec. 1545 | 6 Feb. 1545 | | | | John, his brother; Nicholas Swalowe, his son-in-law |
| Este, John, husbandman | 20 Mar. 1530 | 10 Dec. 1530 | Joan | John Henry** | | his mother; Edward Este; Richard Este; John Clerk; Henry Frere; John Seward |
| Este, Henry, husbandman | 17 Nov. 1558 | 3 Mar. 1557 | Margaret | Thomas* | Joan | his mother; his wife's mother |
| Felde, John, goldsmith | 26 Feb. 1485 | 6 Oct. 1486 | Isabella** | | Joan | |
| Freman, William sr. | 3 May 1545 | 9 July 1545 | Anne** | Thomas William | Elena Joan | William Everard, godson; William son of Thomas |
| Frere (Fryer) William | 15 May 1498 | 30 Nov. 1498 | Elena** | | | |
| Frere, William | 3 June 1545 | 9 July 1545 | Alice** | | Sybel Stevenson | Anne, Henry, John, Sybel, Thomas, Thomas jr. and William Stevenson, his grandchildren; Margaret Upchurche |
| Frere, John | 1 Mar. 1547 | 17 July 1547 | Margaret | Thomas | | Anne Frere, daughter of Thomas; Joan, wife of Thomas Frere; Margaret Granger, his sister; Ursula, daughter of Thomas Bowthe; Katherine Senowis, wife of (?); Margaret Morgayn, his servant; Richard Prior jr. |

| | | | | | | |
|---|---|---|---|---|---|---|
| FROST, Thomas | 10 May 1491 | 20 June 1491 | | | Margaret | William Basse; *Alice, daughter of John Frost; Henry Frost; sister of Henry Frost; John Frost of Needingworth |
| FROST, William, sr. | 6 Oct. 1519 | 24 Dec. 1519 | Elena** | John jr. Robert William jr. | | William Nebbis, her son-in-law; children of William Nebbis; Robert Frost; child of William Frost John Ilche** |
| FROST, Alice, widow | 25 Apr. 1538 | 3 June 1538 | Agnes** | | Margaret Nebbis | Jane and Robert, children of Henry Asplond; Robert Holt of St. Neots |
| FULLER, Thomas late of Cottenham, Cambridge | 1550[4] | 11 May 1550 | | *William | | |
| GADDIBYRE, Thomas | 11 Mar. 1547 | 13 Apr. 1548 | Agnes** (nee Stukeley) | | | William, his brother |
| GARLOND, John | 28 July 1537 | 17 Sept. 1537 | Elizabeth** | John sr. John jr. Steven Thomas | Jane | **William Clerk and wife Alice; Alice Gillam, his sister; William Greatham; Thomas and Alice his parents; **Alice wife of Thomas, son of John; William Birdere |
| GARLOP, John | 5 Apr. 1524 | 11 May 1524 | Joan** | | | Marion, his daughter-in-law; John son of Edmund Gybbys |
| GIBBYS, Henry | 15 Aug. 1546 | 23 May 1547 | Elizabeth I (nee Grene[5]) | Edmund John John | Elisabeth Pete | John Bele, his servant; Brigette and Thomas Bele; Cristina Parysh; William Skelton |
| GOODWYN, John | 11 July 1551 | 15 Sept. 1551 | Margaret** | | | |
| GOODWYN, William | 4 Oct. 1550 | 14 Oct. 1550 | Elizabeth** | | | |

[4] Exact date not known
[5] Although not noted in manuscript as nee Grene, Elizabeth daughter of Richard Grene was the wife of Henry Gybbys.

| Testator | Date of Will | Date of Probate | Wife | Son(s) | Daughter(s) | Others |
|---|---|---|---|---|---|---|
| GRANGER, John, sr. | 7 Nov. 1538 | 18 Jan. 1539 | | | | John and Thomas, his brothers; Simon and William Granger; Margaret Bawyne, his servant |
| GRENE, Agnes, widow | 5 July 1544 | 8 Aug. 1544 | | George** | Agnes | Dorothy King, fiance of George Grene; Alice, Agnes, Anne and John Farmer; Elizabeth Howson; Margaret King; Robert Cot |
| GRENE, Richard | 23 Feb. 1535 | 11 Nov. 1535 | Agnes** | George William | Agnes jr. Agnes Alene of London Agnes Gybbys Jane Gyttons | |
| GRANGER, Thomas | 16 Nov. 1544 | 20 July 1545 | Margaret** (nee Frere) | John | | Giles son of John Granger, son of Thomas; Leonard Gyttons, son of Jane |
| GYDE, William, labourer HAWDWYN (AWDWEN), Marion—see AWDWEN | 30 Nov. 1529 23 May 1546 | 26 Mar. 1530 10 June 1546 | | John** | Agnes | Richard Clerk; Elizabeth Clerk her daughter-in-law; Sir John Anderson; John and Elena Hawdwyn; Anne Vyntner, wife of Robert; Jane Vyntner; to each child of Robert Vynter Brother John Anderson |
| HAYS, George | 31 Dec. 1534 | last day of Feb. 1535? | Katherine** | | | |
| HAYS, Katherine | 7 Sept. 1540 | 6 Nov. 1540 | | | | Sir Edward Archbould; William and Katherine Omers; William Lord; William Ostler |
| HEDLEY, Robert, labourer | 12 Mar. 1545 | 10 Apr. 1546 | Anne** | | | **John Scot |

|  | | | | | | |
|---|---|---|---|---|---|---|
| HEDLEY, Anne, formerly the wife of John Scot | 30 May 1546 | 10 June 1546 | | John** | Katherine Knowliss, Joan Bell[8], Alice Mordok | Sir Edward Archbould; Elena Knowliss, grandchild; Anne, Alice, Elizabeth and Margaret Scot |
| HERMAN, Thomas | 31 July 1546 | 15 Sept. 1546 | | | | William, his brother; Ursula Vyntner his sister; Elizabeth Croft, his sister; **Robert Croft, husband of Elizabeth |
| HEYWORTH, Hewgene | 23 Aug. 1545 | 3 Oct. 1545 | Margaret** | | Alice*, Elizabeth*, Joan* | Thomas Aplond; William Barnard of East St.; John William |
| HODGSON, John | 23 June 1547 | 29 July 1547 | Margaret** | Raffe** | | |
| HUGGYN, John | 18 Nov. 1545 | 6 Feb. 1546 | Margaret** | John, John of Abbotsley, Nicholas, Robert | Beatrice | |
| HUGGYN, Margaret, widow | 17 Apr. 1558 | 17 Sept. 1558 | | | | |
| HUNT, Richard | 20 June 1528 | 7 July 1528 | Joan** | | Elena | |
| INGRAM, William | 10 Jan. 1557 | 10 Jan. 1557 | Edith** | | Isabella, Margery, Elizabeth | |
| JONSON, Margaret[6] | 14 Jan. 1527 | 4 Apr. 1528 | | Robert Mayle, her son; **William Mayle, her son | | |
| KING, William | 7 Jan. 1530 | 31 Jan. 1530 | Agnes[7], Agnes | Richard, Robert | | children of Richard King; children of Thomas Pacy |
| LANE, Agnes, widow of Thomas | 5 Aug. 1483 | 25 Oct. 1483 | | | Agnes Shalford | John Bonsay, son of Agnes Lynsey; Agnes Lynsey; John son of Richard Motte; **Agnes daughter of John Stukeley; John Page sr. |

[6] Very likely her maiden name

[7] William King was married twice, and both his wives' names were Agnes.

[8] See Bell family.

| TESTATOR | DATE OF WILL | DATE OF PROBATE | WIFE | SON(S) | DAUGHTER(S) | OTHERS |
|---|---|---|---|---|---|---|
| LAWE, Thomas | 23 Feb. 1518 | 31 Jan. 1518 (sic)? | Elizabeth** | | | Emma Stowe |
| LAXTON, Elizabeth, wife of John | 20 Apr. 1529 | 3 July 1529 | | Robert, and Christopher Hatch, Elizabeth's children | | John, her husband |
| LAXTON, John | 16 Dec. 1539 | 17 Jan. 1540 | | Thomas | | **William son of Thomas Laxton |
| LOCKYNGTON, Alice, widow | 2 Dec. 1545 | 6 Feb. 1546 | | Edmund George John** Richard Robert Thomas** | Anne | |
| LOCKYNGTON, Thomas, son of John | 5 Apr. 1544 | 20 Apr. 1544 | Alice** | | | |
| LOCKYNGTON, Edmund | 17 Jan. 1559 | 27 Jan. 1559 | Katherine** | | | John, his brother |
| LOVEDAY, William | 8 Sept. 1537 | 19 Jan. 1539 | Maude** | | Elyne Richmond Anne Allbour Joan Freman Alice Martyn | William Richmond jr.; William Richmond, his son-in-law |
| LOVELL, Alice, formerly the wife of William Melbourne | 3 Jan. 1543 | 8 Aug. 1543 | | | Alice | Thomas, her husband |
| MANDERSTON, Thomas | 8 Oct. 1536 | 6 Nov. 1536 | Agnes** | John | | |
| MARSHALL, John | 16 Apr. 1544 | 26 June 1544 | Anne (nee Pelle) | Thomas | | Robert Pelle, his father-in-law; John Lockington; William Marshall of Woolley |
| MARSHALL, Thomas | 10 Nov. 1507 | 12 Dec. 1507 | Margaret** | Robert | | |

| Name | Date | Date | | | | Other persons named |
|---|---|---|---|---|---|---|
| MARYOT, Edmund | ?1519 | 24 Dec. 1519 | Agnes** | Richard, William | | |
| MAYHEWE, John | 22 Sept. 1559 | 10 Dec. 1559 | Joan** | Benet, John, Robert | Elizabeth, Jane | |
| MAYLE, Thomas | 5 July 1500 | 8 Oct. 1500 | Alice** | John, John** | | William, his brother |
| MAYLE, Robert | 2 July 1542 | 14 Oct. 1542 | Alice** | Henry, Henry**, John**, Thomas** | Elizabeth, Joan | **Sir Robert Mayle |
| MAYLE, William, husbandman | 9 May 1549 | 3 July 1549 | Alice | | | |
| MONYMENT, Thomas | 4 June 1524 | 24 Nov. 1524 | Katherine** | | | William Pennymaker, his brother; Agnes Stamford |
| MYNT, William | 20 June 1522 | ? | Elizabeth | William** | Agnes, Joan | |
| NELSON, John | 10 Feb. 1558 | 30 June 1559 | Margaret** | Robert*, Robert, Thomas | | **Edmund Cook |
| NELSON, Margaret, widow | 17 Apr. 1559 | 30 June 1559 | | | | |
| NEWMAN, Thomas | 8 Nov. 1485 | 5 Dec. 1495 | Joan** | John** | Agnes | Lord Robert Dobbyn; William Lincoln; John Taylor |
| OSTELER, William | 5 Apr. 1557 | ? Apr. 1557 | | | | |
| PAGE, John | 24 Feb. 1489 | 8 May 1500 | Agnes** | Edward*, William** | | |
| PAXTON, William | 5 Apr. 1559 | 30 June 1559 | Margery** | | | Thomas Elways, his servant; Henry Frere; Edward Menell, his servant; Agnes Marshall; John Marshall, husband of Agnes |
| PELLE, Robert, husbandman | 20 Apr. 1539 | 9 June 1539 | Alice | | | |
| PELLE, William | 22 May 1539 | 20 Aug. 1539 | Agnes** | | | |
| PELMAN, William | 20 Oct. 1529 | 26 Mar. 1530 | Joan** | | | John Goodwyn |
| PELMAN, Joan, widow | 20 May 1551 | 4 Feb. 1552 | | John | | John Pryor, brother's son |
| PRYOR, Thomas | 7 July 1554 | 11 Oct. 1554 | Agnes | Henry | Elizabeth | Margaret Stodale, his mother-in-law; Thomas, his brother; Dorothy Punt |
| PUNT, John, husbandman | 13 Feb. 1532 | 31 Mar. 1533 | Margaret** (nee Stodale) | John, Thomas | | |

| TESTATOR | DATE OF WILL | DATE OF PROBATE | WIFE | SON(S) | DAUGHTER(S) | OTHERS |
|---|---|---|---|---|---|---|
| RELTON, Bryant | 19 Aug. 1553 | 20? Oct. 1553 | Agnes** | sons | Agnes sr. | Thomas Parker |
| SANDEN, John sr. | 25 May 1546 | 15 Sept. 1546 | | John** Robert | Elena Wythanhole Marion Morland | John Nele; two children of Elena |
| SCOTTE, John, see Hedley | 4 June 1544 | 26 June 1544 | Anne** | John | Katherine | John Mordoke; Christopher Mordoke |
| SEWARD, William, labourer | 10 Mar. 1529 | 26 Mar. 1530 | Agnes** | William | | |
| SCHACHERE, William | 21 Sept. 1553 | 21 Oct. 1553 | Emma** | John Thomas William | Marion | |
| SMYTH, Richard | 2 Jan. 1512 | 8 Mar. 1512 | Agnes** | | Dorothy | |
| SNELL, Robert | 2 Nov. 1509? | 30 July 1528 | Joan** | | | |
| STELTON, William | 20 Aug. 1538 | 6 Nov. 1540 | Elizabeth** | John | Agnes Elena | |
| STEVEN, John | 20 Apr. 1535 | 27 Sept. 1535 | Joan** | | Anne Elena | |
| STEYLTON, William | 19 Aug. 1535 | 27 Sept. 1535 | Agnes** | Richard | | |
| STUKELEY, Margaret, widow of John | 20 Aug. 1541 | 6 May 1542? | | | **Agnes Gaddibyre Agnes Jane | Elizabeth Punt; Dorothy Sudbury; Thomas Gaddibyre, husband of Agnes |
| TREGE, Thomas | 21 July 1548 | 15 Sept. 1548 | Florence** | Thomas** | Elizabeth | Elizabeth wife of Thomas son of Thomas; Elizabeth daughter of Thomas, son of Thomas; John and William sons of Awdery Trege; Richard Pacy, William Stevenson, Steven Faldyng, godsons |
| TOWNSHENDE (TURNE-SKEWE), John | 22 Mar. 1505 | 28 July 1506 | Joan** | | | |

|  | | | | | | |
|---|---|---|---|---|---|---|
| UPCHURCHE, John | 24 July 1553 | 20 Oct. 1553 | Margaret** | Henry<br>John<br>William | Elizabeth | John son of John son of Thomas; Alice sister of Thomas |
| UPCHURCHE, Thomas | 22 Sept. 1545 | 1 Dec. 1545 | Anne** | John<br>Richard<br>Thomas | Alice<br>Margaret | |
| VYNTNER, John | 12 July 1543 | 17 Oct. 1543 | Joan[9]<br>Marion | John<br>Robert** | | children of Richard Clerk; William and wife Elizabeth, John's parents; *Robert son of John son of John; *John son of John son of John; Anne and Jane daughters of John; Anne and Jane daughters of Robert, son of John; John son of Robert son of John; Alice, Anne and Joan daughters of John, son of John; Dorothy, Robert and Thomas jr. Pacy |
| VYNTNER, Robert, husbandman | 5 June 1530 | 23 July 1530 | Joan | Thomas* | | Robert son of John Vyntner sr.; Robert son of John Vyntner jr.; **John Vynter, his brother; every child of Thomas Pacy; Alice and Joan daughters of Thomas Bell; John Robyn |
| WARDE, Robert | 17 May 1546 | 10 June 1546 | Alice** | | Anne | Thomas Warde, his kinsman; Anne daughter of Thomas Warde |

[9] John Vynter was married twice.

| Testator | Date of Will | Date of Probate | Wife | Son(s) | Daughter(s) | Others |
|---|---|---|---|---|---|---|
| West, Alice,[10] widow | 10 Dec. 1532 | 27 Jan. 1533 | | | | John Borowe, her kinsman; Thomas Borowe sr.; Alice Cromwell, her servant; John Grace her brother-in-law; William Grace; wife of Robert Butcher; Robert Howis; William Granger; John Miles; Thomas Morgrove; John Robyns; Dorothy Robyns and her sister Agnes; Elizabeth Robyns; Agnes Richardson, her servant; Salman, wife of Stratam?; Agnes Sym |
| White, Robert | 12 Oct. 1543 | 10 Dec. 1543 | Elizabeth | William* | Elyn* | Edward Jonson, son of wife |
| Whitlocke, Thomas | 27 Mar. 1545 | 20 July 1545 | Joan** | | | |

[10] Alice reverts back to her maiden name; she was married to John Brandon.

| | | | | | | |
|---|---|---|---|---|---|---|
| WOODE, Henry | 2 Apr. 1543 | 17 Oct. 1543 | Margaret** (nee Leffyn) | | Alice<br>Anne<br>Jane jr.<br>Joan<br>Margaret<br>Margery<br>Parnell | John, his brother; Roger, his brother; William Leffyn, his father-in-law; Arnold and William Varnham |
| WRIGHT, John | 26 Oct. 1550 | 20 Nov. 1550 | Agnes** | Thomas* | Agnes<br>Anne<br>Annes<br>Agnes<br>Emma | Elena Ede |
| WYLDE, John sr. | 28 Nov. 1531 | 4 May 1532 | Anne** | | | |
| WYLDE, Marion | 23 Jan. 1505 | 25 Feb. 1505 | | | | |
| WYNTNER (VYNTNER)? Richard | 17 May 1546 | 10 June 1546 | | | | Robert Harbour and wife Marion; **William Ibott; Richard and William Sanden Alice and Joan Harson; **Robert Smyth; Richard Stilton; Cecilia, Elizabeth and Fran Stilton John Schanber |

# Appendix 9

## The Involvement of Godmanchester People in the Money Market

The figures in parentheses indicate the number of times a suit appears in the court records. An asterisk when two people are noted together indicates that they shared the debt, very likely as custodians of the guild.

| LENDER | BORROWER | LENDER BORROWED FROM |
|---|---|---|
| Acton, Henry, chaplain | 1503 Robert Chandeler | |
| | Elena Fryre | |
| Acton, Robert, vicar | 1503 John Couper (4)[1] | |
| Adams, John | 1501 John Stacy (2) | |
| Alam, Thomas | 1502 William Henby | 1500 Thomas Mounford |
| Aleyff, Robert | 1501 John Snell | |
| Almouth, John | 1502 William Couper | |
| Archebould, Robert | 1490 William Melbourne | |
| Arnold, Austin | 1491 William Godwyn | 1487 Thomas Bennet |
| | John Smith, labourer | |
| Arnowe, William | 1498 Simon Prestwode | |
| Ascheman, Thomas de (King's?) Lynne | 1500 John Nottingham | |
| Aspenc', John | 1496 Henry Gydding | |
| Asshe, John | 1489 John Grace and Joan executors of William Hildemar | |
| | 1502 William Norman | |
| Aylmar, John | 1493 Thomas Faldyng | |
| Aylred, John | 1484 John Monk | |
| | 1485 William Blokke | |
| | 1486 John Gredley | |
| | Thomas Bennet | |
| | William Mounford | |
| | William Wright | |
| | Roger Cook | |
| | John Sparowe | |
| | 1487 John Barnard | |
| | 1489 Thomas Reynold | 1489 John Bayous sr. |
| | 1490 Thomas Newman | |
| | John Barnard sr.[1] | |

[1] This debts was for oxen and cattle.

| Lender | Borrower | Lender Borrowed from |
|---|---|---|
| | 1491 Thomas Newman | |
| | Thomas Cokman | |
| | 1492 Richard Legge | |
| | John Lawman | |
| | John Matthew | |
| | 1493 Henry Este | |
| | John Glover | |
| | Richard West | |
| | 1494 John Barnard | |
| | William Barnard, wright | |
| | John Foster | |
| | Richard West | |
| | 1495 John Custauns | |
| | William Diggby and | |
| | William Melbourne | |
| | Robert Leveret | |
| | 1496 William Walcar | |
| | John Vincent | |
| | Robert Vont | |
| | Robert Leveret | |
| | 1497 John Gredley | |
| | 1498 Thomas Faldyng | 1498 Thomas Faldyng |
| | 1499 John Mayle | 1499 William Basse |
| | John Gredley | |
| | John Couper | |
| | 1500 Thomas Judd | 1500 Robert Chandeler |
| | William Hilton | John Stokis |
| | John Stokys | |
| | 1501 William Browne jr. | |
| | John Mayle | |
| | Richard West | |
| | 1502 William Pelman | |
| Alde, John | 1493 Thomas Faldyng | |
| Aylred, William | 1487 William Gyle | |
| | John Longe | |
| Bailey, Thomas | | 1489 John Minsterchambre |
| | | 1491 Thomas Cokman |
| | | John Bailey |
| | | 1495 William Melbourne |
| | 1492 William Manipenny (2) | 1496 William Manipenny (2) |
| Bell, Aliswandry | 1496 Richard Clerk | |
| | William Broughton | |
| | 1497 Thomas May | |
| | 1500 Richard Chycheley | |
| Balle, Thomas de Kakakton | 1501 Walter Beny | 1501 Walter Beny |
| Balle, Thomas | 1484 William Edmond | |
| | 1485 Simon Prestwode | |
| | 1486 John Martin (2) | 1495 William Manipenny |
| Ballard, Robert | 1497 John Page | 1498 John Snell |
| Barber, John | 1500 Richard Rit' | |

| LENDER | BORROWER | LENDER BORROWED FROM |
|---|---|---|
| Barnard, John, artisan | 1486 John Gredley | 1487 John Aylred |
|  |  | Robert Conys |
|  | 1488 William Nottingham | 1488 William Parker |
|  | 1489 Richard Holme | 1489 John Holme |
|  |  | Richard Holme |
|  |  | William Manipenny |
|  |  | Thomas Norton |
|  | 1490 Roger Cook |  |
|  | William Godwyn |  |
|  | 1492 Robert Nicholas |  |
| Barnard, John jr. | 1488 Richard Kyng |  |
|  | John Snell (2) | 1489 Thomas Frost |
|  | 1491 Thomas Cokman | 1491 Thomas Cokman |
|  | 1493 Patrick Michelson | 1495 William Basse |
|  |  | 1496 William Mynt |
|  |  | 1501 Robert Chandeler (2) |
|  | 1502 William Gonell | 1502 John Tychemarsh |
|  |  | 1503 William Gonell |
|  |  | Thomas Lockyngton |
|  |  | and Thomas Maryot |
| Barnard, John sr., wright | 1497 John Dey sr. | 1494 John Aylred |
|  | 1498 John Bryte |  |
| Barnard, John, sr. | 1487 John Bayous | 1487 John Bayous |
|  | 1489 Thomas Faldyng | 1489 John Clark, servant of |
|  |  | John Draper |
|  |  | Thomas Faldyng |
|  |  | 1490 John Aylred |
|  |  | 1497 Robert Chandeler |
|  |  | 1499 John Stukeley |
|  |  | 1501 William Goslow |
|  |  | William Gonell |
|  |  | 1502 William Dorraunt |
|  |  | John Lockyngton |
|  |  | John Stukeley |
| Barnard, John, labourer | 1497 William Holme | 1489 John Pescode |
|  | 1498 John and Alice | 1498 *John Lockyngton and |
|  | Lockyngton | William Manipenny |
|  | 1499 Henry Smyth | Robert Mayle |
| Barnard, John, candlemaker |  | 1492 Thomas Faldyng |
|  |  | Robert Nicholas |
|  | 1493 Richard Stevens (2) | 1493 Richard Stevens |
|  |  | 1494 Richard Motte |
|  |  | John Aldred |
|  |  | 1497 John Stukeley |
|  |  | 1498 William Dey |
|  | 1501 John Stokys (2) | 1499 John Snell |
|  | 1502 Thomas Burton (2) | 1502 Thomas Burton (2) |
|  |  | John Lockyngton |
| Barnard, John, husbandman |  | 1490 John Bonfay |

| Lender | Borrower | Lender Borrowed from |
|---|---|---|
| Barnard, John, carpenter | | 1495 Alice Sent |
| Barnard, John | 1501 John Couper | |
| | John Lawman | |
| Barnard, John, sub-bailiff | | 1499 William Orwell |
| | | 1500 John Taylor |
| | | 1501 William Orwell |
| | | Richard Stevens |
| | | John Stokys |
| Barnard, William | 1501 John Snell | |
| Baroun, John | 1489 John Sent, artificer | |
| Baroun, William | 1502 Richard Fawn | |
| Barre, Alice | 1501 John Foster | |
| Barre, Edward | 1485 John Wright, servant of | |
| | John Cony | |
| | 1490 John Page sr. | |
| | 1491 Roger Cook | |
| | 1492 William Nicholl | |
| Barre, John | 1495 Thomas Bennet | |
| Basse, William | 1497 Henry Acorne | |
| | 1498 John Bryte | |
| | John Holme | |
| | 1499 William Hilton | |
| | Thomas Syward | |
| | Anna Gravy | 1499 John Bayous sr. |
| | John Aylred | |
| | Thomas Baker | |
| | John Bayous | |
| | John Foster | |
| | John Gredley | |
| | William Lord | |
| | 1500 Richard Fawne | |
| | John Holme | |
| | John Stokys, miller | 1500 Elena Frost |
| | 1501 John Custauns | |
| | 1502 John Couper | |
| | William Henby | 1503 John Couper (3) |
| Bate, Thomas | 1488 Helen Ermyng | 1487 George Hanson |
| | | William Horn (4) |
| | 1488 Thomas Batey | |
| | 1489 Thomas Faldyng | |
| Bayous, John sr. | 1489 John Alred | 1490 Richard Stevens |
| | 1491 Richard Stevens (2) | |
| | 1498 John Bailey, sr. | 1498 William Manipenny |
| | | William Melbron |
| | 1499 William Basse | |
| | John Smyth, de | |
| | Graveley | |
| Bayous, John | 1485 William Mounford | |
| | 1487 Paul Folkys | |
| | 1488 John Gredley | |

| LENDER | BORROWER | LENDER BORROWED FROM |
|---|---|---|
| | 1489 John Barnard, sr. | 1487 John Barnard sr. |
| | 1490 William Hilton | 1495 John Taylor |
| | | 1496 John Dey |
| | 1498 Thomas Porcar (2) | 1499 William Basse |
| | 1500 Thomas Massey | 1500 John Stokys |
| | | 1501 John Stukeley |
| | | 1502 Thomas Ripisle |
| | | William Wolfe |
| Bayous, John jr. | 1489 Matthew Hedley (2) | |
| | 1492 Thomas Cokman and | 1495 John Brite |
| | his son John | 1498 Thomas Gybbys |
| | | William Manipenny |
| Bayous, Robert | 1500 William Kyng (2) | 1500 William Kyng (2) |
| Bennet, Thomas | | 1484 John Turneskewe |
| | | 1485 John Aldred |
| | 1487 Austin Arnold | 1487 William Nottyngham |
| | Godfrey Wright | Godfrey Wright |
| | | 1489 Robert Dobbyn |
| | | William Hangar |
| | | Thomas Weyther |
| | 1490 Richard More | 1490 Richard More |
| | | John Smyth |
| | | 1491 Richard West |
| | 1494 John Gredley | 1494 Thomas Boswell |
| | Richard Sheter | William Mynt |
| | 1495 William Basse | William Willem |
| | John Halle | 1495 John Barre |
| | 1498 John Gredley | Richard Willem |
| | 1499 Cristina Broughton and | 1498 Thomas Fecas |
| | William Hilgar (2) | William Loveday |
| | | William Mynt |
| Bennet, William | 1498 Roger Cook | |
| Bigge, Alice, executor of John | 1488 Richard West | |
| Blokke, William | 1489 Richard Chycheley | 1485 John Aldred |
| | William Gyle | |
| | John Sent, artificer | 1489 Henry Trayley |
| | 1500 William Clark, de Hunts | 1491 William Wright, de St. Ives |
| | John Sadlow, de Hunts | |
| | William Swetnam | |
| Blokke, Agnes, wife of William | | 1489 Henry Trayley |
| Bonsay (Bonfay), John | 1490 John Barnard sr. | |
| | 1491 Thomas Bailey | |
| | Thomas Cokman | |
| | 1492 John Matthews | |
| | Thomas Newman | |
| | 1495 Simon Granger | |
| | 1498 John Gredley | |

| LENDER | BORROWER | LENDER BORROWED FROM |
|---|---|---|
| Boswell, Thomas | 1494 Thomas Bennet | 1491 Thomas Massey |
| Bould, John | 1489 John Gredley | |
| | 1494 John Holme | |
| | Robert Wright | |
| | 1496 Thomas Wilson | |
| | 1498 John Custauns | |
| | John Gredley | |
| | 1500 William Diggby | |
| | William Hilton | |
| | 1503 John Gybbys | |
| Bour, John | 1488 William Gardener (3) | 1488 John Gybbys |
| | 1489 John Gredley | 1489 John Gredley |
| | 1491 William Manipenny | 1490 Thomas Frost |
| | 1492 William Nichol | 1492 John Mannyng |
| | | 1494 Richard Motte |
| | | 1495 William Manipenny (?) |
| | | Martin |
| Bour, William | 1492 Robert Vont (2) | |
| Brandon, John | 1496 Richard Clark | 1495 William Grym |
| | 1499 William W[er]yng | |
| | Thomas Saby | |
| | 1500 Thomas Burton | 1500 Thomas Burton |
| | 1501 John Shetford and wife | 1502 William Mounford |
| | Agnes | |
| Brandon, Watkyn | | 1501 John Taylor |
| Bray, Reynold, miles | 1503 Richard Chycheley | |
| Brewster, John | | 1487 Richard Whitford |
| | | 1488 Bartholomew [Lucas] |
| | | 1489 John Cave |
| | | 1491 William Gonell |
| | | 1498 Thomas Faldyng |
| | | 1500 Robert Marshall |
| | 1501 John Nottyngham | |
| | 1502 Robert Porter | |
| | | 1502 Henry Gybbys |
| | 1503 Richard Chycheley | |
| | William Manipenny | |
| | John Nottyngham | |
| Brewster, Richard | | 1500 John Snell |
| Brithwell, Thomas | 1486 Richard Wilson | |
| Brite, John | | 1492 John Nicoll |
| | | 1493 Robert Lemyng |
| | 1494 John Bayous jr. | 1494 Thomas Cokman |
| | | John Snell |
| | 1495 John Taylor | William Seward |
| Broughton, Cristina, | 1490 William Gardener | |
| widow, executor of | 1494 John Granger | |
| John's will | John Taylor | |
| | 1495 William Walker | |
| | 1496 Thomas Faldyng | 1498 Thomas Bennet |

| Lender | Borrower | Lender Borrowed from |
|---|---|---|
| | | 1499 Thomas Bennet |
| | | Thomas Lockyngton |
| Broughton, William | | 1496 Aliswandry Bell |
| Browne (Broun), John, miller | 1500 John Snell | |
| Browne, Richard | 1490 John Bulward | |
| Browne, William, gentleman | 1502 John Stokys | |
| Browne, William, shepherd | | 1495 John Garlop |
| | | 1497 Roger Cook |
| Browne, William jr. | | 1501 John Aldred |
| Browne, Nicholas | | 1492 William Manipenny |
| Bryon, John de Sledyng-worth [Needingworth?] | 1495 John Gredley | |
| Bulward, John | 1499 William Hilton | 1490 William Browne |
| Burton, Thomas | 1497 Joan Newman (2) | |
| | 1498 John Custauns | 1498 John Custauns |
| | | William Diggby and Thomas Fecas |
| | | William Gonell |
| | | John Lockyngton |
| | | Thomas May |
| | 1500 John Brandon | 1500 John Brandon (2) |
| | | 1501 John Foster |
| | 1502 John Barnard, candlemaker (2) | 1502 John Barnard candlemaker (2) |
| Cave, Alice | 1498 John Lawman, sr. | |
| Cave, Joan | 1498 John Gredley | |
| Cave, John | 1485 John Brewster | |
| | John Capelle | |
| Chandeler, Robert | 1495 Richard Sheter | |
| | 1496 William Holme | |
| | 1497 John Barnard sr. (2) | |
| | William Mounford | |
| | 1498 John Gredley (2) | |
| | 1499 William W[er]yngs | |
| | Thomas Judd | |
| | Thomas Saby | |
| | 1500 John Aldred | |
| | 1501 John Avery | |
| | John Barnard, jr. | |
| | Henry Houghton, chaplain | |
| | John Stokys | |
| | 1502 William Diggby | |
| | John Gybbys | 1503 Henry Acton |
| Chaplain, Thomas | 1503 Richard Fawne | |
| Chese, John, executor of William's will | | 1493 William Lessy |
| Chese, William | 1485 Roger Cook | |

| Lender | Borrower | Lender Borrowed from |
|---|---|---|
| Clark, John, miller | 1501 John Barnard | |
| | John Couper | 1503 John Couper |
| Clark, John | 1495 John Hatley, de Hunts | |
| | 1497 Anna Gravy | |
| | 1498 William Fryre | |
| | 1501 John Gredley | |
| | William Lord | |
| | Thomas Pasgod | |
| | 1503 John Mayle (3) | |
| Clark, John de Brampton | 1488 William Nicholl | |
| Clark, John, servant of John Draper | 1489 John Barnard sr. | |
| Clark, John, de Buckden | | 1487 Thomas Syward |
| Clark, Richard | 1494 Richard Holme | 1494 Richard Holme |
| | | 1495 John Miles |
| | | Richard Watson |
| | | 1496 Aliswandry Bell |
| | | John Brandon |
| | | William Pacy |
| Clark, Steven | 1488 Thomas Faldyng (2) | 1488 Thomas Faldyng |
| | John Miles (2) | |
| | 1493 Thomas Faldyng (4) | 1494 Thomas Faldyng |
| | 1498 John Gredley | |
| Clark, William, de Hunts | | 1494 William Diggby |
| | | 1500 William Blokke |
| Cokman, Thomas | | 1486 Richard Motte (2) |
| | 1488 Richard West | 1488 *Richard Samt |
| | 1489 Richard West (2) | Thomas Reynold |
| | 1491 Thomas Bailey | 1490 William Gonell |
| | John Barnard jr. | 1491 Thomas Fecas |
| | | John Aldred |
| | | John Barnard jr. |
| | | John Bayous jr. |
| | | John Bonfay |
| | 1494 John Brite | 1493 William Lessy |
| | | Richard Motte |
| | | 1494 William Lessy |
| Cokman, John son of Thomas | | 1492 John Bayous jr. |
| | | 1502 Thomas Manchester |
| Colby, William and wife Elizabeth | 1503 William Manipenny | |
| Conys, Robert | 1484 William Wright | |
| | 1487 John Barnard | |
| Cook, Agnes, widow of Thomas | 1492 Robert Vont (3) | |
| Cook, John | | 1503 Margaret Pope |
| Cook, Roger | | 1484 John Lockyngton |
| | | 1485 William Chese |
| | | John Lockyngton |
| | | Thomas Lockyngton |

| LENDER | BORROWER | LENDER BORROWED FROM |
|---|---|---|
| | | 1486 John Aldred |
| | | 1487 John Manipenny |
| | | 1488 John Gybbys |
| | | John Smyth |
| | | 1489 John Gybbys |
| | | Robert Marshall |
| | | John Turneskewe |
| | | William Polle |
| | | 1490 John Barnard |
| | | Edward Barre |
| | | John Foster |
| | | Richard Kyng |
| | 1491 Thomas Frost | John Snell |
| | | 1492 John Foster |
| | | William Mounford |
| | | 1493 Robert Nicholas |
| | | John Stukeley |
| | | Richard Stukeley |
| | | 1496 William Pacy |
| | 1497 William Brown, | 1497 John Garlop (2) |
| | shepherd | 1498 William Bennet |
| | | John Garlop jr. |
| | | William Loveday |
| | | William Mynt |
| | | John Snell |
| | | 1499 Henry Gybbys |
| | | 1500 William Orwell |
| | | 1501 William Goslow |
| | | John Robyns jr. |
| | | 1502 Thomas Lockyngton |
| | | William Mounford |
| | | Richard Stukeley |
| Couper, John, butcher | | 1497 John Stukeley |
| | | 1498 William Mayle |
| | | John Turneskewe |
| | 1499 William Ellington | 1499 John Aylred |
| | John Snell | John Granger |
| | | Robert Houghton |
| | | John and Thomas |
| | | Lockyngton |
| | | John Lockyngton |
| | | John Stukeley |
| | 1500 William Godard, de | 1500 William Ede |
| | Hunts (2) | |
| | William Ede | John Gonell |
| | John Gonell | William Kyng |
| | John Mygton | John Laxton |
| | William Pelle (2) | Richard Motte |
| | John Stokys (2) | John Mygton |

| LENDER | BORROWER | LENDER BORROWED FROM |
|--------|----------|----------------------|
| | Richard Stuleley | John Robyns jr. |
| | | John Stokys (2) |
| | | Richard Stukeley (2) |
| | 1501 John Edward | 1501 John Barnard |
| | Robert Ingyll | John Clark, miller |
| | | William Diggby |
| | | Thomas Gonell, vicar de |
| | | Hemingford Abbots |
| | | William Manipenny (2) |
| | | John Wynde (2) |
| | | 1502 William Basse |
| | | John Lockyngton and |
| | | John Stukeley |
| | 1503 Robert Acton | John Stukeley (2) |
| | William Basse (2) | 1503 Robert Acton (2) |
| | John Clark, miller | Thomas Gybbys |
| | John Elys | Robert Nicholas |
| | Robert Nicholas | John Mordannt |
| | John Tame | |
| Couper, John, labourer | | 1498 Annet Yatys |
| Couper, William | 1500 John Dyvat | 1502 John Almouth |
| | | Thomas Lockyngton |
| Crook, Joan | 1493 Patrick Michelson | |
| Custauns, John | | 1494 Anna Mynsterchambre |
| | | 1495 John Aylred |
| | | 1496 John Dey (2) |
| | | William Mounford |
| | | John Stukeley |
| | | 1497 William Lessy |
| | | William Orwell |
| | | William Pelman |
| | 1498 Thomas Burton | 1498 John Bould and John |
| | | Smyth |
| | John Mayle | Thomas Burton |
| | | John Dey |
| | | John Divet |
| | | Thomas Fecas |
| | | Henry Gybbys |
| | | William Manipenny and |
| | | John Lockyngton |
| | | William Mynt |
| | | John Stokys |
| | | John Stukeley |
| | | 1500 Thomas Gybbys |
| | | 1501 William Basse |
| | | 1502 John Stukeley |
| | | 1503 John Sudbury |
| Dalicote, Henry | 1486 Thomas Ledon | |
| Dalton, John | 1485 Thomas Reynold | |
| | 1486 William Jarnok | |

| Lender | Borrower | Lender Borrowed from |
|---|---|---|
| | 1487 John Lucas | |
| | John Lincoln | |
| | John Schylling | |
| | 1494 Robert Dykes | |
| Dalton, John, de Brampton | | 1498 Thomas Gybbys |
| Dalton, William | 1500 John Vincent (2) | |
| | 1502 John Garlop, wright and wife Jane | |
| | John Stokys | |
| Davy, John | 1492 William Kyng and William Manipenny | |
| | 1495 John Snell | 1502 Thomas Monyment and Richard West |
| Davyson, Henry | 1487 William Wright | |
| Dey, John | 1496 John Boys | |
| | John Custauns (2) | |
| | 1497 Thomas Faldyng | |
| | John Garlop | |
| | 1498 John Foster | |
| | 1499 John Dey | 1500 William Mounford |
| | | 1502 Thomas Osse |
| Dey, John jr. | 1499 Benedict Grey | |
| | John Stokys | |
| Dey, William | 1498 John Barnard, candlemaker | |
| | 1500 Thomas Page | |
| Diggby, William | 1494 William Clark, de Hunts | 1485 William Nottyngham |
| | | 1486 William Orwell |
| | 1495 Thomas Emlyn | 1495 John Aylred (2) |
| | | John Gredley |
| | 1496 Robert Porter | |
| | 1498 Thomas Breton | |
| | 1500 John Stokys, miller | 1500 John Stukeley and John Bould |
| | John Couper (2) | |
| | | 1502 Robert Chandeler |
| | | 1503 Hugh Hay |
| Divet, John | 1498 John Custauns | 1500 William Couper |
| Dobby, Robert, chaplain | 1485 Thomas Faldyng | |
| | 1488 Thomas Reynold | |
| | 1489 Thomas Bennet | |
| | John Stukeley | |
| | 1491 Simon Granger | |
| Dorraunt, Thomas | 1497 Richard Archdekyn | |
| | 1503 Robert Hunte | |
| Dorraunt, William | 1502 John Barnard sr. (2) | |
| Ede, William | 1494 Richard Sheter | 1496 Thomas Page |
| | 1500 John Couper | 1498 John Stukeley |
| | | 1500 John Couper |
| | | 1501 Anna Lockyngton |
| | | Thomas Lockyngton |

| LENDER | BORROWER | LENDER BORROWED FROM |
|---|---|---|
| Elys, Thomas | 1493 William Gardener | 1492 Richard Pernel |
| Emlyn, Thomas | 1486 Thomas son of William Page / Fulbourne, custodian of the cows | 1486 John Lockyngton |
| | 1487 Matilda Watson | 1487 William Orwell |
| | | 1488 William Manipenny / John Stukeley |
| | | 1489 Thomas Lockyngton / Richard Mounford |
| | 1491 William Nicoll | 1491 John Herforth |
| | | 1493 John Snell |
| | | 1495 William Diggby and John Smyth |
| Emson, Richard | 1503 Richard Chycheley | |
| English, John | 1484 Thomas Faldyng | |
| | 1485 John Schylling | |
| Enby, William | 1501 Jacob Syward | |
| Ermyn, Helen | 1488 Thomas Bate / Roger Manning | |
| Este, Henry | 1502 Robert Johnson | |
| Edmond, William | 1484 Robert Nicholas | 1484 Thomas Balle |
| Faldyng, Thomas | | 1484 John English |
| | 1485 William Nicoll | 1485 Robert Dobbyn / Richard Whitford |
| | 1487 William Hilton | |
| | 1489 John Barnard sr. | 1488 Steven Clark (3) / John Stukeley and John Smith |
| | | 1489 John Barnard sr. / Thomas Bate / William Nicholl / John Page / Thomas Ripley / John Tychemarsh |
| | | 1490 John Smyth / William Swettonham |
| | | 1491 Richard Stevens |
| | 1492 John Barnard, candlemaker / Roger Gould / Thomas Newman | 1492 John Aylmar / Steven Clark (2) |
| | 1493 John Alde | |
| | 1494 Steven Clark / Henry Grene / Thomas Mayle | 1494 Steven Clark |
| | 1496 John Gredley / Isabella Hilton | 1495 Richard Motte |
| | | 1496 Cristina Broughton |
| | 1497 Robert Cawdwell / William Gedney / John Gony | 1497 John Dey |

| Lender | Borrower | Lender Borrowed from |
|---|---|---|
| | 1498 John Aylred | 1498 John Aylred |
| | John Brewster | Thomas Mayle |
| | | William Orwell |
| | 1499 William Hilton (2) | 1499 John Lockyngton |
| | Thomas Judd | Thomas Mayle |
| | Thomas Mays | Richard Motte |
| | 1500 William Goodwyn | 1500 Richard Sate de |
| | | Coppingford |
| | William Vyntner | John Turneskewe |
| | 1501 William Goslow | |
| | Richard Holme | |
| | John Punt | 1502 William Kyng |
| | 1503 Richard Stevens | 1503 Richard Stevens |
| Fawn, Richard | | 1494 Thomas Wyddar |
| | | 1500 William Basse |
| | 1501 Thomas Pasgood | 1501 William Orwell and John |
| | | Robys |
| | | John Stokys |
| | | Thomas Wyddar (2) |
| | | Thomas Pasgood |
| | | 1502 William Baron and |
| | | Richard Fawn (2) |
| | | 1503 Thomas Capell |
| | | John Miller |
| Fecas, Thomas | 1488 John Martyn (2) | |
| | 1490 William Mundeford | |
| | William Pelman | |
| | 1491 Thomas Cokman | |
| | | 1493 William Manipenny (8) |
| | 1497 Joan Newman | 1497 William Manipenny |
| | 1498 Thomas Bennet | |
| | Thomas Breton | |
| | John Custauns | |
| | 1500 William Hilton | |
| | 1502 William Hilton | |
| | John Wylde | |
| Feltwelle, John | 1503 John Nottyngham | |
| Foly (Folkys), Paul | | 1487 John Baynes |
| | | John Schylling |
| | 1502 Thomas Squier and wife | 1489 Richard Kyng |
| | Margaret | 1503 John Laxton |
| Folifote, William | 1497 Thomas Kendale | |
| Foster, Richard | 1496 William Godwyn | 1493 Thomas Marshall |
| | 1499 Thomas Bacar | 1494 John Foster |
| | 1501 Thomas Breton | |
| | 1503 Henry Cranfield | |
| Forster, John | 1484 Richard Fratis | 1492 Roger Cook |
| | 1488 John Schylling | 1494 John Aldred |
| | 1490 Roger Cook | John Stukeley |
| | | 1495 Thomas Lockyngton |

| LENDER | BORROWER | LENDER BORROWED FROM |
|---|---|---|
| | 1492  Anna Mynsterchambre | 1496  William Orwell |
| | | 1498  William Dey |
| | William Nichol | 1499  William Basse |
| | | John Stukeley |
| | | John Taylor |
| | | 1501  Alice Barre |
| | | Richard Holme |
| | | Thomas Smyth |
| Fote, Robert | 1495  William Hilton | 1496  John Aldred |
| | 1496  Robert Houghton | |
| Frere (Fryre), William jr. | 1498  John Chert | |
| Frost, Elena | | 1494  John Ordney |
| | 1497  Simon Prestwode | |
| | 1500  William Basse | |
| Frost, Thomas | 1486  Fulbourne, custodian of the cows | |
| | John Page sr. | |
| | 1487  John Kyng, textor | |
| | Henry Paten | |
| | Simon Granger | |
| | 1488  William Ibott | |
| | Richard Stukeley | |
| | 1489  John Barnard jr. | |
| | William Frost | |
| | 1490  John Bowr | 1490  William Frost |
| | | William Goneld |
| | 1491  Roger Cook | |
| | Isabella Wright | |
| Frost, William sr. | | 1489  Thomas Frost |
| | | John Gredley |
| | 1490  Thomas Frost | 1498  John Stukeley |
| | | 1503  William Kyng |
| Frost, William jr. | 1497  John Mayle | |
| Garlop, John jr. | 1498  Roger Cooke | 1498  William Lessy |
| Garlop, John, labourer | 1499  John Lawman, sr. | |
| | John Stokys | |
| | 1500  Richard Chycheley | |
| Garlop, John sr., husbandman | 1500  Thomas Gybbys | |
| Garlop, John, husbandman | 1489  John Lumbard | |
| | 1495  William Brown, shepherd | |
| Gardener, Agnes | 1485, 1486  William Nicholl (2) | 1493  Anna Mynsterchambre |
| Gardener, John | 1487  Richard West | 1487  William Loveday and Robert Stevenson |
| | | John Matthew |
| Gardener, Thomas | 1501, 1502  John Chycheley | |
| Gardener, William | 1488  John Gredley | 1488  John Bour (3) |
| | William Mounford | William Mounford |
| | | William Nicoll |

| LENDER | BORROWER | LENDER BORROWED FROM |
|---|---|---|
|  | William Nicoll | 1489 John Mynsterchambre |
|  | William Orwell | John Tychemarsh |
|  | 1490 William Hilton | 1490 Cristina Broughton |
|  | Thomas Smyth |  |
|  | 1491 William Hilton | 1491 Richard West |
|  | 1492 William Godwyn | 1492 Richard West |
|  | Richard West |  |
|  | 1493 Thomas Elys | 1493 Richard Stukeley |
|  | Richard Stukeley |  |
|  | 1494 William Manipenny |  |
|  | 1496 John Gybbys and |  |
|  | Thomas Lockyngton |  |
|  | (2) |  |
| Garnet, Elizabeth | 1502 John Holme |  |
| Geyssyn, Edward | 1490 William Benson |  |
| Gilby, Richard | 1494 John Gybbys | 1500 John Stukeley |
| Gilby, Thomas | 1499 Anna Gravy |  |
| Gilby, Margaret, daughter | 1499 Anna Gravy |  |
| of Thomas |  |  |
| Gile (Gyle), William | 1484, 1485 John Glover |  |
|  | 1486 William Nicholl | 1487 William Aldred |
|  |  | William Godwyn |
|  |  | Thomas Warde |
|  | 1488 William Hilton | 1488 John Tychemarsh |
|  | Thomas Warde |  |
|  | 1489 John Stukeley | 1489 William Bloke and |
|  |  | Agnes Rede |
| Goldyng, William | 1499 John Gredley |  |
| Gonell, Thomas | 1500 John Couper | 1500 John Couper |
|  | William Lane, chaplain | William Melbron |
|  |  | 1503 Margaret Lawe |
|  |  | Thomas Massey |
|  |  | John Smyth (2) |
| Gonell, Thomas, de | 1501 John Couper |  |
| Hemingford, vicar | John Smyth (2) |  |
| Gonell, William | 1490 Thomas Cokman |  |
|  | Thomas Frost |  |
|  | 1491 John Brewster |  |
|  | John Gredley |  |
|  | Thomas Newman |  |
|  | 1494 John Gredley |  |
|  | 1495 Thomas Bacar |  |
|  | William Massey |  |
|  | 1497 John Holme |  |
|  | 1498 Thomas Breton and |  |
|  | Richard Chycheley |  |
|  | Elena Fryre |  |
|  | John Gybbys |  |
|  | William Vyntner |  |
|  | 1499 Richard Chycheley |  |
|  | John Stokys |  |

| Lender | Borrower | Lender Borrowed from |
|---|---|---|
| | 1500 John Stokys | |
| | John Stukeley | |
| | 1501 John Barnard sr. | |
| | John Gybbys (2) | |
| | William Mynt | |
| | John Stokys | |
| | 1502 John Barnard jr. | |
| | Henry Gybbys | |
| | William Henby | |
| | William Lord | |
| Gony, John | 1487 Simon Prestwode | 1488 William Mounford |
| | 1490 William Nicholl | 1497 Thomas Faldyng |
| | 1491 John Hermyn | |
| Godwyn, William | 1487 William Gile | 1490 Richard Pelle |
| | | John Stukeley |
| | | Richard West |
| | | 1491 John Gybbys |
| | | 1492 Austin Arnold |
| | | John Barnard |
| | | William Gardener |
| | | William Kyng |
| | | William Orwell |
| | | 1496 Richard Forster |
| | | William Orwell |
| | | Agnes Pacy |
| | 1497 Robert Nicholas | 1497 William Mounford |
| | | John Stukeley |
| | | 1498 Henry Gybbys |
| | | William Mayle |
| | | 1500 Thomas Faldyng |
| | | Thomas Wyddar |
| | 1502 William Manipenny | |
| Goslow, William, de Ramsey | 1501 John Barnard sr. | 1501 Thomas Faldyng |
| | Roger Cook | |
| | Alice Mayle | |
| Gould, Roger | 1492 Thomas Faldyng | |
| Grandon, Isabella | 1486 Thomas Mayle (2) | |
| Granger, John | 1488 William Hely and | |
| | Margaret Lokyar | |
| | 1499 John Couper | 1494 Cristina Broughton |
| Granger, Simon | | 1487 Thomas Frost |
| | | 1489 Robert Marshall |
| | | 1491 Robert Dobbyn |
| | 1492 Margaret Paslowe | 1493 John Snell |
| | William Pelman (2) | 1495 John Boleyn |
| | 1499 Robert Nelson | 1498 William Melbron |
| Granger, Thomas | 1498 Richard Miller | |
| | 1501 Thomas Wyng' | |
| Granger, William | 1502 Thomas Smyth jr. | 1493 John Page sr. |
| Gravy, Anna | | 1497 John Lockyngton |

| Lender | Borrower | Lender Borrowed from |
|---|---|---|
| | 1498 Richard Motte | 1498 Richard Motte |
| | | William Longe |
| | 1499 William Lessy | 1499 Thomas Gilby and |
| | | daughter Margaret |
| | | William Basse |
| Gray, Benedict | 1490 John Ussher | 1489 William Pelle |
| | | 1492 Thomas Newman |
| | | 1498 John Dey jr. |
| Gredley, John, butcher | | 1485 John Lockyngton |
| | | Thomas Lockyngton |
| | 1486 William Mayle | 1486 John Aldred |
| | | John Barnard |
| | | Thomas Reynold |
| | | John Turneskewe (2) |
| | 1487 Thomas Reynold | 1487 John Barnard |
| | 1488 William Mayle | 1488 John Bayous |
| | Thomas Reynold | John Gardener (2) |
| | | William Gardiner |
| | | Thomas Lockyngton |
| | | John Lumbard (2) |
| | | William Manipenny |
| | | William Mayle |
| | | William Orwell (2) |
| | | John Page, sr. |
| | | Thomas Reynold |
| | | 1489 John Bould |
| | | John Bour and William |
| | | Frost |
| | | Richard Mounford |
| | | John Mynsterchambre |
| | | John Page, sr. |
| | | Richard Smyth |
| | | Henry Trayley |
| | | John Turneskewe |
| | | 1490 John Smyth |
| | | 1491 William Gonell |
| | | 1492 John Gybbys |
| | | Henry Gybbys |
| | | John Lockyngton |
| | | Richard Lockyngton |
| | | Thomas Lockyngton |
| | | Richard Motte |
| | | William Orwell |
| | | Richard Samt |
| | 1493 William Holme | 1493 William Basse (3) |
| | | Anna Samt |
| | | John Ussher (2) |
| | | 1494 Thomas Bennet |
| | | Helen Frost |
| | | William Goneld |

| LENDER | BORROWER | LENDER BORROWED FROM |
|---|---|---|
| | | John Lockyngton |
| | | Thomas Lockyngton |
| | 1495 John Mileward | 1495 John Bryan de |
| | | Sledyngworth |
| | | (Needingworth?) |
| | | William Diggby |
| | | Anna Lockyngton |
| | | William Mounford |
| | | John Turneskewe |
| | | 1496 Thomas Faldyng |
| | | William Kyng |
| | | William Lane |
| | | Robert Leverett |
| | | Thomas Monyment |
| | 1497 Robert Levrett (2) | 1497 John Aylred |
| | Thomas Lockyngton (2) | Thomas Lockyngton (2) |
| | John Smyth (3) | Thomas Massey |
| | | 1498 John Bonsay |
| | | John Boulde |
| | | Joan Cave |
| | | Robert Chandeler (2) |
| | | Steven Clarke |
| | | Henry Gybbys |
| | | Richard Stukeley |
| | 1499 John Porcar jr. | 1499 John Aylred |
| | | William Basse |
| | | William Goldyng |
| | | Thomas Lockyngton |
| | | 1500 John Laxton |
| | | John Myghton |
| | 1502 John Newton, de | 1501 John Clarke, miller |
| | Willingham | Richard Motte |
| | 1503 William Manipenny (2) | Adam Page |
| | | 1502 Thomas Manchester |
| Grene, Richard | 1498 Robert Nicholl and wife | |
| | Elena (2) | |
| Grym, William, merchant | 1495 John Brandon and wife | |
| | Alice | |
| Grysson, Edward | 1490 William Benson | |
| Gybbys, John de Sutton | | 1494 Richard Gilby |
| Gybbys, John | 1485 John Stokys (2) | |
| | 1488 John Bour | |
| | Roger Cook | |
| | Richard Kyng | |
| | 1489 Roger Cook | 1490 Thomas Newman |
| | 1491 William Godwyn | |
| | 1492 John Gredley | |
| | 1494 Richard Chycheley | |
| | 1495 John Custauns | |
| | 1496 John Abenerly | 1496 John Gardiner and |
| | | William Manipenny |

| Lender | Borrower | Lender Borrowed from |
|---|---|---|
| | 1497 Roger Cook (2) | 1497 John Dey |
| | 1498 Thomas Lockyngton (2) | William Kyng and John Stukeley |
| | 1499 Thomas Monyment | 1498 William Gonell |
| | 1500 Thomas Lockyngton (2) | Thomas Lockyngton |
| | 1502 Thomas Bawdwyne | 1501 Robert Chandeler |
| | | William Gonell |
| | | 1502 William Ibott |
| | | John Laxton |
| | | John Lockyngton and John Bould |
| | | John Page jr. |
| Gybbys, Henry | 1492 John Gredley | |
| | 1498 John Chert | |
| | William Godwyn | |
| | John Gredley | |
| | 1499 Roger Cook (2) | |
| | John Custauns | |
| | John Vyntner | |
| | William Vyntner | |
| | 1500 Thomas Judd | |
| | John Stokys | |
| | Thomas Pasgood | |
| | 1502 John Brewster | 1501 William Gonell |
| Gybbys, Thomas | 1498 John Bayous jr. | |
| | John Dalton, de Brampton | |
| | 1500 John Custauns | 1500 John Garlop sr. |
| | 1501 William Pelle, de Houghton | 1501 William Ibott |
| | 1503 John Couper | |
| Gurne, John | 1501 John Couper (2) | |
| Haghton (Houghton), Robert, clerk | 1499 John Couper | 1496 Robert Fote |
| | | 1501 Robert Chandeler |
| Haghton (Houghton), servant of Robert | 1501 John Holme | |
| Hanger, William, de Swynshed | 1489 Thomas Bennet | |
| Hanson, George | 1485 John Rede and wife Agnes | 1484 Richard Lockyngton |
| | 1487 Thomas Bate | |
| Hatley, John de Hunts | 1495 John Clerk | 1497 John Holme |
| Hay, Hugh | 1503 William Diggby | |
| Hedley, Matthew | 1489 John Bayous jr. (4) | |
| Helgey, John de Cambs | 1499 William Alenson | |
| Herforth, John | 1491 Thomas Emlyn | |
| Holme, John | | 1491 William Manipenny |
| | | Thomas Norton |
| | 1493 John Miles | 1492 Richard Holme |
| | | 1494 John Bould |

| Lender | Borrower | Lender Borrowed from |
|---|---|---|
| | | 1497 William Gonell |
| | | 1498 William Basse |
| | | 1499 John Page son of John Davy |
| | | John Taylor |
| | | 1500 William Basse |
| | | John Lockyngton |
| | | Richard Motte |
| | | John Stukeley |
| | | John Turneskewe |
| | | 1501 servant of Henry Houghton |
| | | 1502 Thomas Monyment and Richard West |
| Holme, Richard | 1489 John Barnard | 1489 John Barnard (2) |
| | 1491 John Schylling (2) | |
| | 1492 John Holme | |
| | 1494 Richard Clark (2) | 1496 Thomas Lockyngton |
| | 1498 John Dey sr. | |
| | 1501 John Foster | 1501 Thomas Faldyng |
| | William Hilton | |
| | 1502 Isabella Wright | |
| Holme, William | | 1489 William Orwell |
| | | 1492 John Gredley |
| | | 1496 Robert Chandeler |
| | 1497 John Hatley (2) | 1497 John Barnard |
| | 1499 John Alenson | 1499 William Mounford |
| | William Alenson | |
| | Ralph Wane | |
| | 1500 Robert Nicholas | 1500 Thomas Judd |
| | John Stokys | Robert Nicholas |
| | Ralph Wane | John Stokys |
| | | 1501 John Sudbury |
| Hooe, Thomas de Amtyll | 1500 John Couper | |
| Horn, William | 1487 Thomas Bate (2) | |
| Horwood, John | 1493 Richard Chycheley | |
| Ibott, William jr. | 1489 John Schylling | |
| Ibott, William | 1491 Robert Porter | |
| | 1495 George Roos | |
| | 1501 John Stokys | 1501 John Stokys |
| | Thomas Gybbys | |
| | John Mynt | |
| | 1503 John Gybys | |
| | Thomas Barber | |
| | John Nottyngham | |
| Iche (Yche), John | 1499 John Stokys | |
| Jatys (Yatys), Anna | 1498 John Couper, labourer | |
| Judd, John | 1495 William Hilton | |
| Judd, Thomas | 1499 Robert Chandeler | 1499 Robert Chandeler |
| | | Thomas Faldyng |
| | | John Nottyngham |

| LENDER | BORROWER | LENDER BORROWED FROM |
|---|---|---|
| | 1500 William Holme | 1500 John Aldred |
| | | Henry Gybbys and |
| | | William Mynt |
| Johnson, Robert | 1499 John Brite | 1497 William Melbron |
| | | 1499 Richard Motte |
| | | 1503 Henry Est |
| | | William Kyng |
| | | John Smyth |
| Kendale, Thomas | 1489 Thomas Baker (4) | 1496 William Longe |
| | | 1495 Roger Manipenny |
| | | 1497 William Folifote |
| | 1498 William Lord | 1498 John Stukeley |
| | William Seward | |
| Kyng, Alice, widow | 1492 Thomas Newman | |
| | 1503 Thomas Barbar | |
| Kyng, Marion, wife of | 1488 William Stodale | |
| Richard | | |
| Kyng, Richard | 1486 John Lumbard | |
| | 1488 John Brewster | 1488 John Barnard jr. |
| | William Hilton | John Gybbys |
| | William Stodale | John Tychemarash |
| | 1489 Paul Foly | 1489 John Matthew (2) |
| | 1490 Roger Cook | 1490 Thomas Norton |
| | 1501 Thomas Lawman | 1491 Richard West |
| | 1502 William Hilton | |
| Kyng, William | 1491 Robert Porter | |
| | 1492 William Nicoll | 1492 John Davy |
| | 1492 William Godwyn | |
| | Richard West | |
| | 1493 Thomas Newman | 1494 Thomas Lockyngton (2) |
| | Isabella Wright (2) | Richard Stukeley |
| | 1495 Thomas Taylor, tanner | |
| | 1496 Henry Frost | |
| | John Gredley | |
| | 1497 William Frere | |
| | John Gybbys | |
| | John Lawman | |
| | 1498 Richard West | |
| | 1499 John Page jr. | 1499 Richard Stukeley |
| | 1500 Robert Bayous | 1500 Robert Bayous (2) |
| | John Couper | |
| | John Nottyngham (2) | |
| | 1501 John Barnard sr. | |
| | Roger Cook | |
| | Alice Mayle, executor of | 1502 Thomas Lockyngton |
| | Thomas Mayle | |
| Lane, William, clerk | 1496 John Gredley | |
| Lawe, Margaret | 1503 John Gonell | |

INVOLVEMENT IN THE MONEY MARKET

| LENDER | BORROWER | LENDER BORROWED FROM |
|---|---|---|
| Lawman, John | | 1497 John Stukeley and William Kyng |
| | 1502 Richard Tanner | 1500 Thomas Mounford |
| Lawrence, John | 1502 William Henby | |
| Laxton, John | 1500 John Couper | |
| | John Gredley | |
| | 1503 Paul Folkys | |
| | John Gybbys | |
| | Thomas Marshall | |
| | 1503 John Smyth de Caxton | |
| | Thomas Squier | |
| Laxton, Thomas | 1493 Thomas Maryot | |
| Legge, Richard | 1491 Thomas Baker | 1492 John Aylred |
| Lemyng, Robert | 1493 John Brite | |
| | 1499 John Latyser, alias Glen | |
| Lessy, William | 1487 William Nicholas | 1487 William Nicoll (2) |
| | 1492 Henry Trayley | |
| | 1493 Thomas Cokman | |
| | John Garlop jr. and John Chese | |
| | 1494 Thomas Cokman | |
| | Richard Sheter | |
| | 1497 John Custauns | |
| Leverett, Robert | 1497 John Aylward | 1497 John Gredley (2) |
| | | 1498 William Manipenny |
| Light, William | 1487 John Mody | |
| Lockyngton, Anna | 1495 John Gredley | |
| | William Mounford | 1495 William Mounford |
| | 1501 William Ede | |
| | John Stokes | |
| Lockyngton, John | 1484 Roger Cook | |
| | 1485 Thomas Emlyn | |
| | John Gredley | |
| | William Wright, butcher | |
| | 1486 William Wright | |
| | 1488 Richard Whitford | |
| | 1492 John Gredley | |
| | 1494 John Gredley | |
| | 1498 John Barnard, labourer | 1498 John Barnard, labourer |
| | Thomas Breton | |
| | John Custauns | |
| | 1499 John Couper (2) | |
| | Thomas Faldyng | |
| | 1500 John Holme | |
| | 1501 John Stokes | |
| | 1502 John Couper | |
| | John Gybbys | |
| Lockyngton, Richard | 1484 George Hansen | |
| | William Wright, butcher | |
| | 1486 Simon Prestwode | |

| LENDER | BORROWER | LENDER BORROWED FROM |
|---|---|---|
| | 1487 John Sent | |
| | 1491 Richard Stukeley | |
| | 1492 John Gredley | |
| Lockyngton, Thomas | 1485 Roger Cook | |
| | John Gredley | |
| | 1487 Thomas Faldyng | |
| | 1488 John Gredley (2) | |
| | 1489 Thomas Emlyn | |
| | Godfrey Wright | |
| | 1491 John Matthew | 1491 John Matthew |
| | 1492 John Gredley | |
| | 1494 John Glover | 1493 Katherine Mayle |
| | John Gredley | 1494 William Kyng |
| | William Kyng | |
| | Robert Vont | |
| | 1495 John Foster | |
| | 1496 William Gardener and | |
| | William Manipenny | |
| | Richard Holme | 1497 John Gredley |
| | 1498 John Gybbys (3) | |
| | Thomas Mounford | |
| | 1499 John Couper | |
| | John Gredley | |
| | William Hilton and | |
| | Cristina Broughton | |
| | William Manipenny (2) | |
| | Thomas Saby | |
| | William W[er]ymms | |
| | 1500 John Gybbys (2) | |
| | 1501 John Avery | |
| | Thomas Milnall | |
| | 1502 John Barnard sr. | 1502 William Manipenny |
| | John Barnard, candle-maker | |
| | Roger Cook | |
| | William Ede | |
| | Edmund Glen' | |
| | William Henby | |
| | William Hilton | |
| | Richard Kyng | |
| | 1503 John Barnard jr. | |
| | John Couper | |
| | John Nottingham | |
| Longe, William | 1486 Thomas Kendale | |
| | 1498 Anna Gravy | |
| Lorydan, Marcus | 1501 John Stokys | |
| Loveday, William | 1487 William Gardener | |
| | 1498 Thomas Bennet | |
| | Roger Cook | |
| Lucas, Barthomomew | 1488 John Brewster | |

| Lender | Borrower | Lender Borrowed from |
|---|---|---|
| Lumbard, John | 1488 John Gredley (2) | 1486 Richard Kyng |
| | | 1489 John Garlop |
| | | William Nicoll (6) |
| | | 1491 John Robinson |
| Manchester, Thomas | 1502 Thomas Cokman | |
| | John Gredley | 1502 John Smyth |
| Manipenny, William | 1486 William Orwell | 1486 William Orwell |
| | 1488 Thomas Emlyn | |
| | John Gredley | |
| | Richard Whitford | |
| | 1489 Robert Barker and wife Agnes | |
| | John Barnard | |
| | 1491 John Holme | |
| | Thomas Newman | |
| | William Pelman | 1491 John Bour |
| | 1492 Nicholas Brown | 1492 John Davy |
| | William Nicholl | |
| | Richard West | |
| | 1493 Thomas Fecas (4) | 1493 Thomas Fecas (3) |
| | John Miles | |
| | 1494 Thomas Fecas (5) | |
| | William Gardener | |
| | Richard Sheter | |
| | John Snell | |
| | Richard Stukeley | |
| | 1495 Thomas Bate | 1495 William Goneld |
| | John Bour | |
| | William Hilton | |
| | 1496 Thomas Bailey (2) | 1496 Thomas Bailey (2) |
| | John Gybbys and Thomas Lockyngton | |
| | Thomas Fecas | |
| | 1498 John Barnard, labourer | |
| | John Bayous, jr. | |
| | John Bayous, sr. | |
| | John Custauns | |
| | Robert Leverett | |
| | 1499 William Alenson | 1499 Thomas Lockyngton and Thomas Maryot |
| | 1500 William Pelman (2) | |
| | 1501 John Couper (2) | 1501 William Godwyn |
| | John Nottyngham (2) | John Stokys |
| | 1502 Richard Chycheley | 1503 John Brewster with |
| | Thomas Lockyngton | William Colne and his |
| | John Stokys | wife Elizabeth |
| Manipenny, John | 1501 Isabella Dey | |
| Manning, John | 1492 John Bour | 1500 John Barnard, |
| | 1501 John Avery | candlemaker |
| Manning, Roger | 1495 Thomas Kendale | |

| Lender | Borrower | Lender Borrowed from |
|--------|----------|---------------------|
| Marshall, Robert | 1489 Richard Cook<br>Simon Granger<br>John Osteler<br>Agnes Wright | |
| Marshall, Robert, alias<br>Wen' | 1501 John Brewster | |
| Marshall, Thomas | 1493 Richard Forster<br>1495 George Roos | 1503 John Laxton (4) |
| Martin, Henry | 1485 William Nicholl | |
| Maryot, Thomas | 1493 Thomas Newman<br>1499 William Manipenny<br>1503 John Barnard jr.<br>John Nottyngham | 1493 Thomas Laxton |
| Massey, Thomas | 1488 John Smyth, labourer<br>1491 Thomas Boswell<br>1497 Robert Copuldyke<br>John Gredley<br>1498 William Farthing<br>1503 John Goneld | 1500 John Bayous<br>John Foster |
| Matthew, John | 1484 Roger Stoke<br>1485 John Goodman de<br>Bedford<br>1487 William Gardener<br>1489 Richard Kyng<br>1491 Thomas Lockyngton<br>Thomas Smyth<br>1492 John Oxen<br>1493 William Bekke | 1491 Thomas Lockyngton<br>1492 John Aylred and John<br>Bonsay |
| May, Thomas | 1498 Thomas Breton<br>Thomas Faldyng<br>Thomas Mounford<br>1499 Thomas Faldyng | 1497 Alyswandr Bell<br>1499 Thomas Faldyng<br>1500 Richard Motte<br>John Stukeley |
| Mayle, John | 1493 William Mounford | 1493 William Mounford<br>1496 William Pacy<br>1497 William Frost jr.<br>William Mynt<br>William Pacy<br>John Stukeley<br>1498 John Custauns<br>1499 John Aldred<br>William Mynt |
| | 1500 John Stokys (2) | 1500 William Porter<br>1501 John Aldred<br>Richard Stevens |
| | 1502 John Garlop, wright | 1503 John Clark (2)<br>John Snell<br>John Stukeley (2) |
| Mayle, Katherine | 1493 Thomas Lockyngton<br>and wife Joan | |

| LENDER | BORROWER | LENDER BORROWED FROM |
|---|---|---|
| Mayle, Robert | 1498 John Barnard, labourer | |
| Mayle, Thomas | 1486 Isabella Crandon (2) | |
| Mayle, William | 1485 Thomas Baker | |
| | Thomas Reginold | |
| | 1496, 1488 John Gredley | 1486, 1488 John Gredley |
| | 1492 William Nicoll | |
| | 1498 John Couper, butcher | |
| | William Godwyn | |
| | William Ingram | |
| | William Mounford (3) | |
| | 1502 John Nicholl | 1502 John Stokys |
| Maynard, Simon | 1487 Simon Prestwode | |
| Melbourne, William | 1488 John Martyn | 1490 Robert Archebould |
| | 1495 Thomas Bailey | 1495 John Aylred (2) |
| | 1497 Robert Johnson | William Pacy |
| | 1498 John Bayous sr. | |
| | John Chert | |
| | Simon Granger | |
| | 1500 Thomas Faldyng | |
| | 1501 John Gonell | |
| Mildenhall, John | 1494 Thomas Weder | 1495 John Gredley |
| | 1501 William Porcar sr. | 1498 William Orwell |
| | 1502 John Page sr. | 1501 Thomas Lockyngton |
| Miles, John | 1495 Richard Clark | 1493 John Holme |
| | | William Manipenny |
| Miller, John | 1498 Richard Fawne | |
| Monke, John | 1484 John Aylred | |
| Monyment, Thomas | 1496 John Gredley | 1499 John Gybbys |
| | 1502 John Davy | |
| | John Holme | |
| | Robert Nelson | |
| Mordaunt, John | 1503 John Couper | |
| Morowe, Robert, de Cambs | 1499 William Alanson | |
| | 1501, 1502 John Nottyngham (3) | |
| More, Richard | 1490 Thomas Bennet | 1490 Thomas Bennet |
| Motte, Alice, wife of Richard | 1485 John Shelley | |
| | 1487 John Woodward | |
| Motte, John | 1488 Richard Motte | |
| Motte, Richard | 1485 John Shelley | |
| | 1486 Thomas Cokman | |
| | William Hilton | |
| | Thomas Cokman and Thomas Reginald | |
| | William Wright | |
| | 1487 John Gredley | 1487 Thomas Newman |
| | Thomas Reginald | |
| | John Woodward | |
| | 1488 John Motte | 1488 John Mynsterchambre |
| | | Thomas Reginald |
| | | Richard Sent |

| Lender | Borrower | Lender Borrowed from |
|---|---|---|
| | 1492 John Gredley | |
| | 1493 Thomas Cokman | |
| | 1494 John Barnard | |
| | John Bowre | |
| | 1495 Thomas Faldyng | 1495 Robert Nicholas |
| | 1497 Anna Mynsterchambre | |
| | John Newman, abbot of the monastery de Woburn | 1498 Anna Gravy |
| | 1498 Anna Gravy | John Page sr. |
| | 1499 Robert Johnson | |
| | 1500 John Couper (5) | |
| | John Holme | |
| | Thomas May | |
| | 1501 John Gredley | |
| Motte, William | 1488 William Marshall, de Papworth Everard (2) | |
| Mounford (Mundeford), Richard | 1489 Thomas Emlyn | |
| | John Gredley | |
| Mounford, Thomas | 1499 John Abekke | 1498 Thomas May |
| | 1500 Thomas Alan | |
| | John Lawman | |
| Mounford, William | 1486 William Godwyn sr. | 1485 John Bayous |
| | John Staylis | 1486 John Aylred |
| | | 1487 John Turneskewe |
| | 1488 Thomas Baker | 1488 William Gardiner |
| | William Brown | 1490 Thomas Fecas |
| | John Gony | |
| | 1491 Richard Pelle | 1491 Richard West |
| | 1492 Roger Cook | 1493 William Nottyngham |
| | 1493 John Mayle | Anna Samt |
| | Robert Porter | 1494 John Mayle |
| | 1495 John Gredley | 1495 Anna Lockyngton |
| | Anna Lockyngton | |
| | 1496 John Custauns (2) | |
| | 1497 William Goodwyn | 1497 Robert Chandeler |
| | 1499 William Holme | 1498 Thomas Lockyngton |
| | | William Mayle (2) |
| | | 1499 John Stokys |
| | 1500 John Dey | |
| | Thomas Rose de St Neots | |
| | 1501 Robert Porter | |
| | 1502 John Branden | |
| | Roger Cook | |
| | William Lane | |
| | 1503 Richard Kellnet | |
| Myghton, John | 1500 John Couper | |
| | John Gredley | 1500 John Couper |

| Lender | Borrower | Lender Borrowed from |
|---|---|---|
| Mynsterchambre, Anna | 1492 John Foster | |
| | 1493 Agnes Gardiner | |
| | John Lawman | |
| | 1494 John Custauns | |
| | Robert Vowght | |
| | 1495 Robert Cawdwell | 1497 Richard Motte |
| Mynsterchambre, John | 1485 Henry Paten | |
| | 1488 Richard Motte | |
| | John Schylling | |
| | 1489 Thomas Bailey | |
| | William Godwyn | |
| | John Gredley | 1491 Thomas Newman |
| | 1491 Henry Trayley | |
| Mynt, William | 1494 Thomas Bennet | |
| | 1496 John Barnard jr. | |
| | 1497 John Custauns | |
| | John Mayle | |
| | 1498 Thomas Bennet | |
| | Richard Cook | |
| | 1499 William Farthyng | |
| | John Mayster | |
| | 1500 Thomas Judd | |
| | John Nottyngham | |
| | Thomas Pasgood | |
| | John Vincent | |
| | 1501 William Ibott | |
| Nelson, Robert | 1501 Henry Crysp | 1499 Simon Granger |
| | | 1502 Thomas Monyment and Richard West |
| Newman, Thomas | 1486 William Wright, butcher | |
| | 1487 Richard Motte (2) | |
| | 1489 William Orwell | 1489 William Orwell |
| | | Richard Pelle |
| | | John Smyth |
| | 1490 John Gybbys | 1490 John Aylred |
| | | 1491 John Aylred |
| | | William Goneld |
| | | William Nicholl |
| | 1492 Benedict Grey | 1492 John Bailey |
| | | Thomas Faldyng |
| | | Alice Kyng |
| | | William Manipenny |
| | | 1493 William Kyng |
| | | Thomas Maryot |
| | | John Oxen |
| | | John Stukeley |
| Nicholl, John | 1492 John Bryte | 1502 William Mayle |
| Nicholas, Robert | 1484 William Edmond | |
| | 1490 John Glover | |
| | 1492 John Barnard | 1492 John Barnard |

| LENDER | BORROWER | LENDER BORROWED FROM |
|---|---|---|
| | 1493 Roger Cook (2) | |
| | 1495 Thomas Baker | |
| | Richard Motte | |
| | 1497 William Goodwyn | 1498 Richard Grene (2) |
| | Thomas Woodcroft | |
| | 1500 William Holme (3) | 1500 William Holme |
| | | 1502 Robert Rodys |
| | 1503 John Couper (2) | 1503 John Couper |
| Nicholl, William | | 1485 Thomas Faldyng |
| | | Agnes Gardener and |
| | | Henry Martin |
| | 1486 John Horwood | 1486 Agnes Gardener (2) |
| | Thomas Lawman | William Gyle |
| | William Lessy (2) | |
| | John Rede and wife | 1487 John Page |
| | Agnes | Agnes Rede |
| | 1488 William Hilton | 1488 John Clark de Brampton |
| | | William Gardiner (3) |
| | 1489 Thomas Faldyng | 1489 John Lumbard (2) |
| | John Lumbard (2) | William Orwell |
| | | Thomas Reginald |
| | | Richard West |
| | 1490 Thomas Newman | 1490 John Gony |
| | 1491 John Brown | John Page jr. |
| | Margaret Frost, servant | 1491 Thomas Emlyn |
| | Richard Mayle | John Turneskewe |
| | Richard Mayle | 1492 Edward Barre |
| | Robert Nicholas | John Bour |
| | 1492 Richard West (2) | John Foster |
| | | William Mayle |
| | | William Manipenny and |
| | | William Kyng |
| | | William Schylling |
| | 1493 Richard West | Richard West |
| Norton, Thomas | 1489 John Barnard | |
| | 1490 Richard Kyng | |
| | 1491 John Holme | |
| Nottyngham, John | 1499 Thomas Judd | 1497 Thomas Smyth |
| | Thomas Pasgood | |
| | Thomas Saby | |
| | William W[er]ymys | |
| | 1500 John Bawdwyn | 1500 Thomas Ascheman |
| | John Stokes, miller | William Mynt |
| | | 1501 John Brewster |
| | | Robert Morowe de |
| | | Cambs (2) |
| | | William Orwell |
| | | John Taylor |
| | | 1502 Robert Morchews |
| | | John Pelle |

| LENDER | BORROWER | LENDER BORROWED FROM |
|---|---|---|
| | 1503 Thomas Barber (2) | 1503 John Feltwelle and John Brewster<br>William Ibott<br>Thomas Lockyngton and Thomas Maryot |
| Nottyngham, William | 1486 William Diggby | |
| | 1487 Thomas Bench | 1488 John Barnard |
| | 1490 Richard West | |
| | 1493 William Mounford | |
| Orston, Richard | 1499 Thomas Faldyng | |
| Orwell, William | 1486 William Diggby | |
| | William Manipenny | |
| | 1487 Thomas Emlyn | |
| | Robert Porter (2) | |
| | John Shalford | |
| | 1488 William Gardener | |
| | John Gredley (2) | |
| | William Hilton | |
| | Roger Manipenny | |
| | John Sent | |
| | 1489 William Holme | |
| | William Nicholl | |
| | Thomas Newman | |
| | 1490 Thomas Baker | |
| | 1491 Agnes Alwright, butcher, widow | |
| | William Est | |
| | 1492 WilliamGodwyn | |
| | John Gredley | |
| | 1495 Robert Caldwell | |
| | 1496 Robert Caldwell | |
| | John Foster | |
| | William Frere | |
| | William Godwyn | |
| | John Vincent | |
| | 1497 John Custauns | |
| | 1498 Thomas Faldyng | |
| | Robert Huston | |
| | John Mildenhall | |
| | 1499 John Barnard, sub-bailiff | |
| | Alice Pelle | |
| | 1500 Roger Cook | |
| | 1501 John Barnard, sub-bailiff | |
| | Richard Fawne | |
| | John Gredley | |
| | John Nottyngham | |
| | John Stacy | |
| Osse, Thomas | 1498 John Stokys | |
| | 1502 John Dey | |
| Osteler, Simon | 1489 Robert Marshall | |

| Lender | Borrower | Lender Borrowed from |
|---|---|---|
| Oxen, Lord John | 1485 John Schylling | |
| | | 1492 William Basse<br>John Matthew |
| | 1493 Thomas Newman | |
| | 1497 John Abernerly | |
| Pacy, Agnes, executor of<br>William's will | 1496 William Godwyn | |
| Pacy, William | 1495 William Melbourne | |
| | 1496 Roger Cook<br>Richard Clerk<br>John Mayle | |
| Page, Adam | 1501 John Gredley | |
| Page, John jr. | 1490 William Nicholl | |
| | 1496 Henry Smyth | 1499 John Ussher and<br>William Manipenny,<br>bailiffs for John Dey |
| | 1502 John Gybbys | |
| Page, John | 1484 John Rede and wife<br>Agnes | |
| | 1487 William Nicholl | |
| | 1489 Thomas Faldyng | |
| Page, John son of John<br>Davy | 1499 John Holme | |
| Page, John sr. | 1488 John Gredley<br>Richard Payne | 1486 Thomas Frost |
| | 1489 John Gredley | |
| | 1490 Edward Barre | |
| | 1491 John Smyth, labourer | |
| | 1494 William Granger | |
| | 1498 Richard Motte | 1502 John Milnall |
| Page, Thomas | 1496 William Ede | 1494 John Turneskewe |
| | | 1497 Robert Ballard<br>John Stukeley |
| | | 1500 William Dey |
| Parker, William | 1485 de uno collar maker | |
| | 1488 John Barnard | |
| Pasgood, Thomas | 1499 John Stokys, butcher | 1499 John Nottyngham |
| | | 1500 Henry Gybbys and<br>William Mynt |
| | 1500 John Saby | 1501 William Mynt |
| | 1501 Richard Fawne | 1501 John Clark, miller<br>Richard Fawne |
| Passelowe, John | 1491 William Este | |
| | 1493 John Fecas | |
| Passelowe, John sr. | 1484 John Sent | |
| Pelle, John | 1502 John Nottyngham | |
| Pelle, John, de Brampton | 1500 John Holme | |
| Pelle, Richard | 1485 Robert Warde | |
| | 1489 Thomas Newman | |
| | 1490 William Godwyn | |

| LENDER | BORROWER | LENDER BORROWED FROM |
|---|---|---|
| | | 1491  William Mounford |
| | 1496  William Hilton | |
| Pelle, William | 1489  Roger Cook | |
| | Benet Grey | |
| | 1500  John Couper | 1500  John Couper |
| | | John Stukeley |
| | | 1501  Thomas Gybbys |
| Pelman, William | 1497  John Custauns | 1490  Thomas Fecas |
| | | 1491  William Manipenny |
| | | 1492  Simon Granger (2) |
| | | 1497  John Stukeley |
| | | 1500  William Manipenny |
| | | 1502  John Aylred |
| Pernell, Richard | 1493  Thomas Elys | |
| | Thomas Perc' | 1497  John Ussher |
| Pescode, John | 1489  John Barnard jr., | 1490  John Barnard, jr., |
| | labourer | labourer |
| Pope, Margaret | 1502  John Cook | |
| Porter, John | 1500  John Mayle | |
| | William Vyntner | 1501  Edmund Rogerson |
| Prestwode, Simon | 1487  John Gony | 1485  Thomas Balle |
| | | 1486  Richard Lockyngton |
| | | 1487  Simon Maynard |
| | | 1497  William Frost |
| | | 1498  William Arnborough |
| Punt, John | 1503  Thomas Bawdwyn | 1501  Thomas Faldyng |
| Rede, Agnes | 1487  William Nicholl | |
| | 1489  Richard Chycheley | |
| | John Sent, artificer | |
| Rede, John | 1485  William Wright | |
| Rede, John and wife Agnes | | 1484  George Hansen |
| | | 1484  John Page |
| | | 1486  William Nicholl |
| Rede, John, mason | 1485  John Shalford and John | |
| | Snell | |
| Reginald, Thomas | 1484  John Schylling | 1485  John Dalton |
| | | William Mayle |
| | 1486  John Gredley | 1486  Richard Motte (2) |
| | | 1487  John Gredley |
| | 1487  William Hilton | Richard Motte |
| | 1488  John Gredley | 1488  John Gredley |
| | Richard Motte | Robert Dobbyn |
| | 1489  Thomas Cokman | 489  John Aylred |
| | William Nicholl | John Schylling |
| | John Schylling | |
| | | 1491  John Smyth |
| Ripley, Thomas | 1489  Thomas Faldyng | |
| | 1502  John Bayns | |
| | Robyns, John | 1501  Richard Fawne |
| Robyns, John jr. | 1500  John Couper | |
| | 1501  Roger Cook | |

| LENDER | BORROWER | LENDER BORROWED FROM |
|---|---|---|
| Robynson, John | 1491 John Lumbard | |
| Rodys, Robert | 1502 Robert Nicholas | |
| Rogerson, Edmund | 1503 John Porter | |
| Roseday, Robert | 1501 John Stokys | |
| Samt (Sent), Alice | 1495 John Barnard sr., carpenter | |
| Samt (Sent), Anna | 1493 John Gredley William Mounford | |
| Samt (Sent, Smyth), Richard | 1487 John Stalys 1488 John Cokman Richard Motte | 1491 John Garlop sr. |
| | 1492 John Gredley | 1492 Robert Symson |
| Samt (Sent), John | 1485 John Passelowe | 1487 Richard Lockyngton 1488 William Orwell 1489 John Baron |
| Samt (Sent), John, artificer | | 1489 William Bloke and wife Agnes |
| Schylling, John | | 1484 Thomas Reginald 1485 John Oxen |
| | 1486 William Hilton (2) 1487 Paul Foly | 1486 John Byglysshe 1487 John Tychemarsh 1488 John Dalton John Foster John Mynsterchambre 1489 William Ibott jr. Thomas Reginald |
| | 1489 Thomas Reginald | 1491 Richard Holme (2) |
| Schylling, William | 1491 Robert Vont 1492 William Nicholl | |
| Scot, Thomas | 1485 John Shelley | |
| Sewale, Thomas | 1494 Richard Sheter (2) | 1493 Richard Sheter |
| Sele, Richard, de Copingford | 1500 Thomas Faldyng | |
| Sheter, Richard | 1493 Thomas Sewale 1494 Thomas Bennet | 1494 William Lessy William Manipenny Thomas Sewale (2) John Ussher |
| | 1495 Richard Wode | 1495 Robert Chandeler |
| Skerw', Robert | 1501 William Godard | |
| Smyth, Henry | 1496 John Page jr. 1501 John Vincent | 1499 John Barnard, labourer |
| Smyth, John, labourer | 1489 Thomas Newman | 1488 Thomas Massey 1490 Richard West |
| Smyth, John | 1488 Roger Cook Thomas Faldyng 1490 Thomas Faldyng 1491 Thomas Reginald | 1491 Austin Arnold John Page sr. Richard West (2) |

| Lender | Borrower | Lender Borrowed from |
|---|---|---|
| | | 1492 William Smyth |
| | | Richard West |
| | 1495 Thomas Emlyn | |
| | 1496 Robert Porter | |
| | 1497 John Gredley | |
| | 1498 John Custauns | |
| | 1499 William Alenson | |
| | Ralph Wane | 1501 Thomas Gonell |
| | 1502 Thomas Manchester | |
| | 1503 John Gonell (2) | |
| | Robert Johnson (2) | |
| Smyth, John, de St. Neots | 1490 Thomas Bennet | |
| Smyth, Richard | 1489 John Gredley | |
| Smyth, Thomas | | 1490 William Gardiner |
| | | 1491 William Matthew |
| | 1494 John Snell | |
| | 1497 Robert Nicholas | |
| | 1497, 1500 John Nottyngham | |
| | 1501 John Foster | |
| Smyth, William, clerk | 1492 John Smyth | |
| | 1497 Robert Nicholas | |
| | John Nottyngham | |
| | 1501 John Foster | |
| Snell, John | | 1485 John Rede, mason |
| | | 1488 John Barnard jr. |
| | | 1489 William Gyle |
| | | Robert Robyn |
| | | John Stukeley |
| | 1490 William Fraunceys jr. | |
| | 1491 Roger Cook | |
| | 1492 Isabell Wright | |
| | 1493 Richard Chycheley | |
| | Thomas Emlyn (2) | |
| | William Hilton | |
| | Simon Granger | |
| | Alice Sent | 1494 William Manipenny |
| | | Thomas Smyth |
| | 1495 John Bryte | 1495 John Davy |
| | 1498 Robert Barland | John Stukeley |
| | Roger Cook | |
| | William Lane, chaplain | |
| | 1499 John Barnard, | 1499 John Couper |
| | candlemaker | |
| | 1500 Richard Brewster | 1500 John Brown, miller |
| | | 1501 William Barnard |
| | | Robert Olyff |
| | 1503 William Hilton | |
| | John Mayle | |
| Staylis, John | 1486 William Mounford | |
| | Richard Stukeley | |

| LENDER | BORROWER | LENDER BORROWED FROM |
|---|---|---|
| | Richard Wyllam | 1486 Richard Stukeley |
| | | 1487 Richard Samt |
| Sterlyng, John | 1495 Henry Frost | |
| Stevens, Richard | 1490 John Bayous sr. | 1491 John Bayous sr. (2) |
| | 1491 Thomas Faldyng | 1493 John Barnard (2) |
| | 1493 John Barnard | |
| | 1497 William Fryre | |
| | 1500 John Stokes, miller | |
| | 1501 John Barnard, sub-bailiff | |
| | John Mayle | |
| | William Vyntner | |
| | 1502 Thomas Faldyng | |
| | William Vyntner | 1503 Thomas Faldyng |
| Stevens, executors of William | 1499 John Mayle | |
| Stevenson, Robert | 1487 William Gardiner | |
| Stokys, John, butcher | | 1485 John Gybbys |
| | 1486 Robert Cawdwell | 1498 Thomas Osse, clerk |
| | | William Wright |
| | 1499 John Custauns | 1499 John Dey jr. |
| | Robert Godard, de | John Garlop, labourer |
| | Hunts | |
| | William Mounford | William Gonell |
| | | John Iche |
| | | Thomas Pasgood |
| | | John Stukeley (2) |
| | 1500 John Aldred | 1500 John Aldred |
| | John Bayous | John Couper (3) |
| | John Couper (2) | William Gonell |
| | William Holme | Henry Gybbys |
| | Thomas Turner | William Holme (2) |
| | William Wolfe, de | |
| | Albursley | |
| | 1501 John Barnard, sub-bailiff | 1501 John Barnard, |
| | John Everard | candlemaker |
| | Richard Fawne | Robert Chandeler |
| | William Henby (2) | William Ibott |
| | William Ibott | Anna Lockyngton |
| | | John Lockyngton |
| | | Marcus Lorydan |
| | | Robert Roseday |
| | 1502 William Manipenny | 1502 Austin Arnold |
| | William Mayle | William Browne |
| | | William Dalton |
| | | William Manipenny |
| Sudbury, John | 1501 William Holme | |
| | 1503 John Custauns | |
| Stukeley, John | 1486 William William | |
| | William Wright | |

| Lender | Borrower | Lender Borrowed from |
|--------|----------|----------------------|
| | 1488 Thomas Emlyn | |
| | Thomas Faldyng | |
| | 1490 William Godwyn | |
| | John Snell | |
| | 1493 Roger Cook | |
| | Thomas Newman | |
| | 1494 John Foster | |
| | John Snell | |
| | 1496 John Custauns | |
| | 1497 John Barnard, | |
| | candlemaker | |
| | John Couper | |
| | William Godwyn | |
| | John Gybbys | |
| | John Lawman | |
| | John Mayle | |
| | Thomas Page | |
| | William Pelman | |
| | 1498 John Averley | |
| | Thomas Byrder | |
| | John Custauns | |
| | William Ede | |
| | William Frost sr. | |
| | Thomas Kendal (2) | |
| | Robert Vont | |
| | 1499 John Barnard sr. | |
| | John Couper (2) | |
| | John Foster | |
| | John Stokys (2) | |
| | 1500 William Diggby | |
| | Richard Gilby | |
| | William Gonell | |
| | John Holme | |
| | Thomas May | |
| | Thomas Pasgood | |
| | William Pelle | |
| | 1501 John Bayous | |
| | John Vincent (2) | |
| | 1502 John Couper (2) | |
| | John Custauns | |
| | 1503 John Barnard sr. | |
| | Robert Hunt | |
| | John Mayle | |
| Stukeley, Richard | 1486 John Stokys | 1486 John Staylis |
| | 1492 Thomas Baker | 1488 Thomas Frost |
| | | 1491 Richard Lockyngton |
| | 1493 Roger Cook | |
| | William Gardener | |
| | William Kyng and | |
| | William Manipenny | |

| LENDER | BORROWER | LENDER BORROWED FROM |
|---|---|---|
| | 1494 executors of Edward Barre | |
| | 1498 John Gredley | |
| | 1499 William Kyng | |
| | 1500 John Couper (2) | 1500 John Couper |
| | 1502 Roger Cook | |
| | William Kyng (2) | 1502 William Kyng (2) |
| Stukeley, William | 1502 William Henby | |
| Swetonham, William | 1490 Thomas Faldyng | 1500 William Bloke |
| Symson, Robert | 1492 Richard Samt | |
| Syward, Thomas jr. | 1487 John Clark | |
| Syward, Thomas | 1495 John Brit | |
| Syward, William | 1498 Thomas Byrder | |
| Tache, William | 1489 John Barnard jr., husbandman | |
| Taylor, John | 1493 William Hilton | 1494 Cristina Broughton |
| | 1495 John Bayous | |
| | John Bryte | |
| | 1497 Robert Stevenson | |
| | Thomas Wilson | |
| | 1499 John Foster | |
| | 1500 John Barnard, sub-bailiff | |
| | John Bryce | |
| | 1501 Watkyn Branden | |
| | John Nottyngham | |
| Thomson, John | 1489 Agnes Wright | |
| Thomson, William, chaplain | 1499 John Fuller, de Hadenham | |
| Trayley, Henry | 1499 William Bloke and wife Agnes | 1491 John Mynt Robert Vont |
| | John Gredley | 1492 William Lessy |
| Turneskewe, John | 1484 Thomas Bennet | 1486 John Gredley (2) |
| | 1487 William Mounford | |
| | 1489 Roger Cook | |
| | John Gredley | |
| | 1490 Godfrey Wright | |
| | 1491 William Nicholl | |
| | 1492 Roger Cook | |
| | 1494 Thomas Mayle | |
| | Thomas Page | |
| | 1495 John Gredley | |
| | 1497 Robert Nicholas, vicar | |
| | 1498 John Couper, butcher | |
| | 1500 Thomas Faldyng | |
| | John Holme | |
| | Thomas Holme | |
| Tychemarsh, John | 1487 William Ponder | |
| | John Schylling | |
| | 1488 John Corby jr., husbandman | |

| Lender | Borrower | Lender Borrowed from |
|---|---|---|
| | William Gyle | |
| | Richard Kyng | |
| | 1489 Thomas Faldyng | |
| | William Gardiner | |
| | 1502 John Barnard | |
| | 1503 Thomas Barber | |
| Ussher, John | 1490 Benedict Grey | |
| | 1493 John Glover | |
| | John Gredley (2) | |
| | 1494 Richard Sheter (2) | 1497 Thomas Perc' |
| | 1499 William Page jr. | 1503 John Laxton |
| Vont, Robert | 1491 Henry Trayley | 1491 William Shylling |
| | | 1492 Agnes Cook and |
| | | William Bowre |
| | | 1498 John Stukeley |
| Vyntner, William | 1497 Robert Lucas | 1498 William Gonell |
| | | 1499 Henry Gybbys |
| | | 1500 Thomas Faldyng |
| | | John Porter |
| | 1502 John Barnard | 1501 Richard Stevens |
| | 1502 William Couper | 1502 Richard Stevens |
| Walton, Richard | 1495 Richard Clark | |
| Wane, Ralph | 1499 John Smyth | 1499, 1501 William Holme |
| Warde, Thomas | 1487 William Gyle | 1488 William Gyle |
| Wattys, John, de Heming- | 1491 Anna Plumpton | |
| ford Abbots | | |
| West, Richard | 1488 Thomas Cokman | 1487 William Gardiner |
| | | 1488 Alice Bigge |
| | | Thomas Cokman |
| | 1489 Thomas Cokman | 1489 Thomas Cokman |
| | William Nicholl (2) | |
| | 1490 Thomas Baker | 1490 William Nottyngham |
| | William Godwyn | |
| | 1491 Thomas Bennet | |
| | Richard Kyng | |
| | William Gardiner | |
| | William Mounford | |
| | John Smyth (2) | |
| | William Snell | |
| | 1492 William Nicholl | 1492 William Gardiner |
| | John Smyth | William Nicholl |
| | | 1493 Richard Kyng and Wil- |
| | | liam Manipenny |
| | | 1494 John Aldred |
| | | 1498 William Kyng |
| | 1501 John Shalford and wife | 1501 John Aldred |
| | Agnes | |
| | 1502 John Davy | |
| | John Holme | |
| | Robert Nelson | |

| LENDER | BORROWER | | LENDER BORROWED FROM | |
|---|---|---|---|---|
| Weyther, Thomas | 1489 | Thomas Bennet | | |
| Whitford, Richard, vicar | 1484 | Thomas Faldyng | 1487 | John Brewster |
| | | | 1488 | John Lockyngton, William Manipenny, and Godfrey and Isabel Wright |
| Wyddyr (Weder), Thomas | 1494 | John Mildenhall | | |
| | 1498 | John Bryte | | |
| | | Richard Fawne | | |
| | 1500 | William Godwyn | | |
| | 1501 | Richard Fawne (2) | | |
| Wyllyam (Wellam), Richard | 1495 | Thomas Bennet | 1486 | John Staylis |
| Wyllyam (Wellam), William | 1494 | Thomas Bennet | 1484 | Robert Conys |
| | | | 1486 | John Stukeley |
| Wolfe, William de Albursley, gentleman | 1502 | John Bayous | 1500 | John Stokys |
| Wright, Godfrey | 1486 | Richard Hodege | | |
| | 1487 | Richard Legge | 1487 | Thomas Bennet |
| | 1488 | Thomas Bennett | | |
| | | Richard Whitford | 1489 | Thomas Lockyngton |
| | | | 1490 | John Turneskewe |
| Wright, Isabella | 1488 | Richard Whitford | 1491 | Thomas Frost |
| | 1491 | Agnes Wright, butcher | 1492 | John Snell |
| | | | 1493 | William Basse (2) |
| | | | | William Kyng |
| Wright, William | | | 1484 | Richard Lockyngton |
| | | | 1485 | Agnes and John Red |
| | | | 1486 | John Aldred and John Lockyngton |
| | | | | Thomas Newman |
| | | | | John Stukeley |
| | 1498 | John Stokys | 1487 | Henry Dawson |
| Wright, William, butcher | | | 1485 | John Lockyngton |
| Wright, William, de St. Ives | 1491 | William Bloke | | |
| Wynge, Thomas, de Hunts | 1495 | John Tanner | | |
| Wyld, John | 1502 | William Henby | 1502 | Thomas Fecas |

# Appendix 10

## Millers' Accounts for Godmanchester

Earliest evidence for the value of Godmanchester mills occurs in the 1279 Hundred Roll. In that record the mills of Godmanchester together with the eight acres of meadow at Holme were said to be worth £15. Since the farm assessment for the meadow would be at eight pence per acre, the Holme assessment would come to 5s.4d. This left the value of revenues from the mills as £14 14s.8d. In short, the mills were expected to pay some nine per cent of the £120 farm to the Crown. From the accounts in Appendix 1 above, it can be found that over the accounting years 1412-1414 the mills returned (*exitus*) only £4 9s.5d. (Easter to Michaelmas, 13s.2d. ; Michaelmas to Easter, £3 16s.3d.). From Michaelmas to Easter, 1445-1446, the return was only £1 7s. As we know from elections on the mid-century frankpledge rolls, the mills were managed by four men, one elected from each street. Apparently one of the steps taken in the accounting reorganization of Godmanchester was to place the mills at farm. From Easter to Michaelmas in 1471 the mills paid a farm of £13. Over the same term in 1483 the farm was £12. As has been noted in Chapter 6, the town had to be responsible for repairs of the mills. In 1478 £3 13s.4d. were requested by Thomas Fecas for this purpose and in 1488 a general request for timber for repair was made by Thomas Balle. And as prominent men took over the farm there is no evidence from the Jurors' Book that any of these ever fell into arrears for the farm of the mill.

In Box 1, Bundle 13 of the Godmanchester Borough Records are two bundles of Millers' Accounts for the fifteenth century. In the full sequence of records from Box 1, miller's accounts are numbered 64A, 65A and 65C. Account 64A has a heading indicating that this account survives for the period before the mills were put at farm. In fact all three records would seem to come from this earlier period and no doubt survived as part of the general dossier of records that we owe to the administrative reform over the third quarter of the century. More precise dating cannot be given for the further reason that relatively few names of Godmanchester residents occur in these accounts. But some of the names for all three records can be found in various documents over the 1460s. Whether most of the Godmanchester people were accounted on some other record, paid for milling by grain or escaped payment (and hence forced the adoption of the farm system) cannot be ascertained.

But these records are valuable indicators of the fact that Godmanchester mills served a considerable region—Hilton, Huntingdon, Offord, Peterborough, Ramsey, Stanton. With so many cited only as 'outsiders', and many names not identifiable as to place, the region served cannot be further specified. These records are presented here to assist someone in the much-needed study of the mills of the Huntingdon section of the Ouse River. Such a study must be undertaken on a regional basis. These records also serve of course to supply data for the milling costs of various types of grain.

Unfortunately the end of the 64A record is decayed so that the total revenues, total number of bushels and several names cannot be found. The legible list of revenues comes to £8 16s.9½d. Despite the incomplete list of names, there is some intimation of the activities of commercial people. For example, Ryse of Huntingdon was likely a baker and his ten entries show the periodic milling, for a total of 12 bushels, usually of wheat, at a total cost of 9s.5d. Robert Dobbyn purchased liberty in 1437 and may have died during the term of this account for his name appears only once and then Isabella Dobbyn has six entries for a total of 21 bushels at 15s.11d. cost. The documents classified as 65A and 65C may be parts of the same account for the pattern of names is very similar. Furthermore, although the heading is gone very little may be torn off since the total of these two records comes to £9 2s.8½d., very close to the total given at the foot of 65C. Among the very interesting items in 65A and 65C is the extensive activities of a piebaker, on one occasion milling peas.

Bundle 13, Roll 64A        MILLERS' ACCOUNTS

The account of Thomas Nichol, John Robyn, Henry Hildemar and Richard Waleys senior, custodians of the mills of the vill of Godmanchester. From feast of Easter to feast of Michaelmas following.

| NAME | BUSHEL(S) | PRODUCT | PRICE |
|------|-----------|---------|-------|
| William Ryse de 'H' | 1 | wheat flour | 1s. 2d. |
| Thomas Edmond | 1 | wheat flour | 1s. 2d. |
| Robert Dobbyn | 4 | wheat | 2s. 8d. |
| a man de Papworth | 1 | wheat | 8d. |
| an outsider de 'H' | 1 | wheat | 9d. |
| Ryse de 'H' | 1 | wheat | 9d. |

| Name | Bushel(s) | Product | Price |
|---|---|---|---|
| Hugh Monye | 2 | wheat | 1s. 6d. |
| Burgeyme de [   ] | 4 | peas | 1s. |
| John Caperon de Hilton | 3 | mixed grain | 1s. 6d. |
| Thomas Edmond de 'H' | 1 | mixed grain | 6d. |
| John Melbourne jr. | 1 | mixed grain | 6d. |
| Beatrix Brabaham | 1 | mixed grain | 6d. |
| Thomas Fuller | 2 | large flour | 1s. 5d. |
| John Clement | 1 | wheat flour | 1s. 2d. |
| Ryse de Huntingdon | 1 | wheat flour | 1s. 2d. |
| John Mokeforde de Hunts | 1 | wheat flour | 1s. 2d. |
| Isabella Dobbyn | 4 | wheat | 3s. |
| and same Isabella | 3 | wheat | 2s. 3d. |
| Richard Conyff | ½ | wheat | 4d. ob. |
| outsiders | 3 | wheat | 2s. 3d. |
| John Melbourne jr. | 1 | mixed grain | 6d. |
| Thomas Tully | ½ | wheat | 3d. |
| William Bennet | 1 | mixed grain | 6d. |
| John Waleys | 1½ | mixed grain | 9d. |
| Thomas Mynsterchambre | 4 | peas | 1s. |
| outsiders | ? | mixed grain, peas, flour | 8s. 1d.ob. |
| outsiders | 2 | large flour | 1s. 6d. |
| outsiders | 2 | mixed grain | 10d. |
| John Reygate | 3 | wheat | 2s. 3d. |
| John Stal' | 4 | wheat | 3s. |
| John Ibott sr. | ½ | wheat | 4d.ob. |
| John White | 1 | mixed grain | 6d. |
| Ryse de 'H' | 1 | mixed grain | 6d. |
| John Stal' | ½ | peas, flour | 2d.ob. |
| William Barber | ? | quisqb' | 2d. |
| Ryse de 'H' | 1 | wheat flour | 1s. 2d. |
| Robert Allyngham | 1 | wheat flour | 1s. 2d. |
| Thomas Edmond | 1 | wheat flour | 1s. 2d. |
| Ryse de 'H' | 1 | wheat flour | 1s. 2d. |
| Thomas Fylle | 1 | wheat | 9d. |
| John Reygate | 1 | wheat | 9d. |
| John Clement | 1 | wheat | 9d. |
| Hugh Monye | 1 | mixed grain | 5d.ob. |
| a man de 'H' | 2 | wheat | 1s. 6d. |
| John Garlop | 1 | mixed grain | 6d. |
| a man de Hilton | 2 | mixed grain | 1s. |
| Ryse de 'H' | 1 | mixed grain | 6d. |
| John Waleys | 1 | mixed grain | 6d. |
| an outsider | 1 | mixed grain | 6d. |
| Thomas Fuller de Ramsey | 1 | large flour | 9d. |
| John Stal' | 4 | wheat | 3s. 4d. |
| Isabella Dobbyn | 4 | wheat | 3s. 4d. |
| the same Isabella | 1 | wheat | 10d. |
| a woman de 'H' | 1 | wheat | 10d. |
| John Robyn | 1 | wheat flour | 1s. 2d. |

| NAME | BUSHEL(S) | PRODUCT | PRICE |
|---|---|---|---|
| Agnes Fisher | 1 | large flour | 4d.ob. |
| Thomas Tully | 1 | peas | 3d. |
| John Garlop [Thakker] | 1 | mixed grain | 6d. |
| John Caperon de Hilton | 1 | mixed grain | 6d. |
| outsiders | 1 | mixed grain | 6d. |
| Ryse de 'H' | 2 | mixed grain | 1s. |
| Richard Caperon | ½ | mixed grain | 3d. |
| John Barre | 1 | wheat | 10d. |
| and same John | 2 | wheat | 1s. 8d. |
| Isabella Dobbyn | 5 | wheat | 4s. 2d. |
| a woman de 'H' | ½ | large flour | 4d.ob. |
| Hugh Monye de 'H' | ½ | peas, flour | 2d.ob. |
| John Garlop, thatcher | 1 | mixed grain | 6d. |
| John Caperon de Hilton | 1 | mixed grain | 6d. |
| outsiders | 1 | mixed grain | 6d. |
| outsiders | 1 | mixed grain | 6d. |
| Richard Cave | 2 | wheat | 1s. 8d. |
| the same Richard | 1 | mixed grain | 6d. |
| the same Richard | | cask of malt | 3s. 4d. |
| John Mase(kin') | 1 | wheat flour | 1s. 2d. |
| John Cossale de 'H' | 1 | wheat flour | 1s. 2d. |
| Ryse de 'H' | 1 | wheat flour | 1s. 2d. |
| Thomas Fuller de Ramsey | 1 | wheat flour | 1s. 2d. |
| Thomas Edmond | 1 | wheat flour | 1s. 2d. |
| John Stal' | 1 quarter | wheat | 5s. 4d. |
| Isabella Dobbyn | 4 | wheat | 2s. 8d. |
| Richard Cave | 1 | wheat flour | 1s. 2d. |
| John Stal' | 3 | wheat | 2s. |
| outsiders | 4 | wheat | 2s. 8d. |
| Thomas Fuller | 1½ | large flour | 9d. + 4d. |
| William Bennet | 1 | mixed grain | 6d. |
| John Caperon de Hilton | 2 | mixed grain | 1s. |
| Thomas Fuller de Ramsey | 1 | mixed grain | 6d. |
| outsiders | 1 | mixed grain | 6d. |
| Beatrix Brabaham | 1 | mixed grain | 6d. |
| John Robyn | 1 | mixed grain | 6d. |
| same John Robyn | ? | ? | 2d. |
| same John Robyn | ? | cask malt | 10s. 8d. |
| Ryse | 2 | mixed grain | 10d. |
| Robert Prop' de Stanton | ? | ? | 3s. |
| Robert Heri | ? | ? | 1s. 3d. |
| John Fuller de Offord | ? | ? | 10d. |
| Thomas Fuller de Ramsey | ? | ? | 3s. |
| John de Stanton | ? | ? | 1s. 10d. |
| Thomas Fisher | ? | ? | 1s. 10d. |

[Doc. 65A]                    [No heading]

| Name | Bushel(s) | Product | Price |
|------|-----------|---------|-------|
| William Miller | 1 | wheat | 7d. |
| Thomas Emerlyn | ½ | wheat | ? |
| Richard Chartre | 1 | wheat | 7d. |
| outsider | 1 | wheat | 7d. |
| Richard Barre | 2 | wheat | 1s. 2d. |
| Harryngton de 'H' | 2 | wheat | 1s. 1d. |
| Margaret Barnard | ½ | wheat | 3d.ob. |
| Richard Newgent | 1 peck | wheat | 1d.ob. |
| Thomas Elsam, bailiff de 'H' | 2 | wheat | 1s. 1d. |
| Piebaker | 2 | wheat | 1s. 2d. |
| Thomas Kopple | 2 | wheat | 1s. 1d. |
| outsiders | ½ | wheat | 3d. |
| Richard Stanlake | 1½ | wheat | 10d.ob. |
| outsiders de 'H' | ½ | wheat | 3d. |
| John Nottyngham | 2 | wheat | 1s. |
| John Harna | 1 | wheat | 6d. |
| William Longe | 2 | wheat | 12d. |
| outsider de 'H' | 1 | wheat | 6d. |
| William Lessy | 1 | mixed grain | 4d. |
| William Longe | ½ | mixed grain | 2d. |
| John Chaunt' | ½ | mixed grain | 2d. |
| Hugh Grona' | ½ | mixed grain | 2d. |
| John Fraunceys | ½ | mixed grain | 2d. |
| outsiders | 4½ | mixed grain | 1s. 6d. |
| Thomas Emerlyn | 3 | mixed grain | 1s. |
| William Miller | 2 | wheat | 1s. 1d. |
| Dawsyn | 2 | wheat | 1s. 1d. |
| Thomas Taylor | 1 quarter | wheat | 4s. 4d. |
| Thomas Bailey | 1 | mixed grain | 4d. |
| William Miller | ½ | mixed grain | 2d. |
| outsider | 2 | peas | 8d. |
| 1 outsider | 2 | wheat | 2d. |
| Piebaker | 2 | wheat | 1s. 2d. |
| Townshende | 1 | wheat | 7d. |
| outsiders | 1½ | wheat | 10d. |
| Thomas Bailey | 1 | wheat | 7d. |
| John Glover | 1 | wheat | 7d. |
| Piebaker | 2 | wheat | 1s. 2d. |
| Thomas Waleys | 1 | [wheat] | 7d. |
| Blo[we] | 1 | wheat | 7d. |
| Thomas Woodward | 2 quarters | wheat | 9s. 4d. |
| William Miller | 1 | wheat | 7d. |
| John Cook | ½ | wheat | 3d.ob. |
| outsiders de 'H' | ½ | wheat | 3d.ob. |
| John Barnard | 1 | mixed grain | 5d. |
| Simon Granger | 1 | mixed grain | 5d. |
| William Barnard | ½ | mixed grain | 2d.ob. |
| Thomas Edenham | ½ | mixed grain | 2d.ob. |
| outsiders | 2 | mixed grain | 9d. |

| Name | Bushel(s) | Product | Price |
|---|---|---|---|
| Thomas Wauk | 1 | peas | 6d. |
| Thomas Edenham | 1 | peas | 6d. |
| Piebaker | 1 | peas | 6d. |
| Perse Hossewet | 2 | peas | 1s. |
| Henry Barnard | 1 | peas | 6d. |
| John Bak | 1 quarter | wheat | 4s. 8d. |
| Bote[lak] de Err're | 1 | wheat | 7d. |
| outsider de 'H' | ½ | wheat | 3d.ob. |
| John Stak' | 5 | wheat | 2s. 10d. |
| Piebaker | 2 | wheat | 1s. 2d. |
| outsiders | ½ | wheat | 3d.ob. |
| John Tully | ½ | wheat | 3d.ob. |
| Ellesam bailiff de 'H' | 1 | wheat | 7d. |
| John Cook | ½ | wheat | 3d.ob. |
| Piebaker | 3 | wheat | 1s. 9d. |
| Thomas Couper | ½ | wheat | 3d. |
| outsiders | 1 | peas | 6d. |
| Andrew Ede, shoemaker | 2 | wheat | 1s. |
| Piebaker | 3 | wheat | 1s. 9d. |
| Roger Marshall | 1 | peas | 7d. |
| John Woodward | 2 quarters | [wheat] | 9s. 4d. |
| outsiders | 1 | wheat | 7d. |
| outsiders | 4 | mixed grain | 1s. 8d. |
| outsiders | 4 | mixed grain | 1s. 8d. |
| William Lessy | 1 | mixed grain | 5d. |
| William Lessy | 2 | mixed grain | 10d. |
| William Longe | 1½ | mixed grain | 7d.ob. |
| outsiders | 4 | mixed grain | 1s. 8d. |
| outsiders | 4 | mixed grain | 1s. 8d. |
| outsiders | 2 | mixed grain | 10d. |
| William Miller | ½ | mixed grain | 3d.ob. |
| Richard Wyllam | 1 | mixed grain | 5d. |
| Richard Wyllam | 1 (quarter) + 5 bushels | peas | 4s. 4d. |
| Thomas Waleys | 1½ | wheat | 10d.ob. |
| Thomas Balle | 1 | wheat | 7d. |
| John Cook de 'H' | 1 | wheat | 7d. |
| John Baker | 1 quarter | wheat | 4s. 7d. |

[Doc. 65C]                    [No heading]

| NAME | BUSHEL(S) | PRODUCT | PRICE | |
|------|-----------|---------|-------|---|
| John Baker | 4 | [wheat] | 2s. | 4d. |
| William Miller | 1 | wheat | | 7d. |
| John Woodward | 1 | wheat | | 7d. |
| Thomas [Wauk] | [10] | wheat | 5s. | 9d. |
| Piebaker | 2 | wheat | 1s. | 2d. |
| John [Baker] | [4] | wheat | 2s. | 4d. |
| William Miller | 1 | wheat | | 7d. |
| Thomas Wett | 1 quarter | wheat | 4s. | 8d. |
| John [Enes'm] | 1 | wheat | | 7d. |
| Piebaker | 3 | wheat | 1s. | 9d. |
| Richard Stanlake | ½ | wheat | | 3d.ob. |
| William Miller | 1 | wheat | | 7d.ob. |
| John Paryche | 1 | wheat | | 7d.ob. |
| Thomas Edenham | 1 | wheat | | 7d.ob. |
| John Edward | 1½ quarter | wheat | 7s. | 6d. |
| John Edward | 1½ cask | malt | 1s. | 10d. |
| Piebaker | 3 | wheat | 1s. | 10d. |
| Piebaker | 3 | wheat | 1s. | 10d. |
| John Batirwyke | 1 | wheat | | 7d.ob. |
| outsiders | 4 | mixed grain | 1s. | 8d. |
| John Pennyman | 1 | mixed grain | | 5d. |
| Henry Paton | 1 | mixed grain | | 5d. |
| Simon Motte | 1 | mixed grain | | 5d. |
| John Barnard | 1 | mixed grain | | 5d. |
| Thomas Couper | 1 | mixed grain | | 5d. |
| and same Thomas | 1 | mixed grain | | 5d. |
| Richard Motte | 1 | mixed grain | | 5d. |
| outsiders | 4 | mixed grain | 1s. | 8d. |
| John Turneskewe | 1 | mixed grain | | 5d. |
| Richard Stanlake | 2 | mixed grain | | 10d. |
| Piebaker | ½ | peas | | 3d. |
| William Bugge | ½ | mixed grain | | 2d. |
| the same William | 1 | wheat | | 8d. |
| John Nottyngham | ½ | peas | | 3d. |
| William William | 2 | mixed grain | | 10d. |
| outsiders | 2 | mixed grain | | 10d. |
| outsiders | 1 | mixed grain | | 5d. |
| Richard Stanlake | 2 | mixed grain | | 10d. |
| Thomas Couper | 1 | wheat | | 7d. |
| and same Thomas | 1 | wheat | | 7d. |
| Thomas Edenham | 1 | wheat | | 7d. |
| William Miller | 2 | wheat | 1s. | 2d. |
| Piebaker | 3 | wheat | 1s. | 9d. |
| Botyrwyke | 2 | wheat | 1s. | 2d. |
| John Baker | 1 quarter | wheat | 4s. | 8d. |
| John Edward | 1 quarter | wheat | 4s. | 8d. |
| John Tully | 1 | wheat | | 7d. |
| John Nottyngham | 1 | peas | | 5d.ob. |
| John Nottyngham | 2 | peas | | 11d. |

| Name | Bushel(s) | Product | Price | |
|---|---|---|---|---|
| Turneskewe | 1 | wheat | | 7d. |
| Richard Fuller | ½ | wheat | | 3d.ob. |
| same Richard | Parr' | | | 3d. |
| same Richard | | for farm aqu' (watermill) | 15s. | |
| same Richard | | cask malt | 7s. | 7d. |
| John Gilby | 1 | mixed grain | | 5d. |
| outsiders | 3 | mixed grain | 1s. | 3d. |
| Piebaker | 4 | wheat | 2s. | 4d. |
| Richard Fuller | ½ | wheat | | 3d.ob. |
| John Gilby | ½ | wheat | | 3d.ob. |
| outsiders | 4 | wheat | 2s. | 4d. |
| outsiders | 1½ | peas | | 8d. |

[ends in middle of parchement]

Sum: £9 13d.ob. ["13d." is stroked out and "£9 10s.4d.ob." is entered; under that is written "£4 16s.4d."]

At the bottom of the parchment is written "John Stokes owes 6s.5d. and William Longe owes 12s.2d. and John Nottyngham [    ] 19d."

# Appendix 11

## References to Outsiders in Property Transactions and Trespass Suits 1400-1547

| | | |
|---|---|---|
| 1400 | Barber, John | St. Ives |
| | Blome, Seman | Huntingdon |
| | Coke, Richard | Huntingdon |
| | Fuller, Adam | Houghton |
| | Leche, Isabella wife of William Couper and daughter of Agnes Millicent | Huntingdon |
| | Thorneby, John | Haryngton |
| | Wynston, Emma wife of Master Roger Wynston and daughter of Agnes Millicent | Huntingdon |
| 1401 | Boys, John | St. Ives |
| | Bryan, John son of William | Yelling |
| | Cobbe, Simon | Caxton |
| | Cook, Lord Thomas rector of church at | Ellington |
| | Est, Walter | Wimpole |
| | Everard, William | Swavesey |
| | Feltwelle, John | Huntingdon |
| | Lyster, John | Huntingdon |
| | Persoun, Hugh | Huntingdon |
| | Tyler, Simon of vill | St. Ives |
| 1402 | Role, John, couper | Offord |
| | Stathern, John, rector | Grafham |
| | Taylor, Walter | Huntingdon |
| 1403 | Cristamasse, Emma | Huntingdon |
| | Ferrour, Richard | Gt. Raveley |
| 1404 | Heed, John | Lollewode |
| | Sayer, John | Huntingdon |
| 1405 | Fuller, Peter | Huntingdon |
| | Over, Henry | Over |
| | Penry, Alice | Offord |
| 1406 | Campion, John | Hilton |
| | Smith, the daughter of William | Brampton |
| | Taylor, John | Huntingdon |
| | Wyllemot, John | St. Ives |
| 1407 | Brendehouse, John | Hemingford Abbots |
| | Taylor, William son of Robert | Brington |

| | | |
|---|---|---|
| 1408 | Nichol, William | Eltisley |
| 1409 | West, Richard | Graveley |
| 1410 | Bocher (Butcher), John | Brampton |
| | Collyson, John | Hartford |
| | Fowler, William | Cambridge (Cambs.) |
| | Frances, John | Offord |
| | Fylle, Thomas | Brampton |
| | Grase, Emma daughter of Amicia | Hemingford |
| | Manning, John | Croxton |
| | Prentys, Thomas | Huntingdon |
| | Robyn, John and son Robert | Hemingford |
| | Slache, Godfrey | Caxton |
| | Swetecock, John | Yelling |
| 1411 | Barber, Thomas | Huntingdon |
| | Chamberlayn, Roger | Huntingdon |
| | Dorraunt, John, malter | Papworth |
| | Frere, John | Stanton Fen |
| | Newman, John | Graveley |
| 1412 | Bek, John | Buckworth |
| | Borele, Thomas | Hemingford Abbots |
| | Hickedon, John | Brampton |
| | Portos, John | Hunts |
| | Wetyng, William | Hartford |
| 1413 | Bedford, John | Huntingdon |
| | Martin, William and wife Agnes | Hemingford Abbots |
| 1415 | Brasier, William | Bury St. Edmunds (Suffolk) |
| | Chamberlayn, John | Fulbourne (Cambs.) |
| | Hesy, John | Grafham |
| | Peyntour, William | Gt. Gransden |
| | Wulston, John | Huntingdon |
| 1416 | Cowper, Isabella | Huntingdon |
| | Taylor, William | Gt. Raveley |
| | Temple, Nicholas | Bayngton |
| 1417 | Fynch, John | Bedford |
| | Ive, John | Hilton |
| | Parys, Galfridus | Offord |
| | Wryght, William | Hemingford Abbots |
| 1418 | Brendehouse, Thomas, alias Almar | Hemingford Abbots |
| | Brendehouse, John son of Robert | Hemingford Abbots |
| | Buckeby, William | Findson (Northants.) |
| | Cowlyngse, Margaret wife of Simon | Croxton |
| | Newell, John | Offord Darcy |
| | Rokeby, Hugh | Brampton |
| | Wranghille, William | Hartford |
| 1419 | Boteler, Robert | Yelling |
| | Colle, Richard | Gamlingay (Cambs.) |
| | Draper, John | St. Ives |
| | Farechyld, Robert | Offord |
| | Fermour, Phillip | Fen Drayton |
| | Galyon, Robert | Offord Darcy |
| | Gatele, John | Huntingdon |
| | Mason, John | Fen Drayton |

|      |                                                    |                              |
|------|----------------------------------------------------|------------------------------|
|      | Roppisley, Robert                                  | Huntingdon                   |
|      | Slade, John                                        | Gamlingay (Cambs.)           |
| 1420 | Borele, Agnes widow of Thomas                      | Hemingford Abbots            |
|      | Cobbe, Simon                                       | Fen Stanton                  |
|      | Grantesden, John, malter                           | Grantesden                   |
| 1421 | Bays, Thomas                                       | Papworth                     |
|      | Parys, Thomas, rector of                           | Graveley                     |
|      | Perkyn, Alan                                       | Offord Darcy                 |
|      | Reed, John                                         | Colchester                   |
|      | Wynne, John                                        | Hamerton                     |
| 1422 | Albotslede, John                                   | Huntingdon                   |
|      | Baly, Thomas                                       | Huntingdon                   |
|      | Brendehouse, Joan wife of Robert and daughter Agnes | Hemingford Abbots           |
|      | Bryan, John                                        | Houghton                     |
|      | Carlton, John                                      | Huntingdon                   |
|      | Fuller, John                                       | St. Ives                     |
|      | Peeke, John                                        | Huntingdon                   |
| 1423 | Bedford, John                                      | Offord Cluny                 |
|      | Brygge, Richard                                    | Huntingdon                   |
|      | Brygge, Thomas                                     | Huntingdon                   |
|      | Bryte, John                                        | Gt. Stukeley                 |
|      | Copionford, John                                   | Huntingdon                   |
|      | Harleston, Richard                                 | Hemingford Grey              |
|      | Walter, John                                       | Buckworth                    |
| 1424 | Aylmar, John                                       | Hemingford Abbots            |
| 1425 | Hoen, Thomas                                       | Buckland (Bucks.)            |
|      | Rownham, Robert                                    | Huntingdon                   |
|      | Warde, John                                        | Hemingford Grey              |
|      | Webester, William                                  | Abbots Ripton                |
| 1428 | Babon, Roger                                       | Newcastle-under-Lyme (Staffs.) |
|      | Chad, Robert                                       | Hemingford Grey              |
|      | Lavenham, Thomas                                   | Gt. Stukeley                 |
|      | Sofham, Bartholomew and son Thomas                 | Cambridge (Cambs.)           |
| 1429 | Baker, Robert                                      | Huntingdon                   |
|      | Evensham, William                                  | Huntingdon                   |
|      | Hardegane, Thomas                                  | Offord Cluny                 |
|      | Laven, Thomas                                      | Offord Cluny                 |
|      | Pulter, Lawrence                                   | Offord                       |
| 1430 | Beper, John, butcher                               | Huntingdon                   |
|      | Ordemer, John                                      | Conington (Cambs.)           |
|      | Hemingford, Thomas                                 | Conington (Cambs.)           |
|      | Plowrighte, Cristina wife of Robert, and daughter of Henry Clerk of Godmanchester | Huntingdon |
|      | Quenyng (Quenyzene), John and wife Cristina        | Buckden                      |
|      | Wilbram, William, Carmelite brother                | Cambridge (Cambs.)           |
| 1432 | Austy, John, squire                                | Cambridge County (Cambs.)    |
|      | Clophill, John                                     | St. Ives                     |
|      | Gottes, William                                    | Huntingdon                   |

|  | Robyn, John | Huntingdon |
|---|---|---|
|  | Smyth, John jr. | Hemingford Abbots |
| 1434 | Almar, John | Huntingdon |
|  | Persey, William | Offord |
| 1435 | Cutte, Thomas | Huntingdon |
|  | Miller, William | Hengton (Hinxton) (Cambs.) |
|  | Mulsco, John | Hartford |
| 1438 | Firmar' (no first name) | Penhyms (?) |
| 1439 | Dobbyn, Robert | Offord |
|  | Hamont, John | Buckden |
|  | Russel, John | Hemingford |
| 1440 | Anton, John | Brampton |
|  | Baron, John | Graveley |
|  | Chetheley, John | Offord Cluny |
|  | (G)unchepe, (no first name) | Offord Cluny |
|  | Miller, John | Offord |
|  | Mystyrthanidyr, Thomas | Huntingdon |
| 1441 | Amyson, John | Wing (Rutland) |
|  | Bakele, John | (H)ampton (Middx.) |
|  | Bryslane, Thomas | Hartford |
|  | Faryes(on), Robert | Offord |
|  | Hare, William sr. | Offord |
|  | Ilger, Thomas | Offord |
|  | Kyng, John | Steeple Gidding |
|  | Miller, William | Howington (?) |
|  | Paryrsch, John | Offord Cluny (also 1443) |
|  | Punte, Thomas | Hilton |
|  | Vyell', John | Offord (also 1452) |
| 1442 | Awbeys, John | Ramsey |
|  | Bocher, Henry | Offord |
|  | Bone, Richard | Elsworth (Cambs.) |
|  | Elys, John, chapman | St. Ives |
|  | Man from | Bassingbourne (Cambs.) |
| 1443 | Banbury, Agnes | Brampton (also 1450, 1452) |
|  | Fuller, John | Offord |
| 1444 | Gydding, John | Huntingdon |
|  | Mayhew, John | Octon (E. Yorks.) (also 1448, 1450) |
|  | Motte, Richard | Huntingdon (also 1459) |
|  | Wythsok, John | Huntingdon |
| 1445 | Robyn, Hugh | Hemingford |
| 1446 | Byrge, John | Hemingford Abbots |
| 1448 | Baker, Cristina | Kymboston (?) |
|  | Judde, the servant of William | Hemingford |
|  | Watt', John | Huntingdon |
|  | Wytnyke, William | Offord |
| 1449 | Bokyngham, Robert | St. Ives |
| 1450 | Abbot, Walter | Yelling |
|  | Birt, John | Hemingford |
|  | Brampton, Thomas | Offord |
|  | Brampton, John | Huntingdon |
|  | Caynhoo, John | Huntingdon |
|  | Parysch, John | Southoe (also 1451, 1452, 1459) |

|      | | |
|------|--------------------------|-----------------------------|
|      | Whytefoote, John         | (Huntingdon)                |
|      | Wylott', Cristina        | Conington                   |
| 1451 | King, John               | Hartford                    |
| 1452 | Vincent, John            | Offord                      |
| 1459 | Clerk, William           | Brampton                    |
|      | Delent, Edmund           | London                      |
|      | Feld, Thomas             | Hemingford                  |
|      | Manipenny, Margaret      | London                      |
|      | Parysch, Edmund          | Offord                      |
| 1461 | Bartholomew de           | Kent                        |
|      | Hemingford, John         | Hemingford                  |
|      | Dorraunt, Joan           | Hemingford                  |
| 1466 | Tailor, John             | Hartford                    |
|      | Watwall (no first name)  | Offord                      |
| 1468 | Kyng, Joan wife of John  | Hartford                    |
|      | Kent, Edmund             | London                      |
| 1469 | Newman, Thomas           | Hemingford                  |
| 1471 | (Am)slee, Walter         | St. Neots                   |
| 1472 | Freman (no first name)   | Hemingford                  |
|      | Mosse, Walter            | Hartford                    |
| 1474 | Melbourne, John          | Houghton                    |
| 1481 | Bonefax (no first name)  | Graveley                    |
|      | Rector of                | Graveley                    |
| 1482 | Adam, John               | Cambridge (Cambs.)          |
|      | Barbour, Thomas          | Hemingford Abbots           |
|      | Pope, Thomas sr.         | Hemingford Abbots           |
| 1483 | Fisher, John             | London                      |
| 1485 | Aleyn, John              | Graveley                    |
|      | Aleyn, William           | Graveley                    |
|      | Goodman, John            | Bedford (Beds.)             |
| 1486 | Aylmar, William          | Hemingford                  |
|      | Crafte, Robert           | Offord                      |
|      | Goneld, William          | Papworth (Cambs.)           |
|      | Whete, Robert            | Graveley                    |
| 1487 | Gardiner, Thomas         | Offord Cluny                |
|      | Whete, John              | Papworth                    |
| 1488 | Baseley, William         | Hemingford                  |
|      | Clerk, John              | Buckden                     |
|      | Clerk, John              | Brampton                    |
|      | Ingyll, Robert           | Hemingford                  |
|      | Marshall, William        | Papworth Everard (Cambs.)   |
| 1489 | Baseley, Thomas          | Offord                      |
|      | Corbygge, John           | Offord                      |
|      | Portas, Robert           | Hemingford                  |
| 1490 | Aleyn, John              | Yelling                     |
|      | Baseley, John            | Hemingford                  |
|      | Lord William, chaplain   | Hemingford                  |
|      | Lucas, William           | Papworth (Cambs.)           |
|      | Lucas, John              | Papworth (Cambs.)           |
|      | Olyver, John             | Papworth (Cambs.)           |
|      | Pulter, Robert           | Offord Cluny                |
|      | Pope, Thomas jr.         | Hemingford Abbots           |
|      | Puntte, Thomas           | Papworth (Cambs.)           |

| | | |
|---|---|---|
| 1491 | Birt, Henry | Offord |
| | Harre, William | Offord |
| | Lawrence, Robert | Offord Cluny |
| | Sterlyng, William | Graveley |
| | Wattys, John | Hemingford Abbots |
| | Wryght, William | St. Ives |
| 1493 | Brown, William | Hereford (Herts.) |
| 1494 | Anton, William | Offord |
| | Baseley, Robert | Hemingford |
| | Birt, John | Offord |
| | Cheven, John | Graveley |
| | Clerk, William | Huntingdon |
| | Dorraunt, John | Hemingford |
| | Ely, John | Hemingford |
| | Feltwelle (no first name) | Huntingdon |
| | Goneld, Richard | Papworth (Cambs.) |
| | Gra(t)e, William | Hemingford |
| | Hardyng, John | Papworth (Cambs.) |
| | Lawrence, John | Offord Cluny |
| | Maddy, John | Papworth |
| | Nottyngham, William | Offord Cluny |
| | Nottyngham, Thomas | Offord Cluny |
| | Outy, Thomas | Hemingford |
| | Pilton, Richard | Hemingford |
| | Portas, William | Papworth (also 1496) |
| | Smyth, William | Graveley (also 1496) |
| | Ulf, John | Offord Cluny |
| | Wryght, William | Papworth |
| | Wryght, Thomas | Graveley |
| | Wylde, William | Offord Cluny |
| 1495 | Seman, Robert | Huntingdon |
| 1496 | Baron, Dunkyn | Graveley |
| | Bryte, John | Offord Cluny |
| | Bryte, Henry | Offord Cluny |
| | Gardiner, John | Offord Cluny |
| | William, clerk de | Hemingford |
| | Hanber, Robert | Offord Cluny |
| | Page, Thomas | Croxton |
| | Pulter, John | Offord Cluny |
| | Pulter, Thomas | Offord Cluny |
| | Smyth, John | Graveley |
| | Tothe, William | Brampton |
| | Watkyn, portas (no first name) | Hemingford |
| | West, Robert | Offord Cluny |
| | Whyghthede, Thomas | Huntingdon (also 1497-1501) |
| | Wolfe, John | Offord Cluny |
| | Wryght, William | Graveley |
| | Wylkynson (no first name) | Papworth |
| 1497 | Abbot of the monastry | Woburn (Beds.) |
| | Dorraunt, Thomas | Hemingford |
| | Herforth, John | Huntingdon |
| | Gonell, John | Croxton |

| 1498 | Bacar, John | Huntingdon |
| 1499 | Helgey, John | Cambs. |
| | Morowse, Robert | Cambridge (Cambs.) |
| 1500 | Hooe, Thomas | Amtyll |
| | Pelle, John | Brampton |
| | Rose, Thomas | St. Neots |
| | Sadlowe, John | Huntingdon |
| | Sate, Robert | Coppingford |
| | Wolffe, William | Albursley |
| 1501 | Balle, Thomas | Kemakton |
| | Gonell, Thomas, vicar of | Hemingford |
| | Polle, Robert | Houghton |
| 1502 | Newton, John | Willingham |
| 1503 | Smyth, John | Caxton |
| 1504 | Paret, John | London |
| 1507 | Feppis, John | Huntingdon |
| 1509 | Lawres, John | Huntingdon |
| 1511 | Ayr, Robert | London |
| 1511 | Feld (no first name) | Hemingford |
| 1512 | Maynner, William | Hilton |
| | Wynge, Thomas | Huntingdon |
| 1513 | Clerk, Richard | Broughton |
| | Coryar, John, butcher | Huntingdon |
| | Kingston, William | Huntingdon |
| 1515 | Baker, Ka | St. Neots |
| 1518 | Halle, Thomas | Huntingdon |
| 1522 | Parker, Thomas | London |
| 1523 | Basse, Robert | Hemingford Abbots |
| | Robert de | Hemingford |
| | Thomas de | Hemingford |
| 1524 | Thasnok, Thomas | Brampton |
| 1525 | Robert de | Huntingdon |
| 1527 | Caldecote, Nicholas, gentleman | London |
| | Taylor, Thomas | Huntingdon |
| | Trevet, John | Stanton |
| 1528 | Same, Robert | Caxton |
| | Whettyng, Thomas | Hemingford |
| 1532 | Beek, William | Stowe |
| | Wolfe, Thomas | Offord Cluny |
| 1533 | Chersey, Robert, alias, Chertsey merchant | London |
| | Crofte, John, grocer | London |
| | Halle, John | Doddington |
| | Pope, John and William sons of Hugh | Hemingford |
| | Ratclyffe, Richard | London |
| | Walis, William | Huntingdon |
| 1535 | May, William | London |
| | Thong, William | Huntingdon |
| 1536 | Dormer, Michael | London |
| | Salmon, John | Diddington |
| | Toronett, John | Huntingdon |
| 1537 | Taylor, Thomas | Offord |

| | | |
|---|---|---|
| 1538 | Feppis, William, pewterer | London |
| | Gaddesby, Thomas | St. Neots |
| | Lawrence, William | Offord |
| | Merpe, Thomas | Ramsey |
| 1539 | Fe(pra), John | London |
| | Gadard, John | Houghton |
| | Horwood, William | Huntingdon |
| 1540 | Tryge (Tryse), Thomas | Brampton |
| 1541 | Dorraunt, John | Houghton |
| | Sandforth, James | Toseland |
| 1542 | Roysley, Robert | Staughton |
| | Smyth, William | Abbots Ripton |
| 1543 | Mustard, William, alias Hamy | Hemingford Grey |
| | Watson, John | Huntingdon |
| 1544 | Regis, John and wife Katherine | St. Ives |
| 1546 | Brown, Florence | Buckworth |
| | Mallory, Alice | Papworth |
| 1547 | Grenold, Thomas | Fletton |
| | Wiseman, Thomas | Graveley |

# Bibliography

A. Manuscript Sources

Huntingdon Record Office
    Godmanchester Borough Records, especially:
    1. Borough Accounts—Box 1, Bundle 10
    2. Borough Rentals—Box 1, Bundle 11
    3. Court Rolls—Box 4, Bundles 4 and 5,
                  Box 6, Bundles 3 and 4,
                  Box 7, Bundles 2 and 3,
                  Box 8, Bundles 3 and 4
    4. Court Books—Box 24, no. 1,
                  Box 27
    5. Views of Frankpledge
    6. Jurors' Book—Box 24, 1488-1635

Huntingdonshire Wills, 1479-1652

London, British Library
    Additional Rolls 34831, 34909, 39477, 39729, 39870
London, Public Record Office
    (Subsidy Rolls) Series E, Portfolio 179 nos. 4, 99, 107, 109, 116, 123, 126,
        135, 137, 141, 146 (sheep tax)
    (Ramsey Court Rolls) Series Sc 2, Portfolio 179 nos. 48, 50, 51, 53, 56, 57,
        59, 60, 61, 62, 65, 66, 67, 68.

B. Secondary Sources

Abel, W. *Agricultural Fluctuations in Europe from the Thirteenth to Twentieth
    Centuries.* Trans. O. Ordisch. London, 1980.
Ault, W. O. "The Village Church and the Village Community in Medieval England."
    *Speculum*, 45 (1970), 197-215.

Bateson, Mary, *Borough Customs.* Seldom Society, 21. London, 1906.
Beckerman, John S. "The Forty-Shilling Jurisdiction Limit in Medieval English
    Personal Actions." In *Legal History Studies*, ed. Dafyyd Jenkins, pp. 110-117.
    Cardiff: University of Wales Press, 1975.
Bennet, Judith, M. "Gender, Family and Community: A Comparative Study of the
    English Peasantry, 1278-1348." Unpublished Ph. D. thesis, University of
    Toronto, 1981.

Beresford, M. W. "The Poll Tax and Census of Sheep, 1549." *The Agricultural History Review*, 2 (1954), 22-28.

Blythe, Ronald. *Akenfield, Portrait of an English Village.* London, 1969.

Bolton, Brenda. *The Medieval Reformation.* London, 1983.

Bowker, Margaret, ed. *An Episcopal Court Book for the Diocese of Lincoln, 1514-1520.* The Lincoln Record Society, vol. 61.

——. *The Henrician Reformation in the Diocese of Lincoln under John Longland, 1521-1547.* Cambridge, 1981.

Britnell, R. H. *Growth and Decline In Colchester, 1300-1525.* New York: Cambridge University Press, 1986.

Butcher, A. F. "English Urban Society and the Revolt of 1381." In *The English Rising of 1381*, eds. R. H. Hilton and T. H. Aston, pp. 84-111. Cambridge, 1984.

Campbell, B. M. S. "The Population of Early Tudor England: Re-evaluation of the 1522 Muster Returns and 1524 and 1525 Lay Subsidies." *Journal of Historical Geography*, 7.2 (1981), 145-154.

Clark, Elaine. "Debt Litigation in a Late Medieval English Vill." In *Pathways to Medieval Peasants*, ed. J. A. Raftis, pp. 265-267. Toronto: Pontifical Institute of Mediaeval Studies, 1981.

Clark, Peter. *The English Alehouse, a Social History 1200-1830.* London, 1983.

Cornwall, Julian. "English Country Towns in the Fifteen Twenties." *The Economic History Review*, 2nd. Series, 15 (1962), 54-69.

DeWindt, Edwin. *Land and People in Holwell-cum-Needingworth.* Toronto: Pontifical Institute of Mediaeval Studies, 1972.

——. *The Liber Gersumarum of Ramsey Abbey.* Toronto: Pontifical Institute of Mediaeval Studies, 1976.

——, and Anne Reiber. *Royal Justice and the Mediaeval English Countryside.* Toronto: Pontifical Institute of Mediaeval Studies, 1981.

Dobson, R. B. "The Risings in York, Beverley and Scarborough, 1380-1381." In *The English Rising of 1381*, eds. R. H. Hilton and T. H. Aston, pp. 112-142. Cambridge, 1984.

Dyer, Christopher. *Lords and Peasants in a Changing Society: The Estates of the Bishopric of Worcester, 680-1540.* Cambridge, 1980.

——. "Warwickshire Farming 1349—c. 1520, Preparation for Agricultural Revolution." In *Dugdale Society Occasional Papers*, no. 27. Oxford, 1981.

Fieldhouse, Roger. "Social Structure from Tudor Lay Subsidies and Probate Inventories: A Case Study: Richmondshire (Yorkshire)." *Local Population Studies*, no. 12 (Spring 1974), 9-24.

Goody, Jack. *The Logic of Writing and the Organization of Society.* Cambridge, 1986.

Gottfried, R. S. *Fifteenth Century England: The Medical Response and the Demographic Consequences.* New Brunswick, NJ: Rutgers University Press, 1949.

——. *Bury St. Edmunds and the Urban Crisis: 1290-1539.* Princeton, 1982.

Green, H. J. M. *Godmanchester.* Cambridge, 1977.

Hajnal, J. "European Patterns in Perspective." In *Population in History*, ed. D. V. Glass and D. E. C. Eversley, pp. 101-143. London, 1965.

Harvey, P. D. A., ed. *The Peasant Land Market in Medieval England.* New York: Clarendon Press and Oxford University Press, 1986.

Herlihy, David. *Medieval Households.* Cambridge, MA and London, 1985.

Hilton, R. H. *The English Peasantry of the Later Middle Ages.* Oxford, 1975.

Howell, Cicely. *Land, Family and Inheritance in Transition: Kibworth Harcourt 1280-1700.* New York: Cambridge University Press, 1983.

Illingworth, W. and J. Caley, eds. *Rotuli Hundredorum.* Publications of the Records Commissioners. 1812-1818.

Jacob, E. F. *The Fifteenth Century, 1399-1485.* Oxford, 1961.

Jones, Andrew. "Bedfordshire: Fifteenth Century." In *The Peasant Land Market in Medieval England*, ed. P. D. A. Harvey, pp. 179-251. New York: Clarendon Press and Oxford University Press, 1986.

Jones, William R. "English Religious Brotherhoods and Medieval Lay Piety: The Inquiry of 1388-1389." *The Historian*, 36 (1974), 646-659.

Kowaleski, Maryanne. "Local Markets and Merchants in Late Fourteenth Century Exeter." Unpublished Ph. D. thesis, University of Toronto, 1982.

Kussmaul, Ann. *Servants in Husbandry in Early Modern England.* Cambridge, 1981.

Le Bras, Gabriel. "Les Confréries Chrétiennes, Problèmes et Propositions." In his *Études de sociologie religieuse*, 2: 423-462. Paris, 1956.

Mackie, J. D. *The Early Tudors 1485-1558.* Oxford, 1952.

McIntosh. Marjorie K. *Autonomy and Community: The Royal Manor of Havering, 1200-1500.* Oxford, 1986.

——. "Servants and the Household Unit in an Elizabethan English Community." *Journal of Family History*, 9 (1984), 3-23.

——. "Local Change and Community Control in England, 1465-1500." *The Huntingdon Library Quarterly*, 49 (1986), 219-242.

Moore, Ellen Wedemeyer. *The Fairs of Medieval England: An Introductory Study.* Toronto: Pontifical Institute of Mediaeval Studies, 1985.

Munro, John H. "The Behaviour of Wages During Deflation in Late-Medieval England and the Low Countries." [Forthcoming study.]

Noble, W. M., comp. *Calendar of Huntingdonshire Wills, 1479-1652.* The British Record Society, Vol. 42 [no date].

Owen, Dorothy M. *Church and Society in Medieval Lincolnshire.* History of Lincolnshire 5. Lincoln, 1971.

Pythian-Adams, Charles. *Desolation of a City, Coventry and the Urban Crisis of the Late Middle Ages.* Cambridge, 1979.

Raban, Sandra. "Mortmain in Medieval England." *Past and Present,* 61 (1) (1974) 3-26.
——. *The Estates of Thorney and Crowland: a Study in Medieval Monastic Land Tenure.* Cambridge, 1977.
Raftis, J. Ambrose. *Estates of Ramsey Abbey.* Toronto: Pontifical Institute of Mediaeval Studies, 1957.
——. *A Small Town in Late Medieval England Godmanchester 1278-1400.* Toronto: Pontifical Institute of Mediaeval Studies, 1982.
——. "Social Change versus Revolution of 1381." In *Social Unrest in the Middle Ages,* ed. F. X. Newman, pp. 3-22. Binghamton, NY, 1986.

Scarisbrick, J. J. *The Reformation and the English People.* Oxford, 1985.
Sheehan, Michael M. *The Will in Medieval England.* Toronto: Pontifical Institute of Mediaeval Studies, 1963.
——. *Family and Marriage in Medieval Europe.* Vancouver, 1986.
Smith, Carol A. "Regional Economic Systems: Linking Geographical Models and Socio-economic Problems." In *Regional Analysis, I, Economic Systems,* ed. Carol A. Smith, pp. 3-59. New York, 1976.
Smith, Richard M. "Kin and Neighbours in a Thirteenth-Century Suffolk Community." *Journal of Family History,* 4 (1979), 219-256.
——. "Modernization and the Corporate Medieval Village Community in England: Some Sceptical Reflections." In *Explorations in Historical Geography: Interpretative Essays,* eds. Alan R. H. Baker and Derek Gregory, pp. 140-179. Cambridge, 1984.
Smith, Toulmin and Lucy Toulmin Smith, eds. *English Gilds: The Original Ordinances of More than 100 English Gilds.* Early English Texts Society, Orig. Ser. 40. London, 1970.
Spufford, M. *Contrasting Communities: English Villagers in the Sixteenth and Seventeenth Centuries.* Cambridge, 1974.

Thrupp, Sylvia. *The Merchant Class of Medieval London.* Ann Arbor, MI 1962.
——. "Gilds." In *The Cambridge Economic History of Europe,* vol. 3, chapter 5. Cambridge, 1953.
Tittler, Robert. "Finance and Politics in English Towns, 1500-1640." [Unpublished paper.]

*Victoria History of the County of Huntingdonshire.* London: Public Record Office, D.L. 38, No. 5.

Wrightson, Keith and David Levine. *Poverty and Piety in an English Village, Terling, 1525-1700.* New York, 1979.
Wrigley, E. A. and R. S. Schofield. *The Population History of England, 1541-1871.* London, 1981.

# Index of Persons

This index does not repeat the alphabetically ordered names of Appendices 4, 5, 7, 8 and 9. As well, names in Appendix 1 and 10 are often too incomplete for inclusion.

292, 293, 295, 299, 300; Thomas 88, 97, 136, 176, 192, 292, 293, 295, 299, 300; William 12, 24, 41, 84, 109, 111, 113, 156, 157, 202, 268, 277, 288, 292, 298, 300

Gransden, John 131

Grantofte, Marv 56

Grase, see Grace

Grasse, see Grace

Gravend, Robert 363

Graveny, Thomas 358

Gravy, Anna 56; John servant of Thomas Gravy 56; Thomas 56, 354

Grawnhurst, John, butcher 66, 346

Gray (Grey), Benet 41, 287, 289; Thomas 351

Greatham, Robert 177; Robert son of William 353; William 24, 110, 111, 170, 192, 193, 222, 271, 276, 285, 286, 298, 300, 353

Gredley, John 54, 74, 152, 153, 173, 174, 175, 178, 180, 182, 300, 355, 356

Greles, John 28, 276

Grene, Agnes widow of Richard 88, 98; Edith 222; Elizabeth daughter of Richard and wife of Henry Gybbys 201; George 31, 98, 113, 222; George, son of Richard 201; Henry 351, 354; John 40, 281, 283; John de London 67, 350; Richard 25, 27, 30, 31, 56, 88, 100, 151, 152, 155, 166, 177, 183, 201, 222, 274, 357; Richard, miller 66, 346; Robert 192, 357; William 25, 170, 191, 276, 360

Greneam, Richard 154, 177, 178, 179, 192

Greneleff, Henry 361

Gressop, John 351

Grey, see Gray

Grigge, John son of Thomas 348; John brother of John son of Thomas 348; Thomas 162, 348

Grimsby, Richard 188; Thomas 188

Grinde, Adam 14

Grome, Richard 347; William 347

Grownde, Margaret wife of Richard de Hemingford Abbots 61; Margaret 65

(Growne), William 65, 191

Gryne, William 357

Gurreny, Robert 352

Gybbys, Agnes 54, 147; Edmund 192; Edmund son of Henry 93, 94; Elizabeth wife of Harry 93, 96; Elizabeth, widow 286; Henry (Harry) 27, 88, 96, 99, 129, 131, 157, 177, 178, 182, 185, 201, 301, 302;

John, grandson of John 87; John 13, 23, 40, 54, 57, 90, 110, 147, 154, 156, 169, 171, 173, 176, 177-180, 182, 186, 263, 269, 301; John, son of Henry 96; Thomas, hayward 32; Thomas 24, 33, 177, 178, 190, 267, 272, 285, 301

Gyde, Agnes daughter of William 129; John son of William 129; William, labourer 129

Gyenessde, Richard 176

Gyldene, Thomas 10

Gyldyrdale, William 356

Gyle, see Gile

Gyleman, John 9; Richard 191, 361

Gyllane, John 351

Gylle, see Gile

Gyttons (and see Granger), Leonard son of Jane Granger 95

Gyune, Robert 292

Habar, John 356

Hacnesse, Arthur 65

Hacon, Joan daughter of Walter de Weston 69; John son of Simon de Weston 69; John son of Walter de Weston, *sutor* 69; Mariota daughter of John de Weston 69; Thomas son of Walter de Weston 69; Thomas naif de Weston 69

Hall, John de Doddington 361; Thomas son of Thomas 363; Thomas 363; wife of John 139

Hallam, William 109

Halton, Joan 139

Hammond, Thomas 363

Hanby, William 146

Hancock, John 346; Thomas 177, 357

Ha(n)le, John 56

Hanson, George 72, 350; Robert 142; Thomas, alias cobbler 138, 364; Thomas 57

Haplond, Thomas 27, 270

Hardyng (Harding), John son of Thomas 364; Thomas 29, 273, 359, 364; Thomas de Hartford 66

Harforth, John 185, 355; Robert de Hunts 165, 360; Robert 169

Harfreyz, Thomas 31

Harleston, Richard, baker 346

Harrowsby, Ralph 25

Harrys, see Harryson

Harryson (Harrys, Harson), John 292; Robert servant of John Boleyn 56, 359; Robert, glover 363; Robert 292, 361; Thomas 153, 178, 180; William 131, 177

# Index of Places

# Subject Index

accounts, see bailiffs accounts
adaptation, Chapter 6 *passim*, 216ff.
administration, Chapter 1
agrarian zone 63
alderman 17
aletoll 8; revenues, Appendix 1
All Saints, Fraternity of, 103
alms 114ff.
almshouses 113ff.
artificer 144-145
assizes: ale, beer, bread 4, 50ff.
*auxiliatrix*, see brewer and sellers of ale

bailiffs accounts, Chapter 1, Appendix 1
baker (*pistor*) 50ff., 147ff.
bellman 3, 13, 32, 101, 140
bells 105
bonds 183ff.
braciator, see brewer
brewer (*braciator*), and sellers 51, 147ff.
bridges 10
butchers (*carnifex*) 51ff., 145ff.
byelaws, see decrees

candlemaker 149ff.
capital, Chapter 6 *passim*; pooling of 208ff.; shortage 211ff.
capital, wealth 98; and see chattels
*carnifex*, see butcher
chantry of Blessed Virgin Mary 105ff.
chantry priest 85; of Corpus Christi 85-86
charters, royal 59
chattels, see household
church wardens 101, 109ff.
*cissor*, see taylor
clerks, Chapter 1 *passim*
cobbler (*sutor*) 51, 69, 138
collector of, farm, rents, ale, church, of the view, Chapter 1 *passim*
commerce 42
constable, Chapter 1 *passim*
conveyance 125; lists by street, Appendix 4; see also land market
coroner, Chapter 1 *passim*

Corpus Christi Fraternity 102ff.
Court Rolls, *passim*
cow herds 55
craftmen 61, 75ff., 90
credits, food trades 145ff., Chapter 6 Section B; money market, Appendix 9
crop revenues, Appendix 1
custodian of church: seals, Chapter 1 *passim*
custodian of Fraternities 103ff.; guardians, keepers 107ff.
custom 59

*De Religiosis*, Statute, 102
debts 6; bailiffs' 19ff.; food trades 145ff.; pleas 170ff., Chapter 6 Section B; money market, Appendix 9
decrees 5
depression 36
ditches 10
diversification 209ff.
draper 66

economic structure 205ff.
election 11ff.
engrossing 162ff.
equality, among heirs 97
executors, see wills

family, estates 48; demography, Chapter 4 Section A; wealthy, local 167ff.; continuity 216ff.; recorded in wills, Appendix 8
farm rentals, Chapter 2 *passim*, 123ff.; lists by street, Appendix 3
farrier (*ferrour*) 66
felony 8
fences 10
fines, entry 123ff.: *gersuma*, Appendix 1; court fines, Appendix 1; and see liberty
fisherman (*piscator*) 66
fishmonger 51ff., 149ff.
foreigner 11, Chapter 2 *passim*; tenants 57-58, 63ff.; and see liberty
Frankpledge rolls, see view of

## DATE DUE

| | | | |
|---|---|---|---|
| | | | |
| | | | |
| | | | |
| | | | |
| | | | |
| | | | |
| | | | |
| | | | |
| | | | |
| | | | |
| | | | |
| | | | |
| | | | |
| | | | |

HIGHSMITH    #LO-45220